UNIX

IN A NUTSHELL

Other resources from O'Reilly

Related titles

Classic Shell Scripting
Effective awk Programming
Essential CVS
Essential System Administration
GDB Pocket Reference
Learning GNU Emacs
Learning the bash Shell
Learning the Korn Shell
Learning the vi Editor
Linux in a Nutshell
Mac OS X Tiger for Unix Geeks
Managing Projects with GNU Make
Running Linux
sed and awk Pocket Reference
TCP/IP Network Administration
The Complete FreeBSD
Unix Power Tools
Using csh & tcsh
Version Control with Subversion

oreilly.com

oreilly.com is more than a complete catalog of O'Reilly books. You'll also find links to news, events, articles, weblogs, sample chapters, and code examples.

Conferences

O'Reilly brings diverse innovators together to nurture the ideas that spark revolutionary industries. We specialize in documenting the latest tools and systems, translating the innovator's knowledge into useful skills for those in the trenches. Visit *conferences.oreilly.com* for our upcoming events.

Safari Bookshelf (*safari.oreilly.com*) is the premier online reference library for programmers and IT professionals. Conduct searches across more than 1,000 books. Subscribers can zero in on answers to time-critical questions in a matter of seconds. Read the books on your Bookshelf from cover to cover or simply flip to the page you need. Try it today for free.

UNIX

IN A NUTSHELL

Fourth Edition

Arnold Robbins

Beijing • Cambridge • Farnham • Köln • Paris • Sebastopol • Taipei • Tokyo

Unix in a Nutshell, Fourth Edition
by Arnold Robbins

Printed in the United States of America.

Published by O'Reilly Media, Inc., 1005 Gravenstein Highway North, Sebastopol, CA 95472.

O'Reilly books may be purchased for educational, business, or sales promotional use. Online editions are also available for most titles (*safari.oreilly.com*). For more information, contact our corporate/institutional sales department: (800) 998-9938 or *corporate@oreilly.com*.

Editor: Mike Loukides
Production Editor: Colleen Gorman
Cover Designer: Edie Freedman
Interior Designer: David Futato
Back Cover Illustration: J.D. "Illiad" Frazer

Printing History:

May 1989: First Edition.
June 1992: Second Edition.
August 1999: Third Edition.
October 2005: Fourth Edition.

ISBN: 0-596-10029-9
ISBN13: 978-0-596-10029-2
[M] [11/06]

To my wife, Miriam. May our dreams continue to come true.

To my children, Chana, Rivka, Nachum, and Malka.

To the memory of Frank Willison.

Table of Contents

Part II. Text Editing and Processing

Part III. Software Development

Part IV. References

Preface

The fourth edition of *Unix in a Nutshell* brings the book into the 21st century. The term "UNIX" is a registered trademark of The Open Group. It is used for branding systems as compliant with the various standards that collectively define the behavior of a modern Unix system. More informally though, many systems in use today are Unix work-alikes, even though their source code base was developed independently from the original Unix systems.

Thus, the goal of this edition to present the broader state of Unix in today's world. In particular, it's important to cover both the commercial variants, and those where source code for the system and the utilities are freely available. To this end, we have chosen to cover these systems, which are representative of "Unix" today:

Solaris 10
: Solaris is the most popular commercial system based on the original Unix System V code base.

GNU/Linux
: GNU/Linux systems have gained a huge foothold in the commercial marketplace. While currently used most heavily for back-end servers, GNU/Linux is also starting to gain ground in the desktop market.

Mac OS X
: Apple's rewrite of their operating system has a core based on Mach and various BSD technologies. The command set is derived from FreeBSD. Thus, besides having an exciting user interface, Mac OS X is representative of the BSD strain of free Unix-like systems.

The commands covered by the current POSIX standard form the core of our presentation. Each specific system has commands that are unique to it; these are covered too. Finally, many important and useful utilities are distributed as Free or Open Source software on the Internet. We have done our best to cover those as well, including presenting the Internet URL from which you can download the source code, in case your particular system doesn't include that utility in its distribution.

This edition has the following new features:

- Covers Solaris 10, the latest version of the SVR4-based operating system from Sun Microsystems,* GNU/Linux, and Mac OS X.
- Chapter 2, *Unix Commands*, has been heavily reorganized and revised, in order to cover the three systems.
- Chapter 3, *The Unix Shell: An Overview*, has been reworked, now covering Bash,† `ksh93`, and `tcsh`.
- Chapter 4, *The Bash and Korn Shells*, now covers the popular Bash shell, along with the 1988 and 1993 versions of `ksh`. Coverage of the vanilla Bourne shell has been dropped.
- Chapter 5, *tcsh: An Extended C Shell*, now covers the widely-used `tcsh` shell instead of the original Berkeley `csh`.
- Chapter 6, *Package Management*, is new. It covers package management programs, which are used for program installation on popular GNU/Linux systems. It also describes similar facilities for Solaris and Mac OS X.
- Chapter 8, *The Emacs Editor*, now covers GNU Emacs Version 21.
- Chapter 9, *The vi, ex, and vim Editors*, now contains merged coverage of the `vi` and `ex` text editors. Important commands and features from the popular `vim` editor are also included.
- Chapter 10, *The sed Editor*, now includes coverage of GNU `sed`.
- The coverage of `awk` in Chapter 11, *The awk Programming Language*, has been updated as well, dropping separate coverage of the original, "old" `awk`.
- Chapter 12, *Source Code Management: An Overview*, which provides an introduction to source code management systems, has been added.
- Chapter 14, *The Concurrent Versions System*, on CVS, has been added.
- Chapter 15, *The Subversion Version Control System*, on the Subversion version control system, is brand new.
- Chapter 16, *The GNU make Utility*, has been revised to focus on GNU Make.
- Chapter 17, *The GDB Debugger*, on the GDB debugger, is brand new.

As time marches on, once-popular or necessary commands fall into disuse. Thus, with the exception of Chapter 18, which describes how to write a manual page, all the material on the venerable `troff` text formatting suite has been removed from the book. We have also removed the previous edition's material on SCCS and on obsolete commands.

Audience

This book should be of interest to Unix users and Unix programmers, as well as to anyone (such as a system administrator) who might offer direct support to users

* The version used for this book was for Intel x86–based systems.

† Because the Free Software Foundation treats "Bash" and "Emacs" as proper nouns, we do too, here and throughout the book.

and programmers. The presentation is geared mainly toward people who are *already* familiar with the Unix system; that is, you know what you want to do, and you even have some idea how to do it. You just need a reminder about the details. For example, if you want to remove the third field from a database, you might think, "*I know I can use the* `cut` *command, but what are the options?*" In many cases, specific examples are provided to show how a command is used.

We have purposely chosen to omit system administration commands. System administration is a complicated topic in its own right, and the Bibliography lists several good books on this important subject.

This reference might also help people who are familiar with some aspects of Unix but not with others. Many chapters include an overview of the particular topic. While this isn't meant to be comprehensive, it's usually sufficient to get you started in unfamiliar territory.

Finally, if you're new to the Unix operating system, and you're feeling bold, you might appreciate this book as a quick tour of what Unix has to offer. The "Beginner's Guide" section in Chapter 1 can point you to the most useful commands, and you'll find brief examples of how to use them, but take note: this book should not be used in place of a good beginner's tutorial on Unix. (You might try *Learning the Unix Operating System* for that.) This reference should be a *supplement*, not a substitute. (There are references throughout the text to other relevant O'Reilly books that will help you learn the subject matter under discussion; you may be better off detouring to those books first. Also, see the Bibliography.)

Scope of This Book

Unix in a Nutshell, Fourth Edition, is divided into four parts:

- Part I (Chapters 1 through 6) describes the syntax and options for Unix commands and for the Bash, Korn, and `tcsh` shells. Part I also covers package management.
- Part II (Chapters 7 through 11) presents various editing tools and describes their command sets (alphabetically and by group). Part II begins with a review of pattern matching, including examples geared toward specific editors.
- Part III (Chapters 12 through 18) summarizes the Unix utilities for software development—RCS, CVS, Subversion, `make` and GDB. It also covers, in brief, what you need to know to write a manual page for your programs.
- Part IV contains a table of ISO Latin-1 characters and equivalent values (*ISO 8859-1 (Latin-1) Character Set*) and a Bibliography of Unix books.

Conventions

This book follows certain typographic conventions, outlined below:

`Constant width`
: is used for directory names, filenames, commands, program names, functions, and options. All terms shown in constant width are typed literally. It is also used to show the contents of files or the output from commands.

`Constant width italic`
: is used in syntax and command summaries to show generic text; these should be replaced with user-supplied values.

`Constant width bold`
: is used in examples to show text that should be typed literally by the user.

Italic
: is used to show generic arguments and options; these should be replaced with user-supplied values. Italic is also used to indicate URLs, macro package names, library names, comments in examples, and the first mention of terms.

`%`, `$`, `#`
: are used in some examples as the C shell prompt (`%`) and as the Bash, Bourne or Korn shell prompts (`$`). `#` is the prompt for the `root` user.

`?`, `>`
: are used in some examples as the C shell secondary prompt (`?`) and as the Bash, Bourne or Korn shell secondary prompts (`>`).

❑, ➔
: are used in some examples to represent the space and tab characters respectively. This is particularly necessary for the examples in the chapters on text editing.

program (*N*)
: indicates the "manpage" for *program* in section *N* of the online manual. For example, *echo* (1) means the entry for the `echo` command.

`[ ]`
: surround optional elements in a description of syntax. (The brackets themselves should never be typed.) Note that many commands show the argument [*files*]. If a filename is omitted, standard input (usually the keyboard) is assumed. End keyboard input with an end-of-file character.

EOF
: indicates the end-of-file character (normally `CTRL-D`).

`^`*`x`*, `CTRL-`*`x`*
: indicates a "control character," typed by holding down the Control key and the *x* key for any key *x*.

`|`
: is used in syntax descriptions to separate items for which only one alternative may be chosen at a time.

A final word about syntax. In many cases, the space between an option and its argument can be omitted. In other cases, the spacing (or lack of spacing) must be followed strictly. For example, `-w`*`n`* (no intervening space) might be interpreted differently from `-w` *`n`*. It's important to notice the spacing used in option syntax.

This icon signifies a tip, suggestion, or general note.

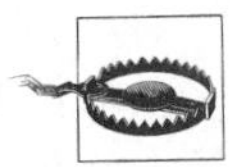

This icon indicates a warning or caution.

Using Code Examples

This book is here to help you get your job done. In general, you may use the code in this book in your programs and documentation. You do not need to contact us for permission unless you're reproducing a significant portion of the code. For example, writing a program that uses several chunks of code from this book does not require permission. Selling or distributing a CD-ROM of examples from O'Reilly books does require permission. Answering a question by citing this book and quoting example code does not require permission. Incorporating a significant amount of example code from this book into your product's documentation does require permission.

We appreciate, but do not require, attribution. An attribution usually includes the title, author, publisher, and ISBN. For example: "*Unix in a Nutshell*, Fourth Edition, by Arnold Robbins. Copyright 2005 O'Reilly Media, Inc., 0-596-10029-9."

If you feel your use of code examples falls outside fair use or the permission given above, feel free to contact us at *permissions@oreilly.com*.

Safari® Enabled

When you see a Safari® enabled icon on the cover of your favorite technology book, that means the book is available online through the O'Reilly Network Safari Bookshelf.

Safari offers a solution that's better than e-books. It's a virtual library that lets you easily search thousands of top tech books, cut and paste code samples, download chapters, and find quick answers when you need the most accurate, current information. Try it free at *http://safari.oreilly.com*.

How to Contact Us

We have tested and verified all of the information in this book to the best of our ability, but you may find that features have changed (or even that we have made mistakes!). Please let us know about any errors you find, as well as your suggestions for future editions, by writing:

O'Reilly Media, Inc.
1005 Gravenstein Highway North
Sebastopol, CA 95472
(800) 998-9938 (in the United States or Canada)
(707) 829-0515 (international/local)
(707) 829-0104 (fax)

You can also send us messages electronically. To be put on the mailing list or request a catalog, send email to:

info@oreilly.com

To ask technical questions or comment on the book, send email to:

bookquestions@oreilly.com

We have a web site for the book, where we'll list examples, errata, and any plans for future editions. You can access this page at:

http://www.oreilly.com/catalog/unixnut4/

Acknowledgments

Thanks again to Yosef Gold for sharing his office with me. Deb Cameron again revised Chapter 8. Thanks to Mike Loukides at O'Reilly Media for his work as editor. Chuck Toporek, also of O'Reilly Media, answered numerous Mac OS X and Macintosh-related questions, for which I'm grateful. J.D. "Illiad" Frazer of User Friendly (see *http://www.userfriendly.org/*) provided the great cartoon on the back cover. It's a relief to finally know the tarsier's name.

Thanks to Jennifer Vesperman for permission to adapt material from *Essential CVS* for Chapter 14. Similarly, Ben Collins-Sussman, Brian W. Fitzpatrick, and C. Michael Pilato gave permission for me to adapt material from *Version Control with Subversion* for Chapter 15, which I greatly appreciate. And thanks to Andy Oram, Ellen Siever, Stephen Figgins and Aaron Weber for making available material from *Linux in a Nutshell* for use in parts of the book.

Thanks to David G. Korn (AT&T Research) and Chet Ramey (Case Western Reserve University) for answering my questions about the Korn shell and Bash. Keith Bostic of Sleepycat Software answered several questions about Berkeley DB. Glenn Barry of Sun Microsystems helped out on the Solaris side.

Thanks to the following people, in alphabetical order, for reviewing the book during its various stages: Nelson H.F. Beebe (University of Utah Mathematics Department), Jon Forrest (University of California, Berkeley, Civil and Environmental Engineering), and Brian Kernighan (Princeton University Computer Science Department). Chet Ramey, co-author and maintainer of Bash, reviewed Chapter 4, and Bram Moolenaar, the author of `vim`, reviewed Chapter 9, for which I thank them.

A special thanks to Dr. Uri Degen, Lev Orpaz, Julio Kadichevski, and Sid Gordon of Ness Technologies, and to Mike Hendrickson and Mike Loukides of O'Reilly Media, for enabling me to finish this edition in a timely fashion.

Once again, thanks to my wife Miriam for her love, patience, and support, and to my children for not giving Mommy (too much) hassle while I was working.

—Arnold Robbins
Nof Ayalon
ISRAEL

I

Commands and Shells

Part I presents a summary of Unix commands of interest to users and programmers. It also describes the major Unix shells, including special syntax and built-in commands. It rounds off with an overview of package management software.

Commands and Shells

[illegible]

Chapter 1, [illegible]

Chapter 2, Unix Commands

Chapter 3, The Unix Shell: An Overview

Chapter 4, The Bash and Korn Shells

Chapter 5, [illegible] Extended C Shell

Chapter 6, Package Management

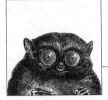

1

Introduction

The Unix operating system originated at AT&T Bell Labs in the early 1970s. System V Release 4 (SVR4) came from USL (Unix System Laboratories) in the late 1980s. Unix source ownership is currently a matter of litigation in U.S. courts. Because Unix was able to run on different hardware from different vendors, developers were encouraged to modify Unix and distribute it as their own value-added version. Separate Unix traditions evolved as a result: USL's System V, the Berkeley Software Distribution (BSD, from the University of California, Berkeley), Xenix, etc.

SVR4, which was developed jointly by USL (then a division of AT&T) and Sun Microsystems, merged features from BSD and SVR3. This added about two dozen BSD commands (plus some new SVR4 commands) to the basic Unix command set. In addition, SVR4 provided a BSD Compatibility Package, a kind of "second string" command group. This package included some of the most fundamental BSD commands, and its purpose was to help users of BSD-derived systems make the transition to SVR4.

Unix in the 21st Century

Today, the specification of what makes a system "Unix" is embodied primarily in the POSIX standard, an international standard based on System V and BSD. Commercial Unix systems, such as Solaris from Sun Microsystems, AIX from IBM, and HP-UX from Hewlett Packard, are standard-adhering direct descendants of the original Unix systems.

A number of other systems are "spiritual" descendents of Unix, even though they contain none of the original Unix source code. The most notable of these systems is GNU/Linux, which has seen a meteoric rise in popularity. However, a large number of systems derived from the 4.4-BSD-Lite distribution are also popular. All of these systems offer standards compliance and compatibility with SVR4 and earlier versions of BSD.

This edition of *Unix in a Nutshell* attempts to define the cross-section of features and commands that "make a Unix system Unix." To that end, it covers three of the most popular and representative systems now available.

Solaris 10
: Solaris 10 is a distributed computing environment from Sun Microsystems. Solaris includes the SunOS 5.10 operating system, plus additional features such as the Common Desktop Environment, GNOME, and Java tools. In addition, the kernel has received significant enhancement to support multiprocessor CPUs, multithreaded processes, kernel-level threads, and dynamic loading of device drivers and other kernel modules. Most of the user-level (and system administration) content comes from SVR4. As a result, Solaris 10 is based on SVR4 but contains additional BSD/SunOS features. To help in the transition from the old (largely BSD-based) SunOS, Solaris provides the BSD/SunOS Compatibility Package and the Binary Compatibility Package.

  Sun has made binary versions of Solaris for the SPARC and Intel architectures available for "free," for noncommercial use. You pay only for the media, shipping, and handling, or you may download installation CD images. To find out more, see *http://www.sun.com/developer*.

  As this book was going to press, Sun announced that it would be making the source code for Solaris available as Open Source. For more details, see *http://www.opensolaris.org*.

Fedora GNU/Linux
: There are many distributions of GNU/Linux (the combination of the GNU utilities with the Linux kernel to make a complete operating environment). We have chosen the Fedora Core 3 system from Red Hat, Inc.* To find out more, see *http://fedora.redhat.com*.

Mac OS X 10.4 (Tiger)
: Mac OS X introduced a revolution into the Macintosh world, with a slick new interface (Aqua) running atop a powerful OS kernel based on Mach and FreeBSD. The shell level utilities are largely from FreeBSD. The 10.4 (a.k.a. "Tiger") release is current as of this writing. To find out more, see *http://www.apple.com/macosx*.

  One important "quirk" of Mac OS X is worth noting. The default HPFS filesystem stores filenames in their original case, but it *ignores* case when looking for files. In practice, this make surprisingly little difference. However, it can occasionally have weird side effects, since things like command completion in the Bash shell are still case-sensitive.

* This is undoubtedly cause to receive hate-mail from the advocates of other distributions. In our defense, we can only claim that it's impossible to cover every GNU/Linux distribution, and that for everyday use with a shell prompt, the systems are all extremely similar.

Obtaining Compilers

If you wish to build programs from source code, you need a compiler. Almost all Unix applications are written in C or C++, with the majority still written in C. This section describes obtaining compilers for the three systems covered in this book.

Solaris

Solaris 10 includes a Java compiler. Earlier versions of Solaris did not come with C or C++ compilers. You had to either buy compilers from Sun, from other third party vendors, or find a binary of some version of GCC for use in bootstrapping the latest version of GCC.

The final version of Solaris 10 now includes GCC (both C and C++ compilers) in `/usr/sfw/bin`. This is true for both the SPARC and Intel x86 versions. You thus have a choice: you may use the supplied GCC, or buy high-quality C and C++ compilers from Sun.

Besides GCC, a very large number of precompiled packages is available from *http://www.sunfreeware.com/*. You should see both the "Download/Install" and "FAQ" sections of that web site.

All the software from *http://www.sunfreeware.com* is in `pkgadd` format and is installable using that command. (See Chapter 6.) We recommend reading the details on the web site, which will always be up to date.

Note that many commands discussed in this book won't be on your system if all you've done is an *end user* install. If you can afford the disk space, do at least a *developer* install. This also installs many of the header files and libraries that you need in order to compile programs from source code.

For support issues and publicly released patches to Solaris, the web starting point is *http://sunsolve.sun.com*.

GNU/Linux

GNU/Linux systems usually install software development tools by default. If your system does not have compiler tools or `make` (see Chapter 16), then you will have to find the appropriate package(s) for your distribution. This is likely to be one or more `.rpm` or `.deb` files on your distribution media (CD or DVD), or you may be able to install it over the Internet, using a package manager such as `apt` or `yum`.

At a minimum, you will need the GNU Compiler Collection (GCC), system header files and libraries, the GNU Binutils (assembler, loader, `ar`, etc.), and `make`.

Mac OS X

Unix-style development tools (compiler, `make`) are included as part of the larger Xcode Tools package. Boxed distributions of Mac OS X include an Xcode Tools CD. The easiest way to install the tools is to insert that CD into your CD drive.

If your version of Mac OS X is that which came with your hardware, you won't have an Xcode Tools CD. Instead, click on `Developer.mpkg` in `/Applications/Installers/Developer Tools`. Doing so installs the development tools.

Building Software

Many of the programs listed in Chapter 2 are available in source code form from the Internet. For GNU/Linux and Mac OS X, you may be able to use a package manager to download and install the software (see Chapter 6). Similarly, for Solaris, you may be able to get a precompiled version of the program from *http://www.sunfreeware.com/*.

However, it's possible, particularly on a commercial Unix system, that you will want (or need) to download the source and build the program yourself if you don't have it, or if you wish to obtain the very latest version. This section outlines the conventional build process.

Most Internet software is written in C or C++. To compile it you will need a compiler. See the previous section for a discussion of where to get a compiler if you don't have one.

Today's programs usually use the GNU Project's Autoconf software suite for managing portability issues. Autoconf generates a shell script named `configure`, which tests various aspects of the target system. The end result of running `configure` is a `Makefile` custom-tuned to the particular system (see Chapter 16), and a header file describing the features available, or missing, from the system. As a result, the recipe for building software is usually quite simple, consisting of the following:

1. Download the software. This can be done with a noninteractive program such as `wget` or `curl` (see their entries in Chapter 2), or interactively using anonymous FTP for programs distributed that way.
2. Decompress and extract the software.
3. Change directory into the program's distribution directory.
4. Run `configure`.
5. Run `make`.
6. Optionally, run the program's self-test suite.
7. Run `make install`, usually as `root`, to install the software.

The following example uses GNU `sed` to illustrate the process. The steps are similar or identical for all GNU software, and for most other freely-available programs as well.

First, we obtain the program using `wget`:

```
$ wget ftp://ftp.gnu.org/gnu/sed/sed-4.1.4.tar.gz  Retrieve the latest version
--15:00:04--  ftp://ftp.gnu.org/gnu/sed/sed-4.1.4.tar.gz
           => `sed-4.1.4.tar.gz'
Resolving ftp.gnu.org... 199.232.41.7
Connecting to ftp.gnu.org[199.232.41.7]:21... connected.
Logging in as anonymous ... Logged in!
```

```
==> SYST ... done.    ==> PWD ... done.
==> TYPE I ... done.  ==> CWD /gnu/sed ... done.
==> PASV ... done.    ==> RETR sed-4.1.4.tar.gz ... done.
Length: 794,257 (unauthoritative)

100%[=================================>] 794,257      60.04K/s    ETA 00:00

15:00:29 (38.86 KB/s) - `sed-4.1.4.tar.gz' saved [794257]
```

The next step is to decompress and extract the software:

```
$ gzip -d < sed-4.1.4.tar.gz | tar -xpvf -          Extract source code
sed-4.1.4/
sed-4.1.4/ABOUT-NLS
sed-4.1.4/AUTHORS
sed-4.1.4/BUGS
...
```

Next we change into the directory and run `configure`:

```
$ cd sed-4.1.4                                       Change directory
$ ./configure && make                                Run configure and make
checking for a BSD-compatible install... /usr/bin/install -c
checking whether build environment is sane... yes
checking for gawk... gawk
checking whether make sets $(MAKE)... yes
...
```

The `&&` construct runs `make` only if `configure` finishes successfully (see Chapter 4).

Next, we run the test suite, to ensure that there were no problems:

```
$ make check                                         Test the build
Making check in intl                                 Lots of output omitted
...
PASS: dc
===================
All 71 tests passed
===================
```

Finally, we install the software. This may require administrative privileges:

```
$ su root                                            Change to superuser
Password:                                            Password is not echoed
# make install                                       Install GNU sed into /usr/local
...
```

What's in the Quick Reference

This guide presents the major features of Solaris, GNU/Linux, and Mac OS X. In addition, this guide presents chapters on Emacs, RCS, CVS, Subversion, GNU Make, and GDB, the GNU debugger. Although they are not part of commercial Unix systems, they are found on many Unix systems because they are useful add-ons.

But keep in mind: if your system doesn't include all the component packages, there will be commands in this book you won't find on your system.

The summary of Unix commands in Chapter 2 makes up a large part of this book. Only user/programmer commands are included; administrative commands are purposely ignored. Chapter 2 describes the following set:

- Commands and options in Solaris, GNU/Linux, and Mac OS X. This includes many "essential" tools for which source and/or binaries are available via the Internet
- Solaris-only tools
- GNU/Linux-only tools
- Mac OS X-only tools
- Java-related tools

Beginner's Guide

If you're just beginning to work on a Unix system, the abundance of commands might prove daunting. To help orient you, the following lists present a small sampling of commands on various topics.

Communication

`ftp`	Interactive file transfer program.
`login`	Sign on to Unix.
`mailx`	Read or send mail.
`slogin`	Sign on to remote Unix using secure shell.
`ssh`	Connect to another system, securely.

Comparisons

`cmp`	Compare two files, byte by byte.
`comm`	Compare items in two sorted files.
`diff`	Compare two files, line by line.
`diff3`	Compare three files.
`dircmp`	Compare directories.
`sdiff`	Compare two files, side by side.

File Management

`cd`	Change directory.
`chgrp`	Change file group.
`chmod`	Change access modes on files.
`chown`	Change file owner.
`cksum`	Print a file checksum, POSIX standard algorithm.
`cp`	Copy files.
`csplit`	Break files at specific locations.
`file`	Determine a file's type.
`head`	Show the first few lines of a file.

`less`	A sophisticated interactive *pager* program for looking at information on a terminal, one screenful (or "page") at a time. The name is a pun on the `more` program.
`ln`	Create filename aliases.
`locate`	Find a file somewhere on the system based on its name. The program uses a database of files that is usually automatically rebuilt, nightly.
`ls`	List files or directories.
`md5sum`	Print a file checksum using the Message Digest 5 (MD5) algorithm.
`mkdir`	Create a directory.
`more`	Display files by screenful.
`mv`	Move or rename files or directories.
`pwd`	Print working directory.
`rm`	Remove files.
`rmdir`	Remove directories.
`scp`	Copy files to remote system securely.
`split`	Split files evenly.
`tail`	Show the last few lines of a file.
`wc`	Count lines, words, and characters.

Miscellaneous

`banner`	Make posters from words.
`bc`	Arbitrary precision calculator.
`cal`	Display calendar.
`calendar`	Check for reminders.
`clear`	Clear the screen.
`info`	The GNU Info system for online documentation.
`man`	Get information on a command.
`nice`	Reduce a job's priority.
`nohup`	Preserve a running job after logging out.
`passwd`	Set your login password.
`script`	Produce a transcript of your login session.
`spell`	Report misspelled words.
`su`	Switch to a different user.

Printing (BSD Commands)

`lpr`	Send to the printer.
`lpq`	Get printer status.
`lprm`	Cancel a printer request.
`pr`	Format and paginate for printing.

Printing (System V Commands)

`cancel`	Cancel a printer request.
`lp`	Send to the printer.
`lpstat`	Get printer status.
`pr`	Format and paginate for printing.

Programming

`cc`	C compiler.
`ctags`	C function references (for `vi`).
`ld`	Loader.
`lex`	Lexical analyzer generator.
`make`	Execute commands in a specified order.
`od`	Dump input in various formats.
`splint`	C program analyzer.
`strace`	Trace signals and system calls.
`strip`	Remove data from an object file.
`truss`	Trace signals and system calls.
`yacc`	Parser generator. Can be used with `lex`.

Searching

`egrep`	Extended version of `grep`.
`fgrep`	Search files for literal words.
`find`	Search the system for filenames matching patterns or attributes.
`grep`	Search files for text patterns.
`strings`	Display text strings found in binary files.

Shells

Bourne family shells:

`bash`	The GNU Project's Bourne Again Shell.
`ksh`	The Korn shell, either an original or clone, depending upon the operating system.
`pdksh`	The Public Domain Korn shell.
`sh`	The original Bourne shell, particularly on commercial Unix systems.
`zsh`	The Z-shell.

C shell family shells:

`csh`	The original BSD C shell.
`tcsh`	The "Tenex" C shell: a much-enhanced version of `csh`.

Shell Programming

`basename`	Print the last component of a pathname, optionally removing a suffix.
`dirname`	Print all but the last component of a pathname.
`echo`	Repeat command-line arguments on the output.
`expr`	Perform arithmetic and comparisons.
`id`	Print user and group ID and name information.
`line`	Read a line of input.
`printf`	Format and print command-line arguments.
`sleep`	Pause during processing.
`test`	Test a condition.

Storage

bunzip2	Expand files compressed with bzip2 (.bz2 files).
bzip2	Very high quality file compression program.
cpio	Copy archives in or out.
gunzip	Expand compressed (.gz and .Z) files.
gzcat	Display contents of compressed files (may be linked to zcat).
gzip	Compress files to free up space.
tar	File tree and tape archiver.
zcat	Display contents of compressed files.

System Status

at	Execute commands later.
crontab	Automate commands.
date	Display or set date.
df	Show free disk space.
du	Show disk usage.
env	Show environment variables.
finger	Display information about users.
kill	Terminate a running command.
ps	Show processes.
stty	Set or display terminal settings.
who	Show who is logged on.

Text Processing

awk	A pattern-matching programming language for working with text files.
cat	Concatenate files or display them.
cut	Select columns for display.
ex	Line editor underlying vi.
fmt	Produce roughly uniform line lengths.
iconv	General-purpose character-encoding conversion tool.
join	Merge different columns into a database.
paste	Merge columns or switch order.
sed	Noninteractive text editor.
sort	Sort or merge files.
tr	Translate (redefine) characters.
uniq	Find repeated or unique lines in a file.
vi	Visual text editor.
xargs	Process many arguments in manageable portions.

Solaris: Standard Compliant Programs

Where the behavior specified by the POSIX standard differs from the historical behavior provided by a command, Solaris provides a different version of the command in either /usr/xpg6/bin or in /usr/xpg4/bin. On Solaris systems, you should place these two directories into your search path *before* the standard /usr/bin directory. Some of these commands are not covered in this book, since they are either administrative commands or are obsolete. Also, today, it is unlikely that the commands in /usr/ucb will be useful; you probably should not have that directory in your search path.

ar	delta	file	kill	nm	tail
awk	df	find	link	nohup	tr
basename	du	get	ln	od	ulimit
bc	ed	getconf	ls	pr	vedit
chgrp	edit	getopts	m4	rm	vi
chown	egrep	grep	make	sccs	view
cp	env	hash	more	sed	wait
ctags	ex	id	mv	sh	who
date	expr	ipcs	nice	sort	xargs
dc	fgrep	jobs	nl	stty	

2

Unix Commands

Introduction

This chapter presents the Unix commands of interest to users and programmers. Most of these commands appear in the "Commands" section of the online manual. With rare exception, this book purposely avoids system administration commands, because system administration is beyond its scope. The focus instead is on everyday commands, those used both interactively and for programming.

Summarizing three operating systems that are similar but not identical is a daunting task. In order to make a coherent presentation, the chapter is organized as follows:

Common Commands
: This section lists commands that should be available on just about any Unix system. We have included here many commands that are downloadable from the Internet and that are standard with GNU/Linux, such as `autoconf` or `wget`, even though they may not come "out of the box" on commercial Unix systems. Wherever possible, we provide a URL from which the source to the command may be downloaded, so that you can build the program yourself if you want it. See the section "Obtaining Compilers" in Chapter 1 for what to do if you don't have a C compiler for your system.

: Additionally, we have made an effort to be as concise as possible. For example, GNU-style long options are listed side-by-side with their standard single-letter counterparts. Similarly, several commands have associated with them additional more specialized commands that are needed only rarely. We simply list such commands as "related," without giving them separate entries. For such commands, you should then see your system's online manual pages or other documentation.

Solaris Commands
: This section lists the important commands that are available only on Solaris.

GNU/Linux Commands
This section lists the important commands that are available only on GNU/Linux.

Mac OS X Commands
This section lists the important commands that are available only on Mac OS X.

Java Commands
The primary commands for doing Java development. These are (essentially) the same across all systems.

Even commands that appear in the section "Alphabetical Summary of Common Commands" are not identical on all systems. Thus, here too we've made an effort to describe the common behavior first, with additional subsections on system specific behavior. This occurs most frequently for the different options that different versions of the commands accept.

In the command summaries, each entry is labeled with the command name on the left-hand edge of the page. The syntax line is followed by a brief description and a list of all available options. Many commands come with examples at the end of the entry. If you need only a quick reminder or suggestion about a command, you can skip directly to the examples.

Some options can be invoked only by a user with special system privileges. Such a person is often called a "superuser." This book uses the term *privileged user* instead.

Typographic conventions for describing command syntax are listed in the Preface. For additional help in locating commands, see the Index.

Finding Commands on Solaris

Solaris systems provide a number of "bin" directories underneath `/usr` for different kinds of commands. For example, `/usr/bin` holds most regular commands, `/usr/java/bin` has the Java commands, and so on. The bin directories are summarized in Table 2-1.

Table 2-1. Solaris bin directories

Directory	Purpose
`/bin`	Symbolic link to `/usr/bin`
`/sbin`	System administration commands
`/usr/sbin`	More system administration commands
`/usr/bin`	Regular commands
`/usr/X/bin`	X Window System utilities
`/usr/ccs/bin`	C Compilation System: compiler-related programs
`/usr/dt/bin`	Common Desktop Environment (CDE) programs
`/usr/java/bin`	Java programs
`/usr/openwin/bin`	OpenWindows programs
`/usr/perl5/bin`	The `perl` command and its related programs
`/usr/sfw/bin`	Additional software from the Internet
`/usr/ucb`	Berkeley Unix compatibility programs

Table 2-1. Solaris bin directories (continued)

Directory	Purpose
/usr/xpg4/bin	Standards-compliant versions of regular utilities
/usr/xpg6/bin	More standards compliant versions of regular utilities

Unix Commands

We strongly recommend placing /usr/xpg6/bin and /usr/xpg4/bin in your shell search path *before* the other directories. Solaris is unique among modern Unix systems in that the versions in /usr/bin continue to be the original System V Release 4 versions of the commands. Today, with just about every other system being POSIX compliant, you should set up your Solaris account to be POSIX compliant too! For Bash or the Korn shell, use something like this in your .profile file:

```
# Use multiple lines to fit on the page:
PATH="/usr/xpg6/bin:/usr/xpg4/bin:/usr/ccs/bin:/usr/bin:/usr/java/bin"
PATH="$PATH:/usr/sfw/bin:/usr/perl5/bin"
PATH="$PATH:/usr/dt/bin:/usr/X/bin:/usr/openwin/bin"
```

The Solaris Software Companion CD contains unsupported copies of many popular Free Software and Open Source programs from the Internet. They install under /opt/sfw. If you install this software, you may wish to add /opt/sfw/bin to your path as well.

Finding Commands on GNU/Linux and Mac OS X

The situation on GNU/Linux and Mac OS X is considerably simpler. For both systems, a path like the following suffices:

```
PATH=/bin:/usr/bin:/usr/X11R6/bin
```

On Mac OS X the default path is /bin:/sbin:/usr/bin:/usr/sbin. You may wish to add the X11 directory to it:

```
PATH=$PATH:/usr/X11R6/bin
```

Essentially every GNU/Linux program accepts long options (such as --fire-phasers) besides the traditional short ones (-F). In addition, just about every GNU/Linux program accepts the options --help and --version, to print a command-line summary and version information respectively. In the interests of brevity, the individual command descriptions omit the --help and --version options, and they omit the statement that long options apply only to GNU/Linux programs.

Alphabetical Summary of Common Commands

This list describes the commands that are common to two or more of Solaris, GNU/Linux, and Mac OS X. It also includes many programs available from the Internet that may not come "out of the box" on all the systems.

On Solaris, many of the Free Software and Open Source programs described here may be found in /usr/sfw/bin or /opt/sfw/bin. Interestingly, the Intel version of

Solaris has more programs in /opt/sfw/bin than does the SPARC version. As mentioned earlier, on Solaris, we recommend placing /usr/xpg6/bin and /usr/xpg4/bin in your PATH *before* /usr/bin.

---

aclocal

aclocal [*options*]

Part of GNU automake. Place m4 macro definitions needed by autoconf into a single file. The aclocal command first scans for macro definitions in m4 files in its default directory (/usr/share/aclocal on some systems) and in the file acinclude.m4. It next scans for macros used in the configure.ac file. It generates an aclocal.m4 file that contains definitions of all m4 macros required by autoconf. See also **automake**.

Options

--acdir=*dir*
: Look for macro files in directory *dir* instead of the default directory.

--force
: Always update the output file.

-I *dir*
: Additionally, search directory *dir* for m4 macro definitions.

--output=*file*
: Save output to *file* instead of aclocal.m4.

--print-ac-dir
: Print the name of the directory to be searched for m4 files, then exit.

--verbose
: Print names of files being processed.

---

apropos

apropos *keywords*

Look up one or more *keywords* in the online manpages. Same as man -k. See also **whatis**.

---

ar

ar *key* [*args*] [*posname*] [*count*] *archive* [*files*]

Maintain a group of *files* that are combined into a file *archive*. Used most commonly to create and update library files as used by the loader (ld). Only one key letter can be used, but each may be combined with additional *args* (with no separations between). *posname* is the name of a file in *archive*. When moving or replacing *files*, you can specify that they be placed before or after *posname*.

On all three systems, *key* and *args* can be preceded with a -, as though they were regular options.

Solaris: ar is found in /usr/ccs/bin.

Key

- `d` Delete *files* from *archive*.
- `m` Move *files* to end of *archive*.
- `p` Print *files* in *archive*.
- `q` Append *files* to *archive*.
- `r` Replace *files* in *archive*.
- `t` List the contents of *archive* or list the named *files*.
- `x` Extract contents from *archive* or only the named *files*.

Common Arguments

- `a` Use with `r` or `m` to place *files* in the archive after *posname*.
- `b` Same as a but before *posname*.
- `c` Create *archive* silently.
- `i` Same as `b`.
- `s` Force regeneration of *archive* symbol table (useful after running `strip`).
- `u` Use with `r` to replace only *files* that have changed since being put in *archive*.
- `v` Verbose; print a description.

Solaris and GNU/Linux Argument

- `V` Print version number.

Solaris and Mac OS X Argument

- `T` Truncate long filenames when extracting onto filesystems that don't support long filenames. Without this operation, extracting files with long filenames is an error.

Solaris Argument

- `C` Don't replace existing files of the same name with the one extracted from the archive. Useful with `T`.

GNU/Linux Arguments

- `f` Truncate long filenames.
- `N` Use the *count* parameter. Where multiple entries with the same name are found, use the *count* instance.
- `o` Preserve original timestamps.
- `P` Use full pathname. Useful for non-POSIX-compliant archives.
- `S` Do not regenerate the symbol table.

Mac OS X Argument

- `L` Provide support for long filenames. This is the default.

Example

Update the versions of object files in `mylib.a` with the ones in the current directory. Only files in the `mylib.a` that are also in the current directory are replaced.

```
ar r mylib.a *.o
```

---

as

`as [options] files`

Generate an object file from each specified assembly language source *file*. Object files have the same rootname as source files but replace the `.s` suffix with `.o`. `as` is usually called by compiler driver programs such as `cc` or `gcc`.

Each system has options specific to it, often too many options to comprehend easily. See your local *as*(1) manpage.

Solaris: `as` is found in `/usr/ccs/bin`.

Common Option

`-o objfile`
: Place output in object file *objfile* (default is *file*`.o`).

---

at

`at options1 time [date] [+ increment]`
`at options2 [jobs]`

Execute commands entered on standard input at a specified *time* and optional *date*. (See also **batch** and **crontab**.) End input with *EOF*. *time* can be formed either as a numeric hour (with optional minutes and modifiers) or as a keyword. *date* can be formed either as a month and date, as a day of the week, or as a special keyword. *increment* is a positive integer followed by a keyword. See the following lists for details.

Common Options1

`-f file`
: Execute commands listed in *file*.

`-m` Send mail to user after job is completed.

Solaris Options1

`-c` Use the C shell to execute the job.

`-k` Use the Korn shell to execute the job.

`-p project`
: Schedule the job under *project*.

`-q queuename`
: Schedule the job in *queuename*. Values for *queuename* are the lowercase letters `a` through `z`. Queue `a` is the default queue for `at` jobs. Queue `b` is the queue for `batch` jobs. Queue `c` is the queue for `cron` jobs.

`-s` Use the Bourne shell to execute the job.

`-t time`
: Run the job at *time*, which is in the same format as allowed by `touch`.

GNU/Linux Options1

-c Display the specified jobs on the standard output. This option does not take a time specification.

-V Display the version number.

Common Options2

-l Report all jobs that are scheduled for the invoking user or, if *jobs* are specified, report only for those. See also **atq**.

Solaris and Mac OS X Options2

-r Remove specified *jobs* that were previously scheduled. To remove a job, you must be a privileged user or the owner of the job. Use -l first to see the list of scheduled jobs. See also **atrm**.

GNU/Linux Options2

-d Same as Solaris or Mac OS X -r.

Time

hh:*mm* [*modifiers*]
: Hours can have one or two digits (a 24-hour clock is assumed by default); optional minutes can be given as one or two digits; the colon can be omitted if the format is *h*, *hh*, or *hhmm*; e.g., valid times are 5, 5:30, 0530, 19:45. If modifier am or pm is added, *time* is based on a 12-hour clock. If the keyword zulu is added, times correspond to Greenwich Mean Time (UTC).

midnight|noon|now
: Use any one of these keywords in place of a numeric time. now must be followed by an *increment*.

Date

month num[, *year*]
: *month* is one of the 12 months, spelled out or abbreviated to their first three letters; *num* is the calendar day of the month; *year* is the four-digit year. If the given *month* occurs before the current month, at schedules that month next year.

day One of the seven days of the week, spelled out or abbreviated to their first three letters.

today|tomorrow
: Indicate the current day or the next day. If *date* is omitted, at schedules today when the specified *time* occurs later than the current time; otherwise, at schedules tomorrow.

Increment

Supply a numeric increment if you want to specify an execution time or day *relative* to the current time. The number should precede any of the keywords minute, hour, day, week, month, or year (or their plural forms). The keyword next can be used as a synonym for + 1.

Examples

In typical usage, you run at and input commands that you want executed at a particular time, followed by *EOF*. The GNU/Linux version prompts for input with at>; the other systems do not.

```
$ at 1:00 am tomorrow
at> ./total_up > output
at> mail joe < output
at> <EOT>                Entered by pressing CTRL-D
job 1 at 2003-03-19 01:00
```

The two commands could also be placed in a file and submitted as follows:

```
$ at 1:00 am tomorrow < scriptfile
```

More examples of syntax follow. Note that the first two commands are equivalent.

```
at 1945 pm December 9
at 7:45pm Dec 9
at 3 am Saturday
at now + 5 hours
at noon next day
```

---

atq

atq [*options*] [*users*]

List jobs created by the at command that are still in the queue. Normally, jobs are sorted by the order in which they execute. Specify the *users* whose jobs you want to check. If no *users* are specified, the default is to display all jobs if you're a privileged user; otherwise, only your jobs are displayed.

Solaris Options

-c
: Sort the queue according to the time the at command was given.

-n
: Print only the total number of jobs in queue.

GNU/Linux and Mac OS X Option

-q *queue*
: Show the jobs in queue *queue*.

GNU/Linux Option

-V
: Print the version number to standard error.

Mac OS X Option

-v
: Show jobs that are completed but not yet removed from the queue.

---

atrm

atrm [*options*] [*users* | *jobIDs*]

Remove jobs queued with at that match the specified *jobIDs*. A privileged user may also specify the *users* whose jobs are to be removed.

Solaris Options

-a Remove all jobs belonging to the current user. (A privileged user can remove *all* jobs.)

-f Remove jobs unconditionally, suppressing all information regarding removal.

-i Prompt for y (remove the job) or n (do not remove).

GNU/Linux and Mac OS X Option

-q *queue*
Remove the jobs in queue *queue*.

GNU/Linux Option

-V Print the version number to standard error.

---

autoconf

autoconf [*options*] [*template_file*]

Generate a configuration script from m4 macros defined in *template_file*, if given, or in a configure.ac or configure.in file in the current working directory. The generated script is almost invariably called configure.

Other related programs come as part of autoconf. They are usually invoked automatically by tools in the autoconf suite. They are:

autoreconf	Update configure scripts by running autoconf, autoheader, aclocal, automake, and libtoolize as needed.
autoscan	Create or maintain a preliminary configure.ac file named configure.scan based on source files in specified *directory*, or the current directory if none given.
autoupdate	Update the configure template file *file*, or configure.ac if no file is specified.

URL: *http://www.gnu.org/software/autoconf*.

Options

-d, --debug
Don't remove temporary files.

-f, --force
Replace files generated previously by autoconf.

-i, --initialization
When tracing calls with the -t option, report calls made during initialization.

-I *dir*, --include=*dir*
Search in directory *dir* for input files.

-o *file*, --output=*file*
Save output to *file*.

-t *macro*, --trace=*macro*
Report the list of calls to *macro*.

`-v, --verbose`
: Verbosely print information about the progress of autoconf.

`-W category, --warnings=category`
: Print any warnings related to *category*. Accepted categories are:

all	All warnings.
cross	Cross compilation.
error	Treat warnings as errors.
no-*category*	Turn off warnings for *category*.
none	Turn off all warnings.
obsolete	Obsolete constructs.
syntax	Questionable syntax.

autoheader

`autoheader [options] [template_file]`

Part of GNU autoconf. Generate a template file of C #define statements from m4 macros defined in *template_file*, if given, or in a configure.ac or configure.in file in the current working directory. The generated template file is almost invariably called config.h.in or config.hin.

Options

`-B dir, --prepend-include=dir`
: Prepend directory *dir* to the search path for input files.

`-d, --debug`
: Don't remove temporary files.

`-f, --force`
: Replace files generated previously by autoheader.

`-I dir, --include=dir`
: Append directory *dir* to the search path for input files.

`-o file, --output=file`
: Save output to *file*.

`-v, --verbose`
: Verbosely print information about the progress of autoheader.

`-V, --version`
: Print version number, then exit.

`-W category, --warnings=category`
: Print any warnings related to *category*. Accepted categories are:

all	All warnings.
cross	Cross compilation.
error	Treat warnings as errors.
gnu	GNU coding standards.
no-*category*	Turn off warnings for *category*.
none	Turn off all warnings.
obsolete	Obsolete constructs.
override	User redefinitions of automake variables or rules.
portability	Portability issues.
syntax	Questionable syntax.
unsupported	Unsupported or incomplete features.

automake `automake [options] [template_file]`

GNU automake tool. Creates GNU standards-compliant `Makefile.in` files from `Makefile.am` template files and can be used to ensure that projects contain all the files and installation options required to be standards-compliant.

URL: *http://www.gnu.org/software/automake*.

Options

`-a, --add-missing`
: Add any missing files automake requires to the directory by creating symbolic links to automake's default versions.

`-c, --copy`
: Used with the -a option. Copy missing files instead of creating symbolic links.

`--cygnus`
: Specifies that the project has a Cygnus-style source tree.

`-f, --force-missing`
: Used with the -a option. Replace required files even if a local copy already exists.

`--foreign`
: Treat project as a non-GNU project. Check only for elements required for proper operation.

`--gnits`
: A stricter version of --gnu, performing more checks to comply with GNU project structure rules.

`--gnu`
: Treat project as a GNU project with the GNU project structure.

`-i, --ignore-deps`
: Disable automatic dependency tracking.

`--include-deps`
: Enable automatic dependency tracking.

`--libdir=dir`
: Used with the -a option. Search in directory *dir* for default files.

`--no-force`
: Update only `Makefile.in` files that have updated dependents.

`-v, --verbose`
: List files being read or created by automake.

`-W category, --warnings=category`
: Print any warnings related to *category*. Accepted categories are:

`all`	All warnings.
`error`	Treat warnings as errors.
`gnu`	GNU coding standards.
`no-category`	Turn off warnings for *category*.
`none`	Turn off all warnings.

`obsolete`	Obsolete constructs.
`override`	User redefinitions of automake variables or rules.
`portability`	Portability issues.
`syntax`	Questionable syntax.
`unsupported`	Unsupported or incomplete features.

awk

`awk [options] [program] [var=value ...] [files]`

Use the pattern-matching *program* to process the specified *files*. *program* instructions have the general form:

`pattern { procedure }`

pattern and *procedure* are optional. When specified on the command line, *program* must be enclosed in single quotes to prevent the shell from interpreting its special symbols.

Two versions of `awk` exist: the original, "old" awk from V7 Unix, circa 1979, and "new" awk, from System V Release 4. POSIX `awk` is based on the new one.

On most systems, `awk` is a POSIX-compliant version, except on Solaris, where you must use `/usr/xpg4/bin/awk` instead of `/usr/bin/awk`. Some systems provide `oawk` and `nawk` commands as well. See Chapter 11 for more information (including examples) on `awk`.

banner

`banner characters`

Print *characters* as a poster on the standard output. Each word supplied must contain 10 characters or less.

The `figlet` program is more useful and flexible (*http://www.figlet.org*).

basename

```
basename pathname [suffix]
basename [-a] [-s suffix] pathname ...
```

Given a *pathname*, strip the path prefix and leave just the filename, which is printed on standard output. If specified, a filename *suffix* (e.g., `.c`) is removed also. `basename` is typically invoked via command substitution (`...`) to generate a filename. See also **dirname**.

Solaris: The version of `basename` in `/usr/bin` allows the suffix to be a pattern of the form accepted by `expr`. See the entry for **expr** for more details. The version is `/usr/xpg4/bin` does not treat the suffix specially.

The second syntax is for Mac OS X.

Mac OS X Options

`-a` Treat every argument as a *pathname*, removing the leading components.

`-s suffix`
Use *suffix* as the suffix to remove from each following *pathname*.

Example

Given the following fragment from a Bourne shell script:

```
ofile=output_file
myname="`basename $0`"
echo "$myname: QUITTING: can't open $ofile" 1>&2
exit 1
```

If the script is called `do_it`, the following message would be printed on standard error:

```
do_it: QUITTING: can't open output_file
```


bash

`bash [`*options*`] [`*file* `[`*arguments*`]]`
`sh [`*options*`] [`*file* `[`*arguments*`]]`

Bash is the GNU Project's Bourne Again shell. On GNU/Linux systems and Mac OS X, it is the standard shell, doing double duty as `/bin/sh`. It is also supplied with Solaris. For more information, see Chapter 4.

URL: *http://www.gnu.org/software/bash*.

batch

`batch [`*options*`] [`*time*`]`

Execute commands entered on standard input. End with *EOF*. Unlike `at`, which executes commands at a specific time, `batch` executes commands one after another (waiting for each one to complete). This avoids the potentially high system load caused by running several background jobs at once. The GNU/Linux and Mac OS X versions allow you to specify *time*, which is when the job should run. See also **at**.

On Solaris, `batch` is equivalent to `at -q b -m now`. It takes no arguments, reading commands from standard input. Instead of the original System V version, Mac OS X uses an earlier version of the same `batch` command found on GNU/Linux. The GNU/Linux version has more options.

On Mac OS X, `at`, `atq`, `atrm` and `batch` are disabled by default. See the *at*(1) manpage for more information.

Solaris Option

`-p` *project*
: Run the job under project *project*.

GNU/Linux and Mac OS X Options

`-f` *file*
: Read the job commands from *file* instead of from standard input.

`-m`
: Send mail to the user when the job is done.

GNU/Linux Options

-q *queue*
: Use job queue *queue*. See the entry for **at** for more information.

-v
: Show the time when the job will run.

-V
: Print version information to standard error before reading the job.

Example

```
$ batch
sort data.raw > data.sorted
troff -Tps -mm thesis.mm > bigfile.ps
EOF
```

bc

bc [*options*] [*files*]

Interactively perform arbitrary-precision arithmetic or convert numbers from one base to another. Input can be taken from *files* or read from the standard input. To exit, type quit or *EOF*.

bc is a language (and compiler) whose syntax resembles that of C, but with unlimited-precision arithmetic. bc consists of identifiers, keywords, and symbols. Examples are given at the end. GNU/ Linux and Mac OS X both use GNU bc.

URL: *http://www.gnu.org/software/bc/*.

Common Option

-l, --mathlib
: Make functions from the math library available. This is the only option required by POSIX.

Solaris Options

-c
: Do not invoke dc; compile only. (On Solaris, and on most commercial Unix systems, bc is a preprocessor for dc, so bc normally invokes dc.)

GNU bc Options

-h, --help
: Print help message and exit.

-i, --interactive
: Interactive mode.

-q, --quiet
: Do not display welcome message.

-s, --standard
: Ignore all extensions, and process exactly as in POSIX.

-v, --version
: Print version number.

-w, --warn
: When extensions to POSIX bc are used, print a warning.

Examples

Note in these examples that when you type some quantity (a number or expression), it is evaluated and printed, but assignment statements produce no display:

```
$ bc                    Stat the program
ibase = 8               Octal input
20                      Evaluate this octal number
16                      Terminal displays decimal value
obase = 2               Display output in base 2 instead of base 10
20                      Octal input
10000                   Terminal now displays binary value
ibase = A               Restore base 10 input
scale = 3               Truncate results to three places
8/7                     Evaluate a division
1.001001000             Oops! Forgot to reset output base to 10
obase = 10              Input is decimal now, so "A" isn't needed
8/7
1.142                   Terminal displays result (truncated)
```

The following lines show the use of functions:

```
$ bc                    Start the program
define p(r,n){          Function p uses two arguments
  auto v                v is a local variable
  v = r^n               r raised to the n power
  return(v)}            Value returned
scale = 5
x = p(2.5,2)            x = 2.5 ^ 2
x                       Print value of x
6.25
length(x)               Number of digits
3
scale(x)                Number of places to right of decimal point
2
```

---

biff

`biff [y | n]`

Turn mail notification on or off. With no arguments, `biff` indicates the current status.

When mail notification is turned on, each time you get incoming mail, the bell rings, and the first few lines of each message are displayed.

Solaris: This command is in `/usr/ucb`.

---

bison

`bison [`*`options`*`]` *`file`*

Given a *file* containing a context-free grammar, convert it into tables for subsequent parsing while sending output to *file.c*. This utility is to a large extent compatible with `yacc`, and in fact is named for it. All input files should use the suffix `.y`; output files will use the original prefix.

URL: *http://www.gnu.org/software/bison*.

Options

-b *prefix*, --file-prefix=*prefix*
: Use *prefix* for all output files.

-d *file*, --defines=*file*
: Generate *file* (usually with a .h suffix), producing #define statements that relate bison's token codes to the token names declared by the user.

-h, --help
: Print a help message and exit.

-k, --token-table
: Include token names and values of YYNTOKENS, YYNNTS, YYNRULES, and YYNSTATES in *file.c*.

-l, --no-lines
: Exclude #line constructs from code produced in *file.c*. (Use after debugging is complete.)

-n, --no-parser
: Suppress parser code in output, allowing only declarations. Assemble all translations into a switch statement body and print it to *file*.act.

-o *file*, --output-file=*file*
: Output to *file*.

-p *prefix*, --name-prefix=*prefix*
: Substitute *prefix* for yy in all external symbols.

-r, --raw
: Use bison token numbers, not yacc-compatible translations, in *file.h*.

-t, --debug
: Compile runtime debugging code.

-v, --verbose
: Verbose mode. Print diagnostics and notes about parsing tables to *file*.output.

-V, --version
: Display version number.

-y, --yacc, --fixed-output-files
: Duplicate yacc's conventions for naming output files.

---

bzip2

```
bzip2 [options] filenames
bunzip2 [options] filenames
bzcat [option] filenames
bzip2recover filenames
```

File compression and decompression utility similar to gzip, but uses a different algorithm and encoding method to get better compression. bzip2 replaces each file in *filenames* with a compressed version of the file and with a .bz2 extension appended. bunzip2 decompresses each file compressed by bzip2 (ignoring other files, except to print a warning). bzcat decompresses all specified files to standard output, and `bzip2recover` is used to try to recover data from damaged files.

Additional related commands include `bzcmp`, which compares the contents of bzipped files; `bzdiff`, which creates diff (difference) files from a pair of `bzip` files; `bzgrep`, to search them; and the `bzless` and `bzmore` commands, which apply the `more` and `less` commands to `bunzip2` output as `bzcat` does with the `cat` command. See **cat**, **cmp**, **diff**, **grep**, **less**, and **more** for information on how to use those commands.

URL: *http://www.bzip.org*.

Options

`--`
: End of options; treat all subsequent arguments as filenames.

`-`*dig*
: Set block size to *dig* × 100KB when compressing, where *dig* is a single digit from 1 to 9.

`--best`
: Same as `-9`.

`-c, --stdout`
: Compress or decompress to standard output.

`-d, --decompress`
: Force decompression.

`--fast`
: Same as `-1`.

`-f, --force`
: Force overwrite of output files. Default is not to overwrite. Also forces breaking of hard links to files.

`-k, --keep`
: Keep input files; don't delete them.

`-L, --license, -V, --version`
: Print license and version information and exit.

`-q, --quiet`
: Print only critical messages.

`-s, --small`
: Use less memory, at the expense of speed.

`-t, --test`
: Check the integrity of the files, but don't actually decompress them.

`-v, --verbose`
: Verbose mode. Show the compression ratio for each file processed. Add more -v's to increase the verbosity.

`-z, --compress`
: Force compression, even if invoked as `bunzip2` or `bzcat`.

cal

```
cal [options] [[month] year]
```

With no arguments, print a calendar for the current month. Otherwise, print either a 12-month calendar (beginning with January) for the given *year* or a one-month calendar of the given *month* and *year*. *month* ranges from 1 to 12; *year* ranges from 1 to 9999.

GNU/Linux and Mac OS X Options

`-j` Display Julian dates (days numbered 1 to 365, starting from January 1).

`-y` Display entire year.

GNU/Linux Options

`-1` Print a one-month calendar. This is the default.

`-3` Print a three-month calendar: previous month, current month, and next month.

`-m` Display Monday as the first day of the week.

`-s` Display Sunday as the first day of the week. This is the default.

Examples

```
cal 12 2007
cal 2007 > year_file
```

calendar

```
calendar [options]
```

Read your `calendar` file and display all lines that contain the current date. The `calendar` file is like a memo board. You create the file and add entries like the following:

```
5/4     meeting with design group at 2 pm
may 6   pick up anniversary card on way home
```

When you run `calendar` on May 4, the first line is displayed. `calendar` can be automated by using `crontab` or `at`, or by including it in your startup files, `.profile` or `.login`.

Solaris Option

`-` Allow a privileged user to invoke `calendar` for all users, searching each user's login directory for a file named `calendar`. Entries that match are sent to a user via mail. This feature is intended for use via `cron`. It is not recommended in networked environments with large user bases.

Mac OS X Options

The Mac OS X version of `calendar` has a number of additional features not described here. See *calendar*(1) for more details.

`-a` Same as the Solaris `-` option, above.

`-A` *count*
: Print lines matching today's date, and for the next *count* days forward.

`-B` *count*
: Print lines matching today's date, and for the previous *count* days backward.

`-d` *MMDD*[[*YY*]*YY*]
: Print entries for the given date. The year may be specified using either two or four digits.

`-f` *file*
: Use *file* instead of `$HOME/calendar`.

`-F` *daynum*
: Day number *daynum* is the "Friday," i.e., the day before the weekend starts. The default is `5`.

`-l` *count*
: Look ahead *count* days and display the entries for that date also.

`-t` *dd*[*.mm*[*.yyyy*]]
: For testing, set the date to the given value.

`-w` *ndays*
: Add *ndays* to the number of "lookahead" days if and only if the originally provided day is a Friday. The default value is `2`, which causes calendars for Fridays to also print entries for the following weekend.

`-W` *count*
: Like `-A`, but do not include weekends in the count of days to look ahead.

---

cancel

`cancel [`*options*`] [`*printer*`]`

Cancel print requests made with `lp`. The request can be specified by its ID, by the *printer* on which it is currently printing, or by the username associated with the request (only privileged users can cancel another user's print requests). Use `lpstat` to determine either the *id* or the *printer* to cancel.

Common Options

id Cancel print request *id*.

`-u` *user*
: Cancel request associated with *user*.

GNU/Linux and Mac OS X Options

GNU/Linux and Mac OS X use CUPS, the Common Unix Printing System. See *http://www.cups.org* for more information. Besides the above options, the CUPS `cancel` command accepts the following:

`-a` Remove all jobs from the given destination.

`-h` *host*
: Treat *host* as the name of the print server. The default is `localhost` or the value of the CUPS_SERVER environment variable.

---

cat

`cat [`*options*`] [`*files*`]`

Read one or more *files* and print them on standard output. Read standard input if no *files* are specified or if `-` is specified as one of the files; end input with *EOF*. Use the > shell operator to combine several files into a new file; >> appends files to an existing file.

Solaris and Mac OS X Options

`-b` Like `-n`, but don't number blank lines.

`-e` Print a `$` to mark the end of each line. Must be used with `-v`.

`-n` Number lines.

`-s` Suppress messages about nonexistent files. (Note: on some systems, `-s` squeezes out extra blank lines.)

`-t` Print each tab as `^I` and each form feed as `^L`. Must be used with `-v`.

`-u` Print output as unbuffered (default is buffered in blocks or screen lines).

`-v` Display control characters and other nonprinting characters.

GNU/Linux Options

`-A, --show-all`
Same as `-vET`.

`-b, --number-nonblank`
Number all nonblank output lines, starting with 1.

`-e` Same as `-vE`.

`-E, --show-ends`
Print $ at the end of each line.

`-n, --number`
Number all output lines, starting with 1.

`-s, --squeeze-blank`
Squeeze down multiple blank lines to one blank line.

`-t` Same as `-vT`.

`-T, --show-tabs`
Print TAB characters as ^I.

`-u` Ignored; retained for Unix compatibility.

`-v, --show-nonprinting`
Display control and nonprinting characters, with the exception of LINEFEED and TAB.

Examples

`cat ch1`	*Display a file*
`cat ch1 ch2 ch3 > all`	*Combine files*
`cat note5 >> notes`	*Append to a file*
`cat > temp1`	*Create file at terminal; end with EOF*
`cat > temp2 << STOP`	*Create file at terminal; end with STOP*

---

cc

`cc [`*`options`*`]` *`files`*

Compile one or more C source files (`.c`), assembler source files (`.s`), or preprocessed C source files (`.i`). `cc` automatically invokes the loader `ld` (unless `-c` is supplied). In some cases, `cc` generates an object file having a .o suffix and a corresponding root name. By default, output is placed in a.out. cc accepts additional system-specific options.

General Notes

- On GNU/Linux and Mac OS X, cc is just a frontend for GCC, the GNU Compiler Collection.
- Options for cc vary wildly across Unix systems. We have chosen here to document only those options that are commonly available. You will need to check your local documentation for complete information.
- Usually, cc passes any unrecognized options to the loader, ld.

Solaris Notes

- Solaris does not come with Sun's C compiler. If you purchase Sun's compiler, it will be installed in /opt/SUNWspro/bin. You should add that directory to your PATH. Solaris does make GCC available in /usr/sfw/bin, so if you installed the optional software, you may choose to use GCC instead.
- The other tools that the C and C++ compilers need (the assembler and loader) are found in /usr/ccs/bin. You should add that directory to your PATH also.

Options

-c
: Suppress loading and keep any object files that were produced.

-D*name*[=*def*]
: Supply a #define directive, defining *name* to be *def* or, if no *def* is given, the value 1.

-E
: Run only the macro preprocessor, sending results to standard output.

-g
: Generate more symbol-table information needed for debuggers.

-I*dir*
: Search for include files in directory *dir* (in addition to standard locations). Supply a -I for each new *dir* to be searched.

-l*name*
: Link source *file* with library files lib*name*.so or lib*name*.a.

-L*dir*
: Like -I, but search *dir* for library archives.

-o *file*
: Send object output to *file* instead of to a.out.

-O
: Optimize object code (produced from .c or .i files). Some compilers accept an additional argument to -O specifying the optimization level.

-p
: Generate benchmark code to count the times each routine is called. File mon.out is created, so prof can be used later to produce an execution profile.

-pg
: Provide profile information for use with gprof.

-P Run only the preprocessor and place the result in *file*.i.

-S Compile (and optimize, if -O is supplied), but don't assemble or load; assembler output is placed in *file*.s.

-U*name*
Remove definition of name, as if through an #undef directive.

Example

Compile xpop.c and load it with the X libraries:

```
cc -o xpop xpop.c -lXaw -lXmu -lXt -lX11
```

cd

cd [*dir*]

Change directory. cd is a built-in shell command. See Chapters 4 and 5.

chgrp

chgrp [*options*] *newgroup files*

Change the group of one or more *files* to *newgroup*. *newgroup* is either a group ID number or a group name located in /etc/group. You must own the file or be a privileged user to succeed with this command.

Common Options

-f, --quiet, --silent
Do not print error messages about files that can't be changed.

-h, --no-dereference
Change the group on symbolic links. Normally, chgrp acts on the file *referenced* by a symbolic link, not on the link itself.

-R, --recursive
Recursively descend through the directory, including subdirectories and symbolic links, setting the specified group ID as it proceeds. The last of -H, -L, and -P take effect when used with -R.

GNU/Linux and Mac OS X Options

-H When used with -R, if a command-line argument is a symbolic link to a directory, recursively traverse the directory. In other words, follow the link.

-L When used with -R, if *any* symbolic link points to a directory, recursively traverse the directory.

-P When used with -R, do not follow any symbolic links. This is the default.

-v, --verbose
Verbosely describe ownership changes.

GNU/Linux Options

-c, --changes
Print information about files that are changed.

--dereference
Change the group of the file pointed to by a symbolic link, not the group of the symbolic link itself. This is the default.

--no-preserve-root
: Do not treat the root directory, /, specially (the default).

--preserve-root
: Do not operate recursively on /, the root directory.

--reference=*filename*
: Change the group to that associated with *filename*. In this case, *newgroup* is not specified.

chmod

`chmod [options] mode files`

Change the access *mode* of one or more *files*. Only the owner of a file or a privileged user may change its mode. Create *mode* by concatenating the characters from *who*, *opcode*, and *permission*. *who* is optional (if omitted, default is a); choose only one *opcode*.

Common Options

-f, --quiet, --silent
: Do not print error messages about files that cannot be changed.

-R, --recursive
: Recursively descend through the directory, including subdirectories and symbolic links, setting the specified group ID as it proceeds. The last of -H, -L, and -P takes effect when used with -R.

GNU/Linux and Mac OS X Option

-v, --verbose
: Verbosely describe ownership changes.

GNU/Linux Options

-c, --changes
: Print information about files that are changed.

--no-preserve-root
: Do not treat the root directory, /, specially (the default).

--preserve-root
: Do not operate recursively on /, the root directory.

--reference=*filename*
: Change the group to that associated with *filename*. In this case, *newgroup* is not specified.

Mac OS X Options

+a, +a#, -a, =a#
: Parse, order, remove or rewrite ACL entries. See the *chmod*(1) manpage for more information.

-C
: Exit nonzero if any files have ACLs in noncanonical order.

-E
: Read new ACL information from standard input. If it parses correctly, use it to replace the existing ACL information.

-H
: When used with -R, if a command-line argument is a symbolic link to a directory, recursively traverse the directory.

`-i` Remove the "inherited" bit from all entries in the ACLs of the given files.

`-I` Remove all "inherited" entries in the ACLs of the given files.

`-L` When used with `-R`, if any symbolic link points to a directory, recursively traverse the directory.

`-P` When used with `-R`, do not follow any symbolic links. This is the default.

Who

`u` User
`g` Group
`o` Other
`a` All (default)

Opcode

`+` Add permission
`-` Remove permission
`=` Assign permission (and remove permission of the unspecified fields)

Permission

`r` Read
`w` Write
`x` Execute
`s` Set user (or group) ID
`t` Sticky bit; save text mode (file) or prevent removal of files by nonowners (directory)
`u` User's present permission
`g` Group's present permission
`o` Other's present permission
`l` Mandatory locking

Alternatively, specify permissions by a three-digit sequence. The first digit designates owner permission; the second, group permission; and the third, others permission. Permissions are calculated by adding the following octal values:

`4` Read
`2` Write
`1` Execute

Note: a fourth digit may precede this sequence. This digit assigns the following modes:

`4` Set user ID on execution
`2` Set group ID on execution or set mandatory locking
`1` Sticky bit

Examples

Add execute-by-user permission to *file*:

```
chmod u+x file
```

Either of the following assigns read-write-execute permission by owner (7), read-execute permission by group (5), and execute-only permission by others (1) to *file*

```
chmod 751 file
chmod u=rwx,g=rx,o=x file
```

Any one of the following assigns read-only permission to *file* for everyone:

```
chmod =r file
chmod 444 file
chmod a-wx,a+r file
```

Set the user ID, assign read-write-execute permission by owner, and assign read-execute permission by group and others:

```
chmod 4755 file
```


---

chown

`chown [options] newowner[:newgroup] files`

Change the ownership of one or more *files* to *newowner*. *newowner* is either a user ID number or a login name located in `/etc/passwd`. The optional *newgroup* is either a group ID number (GID) or a group name located in the `/etc/group` file. When *newgroup* is supplied, the behavior is to change the ownership of one or more *files* to *newowner* and make it belong to *newgroup*.

Note: some systems accept a period as well as the colon for separating *newowner* and *newgroup*. The colon is mandated by POSIX; the period is accepted for compatibility with older BSD systems.

Common Options

`-f, --quiet, --silent`
: Do not print error messages about files that cannot be changed.

`-h, --no-dereference`
: Change the owner on symbolic links. Normally, `chown` acts on the file *referenced* by a symbolic link, not on the link itself.

`-R, --recursive`
: Recursively descend through the directory, including subdirectories and symbolic links, setting the specified group ID as it proceeds. The last of `-H`, `-L`, and `-P` takes effect when used with `-R`.

GNU/Linux and Mac OS X Options

`-H`
: When used with `-R`, if a command-line argument is a symbolic link to a directory, recursively traverse the directory. In other words, follow the link.

`-L`
: When used with `-R`, if *any* symbolic link points to a directory, recursively traverse the directory.

`-P` When used with `-R`, do not follow any symbolic links. This is the default.

`-v, --verbose`
: Verbosely describe ownership changes.

GNU/Linux Options

`-c, --changes`
: Print information about files that are changed.

`--dereference`
: Change the group of the file pointed to by a symbolic link, not the group of the symbolic link itself. This is the default.

`--from=`*`old-owner`*`:`*`old-group`*
: Change the owner/group of the file to the new values only if the original values of the owner/group match *old-owner* and *old-group*. Either one may be omitted.

`--no-preserve-root`
: Do not treat the root directory, `/`, specially (the default).

`--preserve-root`
: Do not operate recursively on `/`, the root directory.

`--reference=`*`filename`*
: Change the owner to that associated with *filename*. In this case, *newowner* is not specified.

---

cksum

`cksum [`*`files`*`]`

Calculate and print a cyclic redundancy check (CRC) sum for each file. The CRC algorithm is based on the polynomial used for Ethernet packets. For each file, `cksum` prints a line of the form:

`sum count filename`

Here, *sum* is the CRC, *count* is the number of bytes in the file, and *filename* is the file's name. The name is omitted if standard input is used.

Mac OS X Option

`-o` *`algorithm`*
: Use a historical algorithm for computing the checksum. Valid values are `1`, for the historic BSD 16-bit `sum` checksum, `2`, for the historic System V 32-bit `sum` checksum, and `3` for a 32-bit CRC that is different from the default algorithm.

---

clear

`clear [`*`term`*`]`

Clear the terminal display. The Solaris version allows an optional terminal name indicating the terminal's type. Normally this value is taken from the TERM environment variable.

cmp

```
cmp [options] file1 file2 [skip1 [skip2]]
```

Compare *file1* with *file2*. Use standard input if *file1* or *file2* is -. (See also **comm** and **diff**.) *skip1* and *skip2* are optional offsets in the files at which the comparison is to start. The exit codes are as follows:

0 Files are identical.
1 Files are different.
2 Files are inaccessible.

Common Options

`-l, --verbose`
: Print offsets and codes of all differing bytes.

`-s, --quiet, --silent`
: Work silently; print nothing, but return exit codes.

GNU/Linux and Mac OS X Options

`-b, --print-bytes`
: Print differing bytes.

`-i num1[:num2], --ignore-initial=num1[:num2]`
: Ignore the first *num1* bytes of input. With *num2*, skip *num1* bytes from the first file and *num2* bytes from the second file.

`-n max, --bytes=max`
: Read and compare no more than *max* bytes.

Example

Print a message if two files are the same (exit code is 0):

```
cmp -s old new && echo 'no changes'
```

comm

```
comm [options] file1 file2
```

Compare lines common to the sorted files *file1* and *file2*. Three-column output is produced: lines unique to *file1*, lines unique to *file2*, and lines common to both *files*. comm is similar to diff in that both commands compare two files. In addition, comm can be used like uniq; that is, comm selects duplicate or unique lines between *two* sorted files, whereas uniq selects duplicate or unique lines within the *same* sorted file.

Options

`-` Read the standard input.

`-1` Suppress printing of Column 1.

`-2` Suppress printing of Column 2.

`-3` Suppress printing of Column 3.

`-12` Print only lines in Column 3 (lines common to *file1* and *file2*).

`-13` Print only lines in Column 2 (lines unique to *file2*).

`-23` Print only lines in Column 1 (lines unique to *file1*).

Example

Compare two lists of top-10 movies and display items that appear in both lists:

```
comm -12 shalit_top10 maltin_top10
```

---

cp

```
cp [options] file1 file2
cp [options] files directory
```

Copy *file1* to *file2*, or copy one or more *files* to the same names under *directory*. If the destination is an existing file, the file is overwritten; if the destination is an existing directory, the file is copied into the directory (the directory is *not* overwritten). If one of the inputs is a directory, use the `-r` option.

Common Options

`-f, --force`
: Remove existing files in the destination.

`-i, --interactive`
: Prompt for confirmation (`y` for yes) before overwriting an existing file.

`-p`
: Preserve the original file's permissions, ownership, and timestamps in the new file.

`-r, -R, --recursive`
: Copy directories recursively. Solaris `-R` replicates named pipes, instead of reading from them.

GNU/Linux and Mac OS X Options

`-H`
: When used with `-R`, if a command-line argument is a symbolic link to a directory, recursively traverse the directory.

`-L, --dereference`
: When used with `-R`, if any symbolic link points to a directory, recursively traverse the directory.

`-P`
: When used with `-R`, do not follow any symbolic links. This is the default.

`-v, --verbose`
: Before copying, print the name of each file.

Solaris Option

`-@`
: Copy extended attributes (ACLs, etc.) along with normal attributes.

GNU/Linux Options

`-a, --archive`
: Preserve attributes of original files where possible. The same as `-dpR`.

`-b`
: Back up files that would otherwise be overwritten.

`--backup[=`*`backup-method`*`]`
: Like `-b`, but accepts an additional specification controlling how the backup copy should be made. Valid arguments are:

`none`, `off`	Never make numbered backups.
`t`, `numbered`	Always make numbered backups.
`nil`, `existing`	Make numbered backups of files that already have them; otherwise, make simple backups.
`never`, `simple`	Always make simple backups.

`--copy-contents`
: Copy the contents of special files when doing a recursive copy.

`-d` Same as `--no-dereference --preserve=links`.

`-l, --link`
: Make hard links, not copies, of nondirectories.

`--no-dereference`
: Do not dereference symbolic links; preserve hard link relationships between source and copy.

`--no-preserve[=`*`items`*`]`
: Do not preserve the given *items* when copying. See `--preserve` for more information.

`--parents`
: Preserve intermediate directories in source. The last argument must be the name of an existing directory. For example, the command:

```
cp --parents jphekman/book/ch1 newdir
```

copies the file `jphekman/book/ch1` to the file `newdir/jphekman/book/ch1`, creating intermediate directories as necessary.

`--preserve[=`*`items`*`]`
: Preserve the given *items* when copying. Possible items are `all`, `link`, `mode`, `mode`, `ownership`, and `timestamps`. Default is same as `-p`.

`--remove-destination`
: Remove each destination file before trying to open it.

`--reply=`*`how`*
: Control handling of queries about removing existing files. Valid values for *how* are yes, `no`, and `query`.

`-s, --symbolic-link`
: Make symbolic links instead of copying. Source filenames must be absolute.

`--sparse=`*`when`*
: Control handling of copying of sparse files. Valid values for *when* are `auto`, `always`, and `never`.

`--strip-trailing-slashes`
: Remove trailing slashes from source file names.

`-S` *`backup-suffix`*`, --suffix=`*`backup-suffix`*
: Set suffix to be appended to backup files. This may also be set with the SIMPLE_BACKUP_SUFFIX environment variable.

The default is ~. You need to explicitly include a period if you want one before the suffix (for example, specify .bak, not bak).

--target-directory=*dir*
: Copy all files into the directory *dir*.

-u, --update
: Do not copy a file to an existing destination with the same or newer modification time.

-x, --one-file-system
: Ignore subdirectories on other filesystems.

-Z *context*, --context=*context*
: Set the security context of the file to *context*. SELinux only.

Mac OS X Options

-n
: Do not overwrite an existing file.

Example

Copy two files to their parent directory (keep the same names):

```
cp outline memo ..
```

---

cpio

cpio *control_options* [*options*]

Copy file archives in from, or out to, tape or disk, or to another location on the local machine. Each of the three control options, -i, -o, or -p accepts different options. (See also **pax** and **tar**.)

cpio -i [*options*] [*patterns*]
cpio --extract [*options*] [*patterns*]
: Copy in (extract) files whose names match selected *patterns*. Each pattern can include filename metacharacters from the Bourne shell. (Patterns should be quoted or escaped so that they are interpreted by cpio, not by the shell.) If no pattern is used, all files are copied in. During extraction, existing files are not overwritten by older versions in the archive (unless -u is specified).

cpio -o [*options*]
cpio --create [*options*]
: Copy out a list of files whose names are given on the standard input.

cpio -p [*options*] *directory*
cpio --create [*options*] *directory*
: Copy (pass) files to another directory on the same system. Destination pathnames are interpreted relative to the named *directory*.

Comparison of Valid Options

Options available to the -i, -o, and -p options are shown respectively in the first, second, and third row below. (The - is omitted for clarity.)

```
-i:    6   b B c C d E f   H I k   m M n r R s S t u v V z Z
-o: 0 a A   B c C         F H     L   M O             v V z Z
-p: 0 a           d             l L m   P   R       u v V
```

Common Options

`-a, --reset-access-time`
: Reset access times of input files.

`-A, --append`
: Append files to an archive (must use with `-O` or `-F`).

`-b, --swap`
: Swap bytes and half-words to convert between big-endian and little-endian 32-bit integers. Words are four bytes.

`-B`
: Block input or output using 5120 bytes per record (default is 512 bytes per record).

`-c`
: Read or write header information as ASCII characters; useful when source and destination machines are different types.

`-C` *n*, `--io-size=`*n*
: Like `-B`, but block size can be any positive integer *n*.

`-d, --make-directories`
: Create directories as needed.

`-E` *file*, `--pattern-file=`*file*
: Extract filenames listed in *file* from the archive.

`-f, --nonmatching`
: Reverse the sense of copying; copy all files *except* those that match *patterns*.

`-H` *type*, `--format=`*type*
: Read or write header information according to *format*. Values for format are `bar` (`bar` format header and file, read-only, Solaris only), `crc` (ASCII header containing expanded device numbers), `odc` (ASCII header containing small device numbers), `ustar` (IEEE/P1003 Data Interchange Standard header), or `tar` (`tar` header). Solaris also allows `CRC`, `TAR`, and `USTAR`.

  Mac OS X allows `tar` and `ustar`, as well as `bcpio` for the original binary `cpio` format, `cpio` for the original octal character (ASCII) `cpio` format, and `sv4cpio` for the System V Release 4 hexadecimal character format.

  GNU/Linux allows `tar` and `ustar`, as well as `bin` for the original binary format, `crc` for the System V Release 4 format with an additional checksum, `hpbin` for the obsolete binary format used by the HP-UX `cpio`, `hpodc` for HP-UX's portable format, `newc` for the System V Release 4 portable (ASCII) format, and `odc` for the old POSIX.1 portable (ASCII) format.

`-I` *file*
: Read *file* as an input archive. As with `-F`, GNU/Linux allows *file* to specify a remote archive.

`-l, --link`
: Link files instead of copying. Can be used only with `-p`.

`-L, --dereference`
: Follow symbolic links.

`-m, --preserve-modification-time`
: Retain previous file-modification time.

`-O` *`file`*
: Direct the output to *file*. As with `-F`, GNU/Linux allows *file* to specify a remote archive.

`-r, --rename`
: Rename files interactively.

`-R` *`ID`*`, -owner` *`ID`*
: Reassign file ownership and group information of extracted files to the user whose login ID is *ID* (privileged users only). GNU/Linux allows *ID* to be of the form `[`*`user`*`][`*`sep group`*`]`, i.e., a user or group name or ID or both. If both, *sep* may be a colon or period. Use a leading separator for just a group. For example: `arnold:users`, `arnold`, or `:users`.

`-s, --swap-bytes`
: Swap bytes of each two-byte half-word.

`-S, --swap-half-words`
: Swap half-words of each four-byte word.

`--sparse`
: For `-o` and `-p`, write files that have large blocks of zeros as sparse files.

`-t, --list`
: Print a table of contents of the input (create no files). When used with the `-v` option, resembles output of `ls -l`.

`-u, --unconditional`
: Unconditional copy; old files can overwrite new ones.

`-v, --verbose`
: Print a list of filenames processed.

`-V, --dot`
: Print a dot for each file read or written (this shows `cpio` at work without cluttering the screen).

Solaris and GNU/Linux Option

`-M` *`msg`*`, --message=`*`msg`*
: Print *msg* when switching media. Use variable `%d` in the message as a numeric ID for the next medium. `-M` is valid only with `-I` or `-O`.

Solaris and Mac OS X Option

`-6`
: Process a PWB Unix Sixth Edition archive format file. Useful only with the `-i` option, mutually exclusive with `-c` and `-H`. Solaris and Mac OS X only.

GNU/Linux and Mac OS X Option

`-F` *`file`*`, --file=`*`file`*
: Same as `-O`. The GNU/Linux version allows *file* to be of the form *`user@host`*`:`*`file`* for accessing a remote archive. The *`user@`* part is optional.

Solaris Options

-k Skip corrupted file headers and I/O errors.

-P Preserve ACLs. Can be used only with -p.

-@ With -o, include extended attributes in the archive. These attributes are stored as special files in the archive. These attributes may be restored upon extraction by using -@ with -i.

GNU/Linux Options

--blocksize=*size*
: Set input or output blocksize to *size* × 512 bytes.

--force-local
: Assume that *file* (provided by -F, -I, or -O) is a local file, even if it contains a colon (:) indicating a remote file.

-n, --numeric-uid-gid
: When verbosely listing contents, show user ID and group ID numerically.

--no-absolute-filenames
: Create all copied-in files relative to the current directory.

--no-preserve-owner
: Make all copied files owned by yourself, instead of the owner of the original. Can be used only if you are a privileged user.

--only-verify-crc
: For a CRC-format archive, verify the CRC of each file; don't actually copy the files in.

--quiet
: Don't print the number of blocks copied.

--rsh-command=*command*
: Tell mt to use *command* for accessing remote archives instead of rsh or ssh.

-0, --null
: (Digit zero.) With -o or -p, read a list of filenames terminated with a NUL byte (all zeros) instead of a newline. This allows archiving files whose names contain newlines. GNU find can produce such a list of names.

Mac OS X Options

-z Compress the archive using gzip.

-Z Compress the archive using the old compress command.

Examples

Generate a list of old files using find; use list as input to cpio:

```
find . -name "*.old" -print | cpio -ocBv > /dev/rmt/0
```

Restore from a tape drive all files whose name contains save (subdirectories are created if needed):

```
cpio -icdv "*save*" < /dev/rmt/0
```

To move a directory tree:

```
find . -depth -print | cpio -padml /mydir
```

crontab

```
crontab [file]
crontab options [user]
```

View, install, or uninstall your current *crontab* file. On Mac OS X and GNU/Linux, a privileged user can run crontab for another user by supplying -u *user*. On Solaris, supply *user* following one of -e, -l, or -r.

A crontab file is a list of commands, one per line, that executes automatically at a given time. Numbers are supplied before each command to specify the execution time. The numbers appear in five fields, as follows:

Minute	0-59
Hour	0-23
Day of month	1-31
Month	1-12
Day of week	0-6, with 0 = Sunday

Use a comma between multiple values, a hyphen to indicate a range, and an asterisk to indicate all possible values. For example, assuming the crontab entries below:

```
59 3 * * 5          find / -print | backup_program
0 0 1,15 * *        echo "Timesheets due" | mail user
```

The first command backs up the system files every Friday at 3:59 a.m., and the second command mails a reminder on the 1st and 15th of each month.

Common Options

-e
Edit the user's current crontab file (or create one).

-l
List the user's file in the crontab directory.

-r
Delete the user's file in the crontab directory.

GNU/Linux and Mac OS X Option

-u *user*
Indicate which *user*'s crontab file will be acted upon.

csh

```
csh [options] [file] [arguments]
```

Command interpreter that uses syntax resembling C. csh (the C shell) executes commands from a terminal or a file. On Mac OS X and most GNU/Linux systems, /bin/csh is a link to tcsh, an enhanced version of the shell. Solaris supplies tcsh as a separate program. See also **tcsh**. See Chapter 5 for information on tcsh, including command-line options.

csplit

```
csplit [options] file arguments
```

Separate *file* into sections and place sections in files named xx00 through xx*n* (*n* < 100), breaking *file* at each pattern specified in *arguments*. A filename of - reads from standard input. See also **split**.

Common Options

`-f` *prefix*, `--prefix=`*prefix*
: Name new files *prefix*`00` through *prefixN* (default is `xx00` through `xx`*n*).

`-k, --keep-files`
: Keep newly created files, even when an error occurs (which would normally remove these files). This is useful when you need to specify an arbitrarily large repeat argument, {*n*}, and you don't want the "out of range" error to remove the new files.

`-n` *num*, `--digits=`*num*
: Use output filenames with numbers *num* digits long. The default is 2.

`-s, --quiet, --silent`
: Suppress all character counts.

GNU/Lnux Options

`-b` *suffix*, `--suffix-format=`*suffix*
: Append *suffix* to output filename. This option causes `-n` to be ignored. *suffix* must specify how to convert the binary integer to readable form by including one of the following: `%d`, `%i`, `%u`, `%o`, `%x`, or `%X`. The value of *suffix* determines the format for numbers as follows:

`%d`, `%i`	Signed decimal.
`%u`	Unsigned decimal.
`%o`	Octal.
`%x`, `%X`	Hexadecimal.

`-q`
: Same as `-s`.

`-z, --elide-empty-files`
: Do not create empty output files. However, number as if those files had been created.

Arguments

Any one or a combination of the following expressions. Arguments containing blanks or other special characters should be surrounded by single quotes.

/*expr*/
: Create file from the current line up to the line containing the regular expression *expr*. This argument takes an optional suffix of the form +*n* or -*n*, where *n* is the number of lines below or above *expr*.

%*expr*%
: Same as /*expr*/, except that no file is created for lines previous to the line containing *expr*.

num
: Create file from current line up to line number *num*.

{*n*}
: Repeat argument *n* times. May follow any of the above arguments. Files will split at instances of *expr* or in blocks of *num* lines. On GNU/Linux, if * is given instead of *n*, repeat argument until input is exhausted.

Examples

Create up to 20 chapter files from the file `novel`:

```
csplit -k -f chap. novel '%CHAPTER%' '{20}'
```

Create up to 100 address files (`xx00` through `xx99`), each four lines long, from a database named `address_list`:

```
csplit -k address_list 4 {99}
```

---

ctags

`ctags [options] files`

Create a list of function and macro names that are defined in the specified C, Pascal, FORTRAN, yacc, or `lex` source *files*. Solaris `ctags` can also process C++ source files. The output list (named `tags` by default) contains lines of the form:

```
name        file        context
```

where *name* is the function or macro name, *file* is the source file in which *name* is defined, and *context* is a search pattern that shows the line of code containing *name*. After the list of tags is created, you can invoke `vi` on any file and type:

```
:set tags=tagsfile
:tag name
```

This switches the `vi` editor to the source file associated with the *name* listed in *tagsfile* (which you specify with `-f`).

GNU/Linux systems often ship with the *Exuberant ctags* (see *http://ctags.sourceforge.net*). That version also understands C++, Java, Perl, Python, `flex`, and `bison`. The Exuberant ctags accepts many more options not listed here, see *ctags*(1) for more information. Of particular note is the `-e` option, which creates tag files usable with Emacs.

Options

`-a`
: Append tag output to existing list of tags.

`-B`
: *context* uses backward search patterns.

`-d`
: Create tags for `#define` macros that don't take arguments (symbolic constants). Mac OS X only.

`-f` *tagsfile*
: Place output in *tagsfile* (default is `tags`).

`-F`
: *context* uses forward search patterns (default).

`-t`
: Include C `typedef`s as tags.

`-u`
: Update tags file to reflect new locations of functions (e.g., when functions are moved to a different source file). Old tags are deleted; new tags are appended.

`-v`
: Produce a listing (index) of each function, source file, and page number (1 page = 64 lines). `-v` is intended to create a file for use with `vgrind` (a `troff` preprocessor for pretty-printing source code).

`-w`
: Suppress warning messages.

`-x`
: Produce a listing of each function, its line number, source file, and context.

Examples

Store tags in Taglist for all C programs:

```
ctags -f Taglist *.c
```

Update tags and store in Newlist:

```
ctags -u -f Newlist *.c
```


curl

curl [*options*] [*URL* ...]

curl retrieves files from the Internet, most often using FTP or HTTP. It has a plethora of options, making it difficult to use easily. One of curl's main strengths is that it may be used to automate file uploading. See also **wget**.

URLs: *http://curl.haxx.se* and *ftp://ftp.sunet.se/pub/www/utilities/curl/*.

Primary Options

For many of the options, using them multiple times toggles the behavior, turning a particular mode off if it was on or vice versa.

--connect-timeout *seconds*
: Limit the connection phase to *seconds* seconds.

-C *offset*, --continue-at *offset*
: Continue a previous file transfer at *offset* bytes. May be used with both downloads and uploads. Use -C - to have curl automatically determine the offset.

--create-dirs
: When used with -o, create local directories as needed.

--disable-epsv
: Do not use the EPSV FTP command for passive FTP transfers. Normally, curl tries the EPSV command before the PASV command.

-f, --fail
: Fail silently upon HTTP server errors. Mainly useful for scripts.

--ftp-pasv
: Use the FTP PASV command. This is the default.

-h, --help
: Print a (relatively) brief help message.

-K *configfile*, --config *configfile*
: Use *configfile* as the configuration file, instead of the default $HOME/.curlrc. Use - to read configuration information from standard input.

--limit-rate *speed*
: Limit transfers to *speed*. The default units is bytes per second, but you may use a trailing k or K for kilobytes, m or M for megabytes, or g or G for gigabytes. The -Y option overrides this option.

--max-filesize *bytes*
: If curl can tell that a file exceeds *bytes* size, it will not download the file. Otherwise, this option has no effect.

`-m seconds, --max-time seconds`
: Do not exceed *seconds* for the entire operation. This prevents batch jobs from hanging due to slow networks or dead links.

`-M, --manual`
: Display the full help text (over 2400 lines!), in the form of a manpage.

`-o file, --output file`
: Write the output to *file* instead of to standard output. See the manpage for more details. See also `--create-dirs`.

`-q`
: When used as the first parameter, do not read `$HOME/.curlrc`.

`-s, --silent`
: Silent mode; do not print a progress meter or any error messages.

`-S, --show-error`
: With `-s`, do display error messages.

`-T file, --upload-file file`
: Upload *file* to the *URL* named on the command line. Use `-` to read standard input. The *URL* must end with a `/` if it's a directory, in which case `curl` will use *file* as the name of the file to create in the remote directory.

`-u user:password, --user user:password`
: Supply *user* and *password* to the server for authentication.

`-U user:password, --proxy-user user:password`
: Supply *user* and *password* for proxy authentication.

`--url URL`
: Retrieve *URL*. This option is mainly for use in a configuration file.

`-v, --verbose`
: Be verbose during file retrieval. Mainly for debugging.

`-V, --version`
: Print version and supported-feature information.

`-x proxyhost[:port], --proxy proxyhost[:port]`
: Use the given *host* and optional *port* as the HTTP proxy. The default port is 1080.

`-#, --progress-bar`
: Print progress information as a progress bar instead of as statistics.

See the manpage for a description of the other options.

---

cut

`cut options [files]`

Select a list of columns or fields from one or more *files*. Either `-c` or `-f` must be specified. *list* is a sequence of integers. Use a comma between separate values and a hyphen to specify a range (e.g., `1-10,15,20` or `50-`). See also **paste** and **join**.

Common Options

`-b` *list*, `--bytes` *list*
: This *list* specifies byte positions, not character positions. This is important when multibyte characters are used. With this option, lines should be 1023 bytes or less in size.

`-c` *list*, `--characters` *list*
: Cut the character positions identified in *list*.

`-d` *c*, `--delimiter` *c*
: Use with `-f` to specify field delimiter as character *c* (default is tab); special characters (e.g., a space) must be quoted.

`-f` *list*, `--fields` *list*
: Cut the fields identified in *list*.

`-n` Do not split characters. When used with `-b`, `cut` doesn't split multibyte characters.

`-s`, `--only-delimited`
: Use with `-f` to suppress lines without delimiters.

GNU/Linux Option

`--output-delimiter=`*string*
: Use *string* as the output delimiter. By default, the output delimiter is the same as the input delimiter.

Examples

Extract usernames and real names from `/etc/passwd`:

```
cut -d: -f1,5 /etc/passwd
```

Find out who is logged on, but list only login names:

```
who | cut -d" " -f1
```

Cut characters in the fourth column of *file*, and paste them back as the first column in the same file. Send the results to standard output:

```
cut -c4 file | paste - file
```

---

date

`date [`*option*`] [+`*format*`]`
`date [`*options*`] [`*string*`]`

In the first form, print the current date and time, specifying an optional display *format*. In the second form, a privileged user can set the current date by supplying a numeric *string*. *format* can consist of literal text strings (blanks must be quoted) as well as field descriptors, whose values will appear as described below (the listing shows some logical groupings).

Format

`%n` Insert a newline.
`%t` Insert a tab.

`%m` Month of year (01–12).
`%d` Day of month (01–31).

`%y` Last two digits of year (00–99).
`%D` Date in `%m/%d/%y` format.

`%b` Abbreviated month name.
`%e` Day of month (1–31); pad single digits with a space.
`%Y` Four-digit year (e.g., 1996).
`%g` Week-based year within century (00–99).
`%G` Week-based year, including the century (0000–9999).

`%h` Same as `%b`.
`%B` Full month name.

`%H` Hour in 24-hour format (00–23).
`%M` Minute (00–59).
`%S` Second (00–61); 61 permits leap seconds and double leap seconds.
`%R` Time in `%H:%M` format.
`%T` Time in `%H:%M:%S` format.
`%k` Hour (24-hour clock, 0–23); single digits are preceded by a space.
`%l` Hour (12-hour clock, 1–12); single digits are preceded by a space.

`%I` Hour in 12-hour format (01–12).
`%p` String to indicate a.m. or p.m. (default is `AM` or `PM`).
`%r` Time in `%I:%M:%S %p` format.

`%a` Abbreviated weekday.
`%A` Full weekday.
`%w` Day of week (Sunday = 0).
`%u` Weekday as a decimal number (1–7), Sunday = 1.
`%U` Week number in year (00–53); start week on Sunday.
`%W` Week number in year (00–53); start week on Monday.
`%V` The ISO-8601 week number (01–53). In ISO-8601, weeks begin on a Monday, and week 1 of the year is the one that includes both January 4th and the first Thursday of the year. If the first Monday of January is the 2nd, 3rd, or 4th, the preceding days are part of the last week of the previous year.
`%j` Julian day of year (001–366).
`%Z` Time-zone name.

`%x` Country-specific date format.
`%X` Country-specific time format.
`%c` Country-specific date and time format (default is `%a %b %e %T %Z %Y`; e.g., `Sun Jul 10 06:00:59 EDT 2005`).
`%F` ISO 8601 date format, equivalent to `%Y-%m-%d`. Not on Solaris.

`%N` The number of nanonseconds within the current second. GNU/Linux only.
`%s` The date and time as seconds since the Epoch. Not on Solaris.

The actual formatting is done by the *strftime*(3) library routine. The country-specific formats depend on the setting of the LC_CTYPE,

LC_TIME, and LC_MESSAGES (and on Solaris, NLSPATH) environment variables.

Common Option

`-u, --utc, --universal`
: Display or set the time using Greenwich Mean Time (UTC).

Solaris Option

`-a` *s.f*
: (Privileged user only.) Gradually adjust the system clock until it drifts *s* seconds away from what it thinks is the "current" time. (This allows continuous micro-adjustment of the clock while the system is running.) *f* is the fraction of seconds by which time drifts. By default, the clock speeds up; precede *s* by a – to slow down.

GNU/Linux Options

`-d` *date*, `--date` *date*
: Display *date*, which should be in quotes and may be in the format *d* `days` or *m* `months` *d* `days` to print a date in the future. Specify `ago` to print a date in the past. You may include formatting (see the previous section).

`-f` *datefile*, `--file=`*datefile*
: Like `-d`, but printed once for each line of `datefile`.

`-I` [*timespec*], `--iso-8601`[=*timespec*]
: Display in ISO-8601 format. If specified, *timespec* can have one of the values `date` (for date only), `hours`, `minutes`, or `seconds` to get the indicated precision.

`-r` *file*, `--reference=`*file*
: Display the time *file* was last modified.

`-R, --rfc-822`
: Display the date in RFC 822 format.

`-s` *date*, `--set` *date*
: Set the date to *date*.

Mac OS X Options

`-n`
: (Privileged user only.) Set the date on the local machine only; do not use *timed*(8) to set the time on all the machines in the local network.

`-r` *seconds*
: Display the time represents by *seconds* seconds since the Epoch.

Strings for Setting the Date

A privileged user can set the date by supplying a numeric *string*. *string* consists of time, day, and year concatenated in one of three ways: *time* or [*day*]*time* or [*day*]*time*[*year*]. Note: don't type the brackets.

time
: A two-digit hour and two-digit minute (*HHMM*); *HH* uses 24-hour format.

day A two-digit month and two-digit day of month (*mmdd*); default is current day and month.

year
The year specified as either the full four digits or just the last two digits; default is current year.

Examples

Set the date to July 1 (0701), 4 a.m. (0400), 1999 (99):

```
date 0701040099
```

Demonstrate the formatting capabilities:

```
$ date +"Hello%t Date is %D %n%t Time is %T"
Hello    Date is 06/26/05
         Time is 11:23:21
```

---

dc

`dc [file]`

An interactive desk calculator program that performs arbitrary-precision integer arithmetic (input may be taken from a *file*). Normally you don't run dc directly, since it's invoked by bc (see **bc**). dc provides a variety of one-character commands and operators that perform arithmetic; dc works like a Reverse Polish calculator; therefore, operators and commands follow the numbers they affect. Operators include `+ - / * % ^` (as in C, although `^` means exponentiation).

GNU/Linux and Mac OS X use the GNU version of dc that accepts a number of options and has additional commands; see *dc*(1) for the details. Some simple commands follow.

- `p` Print current result.
- `q` Quit dc.
- `c` Clear all values on the stack.
- `v` Take square root.
- `i` Change input base; similar to bc's `ibase`.
- `o` Change output base; similar to bc's `obase`.
- `k` Set scale factor (number of digits after decimal); similar to bc's `scale`.
- `!` Remainder of line is a Unix command.

Examples

```
$ dc
3 2 ^ p          Evaluate 3 squared, then print result
9
8 * p            Current value (9) times 8, then print result
72
47 - p           Subtract 47 from 72, then print result
25
v p              Square root of 25, then print result
5
2 o p            Display current result in base 2
101
```

Note: spaces are not needed except between numbers.

dd

`dd [option=value]`

Make a copy of an input file (`if=`), or standard input if no named input file, using the specified conditions, and send the results to the output file (or standard output if `of` is not specified). Any number of options can be supplied, although `if` and `of` are the most common and are usually specified first. Because `dd` can handle arbitrary block sizes, it is useful when converting between raw physical devices.

Although `dd` provides options for ASCII/EBCDIC conversions, `iconv` is better suited to that task.

Options

`bs=`*n*
: Set input and output block size to *n* bytes; this option supersedes `ibs` and `obs`.

`cbs=`*n*
: Set the size of the conversion buffer (logical record length) to *n* bytes. Use only if the conversion *flag* is `block` or `unblock`, or one of the ASCII/EBCDIC conversions.

`conv=`*flags*
: Convert the input according to one or more (comma-separated) *flags* listed below. The first nine *flags* are mutually exclusive. The next two are mutually exclusive with each other, as are the following two.

`ascii`	EBCDIC to ASCII.
`asciib`	EBCDIC to ASCII, using BSD-compatible conversions. Solaris only.
`oldascii`	EBCDIC to ASCII, using BSD-compatible conversions. Mac OS X only.
`ebcdic`	ASCII to EBCDIC.
`ebcdicb`	ASCII to EBCDIC, using BSD-compatible conversions. Solaris only.
`oldebcdic`	ASCII to EBCDIC, using BSD-compatible conversions. Mac OS X only.
`ibm`	ASCII to EBCDIC with IBM conventions.
`ibmb`	ASCII to EBCDIC with IBM conventions, using BSD-compatible conversions. Solaris only.
`oldibm`	ASCII to EBCDIC with IBM conventions, using BSD-compatible conversions. Mac OS X only.
`block`	Variable-length records (i.e., those terminated by a newline) to fixed-length records.
`unblock`	Fixed-length records to variable-length.
`lcase`	Uppercase to lowercase.
`ucase`	Lowercase to uppercase.

noerror	Continue processing when errors occur (up to five in a row).
notrunc	Do not truncate the output file. This preserves blocks in the output file that this invocation of dd did not write. Solaris only.
sparse	When input blocks consist only of zero bytes, try to seek on the output file, creating a sparse file. Mac OS X only.
swab	Swap all pairs of bytes.
sync	Pad input blocks to ibs.

count=*n*
: Copy only *n* input blocks.

files=*n*
: Copy *n* input files (e.g., from magnetic tape), then quit.

ibs=*n*
: Set input block size to *n* bytes (default is 512).

if=*file*
: Read input from *file* (default is standard input).

obs=*n*
: Set output block size to *n* bytes (default is 512).

of=*file*
: Write output to *file* (default is standard output).

iseek=*n*
: Seek *n* blocks from start of input file (like skip but more efficient for disk file input). Solaris and Mac OS X only.

oseek=*n*
: Same as seek. Solaris and Mac OS X only.

seek=*n*
: Seek *n* blocks from start of output file.

skip=*n*
: Skip *n* input blocks; useful with magnetic tape.

You can multiply size values (*n*) by a factor of 1024, 512, or 2 by appending the letters k, b, or w, respectively. You can use the letter x as a multiplication operator between two numbers.

Examples

Convert an input file to all lowercase:

```
dd if=caps_file of=small_file conv=lcase
```

Retrieve variable-length data; write it as fixed-length to out:

```
data_retrieval_cmd | dd of=out conv=sync,block
```

---

df

df [*options*] [*name*]

Report the number of free disk blocks and inodes available on all mounted filesystems or on the given *name*. (On Solaris unmounted filesystems are checked with -F.) *name* can be a device name (e.g., /dev/dsk/0s9), the directory name of a mount point (e.g., /usr), a directory name, or a remote filesystem name (e.g., an NFS filesystem). Besides the options listed, there are additional options specific to different filesystem types or df modules.

On Solaris and Mac OS X, the default block size is the historic 512 bytes. On GNU/Linux it's 1024 bytes. Furthermore, the output format and option availability both vary wildly among the different systems, as well as between `/usr/bin/df` and `/usr/xpg4/bin/df` on Solaris. The end result is that it's hard to use `df` portably in shell scripts.

Common Options

`-a, --all`
: Provide information about all filesystems, even ones usually marked in `/etc/mnttab` to be ignored.

`-h, --human-readable`
: Like `-k`, but in a more "human readable" format, with one line per filesystem.

`-i, --inodes`
: Solaris `/usr/ucb/df`, Mac OS X, GNU/Linux. Show the number of used and available inodes in a format similar to `df -k`.

`-k, --kilobytes`
: Print allocation in kilobytes (typically used without other options). This option produces output in the format traditionally used by the BSD version of `df`.

`-l, --local`
: Report only on local filesystems.

`-o` *suboptions*
: Supply a comma-separated list of *type*-specific *suboptions*.

`-P, --portability`
: Solaris `/usr/xpg4/bin/df` and Mac OS X: like `-k`, but use units of 512-byte blocks. On GNU/Linux, this still uses 1024-byte blocks, but the output format conforms to POSIX. (Set POSIXLY_CORRECT in the environment to force GNU `df` to use 512-byte blocks.)

GNU/Linux and Mac OS X Options

`-H, --si`
: Like `-h`, but use base 10 for sizes, not base 2.

`-m, --megabytes`
: Use 1048576-byte (1-Mbyte) blocks instead of the default. On Mac OS X, overrides the BLOCKSIZE environment variable.

`-t` *type*, `--type=`*type*
: Show only *type* filesystems. (Mac OS X in legacy mode.)

Solaris Options

`-b` Print only the number of free kilobytes.

`-e` Print only the number of free files.

`-F` *type*
: Report on an unmounted filesystem specified by *type*. Available *types* can be seen in the file `/etc/vfstab`.

`-g` Print the whole `statvfs` structure, overriding other print options.

-n Print only the filesystem *type* name; with no other arguments, -n lists the types for all mounted filesystems.

-t Report total allocated space as well as free space.

-v /usr/bin/df only. Like -k, but the size unit is the smallest block size supported by each filesystem.

-V Echo command line but do not execute command.

-Z Display mounts in all visible zones. The default is to provide information only about filesystems mounted in the local zone.

GNU/Linux Options

-B *n*, --block-size=*n*
: Show space as *n*-byte blocks.

--no-sync
: Show results without invoking sync first (i.e., without flushing the buffers). This is the default.

--sync
: Invoke sync (flush buffers) before getting and showing sizes.

-T, --print-type
: Print the type of each filesystem in addition to the sizes.

-x *type*, --exclude-type=*type*
: Show only filesystems that are not of type *type*.

Mac OS X Options

-b Use 512-byte blocks instead of the default. Overrides the BLOCKSIZE environment variable.

-g Use 1073741824-byte (1-Gigabyte) blocks instead of the default. Overrides the BLOCKSIZE environment variable.

-n Print out saved information about each filesystem instead of requesting the information anew.

-T *type*
: Prints statistics only for the given filesystem types.

---

diff

diff [*options*] [*diroptions*] *file1 file2*

diff reports lines that differ between *file1* and *file2*. Output consists of lines of context from each file, with *file1* text flagged by a < symbol and *file2* text by a > symbol. Context lines are preceded by the ed command (a, c, or d) that converts *file1* to *file2*. If one of the files is -, standard input is read. If one of the files is a directory, diff locates the filename in that directory corresponding to the other argument (e.g., diff my_dir junk is the same as diff my_dir/junk junk). If both arguments are directories, diff reports lines that differ between all pairs of files having equivalent names (e.g., olddir/program and newdir/program); in addition, diff lists filenames unique to one directory, as well as subdirectories common to both. See also **cmp**, **comm**, **diff3**, **dircmp**, and **sdiff**.

GNU/Linux and Mac OS X use GNU diff. See *http://www.gnu.org/software/diffutils*.

Common Options

Options -c, -C, -D, -e, -f, -h, -n, -u cannot be combined with each other (they are mutually exclusive).

-b, --ignore-space-change
: Ignore repeating blanks and end-of-line blanks; treat successive blanks as one.

-c
: Produce output in "context diff" format, with three lines of context.

-C *n*, --context=*n*
: Like -c, but produce *n* lines of context.

-D *symbol*, --ifdef=*symbol*
: Merge *file1* and *file2* into a single file containing conditional C preprocessor directives (#ifdef). Defining *symbol* and then compiling yields *file2*; compiling without defining *symbol* yields *file1*.

-e, --ed
: Produce a script of commands (a, c, d) to re-create *file2* from *file1* using the ed editor.

-f, --forward-ed
: Produce a script to re-create *file1* from *file2*; the script is in the opposite order, so it isn't useful to ed.

-h
: Do a half-hearted (but hopefully faster) comparison; complex differences (e.g., long stretches of many changes) may not show up; -e and -f are disabled. GNU diff ignores this option.

-i, --ignore-case
: Ignore uppercase and lowercase distinctions.

-n, --rcs
: Like -f, but counts changed lines. rcsdiff works this way.

-t, --expand-tabs
: Expand tabs in output lines; useful for preserving indentation changed by -c format.

-u
: Produce output in "unified diff" format, with three lines of context.

-U *n*, --unified=*n*
: Like -u, but produce *n* lines of context.

-w, --ignore-all-space
: Like -b, but ignores all spaces and tabs; e.g., a + b is the same as a+b.

Diroptions (Common)

The *diroptions* are valid only when both file arguments are directories.

-l, --paginate
: Long format; output is paginated by pr so that diff listings for each file begin on a new page; other comparisons are listed afterward.

-r, --recursive
: Run diff recursively for files in common subdirectories.

`-s, --report-identical-files`
: Report files that are identical.

`-S` *`filename`*`, --starting-file=`*`filename`*
: Begin directory comparisons with *file*, skipping files whose names alphabetically precede *file*.

Options for GNU diff

`-a, --text`
: Treat all files as text files. Useful for checking to see if binary files are identical.

`--binary`
: Read and write data in binary mode.

`-B, --ignore-blank-lines`
: Ignore blank lines in files.

`-d, --minimal`
: To speed up comparison, ignore segments of numerous changes and output a smaller set of changes.

`-E, --ignore-tab-expansion`
: Ignore differences due to expanding tabs.

`--from-file=`*`file`*
: Compare *file* to each operand. *file* may be a directory.

`-F` *`regexp`*`, --show-function-line=`*`regexp`*
: For context and unified diffs, show the most recent line containing *regexp* before each block of changed lines.

`--horizon-lines=`*`n`*
: In an attempt to find a more compact listing, keep *n* lines on both sides of the changed lines when performing the comparison.

`-H, --speed-large-files`
: Speed output of large files by scanning for scattered small changes; long stretches with many changes may not show up.

`--ignore-file-name-case`
: Ignore case in filenames during a recursive directory comparison.

`-I` *`regexp`*`, --ignore-matching-lines=`*`regexp`*
: Ignore lines in files that match the regular expression *regexp*.

`-L` *`label`*`, --label` *`label`*`, --label=`*`label`*
: For context and unified diffs, print *label* in place of the filename being compared. The first such option applies to the first filename and the second option to the second filename.

`--left-column`
: For two-column output (-y), show only the left column of common lines.

`--no-ignore-file-name-case`
: Cancel the effect of a previous `--ignore-file-name-case` option.

`-n, --normal`
: Produce a normal (default style) diff.

`-N, --new-file`
: Treat nonexistent files as empty.

`-p, --show-c-function`
: When handling files in C or C-like languages such as Java, show the function containing each block of changed lines. Assumes `-c`, but can also be used with a unified diff.

`-q, --brief`
: Output only whether files differ.

`--sdiff-merge-assist`
: Produce `sdiff`-style output. Used by GNU `sdiff` when invoking `diff`.

`--strip-trailing-cr`
: Remove carriage return characters at the end of input lines.

`--to-file=`*`file`*
: Compare each operand to *file*. *file* may be a directory.

`--suppress-common-lines`
: For two-column output (-y), do not show common lines.

`-T, --initial-tab`
: Insert initial tabs into output to line up tabs properly.

`--unidirectional-new-file`
: When doing directory comparisons, if a file is found only in the second directory, pretend it is present but empty in the first one.

`-v, --version`
: Print version number of `diff`.

`-W` *`n`*`, --width=`*`n`*
: For two-column output (-y), produce columns with a maximum width of *n* characters. Default is 130.

`-x` *`regexp`*`, --exclude=`*`regexp`*
: Do not compare files in a directory whose names match *regexp*.

`-X` *`filename`*`, --exclude-from=`*`filename`*
: Do not compare files in a directory whose names match patterns described in the file *filename*.

`-y, --side-by-side`
: Produce two-column output.

GNU diff Group Format Options

When merging files, you may wish to have an if-then-else pattern of lines in the result: i.e., one group of lines used in one case, and another group in another case. The options below give you control over the format of such groups.

`--changed-group-format=`*`format`*
: Use *format* for changed lines in if-then-else format.

`--new-group-format=`*`format`*
: Use *format* for lines from the second file in if-then-else format.

`--old-group-format=`*`format`*
: Use *format* for lines from the first file in if-then-else format.

`--unchanged-group-format=`*`format`*
: Use *format* for lines common to both files in if-then-else format.

Within the *format* strings, special conversion specifiers give you control over the placement of the input text lines in the output.

`%<`
: Lines from the first file, including the final newline. Each line is formatted according to the old line format.

`%>`
: Lines from the second file, including the final newline. Each line is formatted according to the new line format.

`%=`
: Lines common to both files, including the final newline. Each line is formatted according to the unchanged line format.

`%%`
: A literal `%` character.

`%c'`*`C`*`'`
: A literal character *C*. Useful for characters special to `diff`.

`%c'\`*`O`*`'`
: The character represented by *O*, which is a string of 1–3 octal digits.

`printf-specline-spec`
: A *printf*(3) format specification followed by a letter indicating a number to be printed. Valid specifications are `%d`, `%o`, `%x`, and `%X`. A field width and precision are allowed, as are the `-`, `0`, and `'` flags. The *line-spec* is one of the letters in the following list. Lowercase letters are used for lines in the first file; uppercase letters represent lines in the second file.

`e`, `E`	The number of the line just before the group.
`f`, `F`	The number of the first line in the group (same as `e` + 1).
`l`, `L`	The number of the last line of the group.
`m`, `M`	The number of the line just after the group (same as `l` + 1).
`n`, `N`	The number of lines in the group (`L` –`F` + 1).

`%(`*`A`*`=`*`B`*`?`*`T`*`:`*`E`*`)`
: Conditional substitution. *A* and *B* are either numbers or letters as just shown. If they are equal, the result is *T*, otherwise the result is *E*. See the Info documentation for GNU `diff` for more information.

GNU diff Line Format Options

Line format options give you control over the output of individual lines within line groups as specified by the line group options. The options are:

`--line-format=`*`format`*
: Apply *format* to all input lines in if-then-else format.

`--new-line-format=`*`format`*
: Apply *format* to input lines from the second file in if-then-else format.

`--old-line-format=`*`format`*
: Apply *format* to input lines from the first file in if-then-else format.

`--unchanged-line-format=`*`format`*
: Apply *format* to lines common to both files in if-then-else format.

Within the *format* strings, special conversion specifiers give you control over the placement of the input text lines in the output. The default line format is `%l` followed by a newline.

`%l`
The input line's contents, not including the newline.

`%L`
The input line's contents, including the trailing newline. If the input line did not have a newline, this format preserves that fact.

`%%`
A literal `%` character.

`%c'C'`
A literal character *C*. Useful for characters special to `diff`.

`%c'\O'`
The character represented by *O*, which is a string of 1–3 octal digits.

printf-specline-spec
The same as described earlier in this entry.

---

diff3

`diff3 [options] file1 file2 file3`

Compare three files and report the differences. No more than one of the files may be given as `-` (indicating that it is to be read from standard input). The output is displayed with the following codes:

`====`	All three files differ.
`====1`	*file1* is different.
`====2`	*file2* is different.
`====3`	*file3* is different.

`diff3` is also designed to merge changes in two differing files based on a common ancestor file (i.e., when two people have made their own set of changes to the same file). `diff3` can find changes between the ancestor and one of the newer files and generate output that adds those differences to the other new file. Unmerged changes occur where both of the newer files differ from each other and at least one of them differs from the ancestor. Changes from the ancestor that are the same in both of the newer files are called *merged changes*. If all three files differ in the same place, it is called an *overlapping change*.

This scheme is used on the command line with the ancestor being *file2*, the second filename. Comparison is made between *file2* and *file3*, with those differences then applied to *file1*.

Common Options

`-e, --ed`
Create an `ed` script to incorporate into *file1* all differences between *file2* and *file3*.

`-E, --show-overlap`
Same as `-e`, but mark with angle brackets any lines that differ between all three files.

`-x, --overlap-only`
Create an `ed` script to incorporate into *file1* all differences between all three files.

`-X` Same as `-x`, but mark with angle brackets any lines that differ between all three files.

`-3, --easy-only`
Create an `ed` script to incorporate into *file1* differences between *file1* and *file3*.

GNU/Linux and Mac OS X Options

`-a, --text`
Treat files as text.

`-A, --show-all`
Create an `ed` script to incorporate all changes, showing conflicts in bracketed format.

`--diff-program=`*prog*
Use *prog* to compare files instead of `diff`.

`-i` Append the `w` (save) and `q` (quit) commands to `ed` script output.

`-L` *label*, `--label=`*label*
Use *label* to replace filename in output.

`-m, --merge`
Create file with changes merged (not an `ed` script).

`-T, --initial-tab`
To line tabs up properly in output, begin lines with a tab instead of two spaces.

`-v, --version`
Print version information and then exit.

dig

```
dig [@server] [options] [name] [type] [class] [query-options]
dig @server name type
dig -h
```

The `dig` command queries DNS servers; it is more flexible than the deprecated `nslookup` command. If you use it without any options or arguments, it searches for the root server. This entry documents the GNU/Linux and Mac OS X version of `dig`; the Solaris version is slightly different and resides in `/usr/sbin`. The standard arguments are:

server
The server to query. If no server is supplied, `dig` checks the name servers listed in `/etc/resolv.conf`. The address may be an IPv4 dotted address or an IPv6 colon-delimited address. It may also be a hostname, which `dig` will resolve (through the name servers in `/etc/resolv.conf`).

name
The domain name to look up.

type
The type of query to perform, such as `A`, `ANY`, `MX`, `SIG`, and so on. The default is `A`, but you may use any valid BIND9 query type.

Options

-b *address*
: Set the source IP address for the query.

-c *class*
: Set the class of query. The default value is IN (Internet), but you can choose HS for Hesiod or CH for CHAOSNET.

-f *filename*
: Operate in batch mode, performing the queries in the file you specify.

-h
: Print a command-line option summary and exit.

-k *filename*
: Specify a TSIG key file; used for signed transactions. You can also use the -y key, although this is less secure.

-p *portnumber*
: Choose the port number for the query. The default value is the standard DNS port, 53.

-t *type*
: Set the type of query, as with the query argument. The default value is A, but you may use any valid BIND9 query.

-x *addr*
: Perform a reverse lookup, specifying an IPv4 or IPv6 address. You don't need the name, class, or type arguments if you use -x.

-y *keyname*:*keyvalue*
: Enter the actual key name and value when conducting a signed transaction. Because the key and value can be seen in the output of ps, this is not recommended for use on multiuser systems; use -k instead.

Query Options

There are a large number of query options for dig. Each query option is preceded by +, and many have an opposite version beginning with no. For example, the tcp flag is passed as +tcp, and negated with +notcp. Because there are so many options, only a few are discussed here. For greater detail, see the *dig*(1) manpage.

+tcp, +notcp
: Use (or do not use) the TCP protocol instead of the default UDP.

+domain=*searchdomain*
: Perform a search in the domain specified; this is equivalent to using the +search option and having *searchdomain* as the sole entry in the search list or domain directive of /etc/resolv.conf.

+search, +nosearch
: Use (or don't use) the search list provided in /etc/resolv.conf. The default is not to use the search list.

+time=*T*
: Timeout for queries, in seconds. The default is five, and the minimum is one.

`+tries=`*N*
: The number of times to retry UDP queries. The default is three, and the minimum is one.

dirname

`dirname` *`pathname`*

Print *pathname*, excluding last level. Useful for stripping the actual filename from a pathname. See also **basename**.

dos2unix

`dos2unix [`*`options`*`]` *`dosfile unixfile`*

Solaris and GNU/Linux only. Convert files using the DOS extended character set to their ISO standard counterparts. If *dosfile* and *unixfile* are the same, the file is overwritten after the conversion is done. See also **unix2dos**.

Solaris Options

`-ascii`
: Remove extra carriage returns and convert (remove) DOS end-of-file characters for use under Unix.

`-iso` Same as the default action.

`-7` Convert 8-bit DOS graphics characters to space characters.

GNU/Linux Options

`-c` *`mode`*`, --convmode` *`mode`*
: Set the conversion mode to *mode*. Possible values are `ASCII`, `7bit`, `ISO`, and `Mac`. The default is `ASCII`. This emulates the Solaris version of `dos2unix`.

`-h, --help`
: Print a command-line summary and exit.

`-k, --keepdate`
: Make the modification date of the output file be the same as that of the input file.

`-n` *`infile outfile`* `...`, `--newfile` *`infile outfile`* `...`
: New file mode. Filenames must be provided in pairs: the first one is the input file, the second is the output file.

`-o` *`file`* `...`, `--oldfile` *`file`* `...`
: Old file mode. Each input file in converted in place. This is the default.

`-q, --quiet`
: Do not print any warnings or messages.

`-V, --version`
: Print version information and exit.

du

`du [`*`options`*`] [`*`directories`*`]`

Print disk usage, i.e., the number of blocks used by each named directory and its subdirectories (default is current directory).

On Solaris and Mac OS X, the default block size is the historic 512 bytes. On GNU/Linux it's 1024 bytes. Furthermore, the option availability and meanings vary wildly among the different systems, as well as between /usr/bin/du and /usr/xpg4/bin/du on Solaris. The end result is that it's hard to use du portably in shell scripts, although du -k seems to be a universal least common denominator.

Common Options

-a, --all
: Print usage for all files, not just subdirectories.

-h, --human-readable
: Print sizes in human-readable format.

-k, --kilobytes
: Print information in units of kilobytes.

-L, --dereference
: For symbolic links, process the file or directory to which the link refers, not the link itself.

-s, --summarize
: Print only the grand total for each named directory.

-x, --one-file-system
: Restrict file size evaluations to files on the same filesystem as the command-line *file* parameter. Not available for Solaris /usr/bin/du.

Solaris Options

-d
: Do not cross filesystem boundaries. /usr/bin/du only.

-H
: When a symbolic link named on the command line refers to a directory, process the linked-to directory instead of the link itself.

-o
: Do not add child-directory statistics to the parent directory's total. No effect if -s is also used. /usr/bin/du only.

-r
: Print a "cannot open" message if a file or directory is inaccessible.

GNU/Linux Options

--apparent-size
: Print the apparent size, not actual disk usage. This may be larger than actual disk usage due to holes in sparse files, as well as other factors.

-b, --bytes
: Print sizes in bytes.

-B, --block-size=*size*
: Use a block size of *size* bytes.

`-c, --total`
: In addition to normal output, print grand total of all arguments.

`-D, --dereference-args`
: Follow symbolic links, but only if they are command-line arguments.

`--exclude=`*`pattern`*
: Exclude files that match *pattern*.

`-H`
: Like `--si`, but also evokes a warning. For standards-compliance, this option will eventually become the same as `-D`.

`-l, --count-links`
: Count the size of all files, whether or not they have already appeared (i.e., via a hard link).

`-P, --no-dereference`
: Do not follow any symbolic links. This is the default.

`--max-depth=`*`num`*
: Report sizes for directories only down to *num* levels below the starting point (which is level 0).

`-m, --megabytes`
: Print sizes in megabytes.

`--si`
: Like `-h`, but show as power of 1000 rather than 1024.

`-S, --separate-dirs`
: Do not include the sizes of subdirectories when totaling the size of parent directories.

`-X, --exclude-from=`*`file`*
: Exclude files that match any pattern in *file*.

`-0, --null`
: End each output line with a binary zero (NUL) character, instead of a newline.

Mac OS X Options

`-c`
: Print a grand total.

`-d` *`depth`*
: Descend only *depth* directories deep.

`-H`
: When a symbolic link named on the command line refers to a directory, process the linked-to directory instead of the link itself.

`-I` *`mask`*
: Ignore files and directories that match *mask*.

`-P`
: Do not follow any symbolic links. This is the default.

`-r`
: Print a "cannot open" message if a file or directory is inaccessible.

echo

`echo [option] [string]`

Echo arguments to standard output. Often used for producing prompts from shell scripts. This is the echo command in the filesystem, not the one built into the shells (see Chapters 4 and 5).

Although echo is conceptually the simplest of all Unix commands, using it in practice is complicated, because of portability and version differences. (Consider using printf instead.) The following sections summarize the differences.

Options

-e Always interpret escape sequences in argument strings.

-E Never interpret escape sequences in argument strings.

-n Do not print the final terminating newline.

Version Differences

Solaris /usr/bin/echo
: Does not accept any options. Interprets the escape sequences described next.

Solaris /usr/ucb/echo
: Accepts the -n option if it's first. Does not interpret escape sequences.

Mac OS X /bin/echo
: Accepts the -n option if it's first, and interprets only the \c escape sequence.

GNU/Linux /bin/echo
: Accepts the -e, -E, and -n options, and the options --help and --version.

Bourne shell echo
: Does not accept the -n option. Interprets the escape sequences described next, except \a.

C shell echo
: Accepts the -n option if it's first. Does not interpret escape sequences. In tcsh, the echo_style shell variable controls emulation of BSD and/or System V echo options and escape sequences.

Korn shell echo
: Searches $PATH and behaves like the first version of echo that it finds.

Bash echo
: Accepts the -e, -E, and -n options.

Escape Sequences

\a	Alert (ASCII BEL). (Not in /bin/sh's echo.)
\b	Backspace.
\c	Suppress the terminating newline (same as -n).
\E	The ASCII ESCAPE character. Bash built-in echo only.
\f	Formfeed.

`\n`	Newline.
`\r`	Carriage return.
`\t`	Tab character.
`\v`	Vertical-tab character.
`\\`	Backslash.
`\0`*nnn*	ASCII character represented by octal number *nnn*, where *nnn* is 1, 2, or 3 digits and is preceded by a 0.

Examples

```
echo "testing printer" | lp
echo "TITLE\nTITLE" > file ; cat doc1 doc2 >> file
echo "Warning: ringing bell \07"
```

---

ed

`ed [`*`options`*`] [`*`file`*`]`

ed is the standard text editor. If the named *file* does not exist, ed creates it; otherwise, the existing *file* is opened for editing. As a line editor, ed is generally no longer used because vi and ex have superseded it. However, it can be useful from a slow dial-in connection or over an intercontinental ssh session when using a screen editor is painful. Some utilities, such as diff, continue to make use of ed command syntax.

URL: *http://www.gnu.org/fun/jokes/ed.msg.html.*

Common Options

-p *string*
: Set *string* as the prompt for commands (default is *). The P command turns the prompt display on and off.

-s
: Suppress character counts, diagnostics, and the ! prompt for shell commands. Earlier versions of ed used plain -; this is still accepted.

System Specific Options

-C
: Same as -x, but assume *file* began in encrypted form. Solaris only.

-G
: Forces backwards compatibility. This affects the commands G, V, f, l, m, t, and !!. GNU/Linux only.

-x
: Supply a key to encrypt or decrypt *file* using crypt. Solaris and Mac OS X only.

---

egrep

`egrep [`*`options`*`] [`*`regexp`*`] [`*`files`*`]`

Search one or more *files* for lines that match a regular expression *regexp*. egrep doesn't support the metacharacters \(, \), *n*, \<, \>, but does support the other metacharacters, as well as the extended set +, ?, |, and ( ). Remember to enclose these characters in quotes. Regular expressions are described in Chapter 6. Exit status is 0 if any lines match, 1 if not, and 2 for errors. See also **grep** and **fgrep**.

Solaris /usr/bin/egrep does not support \{, or \}. Mac OS X and GNU/Linux use GNU egrep.

Common Options

-c, --count
: Print only a count of matched lines.

-e *regexp*, --regexp=*regexp*
: Use this if *regexp* begins with -.

-f *file*, --file=*file*
: Take expression from *file*. Multiple expressions may be provided, one per line, in which case any of them may match.

-i, --ignore-case
: Ignore uppercase and lowercase distinctions.

-h, --no-filename
: Do not print the names of matching files, just the matched lines.

-l, --files-with-matches
: List filenames but not matched lines.

-n, --line-number
: Print lines and their line numbers.

-s, --no-messages
: Silent mode: print only error messages, and return the exit status.

-v --invert-match
: Print all lines that *don't* match *regexp*.

-x, --line-regexp
: Select only those matches that exactly match the whole line. (Only /usr/xpg4/bin/egrep on Solaris, not /usr/bin/egrep.)

GNU grep, egrep, and fgrep Options

-a, --text
: Treat a binary file as text. Same as --binary-files=text.

-A *count*, --after-context=*count*
: Print *count* lines of trailing context. This places a -- between contiguous groups of matches.

-b, --byte-offset
: Before each output line, print the byte offset within the file.

--binary-files=*type*
: egrep examines the first few bytes of a file. If this examination indicates that the file is binary, this option tells egrep what to do. Values for *type* are: binary, which gives the default behavior of printing a message that the file does (or does not) match; without-match to indicate that the file does not match, or text, which causes egrep to attempt to print the matching line.

-B *count*, --before-context=*count*
: Print *count* lines of leading context. This places a -- between contiguous groups of matches.

`--color[=when], --colour[=when]`
: Highlight matching text with color as provided by the GREP_COLOR environment variable. *when* may be `always`, `auto`, or `never`.

`-C count, --context=count`
: Print *count* lines of output context. This places a `--` between contiguous groups of matches.

`-d action, --directories=action`
: Use *action* to process directories. Possible values are: `read`, which means to read the directory as if it was a file; `skip`, to skip processing the directory; or `recurse`, to enter it and process its files recursively (equivalent to `-r`).

`-D action, --devices=action`
: Use *action* to process device, FIFO, or socket special files. Possible values are: `read`, which means to read the file; and `skip`, to skip processing the file.

`--exclude=pattern`
: During recursive directory processing, skip files whose names match *pattern*.

`-E, --extended-regexp`
: Treat the search pattern as an Extended Regular Expression (ERE). See Chapter 7. This is the default for egrep.

`-F, --fixed-strings`
: Treat the *regexp* argument as a list of fixed strings, separated by newlines. Any of the strings may match. This is the default for fgrep.

`-G, --basic-regexp`
: Treat the search pattern as an Basic Regular Expression (BRE). See Chapter 7. This is the default for grep.

`-H, --with-filename`
: Always print the name of matching files. (Normally, grep, egrep, and fgrep print the name of the matching file only if more than one filename is listed on the command line.)

`--include=pattern`
: During recursive directory processing, only process files whose names match *pattern*.

`-I` Same as `--binary-files=without-match`.

`-L, --files-without-match`
: The inverse of `-l`: print just the names of files that do *not* match *regexp*.

`-m count, --max-count=count`
: Stop reading each input file after matching *count* lines. With `-v`, stop after *count* nonmatching lines.

`--mmap`
: Use the *mmap*(2) system call for reading input, if possible. This can provide a performance improvement.

`--label=`*label*
: Use *label* for the name of standard input instead of `(standard input)`.

`--line-buffered`
: Use line buffering. This may decrease performance.

`-o, --only-matching`
: Display only the part of the line that matches *regexp*.

`-P, --perl-regexp`
: Treat *regexp* as a Perl regular expression. This option is experimental, don't use it for production shell scripts.

`-q, --quiet, --silent`
: Be quiet; do not produce any output. egrep exits immediately with a zero status if any match is found, even if there were previous errors. See also the `-s` option.

`-r, -R, --recursive`
: When given a directory, process it recursively, searching the contained files and directories for matches.

`-u, --unix-byte-offsets`
: For MS-DOS and MS-Windows platforms, report byte offsets as if reading a Unix text file. In other words, ignore the carriage return characters. Must be used together with `-b`.

`-U, --binary`
: For MS-DOS and MS-Windows platforms, force egrep to treat the file as binary data. This prevents the default automatic removal of carriage return characters on that platform.

`-V, --version`
: Print version information to standard output and exit.

`-w, --word-regexp`
: Perform a word match on *regexp*. The match must be at the beginning of a line or preceded by a non-word-constituent character. The matching text must also be either at the end of the line or be followed by a non-word–constituent character. Word-constituent characters are letters, digits, and the underscore.

`-y`
: An obsolete synonym for `-i`.

`-Z, --null`
: Use a zero byte (ASCII NUL) instead of the colon that usually follows a filename. Intended for use with `-l` to produce an unambiguous list of filenames that can be processed by programs like `xargs -0` or `sort -z`. This allows easy processing of filenames that contain unusual characters, such as newlines.

Examples

Search for occurrences of `Victor` or `Victoria` in *file*:

```
egrep 'Victor(ia)?' file
egrep '(Victor|Victoria)' file
```

Find and print strings such as `old.doc1` or `new.doc2` in *files*, and include their line numbers:

```
egrep -n '(old|new)\.doc?' files
```

eject

```
eject [options] [media]
```

Solaris and GNU/Linux only. Eject removable media, such as a floppy disk or CD-ROM. On Solaris, necessary for media being managed by `vold`, or for media without an eject button, such as the floppy drives on some Sun SPARC systems. *media* is either a device name or a nickname, such as `floppy` or `cdrom`.

With volume management available, `eject` unmounts any filesystems mounted on the named *media*. In this case, it also displays a pop-up dialog if a window system is running. Without volume management, it simply sends an "eject" command to the given device.

On GNU/Linux, the default device is `cdrom`. A device name or mount point may be supplied.

Solaris Options

`-d` Print the name of the default device to be ejected.

`-f` When volume management is not in effect, force the eject, even if the device is busy.

`-n` Display the list of nicknames and their corresponding real devices.

`-p` Do not use a windowing pop-up dialog.

`-q` Query to see if the device has media. Use the exit status to determine the answer.

GNU/Linux Options

`-a on|1|off|0, --auto on|1|off|0`
Set the auto-eject mode to on or off (equivalent to 1 or 0). If auto-eject mode is on, the device is ejected when closed or unmounted.

`-c` *`slotnumber`*`, --changerslot` *`slotnumber`*
If using a CD-ROM changer, select a CD from one of the slots. Slots are enumerated starting with 0, and the CD-ROM drive must not be playing music or mounted to read data.

`-d, --default`
List the default device name rather than doing anything.

`-f, --floppy`
Use floppy commands to eject the drive. Normally, the system will try all methods (CD-ROM, SCSI, floppy, tape) to eject.

`-h, --help`
Display help information.

`-n, --noop`
Do not perform any actions; merely display the actions that would be performed.

`-p, --proc`
Use the mounted files listed in `/proc/mounts` rather than the ones in `/etc/mtab`.

`-q, --tape`
: Use tape commands to eject the drive. Normally, the system will try all methods (CD-ROM, SCSI, floppy, tape) to eject.

`-r, --cdrom`
: Use CD-ROM commands to eject the drive. Normally, the system will try all methods (CD-ROM, SCSI, floppy, tape) to eject.

`-s, --scsi`
: Use SCSI commands to eject the drive. Normally, the system will try all methods (CD-ROM, SCSI, floppy, tape) to eject.

`-t, --trayclose`
: Close the CD-ROM drive. Not all drives will respond to this command.

`-v, --verbose`
: Verbose mode: display additional information about actions.

`-V, --version`
: Display version information, then quit.

`-x` *`speed`*`, --cdspeed` *`speed`*
: Set the speed multiplier for the CD-ROM to an integer, usually a power of 2. Not all devices support this command. Setting the speed to 0 indicates that the drive should operate at its maximum speed.

---

emacs

`emacs [`*`options`*`] [`*`files`*`]`

A text editor and all-purpose work environment. For more information, see Chapter 8.

---

env

`env [`*`options`*`] [`*`variable=value ...`*` ] [`*`command`*`]`

Display the current environment or, if environment *variables* are specified, set them to a new *value* and display the modified environment. If *command* is specified, execute it under the modified environment.

Options

`-, -i, --ignore-environment`
: Ignore current environment entirely.

`-u` *`name`*`, --unset` *`name`*
: Unset the specified variable.

---

etags

`etags [`*`options`*`]` *`files`*

Create a list of function and macro names defined in a programming source *file*. etags generates tags for use by emacs. (ctags produces an equivalent tags file for use with vi.) More than one file may be specified. etags understands many programming languages, including Ada, bison, C++, C, Cobol, Emacs Lisp/Common Lisp,

Erlang, flex, Fortran, Java, Perl, Python, Scheme, TeX, and yacc. The output list (named TAGS by default) contains lines of the form:

```
name     file     context
```

where *name* is the function or macro name, *file* is the source file in which *name* is defined, and *context* is a search pattern that shows the line of code containing *name*. After the list of tags is created, you can invoke Emacs on any file and type:

```
M-x visit-tags-table
```

You will be prompted for the name of the tag table; the default is TAGS. To switch to the source file associated with the *name* listed in *tagsfile*, type:

```
M-x find-tag
```

You will be prompted for the tag you would like Emacs to search for.

This entry documents the etags program shipped with GNU Emacs. A related ctags program is also included for generating a tags file for vi. Some of the options below only work with GNU ctags. The **ctags** entry in this chapter documents a different version of ctags, the Exuberant ctags.

Options

`-a, --append`
: Append tag output to existing list of tags.

`-C, --c++`
: Expect `.c` and `.h` files to contain C++, not C, code.

`-d, --defines`
: Include tag entries for C preprocessor definitions.

`--declarations`
: Create tags for function declarations and `extern` variables for C and similar languages.

`-D, --no-defines`
: Do not include tag entries for C preprocessor definitions.

`-g, --globals`
: In C, C++, Objective C, Java, and Perl, create tags for global variables. This is the default for etags.

`-G, --no-globals`
: In C, C++, Objective C, Java, and Perl, do not create tags for global variables. This is the default for ctags.

`-h, -H, --help`
: Print usage information.

`-i` *`file`*`, --include=`*`file`*
: Add a note to the tags file that *file* should be consulted in addition to the normal input file.

`--ignore-case-regex=`*`regexp`*
: Similar to `--regex`, except that case is not significant.

`-I, --ignore-indentation`
Do not assume that a closing brace in the first column ends a function or structure definition for C and C++.

`-l` *`language`*`, --language=`*`language`*
Consider the files that follow this option to be written in *language*. Use the `-h` option for a list of languages and their default filename extensions.

`-m, --members`
Create tags for members of `structs` and similar constructs in C++, Objective C and Java.

`-M, --no-members`
Do not create tags for members of `structs` and similar constructs in C++, Objective C and Java. This is the default.

`-o` *`file`*`, --output=`*`file`*
Write to *file*.

`-r` *`regexp`*`, --regex=`*`regexp`*
Include a tag for each line that matches *regexp* in the files following this option.

`-R, --noregex`
Don't include tags based on regular-expression matching for the files that follow this option.

`-V, --version`
Print the version number.

GNU ctags Options

`-B, --backward-search`
Create tags files using the `?` backward search character, instead of the default `/` forward search character.

`-t, --typedefs`
Include `typedef`s in C. etags does this by default.

`-T, --typedefs-and-c++`
Include tags for `typedefs`, `struct`, `enum`, and `union` tags, and C++ member functions. etags does this by default.

`-u, --update`
Update the entries just for the named files, leaving other entries in place. It is likely to be faster to simply rebuild the entire tags file.

`-v, --vgrind`
Do not create a tags file. Instead, write the index in `vgrind` format. This is a rather obsolete option.

`-w, --no-warn`
Do not warn about duplicate entries.

`-x, --cxref`
Do not create a tags file. Instead, write a cross reference in `cxref` format to standard output. This option is also of only marginal use, as there is no standard cross-platform `cxref` program.

evim

```
evim [options] [file ...]
eview [options] [file ...]
```

evim starts the graphical version of vim in "easy mode," whereby editing uses point-and-click. This makes vim feel like the very simple text editor found on some non-Unix operating systems. It should be used only by people who can't handle regular vim. eview is the same as evim but it starts up in read-only mode (equivalent to the -R option). See also **vim** and Chapter 9.

Solaris supplies evim in /opt/sfw/bin, and evim is installed by default if you build vim from source. On GNU/Linux, you can make a symbolic link named evim to gvim and it will work. On Mac OS X, you can link regular vim to evim, and it will work inside a terminal window. To access the ex prompt (so that you can exit, for example), type CTRL-O :.

URL: *http://www.vim.org*.

ex

```
ex [options] files
```

A line-oriented text editor; a superset of ed and the root of vi. See Chapter 9 for more information.

expand

```
expand [options] [files]
```

Expand tab characters into appropriate number of spaces. expand reads the named *files* or standard input if no *files* are provided. See also **unexpand**.

Options

-*n* Set the tabstops every *n* characters. The default is 8.

-*tablist*
: Interpret tabs according to *tablist*, a space- or comma-separated list of numbers in ascending order, that describe the "tabstops" for the input data.

-i, --initial
: Convert tabs only at the beginning of lines.

-t *tablist*, --tabs *tablist*
: Interpret tabs according to *tablist*, a space- or comma-separated list of numbers in ascending order, that describe the "tabstops" for the input data.

Example

Cut columns 10–12 of the input data, even when tabs are used:

```
expand data | cut -c 10-12 > data.col2
```

expr

```
expr arg1 operator arg2 [ operator arg3 ... ]
```

Evaluate arguments as expressions and print the result. Strings can be compared and searched. Arguments and operators must be separated by spaces. In most cases, an argument is an integer, typed literally or represented by a shell variable. There are three types of operators: arithmetic, relational, and logical. Exit status for expr is 0 (expression is nonzero and nonnull), 1 (expression is 0 or null), or 2 (expression is invalid).

expr is typically used in shell scripts to perform simple arithmetic, such as addition or subtraction. It is made obsolete in modern shells that have built-in arithmetic capabilities.

Arithmetic Operators

Use the following operators to produce mathematical expressions whose results are printed:

+	Add *arg2* to *arg1*.
-	Subtract *arg2* from *arg1*.
*	Multiply the arguments.
/	Divide *arg1* by *arg2*.
%	Take the remainder when *arg1* is divided by *arg2*.

Addition and subtraction are evaluated last, unless they are grouped inside parentheses. The symbols *, (, and) have meaning to the shell, so they must be escaped (preceded by a backslash or enclosed in single or double quotes).

Relational Operators

Use relational operators to compare two arguments. Arguments can also be words, in which case comparisons assume `a < z` and `A < Z`. If the comparison statement is true, the result is 1; if false, the result is 0. Symbols < and > must be escaped.

=	Are the arguments equal?
!=	Are the arguments different?
>	Is *arg1* greater than *arg2*?
>=	Is *arg1* greater than or equal to *arg2*?
<	Is *arg1* less than *arg2*?
<=	Is *arg1* less than or equal to *arg2*?

Logical Operators

Use logical operators to compare two arguments. Depending on the values, the result can be *arg1* (or some portion of it), *arg2*, or 0. Symbols | and & must be escaped.

|
: Logical OR; if *arg1* has a nonzero (and nonnull) value, the result is *arg1*; otherwise, the result is *arg2*.

&
: Logical AND; if both *arg1* and *arg2* have a nonzero (and nonnull) value, the result is *arg1*; otherwise, the result is 0.

: Similar to grep; *arg2* is a pattern to search for in *arg1*. *arg2* must be a regular expression in this case. If the *arg2* pattern is enclosed in `\(   \)`, the result is the portion of *arg1* that matches; otherwise, the result is simply the number of characters that match. By default, a pattern match always applies to the beginning of the first argument (the search string implicitly begins with a ^). To match other parts of the string, start the search string with `.*`.

Keywords

The GNU/Linux version accepts additional keyword commands. Some Unix versions of `expr` also accept the `index`, `length`, and `substr` keywords.

`+` *`token`*
: Treat *token* as a string, even if it would normally be a keyword or an operator.

`index` *`string character-list`*
: Return the first position in *string* that matches the first possible character in *character-list*. Continue through *character-list* until a match is found, or return 0.

`length` *`string`*
: Return the length of *string*.

`match` *`string regex`*
: Same as *string* : *regex*.

`substr` *`string start length`*
: Return a section of *string*, beginning with *start*, with a maximum length of *length* characters. Return null when given a negative or nonnumeric *start* or *length*.

Examples

Division happens first; result is 10:

```
expr 5 + 10 / 2
```

Addition happens first; result is 7 (truncated from 7.5):

```
expr \( 5 + 10 \) / 2
```

Add 1 to variable `i`; this is how variables are incremented in shell scripts:

```
i=`expr $i + 1`
```

Print 1 (true) if variable `a` is the string "hello":

```
expr $a = hello
```

Print 1 (true) if variable `b` plus 5 equals 10 or more:

```
expr $b + 5 \>= 10
```

In the following examples, variable `p` is the string `"version.100"`. This command prints the number of characters in `p`:

```
expr $p : '.*'              Result is 11
```

Match all characters and print them:

```
expr $p : '\(.*\)'          Result is "version.100"
```

Print the number of lowercase letters at the beginning of p:

```
expr $p : '[a-z]*'        Result is 7
```

Match the lowercase letters at the beginning of p:

```
expr $p : '\([a-z]*\)'  Result is "version"
```

Truncate $x if it contains five or more characters; if not, just print $x. (Logical OR uses the second argument when the first one is 0 or null; i.e., when the match fails.) Double-quoting is a good idea, in case $x contains whitespace characters:

```
expr "$x" : '\(.....\)' \| "$x"
```

In a shell script, rename files to their first five letters:

```
mv "$x" `expr "$x" : '\(.....\)' \| "$x"`
```

(To avoid overwriting files with similar names, use `mv -i`.)

---

factor

`factor [num]`

Solaris and GNU/Linux only. Produce the prime factors of *num* or read numbers from input.

---

false

`false`

A do-nothing command that returns an unsuccessful (nonzero) exit status. Normally used in Bourne shell scripts. See also **true**.

`false` is built into most modern shells.

Examples

```
# This loop never executes
while false
do
        commands
done

# This loop executes forever
until false
do
        commands
done
```

---

fdformat

`fdformat [options] [device]`

Solaris and GNU/Linux only.[*] Format floppy disks and PCMCIA memory cards. *device* is the name of the appropriate device to format, and varies considerably based on the density of the media, the capability of the disk drive, and—on Solaris—whether or not volume management is in effect.

[*] As Macintosh systems don't have floppy disk drives, this command would be of no use, anyway.

Solaris Options

`-b` *`label`*
: Apply the *label* to the media. SunOS labels may be up to 8 characters; DOS labels may be up to 11 uppercase characters.

`-B` *`file`*
: Install bootloader in *file* on an MS-DOS diskette. Can only be used with `-d` or `-t dos`.

`-D` Format a 720KB (3.5 inch) or 360KB (5.25 inch) double-density diskette. Use on high- or extended-density drives.

`-e` Eject floppy disk when done.

`-E` Format a 2.88MB (3.5 inch) extended-density diskette.

`-f` Force. Do not prompt for confirmation before formatting.

`-H` Format a 1.44MB (3.5 inch) or 1.2MB (5.25 inch) high-density diskette. Use on extended-density drive.

`-M` Use a 1.2MB (3.5 inch) medium-density format on a high-density diskette. Use only with the `-t nec` option.

`-q` Quiet mode. Don't print status messages.

`-t dos`
: Install an MS-DOS filesystem and boot sector formatting.

`-t nec`
: Install an NEC-DOS filesystem and boot sector after formatting. Use only with `-M`.

`-U` Unmount any filesystems on the media, and then format.

`-v` Verify each block on the media after formatting.

`-x` Don't format, just write a SunOS label or MS-DOS filesystem.

Solaris Compatibility Options

These options are for compatibility with previous versions of `fdformat`. Their use is discouraged.

`-d` Same as `-t dos`.

`-l` Same as `-D`.

`-L` Same as `-D`.

`-m` Same as `-M`.

GNU/Linux Option

`-n` Do not verify format after completion.

---

fgrep

`fgrep [`*`options`*`] [`*`pattern`*`] [`*`files`*`]`

Search one or more *files* for lines that match a literal, text-string *pattern*. Because `fgrep` does not support regular expressions, it is potentially faster than `grep` (hence `fgrep`, for fast grep). Exit status is 0 if any lines match, 1 if not, and 2 for errors. See also **egrep** and **grep**.

The *options* for `fgrep` are the same as for `egrep`, including the Solaris versus GNU differences. See **egrep** for the full list.

Examples

Print lines in *file* that don't contain any spaces:

```
fgrep -v ' ' file
```

Print lines in *file* that contain the words in spell_list:

```
fgrep -f spell_list file
```

file

```
file [options] files
```

Classify the named *files* according to the type of data they contain. file checks the magic file (usually /etc/magic) to identify many common file types.

Many file types are understood. Output lists each filename, followed by a brief classification such as:

```
ascii text
c program text
c shell commands
data
empty
iAPX 386 executable
directory
[nt]roff, tbl, or eqn input text
shell commands
symbolic link to ../usr/etc/arp
```

Mac OS X and GNU/Linux use the freely-available version of file from *ftp://ftp.astron.com/pub/file/*.

Solaris Options

-c
: Check the format of the magic file (*files* argument is invalid with -c).

-d
: Apply any default system tests that are position-dependent or context-dependent to the file.

-f *listfile*
: Run file on the filenames in *listfile*.

-h
: Do not follow symbolic links.

-i
: For regular files, do not attempt to classify the file further. Instead, just print the message "regular file."

-m *file*
: /usr/xpg4/bin/magic: same as -M.

  /usr/bin/magic: use *file* as the magic file instead of /etc/magic.

-M *file*
: *file* contains position-dependent or context-sensitive tests to apply.

Astron.com file Options

-b, --brief
: Brief mode; do not prepend filenames to output lines.

-c, --checking-printout
: Check the format of the magic file (*files* argument is invalid with -c). Usually used with -m.

`-C, --compile`
: Create a `magic.mgc` file, which is a preparsed version of the `magic` file.

`-f` *`file`*`, --files-from` *`file`*
: Read the names of files to be checked from *file*.

`-F` *`sep`*`, --separator` *`sep`*
: Use *sep* as the separator between the filename and the type. The default is `:`.

`-i, --mime`
: Produce MIME type strings instead of the traditional output.

`-k, --keep-going`
: Keep going after the first match.

`-L, --dereference`
: Follow symbolic links. By default, symbolic links are not followed.

`-m` *`filelist`*`, --magic-file` *`filelist`*
: Search for file types in *filelist* instead of `/usr/share/magic`. *filelist* may be a single filename or a colon-separated list of files. If a compiled magic file is found, it is used. With `-i`, `file` appends `.mime` to each filename.

`-n, --no-buffer`
: Flush standard output after checking a file.

`-N, --no-pad`
: Do not pad filenames to make them align in the output.

`-p, --preserve-date`
: Attempt to preserve the access times of read files so that it looks as if `file` never read them.

`-r, --raw`
: Do not translate unprintable characters into their octal equivalents.

`-s, --special-files`
: Read the contents of block or character device special files, instead of being merely content to display their type.

`-v, --version`
: Print the version and exit.

`-z, --uncompress`
: Attempt checking of compressed files.

Example

List all files that are deemed to be HTML input:

```
file * | grep -i HTML
```

find

`find [`*`options`*`]` *`pathname(s) condition(s)`*

An extremely useful command for finding particular groups of files (numerous examples follow this description). `find` descends the directory tree beginning at each *pathname* and locates files that meet the specified *conditions*. At least one *pathname* must be specified. The most useful conditions include -print, -name, and -type (for general use), -exec and -size (for advanced users), and -mtime and -user (for administrators).

On very old systems, you must supply at least one *condition*. If you don't, find traverses the *pathnames* but doesn't produce any output. Therefore, for highest portability, always provide -print.

Conditions may be grouped by enclosing them in \(\) (escaped parentheses), negated with ! (use \! in the C shell), given as alternatives by separating them with -o, or repeated (adding restrictions to the match; usually only for -name, -type, and -perm).

The find command can often be combined with the xargs command when there are too many files for naming on the command line. (See **xargs**.)

find is yet another example of a Unix command that has a core set of common abilities, with many system-specific extensions. Take careful note of which systems support which conditions.

Solaris and Mac OS X Options

-H
: Only for files named on the command line, follow symbolic links, working with the information about the linked-to file, instead of the symbolic link itself.

-L
: For all symbolic links, follow the link, working with the information about the linked-to file, instead of the symbolic link itself.

GNU/Linux Option

-daystart
: Calculate times from the start of the day today, not 24 hours ago.

Mac OS X Options

-d
: Do a depth-first traversal, directories being visited after their children (postorder). The default is a preorder traversal, with directories being visited before their children.

-E
: Interpret regular expressions for -regex and -iregex as Extended Regular Expressions. (See Chapter 7.)

-f *pathname*
: Descend *pathname*.

-P
: For symbolic links, use information about the link itself, not the linked-to file. This is the default.

-s
: Traverse file hierarchies in lexicographical order.

-x
: Do not descend into directories on different devices (filesystems) from the one where the descent began.

-X
: For use with xargs, complain if the filename contains an xargs delimiter character (any of single quote, double quote, backslash, space, tab, or newline). Such files are skipped.

Common Conditions

`-atime` *+n* | *-n* | *n*
: Find files that were last accessed more than *n* (+*n*), less than *n* (-*n*), or exactly *n* days ago. Note that `find` will change the access time of directories supplied as *pathnames*.

`-ctime` *+n* | *-n* | *n*
: Find files that were changed more than *n* (+*n*), less than *n* (-*n*), or exactly *n* days ago. Change refers to modification, permission or ownership changes, etc.; therefore, `-ctime` is more inclusive than `-atime` or `-mtime`.

`-depth`
: Descend the directory tree, skipping directories and working on actual files first (and *then* the parent directories). Useful when files reside in unwritable directories (e.g., when using `find` with `cpio`).

`-exec` *command* `{} \;`
: Run the Unix *command* on each file matched by `find`, provided *command* executes successfully on that file; i.e., returns a 0 exit status. When *command* runs, the argument `{}` is replaced with the name of the current file. Follow the entire sequence with an escaped semicolon (`\;`).

`-follow`
: Follow symbolic links and track the directories visited (don't use this with `-type l`).

`-fstype` *type*
: Find files that reside on filesystems of type *type*.

`-group` *gname*
: Find files belonging to group *gname*, which can be a group name or a group ID number.

`-inum` *n*
: Find files whose inode number is *n*.

`-links` *n*
: Find files having *n* links.

`-ls`
: Display matching files with associated statistics (as if run through `ls -lids`).

`-mount`
: Search for files that reside only on the same filesystem as *pathname*. Solaris and GNU/Linux only. (On Mac OS X, use `-xdev` instead.)

`-mtime` *+n* | *-n* | *n*
: Find files that were last modified more than *n* (+*n*), less than *n* (-*n*), or exactly *n* days ago.

`-name` *pattern*
: Find files whose names match *pattern*. Filename metacharacters may be used, but should be escaped or quoted.

`-newer` *file*
: Find files that have been modified more recently than *file*; similar to `-mtime`.

`-nogroup`
: Find files belonging to a group *not* in `/etc/group`.

`-nouser`
: Find files owned by a user *not* in `/etc/passwd`.

`-ok` *command* `{} \;`
: Same as `-exec`, but user must respond (with a `y`) before *command* is executed.

`-perm` *nnn*
: Find files whose permission settings (e.g., `rwx`) match octal number *nnn* exactly (e.g., 664 matches `-rw-rw-r--`). Use a minus sign to make a wildcard match of any specified bit (e.g., `-perm -600` matches `-rw*******`, where * can be any mode). Some systems also allow *+nnn* for this purpose.

  Solaris allows *nnn* to be a symbolic mode in the same form as allowed by `chmod`.

`-print`
: Print the matching files and directories, using their full pathnames. On modern systems, this is the default action.

`-prune`
: "Prune" the directory tree of unwanted directory searches; that is, skip the directory most recently matched.

`-size` *n*`[c]`
: Find files containing *n* blocks, or, if `c` is specified, files that are *n* characters (bytes) long. (One block = 512 bytes). Some systems allow *n*`k` to specify the size in kilobytes.

`-type` *c*
: Find files whose type is *c*. *c* can be:

`b`	Block special file
`c`	Character special file
`d`	Directory
`D`	Door special file, Solaris and GNU version only
`f`	Plain file
`l`	Symbolic link
`p`	Fifo or named pipe
`s`	Socket

`-user` *user*
: Find files belonging to a *user* name or ID.

`-xdev`
: Same as `-mount`.

GNU/Linux and Mac OS X Conditions

`-amin` *+n* | *-n* | *n*
: Find files last accessed more than *n* (*+n*), less than *n* (*-n*), or exactly *n* minutes ago.

`-anewer` *file*
: Find files that were accessed after *file* was last modified. Affected by `-follow` when after `-follow` on the command line.

`-cmin` *+n* | *-n* | *n*
: Find files last changed more than *n* (+*n*), less than *n* (-*n*), or exactly *n* minutes ago.

`-cnewer` *file*
: Find files that were changed after they were last modified. Affected by `-follow` when after `-follow` on the command line.

`-empty`
: Continue if file is empty. Applies to regular files and directories.

`-false`
: Return false value for each file encountered.

`-iname` *pattern*
: A case-insensitive version of `-name`.

`-ipath` *pattern*
: A case-insensitive version of `-path`.

`-iregex` *pattern*
: A case-insensitive version of `-regex`.

`-maxdepth` *num*
: Do not descend more than *num* levels of directories.

`-mindepth` *num*
: Begin applying tests and actions only at levels deeper than *num* levels.

`-mmin` *+n* | *-n* | *n*
: Find files last modified more than *n* (+*n*), less than *n* (-*n*), or exactly *n* minutes ago.

`-not` *expr*
: Same as `!` *expr*.

`-path` *pattern*
: Find files whose names match *pattern*. Expect full pathnames relative to the starting pathname (i.e., do not treat `/` or `.` specially).

`-print0`
: Like `-print`, but terminate the pathname with a zero byte. This allows programs that read filenames to interpret them unambiguously. See also **xargs**.

`-regex` *pattern*
: Like `-path`, but uses grep-style regular expressions instead of the shell-like globbing used in `-name` and `-path`.

Solaris Conditions

`-acl` True if the file has ACLs (Access Control Lists) defined.

`-cpio` *dev*
: Take matching files and write them on device *dev*, using `cpio`. Obsolete.

`-local`
: Find files that physically reside on the local system.

`-ncpio` *dev*
: Take matching files and write them on device *dev*, using `cpio -c`. Obsolete.

`-xattr`
: True if the file has extended attributes.

GNU/Linux Conditions

`-context` *scontext*, `--context` *scontext*
: File has security context *scontext*. SELinux only.

`-fls` *file*
: Like `-ls`, but send output to *file*.

`-fprint` *file*
: Like `-print`, but send output to *file*.

`-fprint0` *file*
: Like `-print0`, but send output to *file*.

`-fprintf` *file format*
: Like `-printf`, but send output to *file*.

`-gid` *num*
: Find files with numeric group ID of *num*.

`-ilname` *pattern*
: A case-insensitive version of `-lname`.

`-lname` *pattern*
: Search for files that are symbolic links, pointing to files named *pattern*. *pattern* can include shell metacharacters and does not treat / or . specially. The match is case-insensitive.

`-noleaf`
: Normally, `find` assumes that each directory has at least two hard links that should be ignored (a hard link for its name and one for "."; i.e., two fewer "real" directories than its hard link count indicates). `-noleaf` turns off this assumption, a useful practice when `find` runs on non-Unix-style filesystems. This forces `find` to examine all entries, assuming that some might prove to be directories into which it must descend (a time-waster on Unix).

`-printf` *format*
: Print using *format* to standard output. Interpret escape sequences and special formatting control sequences that begin with `%`. See the manpage for the full details.

`-true`
: Return true value for each file encountered.

`-uid` *num*
: Find files with numeric user ID of *num*.

`-used` *num*
: File was accessed *num* days after it was modified.

`-xtype` *c*
: Like `-type` except for symbolic links. For symbolic links, this checks the type of the linked-to file. However, with `-follow`, `find` checks the link itself, and this condition will be true only if *c* is `l`.

Mac OS X Conditions

-delete
: Delete found files or directories. Always returns true. Use with extreme caution.

-execdir *command* { } \;
: Like -exec, but execute the command from within the directory holding the current file. The filename substituted for { } is *not* fully qualified.

-flags [+|-]*flags,notflags*
: Check that the given *flags* are set and that the *notflags* (flag names prefixed with no) are not set. The flags are those managed by chflags. With a leading -, the condition evaluates to true if at least all the bits in *flags* must be set and all the bits in *notflags* must be clear. With a leading +, the condition evaluates to true if any of the bits in *flags* are set and any of the bits in *notflags* are clear. Otherwise, the file's flags must exactly match the combination of *flags* and *notflags*.

-mnewer *file*
: Same as -newer.

-newer*XY* *file*
: Compare the attribute *X* of the current file against the attribute *Y* of *file*. Values for *X* and *Y* may be a for the access time, c for the inode change time, or m for the modification time. Additionally, *Y* may be t, in which case *file* is expected to be a date specification as understood by CVS. (See Chapter 14.)

-okdir *command* { } \;
: Like -ok, but execute the command from within the directory holding the current file. The filename substituted for { } is *not* fully qualified.

Examples

List all files (and subdirectories) in your home directory:

```
find $HOME -print
```

List all files named chapter1 underneath the /work directory:

```
find /work -name chapter1 -print
```

List "memo" files owned by ann (note the use of multiple starting paths):

```
find /work /usr -name 'memo*' -user ann -print
```

Search the filesystem (begin at root) for manpage directories:

```
find / -type d -name 'man*' -print
```

Search the current directory, look for filenames that don't begin with a capital letter, and send them to the printer:

```
find . \! -name '[A-Z]*' -exec lp { } \;
```

Find and compress files whose names don't end with .gz:

```
gzip `find . -type f \! -name '*.gz' -print`
```

Remove all empty files on the system (prompting first):

```
find / -size 0 -ok rm { } \;
```

Skip RCS directories, but list remaining read-only files:

```
find . -name RCS -prune -o -perm 444 -print
```

Search the system for files that were modified within the last two days (good candidates for backing up):

```
find / -mtime -2 -print
```

Recursively grep for a pattern down a directory tree:

```
find /book -print | xargs grep '[Nn]utshell'
```


---

finger

`finger [options] users`

Display data about one or more *users*, including information listed in the files `.plan` and `.project` in *user*'s home directory. You can specify each *user* either as a login name (exact match) or as a first or last name (display information on all matching names). Networked environments recognize arguments of the form *user@host* and *@host*. (Today, many systems on the Internet disallow connections from `finger` requests.)

Common Options

`-l` Force long format (default).

`-m` *users* must match usernames exactly, instead of also searching for a match of first or last names.

`-p` Omit `.plan` file from display. On Mac OS X, this also omits the `.forward`, `.project`, and `.pubkey` files.

`-s` Show short format.

Solaris Options

`-b` Omit user's home directory and shell from display.

`-f` Used with `-s` to omit heading that normally displays in short format.

`-h` Omit `.project` file from display.

`-i` Show "idle" format, a terse format (like `-s`).

`-q` Show "quick" format, the tersest of all (requires an exact match of username).

`-w` Use with `-s` to omit user's full name that normally displays in short format.

Mac OS X Options

`-4` Use only IPv4 addresses.

`-6` Use only IPv6 addresses.

`-g` Display only the user's real name from the *gecos* information.

`-h` Together with `-s`, display the remote host information instead of the office information.

`-o` Together with `-s`, display only the office information.

`-T` Don't piggyback data with the initial connection request. Needed for some servers with broken TCP/IP implementations.

flex

`flex [options] [file]`

flex (Fast Lexical Analyzer Generator) is a faster variant of lex. It generates a lexical analysis program (named *lex.yy.c*) based on the regular expressions and C statements contained in one or more input *files*. See also **lex**, **bison**, **yacc**, and *lex & yacc*, cited in the Bibliography.

URL: *http://www.gnu.org/software/flex*.

Options

`-b` Generate backup information to `lex.backup`.

`-B` Generate a batch (noninteractive) scanner.

`-c` Ignored; for POSIX compliance only.

`-C` Compress scanner tables but do not use equivalence classes or metaequivalence classes.

`-Ca` Align tables for memory access and computation. This creates larger tables but gives faster performance.

`-Ce` Construct equivalence classes. This creates smaller tables and sacrifices little performance (default).

`-Cf` Generate full scanner tables, not compressed.

`-CF` Generate faster scanner tables, like `-F`.

`-Cm` Construct metaequivalence classes (default).

`-Cr` Bypass use of the standard I/O library; use *read*(2) system calls instead.

`-d` Debug mode.

`-f` Create a faster but larger scanner.

`-F` Use the fast scanner table representation.

`-h, -?, --help`
Help summary.

`-i` Create a case-insensitive scanner.

`-I` Generate an interactive scanner (default).

`-l` Maximum `lex` compatibility.

`-L` Suppress `#line` directives in `lex.yy.c`.

`-n` Ignored; for POSIX compliance only.

`-o file`
Write output to *file* instead of `lex.yy.c`.

`-p` Print performance report to standard error.

`-P prefix`
Change default yy prefix to *prefix* for all globally visible variable and function names.

`-s` Create a scanner that exits if it encounters input that does not match any of its rules.

`-S skeleton_file`
Use *skeleton_file* for the code skeleton, instead of the default file. This option is mainly for use by the `flex` maintainers.

-t Print to standard output. (By default, flex prints to lex.yy.c.)

-T Run in trace mode. This produces considerable output, which is mainly of use to the flex maintainers.

-v Print a summary of statistics to standard error.

-V, --version
Print version information and exit.

-w Suppress warning messages.

-7 Generate a seven-bit scanner.

-8 Generate an eight-bit scanner (default).

-+ Generate a C++ scanner class.

fmt

fmt [*options*] [*files*]

Fill and join text, producing lines of roughly the same length. (Unlike nroff, the lines are not justified.) fmt ignores blank lines and lines beginning with a dot (.) or with "From:". The emacs editor uses ESC-q to join paragraphs, so fmt is useful for other editors, such as vi. The following vi command fills and joins the remainder of the current paragraph:

```
!}fmt
```

Solaris Options

-c Don't adjust the first two lines; align subsequent lines with the second line. Useful for paragraphs that begin with a hanging tag.

-s Split long lines but leave short lines alone. Useful for preserving partial lines of code.

-w *n* Create lines no longer than *n* columns wide. Default is 72. (Can also be invoked as -*n* for compatibility with BSD.)

GNU/Linux Options

-c, --crown-margin
Crown margin mode. Do not change indentation of each paragraph's first two lines. Use the second line's indentation as the default for subsequent lines.

-p *prefix*, --prefix=*prefix*
Format only lines beginning with *prefix*.

-s, --split-only
Suppress line-joining.

-t, --tagged-paragraph
Tagged paragraph mode. Same as crown mode when the indentations of the first and second lines differ. If the indentation is the same, treat the first line as its own separate paragraph.

-u, --uniform-spacing
Reduce spacing to a maximum of one space between words and two between sentences.

-w *width*, --width=*width*
Set output width to *width*. The default is 75.

Mac OS X Options

-c Center each line of text. Most other options are ignored, and no splitting or joining of lines is done.

-d *charlist*
: Treat the characters in *charlist* as sentence-ending characters. The default list is `.?!` (period, question mark, and exclamation mark).

-l *count*
: Replace each *count* spaces at the beginning of a line with a tab character. The default is eight. If *count* is zero, spaces are preserved.

-m Attempt to sensibly format mail header lines.

-n Format lines that begin with `.` (dot). Normally, for `nroff` compatibility, `fmt` leaves such lines alone.

-p Allow indented paragraphs. Normally changes in leading whitespace start a new output paragraph. This option disables that behavior.

-s Condense multiple whitespace characters inside lines into single spaces.

-t *count*
: Assume that input files use *count* spaces per tab stop. The default is eight.

---

ftp

`ftp [`*options*`] [`*hostname*`]`

Transfer files to and from remote network site *hostname*. `ftp` prompts the user for a command. Type `help` to see a list of known commands.

Common Options

-d Enable debugging.

-e Disable command-line editing and history. GNU/Linux and Mac OS X only.

-g Disable filename expansion (*globbing*).

-i Turn off interactive prompting.

-n No auto-login upon initial connection.

-p Use passive mode for transfering data.

-v Verbose on. Show all responses from remote server.

Solaris Options

-a Use GSSAPI authentication. If authentication fails, close the connection.

-v Forward local security credentials to the server.

-m *GSSAPI-mech*
: Use the provided GSSASPI mechanism. For details see *mech*(4).

-t Enable packet tracing. This option is not yet implemented.

`-T` *timeout*
Use *timeout* in seconds for the global connection timer.

`-x` Use GSSAPI for authentication and encryption.

Mac OS X Options

`-4` Use only IPv4 addresses.

`-6` Use only IPv6 addresses.

`-a` Use anonymous login instead of the normal login procedure.

`-A` Force active mode FTP. The default is passive mode.

`-f` Force a cache reload when a transfer goes through an FTP or HTTP proxy.

`-N` *netrc-file*
Use the given file instead of `$HOME/.netrc`.

`-o` *file*
Save the first automatically retrieved file to *file*, unless file is `-` or starts with `|`. See the manpage for more details.

`-P` *port*
Use port number *port*.

`-r` *count*
When a connection attempt fails, wait *count* seconds and then retry.

`-R` Restart all nonproxied auto-fetches.

`-t` Enable packet tracing.

`-T` *direction*,*max*[,*incr*]
Set the maximum transfer rate in *direction* to *max* bytes/second. If given, set the increment to *incr*. See the manpage for more information.

`-u` *url file ...*
Upload one or more *files* to *url*.

`-v` Enable the `verbose` and `progress` commands. This is the default when output is to a terminal.

`-V` Disable the `verbose` and `progress` commands.

---

g++

`g++ [`*options*`]` *files*

Invoke gcc with the options necessary to make it recognize C++. g++ recognizes all the file extensions gcc does, in addition to C++ source files (`.C`, `.cc`, `.cpp`, or `.cxx` files) and C++ preprocessed files (`.ii` files). See also **gcc**.

---

gcc

`gcc [`*options*`]` *files*

GNU Compiler Collection. gcc, formerly known as the GNU C Compiler, compiles multiple languages (C, C++, Objective-C, Ada, Fortran, and Java) to machine code. Here we document its use to compile C, C++, or Objective-C code. gcc compiles one or more program source files; for example, C source files (`file.c`), assembler source files (file.s), or preprocessed C source files (file.i). If the file suffix is not recognizable, assume that the file is an object file or library. gcc normally invokes the C preprocessor, compiles the preprocessed code to assembly language code, assembles it, and then links it with the linker. This process can be stopped at one of these stages using the -c, -S, or -E option. The steps may also differ depending on the language being compiled. By default, output is placed in a.out. In some cases, gcc generates an object file having a .o suffix and a corresponding root name.

Preprocessor and linker options given on the gcc command line are passed on to these tools when they are run. These options are briefly described here, but some are more fully described under the entry for ld. The options that follow are divided into general, preprocessor and linker options. We have included only the most generally useful options. gcc accepts many, many more options not covered here.

gcc is the GNU form of cc; on most Linux systems, the command cc invokes gcc. The command g++ invokes gcc with the appropriate options for interpreting C++; see g++.

URL: *http://gcc.gnu.org*.

General options

-a
: Provide profile information for basic blocks.

-ansi
: Enforce full ANSI conformance.

-c
: Create linkable object file for each source file, but do not call the linker.

-E
: Preprocess the source files, but do not compile. Print result to standard output. This option is useful to meaningfully pass some cpp options that would otherwise break gcc, such as -C, -M, or -P.

-f*option*
: Set the specified compiler *option*. Many of these control debugging, optimization of code, and special language options. Use the --help -v options for a full listing.

-g
: Include debugging information for use with gdb.

-g*level*
: Provide *level* amount of debugging information. *level* must be 1, 2, or 3, with 1 providing the least amount of information. The default is 2.

--help
: Print most common basic options, then exit. When used with option -v, print options for all of gcc's subprocesses. For options specific to a target, use --target-help.

-m*option*
: Set the specified machine specific *option*. Use the --target-help option for a full listing.

`-o` *file*
: Specify output file as *file*. Default is *a.out*.

`-O[`*level*`]`
: Optimize. *level* should be 1, 2, 3, or 0 (the default is 1). 0 turns off optimization; 3 optimizes the most.

`-p` Provide profile information for use with `prof`.

`-pedantic`
: Warn verbosely.

`-pg` Provide profile information for use with `gprof`.

`-std=`*standard*
: Specify C *standard* of input file. Accepted values are:

`iso9899:1990`, `c89`	1990 ISO C standard.
`iso9899:199409`	1994 amendment to the 1990 ISO C standard.
`iso9899:1999`, `c99`, `iso9899:199x`, `c9x`	1999 revised ISO C standard.
`gnu89`	1990 C Standard with GNU extensions (the default value).
`gnu99`, `gnu9x`	1999 revised ISO C standard with GNU extensions.

`-S` Compile source files into assembler code, but do not assemble.

`-v` Print version information.

`-V` *version*
: Attempt to run gcc version *version*.

`-w` Suppress warnings.

`-W` Warn more verbosely than normal.

`-Wall`
: Enable almost all possible warnings. See the manpage for a detailed list of available warnings.

`-x` *language*
: Expect input file to be written in *language*, which may be `c`, `objective-c`, `c-header`, `c++`, `ada`, `f77`, `ratfor`, `assembler`, `java`, `cpp-output`, `c++-cpp-output`, `objc-cpp-output`, `f77-cpp-output`, `assembler-with-cpp`, or `ada`. If `none` is specified as *language*, guess the language by filename extension.

Preprocessor options

gcc passes the following options to the preprocessor:

`-D`*name*`[=`*def*`]`
: Define *name* with value *def* as if by `#define`. If no =*def* is given, *name* is defined with value 1. `-D` has lower precedence than `-U`.

`-I`*dir*
: Include *dir* in list of directories to search for include files. If *dir* is `-`, search those directories specified by `-I` before the `-I-` only when `#include "`*file*`"` is specified, not `#include <`*file*`>`.

`-M, -MG, -MF, -MD, -MMD, -MQ, -MT`
: Suppress normal output and print Makefile rules describing file dependencies. Print a rule for `make` that describes the main source file's dependencies. If `-MG` is specified, assume that missing header files are actually generated files, and look for them in the source file's directory. Most of these options imply `-E`.

`-trigraphs`
: Convert special three-letter sequences, meant to represent missing characters on some systems, into the single character they represent.

`-U`*name*
: Remove definition of symbol *name*.

Linker options

gcc passes the following options to the linker:

`-l`*lib*
: Link to *lib*.

`-L`*dir*
: Search *dir* in addition to standard directories for libraries.

`-s`
: Remove all symbol table and relocation information from the executable.

`-u` *symbol*
: Force the linker to search libraries for a definition of *symbol*, and to link to the libraries found.

---

gcore

`gcore [`*option*`]` *process_ids*

Solaris and GNU/Linux only. Create ("get") a core image of each running process specified. The core image can be used with a debugger. You must own the running process or be a privileged user to use this command.

Common Option

`-o` *file*
: Place the output in a file named *file.process_id* (default is `core.`*process_id*).

Solaris Options

`-c` *content*
: Place *content* in the core file. See *coreadm*(1M) for details on the values of `content`.

`-F`
: Force; take control of *pid* even if another process had control of it.

`-g`
: Produce a core file in the global repository with global content as configured via *coreadm*(1M). You must have permission to create files in the global core repository.

`-p`
: Produce a core file in the process-specific repository with process-specific content as configured via *coreadm*(1M). You must have permission to create files in the process-specific core repository.

gdb

`gdb [options] [program [core | pid]]`

GDB (the GNU DeBugger) allows you to step through the execution of a program in order to find the point at which it breaks. It supports a number of languages. The program to be debugged is normally specified on the command line; you can also specify a core file or, if you want to investigate a running program, a process ID. For more information, see Chapter 17.

getconf

```
getconf [-v spec] system_var
getconf [-v spec] path_var path
getconf -a
```

This command is specified by POSIX as a portable way of determining system limits. In the first form, print the value of system configuration variables. In the second, print the value of filesystem-related parameters. In the third, print the values of all system configuration variables.

Options

`-a` Print the names and values of all system configuration variables. Solaris only.

`-v` *spec*
Use *spec* to govern the selection of values for configuration variables.

getopts

`getopts string name [arg]`

Same as built-in Bash and `ksh` shell command `getopts`. See Chapter 4.

gettext

`gettext [options] [domain] string`

Solaris and GNU/Linux only. Retrieve and print the translated version of *string*. This provides shell-level access to the facilities of *gettext*(3C). Translations are looked up in the file *lang*/LC_MESSAGES/*domain*.mo in the system's translation directory. *lang* is the current locale (e.g., en_US). If *domain* is not supplied, the value of $TEXTDOMAIN is used instead. Without a domain, or if no translation can be found, gettext simply prints *string*. If $TEXTDOMAINDIR exists, its value is used instead of the system default.

The GNU version of gettext and the accompanying commands and library functions are an extension of the original Solaris design from the early 1990s. Modern Solaris versions of the commands have picked up some of the features first developed for the GNU version. Thus, for example, even the Solaris version of this command accepts long options.

URL: *http://www.gnu.org/software/gettext.*

Options

`-d` *domain*, `--domain=`*domain*
: Retrieve messages from the *domain* text domain.

`-e` Enable expansion of some escape sequences. Use with `-s`.

`-h`, `--help`
: Print a command-line summary and exit. GNU/Linux only.

`-n` Don't print the trailing newline. Use with `-s`.

`-s` Enable echo-like features (`-e` and `-n`).

`-V`, `--version`
: Print version information and exit. GNU/Linux only.

---

ghostscript

`ghostscript [`*options*`]` *files*

GhostScript, an interpreter for Adobe Systems' PostScript and PDF (Portable Document Format) languages. Used for document processing. With `-` in place of *files*, standard input is used. The usual name is gs; see **gs**.

---

gprof

`gprof [`*options*`] [`*objfile* `[`*pfile*`]]`

Display call-graph profile data of C programs. Programs compiled with the `-xpg` option of Sun's `cc` (`-pg` on other compilers) produce a call-graph profile file *pfile*, whose default name is `gmon.out`. The specified object file *objfile* (`a.out` by default) contains a symbol table that is read and correlated with *pfile*.

URL: *http://www.gnu.org/software/binutils* for the GNU version of `gprof`.

Common Options

`-a`, `--no-static`
: Don't print statically declared functions.

`-b`, `--brief`
: Brief; don't print field descriptions in the profile.

`-c`, `--static-call-graph`
: Find the program's static call-graph. Call counts of 0 indicate static-only parents or children.

`-e` *name*
: Don't print the graph profile entry for the routine *name*. `-e` may be repeated.

`-E` *name*
: Like `-e`. In addition, during time computations, omit the time spent in *name*.

`-f` *name*
: Print the graph profile entry only for routine *name*. `-f` may be repeated.

`-F name`
: Like `-f`. In addition, during time computations, use only the times of the printed routines. `-F` may be repeated, and it overrides `-E`.

`-s, --sum`
: With this option, you supply one or more existing *pfiles*. Sum the information in all specified profile files and send it to a profile file called `gmon.sum`. Useful for accumulating data across several runs.

`-z, --display-unused-functions`
: Show routines that have zero usage. Useful with `-c` to find out which routines were never called.

Solaris Options

`-n` Only print the top *n* functions.

`-C` Demangle C++ symbol names before printing them out.

`-D` With this option, you supply one or more existing *pfiles*. Process the information in all specified profile files and produce a profile file called `gmon.sum` that shows the difference between the runs. See also the `-s` option.

`-l` Don't print entries for local symbols.

GNU/Linux Options

`-A[symspec], --annotated-source[=symspec]`
: Print annotated source code.

`-C[symspec], --exec-counts[=symspec]`
: Print statistics on the number of times each function is called. When used with option `-l`, count basic-block execution.

`-d [num], --debug[=num]`
: Turn on debugging. Use *num* to specify specific debugging features; otherwise enable all debugging. See the `gprof` Info file for more information.

`-D, --ignore-non-functions`
: Ignore symbols that are not known functions. This produces more accurate profiles.

`--demangle[=style], --no-demangle`
: Specify whether C++ symbols should be demangled or not. They are demangled by default. If profiling a program built by a different compiler, you may need to specify the mangling style.

`--file-ordering file`
: Print suggested link line order for `.o` files based on profiling data. Read function name to object file mappings from *file*. This file can be created using the `nm` command.

`--function-ordering`
: Print suggested function order based on profiling data.

`-i, --file-info`
: Print summary information on data files, then exit.

`-I` *dirs*, `--directory-path=`*dirs*
: Set directory path to search for source files. The *dirs* argument may be given as a colon-separated list of directories.

`-J[`*symspec*`]`, `--no-annotated-source[=`*symspec*`]`
: Don't print annotated source code.

`-k` *from/to*
: Remove arcs between the routines *from* and *to*.

`-l`, `--line`
: Generate line-by-line profiles. This can increase gprof's running time and may be less statistically accurate.

`-L`, `--print-path`
: Print the path information when printing filenames.

`-m` *n*, `--min-count[=`*n*`]`
: Don't print count statistics for symbols executed less than *n* times.

`-n[`*symspec*`]`, `--time[=`*symspec*`]`
: Propagate time statistics in call graph analysis.

`-N[`*symspec*`]`, `--no-time[=`*symspec*`]`
: Don't propagate time statistics in call graph analysis.

`-O` *format*, `--file-format[=`*format*`]`
: Use *format* for the output file format. Acceptable values are `auto` (the default), `bsd`, `4.4bsd`, `magic`, and `prof` (not yet implemented).

`-p[`*symspec*`]`, `--flat-profile[=`*symspec*`]`
: Print profile statistics.

`-P[`*symspec*`]`, `--no-flat-profile[=`*symspec*`]`
: Don't print profile statistics.

`-q[`*symspec*`]`, `--graph[=`*symspec*`]`
: Print call graph analysis.

`-Q[`*symspec*`]`, `--no-graph[=`*symspec*`]`
: Don't print call graph analysis.

`-T`, `--traditional`
: Print output in BSD style.

`-v`, `--version`
: Print version and exit.

`-w` *n*, `--width=`*n*
: Print function index formatted to width *n*.

`-x`, `--all-lines`
: When printing annotated source, annotate every line in a basic block, not just the beginning.

`-y`, `--separate-files`
: Print annotated-source output to separate files instead of standard output. The annotated source for each source file is printed to *filename*`-ann`.

`-Z[`*symspec*`]`, `--no-exec-counts[=`*symspec*`]`
: Don't print statistics on the number of times each function is called.

Mac OS X Options

-S Create the "order" files gmon.order, callf.order, callo.order, and time.order, for use with ld. To include library functions in the files, you must have a whatsloaded file from ld in the current directory. For more details see *ld*(1).

grep

`grep [options] regexp [files]`

Search one or more *files* for lines that match a regular expression *regexp*. Regular expressions are described in Chapter 7. Exit status is 0 if any lines match, 1 if not, and 2 for errors. See also **egrep** and **fgrep**.

Options

The *options* for grep are the same as for egrep, including the Solaris versus GNU differences. For Solaris, there is an exception: /usr/xpg4/bin/grep also accepts the -q option. See **egrep** for the full list.

Examples

List the number of users who use the C shell:

```
grep -c /bin/csh /etc/passwd
```

List header files that have at least one #include directive:

```
grep -l '^#include' /usr/include/*
```

List files that don't contain *pattern*:

```
grep -c pattern files | grep :0
```

groff

`groff [options] [files]`

The GNU version of troff. Formats documents to screen or for laser printing. See Chapter 18.

groups

`groups [options] [user]`

Show the groups that *user* belongs to (default is your groups). Groups are listed in /etc/passwd and /etc/group.

gs

`gs [options] [files]`

Solaris (in /usr/sfw/bin), and GNU/Linux only. GhostScript, an interpreter for Adobe Systems' PostScript and PDF (Portable Document Format) languages. Used for document processing. With - in place of *files*, standard input is used.

URLs: *http://www.gnu.org/software/ghostscript* and *http://www.cs.wisc.edu/~ghost/*.

Options

`--` *`filename arg1 ...`*
: Take the next argument as a filename, but use all remaining arguments to define `ARGUMENTS` in `userdict` (not `systemdict`) as an array of those strings before running the file.

`-D`*`name`*`=`*`token`*`, -d`*`name`*`=`*`token`*
: Define a name in `systemdict` with the given definition. The token must be exactly one token (as defined by the token operator) and must not contain any whitespace.

`-D`*`name`*`, -d`*`name`*
: Define a name in `systemdict` with a null value.

`-g`*`number1`*`x`*`number2`*
: Specify width and height of device; intended for systems like the X Window System.

`-I`*`directories`*
: Add the designated list of directories at the head of the search path for library files.

`-q` Quiet startup.

`-r`*`number`*`, -r`*`number1`*`x`*`number2`*
: Specify X and Y resolutions (for the benefit of devices, such as printers, that support multiple X and Y resolutions). If only one number is given, it is used for both X and Y resolutions.

`-S`*`name`*`=`*`string`*`, -s`*`name`*`=`*`string`*
: Define a name in `systemdict` with a given *string* as value.

Special names

`-dDISKFONTS`
: Causes individual character outlines to be loaded from the disk the first time they are encountered.

`-dNOBIND`
: Disables the `bind` operator. Useful only for debugging.

`-dNOCACHE`
: Disables character caching. Useful only for debugging.

`-dNODISPLAY`
: Suppresses the normal initialization of the output device. May be useful when debugging.

`-dNOPAUSE`
: Disables the prompt and pause at the end of each page.

`-dNOPLATFONTS`
: Disables the use of fonts supplied by the underlying platform (e.g., the X Window System).

`-dSAFER`
: Disables the `deletefile` and `renamefile` operators and the ability to open files in any mode other than read-only.

`-dWRITESYSTEMDICT`
: Leaves `systemdict` writable.

`-sDEVICE=`*device*
: Selects an alternate initial output device.

`-sOUTPUTFILE=`*filename*
: Selects an alternate output file (or pipe) for the initial output device.

---

gunzip

`gunzip [`*gzip options*`] [`*files*`]`

Identical to `gzip -d`. Typically provided as a hard link to `gzip`. The `-1` ... `-9` and corresponding long-form options are not available with `gunzip`; all other `gzip` options are accepted. See **gzip** for more information.

---

gzcat

`gzcat [`*gzip options*`] [`*files*`]`

A link to `gzip` instead of using the name `zcat`, which preserves `zcat`'s original link to the old `compress` command. Its action is identical to `gunzip -c`. May be installed as `zcat` on some systems. See **gzip** for more information.

---

gzip

`gzip [`*options*`] [`*files*`]`

GNU Zip. Reduce the size of one or more *files* using Lempel-Ziv (LZ77) coding, and move to *file*`.gz`. Restore with `gunzip`. With a filename of `-`, or with no *files*, `gzip` reads standard input. Usually, compression is considerably better than that provided by the old `compress` command. Furthermore, the algorithm is patent-free. Today, `gzip` is the de-facto compression software used throughout the Internet. (Although `bzip2` is also popular, see **bzip2**.)

`gzip` ignores symbolic links. The original file's name, permissions, and modification time are stored in the compressed file, and restored when the file is uncompressed. `gzip` is capable of uncompressing files that were compressed with `compress`, `pack`, or the BSD `compact`. Default options may be placed in the environment variable GZIP.

`gunzip` is equivalent to `gzip -d`. It is typically a hard link to the `gzip` command. `gzcat` and `zcat` are equivalent to `gunzip -c`, and are also often hard links to `gzip`.

Additional related commands include `gzcmp`, which compares the contents of gzipped files; `gzdiff`, which creates diff (difference) files from a pair of `gzip` files; `gzgrep`, to search them; and the `gzless` and `gzmore` commands, which apply the `more` and `less` commands to `gzip` output as `gzcat` does with the `cat` command. See **cat**, **cmp**, **diff**, **grep**, **less**, and **more** for information on how to use those commands.

URL: *http://www.gzip.org*.

Options

-a, --ascii
: ASCII text mode: convert end-of-lines using local conventions. Not supported on all systems.

-c, --stdout, --to-stdout
: Write output on standard output; keep original files unchanged. Individual input files are compressed separately; for better compression, concatenate all the input files first.

-d, --decompress, --uncompress
: Decompress.

-f, --force
: Force. The file is compressed or decompressed, even if the target file exists or if the file has multiple links.

-h, --help
: Display a help screen and exit.

-l, --list
: List the compressed and uncompressed sizes, the compression ratio, and the original name of the file for each compressed file. With --verbose, also list the compression method, the 32-bit CRC, and the original file's last-modification time. With --quiet, the title and totals lines are not displayed.

-L, --license
: Display the gzip license and quit.

-n, --no-name
: For gzip, do not save the original filename and modification time in the compressed file. For gunzip, do not restore the original name and modification time; use those of the compressed file (this is the default).

-N, --name
: For gzip, save the original filename and modification time in the compressed file (this is the default). For gunzip, restore the original filename and modification time based on the information in the compressed file.

-q, --quiet
: Suppress all warnings.

-r, --recursive
: Recursively walk the current directory tree and compress (for gunzip, uncompress) all files found.

--rsyncable
: Make an archive that is "friendly" to rsync. Not supported on all systems.

-S *.suf*, --suffix *.suf*
: Use *.suf* as the suffix instead of .gz. A null suffix makes gunzip attempt decompression on all named files, no matter what their suffix.

`-t, --test`
: Check the compressed file integrity.

`-v, --verbose`
: Display the name and percentage reduction for each file compressed or decompressed.

`-V, --version`
: Display the version number and compilation options, and then quit.

`-n, --fast, --best`
: Control the compression method. *n* is a number between 1 and 9. `-1` (same as `--fast`) gives the fastest, but least compressed method. `-9` (same as `--best`) gives the best compression, but is slower. Values between 1 and 9 vary the tradeoff in compression method. The default compression level is `-6`, which gives better compression at some expense in speed. In practice, the default is excellent, and you should not need to use these options.

---

head

`head [options] [files]`

Print the first few lines of one or more *files* (default is 10).

Common Options

`-n`
: Print the first *n* lines of the file. This is traditional `head` behavior, although it is not blessed by all versions of the POSIX standard.

`-n n`
: Print the first *n* lines of the file.

GNU/Linux Options

`-c num[b|k|m], --bytes num[b|k|m]`
: Print first *num* bytes or, if *num* is followed by `b`, `k`, or `m`, first *num* 512-byte blocks, 1-kilobyte blocks, or 1-megabyte blocks.

`--lines num`
: Same as `-n`.

`-q, --quiet, --silent`
: Quiet mode; never print headers giving filenames.

`-v, --verbose`
: Print filename headers, even for only one file.

Examples

Display the first 20 lines of `phone_list`:

```
head -n 20 phone_list
```

Display the first 10 phone numbers having a 202 area code:

```
grep '(202)' phone_list | head
```

hexdump

`hexdump [options] file`

GNU/Linux and Mac OS X only. Display specified file or input in hexadecimal, octal, decimal, or ASCII format. Option flags specify the display format.

Options

-b
: Use a one-byte octal display, meaning the input offset is in hexadecimal and followed by sixteen three-column octal data bytes, filled in with zeroes and separated by spaces.

-c
: Use a one-byte character display, meaning the input offset is in hexadecimal and followed by sixteen three-column entries, filled in with zeroes and separated with spaces.

-C
: Canonical mode. Display hexadecimal offset, two sets of eight columns of hexadecimal bytes, then a | followed by the ASCII representation of those same bytes.

-d
: Use a two-byte decimal display. The input offset is again in hexadecimal, but the display has only eight entries per line, of five columns each, containing two bytes of unsigned decimal format.

-e *format_string*
: Choose a format string to be used to transform the output data. Format strings consist of:

  Iteration count
  : The iteration count is optional. It determines the number of times to use the transformation string. The number should be followed by a slash character (/) to distinguish it from the byte count.

  Byte count
  : The number of bytes to be interpreted by the conversion string. It should be preceded by a slash character to distinguish it from the iteration count.

  Format characters
  : The actual format characters should be surrounded by quotation marks and are interpreted as *printf*(3) formatting strings (see also **printf**), although the *, h, l, n, p, and q options will not work as expected. Format string usage is discussed at greater length in the hexdump manpage.

-f *filename*
: Choose a file that contains several format strings. The strings should be separated by newlines; the # character marks a line as a comment.

-n *length*
: Limit the number of bytes of input to be interpreted.

-o
: Two-byte octal display, meaning a hexadecimal offset followed by eight five-column data entries of two bytes each, in octal format.

`-s` *offset*
: Skip to specified *offset*. The offset number is assumed to be decimal unless it starts with `0x` or `0X` (hexadecimal), or `0` (octal). Numbers may also be designated in megabytes, kilobytes, or half-kilobytes with the addition of `m`, `k`, or `b` at the end of the number.

`-v`
: Display all input data, even if it is the same as the previous line. Normally, a duplicate line is replaced by an asterisk (*).

`-x`
: Display data in a two-byte hexadecimal format. The offset is, as usual, in hexadecimal, and is followed by eight space-separated entries, each of which contains four-column, two-byte chunks of data in hexadecimal format.

---

hostname

`hostname [`*option*`] [`*nameofhost*`]`

Set or print name of current host system. A privileged user can set the hostname with the *nameofhost* argument.

Mac OS X accepts the `-s` option.

GNU/Linux Options

`-a, --alias`
: Display the alias name of the host (if used).

`-d, --domain`
: Print DNS domain name.

`-f, --fqdn, --long`
: Print fully qualified domain name.

`-F` *file*`, --file` *file*
: Consult *file* for hostname.

`-i, --ip-address`
: Display the IP address(es) of the host.

`-n, --node`
: Display or set the DECnet node name. Not available on all systems. (And not terribly useful even on those systems that have it.)

`-s, --short`
: Trim domain information from the printed name.

`-v, --verbose`
: Verbose mode.

`-y, --yp, --nis`
: Display the NIS domain name. A privileged user can set a new NIS domain name with *nameofhost*.

---

iconv

`iconv [`*options*`] -f` *from_encoding* `-t` *to_encoding* `[`*file*`]`

Convert the contents of *file* from one character set to another.

Common Options

`-c` Omit invalid output characters.

`-f` *`code1`*`, --from-code=`*`code1`*
: Convert input characters from the *code1* encoding.

`-l, --list`
: Print a list of valid encodings to standard output.

`-s, --silent`
: Operate silently; don't print warning messages.

`-t` *`code2`*`, --to-code=`*`code2`*
: Convert input characters to the *code2* encoding.

GNU/Linux Options

`-o` *`file`*`, --output=`*`file`*
: Write the converted output to *file* instead of standard output.

`--usage`
: Print a brief usage message showing only the command syntax and then exit.

`-V, --version`
: Print version information and exit.

`--verbose`
: Operate verbosely; print progress messages.

`-?, --help`
: Print a help message and exit.

---

id

`id [`*`options`*`] [`*`username`*`]`

Display information about yourself or another user: user ID, group ID, effective user ID and group ID if relevant, and additional group IDs.

Common Options

`-g, --group`
: Print group ID only.

`-G, --groups`
: Print supplementary groups only.

`-n, --name`
: With `-u`, `-g`, or `-G`, print user or group name, not number.

`-r, --real`
: With `-u`, `-g`, or `-G`, print real, not effective, user ID or group ID.

`-u, --user`
: Print user ID only.

Solaris Option

`-a` `/usr/bin/id`: list all groups.

GNU/Linux Options

`-a` Ignored; for compatibility with other systems.

`-Z, --context`
: Print the security context. SELinux only.

Mac OS X Option

`-P` Print information as an `/etc/passwd` entry.

info

`info [options] [topics]`

GNU hypertext documentation reader. Display online documentation previously built from Texinfo input. Info files are arranged in a hierarchy and can contain menus for subtopics. When entered without options, the command displays the top-level Info file (usually `/usr/local/info/dir`). When *topics* are specified, find a subtopic by choosing the first *topic* from the menu in the top-level Info file, the next *topic* from the new menu specified by the first *topic*, and so on. The initial display can also be controlled by the `-f` and `-n` options. If a specified *topic* has no Info file but does have a manpage, `info` displays the manpage; if there is neither, the top-level Info file is displayed.

URL: *http://www.gnu.org/software/texinfo*.

Options

`--apropos` *string*
: Find *string* in the indexes of all manuals.

`-d` *directories*, `--directory` *directories*
: Search *directories*, a colon-separated list, for info files. If this option is not specified, use the INFOPATH environment variable or the default directory (usually `/usr/share/info` or `/usr/local/info`).

`--dribble` *file*
: Store each keystroke in *file*, which can be used in a future session with the `--restore` option to return to this place in `info`.

`-f` *file*, `--file` *file*
: Display specified Info file.

`--index-search` *string*
: Find the index entry *string* and go to the node it points to.

`-n` *node*, `--node` *node*
: Display specified node in the Info file.

`-o` *file*, `--output` *file*
: Copy output to *file* instead of displaying it at the screen.

`-O`, `--show-options`, `--usage`
: Go to the node for command-line options.

`--restore` *file*
: When starting, execute keystrokes in *file*.

`-R`, `--raw-escapes`
: Do not remove formatting escape sequences from manpages.

`--subnodes`
: Display subtopics.

`--vi-keys`
: Use vi-like key bindings.

join

`join [options] file1 file2`

Join the common lines of sorted *file1* and sorted *file2*. Read standard input if *file1* is -. The output contains the common field and the remainder of each line from *file1* and *file2*. In the options below, *n* can be 1 or 2, referring to *file1* or *file2*.

Common Options

-a *filenum*
: List unpairable lines in file *filenum*. Use -a 1 -a 2 to list unpairable lines from both files.

-e *string*
: Replace any empty output field with the string *string*.

-o *n.m*
: Each output line contains fields specified by file number *n* and field number *m*. The common field is suppressed unless requested.

-t*c*
: Use character *c* as field separator for input and output.

-v *n*
: Print only the unpairable lines in file *n*. With both -v 1 and -v 2, all unpairable lines are printed.

-1 *m*
: Join on field *m* of file 1. Fields start with 1.

-2 *m*
: Join on field *m* of file 2. Fields start with 1.

Solaris and GNU/Linux Option

-j *fieldnum*
: Equivalent to -1*fieldnum* -2*fieldnum*.

Solaris Options

-j1 *fieldnum*
: Equivalent to -1*fieldnum*.

-j2 *fieldnum*
: Equivalent to -2*fieldnum*.

GNU/Linux Option

-i, --ignore-case
: Ignore case differences when comparing keys.

Examples

Assuming the following input files:

```
$ cat score
olga    81      91
rene    82      92
zack    83      93
$ cat grade
olga    B       A
rene    B       A
```

List scores followed by grades, including unmatched lines:

```
$ join -a1 score grade
olga 81 91 B A
rene 82 92 B A
zack 83 93
```

Pair each score with its grade:

```
$ join -o 1.1 1.2 2.2 1.3 2.3 score grade
olga 81 B 91 A
rene 82 B 92 A
```


kill

`kill [options] IDs`

Terminate one or more process *IDs*. You must own the process or be a privileged user. This command is similar to the `kill` command that is built in to the Bash, Korn, and C shells. A minus sign before an *ID* specifies a process group ID. (The built-in version doesn't allow process group IDs, but it does allow job IDs.)

The command `kill -l` prints a list of the available signal names. The list varies by system architecture; for a PC-based system, it looks like this:

From Bash on GNU/Linux

```
$ kill -l
 1) SIGHUP       2) SIGINT       3) SIGQUIT      4) SIGILL
 5) SIGTRAP      6) SIGABRT      7) SIGBUS       8) SIGFPE
 9) SIGKILL     10) SIGUSR1     11) SIGSEGV     12) SIGUSR2
13) SIGPIPE     14) SIGALRM     15) SIGTERM     17) SIGCHLD
18) SIGCONT     19) SIGSTOP     20) SIGTSTP     21) SIGTTIN
22) SIGTTOU     23) SIGURG      24) SIGXCPU     25) SIGXFSZ
26) SIGVTALRM   27) SIGPROF     28) SIGWINCH    29) SIGIO
30) SIGPWR      31) SIGSYS      33) SIGRTMIN    34) SIGRTMIN+1
35) SIGRTMIN+2  36) SIGRTMIN+3  37) SIGRTMIN+4  38) SIGRTMIN+5
39) SIGRTMIN+6  40) SIGRTMIN+7  41) SIGRTMIN+8  42) SIGRTMIN+9
43) SIGRTMIN+10 44) SIGRTMIN+11 45) SIGRTMIN+12 46) SIGRTMIN+13
47) SIGRTMIN+14 48) SIGRTMIN+15 49) SIGRTMAX-15 50) SIGRTMAX-14
51) SIGRTMAX-13 52) SIGRTMAX-12 53) SIGRTMAX-11 54) SIGRTMAX-10
55) SIGRTMAX-9  56) SIGRTMAX-8  57) SIGRTMAX-7  58) SIGRTMAX-6
59) SIGRTMAX-5  60) SIGRTMAX-4  61) SIGRTMAX-3  62) SIGRTMAX-2
63) SIGRTMAX-1  64) SIGRTMAX
```

The signals and their numbers are defined in the C `<signal.h>` header file. This file may include others, thus the actual location varies across systems. They are shown in the following table. (Note: you should not include these files directly; rather, always use `<signal.h>` in your C or C++ programs.) Look in your system's file to find the signals that apply to your system.

System	File
Solaris	`/usr/include/sys/iso/signal_iso.h`
GNU/Linux	`/usr/include/bits/signum.h`
Mac OS X	`/usr/include/sys/signal.h`

Common Options

`-l [status]`
: List the signal names. (Used by itself.) The optional *status* is a numeric exit value from a process killed by a signal; `kill` will indicate which signal it was.

`-s signal`
: Send signal *signal* to the given process or process group. The signal number (from `<signal.h>`) or name (from `kill -l`). With a signal number of 9, the kill is absolute.

`-signal`
: Send signal *signal* to the given process or process group. *signal* may be either a signal name or a signal number.

GNU/Linux Options

`-a` Kill all processes of the given name (if privileges allow), not just processes with the same UID. To use this option, specify the full path (e.g., `/bin/kill -a gcc`).

`-p` Print the process ID of the named process, but do not send it a signal. In order to use this option, specify the full path (e.g., `/bin/kill -p`).

ksh

`ksh [options] [arguments]`

Korn shell command interpreter. See Chapter 4 for more information, including command-line options.

ld

`ld [options] objfiles`

Combine several *objfiles*, in the specified order, into a single executable object module (`a.out` by default). `ld` is the loader and is usually invoked automatically by compiler commands such as `cc`.

Solaris: `ld` is in `/usr/ccs/bin`.

Options for `ld` vary wildly across systems. Furthermore, in the 21st century, no matter what system you work on, the loader is one of the most complicated commands. We have chosen here to document only those options that are commonly available. You will need to check your local documentation for complete information.

Options

`-e symbol`
: Set *symbol* as the address of the output file's entry point.

`-lx` Search a library named `libx.so` or `libx.a` (the placement of this option on the line affects when the library is searched).

`-L dir`
: Search directory *dir* before standard search directories (this option must precede `-l`).

`-o` *file*
Send the output to *file* (default is `a.out`).

`-r` Allow output to be subject to another `ld`. (Retain relocation information.)

`-R` *path*
Record the colon-separated list of directories in *path* in the object file for use by the runtime loader. Multiple instances may be supplied; the values are concatenated together.

`-s` Remove (strip) symbol table and relocation entries.

`-u` *symbol*
Enter *symbol* in symbol table; useful when loading from an archive library. *symbol* must precede the library that defines it (so `-u` must precede `-l`).

---

ldd

`ldd [options] file`

Solaris and GNU/Linux only. List dynamic dependencies: that is, list shared objects that would be loaded if *file* were executed. (If a valid *file* needs no shared objects, `ldd` succeeds but produces no output.) In addition, `ldd`'s options can show unresolved symbol references that result from running *file*.

Options

Specify only one of these options:

`-d, --data-relocs`
Check references to data objects only.

`-r, --function-relocs`
Check references to data objects and to functions.

Solaris Options

`-c` Disables the use of configuration files; see *crle*(1).

`-e` *envar*
Set the environment variable *envar*. Useful for experimenting with environment variables that affect `ldd` without having to change the global environment.

`-f` Force checking of nonsecure executables. This option is dangerous if running as a privileged user.

`-i` Print the execution order of initialization sections.

`-l` Do immediate processing of any filters, to list all "filtees" and their dependencies.

`-L` Enable lazy loading.

`-s` Display the search path for shared object dependencies.

`-u` Display unused objects. Mutually exclusive with `-U`.

`-U` Display unused objects and dependencies. This is a superset of `-u` and is mutually exclusive with it.

`-v` Display all dependency relationships and version requirements.

GNU/Linux Options

`-v, --verbose`
: Print all information.

`-V, --version`
: Display `ldd`'s version.

less

`less [options] [filename]`

`less` is a program for paging through files or other output. It was written in reaction to the perceived primitiveness of `more` (hence its name). Some commands may be preceded by a number.

URL: *http://www.greenwoodsoftware.com/less*.

The `lesskey` command configures keybindings for `less`. See *lesskey*(1) for more information on it.

Options

`-[z]num, --window=num`
: Set number of lines to scroll to *num*. Default is one screenful. A negative *num* sets the number to *num* lines less than the current number.

`+[+]command`
: Run *command* on startup. If *command* is a number, jump to that line. The option ++ applies this command to each file in the command-line list.

`-?, --help`
: Print help screen. Ignore all other options; do not page through file.

`-a, --search-screen`
: When searching, begin after last line displayed. (Default is to search from second line displayed.)

`-bbuffers, -buffers=buffers`
: Use *buffers* buffers for each file (default is 10). Buffers are 1 KB in size.

`-B, --auto-buffers`
: Do not automatically allocate buffers for data read from a pipe. If `-b` specifies a number of buffers, allocate that many. If necessary, allow information from previous screens to be lost.

`-c, --clear-screen`
: Redraw screen from top, not bottom.

`-C, -CLEAR-SCREEN`
: Redraw screen by clearing it and then redrawing from top.

`-d, --dumb`
: Suppress dumb-terminal error messages.

`-e, --quit-at-eof`
: Automatically exit after reaching EOF twice.

`-E, --QUIT-AT-EOF`
: Automatically exit after reaching EOF once.

`-f, --force`
: Force opening of directories and devices; do not print warning when opening binaries.

`-F, --quit-if-one-screen`
: Exit without displaying anything if first file can fit on a single screen.

`-g, --hilite-search`
: Highlight only string found by past search command, not all matching strings.

`-G, --HILITE-SEARCH`
: Never highlight matching search strings.

`-h`*`num`*`, --max-back-scroll=`*`num`*
: Never scroll backward more than *num* lines at once.

`-i, --ignore-case`
: Make searches case-insensitive, unless the search string contains uppercase letters.

`-I, --IGNORE-CASE`
: Make searches case-insensitive, even when the search string contains uppercase letters.

`-j`*`num`*`, --jump-target=`*`num`*
: Position target line on line *num* of screen. Target line can be the result of a search or a jump. Count lines beginning from 1 (top line). A negative *num* is counted backward from bottom of screen.

`-J, --status-column`
: Used with `-w` or `-W`, highlight a single column on the left edge of the screen instead of the whole text of an unread line.

`-k`*`file`*`, --lesskey-file=`*`file`*
: Read *file* to define special key bindings.

`-K`*`charset`*
: Use the specified *charset*.

`-m, --long-prompt`
: Display more-like prompt, including percent of file read.

`-M`
: Prompt more verbosely than with `-m`, including percentage, line number, and total lines.

`-n, --line-numbers`
: Do not calculate line numbers. Affects `-m` and `-M` options and `=` and `v` commands (disables passing of line number to editor).

`-N, --LINE-NUMBERS`
: Print line number before each line.

`-o`*`file`*`, --log-file=`*`file`*
: When input is from a pipe, copy output to *file* as well as to screen. (Prompt for overwrite authority if *file* exists.)

`-O`*`file`*`, --LOG-FILE=`*`file`*
: Similar to `-o`, but do not prompt when overwriting file.

`-ppattern, --pattern=pattern`
: At startup, search for first occurrence of *pattern*.

`-P[mM=]prompt`
: Set the prompt displayed by `less` at the bottom of each screen to *prompt*. The `m` sets the prompt invoked by the `-m` option, the `M` sets the prompt invoked by the `-M` option, and the `=` sets the prompt invoked by the `=` command. Special characters (described in the manpage for `less`), can be used to print statistics and other information in these prompts.

`-q, --quiet, --silent`
: Disable ringing of bell on attempts to scroll past *EOF* or before beginning of file. Attempt to use visual bell instead.

`-Q, --QUIET, --SILENT`
: Never ring terminal bell.

`-r, --raw-control-chars`
: Display "raw" control characters instead of using ^*x* notation. This sometimes leads to display problems, which might be fixed by using `-R` instead.

`-R, --RAW-CONTROL-CHARS`
: Like `-r`, but adjust screen to account for presence of control characters.

`-s, --squeeze-blank-lines`
: Print successive blank lines as one line.

`-S, --chop-long-lines`
: Cut, do not fold, long lines.

`-ttag, --tag=tag`
: Edit file containing *tag*. Consult `./tags` (constructed by `ctags`).

`-Tfile, --tag-file=file`
: With the `-t` option or `:t` command, read *file* instead of `./tags`.

`-u, --underline-special`
: Treat backspaces and carriage returns as printable input.

`-U, --UNDERLINE-SPECIAL`
: Treat backspaces and carriage returns as control characters.

`-V, --version`
: Display version and exit.

`-w, --hilite-unread`
: Show the line to which a movement command has skipped, phrases displayed by a search command, or the first unread line during a normal scroll by highlighting text in reverse video.

`-W, --HILITE-UNREAD`
: Show phrases displayed by a search command, or the first unread line of any forward movement that is more than one line, by highlighting text in reverse video.

`-xn, --tabs=n`
: Set tab stops to every *n* characters. Default is 8.

`-X, --no-init`
: Do not send initialization and deinitialization strings from termcap to terminal.

`-yn, --max-forw-scroll=n`
: Never scroll forward more than *n* lines at once.

Prompts

The prompt interprets certain sequences specially. Those beginning with `%` are always evaluated. Those beginning with `?` are evaluated if certain conditions are true. Some prompts determine the position of particular lines on the screen. These sequences require that a method of determining that line be specified. See the `-P` option and the manpage for more information.

---

lex

`lex [options] [files]`

Generate a lexical analysis program (named `lex.yy.c`) based on the regular expressions and C statements contained in one or more input *files*. On GNU/Linux and Mac OS X, `lex` is actually `flex`. See also **yacc**, **bison**, **flex**, and *lex & yacc*, which is listed in the Bibliography.

Options

The `-e` and `-w` options may not be available on other Unix systems where `lex` is the original Unix version.

`-c`
: *file*'s program statements are in C (default).

`-e`
: Handle EUC (Extended Unix Code, i.e., eight-bit) characters. Mutually exclusive with `-w`. This gives `yytext[ ]` type `unsigned char`.

`-n`
: Suppress the output summary.

`-Qc`
: Print version information in `lex.yy.c` (if *c* = `y`) or suppress information (if *c* = `n`, the default).

`-t`
: Write program to standard output, not `lex.yy.c`.

`-v`
: Print a summary of machine-generated statistics.

`-V`
: Print version information on standard error.

`-w`
: Handle EUC (eight-bit or wider) characters. Mutually exclusive with `-e`. This gives `yytext[ ]` type `wchar_t`.

---

link

`link file1 file2`

Create a link between two files. This is the same as the `ln` command, but it has no error checking because it uses the *link*(2) system call directly.

ln

```
ln [options] existing new
ln [options] files directory
```

Create pseudonyms (links) for files, allowing them to be accessed by different names. In the first form, link *existing* to *new*, where *new* is usually a new filename. If *new* is an existing file, it is removed first; if *new* is an existing directory, a link named *existing* is created in that directory. In the second form, create links in *directory*, each link having the same name as the file specified.

Common Options

`-f, --force`
: Force the link to occur (don't prompt for overwrite permission).

`-s, --symbolic`
: Create a symbolic link. This lets you link across filesystems and also see the name of the link when you run `ls -l`. (Otherwise, you have to use `find -inum` to find any other names a file is linked to.)

Solaris Option

`-n` `/usr/bin/ln`: Do not overwrite existing files.

GNU/Linux and Mac OS X Options

`-i, --interactive`
: Prompt for permission before removing files.

`-v, --verbose`
: Verbose mode. List files as they are processed.

GNU/Linux Options

`-b, --backup[=control]`
: Back up any existing files. When using the long version of the option, the optional *control* parameter controls the kind of backup. When no control is specified, `ln` attempts to read the control value from the VERSION_CONTROL environment variable. Accepted values are:

`none`, `off`	Never make backups.
`numbered`, `t`	Make numbered backups.
`existing`, `nil`	Match existing backups, numbered or simple.
`simple`, `never`	Always make simple backups.

`-d, -F, --directory`
: Allow hard links to directories. Available to privileged users.

`-n, --no-dereference`
: Replace symbolic links to directories instead of dereferencing them. `--force` is useful with this option.

`-S suffix, --suffix=suffix`
: Append *suffix* to files when making backups, instead of the default ~.

`--target-directory=directory`
: Create links in the specified *directory*.

Mac OS X Options

-h
: Do not follow symbolic links for the target file or directory. Useful with -f to replace a symbolic link that may point to a directory.

-n
: Same as -h.

locale

`locale [options] [name ...]`

Print locale-specific information. With no arguments, locale summarizes the current locale. Depending on the arguments, locale prints information about entire locale categories or the value of specific items within a locale. A *public* locale is one an application can access.

Options

-a, --all-locales
: Print information about all available public locales. The POSIX locale should always be available.

-c, --category-name
: Provide information about the locale category *name*. Useful with or without -k.

-k, --keyword-name
: Print the names and values of the given locale keywords.

-m, --charmaps
: Print the names of the available charmaps.

Environment variables

LANG
: The default value for unset internationalization variables. If not set, the system's default value is used.

LC_ADDRESS
: Postal settings, country, and language names and abbreviation.

LC_ALL
: When set, overrides the values of all other internationalization variables.

LC_COLLATE
: String and character sorting and comparison settings.

LC_CTYPE
: Character attributes, including case conversion mappings, and categories of characters (whitespace, digit, lower, upper, punctuation, etc.).

LC_IDENTIFICATION
: Information related to the current locale definition, including its title, source, revision, and contact information for its author.

LC_MEASUREMENT
: Measurement units, metric or other.

LC_MESSAGES
: Settings for yes/no prompts and other informative and diagnostic messages.

LC_MONETARY
: Currency formats and symbols.

LC_NAME
: Formats for names and honorifics.

LC_NUMERIC
: Nonmonetary number formats.

LC_PAPER
: Default paper sizes for printing and pagination.

LC_TELEPHONE
: Telephone number formats.

LC_TIME
: Date and time formats.

NLSPATH
: The path for finding message catalogues used in processing messages.

Examples

Print the category name and all keywords for date and time settings:

```
locale -ck LC_TIME
```

Print the strings used for days of the week and months of the year:

```
locale day mon
```

locate

`locate [options] [pattern]`

Search database(s) of filenames and print matches. *, ?, [, and] are treated specially; `/` and `.` are not. Matches include all files that contain *pattern* unless *pattern* includes metacharacters, in which case `locate` requires an exact match.

Solaris does not provide this command. Mac OS X uses the original BSD version of this command that takes no options. For details on the GNU/Linux version of this command, see the **slocate** entry in the later section "Alphabetical Summary of GNU/Linux Commands."

logger

`logger [options] [messages]`

Log messages to the system log. Command-line messages are logged if provided. Otherwise, messages are read and logged, line-by-line, from the file provided via `-f`. If no such file is given, `logger` reads messages from standard input.

Common Options

-f *file*
: Read and log messages from *file*.

-i
: Log the process ID of the logger process with each message.

-p *priority*
: Log each message with the given *priority*. Priorities have the form *facility.level*. The default is user.notice. See *syslog*(3) for more information.

-t *tag*
: Add *tag* to each message line.

Mac OS X and GNU/Linux Option

-s
: Send the message to standard error, in addition to sending it to the system log.

GNU/Linux Options

-d
: When using a specified socket with -u, use a datagram socket instead of stream socket.

-u *socket*
: Write to *socket* instead of to the system log.

Example

Warn about upcoming trouble:

```
logger -p user.emerg 'Incoming Klingon battleship!'
```

---

login

login [*options*] [*user*]

Sign on and identify yourself to the system. At the beginning of each terminal session, the system prompts you for your username and, if relevant, a password. The options aren't normally used.

Bash, the Korn shell, and the C shell have their own, built-in versions of login. See Chapters 4 and 5 for more information.

Common Options

-h *host* [*term*]
: Used for remote logins via telnet to indicate the login is from host *host* and that the user's terminal type is *term*.

-p
: Pass the current environment to the new login session.

Solaris Options

user
: Sign on as *user* (instead of being prompted).

-d *tty*
: Specify the pathname of the *tty* that serves as the login port.

-r *host*
: Used for remote logins via rlogin to indicate the login is from host *host*.

`-R` *`repository`*
: Use the PAM repository *repository* for the *identity* provided with `-u`.

`-s` *`service`*
: Use the PAM service *service*. Usually not needed, but is useful, for example, with Kerberized logins.

`-u` *`identity`*
: Provides the identity string for the user; this is usually different from the login name. In Kerberos it's the user's principal name.

`-U` *`ruser`*
: The name of the remote person attempting a remote login. Used by `in.rlogind` in Kerberized mode.

`var=value`
: When specified after the username, assign a *value* to one or more environment variables. PATH and SHELL can't be changed.

`value`
: Pass values into the environment. Each value that does not contain an `=` is assigned to a variable of the form `L`*n*, where *n* starts at 0 and increments by one.

Mac OS X and GNU/Linux Option

`-f` Assume authentication has already been done. May be used only by a privileged user. The GNU/Linux *login*(1) manpage indicates that this option does not work well under GNU/Linux.

---

logname

```
logname
```

Display your login name. The command looks the user up in the system's database of currently logged in users. It ignores both the LOGNAME and USER environment variables. See also **whoami**.

---

look

`look [`*`options`*`]` *`string`* `[`*`file`*`]`

Look through a sorted file and print all lines that begin with *string*. *string* may be up to 256 characters long. This program is potentially faster than `fgrep` because it relies on the *file* being already sorted, and can thus do a binary search through the file, instead of reading it sequentially from beginning to end.

With no *file*, `look` searches `/usr/share/lib/dict/words` (the spelling dictionary) with options `-df`.

Common Options

`-d` Use dictionary order. Only letters, digits, space, and tab are used in comparisons.

`-f` Fold case; ignore case distinctions in comparisons.

`-t` *char*
: Use *char* as the termination character, i.e., ignore all characters to the right of *char*.

GNU/Linux Option

`-a` Use alternate dictionary `/usr/share/dict/web2`.

lp

`lp [options] [files]`

Send *files* to the printer. With no arguments, prints standard input. To print standard input along with other files, specify - as one of the *files*.

Common Options

`-c` Copy *files* to print spooler; if changes are made to *file* while it is still queued for printing, the printout is unaffected.

`-d` *dest*
: Send output to destination printer named *dest*.

`-d any`
: Used after `-f` or `-S` to print the request on any printer that supports the given form or character set.

`-H` *action*
: Print according to the named *action*: `hold` (notify before printing), `resume` (resume a held request), `immediate` (print next; privileged users only). Mac OS X and GNU/Linux also allow `restart` with `-i` to restart a completed job.

`-i` *IDs*
: Override `lp` options used for request *IDs* currently in the queue; specify new `lp` options after `-i`. For example, change the number of copies sent.

`-m` Send mail after *files* are printed.

`-n` *number*
: Specify the *number* of copies to print.

`-o` *options*
: Set one or more printer-specific *options*. Standard options include:

`cpi=`*n*	Print *n* characters per inch. *n* can also be `pica`, `elite`, or `compressed`.
`lpi=`*n*	Print *n* lines per inch.
`length=`*n*	Print pages *n* units long; e.g., `11i` (inches), `66` (lines).
`nobanner`	Omit banner page (separator) from request.
`nofilebreak`	Suppress formfeeds between files.
`width=`*n*	Print pages *n* units wide; e.g., `8.5i` (inches), `72` (columns).
`stty=`*list*	Specify a quoted *list* of `stty` options.

-P *list*
: Print only the page numbers specified in *list*.

-q *n* Print request with priority level *n* (39 = lowest).

-s Suppress messages.

-t *title*
: Use *title* on the printout's banner page.

-w Write a message on the user's terminal after *files* are printed (same as -m if user isn't logged on).

Solaris Options

-f *name*
: Print request on preprinted form *name*. *name* references printer attributes set by the administrative command lpforms.

-p Enable notification of completion of the print job.

-r Don't adapt request if *content* isn't suitable; reject instead. (Obscure; used only with -T.)

-S *name*
: Use the named print wheel or character set for printing.

-T *content*
: Send request to a printer that supports *content* (default is simple; an administrator sets *content* via lpadmin -I).

-y *modes*
: Print according to locally defined *modes*.

GNU/Linux and Mac OS X Options

GNU/Linux and Mac OS X use CUPS, the Common Unix Printing System. See *http://www.cups.org* for more information. Besides the common options, the CUPS lp accepts the following:

-E Use encryption when connecting to the server.

-h *host*
: Provide the print server hostname. The default is localhost or the value of $CUPS_SERVER.

Examples

Send mail after printing five copies of report:

```
lp -n 5 -m report
```

Format and print thesis; print title too:

```
nroff -ms thesis | lp - title
```

lpq

lpq [*options*] [*jobid*]

Check the print spool queue for status of print jobs. For each job, display username, rank in the queue, filenames, job number, and total file size (in bytes).

On Solaris, this is the original BSD interface, in /usr/ucb/lpq; see *lpq*(1B) for more information. This entry documents the CUPS version, which is used on GNU/Linux and Mac OS X. See also **lpr**.

Options

-a
: Report on all printers.

-E
: Encrypt the connection to the server.

-l
: Verbose mode. Print information about each file comprising a job. Use -l multiple times to increase the information provided.

-P *printer*
: Specify which printer to query. Without this option, lpq uses the printer set in the PRINTER or other printer-related environment variables or the default system printer.

+*interval*
: Print the status every *interval* seconds until the queue is empty.

---

lpr

lpr [*options*] [*files*]

Send *files* to the printer. On Solaris, this is the original BSD interface, in /usr/ucb/lpr; see *lpr*(1B) for more information. This entry documents the CUPS version, which is used on GNU/Linux and Mac OS X.

URL: *http://www.cups.org*. By default, CUPS makes its online documentation available via web browser at *http://localhost:631/documentation.html*.

Options

-# *count*
: Print *count* copies (100 maximum).

-C *name*
: Set the job name.

-E
: Encrypt the connection to the server.

-J *name*
: Same as -C.

-l
: The print file is in binary form, ready to be printed. Do not apply any filtering. Equivalent to -oraw.

-o *option*
: Set a job option. See the online documentation for more details.

-p
: Supply a shaded header with the date, time, job name, and page number. Equivalent to -oprettyprint.

-P *destination*
: Print files to the named printer.

-r
: Remove the files after printing them.

-T *name*
: Same as -C.

The original BSD and LPRng lpr options -c, -d, -f, -g, -i, -m, -n, -t, -v, and -w are not supported and produce a warning message if used.

lprm

`lprm [options] [jobid]`

Remove a print job from the print spool queue. You must specify a job number or numbers, which can be obtained from `lpq`. Only a privileged user may remove files belonging to another user.

On Solaris, this is the original BSD interface, in `/usr/ucb/lprm`; see *lprm*(1B) for more information. This entry documents the CUPS version, which is used on GNU/Linux and Mac OS X. See also **lpr**.

Options

`-E`
: Encrypt the connection to the server.

`-P printer`
: Specify printer queue. Normally, the default printer or printer specified in the PRINTER environment variable is used.

`-`
: Cancel all jobs.

lpstat

`lpstat [options]`

Print the `lp` print queue status. With options that take a *list* argument, omitting the list produces all information for that option. *list* can be separated by commas or, if enclosed in double quotes, by spaces.

Common Options

`-a [list]`
: Show if the *list* of printer or class names is accepting requests.

`-c [list]`
: Show information about printer classes named in *list*.

`-d`
: Show the default printer destination.

`-l`
: Use after `-f` to describe available forms, after `-p` to show printer configurations, or, on Solaris, after `-S` to describe printers appropriate for the specified character set or print wheel.

`-o [list]`
: Show the status of output requests. *list* contains printer names, class names, or request IDs.

`-p [list]`
: Show the status of printers named in *list*.

`-r`
: Show whether the print scheduler is on or off.

`-R`
: Show the job's position in the print queue.

`-s`
: Summarize the print status (shows almost everything).

`-t`
: Show all status information (reports everything).

`-u [list]`
: Show request status for users on *list*. *list* can be:

`user`	*user* on local machine
`all`	All users on all systems
`host!user`	*user* on machine *host*
`host!all`	All users on *host*
`all!user`	*user* on all systems
`all!all`	All users on all systems

`-v [list]`
: Show device associated with each printer named in *list*.

Solaris Options

`-D` Use after `-p` to show a brief printer description.

`-f [list]`
: Verify that the *list* of forms is known to `lp`.

`-S [list]`
: Verify the *list* of character sets or print wheels is known to `lp`.

GNU/Linux and Mac OS X Options

GNU/Linux and Mac OS X use CUPS, the Common Unix Printing System. See *http://www.cups.org* for more information. Besides the common options, the CUPS `lpstat` accepts the following:

`-E` Use encryption when connecting to the server.

`-h host`
: Provide the print server hostname. The default is `localhost` or the value of $CUPS_SERVER.

`-W which`
: Show *which* jobs. The valid values include `completed` and `not-completed`. Use before `-o` and/or any printer names.

---

ls

`ls [options] [names]`

If no *names* are given, list the files in the current directory. With one or more *names*, list files contained in a directory *name* or that match a file *name*. The options let you display a variety of information in different formats. The most useful options include `-F`, `-R`, `-a`, `-l`, and `-s`. Some options don't make sense together; e.g., `-u` and `-c`.

Modern versions of `ls` pay attention to the LC_COLLATE environment variable. Its default value, `en_US`, (in the United States) causes `ls` to sort in dictionary order (i.e., ignoring case). You may prefer to set LC_COLLATE to `C` to restore the traditional Unix behavior of sorting in ASCII order.

Common Options

`-a, --all`
: List all files, including the normally hidden `.` files.

`-A, --almost-all`
: Like `-a`, but exclude `.` and `..` (the current and parent directories).

`-b, --escape`
: Show nonprinting characters in octal.

`-c, --time-ctime, --time=status`
: List files by inode modification time.

`-C, --format=vertical`
: List files in columns (the default format, when displaying to a terminal device).

`-d, --directory`
List only the directory's information, not its contents. (Most useful with `-l` and `-i`.)

`-f` Interpret each *name* as a directory (files are ignored).

`-F, --classify, --indicator-style=classify`
Flag filenames by appending `/` to directories, `>` to doors (Solaris only), `*` to executable files, `|` to FIFOs, `@` to symbolic links, and `=` to sockets.

`-g` Like `-l`, but omit owner name (show group).

`-h` Produce "human-readable" output, using abbreviations for kilobyte, megabyte, and so on.

`-H, --dereference-command-line`
If an argument on the command line is a symbolic link, list the file or directory referenced by a symbolic link rather than the link itself.

`-i, --inode`
List the inode number for each file.

`-l, --format=long, --format=verbose`
Long format listing (includes permissions, owner, size, modification time, etc.).

`-L` List the file or directory referenced by a symbolic link rather than the link itself.

`-m, --format=commas`
Merge the list into a comma-separated series of names.

`-n, --numeric-uid-gid`
Like `-l`, but use user ID and group ID numbers instead of owner and group names.

`-p, --filetype, --indicator-style=file-type`
Mark directories by appending `/` to them. GNU/Linux also appends `|` to FIFOs, `@` to symbolic links, and `=` to sockets. (Almost, but not quite, the same as `-F`.)

`-q, --hide-control-chars`
Show nonprinting characters as ?.

`-r, --reverse`
List files in reverse order (by name or by time).

`-R, --recursive`
Recursively list subdirectories as well as current directory.

`-s, --size`
Print sizes of the files in blocks.

`-t, --sort=time`
List files according to modification time (newest first).

`-u, --time=atime, --time=access, --time=use`
List files according to the file access time.

`-x, --format=across, --format=horizontal`
List files in rows going across the screen.

`-1, --format=single-column`
Print one entry per line of output.

Solaris and GNU/Linux Option

-o Like -l, but omit group name (show owner).

Solaris Options

-e Like -l, but use the same format for times regardless of age: mmm dd hhh:mm:ss yyyy.

-E Like -l, but use the ISO 8601 format for times regardless of age: yyyy-mm-dd hh:mm:ss.nnnnnnnnn.

-@ Like -l, but extended attribute information supersedes ACL information. ls places an @ after the permission bits for files with extended attributes.

GNU/Linux Options

--author
: Print the author of each file. On GNU/Hurd systems, the author is different than the owner. On all other systems, this prints the file's owner.

--block-size=*size*
: Use blocks of *size* bytes.

-B, --ignore-backups
: Do not list files ending in ~ unless given as arguments.

--color[=*when*]
: Colorize the names of files depending on the type of file. Accepted values for *when* are never, always, or auto.

--dereference-command-line-symlink-to-dir
: Follow command-line argument symbolic links that point to directories.

-D, --dired
: List in a format suitable for Emacs dired mode.

--full-time
: List times in full, rather than using the standard abbreviations.

-G, --no-group
: In long format, do not display group name.

--indicator-style=*style*
: Add trailing indicators to filenames according to *style*. Possible values are none, classify (same as -F), and file-type (same as -p). Default is none.

-I *pattern*, --ignore *pattern*
: Do not list files whose names match the shell pattern *pattern* unless they are given on the command line.

-k, --kilobytes
: If file sizes are being listed, print them in kilobytes. This option overrides the environment variable POSIXLY_CORRECT.

--lcontext
: Display the full security context. Implies -l. SELinux only.

-N, --literal
: Display special graphic characters that appear in filenames.

`--quoting-style=style`
Use the *style* quoting style. Possible values are: `c`, `escape`, `literal`, `locale`, `shell`, and `shell-always`.

`-Q, --quote-name`
Quote filenames with "; quote nongraphic characters.

`--scontext`
Display only the filename and the security context. SELinux only.

`--show-control-chars`
Show nonprinting characters verbatim (default for printing to a file).

`--si` Similar to `-h`, but uses powers of 1000 instead of 1024.

`--sort=criteria`
Sort by the given *criteria*. Possible values and their corresponding options are: `access` (`-u`), `atime` (`-u`), `extension` (`-X`), `none` (`-U`), `size` (`-S`), `status` (`-c`), `time` (`-t`), `use` (`-u`), and `version` (`-v`).

`-S, --sort=size`
Sort by file size, largest to smallest.

`--time=filetime`
Show the given time attribute of the file instead of the modification time. Allowed values are: `atime`, `access`, `use`, `ctime`, and `status`. The time attribute is used for sorting with `--sort=time`.

`--time-style=style`
Format times according to the given *style*. If *style* is preceded by `posix-`, then the style is used only if not in the `POSIX` locale. Allowed values are: `full-iso`, `iso`, `locale`, `long-iso`, and `+format`.

For `+format`, the *format* is interpreted as for `date` (see **date**). Two formats may be provided separated by a newline. In this case, the first one applies to nonrecent files, and the second one applies to recent files.

`-T ncols, --tabsize=ncols`
Set tab stops at *ncols* columns.

`-U, --sort=none`
Do not sort files.

`-v, --sort=version`
Interpret the digits in names such as *file.6* and *file.6.1* as versions, and order filenames by version.

`-w n, --width=n`
Format output to fit *n* columns.

`-X, --sort=extension`
Sort by file extension, then by filename.

`-Z, --context`
Display the security context so that it will fit on the screen. The information given is the mode, user, group, security context, and filename. SELinux only.

Mac OS X Options

-B Print nonprintable characters as an octal escape: *nnn*.

-e Print the Access Control List (ACL) of the file, if any.

-G Enable colorized output.

-k For use with -s; print file sizes in kilobytes, not blocks. Overrides the BLOCKSIZE environment variable.

-o Include the file flags in the long format listing (-l).

-P Cancel the -H and -L options, causing ls to list information about symbolic links, not the files they point to.

-S Sort files by their size.

-T Use with -l. Print complete time information, including month, day, hour, minute, second, and year.

-w Print nonprintable characters verbatim. This is the default if the output is not a terminal.

-W Display whiteout entries when scanning directories.

-v Print nongraphic characters verbatim. This is the default if the output is not a terminal.

Examples

List all files in the current directory and their sizes; use multiple columns and mark special files:

```
ls -asCF
```

List the status of directories /bin and /etc:

```
ls -ld /bin /etc
```

List C source files in the current directory, the oldest first:

```
ls -rt *.c
```

Count the files in the current directory:

```
ls | wc -l
```

---

m4

m4 [*options*] [*files*]

General purpose macro processor. On Solaris, m4 is found in /usr/ccs/bin and is the original Unix version. GNU/Linux and Mac OS X use the GNU version of m4. (On Solaris, GNU m4 is in /usr/sfw/bin/gm4.)

URL: *http://www.gnu.org/software/m4*.

Common Options

-B*n* Set push-back and argument collection buffers to *n* (default is 4096). Ignored by GNU m4.

-D*name*[=*value*], --define=*name*[=*value*]
Define *name* as *value* or, if *value* is not specified, define *name* as null.

-e, --interactive
Operate interactively, ignoring interrupts.

`-Hn, --hashsize=n`
: Set symbol table hash array size to *n* (default is 199 on Solaris, 509 for GNU `m4`).

`-s, --synclines`
: Enable line-sync output (`#line` directives) for the C preprocessor.

`-Sn`
: Set call stack size to *n* (default is 100 slots). Ignored by GNU `m4`.

`-Tn`
: Set token buffer size to *n* (default is 512 bytes). Ignored by GNU `m4`.

`-Uname, --undefine=name`
: Undefine *name*.

GNU m4 Options

`-d [flags], --debug[=flags]`
: Specify *flag*-level debugging. Default is flags `aeq`.

`-E, --fatal-warnings`
: Consider all warnings to be fatal, and exit after the first of them.

`-F file, --freeze-state=file`
: Record `m4`'s frozen state in *file* for later reloading.

`-G, --traditional`
: Behave like traditional `m4`, ignoring GNU extensions.

`-I directory, --include=directory`
: Search *directory* for include files.

`-l n, --arglength=n`
: Specify the length of debugging output.

`-L n, --nesting-limit=n`
: Limit the textual nesting of macros calls to *n*. The default is 250. Useful for some machine-generated input.

`-o file, --error-output=file`
: Place output in *file*. Despite the option's name, print error messages on standard error.

`-P, --prefix-built-ins`
: Prepend `m4_` to all built-in macro names.

`-Q, --quiet, --silent`
: Suppress warning messages.

`-R file, --reload-state=file`
: Load state from *file* before starting execution.

`-t name, --trace=name`
: Insert *name* into symbol table as undefined. Trace macro from the point it is defined.

mail

`mail [options] [users]`

Read mail (if no *users* listed), or send mail to other *users*. Type ? for a summary of commands. Esoteric debugging options exist (not listed) for system administrators. See also **mailx**, and **vacation** in the later section "Alphabetical Summary of Solaris Commands."

This is the original V7 Unix `mail` program. On Mac OS X and GNU/Linux, `mail` is really `mailx`. See **mailx**.

Options for Sending Mail

`-m` *type*
: Print a "Message-type:" line at the heading of the letter, followed by *type* of message.

`-t`
: Print a "To:" line at the heading of the letter, showing the names of the recipients.

`-w`
: Force mail to be sent to remote users without waiting for remote transfer program to complete.

Options for Reading Mail

`-e`
: Test for the existence of mail without printing it. Exit status is 0 if mail exists; otherwise 1.

`-f` *file*
: Read mail from alternate mailbox *file*.

`-h`
: Display a window of messages rather than the latest message.

`-p`
: Print all messages without pausing.

`-P`
: Print messages with all header lines displayed.

`-q`
: Terminate on an interrupt.

`-r`
: Print oldest messages first.

mailx

```
mailx [options] [users]
Mail [options] [users]
```

Read mail, or send mail to other *users*. For a summary of commands, type ? in command mode (e.g., when reading mail) or ~? in input mode (e.g., when sending mail). The start-up file `.mailrc` in the user's home directory is useful for setting display variables and for defining alias lists.

Version Names

The original V7 Unix `mail` program provided a very spartan interactive user interface.* This inspired the creation of Berkeley Mail, a more capable mail-reading program for BSD Unix. Not surprisingly, and because Unix systems distinguish between uppercase and lowercase, the program was named `Mail`, and it lived in the `/usr/ucb` directory. When the System V developers imported Berkeley Mail,

* This program survives on commercial Unix systems as `/bin/mail`; its primary use these days is by Mail Transport Agents, such as Sendmail, for physical delivery of mail into a user's mailbox. Even long-time Unix veterans do not use it interactively.

they renamed it `mailx`, to avoid the case-distinction problem. By that name the command was standardized in POSIX. Today, just to keep life interesting, different systems offer the program under multiple names and locations, as follows:

Solaris
: The program is in `/usr/bin/mailx`. `/usr/ucb/mail` and `/usr/ucb/Mail` are symbolic links to it.

GNU/Linux
: The program is in `/bin/mail`. `/usr/bin/Mail` is a symbolic link to it. There is no `mailx` command.

Mac OS X
: The program is in `/usr/bin/mailx`. `/usr/bin/mail` is a hard link to it. Because the Mac OS X HFS filesystem ignores case, `/usr/bin/Mail` is the same as `/usr/bin/mail` (i.e., typing `Mail` at a shell prompt runs `/usr/bin/mail`).

Common Options

`-b` *address*
: Send blind carbon copies to *address*. Quote the list if there are multiple recipients.

`-c` *address*
: Send carbon copies to *address*. Quote the list if there are multiple recipients.

`-d` Set debugging.

`-f` [*file*]
: Read mail in alternate *file* (default is `mbox`).

`-i` Ignore interrupts (useful on modems); same as `mailx` option `ignore`.

`-I` Use with `-f` when displaying saved news articles; newsgroup and article ID headers are included.

`-n` Do not read the system startup `mailx.rc` or `Mail.rc` file(s).

`-N` Don't print mail header summary.

`-s` *sub*
: Place string *sub* in the `Subject:` header field. *sub* must be quoted if it contains whitespace.

`-u` *user*
: Read *user*'s mail.

`-v` Verbose mode; displays delivery details.

Solaris and Mac OS X Options

`-e` Test for the existence of mail without printing it. Exit status is 0 if mail exists; otherwise 1.

`-F` Store message in a file named after the first recipient.

`-H` Print mail header summary only.

Solaris Options

`-B` Do not buffer standard input or standard output.

`-H` Print mail header summary only.

`-r` *address*
: Specify a return *address* for mail you send.

`-t` Use `To:`, `Cc:`, and `Bcc:` headers in the input to specify recipients instead of command-line arguments.

`-T` *file*
: Record message IDs and article IDs (of news articles) in *file*.

`-U` Convert uucp-type addresses to Internet format.

`-V` Print version number of `mailx` and exit.

`-~` Process tilde escapes, even if not reading from a terminal.

Mac OS X Option

`-E` Do not send messages with an empty body. Useful for receiving output from cron scripts.

---

make

`make [options] [targets]`

Update one or more *targets* according to dependency instructions in a description file in the current directory. By default, this file is called `makefile` or `Makefile`.

On Solaris `make` is found in `/usr/ccs/bin`, and GNU `make` is in `/usr/sfw/bin/gmake`. GNU/Linux and Mac OS X use GNU `make`. See Chapter 16 for more information on GNU `make`, including Internet download information. See also *Managing Projects with GNU make*, listed in the Bibliography.

---

man

`man [options] [[section] subjects]`

Display information from the online reference manual. Each *subject* is usually the name of a command from Section 1 of the online manual, unless you specify an optional *section* from 1 to 8. If you don't specify a *subject*, you must supply either a keyword (for `-k`) or a file (for `-f`). No options except `-M` can be used with `-k` or `-f`. The MANPATH environment variable defines the directories in which `man` searches for information (default is `/usr/share/man`). PAGER defines how output is sent to the screen. Note: in Solaris, *section* must be preceded by `-s`. GNU/Linux and Mac OS X use the same `man` program.

Options

`-a` Show all pages matching *subject*.

`-d` Debug; evaluate the `man` command and print debugging information, but don't execute.

`-f` *files*
: Display a one-line summary of one or more reference *files*. Same as `whatis`.

`-k` *keywords*
: Display any header line that contains one of the specified *keywords*. Same as `apropos`.

`-M` *path*
: Search for online descriptions in directory *path* instead of default directory. `-M` overrides MANPATH.

`-t` Format the manpages with `troff`.

Solaris Options

`-` Pipe output through `cat` instead of `more -s`.

`-F` Search MANPATH directories, not `windex` database.

`-l` Like `-a`, but list only the pages.

`-r` Reformat but don't display manpage. Same as `man - -t`.

`-s` *section*
: Specify the section of the manpage to search in. Required for anything that isn't a command.

`-T` *mac*
: Display information using macro package *mac* instead of `tmac.an` (the *man* macros).

GNU/Linux and Mac OS X Options

`-c` Reformat the source file, even if a preformatted manual page exists.

`-C` *file*
: Use an alternate configuration file.

`-D` Like `-d`, but also print the manual page.

`-F` Format only, do not display the formatted pages.

`-h, --help`
: Print a command-line summary and exit.

`-K` Search for a string in *all* manpages.

`-m` *system*
: Search an alternate set of manpages based on the *system* name.

`-p` *letters*
: Specify the order in which to run various `troff` preprocessors based on `letters`. The letters and their program are:

e: eqn or neqn	p: pic	t: tbl
g: grap	r: refer	v: vgrind

`-P` *program*
: Use *program* as the pager.

`-w, --path`
: Print the location of the manpage that would be displayed. With no argument, print the list of directories to be searched.

`-W` Like `-w`, but print names one per line.

Examples

Save documentation on the `mv` command (strip overstruck characters):

```
man mv | sed 's/.^H//g' > mv.txt
```

Display commands related to linking and compiling:

```
man -k link compile | more
```

Display a summary of all `intro` files:

```
man -f intro
```

Look up the `intro` page from Section 3M (the math library):

```
man 3m intro             In most systems
man -s 3m intro          In Solaris
```


mesg

`mesg [options]`

Change the ability of other users to use `talk`, or to send `write` messages to your terminal. With no options, display the permission status.

Options

`n` Forbid `write` messages.

`y` Allow `write` messages (the default).

Solaris allows you to supply a leading - (i.e., -n, -y).

mkdir

`mkdir [options] directories`

Create one or more *directories*. You must have write permission in the parent directory in order to create a directory. See also **rmdir**.

Common Options

`-m, --mode mode`
Set the access *mode* for new directories.

`-p, --parents`
Create intervening parent directories if they don't exist.

GNU/Linux Options

`-v, --verbose`
Print directory names as they are created.

`-Z context, --context context`
Set the security context. SELinux only.

Mac OS X Option

`-v` Print directory names as they are created.

Examples

Create a read/execute-only directory named `personal`:

```
mkdir -m 555 personal
```

The following sequence:

```
mkdir work; cd work
mkdir junk; cd junk
mkdir questions; cd ../..
```

could be accomplished by typing this:

```
mkdir -p work/junk/questions
```

mkisofs

```
mkisofs [options] -o file pathspecs
```

Solaris and GNU/Linux only. Generate an ISO9660/Joliet/HFS filesystem for writing to a CD with a utility such as `cdrecord`. (HFS is the native Macintosh Hierarchical File System.) `mkisofs` takes a snapshot of a directory tree and generates a binary image that corresponds to an ISO9660 or HFS filesystem when it is written to a block device. Each specified *pathspec* describes the path of a directory tree to be copied into the ISO9660 filesystem; if multiple paths are specified, the files in all the paths are merged to form the image.

Options

`-abstract` *file*
: Specify the abstract filename. Overrides an `ABST=`*file* entry in `.mkisofsrc`.

`-allow-leading-dots, -ldots`
: Allow ISO9660 filenames to begin with a period.

`-allow-lowercase`
: Allow ISO9660 filenames to be lowercase. Violates the ISO9660 standard.

`-allow-multidot`
: Allow more than one dot in ISO9660 filenames. Violates the ISO9660 standard.

`-A` *id*, `-appid` *id*
: Specify a text string *id* that describes the application to be written into the volume header.

`-b` *image*, `-eltorito-boot` *image*
: Specify the path and filename of the boot image to be used for making a bootable CD based on the El Torito specification.

`-B` *sun-images*, `-sparc-boot` *sun-images*
: Specify a comma-separated list of boot images needed to make a bootable CD for a Sun Sparc system.

`-biblio` *file*
: Specify bibliographic filename. Overrides a `BIBLIO=`*file* entry in `.mkisofsrc`.

`-boot-info-table`
: Specify that a 56-byte table with information on the CD layout is to be patched in at offset 8 of the boot file. If specified, the table is patched into the source boot file, so make a copy if the file isn't recreatable.

`-boot-load-seg` *addr*
: Specify the load segment address of the boot image for a no-emulation El Torito CD.

`-boot-load-size` *size*
: Specify the number of virtual 512-byte sectors to load in no-emulation mode. The default is to load the entire boot file. The number may need to be a multiple of four to prevent problems with some BIOSes.

`-c` *catalog*, `--eltorito-catalog` *catalog*
: Specify the path, relative to the source *pathspec*, and the filename of the boot catalog for an El Torito bootable CD. Required for making a bootable CD.

`-cache-inodes, -no-cache-inodes`
: Cache [do not cache] inode and device numbers to find hard links to files. The default on Linux is to cache. Use `-no-cache-inodes` for filesystems that do not have unique inode numbers.

`-check-oldnames`
: Check all filenames imported from old sessions for `mkisofs` compliance with ISO9660 file-naming rules. If not specified, check only those files with names longer than 31 characters.

`-check-session` *file*
: Check all old sessions for `mkisofs` compliance with ISO9660 file-naming rules. This option is the equivalent of:

```
-M file -C 0,0 -check-oldnames
```

where *file* is the pathname or SCSI device specifier that would be specified with `-M`.

`-chrp-boot`
: Add a CHRP boot header.

`-copyright` *file*
: Specify the name of the file that contains the copyright information. Overrides a `COPY=`*file* entry in `.mkisofsrc`.

`-C` *last-start,next-start*
`-cdrecord-params` *last-start,next-start*
: Required for creating a CDExtra or a second or higher-level session for a multisession CD. *last-start* is the first sector number in the last session on the disk, and *next-start* is the first sector number for the new session. Use the command:

```
cdrecord -msinfo
```

to get the values. Use `-C` with `-M` to create an image that is a continuation of the previous session; without `-M`, create an image for a second session on a CDExtra (a multisession CD with audio data in the first session and an ISO9660 filesystem image in the second).

`-d, -omit-period`
: Omit trailing period from files that do not have one. Violates the ISO9660 standard, but works on many systems.

`-debug`
: Enable debugging.

`-dev` *device*
: For use with `-C` and `-M`, *device* is the device name from which to read the previous session of a multisession CD.

`-D, -disable-deep-relocation`
: Do not use deep directory relocation. Violates the ISO9660 standard, but works on many systems.

`-dir-mode` *mode*
: Specify the mode for directories used to create the image. Automatically enables the Rock Ridge extensions.

`-dvd-video`
: Generate a UDF filesystem compliant with DVD videos.

`-eltorito-alt-boot`
: Start with a new set of El Torito boot parameters. Allows putting more than one El Torito boot image on a CD (maximum is 63).

`-exclude-list` *file*
: Check filenames against the globs contained in the specified file and exclude any that match.

`-f, -follow-links`
: Follow symbolic links when generating the filesystem.

`-file-mode` *mode*
: Specify the mode for files used to create the image. Automatically enables the Rock Ridge extensions.

`-force-rr`
: Do not use automatic Rock Ridge detection for the previous session.

`-G` *image*, `--generic-boot` *image*
: Specify the path and filename of the generic boot image for making a generic bootable CD.

`-gid` *gid*
: Set the group ID to *gid* for the source files. Automatically enables the Rock Ridge extensions.

`-graft-points`
: Allow the use of graft points for filenames, which permits paths to be grafted at locations other than the root directory. `-graft-points` checks all filenames for graft points and divides the filename at the first unescaped equals sign (`=`).

`-gui`
: Switch the behavior for a GUI. Currently, the only effect is to make the output more verbose.

`-hard-disk-boot`
: Specify that the boot image to be used to create an El Torito bootable CD is a hard disk image and must begin with a master boot record containing a single partition.

`-help`
: Print a help message.

`-hidden` *glob*
: Set the hidden (existence) ISO9660 directory attribute for paths or filenames matching the shell-style pattern *glob*. To match a directory, the path must not end with a trailing `/`.

`-hidden-list` *file*
: Specify a file containing a list of *globs* that are to be hidden with `-hidden`.

`-hide` *glob*
: Find paths or files that match the shell-style pattern *glob* and hide them from being seen on the ISO9660 or Rock Ridge directory. The files are still included in the image file. If the pattern matches a directory, the contents of the directory are hidden. To match a directory, the path must not end with a trailing `/`. Use with the `-hide-joliet` option.

`-hide-joliet` *glob*
: Hide paths or files that match the shell-style pattern *glob* so they will not be seen in the Joliet directory. If the pattern matches a directory, the contents of the directory are hidden. To match a directory, the path must not end with a trailing `/`. Should be used with `-hide`.

`-hide-joliet-list` *file*
: Specify a file with a list of *globs* to be hidden with `-hide-joliet`.

`-hide-joliet-trans-tbl`
: Hide the `TRANS.TBL` files from the Joliet tree.

`-hide-list` *file*
: Specify a file containing a list of *globs* to be hidden with `-hide`.

`-hide-rr-moved`
: Rename the directory `RR_MOVED` to `.rr_moved` to hide it as much as possible from the Rock Ridge directory tree. Use the `-D` option to omit the file entirely.

`-input-charset` *charset*
: Specify the character set for characters used in local filenames. Specify `help` in place of a *charset* for a list of valid character sets.

`-iso-level` *level*
: Set the ISO9660 conformance level. Possible values are:

1	Filenames are restricted to 8.3 characters and files may have only one section.
2	Files may have only one section.
3	No restrictions.

`-jcharset` *charset*
: The equivalent of `-input-charset -J`.

`-J`, `-joliet`
: Generate Joliet directory records in addition to regular ISO9660 filenames.

`-joliet-long`
: Allow Joliet filenames to be up to 103 Unicode characters. This breaks the Joliet specification but apparently works.

`-l`, `-full-iso9660-filenames`
: Allow full 31-character filenames instead of restricting them to the MS-DOS-compatible 8.3 format.

`-log-file` *file*
: Send all messages to the specified log file.

`-m` *glob*, `-exclude` *glob*
: Exclude files matching the shell-style pattern *glob*.

`-max-iso9660-filenames`
: Allow up to 37 characters in ISO9660 filenames. Forces `-N`. Violates the ISO9660 standard.

`-M` *path*, `-prev-session` *path*
: Specify the path to an existing ISO9660 image to be merged. *path* can also be a SCSI device specified in the same syntax as `cdrecord`'s `dev=` parameter. May be used only with `-C`.

`-new-dir-mode` *mode*
: Specify the mode to use for new directories in the image. The default is 0555.

`-nobak`, `-no-bak`
: Do not include backup files on the ISO9660 filesystem.

`-no-boot`
: Mark the El Torito CD to be created as not bootable.

`-no-emul-boot`
: Specify that the boot image for creating an El Torito bootable CD is a no-emulation image.

`-no-iso-translate`
: Do not translate the `#` and `~` characters. Violates the ISO9660 standard.

`-no-rr`
: Do not use Rock Ridge attributes from previous sessions.

`-no-split-symlink-components`
: Do not split symlink components.

`-no-split-symlink-fields`
: Do not split symlink fields.

`-N`, `-omit-version-number`
: Omit version numbers from ISO9660 filenames. Violates the ISO9660 standard. Use with caution.

`-old-root` *dir*
: Specify *dir* as the root used with `-root` for a previous session. Used for doing incremental backups.

`-output-charset` *charset*
: Specify the output character set for Rock Ridge filenames. The default is the input character set.

`-p` *prepid*, `-preparer` *prepid*
: Specify a text string of up to 128 characters describing the preparer of the CD. Overrides a `PREP=` parameter set in the file `.mkisofsrc`.

`-publisher` *pubid*
: Specify a text string of up to 128 characters describing the publisher of the CD to be written to the volume header. Overrides a `PUBL=` parameter set in `.mkisofsrc`.

`-pad, -no-pad`
: Pad [do not pad] the ISO9660 filesystem by 16 sectors (32KB). If the resulting size is not a multiple of 16 sectors, add sectors until it is. The default is `-pad`.

`-path-list` *`file`*
: Specify a file that contains a list of *pathspec* directories and filenames to add to the ISO9660 filesystem. Note that at least one *pathspec* must be given on the command line.

`-print-size`
: Print estimated filesystem size and exit.

`-quiet`
: Run in quiet mode; do not display progress output.

`-r, -rational-rock`
: Like `-R`, but set UID and GID to zero, set all file read bits to on, and turn off all file write bits. If any execute bit is set for a file, set all execute bits; if any search bit is set for a directory, set all search bits; if any special mode bits are set, clear them.

`-relaxed-filenames`
: Allow ISO9660 filenames to include seven-digit ASCII characters except lowercase characters. Violates the ISO9660 standard.

`-root` *`dir`*
: Makes *dir* be the root of the filesystem on the image. Similar to `-graft-points`.

`-R, -rock`
: Generate SUSP (System Use Sharing Protocol) and Rock Ridge records using the Rock Ridge protocol.

`-sort` *`file`*
: Sort file locations according to the rules in the specified file, which contains pairs of filenames and weights, with one space or tab between them. A higher weight puts the file closer to the beginning of the media.

`-sparc-label` *`text`*
: Set the Sun disk label to *text*.

`-split-output`
: Split the output into files approximately one gigabyte in size. Useful for creating DVDs on operating systems that don't support large files.

`-stream-file-name` *`name`*
: Reserved for future use.

`-stream-media-size` *`size`*
: Operate in streaming mode, with *size* as the media size in sectors. This creates a simple ISO9660 archive named `STREAM.IMG`. See the manpage for details.

`-sunx86-boot` *`files`*
: Use *files* to create a Solaris x86 bootable CD.

`-sunx86-label` *`text`*
: Set the System V Release 4 disk label on a Sun x86 CD to *text*.

-sysid *id*
: Specify the system ID. Overrides a SYSI= parameter set in the file .mkisofsrc.

-table-name *table*
: Use *table* as the translation table name instead of TRANS.TBL. Implies -T. For a multisession image, the table name must be the same as the previous session.

-T, -translation-table
: Generate the file TRANS.TBL in each directory for establishing the correct filenames on non-Rock Ridge-capable systems.

-ucs-level *num*
: Set the Unicode conformance level to the specified number, which can be between 1 and 3 (default is 3).

-udf
: Produce a UDF filesystem.

-uid *uid*
: Set the user ID to *uid* for the source files. Automatically enables the Rock Ridge extensions.

-use-fileversion *level*
: Use file version numbers from the filesystem. The version number is a string from 1 to 32767. The default is to set a version of 1.

-U, -untranslated-filenames
: Allow untranslated filenames. Violates the ISO9660 standard. Forces the options -d, -l, -N, -relaxed-filenames, -allow-lowercase, -allow-multidot, and -allow-leading-dots. Use with extreme caution.

-v, -verbose
: Run in verbose mode. Specify twice to run even more verbosely.

-version
: Print version information.

-volset *id*
: Specify the volume set ID. Overrides a VOLS= parameter specified in .mkisofsrc.

-volset-seqno *num*
: Set the volume set sequence number to *num*. Must be specified after -volset-size.

-volset-size *num*
: Set the volume set size (the number of CDs in a set) to *num*. Must be specified before -volset-seqno.

-V *volid*, -volid *volid*
: Specify the volume ID (volume name or label) to be written to the master block. Overrides a VOLI= parameter specified in the file .mkisofsrc.

`-x` *path*, `-old-exclude` *path*
: Exclude *path* from being written to the CD, where *path* is the complete pathname derived from the concatenation of the pathname from the command line and the path relative to this directory. May be specified more than once to exclude multiple paths.

`-z`, `-transparent-compression`
: Generate RRIP records for transparent compression. Violates the ISO9660 standard. Must be used with `-r` or `-R`. Such CDs are only transparently readable under GNU/Linux.

HFS options

`-auto` *file*
: Set *file* as the Autostart file to make the HFS CD use the QuickTime 2.0 Autostart feature. *file* must be the name of an application or document at the top level of the CD and must be less than 12 characters long.

`-boot-hfs-file` *file*
: Install *file* as the driver file that may make the CD bootable on a Macintosh.

`-cluster-size` *size*
: Specify the size in bytes of a cluster or allocation units of PC Exchange files. Implies the use of `--exchange`.

`-g`, `-apple`
: Create an ISO9660 CD with Apple's extensions.

`-h`, `-hfs`
: Create a hybrid ISO9660/HFS CD. Use with `-map`, `-magic`, and/or the various HFS options.

`-hfs-bless` *folder*
: "Bless" the specified directory (folder), specified as the full pathname to `mkisofs`. This is usually the System Folder and is used in creating HFS bootable CDs. The pathname must be in quotes if it contains spaces.

`-hfs-creator` *creator*
: Set the four-character default creator for all files.

`-hfs-parms` *parameters*
: Override certain HFS filesystem parameters. The manpage points you to a file in the source code for more details.

`-hfs-type` *type*
: Set the four-character default type for all files.

`-hfs-unlock`
: Leave the HFS volume unlocked so other applications can modify it. The default is to lock the volume.

`-hfs-volid` *id*
: Specify the volume name for the HFS partition. This name is assigned to the CD on a Macintosh and replaces the ID set with the `-V` option.

`-hide-hfs` *glob*
: Hide files or directories matching the shell-style pattern *glob* from the HFS volume, although they still exist in the ISO9660 and/or Joliet directory. May be specified multiple times.

`-hide-hfs-list` *file*
: The specified file contains a list of globs to be hidden.

`-icon-position`
: Use the icon position from the HFS file. This is an experimental option.

`-input-hfs-charset` *charset*
: Specify the input character set used for HFS filenames when used with the `-mac-name` option. The default is cp10000 (Mac Roman).

`-mac-name`
: Use the HFS filename as the starting point for the ISO9660, Joliet, and Rock Ridge filenames.

`-magic` *file*
: Use the specified magic file to set a file's creator and type information based on the file's *magic number*, which is usually the first few bytes of the file. The magic file contains entries consisting of four tab-separated columns specifying the byte offset, type, test, and a message.

`-map` *file*
: Use the specified mapping file to set a file's creator and type information based on the filename extension. Only files that are not known Apple or Unix file types need to be mapped. The mapping file consists of five-column entries specifying the extension, file translation, creator, type, and a comment. Creator and type are both four-letter strings.

`-no-desktop`
: Do not create empty Desktop files. The default is to create such files.

`-output-hfs-charset` *charset*
: Specify the output character set used for HFS filenames. Defaults to the input character set.

`-part`
: Generate an HFS partition table. The default is not to generate the table.

`-prep-boot` *file*
: PReP boot file. Up to four may be provided. Experimental option.

`-probe`
: Search the contents of files for known Apple or Unix file types.

`-root-info` *file*
: Set the information for the root folder from *file*. Experimental option.

`--format`
: Look for Macintosh files of the specified file format type. The valid formats are `cap` (Apple/Unix File System (AUFS) CAP files), `dave`, `double`, `ethershare`, `exchange`, `macbin`, `netatalk`, `osx-double`, `osx-hfs`, `sfm`, `sgi`, `single`, `ushare`, and `xinet`.

mktemp

`mktemp [options] template`

Generate a unique temporary filename for use in a script. The filename is based on the specified template, which may be any filename with at least six Xs appended (e.g., `/tmp/mytemp.XXXXXX`). `mktemp` replaces the Xs with the current process number and/or a unique letter combination. The file is created with mode 0600 (unless `-u` is specified) and the filename is written to standard output.

Common Options

`-d` Make a directory, not a file.

`-q` Fail silently in case of error. Useful to prevent error output from being sent to standard error.

`-u` Operate in "unsafe" mode and unlink the temporary file before `mktemp` exits. Use of this option is not recommended.

Solaris and GNU/Linux Options

`-p` *prefix*
: Use *prefix* as the directory for the temporary filename. The TMPDIR environment variable overrides this option. Implies `-t`.

`-t` Create a path in a temporary directory. The directory name is the first of: the TMPDIR environment variable; the value of *prefix* given to `-p`; or `/tmp`.

GNU/Linux Option

`-V` Print version information and exit.

Mac OS X Option

`-t [prefix]`
: Like Solaris `-p`, except that the *prefix* is optional.

more

`more [options] [files]`

Display the named *files* on a terminal, one screenful at a time. After each screen is displayed, press the ENTER key to display the next line or press the spacebar to display the next screenful. Press `h` for help with additional commands, `q` to quit, `/` to search, or `:n` to go to the next file. `more` can also be invoked using the name `page`.

The Mac OS X `more` is a hard link to `less`; see **less** for more information.

Common Options

-c Page through the file by clearing the screen instead of scrolling. This is often faster and is much easier to read.

-d Display the prompt `Press space to continue, 'q' to quit.`

-f Count logical rather than screen lines. Useful when long lines wrap past the width of the screen.

-l Ignore formfeed (^L) characters.

-s Squeeze; display multiple blank lines as one.

-u Suppress underline characters and backspace (^H).

-*n* Use *n* lines for each "window" (default is a full screen).

+*num*
: Begin displaying at line number *num*.

+/*pattern*
: Begin displaying two lines before *pattern*.

Solaris /usr/xpg4/bin/more Options

-e Exit after writing the last line of the last file, instead of prompting.

-i Ignore case when searching.

-n *n* Use *n* lines for each "window" (default is a full screen).

-p *command*, +*command*
: Execute more command *command* before showing each file.

-t *tagstring*
: Display the screenful of the file containing the tag *tagstring* as defined by ctags. Processed before -p if both are given.

Solaris /usr/bin/more Options

-r Force display of control characters, in the form ^*x*.

-w Wait for a user keystroke before exiting.

GNU/Linux Option

-p Do not scroll; clear the screen and then show the text.

Examples

Page through *file* in "clear" mode, and display prompts:

```
more -cd file
```

Format doc to the screen, removing underlines:

```
nroff doc | more -u
```

View the manpage for the grep command; begin near the word "BUGS" and compress extra whitespace:

```
man grep | more +/BUGS -s
```

mount

mount [*options*] [*arguments*]

Mount a filesystem. This command is very system-specific. See the **mount** entries in the sections for each operating system.

msgfmt

`msgfmt [options] pofiles`

Solaris and GNU/Linux only. `msgfmt` translates "portable object files" (`.po` files) into loadable message files that can be used by a running application via the *gettext*(3C) and *dgettext*(3C) library functions.

Portable object files are created using `xgettext` from the original C source code files. A translator then edits the `.po` file, providing translations of each string (or "message") in the source program. The format is described in the *msgfmt*(1) manpage.

Once compiled by `msgfmt`, the running program uses the translations for its output when the locale is set up appropriately.

The Solaris version of this command has picked up some features from the GNU version; see **gettext** for more discussion of this fact and for a URL reference. The Solaris version can create both Solaris format output files and GNU format output files.

Unix Commands

Common Options

`-D` *dir*, `--directory=`*dir*
: Add *dir* to the list of directories searched for input files.

`-f, --use-fuzzy`
: Place fuzzy entries in the output.

`-o` *file*, `--output=`*file*
: Place the output in *file*. This option ignores `domain` directives and duplicate `msgid`s.

`--strict`
: Enable strict Uniforum compliance: append the `.mo` suffix if not already present. The Solaris version ignores this option for Solaris output format files.

`-v, --verbose`
: Be verbose. Duplicate message identifiers are listed, but message strings are not redefined.

Solaris Options

`-g` Generate GNU format output files. Mutually exclusive with `-s`.

`-s` Generate Solaris format output files. Mutually exclusive with `-g`.

GNU/Linux Options

The GNU gettext package continues to acquire features over time. The following list may thus be incomplete; check *msgfmt*(1) for the full story.

`-a` *count*, `--alignment=`*count*
: Align strings to *count* bytes (default is one).

`-c, --check`
: Do all of `--check-domain`, `--check-format`, and `--check-header`.

`--check-accelerators[=`*char*`]`
: Verify translation of menu-item keyboard-accelerator strings. Such strings are assumed to use `&` as the "marker" for

accelerator keys; this option verifies that the translation only has one & character. With *char*, use that character instead of &.

`--check-domain`
: Check for conflicts between the `-o` option and domain directives.

`--check-format`
: Check language-dependent format strings.

`--check-header`
: Check for the presence of the header entry, and verify its contents.

`--csharp`
: C# mode: Create a .NET `.dll` file.

`--csharp-resources`
: Create a .NET `.resources` file.

`--C, --check-compatibility`
: Be compatible with the X/Open `msgfmt`. This produces errors if any GNU extensions are used.

`-d` *`dir`*
: Place generated files for C#, Java and Tcl underneath *dir*.

`-h, --help`
: Print a command-line summary and exit.

`-j, --java`
: Java mode: create a Java `ResourceBundle` class.

`--java2`
: Like `-j`, but assume JDK 1.2 or higher.

`-l` *`locale`*`, --locale=`*`locale`*
: Specify the locale for C#, Java and Tcl modes.

`--no-hash`
: Do not include the hash table in the binary file.

`-P, --properties-input`
: The input files use Java `.properties` syntax.

`--qt` Qt mode: create a Qt `.qm` file.

`-r` *`resource`*`, --resource=`*`resource`*
: Specify the resource name for C# and Java modes.

`--statistics`
: Print translation statistics.

`--stringtable-input`
: The input files use NeXTstep/GNUstep `.strings` syntax.

`--tcl`
: Tcl mode: create a `tcl/msgcat .msg` file.

`-V, --version`
: Print version information and exit.

---

mv

`mv [`*`options`*`]` *`sources target`*

Basic command to move files and directories around on the system or to rename them. `mv` works as the following table shows.

Source	Target	Result
File	*name*	Rename file as *name*.
File	Existing file	Overwrite existing file with source file.
Directory	*name*	Rename directory as *name*.
Directory	Existing directory	Move directory to be a subdirectory of existing directory.
One or more files	Existing directory	Move files to directory.

Common Options

`--`
: Use this when one of the names begins with a `-`. For compatibility with old programs, a plain `-` also works.

`-f, --force`
: Force the move, even if *target* file exists; suppress messages about restricted access modes.

`-i, --interactive`
: Inquire; prompt for a `y` (yes) response before overwriting an existing target.

GNU/Linux Options

`-b, --backup[=`*`control`*`]`
: Back up any existing files. When using the long version of the option, the optional *control* parameter controls the kind of backup. When no control is specified, `mv` attempts to read the control value from the VERSION_CONTROL environment variable. Accepted values are:

`none`, `off`	Never make backups.
`numbered`, `t`	Make numbered backups.
`existing`, `nil`	Match existing backups, numbered or simple.
`simple`, `never`	Always make simple backups.

`--reply=`*`type`*
: Set the default behavior that is used for overwriting existing files. `--replay=yes` is the same as `--force`. `--replay=query` is the same as `--interactive`. `--replay=no` skips existing files.

`--strip-trailing-slashes`
: Removes trailing slashes from each *source* argument. This is needed on many systems for symbolic links that point to directories; on POSIX systems, running `mv` on such a link terminated with a trailing slash moves the *pointed-to directory* and not the link itself.

`-S` *`suffix`*`, --suffix=`*`suffix`*
: Override the SIMPLE_BACKUP_SUFFIX environment variable, which determines the suffix used for making simple backup files. If the suffix is not set either way, the default is a tilde (~).

--target-directory=*dir*
: Move all *sources* into *dir*. This allows you to use mv together with xargs, which otherwise does not work, since the final argument would be the target.

-u, --update
: Do not remove a file or link if its modification date is the same as or newer than that of its replacement.

-v, --verbose
: Print the name of each file before moving it.

Mac OS X Options

-n
: Do not overwrite an existing file. Overrides a previous -f or -i.

-v
: Verbose; print filenames as they are moved.

---

nawk

nawk [*options*] [*program*] [*var*=*value* ...] [*files*]

New version of the awk programming language. For more information see **awk** and Chapter 11.

---

nice

nice [*options*] *command* [*arguments*]

Execute a *command* and *arguments* with lower priority (i.e., be "nice" to other users). Also built-in to the C shell, with a different command syntax (see Chapter 5).

Options

-*n*
: Run *command* with a niceness of *n* (1–19); default is 10. Higher *n* means lower priority. A privileged user can raise priority by specifying a negative *n* (e.g., –5). nice works differently in the C shell (see Chapter 5). +*n* raises priority, -*n* lowers it, and 4 is the default.

-n *n*, --adjustment=*n*
: Same as -*n*.

---

nl

nl [*options*] [*file*]

Number the lines of *file* in logical page segments. Numbering resets to 1 at the start of each logical page. Pages consist of a header, body, and footer; each section may be empty. It is the body that gets numbered. The sections are delimited by special standalone lines as indicated next; the delimiter lines are copied to the output as empty lines.

Section Delimiters

\:\:\:	Start of header
\:\:	Start of body
\:	Start of footer

Common Options

`-b type, --body-numbering=type`
: Number lines according to *type*. Values are:

`a`	All lines.
`n`	No lines.
`t`	Text lines only (the default).
`p"exp"`	Lines matching the regular expression *exp* only.

`-d xy, --section-delimiter=xy`
: Use characters *xy* to delimit logical pages (default is `\:`).

`-f type, --footer-numbering=type`
: Like `-b`, but number footer (default *type* is `n`).

`-h type, --header-numbering=type`
: Like `-b`, but number header (default *type* is `n`).

`-i n, --page-increment=n`
: Increment each line number by *n* (default is 1).

`-l n, --join-blank-lines=n`
: Count *n* consecutive blank lines as one line.

`-n format, --number-format=format`
: Set line number *format*. Values are:

`ln`	Left-justify, omit leading zeros.
`rn`	Right-justify, omit leading zeros (default).
`rz`	Right-justify.

`-p, --no-renumber`
: Do not reset numbering at start of pages.

`-s c, --number-separator=string`
: Separate text from line number with character(s) *c* (default is a tab).

`-v n, --first-page=n`
: Number each page starting at *n* (default is 1).

`-w n, --number-width=n`
: Use *n* columns to show line number (default is 6).

Examples

List the current directory, numbering files as `1)`, `2)`, etc.:

```
ls | nl -w3 -s')  '
```

Number C source code and save it:

```
nl prog.c > print_prog
```

Number only lines that begin with `#include`:

```
nl -bp"^#include" prog.c
```

nm

`nm [options] objfiles`

Print the symbol table (name list) in alphabetical order for one or more object files (usually ELF or COFF files), shared or static libraries, or binary executable programs. Output includes each symbol's value, type, size, name, etc. A key letter categorizing the symbol can also be displayed. You must supply at least one object file.

On Solaris, `nm` is in `/usr/ccs/bin` and `/usr/xpg4/bin`.

Common Options

`-A, --print-file-name`
: Write the full pathname or library name on each line.

`-g, --extern-only`
: Write only external (global) symbol information.

`-P, --portability`
: Print output in the POSIX portable format.

`-t` *radix*, `--radix=`*radix*
: Write numeric values in the specified *radix*: `d` for decimal, `o` for octal, and `x` for hexadecimal.

`-u, --undefined-only`
: Report only the undefined symbols.

Solaris and GNU/Linux Options

`-C, --demangle[=`*style*`]`
: Print demangled C++ symbol names. GNU/Linux lets you supply the appropriate demangling style.

`-D, --dynamic`
: Print dynamic, not normal, symbols. Useful only when working with dynamic objects (some kinds of shared libraries, for example).

`-V, --version`
: Print `nm`'s version number on standard error.

GNU/Linux and Mac OS X Options

`-a, --debug-syms`
: Print debugger symbols.

`-n, --numeric-sort`
: Sort the external symbols numerically, not by name.

`-p, --no-sort`
: Don't sort the symbols; print them in the order they are found in the object file.

`-r, --reverse-sort`
: Sort in reverse order.

Solaris Options

`-e` Report only external and static symbols; obsolete.

`-f` Report all information; obsolete.

`-h` Suppress the header.

-l Use with -p; indicate WEAK symbols by appending an asterisk (*) to key letters.

-n Sort the external symbols by name.

-o Report values in octal.

-p Precede each symbol with its key letter (used for parsing).

-r Report the object file's name on each line.

-R Print the archive name (if present), followed by the object file and symbol name. -r overrides this option.

-s Print section name instead of section index.

-T Truncate the symbol name in the display; obsolete.

Solaris /usr/xpg4/bin/nm Options

-u Print output in long format.

-v Sort the external symbols by value.

-x Report values in hexadecimal.

GNU/Linux Options

-B Same as --format=bsd (for compatibility with MIPS).

--defined-only
: Display only defined symbols.

-f *format*, --format=*format*
: Specify output format (bsd, sysv, or posix). Default is bsd.

-l, --line-numbers
: Use debugging information to try to find line numbers for each symbol.

--no-demangle
: Do not demangle C++ symbols.

-o Same as -a.

-s, --print-armap
: Print the index of files and symbols in ar archives.

--size-sort
: Sort by size.

-S, --print-size
: Print the size of defined symbols.

--target=*bfdname*
: Use object code format *bfdname*, not the system default.

-v Same as -n.

-X 32_64
: For compatibility with AIX nm. Ignored.

Mac OS X Options

--arch *type*
: Display information about only architecture *type* when running nm on a "fat" binary. Use all to see information about all architectures.

-f Display the symbol table of a shared library as if it were a flat file.

-j Display just the symbol names.

-l Show a pseudo-symbol .section_start if no such symbol exists. Use together with -s.

-m Display N_SECT (Mach-O) symbols with segment and section names and their status as external, nonexternal, undefined, common, absolute, or indirect.

-o Include the filename or archive element name on each output line.

-s *segname sectname*
List only the symbols in (*segname*, *sectname*).

-x Print entries in hexadecimal, with the name as a string.

Solaris Key Letters

Uppercase letters are used for GLOBAL and WEAK symbols. Lowercase letters are used for LOCAL symbols.

A Absolute symbol.
B BSS (uninitialized data space).
C Common symbol.
D Data object symbol.
F File symbol.
L Thread local storage.
N Symbol with no type.
S Section symbol.
T Text symbol.
U Undefined symbol.

nohup

nohup *command* [*arguments*] &

Continue to execute the named *command* and optional command *arguments* after you log out (make command immune to hangups; i.e., **no hangup**). In the C shell, nohup is built in. In the Korn and Bash shells, nohup allows output redirection; output goes to nohup.out by default. In the Korn shell, nohup is an alias that allows the command it runs to also be aliased. (See Chapters 4 and 5.)

The Solaris /usr/bin/nohup accepts some rather specialized options; see the manpage for details.

nroff

nroff [*options*] [*files*]

Format documents to line printer or to screen. See Chapter 18.

od

od [*options*] [*file*] [[+] *offset*[. | b]]

Octal dump; produce a dump (normally octal) of the named *file*. *file* is displayed from its beginning, unless you specify an *offset* (normally in octal bytes). In the following options, a "word" is a 16-bit unit.

Common Options

`-A` *base*, `--address-radix=`*base*
: Indicate how the offset should be written. Values for *base* are `d` for decimal, `o` for octal, `x` for hexadecimal, or `n` for no offset.

`-b` Display bytes as octal.

`-c` Display bytes as ASCII.

`-d` Display words as unsigned decimal.

`-f` Display 32-bit words as floating point.

`-j` *skip*, `--skip-bytes=`*skip*
: Jump over *skip* bytes from the beginning of the input. *skip* can have a leading `0` or `0x` for it to be treated as an octal or hexadecimal value. It can have a trailing `b`, `k`, or `m` to be treated as a multiple of 512, 1024, or 1,048,576 bytes.

`-N` *count*, `--read-bytes=`*count*
: Process up to *count* input bytes.

`-o` Display words as unsigned octal (the default).

`-t` *type_string*, `--format=`*type_string*
: Specify one or more output types. See the "Common Type Strings" section later in this entry.

`-v`, `--output-duplicates`
: Verbose; show all data. Without this, duplicate lines print as *.

`-x` Display words as hexadecimal.*

`+` Required before *offset* if *file* isn't specified.

Solaris and Mac OS X Options

`-D` Display 32-bit words as unsigned decimal.

`-F` Display 64-bit words as extended precision.

`-O` Display 32-bit words as unsigned octal.

`-s` Display words as signed decimal.

`-X` Display 32-bit words as hexadecimal.

GNU/Linux and Mac OS X Options

`-a` Same as `-t a`.

`-h` Same as `-t x2`.

Solaris Options

`-C` Interpret bytes as characters based on the setting of LC_CTYPE.

`-S` Display 32-bit words as signed decimal.

GNU/Linux Options

`-i` Same as `-t d2`.

`-l` Same as `-t d4`.

* `od -x` is the canonical Unix oxymoron.

`-s bytes, --strings[=bytes]`
: Output strings that are at least *bytes* ASCII graphic characters long (default is 3 if *bytes* is not specified for `--strings`).

`--traditional`
: Accept arguments in the traditional form, which takes a single file specification with an optional offset and label. *offset* is an octal number indicating how many input bytes to skip over. *label* specifies an initial pseudo-address, which is printed in parentheses after any normal address. Both the offset and the label can begin with an optional plus sign (+), and can have a trailing decimal point (.) to force the offset to be interpreted as a decimal number and/or a trailing `b` to multiply the number of bytes skipped by *offset* by 512.

`-w [bytes], --width[=bytes]`
: Dump *bytes* input bytes to each output line. Defaults to 16 if this option is omitted. If `--width` is specified but *bytes* is omitted, the default is 32.

Mac OS X Options

`-B` Same as `-o`.

`-e` Same as `-F`.

`-H` Same as `-X`.

`-i` Same as `-t dI`.

`-I, -l, -L`
: Same as `-t dL`.

Modifiers for offset

`.` *offset* value is decimal.

`b` *offset* value is 512-byte blocks. Solaris and Mac OS X also allow `B`.

Common Type Strings

Type strings can be followed by a decimal number indicating how many bytes to process.

`a`	ASCII named characters (e.g., BEL for `\007`)
`c`	Single- or multibyte characters
`d, o, u, x`	Signed decimal, unsigned octal, decimal, and hexadecimal
`f`	Floating point

passwd

`passwd [options] [user]`

Create or change a password associated with a *user* name. Only the owner or a privileged user may change a password. Owners need not specify their *user* name.

Solaris and GNU/Linux Privileged User Options

`-d, --delete`
: Delete password; *user* is no longer prompted for one.

`-f, --force`
: Force expiration of *user*'s password; *user* must change password at next login.

`-l, --lock`
: Lock *user*'s password; mutually exclusive with `-d` and `-u`.

`-n` *days*, `--minimum=`*days*
: Set the minimum number of days that must pass before user can change his password.

`-u, --unlock`
: Unlock *user*'s password; mutually exclusive with `-l`.

`-w` *days*, `--warning=`*days*
: Give *user* a warning beginning *days* days before his password is due to expire.

`-x` *days*, `--maximum=`*days*
: Set the number of days before the password expires. Use a value of –1 (minus one) to disable password aging, 0 to force expiration like `-f`.

Solaris Options

Normal users may change the so-called *gecos* information (user's full name, office, etc.) and login shell when using NIS or NIS+; otherwise only privileged users may change the following:

`-D` *domain*
: Use the `passwd.org_dir` database in the NIS+ domain *domain*, instead of in the local domain.

`-e`
: Change the login shell.

`-g`
: Change the *gecos* information.

`-r` *db*
: Change the password in password database *db*, which is one of `files`, `ldap`, `nis`, or `nisplus`. Only a privileged user may use `files`.

`-s`
: Display password information:

1. *user* name.
2. Password status (`NP` for no password, `PS` for password, `LK` for locked).
3. The last time the password was changed (in *mm/dd/yy* format).
4. Number of days that must pass before *user* can rechange the password.
5. Number of days before the password expires.
6. Number of days prior to expiration that *user* is warned of impending expiration.

The following may be used only by privileged users.

`-a` Use with `-s` to display password information for all users. *user* should not be supplied.

`-h` Change the home (login) directory.

`-N` Disable *user*'s password without locking it; mutually exclusive with `-d`.

GNU/Linux Options

`-k, --keep-tokens`
: Keep authentication tokens that have not expired.

`-i` *days*`, --inactive=`*days*
: After *days* days, disable inactive accounts.

`--stdin`
: Read new password information from standard input.

`-S, --status`
: Print a short status about *user*'s password entry.

`-?, --help, --usage`
: Print a command-line summary and exit.

Mac OS X Options

`-i` *db*
: Change the password in *db*, which may be one of `file`, `netinfo`, `nis`, or `opendirectory`.

`-l` *location*
: Change the password in *location*. Valid values vary based on the argument to `-i`:

`file`	A filename. Default is `/etc/master.passwd`.
`netinfo`	A domain name or server/tag pair.
`nis`	An NIS domain name.
`opendirectory`	A directory node name.

paste

`paste [`*options*`]` *files*

Merge corresponding lines of one or more *files* into vertical columns, separated by a tab. See also **cut**, **join**, and **pr**.

Options

`-` Replace a filename with the standard input.

`-d` *char*`, --delimiters=`*char*
: Separate columns with *char* instead of a tab. *char* can be any regular character or the following escape sequences:

`\n`	Newline
`\t`	Tab
`\\`	Backslash
`\0`	Empty string

Note: you can separate columns with different characters by supplying more than one *char*.

`-s, --serial`
Merge subsequent lines from one file.

Examples

Create a three-column result file `results` from the files `in1.data`, `in2.data`, and `in3.data`:

```
paste in1.data in2.data in3.data > results
```

List users in two columns:

```
who | paste - -
```

Merge each pair of lines into one line:

```
paste -s -d"\t\n" list
```

---

patch

`patch [options] [original [patchfile]]`

Apply the patches specified in *patchfile* to *original*. Replace the original with the new, patched version; move the original to *original*.orig or *original*~. The patch file is a difference listing produced by the `diff` command. On Solaris, this command is named gpatch.

URL: *http://www.gnu.org/software/patch*.

Options

`-b, --backup`
Back up the original file.

`--backup-if-mismatch, --no-backup-if-mismatch`
When not backing up all original files, these options control whether a backup should be made when a patch does not match the original file. The default is to make backups unless `--posix` is specified.

`--binary`
Read and write files as binary. Has no effect on a Unix system.

`-B prefix, --prefix=prefix`
Prepend *prefix* to the backup filename.

`-c, --context`
Interpret *patchfile* as a context diff.

`-d dir, --directory=dir`
cd to *directory* before beginning patch operations.

`--dry-run`
Print the results of applying a patch, but don't change any files.

`-D string, --ifdef=string`
Mark all changes with:

```
#ifdef string
   ...
#endif
```

`-e, --ed`
: Treat the contents of *patchfile* as `ed` commands.

`-E, --remove-empty-files`
: If `patch` creates any empty files, delete them.

`-f, --force`
: Force all changes, even those that look incorrect. Skip patches if the original file does not exist; force patches for files with the wrong version specified; assume patches are never reversed.

`-F` *`num`*`, --fuzz=`*`num`*
: Specify the maximum number of lines that may be ignored (fuzzed over) when deciding where to install a hunk of code. The default is 2. Meaningful only with context diffs.

`-g` *`num`*`, --get` *`num`*
: Specify whether to check the original file out of source control if it is missing or read-only. If *num* is a positive number, get the file. If it is negative, prompt the user. If it is 0, do not check files out of source control. The default is negative or the value of the PATCH_GET environment variable when set, unless the `--posix` option is given. Then the default is 0.

`-i` *`file`*`, --input=`*`file`*
: Read patch from *file* instead of standard input.

`-l, --ignore-whitespace`
: Ignore whitespace while pattern matching.

`-n, --normal`
: Interpret patch file as a normal diff.

`-N, --forward`
: Ignore patches that appear to be reversed or to have already been applied.

`-o` *`file`*`, --output=`*`file`*
: Print output to *file*.

`-p[`*`num`*`], --strip[=`*`num`*`]`
: Specify how much of preceding pathname to strip. A *num* of 0 strips everything, leaving just the filename. 1 strips the leading `/`. Each higher number after that strips another directory from the left.

`--posix`
: Conform more strictly to the POSIX standard.

`--quoting-style=`*`style`*
: Set the quoting style used when printing names. The default style is `shell` unless set by the environment variable QUOTING_STYLE. *style* may be one of the following:

`c`	Quote as a C language string.
`escape`	Like `c`, but without surrounding double-quote characters.
`literal`	Print without quoting.
`shell`	Quote for use in shell when needed.
`shell-always`	Quote for use in shell even if not needed.

-r *file*, --reject-file=*file*
  Place rejects (hunks of the patch file that patch fails to place within the original file) in *file*. Default is *original*.rej.

-R, --reverse
  Do a reverse patch: attempt to undo the damage done by patching with the old and new files reversed.

-s, --silent, --quiet
  Suppress commentary.

-t, --batch
  Skip patches if the original file does not exist.

-T, --set-time
  When original file timestamps match the times given in the patch header, set timestamps for patched files according to the context diff headers. Use option -f to force date changes. Assume timestamps are in local time.

-u, --unified
  Interpret patch file as a unified context diff.

-v, --version
  Print version number and exit.

--verbose
  Verbose mode.

-V *method*, --version-control=*method*
  Specify method for creating backup files (overridden by -B):

t, numbered	Make numbered backups.
nil, existing	Back up files according to preexisting backup schemes, with simple backups as the default. This is patch's default behavior.
never, simple	Make simple backups.

-Y *prefix*, --basename-prefix=*prefix*
  Use the specified *prefix* with a file's basename to create backup filenames. Useful for specifying a directory.

-z *suffix*, --suffix=*suffix*
  Back up the original file in *original.suffix*.

-Z, --set-utc
  When original file timestamps match the times given in the patch header, set timestamps for patched files according to the context diff headers. Use option -f to force date changes. Assume timestamps are in Coordinated Universal Time (UTC).

Example

Update a software distribution:

```
$ cd whizprog-1.1
$ patch --verbose --backup -p1 < whizprog-1.1-1.2.diff
Lots of messages here as patch works
$ find . -name '*.orig' -print | xargs rm
$ cd ..
$ mv whizprog-1.1 whizprog-1.2
```

pathchk

`pathchk [-p] pathnames`

Check pathnames. This command verifies that the file(s) named by *pathnames* do not violate any constraints of the underlying filesystem (such as a name that might be too long), and that the files could be accessed (e.g., if an intermediate directory lacks search permission, it is a problem). The `-p` option provides additional portability checks for the *pathnames*. GNU/Linux provides `--portability` as another name for `-p`.

pax

`pax [options] [patterns]`

Portable Archive Exchange program. When members of the first POSIX 1003.2 working group could not standardize on either `tar` or `cpio`, they invented this program.* (See also **cpio** and **tar**.)

GNU/Linux and Mac OS X use almost identical versions of `pax`, developed by the OpenBSD team, based on the original freely available version by Keith Muller.

`pax` operates in four modes, depending on the combinations of `-r` and `-w`:

List mode
: No `-r` and no `-w`. List the contents of a `pax` archive. Optionally, restrict the output to filenames and/or directories that match a given pattern.

Extract mode
: `-r` only. Extract files from a `pax` archive. Intermediate directories are created as needed.

Archive mode
: `-w` only. Archive files to a new or existing `pax` archive. The archive is written to standard output; it may be redirected to an appropriate tape device if needed for backups.

Pass-through mode
: `-r` and `-w`. Copy a directory tree from one location to another, analogous to `cpio -p`.

Common Options

Here are the options available in the four modes:

```
None:       c d f           n   s   v
-r:         c d f   i k     n o p s   u v
-w:     a b   d f H i     L   o   s t u v x X
-rw:          d   H i k l   n   p s t u v   X
```

`-a` Append files to the archive. This may not work on some tape devices.

* This period in Unix history is known as the "tar wars." :-)

`-b size`
: Use *size* as the blocksize, in bytes, of blocks to be written to the archive.

`-c`
: Complement. Match all file or archive members that do *not* match the patterns.

`-d`
: For files or archive members that are directories, extract or archive only the directory itself, not the tree it contains.

`-f archive`
: Use *archive* instead of standard input or standard output.

`-H`
: Follow symbolic links named on the command line, archiving the pointed-to file or directory.

`-i`
: Interactively rename files. For each file, `pax` writes a prompt to `/dev/tty` and reads a one-line response from `/dev/tty`. The responses are as follows:

ENTER	Skip the file.
A period	Take the file as is.
new name	Anything else is taken as the new name to use for the file.
EOF	Exit immediately with a nonzero exit status.

`-k`
: Do not overwrite existing files.

`-l`
: Make hard links. When copying a directory tree (`-rw`), make hard links between the source and destination hierarchies wherever possible.

`-L`
: Follow all symbolic links, archiving the pointed-to file or directory.

`-n`
: Choose the first archive member that matches each pattern. No more than one archive member will match for each pattern.

`-o options`
: Reserved for format-specific options.

`-p privs`
: Specify one or more privileges for the extracted file. *privs* specify permissions or other characteristics to be preserved or ignored, as follows:

`a`	Do not preserve file access times.
`e`	Retain the user and group IDs, permissions (mode), and access and modification time.
`m`	Do not preserve the file modification time.
`o`	Retain the user and group ID.
`p`	Keep the permissions (mode).

`-r`
: Read an archive and extract files.

`-s replacement`
: Use *replacement* to modify file or archive member names. This is a string of the form `-s/old/new/[gp]`. This is similar to the substitution commands in `ed`, `ex`, and `sed`. *old* is a regular

expression, and *new* may contain & to mean the matched text and *n* for subpatterns. The trailing g indicates the substitution should be applied globally. A trailing p causes pax to print the resulting new filename. Multiple -s options may be supplied. The first one that works is applied. Any delimiter may be used, not just /, but in all cases it is wise to quote the argument to prevent the shell from expanding wildcard characters.

-t
: Reset the access time of archived files to what they were before being archived by pax.

-u
: Ignore files older than preexisting files or archive members. The behavior varies based on the current mode.

    Extract mode
    : Extract the archive file if it is newer than an existing file with the same name.

    Archive mode
    : If an existing file with the same name as an archive member is newer than the archive member, supersede the archive member.

    Pass-through mode
    : Replace the file in the destination hierarchy with the file in the source hierarchy (or a link to it) if the source hierarchy's file is newer.

-v
: In list mode, print a verbose table of contents. Otherwise, print archive member names on standard error.

-w
: Write files to standard output in the given archive format.

-x *format*
: Use the given *format* for the archive. The value of *format* is one of cpio, pax, or ustar. The details of the formats are provided in the IEEE 1003.1 (2004) POSIX standard. The formats are mutually incompatible; attempting to append using one format to an archive using another is an error.

    Solaris provides the xustar format, which allows archiving files over 8GB in size.

    Mac OS X and GNU/Linux provide the bcpio, sv4cpio, sv4crc, and tar formats, which provide compatibility with various historical versions of tar and cpio.

-X
: When traversing directory trees, do not cross into a directory on a different device (the st_dev field in the stat structure, see *stat*(2); similar to the -mount option of find).

Solaris Options

-@
: Archive or extract extended attributes.

GNU/Linux and Mac OS X Options

-B *bytes*
: Write no more than *bytes* bytes for each volume. Intended for use on tape media, not recommended for floppies or hard disks. *bytes* may be suffixed with m, k, or b to specify units of megabytes, kilobytes, or 512-byte blocks, respectively.

-D Like -u, but check the file's inode-change time instead of the modification time.

-E *count*
Retry failed reads no more than *count* times. A limit of 0 causes pax to stop after the first read failure. A limit of NONE causes pax to retry forever, which could cause an infinite loop when reading from very poor media.

-G *group*
Select files based on the group ownership. Use #*number* to supply a numeric GID. Use \# if the group name contains a literal # character. Multiple -G options may be supplied.

-P Do not follow any symbolic links. This is the default.

-T [*from_date*][,*to_date*][/[c][m]]
Choose files based on modification time or inode change time whose times fall within a specified range. With just *from_date*, select files of same age or younger. With just *to_date*, select files of same age or older. With both, choose files falling within the given dates. If the two dates are equal, the file's time must exactly match the given date. The trailing c and m let you specify which timestamp to compare against: inode change time or modification time, respectively. If both are used, both times are compared. The default is the modification time. Multiple -T options may be provided; the first one that matches a given file is used.

The time is specified as [*yy*[*mm*[*dd*[*hh*]]]]*mm*[.*ss*]. Only the minutes (*mm*) field is required. Other fields may be added, but no intervening fields may be omitted (e.g., you can't provide the day of the month without also providing the hour). Times are relative to the current time; thus an *hhmm* specification is relative to today.

-U *user*
Select files based on the user. Use #*number* to supply a numeric UID. Use \# if the username contains a literal # character. Multiple -U options may be supplied.

-Y Like -D, but check the inode change time of the pathname created after all filename substitutions have occurred.

-z Use gzip to compress/decompress the archive when writing/reading. Mutually exclusive with -a.

-Z Like -u, but check the modification time of the pathname created after all filename substitutions have occurred.

Examples

Copy the current directory to tape:

```
pax -x ustar -w -f /dev/rmt/0m .
```

Copy a home directory to a different directory (presumably on a bigger disk).

```
# cd /home
# pax -r -w arnold /newhome
```

perl

perl [*options*] [*programfile*] [*files*]

perl is the interpreter for the Perl programming language (the Swiss Army knife of Unix programming tools). The Perl program is provided via one or more -e options. If no -e options are used, the first file named on the command line is used for the program. See *perlrun*(1) for the full list of options.

For more information about Perl, see *Learning Perl*, *Programming Perl*, and *Advanced Perl Programming*, all listed in the Bibliography.

URLs: *http://www.perl.org* and *http://www.perl.com*.

pr

pr [*options*] [*files*]

Format one or more *files* according to *options* to standard output. Each page includes a heading that consists of the page number, filename, date, and time. When files are named directly, the date and time are those of the file's modification time. Otherwise, the current date and time are used.

Common Options

-a, --across
: Multicolumn format; list items in rows going across.

-d, --double-space
: Double-spaced format.

-e[*tab-char*[*width*]], --expand-tabs=[*tab-char*[*width*]]
: Convert tabs (or *tab-chars*) to spaces. If *width* is specified, convert tabs to *width* characters (default is 8).

-F, --form-feed
: Separate pages with form feeds, not newlines. (Solaris /usr/bin/pr folds input lines, avoiding truncation by -a or -m.)

-h *str*, --header=*str*
: Replace default header with string *str*.

-i[*out-tab-char*[*out-tab-width*]]
--output-tabs[=*out-tab-char*[*out-tab-width*]]
: Replace spaces with tabs on output. Can specify alternative tab character (default is tab) and width (default is 8).

-l *n*, --length=*n*
: Set page length to *n* lines (default is 66).

-m, --merge
: Merge files, printing one in each column (can't be used with -*n* and -a). Text is chopped to fit. See also **paste**.

-n[*delimiter*[*digits*]], --number-lines[=*delimiter*[*digits*]]
: Number columns, or, with the -m option, number lines. Append *delimiter* to each number (default is a tab) and limit the size of numbers to *digits* (default is 5).

`-o n, --indent=n`
: Offset each line *n* spaces (default is 0).

`-r, --no-file-warnings`
: Suppress messages for files that can't be found.

`-s[delimiter], --separator[=delimiter]`
: Separate columns with *delimiter* (default is a tab).

`-t, --omit-header`
: Omit the page header and trailing blank lines.

`-w n, --width=n`
: Set line width to *n* (default is 72).

`+beg_page[:end-page], --pages=[beg_page[:end-page]`
: Begin printing at page *beg_page* (default is 1). The GNU/Linux version supports supplying an end page *end_page* also.

`-n, --columns=n`
: Produce output having *n* columns (default is 1); tabs are expanded as with `-i`.

Solaris Options

`-f` Separate pages using a formfeed character (`^L`) instead of a series of blank lines.

`-p` Pause before each page.

GNU/Linux Options

`-c, --show-control-chars`
: Convert control characters to hat notation (such as `^C`), and other unprintable characters to octal backslash format.

`-D format, --date-format=format`
: Format the header date using *format*. See the `date` command for the possible formats.

`-f` Same as `-F`.

`-J, --join-lines`
: Merge full lines; ignore `-W` if set.

`-N num, --first-line-number=num`
: Start counting with *num* at the first line of the first page printed. Also see *+beg_page*.

`-S[string], --sep-string[=string]`
: Separate columns with *string*. Default is a tab with `-J` and a space otherwise.

`-T, --omit-pagination`
: Like `-t` but also suppress form feeds.

`-v, --show-non-printing`
: Convert unprintable characters to octal backslash format.

Mac OS X Options

`-f` Like `-F`, but pause before printing the first page.

`-L locale`
: Use *locale* for the locale, instead of what's in the environment.

`-p` Pause before each page.

Examples

Print a side-by-side list, omitting heading and extra lines:

```
pr -m -t list.1 list.2 list.3
```

Alphabetize a list of states; number the lines in five columns:

```
sort states_50 | pr -n -5
```

printenv

`printenv [variable]`

Print values of all environment variables or, optionally, only the specified *variable*. The more standard alternative, env, doesn't let you view just one variable, but it lets you redefine them. On Solaris, printenv is in /usr/ucb.

printf

`printf formats [strings]`

Print *strings* using the specified *formats*. *formats* can be ordinary text characters, C-language escape characters, *printf*(3S) format conversion specifiers, or, more commonly, a set of conversion *arguments* listed next.

printf is built into Bash and ksh93 (see Chapter 4); this entry describes the external version in /usr/bin/printf.

Common Arguments

%b
: Process a string argument for backslash escapes (not in *printf*(3S)). See the description of allowed escapes under **echo**.

%s
: Print the next *string*.

%[-]*m*[.*n*]s
: Print the next *string*, using a field that is *m* characters wide. Optionally limit the field to print only the first *n* characters of *string*. Strings are right-adjusted unless the left-adjustment flag - is specified.

Solaris Argument

%*n*$s Print the *n*th *string*.

Examples

```
$ printf '%s %s\n' "My files are in" $HOME
My files are in /home/arnold
$ printf '%-25.15s %s\n' "My files are in" $HOME
My files are in           /home/arnold
```

ps

`ps [options] [arguments]`

Process status. This command is very system-specific. See the **ps** entries in the sections for each operating system.

pwd

`pwd`

Print the full pathname of the current directory. (Command name stands for "print working directory.") Note: the built-in versions, `pwd` (Bash and Korn shells) and `dirs` (C shell), are faster, so you might want to define the following C shell alias:

```
alias pwd dirs -l
```

python

`python`

A powerful object-oriented scripting language often compared to Perl or Java. `python` drives many of the configuration scripts used in Red Hat and other Linux distributions. For more information, see *Learning Python* and *Programming Python*.

URL: *http://www.python.org*.

r Commands

```
rcp [options] file1 file2
rcp [options] file ... directory
rlogin [options] rhost
rsh [options] host [command]
```

The BSD "r" commands provide remote file copy, remote login, and remote command execution across a TCP/IP network. In the 21st century these commands are considered to be terribly insecure, and *you should never use them*. Instead, consider the secure versions that come as part of the Secure Shell: `scp`, `slogin`, and `ssh` (see **ssh**).

rcs

`rcs [options] files`

The Revision Control System (RCS) keeps track of multiple versions of files, letting you store and retrieve revisions and track the history of the files. The `rcs` command creates new RCS files and modifies attributes of existing files. See Chapter 13 for more information on RCS and its commands.

reset

`reset [options] [terminal]`

Clear screen (reset terminal). If *terminal* is specified on the command line, the value is used as the terminal type. `reset` is a symbolic link to the `tset` command. Invoking the command as `reset` is useful for clearing your terminal when a program dies and leaves the terminal in an abnormal state. You may have to run the command with a linefeed character (usually CTRL-J) before and after it:

```
CTRL-JresetCTRL-J
```

On Solaris, this command is found is `/usr/ucb`. See the **tset** entry for the available options.

rm

`rm [options] files`

Delete one or more *files*. To remove a file, you must have write permission on the directory that contains the file, but you need not have permission on the file itself. If you do not have write permission on the file, you are prompted (y or n) to override.

Common Options

`-f, --force`
: Force. Remove write-protected files without prompting.

`-i, --interactive`
: Prompt for y (remove the file) or n (do not remove the file). Overrides -f.

`-r, -R, --recursive`
: If *file* is a directory, remove the entire directory and all its contents, including subdirectories. Be forewarned: use of this option can be dangerous.

`--`
: Mark the end of options (rm still accepts -, the old form). Use this when supplying a filename beginning with -.

GNU/Linux and Mac OS X Options

`-d, --directory`
: Remove directories, even if they are not empty. Available only to a privileged user.

`-v, --verbose`
: Verbose mode (print the name of each file before removing it).

GNU/Linux Options

`--no-preserve-root`
: Do not treat the root directory, /, specially.

`--preserve-root`
: Do not operate recursively on the root directory, /.

Mac OS X Options

`-P`
: Overwrite the contents of the to-be-removed files before deleting them. Each file is written with three different bit patterns: 0xff, 0x00, and then 0xff again.

`-W`
: Undelete the named files. Only works for files covered by whiteouts.

rmdir

`rmdir [options] directories`

Delete the named *directories* (the directory itself, not the contents). *directories* are deleted from the parent directory and must be empty (if not, rm -r can be used instead). See also **mkdir**.

Common Option

`-p, --parents`
: Remove *directories* and any intervening parent directories that become empty as a result; useful for removing subdirectory trees.

Solaris Option

`-s` Suppress standard error messages caused by `-p`.

GNU/Linux Options

`--ignore-fail-on-non-empty`
: Ignore failure to remove directories that are not empty.

`-v, --verbose`
: Verbose mode; print a message for each directory as it is processed.

---

rsync

`rsync [options] source ... dest`

rsync synchronizes files across a network connection. It is particularly good for high-latency connections, and for synchronizing entire directory trees across machines. On Solaris, rsync is in /opt/sfw/bin; it may not be installed on your system. However, you can download it and compile and install it. This entry documents rsync 2.6.5, which is the most recent as of the time of this writing.

URL: *http://rsync.samba.org/*.

Source and destination specifications take three forms:

Pathname
: A regular Unix pathname, representing a local file.

`[user@]host:[path]`
: The file or directory *path* on remote host *host* as remote user *user*. With a single colon, rsync uses a remote shell such as ssh or rsh for its transfer mechanism. The remote username is optional, and the remote path defaults to the current users's home directory on the remote system. A relative *path* (one that does not start with /) is relative to the home directory on the remote system.

`[user@]host::[path]`
: The file or directory *path* on remote host *host* as remote user *user*. With a double colon, rsync makes a direct TCP connection to port 873 on the remote machine, and expects to talk to another copy of rsync running in daemon mode.

If both source and destination are local pathnames, rsync synchronizes the two local files or directory trees. You may not specify a remote source together with a remote destination.

Using a trailing / on a directory name causes rsync to work on the contents of that directory, instead of starting with and copying the directory itself.

Primary Options

rsync has a large number of options. We document the most useful ones here; see the manpage for more information.

`-a, --archive`
: Same as `-rlptgoD`. This provides recursion and synchronizes almost everything. Add `-H` to preserve hard links.

`-b, --backup`
: Backup preexisting files before copying them.

`--backup-dir=`*dir*
: With `-b`, indicates that backup copies should be stored in *dir*.

`-c, --checksum`
: Use 128-bit MD4 checksums during the transfer. This increases reliability but severely slows down the synchronization.

`-C, --cvs-exclude`
: Ignore the same files that CVS would. rsync starts with this list:

```
RCS SCCS CVS CVS.adm RCSLOG cvslog.* tags TAGS .make.
state .nse_depinfo *~ #* .#* ,* _$* *$ *.old *.bak .BAK
*.orig *.rej .del-* *.a *.olb *.o *.obj *.so *.exe *.Z
*.elc *.ln core .svn/
```

It then adds files listed `$HOME/.cvsignore` and those in the CVSIGNORE environment variable. As it traverse directories, when it finds a `.cvsignore` file, rsync also ignores files listed therein. These rules are applied *after* `--filter` rules you supply.

`--delete`
: Delete files on the receiving side that are not on the sending side. This applies only for recursive directory copies, not for individual files. *Use with caution*. You may wish to use `-n` first. See the manpage for details on this and other related options.

`-e` *program*, `--rsh=`*program*
: Use *program* as the remote shell for communication with the remote system. By default, modern versions of rsync use ssh, the Secure Shell, but it's possible that rsync was configured differently. If you provide *program* as a quoted argument, you can include command-line arguments for it.

`--exclude=`*pattern*
: Exclude files matching *pattern*. You can usually think of *pattern* as a shell-style wildcard; however, much more powerful patterns are possible; see the manpage for more information.

`-g, --group`
: Make the group of the destination file be the same as the group of the source file. Only groups in the remote user's group set may be used. The default is to use group names, but sometimes numeric GID values are used; see the manpage for the details.

`-h, --help`
: Print a command-line summary and exit.

`-H, --hard-links`
: Preserve hard link information when copying files. This only works if both links are in the files being copied. This option can be slow, since rsync must keep track of more information.

`--include=`*pattern*
: Include only files matching *pattern*. You can usually think of *pattern* as a shell-style wildcard; however, much more powerful patterns are possible; see the manpage for more information.

`-l, --links`
: Re-create source symbolic links as symbolic links on the destination system.

`-L, --copy-links`
: Follow symbolic links, copying the files they point to, not the symbolic links themselves.

`-n, --dry-run`
: Do not actually transfer any files, just report what would happen.

`-o, --owner`
: Make the owner of the destination file be the same as the owner of the source file. Often, changing ownership is a privileged operation, so this may not always work. The default is to use usernames, but sometimes numeric UID values are used; see the manpage for the details.

`-p, --perms`
: Make the destination permissions be the same as the source permissions. Normally permissions on existing files are not changed.

`--progress`
: Print running progress information during the transfer.

`-q, --quiet`
: Decrease information during a transfer. Useful if invoking `rsync` from `cron`.

`-r, --recursive`
: Copy directories recursively.

`--rsync-path=`*program*
: Specify the path to the remote copy of `rsync`. Use this when `rsync` is not included in the PATH of the remote shell. The *program* is run on the remote system by a real shell, so it can be a (small) shell script; just be careful that it does not produce any output or read any input, so that `rsync`'s communications are not affected.

`-S, --sparse`
: Attempt to be efficient when transfering sparse files (those with holes in them) so that they take up less space on the destination system. Note: the manpage warns against using this option for destinations on Solaris `tmpfs` filesystems.

`-t, --times`
: Make the modification time of the destination file be the same as that of the source file. You should always do this; it enables optimizations within rsync that make subsequent updates go faster.

`-u, --update`
: Skip any destination files that have a newer modification time than the source file. Note, however, that the modification time doesn't matter if the files have a different type, for example a symbolic link source and a regular file destination; in such a case the update is always done.

`-v, --verbose`
: Increase information during a transfer. Repeating the option increases verbosity; however, more than two `-v` options is useful only for debugging.

`-x, --one-file-system`
: Do not cross filesystem boundaries when recursively copying directory trees.

`-z, --compress`
: Compress file data as it's sent. Due to the way rsync works, this can achieve better performance than just using a remote shell that compresses data.

`-0, --from0`
: Filenames read from a file are terminated with the zero byte, instead of a newline. This provides unambiguous interpretation of filenames. It does not apply to `.cvsignore` files.

See the manpage for a description of the other options.

Examples

Mirror a directory tree from an rsync server:

```
rsync -avz archive.example.com::Cool_Stuff .
```

Synchronize the home directory on your laptop with that of your desktop system. Assume that the full path to your home directory is the same on both, and that you're using Bash or the Korn shell:

```
laptop$ cd $HOME
laptop$ rsync -aHzv --delete desktop.example.com:$PWD/ ./
```

---

samba — Samba Tools For Working With SMB Filesystems

The Samba suite allows you to serve Unix filesystems to MS-Windows clients. It also allows you to make Unix printers available to MS-Windows systems. It provides considerable interoperability with those systems. Samba comes with GNU/Linux, and GNU/Linux systems can also mount SMB fileshares.

URL: *http://www.samba.org*.

scp `scp [options] file1 [...] file2`

Securely copy files between hosts on a network, using ssh. Part of the OpenSSH suite of network tools. (See also **ssh** and **sftp**.) scp requests a password or passphrase if required. The transfer can be between two remote hosts. If more than one file is specified for *file1*, *file2* should be a directory; otherwise, only the last file in the list is copied. *file1* and *file2* can be specified in any of the following ways:

```
file
host:file
user@host:file
```


Common Options

`-4` Use IPv4 addresses.

`-6` Use IPv6 addresses.

`-B` Run in batch mode. Don't ask for passwords or passphrases.

`-c` *cipher*
: Specify the *cipher* to be used for encrypting the data.

`-C` Enable ssh compression.

`-F` *file*
: Use *file* as the per-user configuration file.

`-i` *file*
: Specify the file that contains the identity (private key) for RSA authentication.

`-o` *option*
: Specify an option to pass to ssh.

`-p` Preserve modification time, access time, and mode.

`-P` *port*
: Connect to *port* on the remote host.

`-q` Don't display the progress meter.

`-r` Copy directories recursively.

`-S` *program*
: Specify the program to use for the encrypted connection. The program must understand ssh options.

`-v` Verbose mode.

GNU/Linux and Mac OS X Options

`-1` Force use of the SSH1 protocol.

`-2` Force use of the SSH2 protocol.

`-l` *count*
: Limit the bandwidth used to *count* Kbits per second.

Mac OS X Option

`-E` Preserve extended attributes, such as resource forks. Both ends of the connection must be running Mac OS X 10.4 or later.

screen

`screen [options] [command [args]]`

Provide ANSI/VT100 terminal emulation, making it possible to run multiple full-screen pseudo-terminals from one real terminal, and letting you manipulate and save your screen input and output, copy and paste between windows, etc. Solaris does not have screen, but you can download and build it.

URL: *http://www.gnu.org/software/screen*.

Options

`-a` Include all capabilities in each window's termcap.

`-A` Adapt all windows to the size of the current terminal. Default is to try to use the previous window size.

`-c` *file*
: Use *file* as the configuration file instead of the default `$HOME/.screenrc`.

`-d` Detach session running elsewhere. With `-r`, reattach to this terminal. With `-R`, reattach to this terminal or create it if it doesn't already exist. With `-RR`, use the first session when reattaching if more than one session is available. With `-m`, start in detached mode.

`-D` Detach session running elsewhere, logging out before detaching. With `-r`, reattach to this terminal. With `-R`, reattach to this terminal or create it if it doesn't already exist. With `-RR`, do whatever is necessary to create a new session. With `-m`, start in detached mode, but don't fork a new process.

`-e` *xy*
: Change command characters. Specify *x* as the command character (default `CTRL-A`) and *y* as the character that generates a literal command character (default `a`). Specify in caret notation (e.g., `^A` for `CTRL-A`).

`-f, -fn, -fa`
: Turn flow control on, off, or to automatic switching mode.

`-h` *num*
: Specify the size of the history scrollback buffer.

`-i` Cause the interrupt key (usually `CTRL-C`) to interrupt the display immediately when flow control is on. Use of this option is discouraged.

`-l, -ln`
: Turn login mode on or off for `/var/adm/utmp` updating. (The actual filename varies from system to system.)

`-ls, -list`
: Print list of *pid.tty.host* strings identifying screen sessions.

`-L` Tell screen that automargin terminal has a writable last position.

`-m` Ignore the $STY environment variable and create a new session. With `-d`, start session in detached mode; useful for scripts. With `-D`, start session in detached mode but don't fork a new process; the command exits if the session terminates.

`-O` Use optimal output mode for terminal rather than true VT100 emulation.

`-p` *window*
Preselect the specified window if it exists.

`-q` Suppress error message printing on startup. Exit with nonzero return code if unsuccessful.

`-r` [*pid.tty.host*]
`-r` *sessionowner/*[*pid.tty.host*]
Resume detached session. No other options except `-d` or `-D` can be specified. With *sessionowner*, resume another user's detached session; requires setuid `root`.

`-R` Attempt to resume the first session found, or start a new session with the specified options. Set by default if `screen` is run as a login shell.

`-s` *shell*
Set the default shell, overriding the $SHELL environment variable.

`-S` *name*
Specify a name for the session being started.

`-t` *name*
Set the window's title.

`-T` *term*
Set $TERM to *term* instead of `screen`.

`-U` Run in UTF-8 mode.

`-v` Print version information and exit.

`-wipe` [*match*]
Like `-ls`, but remove destroyed sessions instead of marking them dead. If a match is specified, it should be in the same form as the argument to the `-r` option.

`-x` Attach to a session that is not detached. Requires multi-display mode.

`-X` Run specified command in specified session. Requires multi-display mode, and session must not be password-protected.

---

script

`script [`*options*`] [`*file*`]`

Create a record of your login session, storing in *file* everything that displays on your screen. The default file is called `typescript`. `script` records nonprinting characters as control characters and includes prompts. This command is useful for beginners or for saving output from a time-consuming command.

Common Option

`-a` Append the script record to *file*.

GNU/Linux Options

-c *command*
: Run *command* instead of creating an interactive shell. Useful for capturing the output of a command that acts differently when it's connected to a terminal.

-f
: Flush output after each write. Useful if another person is monitoring the output file.

-q
: Operate in quiet mode.

-t
: Write timing data to standard error. Each entry has two fields: the first is the elapsed time since the last output, and the second is the number of characters in the current output.

---

sdiff

`sdiff [options] file1 file2`

Produce a side-by-side comparison of *file1* with *file2*. Output is:

text text
: Identical lines.

text <
: Line that exists only in *file1*.

> *text*
: Line that exists only in *file2*.

text | *text*
: Lines that are different.

GNU/Linux and Mac OS X both use the GNU version of `sdiff`.

Common Options

-l, --left-column
: List only lines of *file1* that are identical.

-o *outfile*, --output=*outfile*
: Send identical lines of *file1* and *file2* to *outfile*; print line differences and edit *outfile* by entering, when prompted, the following commands:

e	Edit an empty file.
e b	Edit both left and right columns.
e l	Edit left column.
e r	Edit right column.
l	Append left column to *outfile*.
q	Exit the editor.
r	Append right column to *outfile*.
s	Silent mode; do not print identical lines.
v	Turn off "silent mode."

-s, --suppress-common-lines
: Do not print identical lines.

-w *cols*, --width=*cols*
: Set line length to *cols* (default is 130).

GNU sdiff Options

`-a, --text`
Treat all files as text and compare line-by-line.

`-b, --ignore-space-change`
Ignore differences in whitespace.

`-B, --ignore-blank-lines`
Ignore added or missing blank lines.

`-d, --minimal`
Use a different algorithm to find fewer changes. This option causes `sdiff` to run more slowly.

`--diff-program=`*`program`*
Use *program* in place of the standard version of `diff`.

`-E, --ignore-tab-expansion`
Ignore changes occurring because of tab expansion.

`-H, --speed-large-files`
Heuristically speed comparison of large files with many small scattered changes.

`-i, --ignore-case`
Ignore case changes.

`--ignore-all-space`
Ignore whitespace when comparing lines.

`-I` *`regexp`*`, --ignore-matching-lines=`*`regexp`*
Ignore any changes that insert or delete lines matching the regular expression *regexp*.

`--strip-trailing-cr`
Ignore Carriage Return characters at the end of input lines.

`-t, --expand-tabs`
Convert tabs to spaces in the output to preserve alignment.

`-v, --version`
Print version information and exit.

`-W, --ignore-all-space`
Ignore horizontal whitespace when comparing lines.

Example

Show differences using 80 columns and ignore identical lines:

```
sdiff -s -w80 list.1 list.2
```

---

sed

`sed [`*`options`*`] [`*`files`*`]`

Stream editor. Edit one or more *files* without user interaction. See Chapter 10 for more information on `sed`. The `-e` and `-f` options may be provided multiple times, and they may be used with each other. See also *sed & awk*, cited in the Bibliography.

Common Options

`-e '`*`instruction`*`', --expression='`*`instruction`*`'`
Apply the editing *instruction* to the files.

-f *script*, --file=*script*
Apply the set of instructions from the editing *script*.

-n, --quiet, --silent
Suppress default output.

GNU/Linux and Mac OS X Option

-i [*suffix*], --in-place=[*suffix*]
Edit files in place, saving each original in a file created by concatenating *suffix* to the filename. A zero length *suffix* does not save a backup copy; this is not recommended.

GNU/Linux Options

-l *count*, --line-length=*count*
Wrap lines at column *count* for the l command.

--posix
Disable all GNU extensions.

-r, --regex-extended
Use Extended Regular Expressions instead of Basic Regular Expressions (see Chapter 7).

-s, --separate
Process each file separately instead of treating them all as one long input stream.

-u, --unbuffered
Do not keep as much data in memory as sed would normally; flush output buffers more often.

Mac OS X Option

-E Use Extended Regular Expressions instead of Basic Regular Expressions (see Chapter 7).

sftp

sftp [*options*] *host*

An interactive file transfer program, similar to ftp except that it uses ssh to perform file transfers securely. sftp connects to *host* and logs in, prompting for a password if required. The host can be specified in the following ways:

host
[*user*@]*host*[:*file* [*file*] ...]
[*user*@]*host*[:*dir*[/]]

If *user* is specified, that username is used for the login. If any files are specified, the sftp client automatically retrieves them after the user has been authenticated and then exits. If a directory *dir* is specified, the client starts in that directory on the remote host. sftp is part of the OpenSSH suite of network tools. See also **ssh** and **scp**.

Options

-1 Use SSH1. The default is to use SSH2.

-b *file*
Run in batch mode, taking commands from the specified file. Requires a noninteractive authentication mechanism.

-B *bytes*
Specify the size of the buffer sftp uses for file transfers. Default is 32768 bytes.

-C Enable compression (uses ssh -C).

-F *file*
Use *file* as the ssh configuration file instead of the default system configuration file. The system-wide file is usually /etc/ssh/ssh_config and per-user files are $HOME/.ssh/config.

-o*option*
Pass an option to ssh. The passed option is in the format used by *ssh_config*(5) (e.g., -oPORT=*nn*, where *nn* is the port number). -o can appear more than once to pass multiple options to ssh. This option is useful for passing options that don't have an equivalent sftp command-line option.

-P *server_path*
Connect directly to the local sftp server specified in *server_path*. Useful for debugging.

-R *num*
Specify the number of requests that may be outstanding at any time (default is 16).

-s *subsys|server_path*
Specify the SSH2 subsystem or path to the sftp server on the remote system. Specifying the path is useful for using sftp via SSH1 or if the remote sshd does not have an sftp subsystem configured.

-S *program*
Specify the name of a program that understands ssh options and that you want to use for the encrypted connection.

-v Raise the logging level.

---

sh

sh [*options*] [*arguments*]

The standard command interpreter that executes commands from a terminal or a file. On commercial Unix systems, /bin/sh is often the original Bourne shell, which lacks features found in Bash and the Korn shell.

On some systems, /bin/sh may be a version of ksh88. (This is true of Solaris's /usr/xpg4/bin/sh.) On GNU/Linux, /bin/sh is a symbolic link to Bash, while on Mac OS X /bin/sh is a separate copy of Bash. See Chapter 4 for more information on Bash, ksh88, and ksh93, including command-line options.

---

size

size [*options*] [*objfile* ...]

Print the (decimal) number of bytes of each section of *objfile*. On many systems, if *objfile* is not specified, a.out is used. Solaris requires the *objfile* name. On Solaris, this program resides in /usr/ccs/bin.

Like the loader ld, this program has diverged across time and platforms, to the point where it's not worthwhile to provide an option list. The output format is also not the same across systems. See the manpage for your local system.

sleep

`sleep seconds`

Wait a specified number of *seconds* before executing another command. Often used in shell scripts. sleep is built in to ksh93.

The GNU/Linux version allows the number to have a suffix: s for seconds (the default), m for minutes, h for hours, and d for days. The value may also be real number, specifying fractional units as well.

soelim

`soelim [files]`

A preprocessor that reads nroff/troff input *files*, resolving and then eliminating .so requests. That is, input lines such as:

```
.so header
```

are replaced by the contents of the file header. Normally, .so requests are resolved by nroff or troff. Use soelim whenever you are preprocessing the input (e.g., passing it through tbl or sed), and the complete text is needed prior to formatting. See also Chapter 18.

Example

Run a sed script on (all) input before formatting:

```
soelim file | sed -e 's/--/\\(em/g' | nroff -mm - | lp
```

sort

`sort [options] [files]`

Sort the lines of the named *files*, typically in alphabetical order. See also **uniq**, **comm**, and **join**.

Mac OS X uses an early version of GNU sort that lacks long options as well as some of the features of the current GNU sort.

Common Options

`-b, --ignore-leading-blanks`
: Ignore leading spaces and tabs.

`-c, --check`
: Check whether *files* are already sorted, and if so, produce no output.

`-d, --dictionary-order`
: Sort in dictionary order (ignore punctuation).

`-f, --ignore-case`
: "Fold"; ignore uppercase/lowercase differences.

`-i, --ignore-nonprinting`
: Ignore nonprinting characters (those outside ASCII range 040-176).

`-k` *`fieldspec`*`, --key=`*`fieldspec`*
: Specify significance of input fields for sorting. See the fuller description below.

`-m, --merge`
: Merge sorted input files.

`-M, --month-sort`
: Compare first three characters as abbreviations for month names (`Jan` < `Feb`, etc.).

`-n, --numeric-sort`
: Sort in arithmetic (numerical) order.

`-o` *`file`*`, --output=`*`file`*
: Put output in *file*.

`-r, --reverse`
: Reverse the order of the sort.

`-t`*`c`*`, --field-separator=`*`c`*
: Fields are separated with *c* (default is any whitespace).

`-T` *`dir`*`, --temporary-directory=`*`dir`*
: Use *dir* for temporary files.

`-u, --unique`
: Identical lines in input file appear only one (**u**nique) time in output.

`+`*`n`* `[-`*`m`*`]`
: Skip *n* fields before sorting, and sort up to field position *m*. If *m* is missing, sort to end of line. Positions take the form *a.b*, which means character *b* of field *a*. If *.b* is missing, sort at the first character of the field. Counting starts at zero. Fields may have optional trailing modifiers, as in the `-k` option. Note: This method of describing fields is considered obsolete. Use `-k` instead.

Solaris Options

`-S` *`kmem`*
: Adjust the amount of swap-based memory (in kilobytes) `sort` uses. Trailing suffixes of `b`, `k`, `m`, `g`, `t`, and `%`, allow specification of memory in bytes, kilobytes, megabytes, gigabytes and terabytes, or as a percentage of physical memory, respectively.

`-y [`*`kmem`*`]`
: Adjust the amount of memory (in kilobytes) `sort` uses. If *kmem* is not specified, allocate the maximum memory. Obsolete: use `-S` instead.

`-z` *`recsz`*
: Provide the maximum number of bytes for any one line in the file. This option prevents abnormal termination of `sort` in certain cases. Solaris `sort` accepts but otherwise ignores this option.

Gnu/Linux and Mac OS X Option

-s, --stable
: Provide a stable sort, which preserves the order of input records that otherwise compare equal.

Gnu/Linux Options

-g, --general-numeric-sort
: Sort in general numeric order.

-S *size*, --buffer-size=*size*
: Like the Solaris -S option. Besides the suffixes listed there, GNU sort allows P, E, Z, and Y, each of which increases the possible amount by even more orders of magnitude.

-z, --zero-terminated
: End lines with a zero byte, not with a newline.

Field Specifications for -k

A *fieldspec* has the form *fieldstart*[*type*][,*fieldend*[*type*]].

fieldstart
: A field number and optional starting character of the form *fnum*[.*schar*]. *fnum* is the field number, starting from 1. *schar*, if present, is the starting character within the field, also counting from 1.

fieldend
: A field number and optional ending character of the form *fnum*[.*echar*]. *fnum* is the field number, starting from 1. *echar*, if present, is the last significant character within the field, also counting from 1.

type
: A modifier, one of the letters b, d, f, i, M, n, or r. The effect is the same as the corresponding option, except that the b modifier only applies to the fields, not the whole line.

Examples

List files by decreasing number of lines:

```
wc -l * | sort -rn
```

Alphabetize a list of words, remove duplicates, and print the frequency of each word:

```
sort -fd wordlist | uniq -c
```

Sort the password file numerically by the third field (user ID):

```
sort -k 3n -t: /etc/passwd
```

Find the top 20 disk hogs on a system:

```
cd /home; du -sk * | sort -nr | head -n 20
```

spell

```
spell [options] [files]
```

Compare the words of one or more named *files* with the system dictionary and report all misspelled words. System files for `spell` reside in `/usr/lib/spell`.

Solaris and commercial Unix systems supply the original Unix version of `spell`. Mac OS X does not have `spell`; however, you can download either `ispell` or `aspell` and use them instead. GNU/Linux supplies both `aspell` and `ispell`, but not necessarily a `spell` command.

Program	URL(s)
`aspell`	*http://aspell.net/* *http://www.gnu.org/software/aspell*
`ispell`	*http://www.gnu.org/software/ispell*

At least one major GNU/Linux system uses the following shell script to emulate `spell`:

```
#!/bin/sh

# aspell -l mimicks the standard unix spell program, roughly.

cat "$@" | aspell -l --mode=none | sort -u
```

See also *Classic Shell Scripting*, cited in the Bibliography, which devotes an entire chapter to the topic of spell checking, including improvements to the previously shown script.

Solaris Options

`-b` Check for British spelling.

`-i` Ignore files included with the `nroff` or `troff .so` request. No effect if `deroff` is unavailable.

`-l` Follow *all* included files (files named in `.so` or `.nx` requests); default is to ignore filenames that begin with `/usr/lib`.

`-v` Include words that are derived from the dictionary list but are not literal entries.

`-x` Show every possible word stem (on standard error).

`+wordlist`
Use the sorted *wordlist* file as a local dictionary to add to the system dictionary; words in *wordlist* are not treated as misspelled.

Example

Run the first pass of `spell`:

```
spell file1 file2 > jargon
```

After editing the `jargon` file, use it as a list of special terms. The second pass of `spell` produces genuine misspellings:

```
spell +jargon file[12] > typos          Solaris spell
```

split

```
split [options] [infile] [outfile]
```

Split *infile* into several files of equal length. *infile* remains unchanged, and the results are written to *outfile*aa, *outfile*ab, etc. (default is xaa, xab, etc.). If *infile* is - (or missing), standard input is read. See also **csplit**.

Common Options

`-n, -l n, --lines=n`
: Split *infile* into files, each *n* lines long (default is 1000).

`-a slen, --suffix-length=slen`
: Use *slen* characters for the filename suffix. Default is 2.

`-b n[m], --bytes=n[m]`
: Split into pieces of size *n* bytes. An optional multiplier *m* may be supplied: k for kilobytes and m for megabytes. GNU/Linux allows b for 512-byte blocks. Mutually exclusive with -l.

GNU/Linux Options

`-C bytes[m], --line-bytes=bytes[m]`
: Put a maximum of *bytes* into file; insist on adding complete lines. *m* is a multiplier: b for 512, k for 1024, and m for one megabyte.

`-d, --numeric-suffixes`
: Use numeric file suffixes instead of alphabetic ones.

`--verbose`
: Print a message for each output file.

Examples

Break *bigfile* into 1000-line segments:

```
split bigfile
```

Join four files, then split them into ten-line files named new.aa, new.ab, etc. Note that without the -, new. would be treated as a nonexistent input file:

```
cat list[1-4] | split -l 10 - new.
```

ssh

```
ssh [options] hostname [command]
slogin [options] hostname [command]
```

Securely log a user into a remote system and run commands on that system. The version of ssh described here is the OpenSSH client. ssh can use either Version 1 (SSH1) or Version 2 (SSH2) of the SSH protocol. SSH2 is preferable, as it provides better encryption methods and greater connection integrity. The hostname can be specified either as *hostname* or as *user@hostname*. If a command is specified, the user is authenticated, the command is executed, and the connection is closed. Otherwise, a terminal session is opened on the remote system. See the "Escape characters" section later in this entry for functions that can be supported through an escape character. The default escape character is a tilde (~). The exit status returned from ssh is the exit status from the remote system or 255 if there was an error. Interestingly enough, Solaris, GNU/Linux, and Mac OS X all use OpenSSH. See also **scp**, **sftp**, and *SSH, The Secure Shell*, cited in the Bibliography.

On GNU/Linux and Mac OS X, slogin is a symbolic link to ssh. It is meant to replace the original BSD rlogin command.

URL: *http://www.openssh.org*.

Options

-1 Try only SSH1.

-2 Try only SSH2.

-4 Use only IPv4 addresses.

-6 Use only IPv6 addresses.

-a Disable forwarding of the authentication agent connection.

-A Allow forwarding of the authentication agent connection. Can also be specified on a per-host basis in a configuration file.

-b *bind_address*
Specify the interface to transmit from when there are multiple available interfaces or aliased addresses.

-c blowfish|3des|des|*ciphers*
Select the cipher for encrypting the session. The default is 3des. For SSH2, a comma-separated list of *ciphers* can also be specified, with the ciphers listed in order of preference. des is supported only for legacy SSH1 compatibility and otherwise should not be used.

-C Enable compression. Useful mainly for slow connections. The default compression level can be set on a per-host basis in the configuration file with the CompressionLevel option.

-D *port*
Enable dynamic application-level port forwarding using *port* on the local side. Can be specified in the configuration file. Only a privileged user can forward privileged ports.

-e *char*|^*char*|none
Set the escape character (default ~). The escape character must be the first character on a line. If none is specified, disable the use of an escape character.

-f Run interactively for user authentication, then go into background mode for command execution. Implies -n.

-F *configfile*
Specify a per-user configuration file (default is $HOME/.ssh/config).

-g Allow remote hosts to connect to local forwarded ports.

-i *idfile*
Use *idfile* to read identity (private key) for RSA or DSA authentication. Default is $HOME/.ssh/id_rsa or $HOME/.ssh/id_dsa for SSH2, or $HOME/.ssh/identity for SSH1. You can specify more than one -i option on the command line or in the configuration file.

`-I` *device*
: Specify a smartcard *device* from which to get the user's private RSA key.

`-k`
: Disable Kerberos ticket and AFS token forwarding. Can be set on a per-host basis in the configuration file.

`-l` *user*
: Log in as *user* on the remote system. Can be specified on a per-host basis in the configuration file.

`-L` *port:host:hostport*
: Forward *port* on the local host to the specified remote host and port. Can be specified in the configuration file. Only a privileged user can forward privileged ports. For IPv6, an alternative syntax is *port/host/hostport*.

`-m` *macspec*
: For SSH2, the contents of *macspec* specify message authentication code (MAC) algorithms to use. *macspec* is a comma-separated list of algorithms in order of preference.

`-n`
: Get standard input as a redirection from `/dev/null`. Used to prevent reading from standard input, which is required when running `ssh` in the background. Useful for running X programs on a remote host.

`-N`
: Do not execute a remote command. Useful with SSH2 for port forwarding.

`-o` *option*
: Specify options in configuration-file format. Useful for specifying options that have no command-line equivalent.

`-p` *port*
: Specify the port on the remote host to which `ssh` is to connect. Can be specified on a per-host basis in the configuration file.

`-q`
: Run quietly, suppressing warnings and error messages.

`-R` *port:host:hostport*
: Forward *port* on the remote host to the local *host:hostport*. Can be specified in the configuration file. You can forward privileged ports only if you are logged in as `root` on the remote host. For IPv6, an alternative syntax is *port/host/hostport*.

`-s`
: For SSH2, request invocation of a subsystem on the remote host to be used for another application such as `sftp`. The desired subsystem is specified as the remote command.

`-t`
: Force pseudo-tty allocation. Multiple `-t` options can be specified to force tty allocation even when `ssh` has no local tty.

`-T`
: Disable pseudo-tty allocation.

`-v`
: Verbose mode. Useful for debugging. Specify multiple `-v` options to increase verbosity.

`-V`
: Display just the version number. GNU/Linux and Mac OS X only.

`-x`
: Disable X11 forwarding.

`-X`
: Enable X11 forwarding. Can be specified on a per-host basis in the configuration file.

Escape characters

~. Disconnect.

~~ Send a single ~.

~# List forwarded connections.

~& Run `ssh` in the background at logout, while waiting for a forwarded connection or X11 sessions to terminate.

~? Display the available escape characters.

~C Open a command line. Useful for adding port forwardings when using the `-L` and `-R` options.

~R Request rekeying of the connection. Useful only for SSH2 and if the peer supports it.

~^Z Suspend the connection.

---

ssh-add

`ssh-add [`*options*`] [`*files*`]`
`ssh-add -e|-s` *reader*

Add RSA or DSA identities to the authentication agent (see **ssh-agent**), which must be running. With no arguments specified, add the files `$HOME/.ssh/id_rsa`, `$HOME/.ssh/id_dsa`, and `$HOME/.ssh/identity`. If any *files* are specified, add those instead, prompting for a passphrase if required.

Options

`-c` Confirm that an added identity should be used for authentication. The confirmation is done by the program named in the SSH_ASKPASS environment variable. GNU/Linux and Mac OS X only.

`-d` Remove an identity from the agent instead of adding one.

`-D` Delete all identities from the agent.

`-e` *reader*
Remove key in specified smartcard reader.

`-l` List fingerprints of all identities known to the agent.

`-L` List public key parameters of all identities known to the agent.

`-s` Add key in smartcard *reader*.

`-t` *life*
Set maximum lifetime when adding identities to an agent. The value of *life* can be in seconds or another time format specified in `sshd`.

`-x` Lock the agent with a password.

`-X` Unlock the agent.

---

ssh-agent

`ssh-agent [`*options*`] [`*command* `[`*arguments*`]]`

Hold private keys used for public key authentication. `ssh-agent` is usually executed at the beginning of an X or login session; then all other windows or programs given as *command* are run as clients of ssh-agent. When a command is specified, the command and any arguments are executed. The agent dies when the command completes. Use ssh-add to add keys to the agent. Operations that require a private key are performed by the agent, which returns the results to the requestor.

Options

`-a` *bind_addr*
: Bind the agent to the socket *bind_addr* (default is /tmp/ssh-*nnnnnnnn*/agent, where *nnnnnnnn* is a generated number).

`-c`
: Write csh commands to standard output. This is the default if the environment variable SHELL looks like a csh-type shell.

`-d`
: Debug mode.

`-k`
: Kill the current agent.

`-s`
: Write Bourne shell commands to standard output. This is the default if the environment variable SHELL does not look like a csh-type command.

`-t` *life*
: Set maximum lifetime when adding identities to an agent. The value of *life* can be in seconds or another time format specified in sshd. GNU/Linux and Mac OS X only.

---

ssh-keygen

ssh-keygen [*options*]

Generate, manage, and convert authentication keys for ssh.

Common Options

`-b` *bits*
: Specify the number of bits in the key. The minimum is 512 and the default is 1024.

`-B`
: Show the bubblebabble digest (a digest represented as a string that looks like real words) for the private or public key file specified with -f.

`-c`
: Change the comment in the private and public key files (for RSA1 keys only).

`-C` *comment*
: Specify the new comment.

`-e`
: Read an OpenSSH private or public key file and write it in SECSH Public Key File Format to standard output for exporting to a commercial SSH.

`-f` *file*
: Specify the filename of the key file.

`-i`
: Read an SSH2-compatible unencrypted private or public key file and write an OpenSSH-compatible key to standard output. Used to import keys from a commercial SSH.

`-l`
: Show fingerprint of public or private RSA1 key file specified with -f.

`-N` *passphrase*
: Specify the new passphrase.

`-p` Change the passphrase for a private key file. Prompt for the file, the old passphrase, and twice for the new passphrase.

`-P` *passphrase*
: Specify the old passphrase.

`-q` Operate in quiet mode.

`-t` *type*
: Specify the type of key to create. Possible values of *type* are `rsa1` for SSH1, and `rsa` or `dsa` for SSH2.

`-y` Read a private OpenSSH-format file and print a public key to standard output.

GNU/Linux and Mac OS X Options

`-D` *reader*
: Download the RSA public key from the smartcard in *reader*.

`-U` *reader*
: Upload an existing RSA private key to the smartcard in *reader*.

Mac OS X Options

`-a` *trials*
: Make *trials* primatlity tests for DH-GEX candidates with `-T`.

`-g` Use generic DNS record format.

`-G` *file*
: Produce candidate primes for DH-GEX to *file*.

`-M` *mem*
: Use *mem* megabytes when generating candidate moduli for DH-GEX.

`-r` *hostname*
: Print DNS resource records using *hostname*.

`-S` *start*
: Start at *start* (in hexadecimal) when generating candidate moduli for DH-GEX.

`-T` *file*
: Test DH group exchange candidate primes for safety. Such primes are generated with `-G`.

`-v` Be verbose. Helpful for debugging moduli generation. May be repeated up to three times to increase verbosity.

`-W` *generator*
: Use *generator* when testing candidate moduli for DH-GEX.

---

strings

`strings [`*options*`]` *files*

Search object or binary *files* for sequences of four or more printable characters that end with a newline or null. See also **od**.

Common Options

-n, -n *n*, --bytes=*n*
: Minimum string length is *n* (default is 4).

-, -a, --all
: Search entire *file*, not just the initialized data portion of object files.

-o
: Display the string's offset position before the string. Solaris and Mac OS X: same as -t d. GNU/Linux: same as -t o.

-t *format*, --radix=*format*
: Specify how to print string offsets. *format* is one of d, o, or x for decimal, octal, or hexadecimal, respectively.

GNU/Linux Options

-e *encoding*, --encoding=*encoding*
: Specify the character encoding of the strings to be found. Possible values are:

b	16-bit big-endian
B	32-bit big-endian
l	16-bit little-endian
L	32-bit little-endian
s	Single-byte character, such as ASCII, ISO-8859, etc. (the default)

--target=*format*
: Specify an alternative object code format to the system default. Any valid BFD target name may be used for *format*.

strip

strip [*options*] *files*

Remove information from ELF object *files* or archive *files*, thereby reducing file sizes and freeing disk space. On Solaris, strip is in /usr/ccs/bin.

Like the loader ld, this program has diverged across time and platforms, to the point where it's not worthwhile to provide an option list. See the manpage for your local system.

stty

stty [*options*] [*modes*]

Set terminal I/O options for the current device. Without options, stty reports the terminal settings, where a ^ indicates the Control key, and ^` indicates a null value. Most modes can be switched using an optional preceding - (shown in brackets). The corresponding description is also shown in brackets. As a privileged user, you can set or read settings from another device using the syntax:

    stty [options] [modes] < device

stty is one of the most complicated Unix commands. The complexity stems from the need to deal with a large range of conflicting, incompatible, and nonstandardized terminal devices—everything from printing teletypes to CRTs to pseudo-terminals for windowing systems. Only a few of the options are really needed for day-to-day use. `stty sane` is a particularly valuable one to remember.

Solaris provides additional hardware flow control modes and clock modes; see the *stty*(1) manpage should you find that you need these features.

Common Options

`-a, --all`
: Report all option settings.

`-g, --save`
: Report current settings.

GNU/Linux Options

`-F` *device*, `--file=`*device*
: Read or change setting of *device* instead of the current terminal.

Mac OS X Options

`-e`
: Print information in BSD `stty everything` format.

`-f` *device*
: Read or change setting of *device* instead of the current terminal.

Many but not all of the following features are shared among all the systems. For brevity, Solaris-only features are marked with an **S**, GNU/Linux-only features are marked with an **L**, and Mac OS X–only features are marked with an **M**. Items without any mark work on all the systems.

Control Modes

`0`
: Hang up connection (set the baud rate to zero).

n
: Set terminal baud rate to *n* (e.g., 19200).

`[-]clocal`
: [Enable] disable modem control.

`[-]cread`
: [Disable] enable the receiver.

`[-]crtscts`
: [Disable] enable output hardware flow control using RTS/CTS.

`[-]crtsxoff`
: [Disable] enable input hardware flow control using RTS. **S**.

`cs`*n*
: Select character size in bits ($5 \leq n \leq 8$).

`[-]cstopb`
: [One] two stop bits per character.

`defeucw`
: Set the width in bytes per character and screen display columns per character, for EUC (Extended Unix Code) characters. **S**.

`[-]hup`
: [Do not] hang up connection on last close.

`[-]hupcl`
: Same as `[-]hup`.

`ispeed` *n*
: Set terminal input baud rate to *n*.

`ospeed` *n*
: Set terminal output baud rate to *n*.

`[-]parenb`
: [Disable] enable parity generation and detection.

`[-]parext`
: [Disable] enable extended parity generation and detection for mark and space parity. **S**.

`[-]parodd`
: Use [even] odd parity.

Input Modes

`[-]brkint`
: [Do not] signal INTR on break.

`[-]icrnl`
: [Do not] map carriage return (`^M`) to newline (`^J`) on input.

`[-]ignbrk`
: [Do not] ignore break on input.

`[-]igncr`
: [Do not] ignore carriage return on input.

`[-]ignpar`
: [Do not] ignore parity errors.

`[-]imaxbel`
: [Do not] echo BEL when input line is too long.

`[-]inlcr`
: [Do not] map newline to carriage return on input.

`[-]inpck`
: [Disable] enable input parity checking.

`[-]istrip`
: [Do not] strip input characters to 7 bits.

`[-]iuclc`
: [Do not] map uppercase to lowercase on input. **S**, **L**.

`[-]ixany`
: Allow [only XON] any character to restart output.

`[-]ixoff`
: [Do not] send START/STOP characters when the queue is nearly empty/full.

`[-]ixon`
: [Disable] enable START/STOP output control.

`[-]parmrk`
: [Do not] mark parity errors.

`[-]tandem`
: Same as `[-]ixoff`. **L**, **M**.

Output Modes

`bsn` Select style of delay for backspaces (n = 0 or 1). **S**, **L**.

`crn` Select style of delay for carriage returns ($0 \leq n \leq 3$). **S**, **L**.

`ffn` Select style of delay for formfeeds (n = 0 or 1). **S**, **L**.

`nln` Select style of delay for linefeeds (n = 0 or 1). **S**, **L**.

`[-]ocrnl`
: [Do not] map carriage return to newline on output.

`[-]ofdel`
: Set fill character to [NULL] DEL. **S**, **L**.

`[-]ofill`
: Delay output with [timing] fill characters. **S**, **L**.

`[-]olcuc`
: [Do not] map lowercase to uppercase on output. **S**, **L**.

`[-]onlcr`
: [Do not] map newline to carriage return-newline on output.

`[-]onlret`
: [Do not] perform carriage return after newline.

`[-]onocr`
: [Do not] output carriage returns at column zero.

`[-]opost`
: [Do not] postprocess output; ignore all other output modes.

`[-]oxtabs`
: [Do not] expand tabs to spaces. **M**.

`tabn`
: Select style of delay for horizontal tabs ($0 \leq n \leq 3$). **S**, **L**.

`vtn` Select style of delay for vertical tabs (n = 0 or 1). **S**, **L**.

Local Modes

`[-]altwerase`
: [Do not] Use an alternate algorithm for processing the "word erase" character. **M**.

`[-]cbreak`
: Opposite of `[-]icanon`. **L**, **M**.

`[-]ctlecho`
: Same as `[-]echoctl`. **L**, **M**.

`[-]crterase`
: Same as `[-]echoe`. **L**, **M**.

`[-]crtkill`
: Same as `[-]echoke`. **L**, **M**.

`[-]echo`
: [Do not] echo every character typed.

`[-]echoctl`
: [Do not] echo control characters as ^*char*, DEL as ^?.

`[-]echoe`
: [Do not] echo ERASE character as BS-space-BS string.

`[-]echok`
: [Do not] echo newline after KILL character.

`[-]echoke`
: [Do not] BS-SP-BS erase entire line on line kill.

`[-]echonl`
: [Do not] echo newline (`^J`).

`[-]echoprt`
: [Do not] echo erase character as character is "erased."

`[-]flusho`
: Output is [not] being flushed. **S**, **M**.

`[-]icanon`
: [Disable] enable canonical input (ERASE and KILL processing).

`[-]iexten`
: [Disable] enable extended functions for input data.

`[-]isig`
: [Disable] enable checking of characters against INTR, QUIT, and SWITCH.

`[-]lfkc`
: Same as `[-]echok`. Obsolete. **S**.

`[-]mdmbuf`
: [Do not] flow control output based on the state of Carrier Detect. **M**.

`[-]noflsh`
: [Enable] disable flush after INTR, QUIT, or SWITCH.

`[-]pendin`
: [Do not] retype pending input at next read or input character. **S**, **M**.

`[-]prterase`
: Same as `[-]echoprt`. **L**, **M**.

`[-]stappl`
: [Line] application mode on a synchronous line. **S**.

`[-]stflush`
: [Disable] enable flush on synchronous line. **S**.

`[-]stwrap`
: [Enable] disable truncation on synchronous line. **S**.

`[-]tostop`
: [Do not] send `SIGTTOU` when background processes write to the terminal.

`[-]xcase`
: [Do not] change case on local output. **S**, **L**.

Control Assignments

`ctrl-char c`
: Set control character to *c*. *ctrl-char* is:

Common	`dsusp`, `eof`, `eol`, `eol2`, `erase`, `intr`, `kill`, `lnext`, `quit`, `rprnt`, `start`, `stop`, `susp`, `werase`
Solaris	`ctab`, `discard`, `reprint`
GNU/Linux	`swtch`
Mac OS X	`brk` (same as `eol`), `erase2`, `flush` (same as `discard`), `reprint`, `status`

`line` *i*
Set line discipline to *i* ($1 \leq i \leq 126$). **S**, **L**.

`min` *n*
With `-icanon`, *n* is the minimum number of characters that will satisfy the `read` system call until the timeout set with `time` expires.

`time` *n*
With `-icanon`, *n* is the number of tenths of seconds to wait before a `read` system call times out. If the minimum number of characters set with `min` has been read, the `read` can return before the timeout expires.

Combination Modes

`all` Like `stty -a`, but print information in the traditional BSD columnar format. **M**.

`async`
Set normal asynchronous communications. **S**.

`cooked`
Same as `-raw`.

`[-]crt`
[Disable] Enable `echoe echok echoke`. **L**, **M**.

`[-]crtbs`
Same as `[-]echoe`. **M**.

`dec` Same as `echoe echoctl echoke -ixany intr ^C erase 0177 kill ^U`. **L**, **M**.

`[-]decctlq`
Converse of `[-]ixany`. **L**, **M**.

`ek` Reset ERASE and KILL characters to system defaults.

`[-]evenp`
Same as `[-]parenb` and `cs7[8]`.

`everything`
Same as `stty all`. **M**.

`[-]extproc`
Indicate that the terminal hardware or the remote side of a pty is [not] doing some of the terminal processing. **M**.

`[-]kerninfo`
[Disable] Enable the system's response to the status character, usually CTRL-T. **M**.

`[-]lcase`
[Un] set `xcase`, `iuclc`, and `olcuc`. **S**, **L**.

`[-]litout`
Converse of `[-]opost`. **L**, **M**.

`[-]LCASE`
Same as `[-]lcase`. **S**, **L**.

`[-]markp`
[Disable] enable `parenb`, `parodd`, and `parext`, and set `cs7[8]`. **S**.

`new` Same as `stty tty`. **M**.

`[-]newcrt`
: Same as `[-]crt`. **M.**

`[-]nl`
: [Un] set `icrnl` and `onlcr`. `-nl` also unsets `inlcr`, `igncr`, `ocrnl`, and `onlret`.

`[-]oddp`
: Same as `[-]parenb`, `[-]parodd`, and `cs7[8]`.

`old` Same as `stty tty`. **M.**

`[-]parity`
: Same as `[-]parenb` and `cs7[8]`.

`[-]pass8`
: Converse of `[-]parity`. **L, M.**

`[-]raw`
: [Disable] enable raw input and output (no ERASE, KILL, INTR, QUIT, EOT, SWITCH, or output postprocessing).

`sane`
: Reset all modes to reasonable values.

`size`
: Print the terminal's size in rows and columns. **L, M.**

`speed`
: Print the terminal's speed (baud rate). **L, M.**

`[-]spacep`
: [Disable] enable `parenb` and `parext`, and set `cs7[8]`. **S.**

`[-]tabs`
: [Expand to spaces] preserve output tabs.

`term`
: Set all modes suitable for terminal type *term* (`tty33`, `tty37`, `vt05`, `tn300`, `ti700`, or `tek`). (These predefined names are all so obsolete as to be useless.) **S.**

`tty` Use the standard line discipline. **M.**

Window size

`columns` *`n`*
: Set size to *n* columns. Can also be given as `cols`.

`rows` *`n`*
: Set size to *n* rows.

`xpixels` *`n`*
: Set size to *n* pixels across. **S.**

`ypixels` *`n`*
: Set size to *n* pixels up and down. **S.**

---

su

`su [option] [user] [shell_args]`

Create a shell with the effective user ID of another *user* (that is, login as *user*). If no *user* is specified, create a shell for a privileged user (that is, become a superuser). Enter *EOF* to terminate. You can run the shell with particular options by passing them as *shell_args* (e.g., if the shell runs sh, you can specify -c *command* to execute *command* via sh, or -r to create a restricted shell).

su will inherit your environment settings. Administrators wishing to switch to a user's setup (perhaps to help them solve a problem) may wish to consider using this sequence:

```
me$ su                    Switch to root
Password:                 Enter root password
# su - user               Switch to other user
user$
```

The sudo program is worth installing if your system doesn't have it. See *http://www.sudo.ws/* and/or *http://www.courtesan.com/sudo*.

Common Option

- Go through the entire login sequence (i.e., change to *user*'s environment).

GNU/Linux and Mac OS X Options

-c *command*, --command=*command*
: Run a single command (by way of sh -c).

-f, --fast
: Pass -f on to csh or tcsh.

-l, --login
: Same as su -.

-m, --preserve-environment
: Preserve the environment.

GNU/Linux Options

-p Same as -m.

-s *shell*, --shell=*shell*
: Use *shell* if *shell* is listed in /etc/shells.

---

tail

tail [*options*] [*file*]

Print the last 10 lines of the named *file*. Use only one of -f or -r.

The GNU/Linux and Mac OS X versions can process multiple files. In that case, the output includes a header at the beginning of each file:

==>*filename*<==

Historic Options

The syntaxes shown here are the historic usage. Currently all systems continue to accept them, but the -c and -n options are preferred.

-*n*[*k*]
: Begin printing at *n*th item from end of file. *k* specifies the item to count: l (lines, the default), b (blocks), or c (characters, i.e., bytes).

-*k* Same as previous, but use the default count of 10.

`+n[k]`
: Like *-n*, but start at *n*th item from beginning of file.

`+k`
: Like *-k*, but count from beginning of file.

Common Options

`-c count, --bytes=count`
: With a leading + on *count*, start *count* bytes from the front of the file. With a leading - or no sign, start from the end of the file.

`-f [follow_spec], --follow[=follow_spec]`
: Don't quit at the end of file; "follow" file as it grows. End with an INTR (usually `^C`).

  Only GNU/Linux allows a *follow_spec*. If the *follow_spec* is `descriptor`, `tail` follows the open file descriptor. This shows the original file, even if it is renamed or removed, and is the command's original, default behavior. If *follow_spec* is `name`, then `tail` periodically reopens the file by name. This is useful in cases where filenames change, such as rotated log files.

`-n count, --lines=count`
: With a leading + on *count*, start *count* lines from the front of the file. With a leading - or no sign, start from the end of the file.

Solaris and Mac OS X Option

`-r`
: Copy lines in reverse order.

GNU/Linux Options

`-F`
: Identical to `--follow=name --retry`.

`--max-unchanged-stats=num`
: Used with `--follow=name` to reopen a file whose size hasn't changed after *num* iterations (default 5), to see if it has been unlinked or renamed (as with rotated log files).

`--pid=pid`
: Used with `-f` to end when process ID *pid* dies.

`-q, --quiet, --silent`
: Suppress filename headers.

`--retry`
: With `-f`, keep trying to open a file even if it isn't accessible when `tail` starts or if it becomes inaccessible later.

`-s sec, --sleep-interval=sec`
: With `-f`, sleep approximately *sec* seconds between iterations. Default is 1 second.

`-v, --verbose`
: With multiple files, always output the filename headers.

Mac OS X Options

`-b` *count*
: With a leading + on *count*, start *count* blocks (512-byte units) from the front of the file. With a leading - or no sign, start from the end of the file.

`-F`
: Like the GNU/Linux `--follow=name`.

Examples

Show the last 20 lines containing instances of `<title>`:

```
grep '<title>' file | tail -n 20
```

Continually track the latest system messages (under GNU/Linux):

```
tail -f /var/log/messages
```

Show the last 10 characters of variable `name`:

```
echo "$name" | tail -c
```

Reverse all lines in `list`:

```
tail -r list
```

---

talk

`talk` *user* [*@hostname*] [*tty*]

Exchange typed communication with another *user* who is on the local machine or on machine *hostname*. `talk` might be useful when you're logged in via modem and need something quickly, making it inconvenient to telephone or send email. `talk` splits your screen into two windows. When connection is established, you type in the top half while *user*'s typing appears in the bottom half. Type `^L` to redraw the screen and `^C` (or interrupt) to exit. If *user* is logged in more than once, use *tty* to specify the terminal line. The *user* needs to have used `mesg y`.

Notes

- There are different versions of `talk` that use different protocols; interoperability across different Unix systems is very limited.
- `talk` is also not very useful if the remote user you are "calling" is using a windowing environment, since there is no way for you to know which *tty* to use to get their attention. The connection request could easily show up in an iconified window! Even if you know the remote *tty*, the called party must have done a `mesg y` to accept the request, and the called system must allow incoming `talk` connections. All in all, this command is not as useful as it once was.

---

tar

`tar` [*options*] [*files*]

Copy *files* to or restore *files* from tape (**t**ape **ar**chive). If any *files* are directories, tar acts on the entire subtree. (See also **cpio** and **pax**.)

Options are supplied as one group, with any arguments placed afterward in corresponding order. Originally, tar did not even accept a leading - on its options. Although the Solaris version allows one, it does not require it. On many other Unix systems, you may use conventional option notation, with each option preceded by a dash and separated from the other options with whitespace. Some systems actually require the use of separate options. Check your local documentation for the final word.

GNU/Linux and Mac OS X both use the GNU version of tar which accepts all the common options, and also has *many* options of its own.

Notes

For the following reasons, tar is best used as a way to exchange file or source code archives over a network. A system administrator performing system backups is advised to use the vendor-supplied backup program (typically called dump or backup; see your local documentation) for backups instead of tar. (Many of these same points apply to cpio and to pax as well.)

- Most Unix versions of tar preserve the leading / from an absolute filename in the archive. This makes it difficult or impossible to extract the files on a different system.
- The tar archive format was designed when Unix file and directory names were short (14 characters maximum). Modern Unix systems allow individual filenames to be up to 255 characters in length, but the tar archive header has a limit of 100 characters for the entire pathname. This makes it difficult or impossible in practice to archive a typical Unix filesystem.
- In general, Unix versions of tar cannot recover from data errors, which are particularly common with tapes. An early tape error can render an entire tar tape useless.
- While tar does checksum the header information describing each archived file, it does not checksum the actual data blocks. Thus, if a data block becomes corrupted on a tape, tar will never notice.

The GNU version of tar has extensions to get around many of these problems, at the cost of portability of the archive format to non-GNU versions. Source code can be obtained from the Free Software Foundation (see *http://www.gnu.org/software/tar*).

Common Control Option

-C *dir files*, --directory=*dir files*
: Change directory to *dir* before adding *files* to the archive. Use relative pathnames. This option makes it possible to archive files that don't share a common ancestor directory.

Solaris Control Options

`-I` *file*
: Read a list of filenames to be archived, one filename per line, from *file*. Useful when there are too many files to name on the command line.

`-X` *file*
: Exclude files. The corresponding file argument is read for a list of relative pathnames, one per line, of files that should not be archived. This option may be provided multiple times with multiple files. Filenames that appear here are excluded even if the same name was provided in a file used with `-I`.

GNU tar Control Options

`-T` *file*, `--files-from=`*file*
: Read a list of filenames to be archived, one filename per line, from *file*. Useful when there are too many files to name on the command line.

`-X` *file*, `--exclude-from=`*file*
: Exclude files. The corresponding file argument is read for a list of relative pathnames, one per line, of files that should not be archived. Each line may be a shell wildcard pattern. This option may be provided multiple times with multiple files.

Common Function Options (Choose One)

`-c, --create`
: Create a new archive.

`-r, --append`
: Append *files* to archive.

`-t, --list`
: Table of contents. Print the names of *files* if they are stored on the archive (if *files* not specified, print names of all files).

`-u, --update`
: Update. Add files if not in archive or if modified.

`-x, --extract, --get`
: Extract *files* from archive (if *files* not specified, extract all files).

GNU tar Function Options (Choose One)

`-A, --catenate, --concatenate`
: Concatenate a second tar file to the end of the first.

`-d, --diff, --compare`
: Compare the files stored in *tarfile* with *other-files*. Report any differences: missing files, different sizes, different file attributes (such as permissions or modification time).

`--delete`
: Delete from the archive. This option cannot be used with magnetic tape.

Common Options

n[*c*] Select tape drive *n* and use speed *c*. *n* is 0–7 (default is 0); *c* is `l` (low), `h` (high), or `m` (medium, the default). Used to modify *arch*. (These are highly system-specific and nonportable: it is much better to always just specify the *arch* explicitly with `-f`.)

`-b` *n*, `--blocking-factor=`*n*
: Use blocking factor *n* (default is 1; maximum is 20). Different Unix systems often allow larger blocking factors.

`-B, --read-full-records`
: Continue reading until logical blocks are full. For use across Ethernet connections with `rsh` or `ssh`. On some systems, enabled by default when reading standard input.

`-f` *arch*, `--file=`*arch*
: Store files in or extract files from archive *arch*; *arch* is usually a device name (default varies from system to system). If *arch* is `-`, standard input or output is used as appropriate (e.g., when piping a `tar` archive to a remote host). GNU `tar` allows remote tape drives, of the form *host*:*device*.

`-h, --dereference`
: Follow symbolic links, archiving the files they point to, not the links themselves.

`-m, --touch`
: Do not restore file modification times; update them to the time of extraction.

`-p, --same-permissions, --preserve-permissions`
: Preserve permissions of extracted files. On Solaris, ACLs are restored if recorded in the archive and are added to the archive when used with `-c`.

`-v, --verbose`
: Print function letter (`x` for extraction or `a` for archive) and name of files. With `-t`, print a listing similar to that of `ls -l`.

`-w, --interactive, --confirmation`
: Wait for user confirmation (y) before taking any actions.

Solaris Options

`-D` Warn about changes in data files instead of treating them as fatal errors; for example, if a file's size changes while it's being archived.

`-e` Exit immediately upon unexpected errors.

`-E` Use an extended header that allows longer filenames, larger files, and other extensions. Not portable.

`-F, -FF`
: With `F`, do not archive `SCCS` and `RCS` directories. With `FF`, also exclude files named `a.out`, `core`, `errs`, and all `.o` files.

`-i` Ignore directory checksum errors.

-k *size*
: Specify the archive size in kilobytes. Archives that are larger than *size* are split across volumes. Useful for fixed-size media, such as floppy disks.

-l
: Print error messages about links that can't be found.

-n
: Archive is not a tape device. This allows tar to seek, instead of doing sequential reads, which is faster.

-o
: Change ownership of extracted files to that of user running program. This is the default for nonprivileged users.

-P
: Do not add a trailing / to directory names in the archive.

-q
: Quit after extracting the first occurrence of the named file. Normally tar continues reading the archive.

-@
: Add Solaris extended file attributes to the archive upon archive creation, or extract them from the archive if extracting. They may only be extracted as part of extracting a file; it is not possible to extract just the extended attributes.

GNU tar Options

--anchored
: Exclude patterns must match the start of the filename (the default).

--atime-preserve
: Preserve original access time on extracted files.

--backup[=*type*]
: Instead of overwriting files upon extraction, back them up. If no backup type is specified, a simple backup is made with ~ as the suffix. (See also --suffix.) The possible values of *type* are:

t, numbered	Make numbered backups.
nil, existing	Make numbered backups if there are already numbered backups, otherwise make simple backups.
never, simple	Always make simple backups.

--check-links
: When creating an archive, if a file has multiple hard links, and not all the file's links were written to the archive, output a warning message.

--checkpoint
: List directory names encountered.

--exclude=*pattern*
: Remove files matching *pattern* from any list of files.

--force-local
: Interpret filenames in the form *hostname:filename* as local files.

--format=*type*
: Create a *type* format archive. Valid values are gnu, oldgnu, posix, ustar, and v7.

`-F` *`script`*, `--info-script=`*`script`*
`--new-volume-script=`*`script`*
: Implies `-M` (multiple archive files). Run *script* at the end of each file.

`-g` *`file`*, `--listed-incremental=`*`file`*
: Create new-style incremental backup.

`--group=`*`group`*
: Use *group* as the group for files added to the archive.

`-G`, `--incremental`
: Create old-style incremental backup.

`-i`, `--ignore-zeros`
: Ignore zero-sized blocks (i.e., EOFs).

`--ignore-case`
: Ignore case when excluding files.

`--ignore-failed-read`
: Ignore unreadable files to be archived. Default behavior is to exit when encountering these.

`--index-file=`*`file`*
: Send verbose output to *file* instead of to standard output.

`-j`, `--bzip2`
: Compress files with `bzip2` before archiving them, or uncompress them with `bunzip2` before extracting them.

`-k`, `--keep-old-files`
: When extracting files, do not overwrite files with identical names. Instead, print an error message.

`-K` *`file`*, `--starting-file=`*`file`*
: Begin `tar` operation at *file* in archive.

`--keep-newer-files`
: If a file being extracted is newer than the one in archive, do not replace it.

`-l`, `--one-file-system`
: Do not archive files from other filesystems. Note: in the future, the meaning of `-l` will change to `--check-links`.

`-L` *`length`*, `--tape-length=`*`length`*
: Write a maximum of *length* × 1024 bytes to each tape.

`--mode=`*`permissions`*
: Use *permissions* when adding files to an archive. The permissions are specified the same way as for the `chmod` command.

`-M`, `--multivolume`
: Expect archive to be multivolume. With `-c`, create such an archive.

`--newer-mtime=`*`date`*
: Add only files whose contents have changed since *date* to the archive.

`--no-anchored`
: Exclude patterns may match after any slash.

`--no-ignore-case`
Do not ignore case when excluding files.

`--no-recursion`
Do not move recursively through directories.

`--no-same-owner`
When extracting, create files with yourself as owner.

`--no-same-permissions`
Do not extract permissions information when extracting files from the archive. This is the default for users, and therefore affects only the superuser.

`--no-wildcards`
Don't use wildcards when excluding files; treat patterns as strings.

`--no-wildcards-match-slash`
Wildcards do not match / when excluding files.

`--null`
Allow filenames to be null-terminated with `-T`. Override `-C`.

`--numeric-owner`
Use the numeric owner and group IDs rather than the names.

`-N` *`date`*, `--newer=`*`date`*, `--after-date=`*`date`*
Ignore files older than *date*.

`-o` If creating an archive, same as `--old-archive`. If extracting, same as `--no-same-owner`.

`--occurrence[=`*`num`*`]`
Process only the *num*th occurrence of each named file. For use with `--delete`, `--diff`, `--extract`, or `--list`.

`--old-archive, --portability`
Create old-style archive in Unix V7 rather than POSIX format.

`--overwrite`
Overwrite existing files and directory metadata when extracting from archive.

`--overwrite-dir`
Overwrite existing directory metadata when extracting from archive.

`--owner=`*`owner`*
Set *owner* as the owner of extracted files instead of the original owner. *owner* is first assumed to be a username, then, if there is no match, a numeric user ID.

`-O, --to-stdout`
Print extracted files to standard output.

`--pax-option=`*`keywords`*
For use with `posix` format archives, process the *keywords* appropriately. See the online Info manual for the (complicated) details.

`--posix`
Create a POSIX-compliant archive.

`--preserve`
Equivalent to invoking both the `-p` and `-s` options.

`-P, --absolute-names`
: Do not remove initial slashes (/) from input filenames.

`--record-size=`*`size`*
: Treat each record as having *size* bytes, where *size* is a multiple of 512.

`--recursion`
: Move recursively through directories.

`--recursive-unlink`
: Remove existing directory hierarchies before extracting directories with the same name.

`--remove-files`
: Remove originals after inclusion in archive.

`--rmt-command=`*`command`*
: Use *command* on a remote host to perform remote file operations instead of `/usr/local/libexec/rmt` (or whatever was configured into `tar` when it was built).

`--rsh-command=`*`command`*
: Do not connect to remote host with `rsh`; instead, use *command*.

`-R, --block-number`
: Display archive's block number in messages.

`-s, --same-order, --preserve-order`
: When extracting, sort filenames to correspond to the order in the archive.

`--same-owner`
: When extracting, create files with the same ownership as the originals.

`--show-defaults`
: Show the default options and exit successfully. For use in shell scripts.

`--show-omitted-dirs`
: List directories being omitted when operating on an archive.

`--strip-path=`*`count`*
: Strip *count* leading components off of archived pathnames before extraction.

`--suffix=`*`suffix`*
: Use *suffix* instead of the default ~ when creating a backup file.

`-S, --sparse`
: Treat sparse files more efficiently when adding to archive.

`--totals`
: Print byte totals.

`--use-compress-program=`*`program`*
: Compress archived files with *program*, or uncompress extracted files with *program*.

`--utc`
: Display file modification times in UTC instead of in local time.

`-U, --unlink-first`
: Remove each existing file from the filesystem before extracting from the archive.

`-v, --verbose`
: Verbose. Print filenames as they are added or extracted.

`--volno-file=`*file*
: Use/update the volume number in *file*.

`-V` *name*, `--label=`*name*
: Name this volume *name*.

`--wildcards`
: Use wildcards when excluding files.

`--wildcards-match-slash`
: Wildcards match / when excluding files.

`-W, --verify`
: Check archive for corruption after creation.

`-z, --gzip, --gunzip, --ungzip`
: Compress files with `gzip` before archiving them, or uncompress them with `gunzip` before extracting them.

`-Z, --compress, --uncompress`
: Compress files with the old `compress` command before archiving them, or uncompress them with `uncompress` before extracting them.

Examples

Create an archive of `/bin` and `/usr/bin` (`c`), show the command working (`v`), and write on the tape in `/dev/rmt/0`:

```
tar -cvf /dev/rmt/0 /bin /usr/bin
```

List the archive's contents in a format like `ls -l`:

```
tar -tvf /dev/rmt/0
```

Extract the `/bin` directory:

```
tar -xvf /dev/rmt/0 /bin
```

Create an archive of the current directory, and store it in a file `/tmp/backup.tar` on the system. (Backing up a directory into a file in that directory almost never works.)

```
tar -cvf /tmp/backup.tar .
```

Similar, but compress the archive file:

```
tar -cvf - . | gzip > /tmp/backup.tar.gz
```

(The `-` tells `tar` to store the directory on standard output, which is then redirected through the pipe.)

Do the same, but using GNU tar:

```
tar -cvzf /tmp/backup.tar.gz .
```

Copy a directory tree from one location to another:

```
# cd olddir; tar -cf - . | (cd newdir; tar -xvpf -)
```

tcsh

`tcsh [options] [file [arguments]]`

An extended version of the C shell, a command interpreter into which all other commands are entered. For more information, see Chapter 5.

tee

`tee [options] [files]`

Duplicate the standard input; send one copy to standard output and another copy to *files*.

Options

`-a, --append`
: Append output to *files*.

`-i, --ignore-interrupts`
: Ignore all interrupts.

Examples

Display a `who` listing on the screen and store it in two files:

```
who | tee userlist ttylist
```

Display misspelled words and add them to existing `typos`:

```
spell ch02 | tee -a typos
```

telnet

`telnet [options] [host [port]]`

Communicate with another *host* using the Telnet protocol. *host* may be either a name or a numeric Internet address (dot format). `telnet` has a command mode (indicated by the `telnet>` prompt) and an input mode (usually a login session on the *host* system). If no *host* is given, `telnet` defaults to command mode. You can also enter command mode from input mode by typing the escape character `^]`. In command mode, type `?` or `help` to list the available commands.

In days of yore, `telnet` used a direct, clear, unencrypted data stream for all information, including login names *and* passwords. Doing so today is terribly insecure, and you should not use `telnet` if you cannot use the encryption facility. (See **ssh** for an alternative.) Nevertheless, `telnet` remains useful for network debugging; for example, connecting directly to SMTP, POP3, or IMAP servers for testing.

Common Options

`-8` Use an eight-bit data path. This negotiates the `BINARY` option for input and output.

`-a` Attempt an automatic login. This is the default on Mac OS X.

`-c` Don't read `$HOME/.telnetrc` at startup.

-d Set the debug option to true.

-e *c* Use *c* as the escape character. The default is ^]. A null value disables the escape character mechanism.

-E Don't have an escape character.

-f If using Kerberos, forward the local credentials to the remote system.

-F Like -f, but includes credentials that were already forwarded to the local system too.

-k *realm*
For Kerberos, obtain a ticket for the remote host from the realm *realm*, instead of the remote host's default realm.

-K Do not allow automatic login to the remote system.

-l *user*
Use the ENVIRON option to pass the value of the USER environment variable.

-L Use an eight-bit data path on output. This negotiates the BINARY option only for output.

-n *file*
Record trace information in *file*.

-r Provide an rlogin-style interface, in which the escape character is ~ and is only recognized after a carriage return. The regular telnet escape character must still be used before a telnet command. "~. ENTER" and "~ ^Z" terminates or stops a session, respectively.

-x Enable encryption if possible. This is the default on Mac OS X.

-X *atype*
Disable authentication type *atype*.

Solaris Host Specification

[[!]@*host1*[@*host2* ...]] *desthost*
Uses loose source routing to *desthost*, sending the connection through *host1*, *host2*, ... With a leading !, uses strict source routing. IPv6 connections may use only loose source routing.

GNU/Linux Options

-7 Strip the eighth bit on input and output.

-b *hostalias*
Use *bind*(2) to bind the local socket to an aliased address or the address of an interface other than the one that would be chosen by *connect*(2).

Mac OS X Options

-4 Use IPv4.

-6 Use IPv6.

-N Do not do IP address to name lookup if the remote *host* is provided as an IP address.

`-s` *`source_address`*
Set the source IP address of the connection to *source_address*. Both IP addresses and hostnames may be used.

`-S` *`tosval`*
Set the IP type-of-service option to *tosval*, which may be numeric, or a symbolic name from `/etc/iptos`, if that file exists.

`-u`
Use a Unix Domain socket, i.e., one accessed as a file pathname.

`-y`
Do not encrypt the data stream.

test

`test` *`expression`*
or
`[` *`expression`* `]`

Evaluate an *expression* and, if its value is `true`, return a zero exit status; otherwise, return a nonzero exit status. In shell scripts, you can use the alternate form `[` *`expression`* `]`. The brackets are typed literally and must be separated from *expression*. Generally, this command is used with conditional constructs in shell programs. See Chapter 4 for more information on `test`.

time

`time [`*`option`*`]` *`command`* `[`*`arguments`*`]`

Execute a *command* with optional *arguments* and print the total elapsed time, execution time, process execution time, and system time of the process (all in seconds). Times are printed on standard error. `time` is a built-in command in all of the Bash, Korn, and C shells. This entry describes the external command that lives in the filesystem.

Common Option

`-p, --portability`
Print the real, user, and system times with a single space separating the title and the value, instead of a tab. (Mac OS X uses a tab.)

GNU/Linux Options

`-a, --append`
Used with `-o` to append the output to *file* instead of overwriting it.

`-f` *`format`*`, --format=`*`format`*
Specify the output format. Overrides any format specified in the TIME environment variable.

`-o` *`file`*`, --output=`*`file`*
Send the output from `time` to the specified file instead of to standard error. If *file* exists, it is overwritten.

-v, --verbose
Give verbose output, providing all available information.

-V, --version
Print version information and exit.

Mac OS X Option

-l Print the contents of the process's `struct rusage` structure. See *getrusage*(2).

touch

`touch [options] [date] files`

For one or more *files*, update the access time and modification timestamp to the current time and date, or update to the optional *date*. *date* is a date and time in the format *mmddhhmm*[*yy*]. `touch` creates the *files* if they don't exist. `touch` is useful in forcing other commands to handle files a certain way; e.g., the operation of `make`, and sometimes `find`, relies on a file's access and modification times.

Common Options

-a, --time=access, --time=atime, --time=use
Update only the access time.

-c, --no-create
Do not create nonexistent files.

-m, --time=modify, --time=mtime
Update only the modification time.

-r *file*, --reference=*file*
Use the access and/or modification times of *file* instead of the current time.

-t *time*
Use the time as it is provided by *time*, which has the form [[*cc*]*yy*]*mmddhhmm*[.*ss*].

GNU/Linux Options

-d *time*, --date=*time*
Change the time value to the specified *time* instead of the current time. *time* can use several formats and may contain month names, time zones, a.m. and p.m. strings, etc.

-f Accepted but ignored.

Mac OS X Option

-f Force; attempt to update the times, even if the file permissions do not allow it.

tr

`tr [options] [string1 [string2]]`

Copy standard input to standard output, performing substitution of characters from *string1* to *string2* or deletion of characters in *string1*. Some older System V systems require that *string1* and *string2* be enclosed in square brackets. (This is true of Solaris's `/usr/bin/tr`, for example.) Most other versions do not have this requirement. POSIX-compliant versions do not have this requirement either.

Common Options

`-c, --complement`
: Complement characters in *string1* with characters in the current character set. The complement is the set of all characters not in *string1*. This option works in terms of byte values.

`-d, --delete`
: Delete characters in *string1* from output.

`-s, --squeeze-repeats`
: Squeeze out repeated output characters in *string2*.

Solaris and Mac OS X Option

`-C` Like `-c`, but work in terms of characters, which may be multibyte values, depending upon the local character set.

GNU/Linux Option

`-t, --truncate-set1`
: Truncate *string1* to the length of *string2* before processing the input.

Mac OS X Option

`-u` Force output to be unbuffered.

Examples

Change uppercase to lowercase in a file:

```
tr  'A-Z'   'a-z'  < file     Modern systems, traditional BSD
tr '[A-Z]' '[a-z]' < file     Old System V systems
```

Modern systems allow the use of character classes:

```
tr '[:upper:]' '[:lower:]' < file
```

Turn spaces into newlines (ASCII code 012):

```
tr ' ' '\012' < file
```

Strip blank lines from `file` and save in `new.file` (or use `\011` to change successive tabs into one tab):

```
tr -s "" "\012" < file > new.file
```

Delete colons from `file`; save result in `new.file`:

```
tr -d : < file > new.file
```

Make long search path more readable:

```
echo $PATH | tr ':' '\n'
```

---

troff

`troff [options] [files]`

Document formatter for laser printer or typesetter. See Chapter 18.

true

`true`

A do-nothing command that returns a successful (zero) exit status. Normally used in Bourne shell scripts. See also **true**.

`true` is built into most modern shells.

tset

`tset [`*options*`] [`*type*`]`

Set terminal modes. Without arguments, the terminal is reinitialized according to the TERM environment variable. `tset` is typically used in startup scripts (`.profile` or `.login`). *type* is the terminal type; if preceded by a `?`, `tset` prompts the user to enter a different type, if needed. Press the ENTER key to use the default value, *type*. On Solaris, this command is found is `/usr/ucb`. See also **reset**.

Common Options

`-`
: Print terminal name on standard output; useful for passing this value to TERM.

`-e` *c*
: Set erase character to *c*; default is `^H` (backspace).

`-i` *c*
: Set interrupt character to *c* (default is `^C`).

`-I`
: Do not output terminal initialization setting.

`-k` *c*
: Set line-kill character to *c* (default is `^U`).

`-m[`*port*`[`*baudrate*`]:`*type*`]`
: Declare terminal specifications. *port* is the port type (usually `dialup` or `plugboard`). *tty* is the terminal type; it can be preceded by `?` as above. *baudrate* checks the port speed and can be preceded by any of these characters:

  - `>` Port must be greater than *baudrate*.
  - `<` Port must be less than *baudrate*.
  - `@` Port must transmit at *baudrate*.
  - `!` Negate a subsequent `>`, `<`, or `@` character.
  - `?` Prompt for the terminal type. With no response, use the given *type*.

`-Q`
: Do not print "Erase set to" and "Kill set to" messages.

`-r`
: Report the terminal type.

`-s`
: Return the values of TERM assignments to shell environment. This is a commonly done via `eval 'tset -s'` (in the C shell, you would surround this with the commands `set noglob` and `unset noglob`).

Solaris Option

`-n`
: Initialize "new" tty driver modes. Useless because of redundancy with the default `stty` settings that incorporate the functionality of the BSD "new" tty driver.

GNU/Linux and Mac OS X Options

-q Print the terminal type on standard output but do not initialize the terminal.

-V Print the version of ncurses used for this program and exit.

Examples

Set TERM to wy50:

```
eval `tset -s wy50`
```

Prompt user for terminal type (default is vt100):

```
eval `tset -Qs -m '?vt100'`
```

Similar to above, but the baudrate must exceed 1200:

```
eval `tset -Qs -m '>1200:?xterm'`
```

Set terminal via modem. If not on a dial-in line, the ?$TERM causes tset to prompt with the value of $TERM as the default terminal type:

```
eval `tset -s -m dialup:'?vt100' "?$TERM"`
```

---

tty

tty [*options*]

Print the device name of your terminal. This is useful for shell scripts and often for commands that need device information.

Common Option

-s, --quiet, --silent
Return only the codes: 0 (a terminal), 1 (not a terminal), 2 (invalid options used).

Solaris Option

-l Print the synchronous line number, if on an active synchronous line.

---

type

type *program* ...

Print a description of *program*, i.e., whether it is a shell built-in, a function, or an external command. type is built into the Bash and Korn shells. See Chapter 4 and also see **which**.

Example

Describe cd and ls:

```
$ type cd ls          From Bash
cd is a shell builtin
ls is hashed (/bin/ls)
```

---

umask

umask [*value*]

Print the current value of the file creation mode mask, or set it to *value*, a three-digit octal code specifying the read-write-execute permissions to be turned off when new files are created. Normally used in `.login` or `.profile`. `umask` is a built-in command in the Bash, Korn, and C shells (see Chapters 4 and 5).

umask number	File permission	Directory permission
0	`rw-`	`rwx`
1	`rw-`	`rw-`
2	`r--`	`r-x`
3	`r--`	`r--`
4	`-w-`	`-wx`
5	`-w-`	`-w-`
6	`---`	`--x`
7	`---`	`---`

Examples

Turn off write permission for others:

`umask 002` *Produces file permission* `-rw-rw-r--`

Turn off all permissions for group and others:

`umask 077` *Produces file permission* `-rw-------`

Note that you can omit leading zeroes.

uname

`uname [options]`

Print the current Unix system name.

Common Options

`-a, --all`
: Report the information supplied by all the other options.

`-m, --machine`
: The hardware name.

`-n, --nodename`
: The node name.

`-p, --processor`
: The host's processor type.

`-r, --kernel-release`
: The operating system release.

`-s, --kernel-name`
: The system name. This is the default action when no options are provided.

`-v, --kernel-version`
: The operating system version.

Solaris and GNU/Linux Option

`-i, --hardware-platform`
: The hardware platform name. (For example on Solaris, `SUNW,Ultra-4`; compare to `sparc` from `-p`.)

Solaris Options

`-S` *name*
: Change the nodename to *name*. Privileged users only.

`-X` Print expanded information as expected by SCO Unix systems.

GNU/Linux Option

`-o, --operating-system`
: Print the operating system name.

---

umount

`umount [`*options*`] [`*arguments*`]`

Unmount a filesystem. This command is very system-specific. See the **umount** entries in the sections for each operating system.

---

unexpand

`unexpand [`*options*`] [`*files*`]`

Convert spaces back into an appropriate number of tab characters. `unexpand` reads the named *files*, or standard input if no *files* are provided. See also **expand**.

Common Options

`-a, --all`
: Replace spaces with tabs everywhere possible, not just leading spaces and tabs.

`-t` *tablist*`, --tabs=`*tablist*
: Interpret tabs according to *tablist*, a space- or comma-separated list of numbers in ascending order that describes the "tabstops" for the input data.

GNU/Linux Option

`--first-only`
: Convert only leading whitespace into tabs. Overrides `-a`.

---

uniq

`uniq [`*options*`] [`*file1* `[`*file2*`]]`

Remove duplicate adjacent lines from sorted *file1*, sending one copy of each line to *file2* (or to standard output). Often used as a filter. Specify only one of `-c`, `-d`, or `-u`. See also **comm** and **sort**.

Common Options

`-c, --count`
: Print each line once, counting instances of each.

`-d, --repeated`
: Print duplicate lines once, but no unique lines.

`-f` *n*`, --skip-fields=`*n*
: Ignore first *n* fields of a line. Fields are separated by spaces or by tabs.

`-s n, --skip-chars=n`
: Ignore first *n* characters of a field.

`-u, --unique`
: Print only unique lines (no copy of duplicate entries is kept).

`-n`
: Like `-f`. This original, pre-POSIX syntax is deprecated; use `-f` instead.

`+n`
: Like `-s`. This original, pre-POSIX syntax is deprecated; use `-s` instead.

GNU/Linux Options

`-D, --all-repeated[=method]`
: Print all duplicate lines. `-D` takes no delimiter method. The delimiter method *method* describes how `uniq` should delimit groups of repeated lines in the output. It takes one of the values `none` (default), `prepend` (output a newline before each group), or `separate` (output a newline after each group).

`-i, --ignore-case`
: Ignore case differences when checking for duplicates.

`-w n, --check-chars=n`
: Compare only first *n* characters per line (beginning after skipped fields and characters).

Examples

Send one copy of each line from `list` to output file `list.new` (`list` must be sorted):

```
uniq list list.new
```

Show which names appear more than once:

```
sort names | uniq -d
```

Show which lines appear exactly three times:

```
sort names | uniq -c | awk '$1 == 3'
```

---

units

```
units
units [options] [from-unit to-unit]
```

Interactively supply a formula to convert a number from one unit to another. Use *EOF* to exit. Known units are maintained in a system table, and the GNU/Linux and Mac OS X versions let you supply your own units file. They also allow you to supply units on the command line, so that the program can be used in a batch fashion.

GNU/Linux and Mac OS X Common Options

`-f file, --file=file`
: Read units from *file*.

`-q, --quiet, --silent`
: Do not prompt, and do not display statistics.

GNU/Linux Options

`-c, --check`
: Verify that all units reduce to primitive units.

`--check-verbose`
: Like `-c`, but list the units as they're checked, for finding infinite loops.

`-e, --exponential`
: Use exponential format output.

`-h, --help`
: Print a command-line summary and exit.

`-o` *format*, `--output-format=`*format*
: Use *printf*(3)-style format *format* for formatting values. *format* should be appropriate for a floating-point value.

`-s, --strict`
: Do not do the reciprocal unit conversion.

`-v, --verbose`
: Be more verbose.

`-V, --version`
: Print version information and exit.

Mac OS X Option

`-v` Print the version number.

---

unix2dos

`unix2dos [`*options*`]` *unixfile dosfile*

Solaris and GNU/Linux only. Convert files using the ISO standard characters to their DOS counterparts. If *unixfile* and *dosfile* are the same, the file is overwritten after the conversion is done. See also **dos2unix**.

For the GNU/Linux version, the options are the same as for `dos2unix`; see the **dos2unix** entry for the list.

Solaris Options

`-ascii`
: Add extra carriage returns for use under DOS.

`-iso` Same as the default action.

`-437` Use the US code page.

`-7` Convert 8-bit Solaris characters to 7-bit DOS characters.

`-850` Use the multilingual code page.

`-860` Use the Portugese code page.

`-863` Use the French Canadian code page.

`-865` Use the Danish code page.

unzip

```
unzip [options[modifiers]] zipfile ... [extraction options]
unzip -Z [zipinfo options] zipfile ...
```

unzip prints information about or extracts files from ZIP format archives. The *zipfile* is a ZIP archive whose filename ends in .zip. The .zip can be omitted from the command line; unzip supplies it. *zipfile* may also be a shell-style wildcard pattern (which should be quoted); all matching files in the ZIP archive will be acted upon. The behavior of *options* is affected by the various *modifiers*.

In the second form, the *options* are taken to be zipinfo options, and unzip performs like that command. See **zipinfo** for more information.

Options may also be included in the UNZIP environment variable, to set a default behavior. Options on the command line can override settings in $UNZIP by preceding them with an extra minus.

When extracting files, if a file exists already, unzip prompts for an action. You may to choose to overwrite or skip the existing file, overwrite or skip all files, or rename the current file.

Notes

- unzip and its companion program zip are part of the InfoZIP project. InfoZIP is an open collaborative compressed archive format, and implementations exist for Unix, Amiga, Atari, VMS and OpenVMS, MS-DOS, Macintosh, Minix, OS/2, Windows NT, and many others. It is the *only* similar format you can expect to port to all of these systems without difficulty. The web home page is *http://www.info-zip.org/*.
- Unlike most Unix tar implementations, zip removes leading slashes when it creates a ZIP archive, so there is never any problem unbundling it at another site.
- The Java Archive format (.jar) is based on ZIP; zip and unzip can process .jar files with no trouble.
- The jar tool may be easier to use for working with .zip files, especially since its options are similar to those of tar.

The following lists intentionally omit obsolete options and those that are specific to non-Unix platforms.

Extraction Options

-d *dir*
: Extract files in *dir* instead of in the current directory. This option need not appear at the end of the command line.

-x *files*
: Exclude. Do not extract archive members that match *files*.

Options

-A
: Print help for the shared library programming interface (API).

-c
: Print files to standard output (the CRT). Similar to -p, but a header line is printed for each file, it allows -a, and

automatically does ASCII to EBCDIC conversion. Not in the unzip usage message.

-f
: Freshen existing files. Only files in the archive that are newer than existing disk files are extracted. unzip queries before overwriting, unless -o is used.

-l
: List archived files, in short format (name, full size, modification time, and totals).

-p
: Extract files to standard output (for piping). Only the file data is printed. No conversions are done.

-q[q]
: Be quiet; suppress most of the informative messages provided during processing. Use -qq to suppress all messages.

-t
: Test the archived files. Each file is extracted in memory, and the extracted file's CRC is compared to the stored CRC.

-T
: Set the timestamp on the archive itself to be that of the newest file in the archive.

-u
: Same as -f, but also extract any files that don't exist on disk yet.

-v
: Be verbose or print diagnostic information. -v is both an option and a modifier, depending upon the other options. By itself, it prints the unzip ftp site information, information about how it was compiled, and what environment variable settings are in effect. With a *zipfile*, it adds compression information to that provided by -l.

-X
: Restore the owner and group (UID and GID) recorded in the archive. The default is to use the UID and GID of the extracting user.

-z
: Only print the archive comment.

-Z
: Run as zipinfo. Remaining options are zipinfo options. See **zipinfo** for more information.

Modifiers

-:
: Allow writing of files outside the directory in which extraction is taking place, via ../ in pathname components. Older versions of unzip allowed this by default; current versions disallow it for safety. This option reenables the original behavior. GNU/Linux and Mac OS X only.

-a[a]
: Convert text files. Normally, files are extracted as binary files. This option causes text files to be converted to the native format (e.g., adding or removing CR characters in front of LF characters). EBCDIC-to-ASCII conversion is also done as needed. Use -aa to force all files to be extracted as text.

-b
: Treat all files as binary.

-B
: Save a backup copy of each overwritten file in *file~*. Only available if compiled with UNIXBACKUP defined.

-C
: Ignore case when matching filenames. Useful on non-Unix systems where filesystems are not case-sensitive.

-j
: "Junk" paths. Extract all files in the current extraction directory, instead of reproducing the directory tree structure stored in the archive.

-L
: Convert filenames to lowercase from archives created on uppercase-only systems. By default, filenames are extracted exactly as stored in the archive.

-M
: Pipe output through the internal pager, which is similar to `more`. Press the ENTER key or spacebar at the `--More--` prompt to see the next screenful.

-n
: Never overwrite existing files. If a file already exists, don't extract it, just continue on without prompting. Normally, `unzip` prompts for an action.

-o
: Overwrite existing files without prompting. Often used together with `-f`. Use with care.

Examples

List the contents of a ZIP archive:

```
unzip -lv whizprog.zip
```

Extract C source files in the main directory, but not in subdirectories:

```
unzip whizprog.zip '*.[ch]' -x '*/*'
```

---

uptime

`uptime`

Print the current time, amount of time the system has been up, number of users logged in, and the system-load averages. This output is also produced by the first line of the `w` command. GNU/Linux accepts `-V` to print the program's version information.

---

users

`users [`*file*`]`

Display the currently logged-in users as a space-separated list. Information is read from a system *file* such as `/var/adm/utmp`, although the location may vary from system to system. On Solaris, this program is in `/usr/ucb`.

---

uudecode

`uudecode [`*options*`] [`*file*`]`

Read a uuencoded file and re-create the original file with the same mode and name.

Common Option

`-o` *file*
: Write output to *file* instead of to the filename recorded in the input. On GNU/Linux, use `-o /dev/stdout` to use `uudecode` in a pipeline.

Solaris and Mac OS X Option

`-p` Write the decoded file to standard output, making it possible to use uudecode in a pipeline.

Mac OS X Options

`-c` Continue; attempt to decode more than one output file from the same input.

`-i` Do not overwrite files.

`-s` Do not strip the final pathname to just the basename. Normally, uudecode removes leading directory components from the output filename for security.

---

vi

`vi [options] [files]`

A screen-oriented text editor based on ex. See Chapter 9 for more information on vi and ex.

---

view

`view [options] [files]`

Same as `vi -R`. See Chapter 9.

---

vim

`vim [options] [files ...]`

An enhanced version of the `vi` screen editor. Both `vi` and `vim` are covered in Chapter 9.

---

vimdiff

```
vimdiff [options] file1 file2 [file3]
gvimdiff [options] file1 file2 [file3]
```

Edit two or three files with `vim`, highlighting the differences. If invoked as `gvimdiff`, the GUI is used instead. This sets the `diff`, `wrap`, and `scrollbind` options. It also sets `foldmethod=diff` and `foldcolumn=2`, which puts ranges of lines that aren't changed into a fold and makes folds easy to spot.

By default, the screen is split vertically, as if with `-O`. Use `-o` to get a horizontal split.

For more information about `vim`, see Chapter 9.

---

w

`w [options] [user]`

Print summaries of system usage, currently logged-in users, and what they are doing. `w` is essentially a combination of `uptime`, `who`, and `ps -a`. Display output for one user by specifying *user*.

Common Option

`-h` Suppress headings and `uptime` information.

Solaris and GNU/Linux Option

-s Display in short format.

Solaris Options

-l Display in long format (the default).

-u Print just the heading line. Equivalent to uptime.

-w Same as -l.

GNU/Linux Options

-f Toggle printing the from (remote hostname) field.

-u Ignore the username while figuring out the current process and CPU times.

-V Display version information.

Mac OS X Options

-d Dump the entire process list per controlling tty, not just the top level process.

-i Sort the output by idle time.

-M *corefile*
Use *corefile* for the name list of the running system instead of /dev/kmem.

-n Don't resolve network addresses to turn them back into hostnames.

-N *system_image*
Use *system_image* for the name list instead of /mach.

---

wait

wait [*n*]

Wait for all background processes to complete and report their termination status. Used in shell scripts. If *n* is specified, wait only for the process with process ID *n*. wait is a built-in command in the Bash, Korn, and C shells. See Chapters 4 and 5 for more information.

---

wc

wc [*options*] [*files*]

Word count. Print a character, word, and line count for *files*. If multiple files, print totals as well. If no *files* are given, read standard input. See other examples under **ls** and **sort**.

Common Options

-c, --bytes
Print byte count only.

-l, --lines
Print line count only.

-m, --chars
Print character count only. This will be different than -c in a multibyte character environment.

-w, --words
Print word count only.

Solaris Option

`-C` Same as `-m`.

GNU/Linux Option

`-L, --max-line-length`
: Print length of longest line.

Examples

Count the number of users logged in:

```
who | wc -l
```

Count the words in three essay files:

```
wc -w essay.[123]
```

Count lines in file named by `$file` (don't display filename):

```
wc -l < $file
```

whatis

`whatis` *`commands`*

Look up one or more *commands* in the online manpages, and display a brief description. Same as `man -f`. The MANPATH environment variable can affect the results obtained with this command. See also **apropos**.

which

`which [`*`options`*`] [`*`commands`*`]`

List which files are executed if the named *commands* are run as a command. `which` reads the user's `.cshrc` file (using the `source` built-in command), checking aliases and searching the `path` variable. Users of the Bourne or Korn shells can use the built-in `type` command as an alternative. (See **type**, Chapters 4 and 5.)

GNU/Linux Options

`-a, --all`
: Print all matches, not just the first.

`-i, --read-alias`
: Read aliases from standard input and write matches to standard output. Useful for using an alias for `which`.

`--read-functions`
: Read shell functions from standard input and report matches to standard output. Useful for also using a shell function for `which` itself.

`--show-dot`
: If a matching command is found in a directory that starts with a dot, print *./cmdname* instead of the full pathname.

`--show-tilde`
: Print a tilde (~) to indicate the user's home directory. Ignored if the user is `root`.

`--skip-alias`
: Ignore `--read-alias` if present. Useful for finding normal binaries while using `--read-alias` in an alias for `which`.

`--skip-dot`
: Skip directories that start with a dot.

`--skip-functions`
: Ignore `--read-functions` if present. Useful when searching for normal binaries while using `--read-functions` in an alias or function for `which`.

`--skip-tilde`
: Skip directories that start with a tilde (~) and executables in $HOME.

`--tty-only`
: Stop processing options on the right if not on a terminal.

`-v, -V, --version`
: Print version information and then exit.

Example

```
$ which file ls
/usr/bin/file
ls:      aliased to ls -sFC
```

---

who

`who [options] [file]`

Display information about the current status of the system. With no options, list the names of users currently logged in to the system. An optional system *file* (the default varies per system) can be supplied to give additional information. `who` is usually invoked without options, but useful options include `am i` and `-u`. For more examples, see **cut**, **line**, **paste**, **tee**, and **wc**.

Common Options

`-H, --heading`
: Print headings.

`-m`
: Report only about the current terminal.

`-q, --count`
: "Quick." Display only the usernames.

`-s, --short`
: List the name, line, and time fields (the default behavior).

`-T, --mesg, --message, --writable`
: Report whether terminals are writable (+), not writable (-), or unknown (?).

`-u, --users`
: Report terminal usage (idle time). A dot (.) means less than one minute idle; `old` means more than 24 hours idle.

`am i`
: Print the username of the invoking user. (Similar to results from id.)

Solaris and GNU/Linux Options

`-a, --all`
: Use the `-b`, `-d`, `-l`, `-p`, `-r`, `-t`, `-T`, and `-u` options.

`-b, --boot`
: Report information about the last reboot.

`-d, --dead`
: Report expired processes.

`-l, --login`
: Report inactive terminal lines.

`-p, --process`
: Report previously spawned processes.

`-r, --runlevel`
: Report the run level.

`-t, --time`
: Report the last change of the system clock (via `date`).

Solaris Option

`-n` *x* Display *x* users per line (works only with `-q`).

GNU/Linux Options

`-i, --idle`
: Present idle time as *`HOURS:MINUTES`*, `.` (dot), or `old`. (Deprecated; use `-u`.)

`--lookup`
: Use DNS to canonicalize hostnames for people logged in remotely.

`-w` Same as `-T`.

Example

This sample output was produced at 8 a.m. on April 17:

```
$ who -uH
NAME    LINE   TIME         IDLE   PID  COMMENTS
martha  ttyp3  Apr 16 08:14 16:25  2240
george  ttyp0  Apr 17 07:33   .   15182
```

Since `martha` has been idle since yesterday afternoon (16 hours), it appears that Martha isn't at work yet. She simply left herself logged in. George's terminal is currently in use. (He likes to beat the traffic.)

---

whoami

`whoami`

Print the username based on effective user ID. On Solaris, this command is in `/usr/ucb`. On GNU/Linux and Mac OS X, it's equivalent to `id -un`.

xargs

`xargs [options] [command]`

Execute *command* (with any initial arguments), but read remaining arguments from standard input instead of specifying them directly. xargs passes these arguments in several bundles to *command*, allowing *command* to process more arguments than it could normally handle at once. The arguments are typically a long list of filenames (generated by `ls` or `find`, for example) that get passed to xargs via a pipe.

Without a *command*, `xargs` behaves similarly to `echo`, simply bundling the input lines into output lines and printing them to standard output.

Common Options

`-E string`
: Stop passing arguments when argument *string* is encountered.

`-I string`
: Pass arguments to *command*, replacing instances of *string* on the command line with the current line of input.

`-L n` Execute *command* for *n* lines of arguments.

`-n count, --max-args=count`
: Execute *command* with up to *count* arguments.

`-p, --interactive`
: Prompt for a `y` to confirm each execution of *command*. Implies `-t`.

`-s max, --max-chars=max`
: Each argument list can contain up to *max* characters. (Older systems limited *n* to 470. The default is system-dependent.)

`-t, --verbose`
: Echo each *command* before executing.

`-x, --exit`
: Exit if argument list exceeds *n* characters (from `-s`); `-x` takes effect automatically with `-i` and `-l`.

Solaris and GNU/Linux Options

`-e[string], --eof[=string]`
: Use *string* as the default logical EOF string (default is underscore). An omitted *string* disables the logical EOF capability.

`-i[string], --replace[=string]`
: Like `-I` but default *string* is { }.

`-l[n], --max-lines[=n]`
: Same as `-L`, but default *n* is 1.

GNU/Linux and Mac OS X Option

`-0, --null`
: Filenames are separated with zero bytes (ASCII NUL) instead of spaces and newlines. For use with `find -print0`.

GNU/Linux Options

`-P` *max*, `--max-procs=`*max*
: Allow no more than *max* processes to run at once. The default is 1. A maximum of 0 allows as many as possible to run at once.

`-r, --no-run-if-empty`
: Do not run command if standard input contains only blanks.

Mac OS X Options

`-J` *string*
: When *string* is found among the arguments on the command line, replace its first occurrence with the current input list. This happens *instead* of appending the list to the given arguments.

`-R` *count*
: Use *count* as the maximum number of arguments in which `-I` will do replacements.

Examples

grep for *pattern* in all files on the system:

```
find / -print | xargs grep pattern > out &
```

Run `diff` on file pairs (e.g., `f1.a` and `f1.b`, `f2.a` and `f2.b` ...):

```
echo "$@" | xargs -n2 diff
```

The previous line could be invoked as a shell script, specifying filenames as arguments.

Display *file*, one word per line:

```
cat file | xargs -n1
```

Move files in `olddir` to `newdir`, showing each command:

```
ls olddir | xargs -i -t mv olddir/{ } newdir/{ }
```

xgettext

```
xgettext [options] files
xgettext -h
```

Solaris and GNU/Linux only. Extract messages (specially marked strings) from C and C++ source files. Place them in a "portable object" file (`.po`) for translation and compilation by `msgfmt`. By default, xgettext extracts strings only inside calls to the *gettext*(3C) and *dgettext*(3C) functions. Source files are named on the command line. A filename of - indicates the standard input. See also **gettext** and **msgfmt**.

GNU gettext extends the original Solaris gettext design and is able to extract strings from source files for a large number of languages. The URL for it is *http://www.gnu.org/software/gettext*.

Common Options

`-a, --extract-all`
: Extract all strings, not just those in calls to gettext or dgettext. (GNU/Linux: applies to languages `C`, `C++`,

ObjectiveC, Shell, Python, Lisp, EmacsLisp, librep, Scheme, Java, C#, awk, Tcl, Perl, PHP, GCC-source, and Glade.)

-c *tag*, --add-comments[=*tag*]
: Copy source file comments marked with *tag* into the .po file as #-delimited comments.

-d *domain*, --default-domain=*domain*
: Use *domain*.po as the output file instead of messages.po.

-h, --help
: Print a help message on the standard output.

-j, --join-existing
: Join (merge) extracted messages with those in the current .po file. Domain directives in the existing .po file are ignored.

-m *prefix*, --msgstrr-prefix=*prefix*
: Fill in each msgstr with *prefix*. Intended for debugging. The GNU version allows *prefix* to be optional.

-M *suffix*, --msgstr-suffix=*suffix*
: Fill in each msgstr with *suffix*. Intended for debugging. The GNU version allows *suffix* to be optional.

-n, --add-location
: Add comments to the .po file indicating the source filename and line number where each string is used.

-p *path*, --output-dir=*path*
: Place output files in the directory *path*.

-s, --sort-output
: Sort the output by msgid (original string), with all duplicates removed.

-x *exfile*, --exclude-file=*exfile*
: *exfile* is a .po file with msgids that are not to be extracted (i.e., to be excluded).

GNU/Linux Options

--copyright-holder=*string*
: Set the copyright holder in the output file.

-C, --c++
: Short for --language=C++.

--debug
: Produce more detailed output, intended for debugging xgettext.

-D *dir*, --directory=*dir*
: Add *dir* to the list of directories searched for input.

-e, --no-escape
: Do not use C escapes in the output (the default).

-E, --escape
: Do use C escapes in the output.

-f *file*, --files-from=*exfile*
: Read list of input files from *file*.

`--force-po`
: Write the `.po` file even if it will be empty.

`--foreign-user`
: Do not place the FSF copyright information into the file.

`--flag=`*`funcname`*`:`*`argnum`*`:`*`flag`*
: Apply *flag* to the *argnum*th argument to function *funcname*. This is a specialized option, see the online Info manual for details. For languages: `C`, `C++`, `ObjectiveC`, `Shell`, `Python`, `Lisp`, `EmacsLisp`, `librep`, `Scheme`, `Smalltalk`, `Java`, `C#`, `awk`, `YCP`, `Tcl`, `Perl`, `PHP`, and `GCC-source`.

`--from-code=`*`encoding`*
: Input files use *encoding*. Not valid for languages `Python`, `Tcl`, or `Glade`.

`-F, --sort-by-file`
: Sort the output by input file location.

`-i, --indent`
: Use an indented style when writing the `.po` file.

`-k [`*`word`*`], --keyword[=`*`word`*`]`
: Additional keyword to search for. Without *word*, do not recognize the default keywords. Valid for languages `C`, `C++`, `ObjectiveC`, `Shell`, `Python`, `Lisp`, `EmacsLisp`, `librep`, `Scheme`, `Java`, `C#`, `awk`, `Tcl`, `Perl`, `PHP`, `GCC-source`, and `Glade`.

`-L `*`lang`*`, --language=`*`name`*
: Source files are in language *lang*. Known languages are `C`, `C++`, `ObjectiveC`, `PO`, `Shell`, `Python`, `Lisp`, `EmacsLisp`, `librep`, `Scheme`, `Smalltalk`, `Java`, `JavaProperties`, `C#`, `awk`, `YCP`, `Tcl`, `Perl`, `PHP`, `GCC-source`, `NXStringTable`, `RST`, and `Glade`.

`--msgid-bugs-address=`*`user@domain`*
: Supply the bug-reporting address for problems with the original `msgid` strings.

`--no-location`
: Do not write `#:` *`filename`*`:`*`line`* lines.

`--no-wrap`
: Do not break long lines.

`-o `*`file`*`, --output=`*`exfile`*
: Write the output to *file*. Use - for standard output.

`--omit-header`
: Do not write a header with a `msgid ""` entry.

`--properties-input`
: Create a `.properties` file.

`--qt`
: Extract Qt format strings. Valid only for `C++`.

`--strict`
: Use the Uniforum format for the `.po` file. Avoid this if possible, it doesn't allow for GNU extensions.

`--stringtable-input`
: Create a NeXTstep/GNUstep `.strings` file.

`-T, --trigraphs`
: Interpret ANSI C trigraphs. Only for `C`, `C++`, and `ObjectiveC`.

`-v, --version`
Print version information and exit.

`-w count, --width=count`
Set the output line width to *count*.

yacc

`yacc [options] file`
`byacc [options] filename`

Given a *file* containing a context-free LALR(1) grammar, convert it to tables for subsequent parsing and send output to `y.tab.c`. This command name stands for **y**et **a**nother **c**ompiler-**c**ompiler. On Solaris yacc is found in `/usr/ccs/bin`. See also **lex**, **flex**, and **bison**, and *lex & yacc*, which is listed in the Bibliography.

Mac OS X uses Berkeley Yacc for yacc, which accepts the traditional options as well as `-o`. GNU/Linux provides Berkeley Yacc under the name byacc.

Common Options

`-d` Generate `y.tab.h`, producing `#define` statements that relate yacc's token codes to the token names declared by the user.

`-l` Exclude `#line` constructs from code produced in `y.tab.c`. (Use after debugging is complete.)

`-t` Compile runtime debugging code by default.

`-v` Generate `y.output`, a file containing diagnostics and notes about the parsing tables.

`-V` Print the version of yacc on standard error. (May not be in all versions.)

GNU/Linux and Mac OS X Option

`-r` Produce separate files for code and tables named *y.code.c* and *y.tab.c*, respectively.

Solaris Options

`-b prefix`
Use *prefix* instead of y for the generated filenames.

`-p prefix`
Use *prefix* instead of yy for all external names in the generated parser.

`-P parser`
Use *parser* instead of `/usr/ccs/bin/yaccpar`.

`-Qc` Place version information about yacc in `y.tab.c` (if *c* = y) or suppress information (if *c* = n, the default).

Berkeley Yacc Option

`-o filename`
Write the generated parser to *filename* instead of to `y.tab.c`.

zcat

`zcat [files]`

Uncompress one or more compressed *files* to the standard output, leaving *files* unchanged. See **bzip2** and **gzip**.

On Solaris, `zcat` is the original version related to `compress`. GNU/Linux and Mac OS X use the version related to `gzip`, which can decompress `.Z` and `.gz` files.

zip

`zip [options] zipfile [files]`

Archive files in InfoZIP format. These files can be retrieved using `unzip`. The files are compressed as they are added to the archive. Compression ratios of 2:1 to 3:1 are common for text files. `zip` may also replace files in an existing archive. With no arguments, display the help information. See also **zipinfo** and **unzip**.

Default options may be placed in the ZIPOPT environment variable, with the exceptions of `-i` and `-x`. Multiple options may be included in ZIPOPT.

The `zip` source code is readily available from *http://www.info-zip.org/*. There are a number of important notes in the **unzip** entry. Go there for more information.

The following list intentionally omits obsolete options and those that are specific to non-Unix platforms.

Options

`-b path`
: Use *path* as the location to store the temporary ZIP archive while updating an existing one. When done, copy the temporary archive over the new one. Useful primarily when there's not enough disk space on the filesystem containing the original archive.

`-c`
: Add one-line comments for each file. `zip` first performs any file operations and then prompts you for a comment describing each file.

`-d`
: Delete entries from a ZIP archive. Filenames to be deleted must be entered in uppercase if the archive was created by PKZIP on an MS-DOS system.

`-D`
: Don't create entries in the archive for directories. Usually entries are created, so that attributes for directories may be restored upon extraction.

`-e`
: Encrypt the archive. `zip` prompts on the terminal for a password and prompts twice, to avoid typing errors. If standard error is not a terminal, `zip` exits with an error.

`-f`
: Freshen (replace) an existing entry in the ZIP archive if the file has a more recent modification time than the one in the archive. This doesn't add files that are not already in the archive: use `-u` for that. Run this command from the same directory where the ZIP archive was created, since the archive stores relative pathnames.

`-F, -FF`
: Fix the ZIP archive. This option should be used with care; make a backup copy of the archive first. The `-FF` version does not trust the compressed sizes in the archive, and instead scans it for special "signatures" that identify the boundaries of different archive members. See the manpage for more information.

`-g` Grow the archive (append files to it).

`-h` Display the `zip` help information.

`-i` *files*
: Include only the specified *files*, typically specified as a quoted shell wildcard-style pattern.

`-j` "Junk" the path; i.e., store just the name of the saved file, not any directory names. The default is to store complete paths, although paths are always relative.

`-J` Strip any prepended data (e.g., an `SFX` stub, for self-extracting executables) from the archive.

`-k` Create an archive that (attempts to) conform to the conventions used under MS-DOS. This makes it easier for PKUNZIP to extract the archive.

`-l` For text files only, translate the Unix newline into a CR-LF pair. Primarily for archives extracted under MS-DOS.

`-ll` For text files only, translate CR-LF into a Unix newline.

`-L` Display the `zip` license.

`-m` "Move" the files into the ZIP archive. This actually deletes the original files and/or directories after the archive has been created successfully. This is somewhat dangerous; use `-T` in conjunction with this option.

`-n` *suffixlist*
: Do not compress files with suffixes in colon-separated *suffixlist*. Useful for sound or image files that often have their own, specialized compression method.

`-o` Set the modified time of the ZIP archive to be that of the youngest file (most recently modified) in the archive.

`-q` Quiet mode. Don't print informational messages and comment prompts. Most useful in shell scripts.

`-r` Recursively archive all files and subdirectories of the named *files*. The `-i` option is also useful in combination with this one.

`-t` *mmddyy*
: Ignore files modified prior to the date given by *mmddyy*.

`-T` Test the new ZIP archive's integrity. If the test fails, an existing ZIP archive is not changed, and with `-m`, no files are removed.

`-u` Update existing entries in the ZIP archive if the named *files* have modification dates that are newer than those in the archive. Similar to `-f`, except that this option adds files to the archive if they aren't already there.

`-v` As the only argument, print help and version information, a pointer to the home and distribution Internet sites, and information about how `zip` was compiled. When used with other options, cause those options to print progress information and provide other diagnostic information.

`-x` *files*
: Exclude the specified *files*, typically specified as a quoted shell wildcard-style pattern.

`-X` Do not save extra file attributes (extended attributes on OS/2, user ID/group ID, and file times on Unix).

`-y` Preserve symbolic links in the ZIP archive, instead of archiving the file the link points to.

`-z` Prompt for a (possibly multiline) comment describing the entire ZIP archive. End the comment with a line containing just a period, or *EOF*.

`-`*n* Specify compression speed: *n* is a digit between 0 and 9. 0 indicates no compression, 1 indicates fast but minimal compression, 9 indicates slowest but maximal compression. Default is `-6`.

`-@` Read standard input for names of files to be archived. Filenames containing spaces must be quoted using single quotes.

Examples

Archive the current directory into `source.zip`, including only C source files:

```
zip source -i '*.[ch]'
```

Archive the current directory into `source.zip`, excluding the object files:

```
zip source -x '*.o'
```

Archive files in the current directory into `source.zip`, but don't compress `.tiff` and `.snd` files:

```
zip source -n '.tiff:.snd' *
```

Recursively archive the entire directory tree into one archive:

```
zip -r /tmp/dist.zip .
```

---

zipinfo

`zipinfo [`*options*`]` *zipfile* ... `[`*exclusion option*`]`

`zipinfo` prints information about ZIP format archives. The *zipfile* is a ZIP archive whose filename ends in `.zip`. The `.zip` can be omitted from the command line; `zipinfo` supplies it. *zipfile* may also be a shell-style wildcard pattern (which should be quoted to protect it from the shell); all matching files in the ZIP archive will be acted upon. See also **zip** and **unzip**.

Exclusion Option

`-x` *files*
: Exclude. Do not extract archive members that match *files*.

Options

-1 Only list filenames, one per line. Nothing else is printed. For use in shell scripts.

-2 Like -1, but also permit headers, trailers, and ZIP archive comments (-h, -t, -z).

-h Print a header line with the archive name, size in bytes, and total number of files.

-l Use "long" format. Like -m, but also print the compressed size in bytes, instead of the compression ratio.

-m Use "medium" format. Like -s, but also include the compression factor (as a percentage).

-M Pipe output through the internal pager, which is similar to more. Press the ENTER key or spacebar at the --More-- prompt to see the next screenful.

-s Use "short" format, similar to ls -l. This is the default.

-t Print totals for all files (number of files, compressed and uncompressed sizes, overall compression factor).

-T Print times and dates in a decimal format (*yymmdd.hhmmss*) that can be sorted.

-v Use verbose, multipage format.

-z Print the archive comment.

Unix Commands

Alphabetical Summary of Solaris Commands

cde

Common Desktop Environment

The Common Desktop Environment (CDE) is one of the graphical user interfaces (GUI) on Solaris systems. Solaris users may choose between CDE and GNOME.

Documenting CDE would require its own book and is beyond the scope of this one. Instead, listed here are some of the more useful individual CDE commands, which are kept in /usr/dt/bin. (Commands for the **D**esk**t**op.) In addition, a number of Open-Windows commands are still useful. See the listing under **openwin**.

Useful CDE Programs

The following CDE and Sun Desktop commands may be of interest. Check the manpages for more information.

answerbook2	Sun hypertext documentation viewer.
dtaction	Invoke CDE actions from within shell scripts.
dtbuilder	CDE applications builder.
dtcalc	Onscreen scientific, logical, and financial calculator.
dtcm	Calendar manager.

`dterror.ds`	`dtksh` script for error notices and dialogues.
`dtfile_error`	`dtksh` script for error dialogues.
`dticon`	Icon editor.
`dtksh`	The "Desktop Korn shell," an early version of `ksh93`.
`dtmail`	Mail reader.
`dtpad`	Simple text editor.
`dtprintinfo`	Print job manager.
`dtscreen`	Screen savers.
`dtterm`	Terminal emulator.
`fdl`	Font downloader utility for PostScript printers.
`sdtconvtool`	GUI for `iconv`.
`sdtfind`	File finder.
`sdtimage`	Image viewer (PostScript, GIF, JPEG, etc.).
`sdtperfmeter`	System performance meter.
`sdtprocess`	Process manager.

cdrw

`cdrw [`*`options`*`]` *`commands`* `|` *`files`*

Read and write CDs and DVDs. `cdrw` can write CD-RW, DVD-RW, and DVD+RW media for data, and read and write audio data for music CDs. Options let you specify devices and control the way in which data are written to writable media. Images for data CDs and DVDs are usually prepared using `mkisofs`.

Without `-C`, the default capacities for writable CD media are assumed to be 74 minutes for an audio CD, 681,984,000 bytes for a data CD, and 4.7 Gbytes for a DVD.

Options

`-a`
: Create an audio CD. Audio CDs are limited to 99 tracks, so no more than 99 files may be provided. Audio files should be in one of the following formats:

AUR	`.aur` files with raw audio data in big-endian format
CDA	`.cda` files with raw audio data (16 bit PCM stereo at 44.1 KHz sample rate, in little-endian format)
RIFF	`.wav` files with data in Red Book CDDA format
Sun	`.au` files with data in Red Book CDDA format

`-b` *`blanktype`*
: Blank (erase) CD-RW and DVD-RW media. The *blanktype* should be one of `all`, `fast`, or `session`. DVD+RW media does not support blanking but can be rewritten without it.

`-c`
: Copy a CD. By default `cdrw` uses the CD writer as the CD reader, and stores the data temporarily on the local hard disk. Use `-s` to specify a different source device.

`-C`
: Use the amount of space reported by the drive as the capacity of the media. Useful when appending to a multisession CD.

`-d` *`device`*
: Use *device* as the CD or DVD writer.

-h Print a usage message.

-i *file*
: Use *file* as the image to write to the media. For best results, the file should be available on a local hard disk, not mounted via NFS.

-l List all CD or DVD writers available on the system.

-L Close the disk. This prevents any further writing. Applies only to CD-RW media.

-m *dir*
: Use *dir* for storing temporary files while copying a CD or DVD, instead of the default temporary directory.

-M Report the media status: blank or not, table of contents, last session start address, and next writable address if the disk is open.

-O Keep the disk open. The session is closed but the disk is left open for addition of another session later, creating a multi-session disk.

-p *speed*
: Set the writing speed of the drive. Usually cdrw uses the drive's default speed. With this option, cdrw attempts to change the speed, but there is no guarantee as to the actual speed used.

-s *device*
: Use *device* as the source for data when copying a CD or DVD.

-S Simulate writing. The drive's laser is turned off; use this option to verify that the system can move data quickly enough.

-T *type*
: Specify the type of audio data. It should be one of aur, cda, wav, or sun. (See the -a option.)

-v Be verbose.

-x Extract audio data from an audio track.

Examples

Extract the second song from an audio CD:

```
cdrw -x 2 three_blind_mice.cda
```

Create a data CD, at speed 40X:

```
cdrw -i -p 40 /bigdisk/tmp/whizprog-dist.iso
```

chkey

chkey [*options*]

Prompt for login password and use it to encrypt a new key. See also **keylogin** and **keylogout**.

Options

-m *mechanism*
: Change or reencrypt the secret key for the specified mechanism. (Mechanisms are those allowed by *nisauthconf*(1).)

-p Reencrypt the existing secret key with the user's login password.

-s *database*
Update the given database, which is one of `files`, `ldap`, `nis`, or `nisplus`.

decrypt

`decrypt [options] [-i infile] [-o outfile]`

Decrypt files encrypted with `encrypt`. `encrypt` and `decrypt` are hard links to each other and accept the same options. See **encrypt** for a full description.

digest

```
digest [-v] -a algorithm [file ...]
digest -l
```

Compute a PKCS#11 message digest of the given *files*. The second form lists the available digest algorithms. See also **decrypt**, **encrypt**, and **mac**.

Options

-a *algorithm*
Use *algorithm* to compute the digest. This option is required. Values for *algorithm* are `sha1` and `md5`.

-l Used by itself to list available digest computation algorithms.

-v Verbose; include algorithm name in the output.

Examples

Calculate MD5 checksums on some start-up files:

```
$ digest -a md5 .profile .login                    Regular results
(.profile) = 74c0f9c28d37f985c3f160efe992e078
(.login) = 05d1f072534b75188bdaba2747d8edaa

$ digest -v -a md5 .profile .login                 Verbose
md5 (.profile) = 74c0f9c28d37f985c3f160efe992e078
md5 (.login) = 05d1f072534b75188bdaba2747d8edaa
```

dircmp

`dircmp [options] dir1 dir2`

Compare the contents of *dir1* and *dir2*. See also **diff** and **cmp**.

Options

-d Execute `diff` on files that differ.

-s Don't report files that are identical.

-w *n* Change the output line length to *n* (default is 72).

dis

`dis [options] files`

Disassemble the object or archive *files*. See also **as**.

Options

-C Display demangled C++ symbol names.

-d *section*
: Disassemble only the specified *section* of data, printing its offset.

-D *section*
: Same as -d, but print the data's actual address.

-F *func*
: Disassemble only the specified function; reuse -F for additional functions.

-l *string*
: Disassemble only the library file *string* (e.g., *string* would be malloc for libmalloc.a).

-L Look for C source labels in files containing debug information (e.g., files compiled with cc -g).

-o Print octal output (default is hexadecimal).

-t *section*
: Same as -d, but print text output.

-V Print version information on standard error.

---

encrypt

encrypt [*options*] [-i *infile*] [-o *outfile*]

Encrypt files using a PKCS#11 algorithm. Files are decrypted with decrypt. encrypt and decrypt are hard links to each other and accept the same options. Both programs read and write standard input and standard output by default. See also **decrypt**, **digest**, and **mac**.

These programs are not related to the original Unix crypt command. That program's encryption algorithm is considered weak by today's standards, and it should not be used.

Options

-a *algorithm*
: Use *algorithm* to encrypt the file. Possible values for *algorithm* are aes, arcfour, des, and 3des.

-i *file*
: Read input data from *file*, instead of from standard input.

-k *keyfile*
: Read the encryption/decryption key from *keyfile*, instead of prompting for it.

-l List available encryption algorithms. This option should be used by itself.

-o *file*
: Write output data to *file*, instead of to standard output.

-v Be verbose. This prints a progress bar.

Examples

Display available algorithms:

```
$ encrypt -l
Algorithm        Keysize:  Min   Max (bits)
------------------------------------------
aes                        128   128
arcfour                      8   128
des                         64    64
3des                       192   192
```

Encrypt a trade secret document, then decrypt it and compare the result to the original:

```
$ encrypt -a aes -i designdoc.txt -o designdoc.txt.aes Encrypt
Enter key:                                   Key is not echoed
$ file design*                               Check results
designdoc.txt:       ASCII text
designdoc.txt.aes: data
$ decrypt -a aes -i designdoc.txt.aes -o designdoc.txt.out Decrypt
Enter key:                                   Enter same key
$ cmp designdoc.txt designdoc.txt.out        Results are identical
$
```

enhance

enhance *command* [*argument* ...]

Provide command-line editing facilities for programs that don't have it, such as ftp. enhance runs the given *command* and *arguments* behind a pseudo-terminal, reading user input, performing editing, and sending final input lines to *command*. enhance uses the *tecla* library; see *tecla*(5) for the details.

filesync

filesync [*options*] [-r *dir* ...]
filesync [*options*] -s *srcdir* -d *dstdir* *filename* ...

Synchronize files and directories (including symbolic links and device files) between two different computer systems. This command is intended for keeping *nomadic* computers, such as laptops or notebook systems, synchronized with server systems. By default, changes are propagated two ways: from both the source system to the destination system, and vice versa. (Typically the server is the source system and the nomadic system is the destination.) Access to the server file tree is via NFS mount on the client, typically managed via the automounter. (Contrast this to the rsync command [see **rsync** in the earlier section "Alphabetical Summary of Common Commands"], where the name of the remote host is provided explicitly.)

filesync synchronizes only the files listed in the $HOME/.packingrules file. See *packingrules*(4) for a description of the file format. The file allows specification of files to be ignored, wildcard patterns, and more. It lists the files and directories that are to be synchronized. Users may edit this file with any text editor in order to adjust filesync's operation. The file $HOME/.filesync-base keeps track of which files are subject to synchronization, and their states when last synchronized. Users should *not* edit this file. Both files should be kept on the nomadic system, which should also be the one where `filesync` is run, in order to avoid problems with multiple nomadic systems synchronizing from a single server.

The first command-line syntax synchronizes files as described by the `.filesync-base` and `.packingrules` files. The `-r` option may be used to restrict synchronization to just the given directory. The second syntax adds new directories to the list of files to be synchronized. This syntax is cumulative; once added, files and directories stay in the synchronization list until explicitly removed (by editing the `.packingrules` file). Specifying a directory copies the directory and the entire file hierarchy under it.

By default `filesync` reports its actions in the form of Unix commands: `mv`, `cp`, etc.

Options

`-a`
: Check, and if possible, reconcile Access Control Lists (ACLs) for files being synchronized.

`-d` *`dstdir`*
: Use *dstdir* as the destination directory into which new files should be synchronized. Use together with `-s` and a *filename* operand.

`-e`
: Report all differences, such as ownership and permissions. `filesync` normally ignores differences it cannot synchronize, such as changing ownership to the original file's owner if not run as a privileged user.

`-f` *`favorite`*
: Favor the system specified by *favorite* when reconciling conflicts between the source and the destination system. Possible values for *favorite* are:

`src`	Favor the source system.
`dst`	Favor the destination system.
`old`	Favor the older version of the file.
`new`	Favor the newer version of the file.

You can use `-f` and `-o` together if they both specify the same preference (`src` or `dst`). If they conflict, `-f` is ignored.

`-h`
: Quit (halt) upon encountering an error. Normally `filesync` continues after errors and attempts to synchronize as many files as possible.

`-m`
: Make sure that both copies of the file have the same modification time.

`-n`
: Dry run option. Do not change any files and do not update the `.packingrules` file.

-o *origin*
One way change. Changes are propagated only from the system specified by *origin*, which is either src or dst, to the other system.

You can use -n and -o together on a disconnected nomadic system to see what changes have been made since the last time files were synchronized.

-q Quiet operation. Suppress the normal report of actions that are being taken.

-r *dir*
Synchronize only the files in directory *dir*. Repeat this option to synchronize multiple directories.

-s *srcdir*
Use *srcdir* as the source directory from which new files should be synchronized. Use together with -d and a *filename* operand.

-v Verbose; display additional information about each file comparison.

-y Assume a "yes" answer to any safety checks, effectively bypassing the checks. Useful if the server has changed to a different mount point and you're sure you know what you're doing when you synchronize; see the *filesync*(1) manpage for more information.

gpatch

gpatch [*options*] [*original* [*patchfile*]]

This is Sun's version of GNU patch. On Solaris, /usr/bin/patch is a much older version of Larry Wall's original patch program. The GNU version is more functional and is generally recommended. For backwards compatibility, the original patch is left in place, and this version is provided for those who want it. For more information, see **patch** in the earlier section "Alphabetical Summary of Common Commands."

keylogin

keylogin [-r]

Prompt user for a password, then use it to decrypt the person's secret key. This key is used by secure network services (e.g., Secure NFS, NIS+). keylogin is needed only if the user isn't prompted for a password when logging in. The -r option updates /etc/.rootkey. Only a privileged user may use this option. See also **chkey** and **keylogout**.

keylogout

keylogout [-f]

Revoke access to (delete) the secret key used by secure network services (e.g., Secure NFS, NIS+). See also **chkey** and **keylogin**.

Option

-f Forget the root key. If specified on a server, NFS security is broken. Use with care.

---

line

```
line
```

Read the next line from standard input and write it to standard output. Exit status is 1 upon *EOF*. Typically used in csh scripts to read from the terminal.

Example

Print the first two lines of output from who:

```
who | ( line ; line )
```

---

listusers

listusers [*options*]

List all users, optionally just by group, or by specific users.

Options

-g *grouplist*
: List all users in the comma-separated list of groups *grouplist*.

-l *users*
: List just the named *users*, sorted by login. A comma-separated list may also be provided.

---

mac

mac [-v] -a *algorithm* [*file* ...]
mac -l

Compute a PKCS#11 message authentication code (MAC) of the given *files*. The second form lists the available MAC algorithms. See also **decrypt**, **digest**, and **encrypt**.

Options

-a *algorithm*
: Use *algorithm* to compute the MAC. This option is required. Values for *algorithm* are des_mac, sha1_hmac, and md5_hmac.

-k *keyfile*
: Read the encryption key from *keyfile*, instead of prompting for it.

-l Used by itself to list available MAC computation algorithms.

-v Be verbose.

Examples

Show available MAC algorithms:

```
$ mac -l
Algorithm       Keysize:  Min   Max (bits)
------------------------------------------
des_mac                    64     64
sha1_hmac                   8    512
md5_hmac                    8    512
```

Generate a MAC for an encrypted version of a trade-secret document:

```
$ mac -a md5_hmac designdoc.txt.aes
Enter key:
277f71848afe07ccbd78bee3bfdf11b8
```

mount

`mount [options] mount_spec ...`

System administration command. Mount a filesystem on a directory. Solaris understands several different kinds of local (hard disk) filesystem structures, as well as supporting network mounts of NFS filesystems and SMB shares. Filesystems and the directories on which to mount them are listed in /etc/vfstab, along with options for each mount. The file /etc/mnttab records which filesystems are actually mounted.

Along with general options, each filesystem may have options specific to it. When run with no options, mount prints the list of currently mounted filesystems.

The *mount_spec* may be either a special file (block device) or mount point listed in /etc/vfstab, in which case it's mounted. Otherwise, you must supply both the device name and the directory on which to mount it. See the Examples.

Options

-a
: Mount all filesystems of the given type. With no type or mount points, attempt to mount every filesystem in /etc/vfstab with yes in the "mount at boot" field.

-F *type*
: The filesystem is of type *type*. Useful types are ufs for the native Unix filesystem format, pcfs for FAT-32 filesystems, cifs for SMB shares, hsfs (High Sierra filesystem) for ISO 9660 CD-ROMs, and nfs for Sun's Network Filesystem.

-g
: Mount the filesystem globally, across all clusters. No effect on nonclustered systems.

-m
: Mount the filesystem without making an entry in /etc/mnttab.

-o *options*
: Supply options for the mount. Multiple options should be comma separated. Following is a list of options supported directly by mount. Each filesystem may have additional options.

  devices, nodevices
  : Allow (disallow) the use of device special files on this filesystem.

  exec, noexec
  : Allow (disallow) the execution of programs on the filesystem. The default is exec.

  nbmand, nonmbmand
  : Allow (disallow) nonblocking mandatory locking. The default is to disallow it. Enabling this option may cause

surprising behavior from applications not expecting non-blocking semantics. Do not use for /, /usr, and /var. Mutually exclusive with -g.

ro, rw
: Mount the filesystem read-only (read-write). The default is read-write. Use ro for read-only media such as CD-ROMs or DVD-ROMs.

setuid, nosetuid
: Allow (disallow) execution of setuid and setgid executables.

suid, nosuid
: The nosuid option is equivalent to nosetuid,nodevices, and is highly recommended for NFS filesystems mounted with the root= option. suid is thus equivalent to setuid,devices.

-O
: Overlay mount. This allows mounting one filesystem on the pre-existing mount point of another filesystem. The pre-existing mount point's files then become inaccessable. Without -O, such a mount is an error.

-p
: Print the list of mounted filesystems in the same format as /etc/vfstab. Must be used by itself.

-r
: Mount the filesystem read-only.

-v
: Print the list of mounted filesystems in verbose format. Must be used by itself.

-V
: Verify. mount prints out what it would do, without actually attempting the mount. This may include the invocation of subsidiary, filesystem-specific mount commands.

Examples

Mounting is usually restricted to privileged users. Here, # is the prompt for the root, the superuser.

Mount a local filesystem. The type is assumed to be ufs:

```
# mount /dev/dsk/c0d0s4 /opt
```

Mount a FAT-32 filesystem:

```
# mount -F pcfs /dev/dsk/c0d1s2 /pcfs
```

Mount a remote NFS filesystem. The *host:file* format of the device indicates that the filesystem is of type NFS:

```
# mount server.example.com:/bigdisk /bigdisk
```

---

nawk

nawk [*options*] ['*program*'] [*files*] [*variable=value*]

New version of awk, with additional capabilities. nawk is a pattern-matching language useful for manipulating data. /usr/xpg4/bin/awk should be used in preference to /usr/bin/nawk. See Chapter 11 for more information on the awk language.

openwin

`/usr/openwin/bin/*`

Programs from the OpenWindows graphical user interface environment. This environment is obsolete; the preferred environments are CDE (the Common Desktop Environment) and GNOME, and you can no longer run OpenWindows directly. However, for compatibility, many OpenWindows programs continue to be shipped with Solaris. The user level programs such as `cmdtool` and `shelltool` are no longer present, although a number of standard X11 programs are to be found in this directory. See also **cde**.

Useful OpenWindows Commands

The following OpenWindows commands may be of interest. Look at the manpages for more information:

`oclock`	A round clock
`xbiff`	Graphical mail arrival watchdog program
`xcalc`	Simple on-screen calculator
`xditview`	Device-independent `troff` output viewer
`xedit`	Simple text editor
`xhost`	Controls permissions for who can connect to display
`xload`	System load monitor
`xlock`	Screen saver/locker
`xmag`	Magnifies portions of the display
`xman`	Viewer for manpages
`xterm`	Standard X Window system terminal emulator

page

`page [`*`options`*`] [`*`files`*`]`

Same as `more`.

ps

`ps [`*`options`*`]`

Report on active processes. In options, *list* arguments should either be separated by commas or put in double quotes. In comparing the amount of output produced, note that `-e` > `-d` > `-a` and `-l` > `-f`. In the BSD version (`/usr/ucb/ps`), options work much differently; you can also display data for a single process.

Options

`-a`
: List all processes except group leaders and processes not associated with a terminal.

`-A`
: Same as `-e`.

`-c`
: List scheduler data set by `priocntl` (an administrative command).

`-d`
: List all processes except session leaders.

`-e`
: List all processes.

`-f`
: Produce a full listing.

`-g` *list*
: List data only for specified *list* of group leader ID numbers (i.e., processes with same ID and group ID).

`-G` *list*
: Show information for processes whose real group ID is found in *list*.

`-j` Print the process group ID and session ID.

`-l` Produce a long listing.

`-L` Print information about lightweight processes.

`-n` *file*
: Use the alternate *file* for the list of function names in the running kernel (default is `/unix`). Accepted for compatibility, but ignored.

`-o` *format*
: Customize information according to *format*. Rarely used.

`-p` *list*
: List data only for process IDs in *list*.

`-P` Print the processor number on which the process or lightweight process is bound.

`-s` *list*
: List data only for session leader IDs in *list*.

`-t` *list*
: List data only for terminals in *list* (e.g., `tty1`).

`-u` *list*
: List data only for usernames in *list*.

`-U` *uidlist*
: Show information for processes whose real user ID is found in *list*.

`-y` With `-l`, omit the `F` and `ADDR` columns and use kilobytes instead of pages for the `RSS` and `SZ` columns.

`-z` *zonelist*
: List only processes in the zones in *zonelist*. Zones may be given using either the zone name or the zone ID. This option is useful only if `ps` is run in the global zone.

`-Z` Add an additional `ZONE` output column showing the zone for each process.

---

rksh

`rksh [`*options*`] [`*arguments*`]`

Restricted version of `ksh` (the Korn shell), used in secure environments. `rksh` prevents you from changing out of the directory or from redirecting output. See Chapter 4.

setpgrp

`setpgrp command [argument ...]`

Become a session leader by setting the process group ID and the session ID to the current process ID, and then using *exec*(2) to run the named *command* and *arguments*.

sotruss

`sotruss [options] program [args ...]`

Shared object library version of truss. sotruss executes *program*, passing it *args*, if any. It then traces calls into and/or out of shared object libraries that are loaded dynamically. See also **truss** and **whocalls**.

Options

-f
: Follow children created by *fork*(2) and print output for each child. Each output line contains the process's process ID.

-F *fromlist*
: Only trace calls from the libraries named in *fromlist*, which is a colon-separated list of libraries. The default is to trace only calls from the main executable.

-o *file*
: Send output to *file*. If used with -f, the process ID of the running program is appended to the filename.

-T *tolist*
: Only trace calls to routines in the libraries named in *tolist*, which is a colon-separated list of libraries. The default is to trace all calls.

timex

`timex [options] command [arguments]`

Execute a *command* with optional *arguments* and print information similar to the time command. Report process data with various options.

Options

-o
: Show total number of blocks and characters used.

-p *suboptions*
: Show process accounting data with possible *suboptions*.

-s
: Show total system activity.

Suboptions for –p

-f
: Include fork/exec flag and system exit status.

-h
: Show "hog" factor (fraction of CPU time used) instead of mean memory size.

-k
: Show total kcore-minutes instead of memory size.

-m
: Show mean core size (this is the default behavior).

-r
: Show CPU use percentage (user time / (system time + user time)).

-t
: Show user and system CPU times.

truss

`truss [options] arguments`

Trace system calls, signals, and machine faults while executing *arguments*. *arguments* is either a Unix command to run or, if -p is specified, a list of process IDs representing the already running processes to trace. The options -m, -r, -s, -t, -v, -w, and -x accept a comma-separated list of arguments. A ! reverses the sense of the list, telling truss to ignore those elements of the list during the trace. (In the C shell, use a backslash before !.) The keyword all can include/exclude all possible elements for the list. The optional ! and corresponding description are shown in brackets. truss also provides tracing of user-level function calls in dynamically loaded shared libraries. See also **sotruss** and **whocalls**.

This command is particularly useful for finding missing files when a third-party application fails. By watching the access and open system calls, you can find where, and which, files the application program expected to find, but did not.

Many systems have similar programs named trace or strace. These programs are worth learning how to use.

Options

-a
: Display parameters passed by each *exec*(2) call.

-c
: Count the traced items and print a summary rather than listing them as they happen.

-d
: Print a timestamp in the output, of the form *seconds.fraction*, indicating the time relative to the start of the trace. Times are when the system call completes, not starts.

-D
: Print a delta timestamp in the output, of the form *seconds.fraction*, indicating the time between events (i.e., the time *not* inside system calls).

-e
: Display values of environment variables passed by each *exec*(2) call.

-E
: Print a delta timestamp in the output, of the form *seconds.fraction*, indicating the time between the beginning and end of a system call. This is the opposite of the -D option.

-f
: Follow child processes. Useful for tracing shell scripts.

-i
: List sleeping system calls only once, upon completion.

-l
: Show the lightweight process ID for a multithreaded process.

-m[!]*faults*
: Trace [exclude from trace] the list of machine *faults*. *faults* are names or numbers, as listed in <sys/fault.h> (default is -mall -m!fltpage).

-M[!]*faults*
: When the traced process receives one of the named faults, truss leaves the process in a stopped state and detaches from it (default is -M!all). The process can subsequently be attached to with a debugger, or with another invocation of truss using different options.

Unix Commands

-o *outfile*
: Send trace output to *outfile*, not standard error.

-p *pidlist*
: Trace one or more running processes instead of a command. Use *pid/lwp* to trace a lightweight process (thread).

-r[!]*file_descriptors*
: Display [don't display] the full I/O buffer of read system calls for *file_descriptors* (default is -r!all).

-s[!]*signals*
: Trace [exclude from trace] the list of *signals*. *signals* are names or numbers, as listed in <sys/signal.h> (default is -sall).

-S[!]*signals*
: When the traced process receives one of the named signals, truss leaves the process in a stopped state and detaches from it (see -M; default is -S!all).

-t[!]*system_calls*
: Trace [exclude from trace] the list of *system_calls*. *system_calls* are names or numbers, as listed in Section 2, "System Calls," of the *UNIX Programmer's Reference Manual* (see *intro*(2)); default is -tall.

-T[!]*system_calls*
: When the traced process executes one of the named system calls, truss leaves the process in a stopped state and detaches from it (see -M; default is -T!all).

-u[!]*lib*,...:[:][!]*func*,...
: Trace user-level function calls, not just system calls. *lib* is a comma-separated list of dynamic library names, without the .so.*n* suffix. *func* is a comma-separated list of names. Shell wildcard syntax may be used to specify many names. (Such use should be quoted to protect it from expansion by the shell.) The leading ! indicates libraries and/or functions to exclude. With :, only calls into the library from outside it are traced; with ::, all calls are traced.

-U[!]*lib*,...:[:][!]*func*,...
: When the traced process executes one of the named user-level functions, truss leaves the process in a stopped state and detaches from it (see -M).

-v[!]*system_calls*
: Verbose mode. Same as -t, but also list the contents of any structures passed to *system_calls* (default is -v!all).

-w[!]*file_descriptors*
: Display [don't display] the full I/O buffer of write system calls for *file_descriptors* (default is -w!all).

-x[!]*system_calls*
: Same as -t, but display the system call arguments as raw code (hexadecimal; default is -x!all).

Examples

Trace system calls access( ), open( ), and close( ) for the lp command:

```
truss -t access,open,close lp files 2> truss.out
```

Trace the make command, including its child processes, and store the output in make.trace:

```
truss -f -o make.trace make target
```


umount

umount [*options*] *device* | *mount_point*

System administration command. Unmount a mounted filesystem. *device* is a device name or other string indicating what is mounted. A *mount_point* is the name of a directory on which a device or other special object is mounted. See also **mount**.

Options

-a
May be used with multiple arguments to cause umount to attempt to do the unmounts in parallel.

-f
Force the unmounting of the filesystem. This option can be dangerous, use with caution.

-o *options*
Provide filesystem-specific options in *options*. This is unusual when unmounting a filesystem. See **mount** for a list of options.

-V
Verify. umount prints out what it would do, without actually attempting the unmount. This may include the invocation of subsidiary, filesystem-specific unmount commands.

vacation

vacation
vacation [*options*] [*user*]

Automatically return a mail message to the sender announcing that you are on vacation.

Use vacation with no options to initialize the vacation mechanism. The process entails several steps.

1. Create a .forward file in your home directory. The .forward file contains:

   ```
   \user, "|/usr/bin/vacation user"
   ```

   user is your login name. The action of this file is to actually deliver the mail to *user* (i.e., you), and to run the incoming mail through vacation. Add any appropriate options to the vacation command line.
2. Create the .vacation.pag and .vacation.dir files. These files keep track of who has sent you messages, so that they only receive one "I'm on vacation" message from you per week.
3. Start an editor to edit the contents of .vacation.msg. The contents of this file are mailed back to whoever sends you

mail. Within its body, `$SUBJECT` is replaced with the contents of the incoming message's `Subject:` line. You should include at least a `Subject:` header line of your own, such as:

```
Subject: I am out of the office until next Wednesday
```

Remove or rename the `.forward` file to disable vacation processing.

You may also create a `.vacation.filter` file that specifies email addresses and/or domains to which `vacation` will send messages. Addresses that don't match will not receive a vacation message. Case is ignored in the `.vacation.filter` file, as are empty lines and lines beginning with `#`.

Options

The `-a`, `-e`, `-f`, `-j`, `-m`, `-s`, and `-t` options are used within a `.forward` file; see the Example.

`-a` *alias*
: Mail addressed to *alias* is actually mail for the *user* and should produce an automatic reply.

`-e` *file*
: Use *file* as the filter file, instead of `.vacation.filter`.

`-f` *file*
: Use *file* as the base name for the database files (`.pag` and `.dir`) instead of `.vacation`.

`-I`
: Reinitialize the `.vacation.pag` and `.vacation.dir` files. Use this right before leaving for your next vacation.

`-j`
: Do not verify that *user* appears in the `To:` or `Cc:` headers.

`-m` *file*
: Use *file* in $HOME as the text of the automatic reply, instead of `~/.vacation.msg`.

`-s` *sender*
: Send replies to *sender* instead of to the address listed in the Unix "`From `" line of the incoming mail.

`-t` *interval*
: By default, no more than one message per week is sent to any sender. This option changes that interval. *interval* is a number with a trailing `s`, `m`, `h`, `d`, or `w` indicating seconds, minutes, hours, days, or weeks, respectively.

Example

Send no more than one reply every three weeks to any given sender:

```
$ cd
$ vacation -I
$ cat .forward
\jp, "|/usr/bin/vacation -t3w jp"
$ cat .vacation.msg
From: jp@wizard-corp.com (J. Programmer, via vacation)
Subject: I'm out of the office ...
```

```
Hi. I'm off on a well-deserved vacation after finishing
up whizprog 2.0. I will read and reply to your mail
regarding "$SUBJECT" when I return.

Have a nice day,

JP
```


volcheck

volcheck [*options*] [*pathnames*]

Check one or more devices named by *pathnames* to see if removable media has been inserted. The default is to check every device being managed by volume management. Most often used with floppies; volume management usually notices when CD-ROMs or DVD-ROMs have been inserted.

Note: use of the -i and -t options, particularly with short intervals, is not recommended for floppy-disk drives.

Options

-i *nsec*
: Check the device(s) every *nsec* seconds. The default is every two seconds.

-t *nsecs*
: Keep checking over the next *nsecs* seconds. Maximum *nsecs* is 28,800 (eight hours).

-v
: Be verbose.

whocalls

whocalls [*options*] *function program* [*arguments* ...]

Run *program* with the given *arguments*. Using facilities of the dynamic loader show which functions call the named *function*. See also **sotruss** and **truss**.

Options

-l *wholib*
: Use *wholib* instead of the standard who.so Link-Auditing library.

-s
: Use the .symtab symbol table in the ELF file for local symbol tables instead of the default .dynsym symbol table. This is more expensive but can provide more detailed stack tracing information.

Example

Show use of *write*(2) system call:

```
$ cat dontpanic.c                         Show program code
#include <unistd.h>

int main(void)
{
        (void) write(1, "Don't panic!\n", 13);
        return 0;
```

```
}
$ cc dontpanic.c -O -o dontpanic            Compile program
$ whocalls write dontpanic                  Run with whocalls
write(0x1, 0x80506cc, 0xd)                  Output from whocalls
        /export/u/guest/arnold/dontpanic:main+0x14
        /export/u/guest/arnold/dontpanic:_start+0x7a
Don't panic!                                Output from dontpanic
```

Alphabetical Summary of GNU/Linux Commands

GNU/Linux programs generally accept `--help` and `--version` options. In the interest of brevity, the individual command descriptions omit listing those options.

aspell

`aspell [`*options*`] [`*files*`]`

`aspell` is intended to be a drop-in replacement for `ispell`, but with more functionality. It thus accepts the same options; see **ispell** for more information. See also **spell** in the earlier section "Alphabetical Summary of Common Commands."

URL: *http://aspell.net/* and *http://www.gnu.org/software/aspell/*.

cdda2wav

`cdda2wav [`*options*`] [`*output.wav*`]`

Convert Compact Disc Digital Audio (CDDA) to the WAV format. This process is often called "ripping" a CD-ROM, and is generally performed before using an encoder to convert the file to a compressed music format such as OGG or MP3. By default, `cdda2wav` reads data from the `/dev/cdrom` device and outputs one WAV file per track.

Options

Some of the following options use sectors as a unit of measurement. Each sector of data on a CD represents approximately 1/75 second of play time.

`-a` *divider*, `--divider` *divider*
: Set rate to 44,100 Hz/*divider*. To get a list of possible values, use the `-R` option.

`-A` *drivename*, `--auxdevice` *drivename*
: Specify a different drive for ioctl purposes.

`-b` *n*, `--bits-per-sample` *n*
: Set the quality of samples to *n* bits per sample per channel. Possible values are 8, 12, and 16.

`-B, --bulk, --alltracks`
: Copy each track into its own file.

`-c` *channels*`, --channels` *channels*
: Set recording channels. Use `1` for mono, `2` for stereo, or `s` for stereo with both channels stopped.

`-C` *endianess*`, --cdrom-endianess` *endianess*
: Set the endianess of the input samples to *endianess*. Possible values are `little`, `big`, or `guess`.

`-d` *amount*`, --duration` *amount*
: Set to a number followed by `f` for frames (sectors) or `s` for seconds. Set time to zero to record an entire track. For example, to copy two minutes, use `120s`.

`-D` *devicename*`, --device` *devicename*`, dev=`*devicename*
: Specify the device. The device must be able to work with the `-I` (`--interface`) setting.

`-e, --echo`
: Copy audio data to a sound device rather than to a file.

`-E` *endianess*`, --output-endianess` *endianess*
: Set the endianess of the output samples to *endianess*. Possible values are `little` or `big`.

`-F, --find-extremes`
: Find extreme amplitudes in samples.

`-g, --gui`
: Format the output for parsing by GUI frontend programs.

`-G, --find-mono`
: Determine if input samples are in mono.

`-h, --help`
: Display version and option summary, and quit.

`-H, --no-infofile`
: Do not write an info file or a CDDB file.

`-i` *n*`, --index` *n*
: Set the start index to *n* when recording.

`-I` *ifname*`, --interface` *ifname*
: Specify the type of interface. For Linux systems, the most appropriate value is usually `cooked_ioctl`.

`-J, --info-only`
: Do not write data to a file; instead just write information about the disc.

`-L` *mode*`, --cddb` *mode*
: Use the CDDB ID to do a `cddbp` album and track title lookup. The *mode* parameter directs handling of multiple entries. Use `0` for interactive choice, or `1` which always takes the first entry. Additional variables may be provided for CDDB server name and port number:

`cddbp-port=`*portnum*	Contact the CDDB server on port number *portnum*.
`cddbp-server=`*server*	Use CDDB server *server*.

`-m, --mono`
: Record in mono. Use `-s` to record in stereo.

`-M` *`count`*`, --md5` *`count`*
: Calculate MD5 checksum for *count* bytes from the beginning of a track.

`-n` *`count`*`, --sectors-per-request` *`count`*
: Read *count* sectors in each request.

`-N, --no-write`
: Do not write data to a file, just read the tracks. For debugging.

`-o` *`n`*`, --offset` *`n`*
: Start recording *n* sectors before the beginning of the first track.

`-O, --output-format`
: Choose the output file format. Normal file options are `wav`, `aiff`, `aifc`, `au`, and `sun`. You can also use `cdr` and `raw` for headerless files dumped into recording devices.

`-p` *`n`*`, --set-pitch` *`n`*
: Adjust the pitch by *n* percent when copying data to an audio device.

`-paranoia`
: Use the *paranoia* library instead of `cdda2wav`'s built-in routines for reading.

`-P` *`n`*`, --set-overlap` *`n`*
: Use *n* sectors of overlap for jitter correction.

`-q, --quiet`
: Quiet mode; the program will not send any data to the screen.

`-Q, --silent-SCSI`
: Do not print SCSI command errors. Mainly for use by GUI frontends.

`-r` *`n`*`, --rate` *`n`*
: Set the sample rate in samples per second. To get a list of possible values, use the `-R` option.

`-R, --dump-rates`
: Output a list of possible sample rates and dividers. This option is typically used alone.

`-s, --stereo`
: Record in stereo. Use `-m` to record in mono.

`-scanbus`
: Scan all SCSI busses for all SCSI devices and print the inquiry strings. Use `dev=`*`device`* to specify devices to scan. For example, `dev=ATA:` for IDE CD Writers using Linux IDE to SCSI emulation.

`-S` *`n`*`, --speed-select` *`n`*
: Specify the speed at which your system will read the CD-ROM. Set the value to the multiple of normal playback speed given as your CD-ROM drive speed (4, 16, 32, and so forth). Setting the speed lower than the maximum can prevent errors in some cases.

`-t tracknumber, --track tracknumber`
Set start track and, optionally, end track. Separate the track numbers with the + character.

`-T, --deemphasize`
Undo pre-emphasis in the input samples.

`-v list, --verbose-level list`
Print information about the CD. *list* is a comma-separated list of one or more of the following options:

`all`	All information
`catalog`	The media catalog number (MCN)
`disable`	No information, but do print warnings
`indices`	Index offsets
`sectors`	Table of contents in start sector notation
`summary`	Summary of the recording parameters
`titles`	Table of contents with track titles (when available)
`toc`	Table of contents
`trackid`	All International Standard Recording Codes (ISRC)

`-V, --verbose-SCSI`
Log SCSI commands to the output. Mainly for debugging.

`-w, --wait`
Wait for a signal before recording anything.

`-x, --max`
Set recording quality (and amount of hard disk usage) to maximum.

Examples

For most systems, you should be able to copy a complete CD to a single WAV file with the following command:

```
cdda2wav
```

To copy a complete CD to a set of WAV files, one per track:

```
cdda2wav -B
```

Scan for IDE CD Writers:

```
$ cdda2wav -scanbus dev=ATA:
scsibus1:
    1,0,0   100) 'ASUS ' 'CRW-5224A  ' '1.20' Removable CD-ROM
    1,1,0   101) *
...
```

cdparanoia

`cdparanoia [options] span [outfile]`

Similar to `cdda2wav`, `cdparanoia` reads Compact Disc audio files as WAV, AIFF, AIFF-C, or raw format files. It uses additional data-verification and sound-improvement algorithms to make the process more reliable, and is used by a number of graphical recording programs as a backend.

Options

`-a, --output-aifc`
: Output in AIFF-C format.

`-B, --batch`
: Split the output into multiple files on track boundaries like `cdda2wav`. Filenames are prefixed with `track#`.

`-c, --force-cdrom-little-endian`
: Force `cdparanoia` to treat the drive as a little-endian device.

`-C, --force-cdrom-big-endian`
: Force `cdparanoia` to treat the drive as a big-endian device.

`-d` *`devicename`*`, --force-cdrom-device` *`devicename`*
: Specify a device name to use instead of the first readable CD-ROM available.

`-e, --stderr-progress`
: Send all progress messages to standard error instead of standard output; used by wrapper scripts.

`-f, --output-aiff`
: Output in AIFF format.

`-g` *`device`*`, --force-generic-device` *`device`*
: Use with -g to set the generic device separately from that of the CD-ROM device. Useful only on nonstandard SCSI setups.

`-h, --help`
: Display options and syntax.

`-n` *`count`*`, --force-default-sectors` *`count`*
: Do atomic reads of *count* sectors per read. Not generally useful.

`-O` *`count`*`, --sample-offset` *`count`*
: Shift sample positions by the given *count*. This shifts track boundaries for the whole disc. May cause read errors or even lockups on buggy hardware.

`-p, --output-raw`
: Output headerless raw data.

`-q, --quiet`
: Quiet mode.

`-Q, --query`
: Display CD-ROM table of contents and quit.

`-r, --output-raw-little-endian`
: Output raw data in little-endian byte order.

`-R, --output-raw-big-endian`
: Output raw data in big-endian byte order.

`-s, --search-for-drive`
: Search for a drive, even if `/dev/cdrom` exists.

`-S` *`n`*`, --force-read-speed` *`n`*
: Set the read speed to *n* on drives that support it. This is useful if you have a slow drive or are low on memory.

`-t n, --toc-offset n`
: Shift the entire disc LBA address by *n*. The amount is added to the beginning offsets in the TOC. `-T` is similar.

`-T, --toc-bias`
: Compensate for the behavior of some drives whereby the actual track beginning offsets are correctly reported in the TOC, but the beginning of track 1 index 1 is treated as sector 0 for reads. May cause read errors or even lockups on buggy hardware.

`-v, --verbose`
: Verbose mode.

`-V, --version`
: Print version information and quit.

`-w, --output-wav`
: Output in WAV format. This is the default.

`-X, --abort-on-skip`
: If a read fails and must be skipped, skip the entire track and delete any partially completed output file.

`-Y, --disable-extra-paranoia`
: Use data verification and correction only at read boundaries. Not recommended.

`-z [retries], --never-skip[=retries]`
: If a read fails (for example, due to a scratch in the disc), try again and again. If you specify a number, `cdparanoia` will try that number of times. If you do not, `cdparanoia` will retry until it succeeds.

`-Z, --disable-paranoia`
: Disable data verification and correction. Causes `cdparanoia` to behave exactly as `cdda2wav` would.

Progress Symbols

The output during operation includes both smiley faces and more standard progress symbols. They are:

`:-)`	Operation proceeding normally.
`:-|`	Operation proceeding normally, but with jitter during reads.
`:-/`	Read drift.
`:-P`	Unreported loss of streaming in atomic read operation
`8-|`	Repeated read problems in the same place.
`:-0`	SCSI/ATAPI transport error (hardware problem not related to the disc itself).
`:-(`	Scratch detected.
`;-(`	Unable to correct problem.
`8-X`	Unknown and uncorrectable error.
`:^D`	Finished.
Blank space	Blank space in the progress indicator means that no corrections were necessary.
`-`	Jitter correction was required.

+	Read errors.
!	Errors even after correction; repeated read errors.
e	Corrected transport errors.
V	An uncorrected error or a skipped read.

The span Argument

The `cdparanoia` command takes exactly one argument, which describes how much of the CD to record. It uses numbers followed by bracketed times to designate track numbers and time within them. For example, the string `1[2:23]-2[5]` indicates a recording from the 2-minute and 23-second mark of the first track up to the fifth second of the second track. The time format is demarcated by colons, *hours:minutes:seconds:.sectors*, with the last item, *sectors*, preceded by a decimal point (a sector is 1/75 of a second). It's best to put this argument within quotes.

If you use the `-B` option, the span argument is not required.

cdrdao

`cdrdao` *`command`* `[`*`options`*`]` *`toc-file`*

Write all content specified in description file *toc-file* to a CD-R disk drive in one step. This is called disk-at-once (DAO) mode, as opposed to the more commonly used track-at-once (TAO) mode. DAO mode allows you to change the length of gaps between tracks and define data to be written in these gaps (like hidden bonus tracks or track intros). The *toc-file* can be created by hand or generated from an existing CD using `cdrdao`'s `read-toc` command. A cue file, as generated by other audio programs, can be used instead of a TOC file. The file format for TOC files is discussed at length in the `cdrdao` manpage.

URL: *http://cdrdao.sourceforge.net/*. (`cdrdao` doesn't come with Fedora Core 3, apparently because `cdrecord` can also do DAO recording.)

Commands

The first argument must be a command. Note that not all options are available for all commands.

`blank`
: Blank a CD-RW disc.

`copy`
: Copy the CD. If you use a single drive, you will be prompted to insert the CD-R after reading. An image file will be created unless you use the `--on-the-fly` flag and two CD drives.

`discid`
: Print out CDDB information for a CD.

`disk-info`
: Display information about the CD-R currently in the drive.

`msinfo`
: Display multisession information. Useful mostly for wrapper scripts.

`read-cd`
: Create a TOC file and read in the audio data on a CD.

`read-cddb`
: Check a CDDB server for data about the CD represented by a given TOC file, then write that data to the TOC file as CD-TEXT data.

`read-test`
: Check the validity of the audio files described in the TOC file.

`read-toc`
: Read from a CD and create a disk image and TOC file that will allow creation of duplicates.

`scanbus`
: Scan the system bus for devices.

`show-data`
: Print out the data that will be written to the CD-R. Useful for checking byte order.

`show-toc`
: Print a summary of the CD to be created.

`simulate`
: A dry run: do everything except write the CD.

`toc-info`
: Print a summary of the TOC file.

`toc-size`
: Print the total number of blocks for the TOC.

`unlock`
: Unlock the recorder after a failure. Run this command if you cannot eject the CD after using `cdrdao`.

`write`
: Write the CD.

Options

`--blank-mode` *mode*
: Set the blanking mode for a rewritable disc. The value for *mode* is either `full` or `minimal`.

`--buffer-under-run-protection` *n*
: Use `0` to disable buffer underrun protection, or `1` to enable it. The default is enabled.

`--buffers` *n*
: Set the number of seconds of data to be buffered. Default is 32; set to a higher number if your read source is unreliable or is slower than the CD-R.

`--capacity` *minutes*
: Set the capacity in minutes for `--full-burn`.

`--cddb-directory` *localpath*
: CDDB data that is fetched will be saved in the directory *localpath*.

`--cddb-servers` *server,server*
: Enter hosts for servers. Servers may include ports, paths, and proxies; you can list multiple servers separated by spaces or commas.

`--cddb-timeout` *s*
: Set the timeout for CDDB server connections to *s* seconds.

`--datafile` *filename*
: When used with the `read-toc` command, specifies the data file placed in the TOC file. When used with `read-cd` and `copy`, specifies the name of the image file created.

`--device` *bus,id,logicalunit*
: Set the SCSI address of the CD-R using the bus number, ID number, and logical unit number.

`--driver` *driver-id*:*option-flags*
: Force `cdrdao` to use the driver you choose with the driver options named, instead of the driver it autodetects.

`--eject`
: Eject the disc when done.

`--fast-toc`
: Do not extract the pre-gaps and the index marks.

`--force`
: Override warnings and perform the action anyway.

`--full-burn`
: Force burning to the outer edge of the disc.

`-h` Print a help summary for individual *commands*.

`--keepimage`
: Used only with the `copy` command. Keeps the image file created during the copy process.

`--multi`
: Record as a multisession disc.

`-n` Do not wait 10 seconds before writing the disc.

`--on-the-fly`
: Do not create an image file: pipe data directly from source to CD-R.

`--overburn`
: If you are using a disc with more storage space than `cdrdao` detects, use this option to keep writing even when `cdrdao` thinks you're out of space.

`--paranoia-mode` *n*
: Specifies *n*, from 0 to 3, for the amount of error correction in the CD read. 0 is none, 3 is full (see **cdparanoia** for information about error correction). Set error correction to a lower number to increase read speed. The default is 3.

`--query-string`
: Just print out the CDDB query.

`--read-raw` *mode*
: Set sub-channel reading mode. Possible values are `rw` or `rw_raw`.

`--read-subchan`
: Used only with the `read-cd` command. Write raw data to the image file.

`--reload`
: Allow the drive to be opened before writing without interrupting the process. Used with simulation runs.

`--save`
: Save current options to the settings file `$HOME/.cdrdao`.

`--session` *n*
: Used only with the `read-toc` and `read-cd` commands when working with multisession CDs. Specifies the number of the session to be processed.

`--simulate`
: Don't actually write data.

`--source-device` *bus,id,logicalunit*
: Used only with the `copy` command. Set the SCSI address of the source device.

`--source-driver` *driver-id*:*option-flags*
: Used only with the `copy` command. Set the source device driver and flags.

`--speed` *value*
: Set the write speed to *value*. The default is the highest available; use a lower value if higher values give poor results.

`--swap`
: Swap byte order for all samples.

`--tao-source`
: For reading or copying, indicates that the source CD was written in TAO mode.

`--tao-source-adjust` *n*
: Use *n* link blocks for TAO source CDs. The default is two.

`--with-cddb`
: Use CDDB to fetch information about the disc and save it as CD-TEXT data. Used with the `copy`, `read-toc`, and `read-cd` commands.

`-write-speed-control` *n*
: If *n* is 0, disable writing speed control by the drive. The default is 1, which enables writing speed control.

`-v` *verbose-level*
: Set the amount of information printed to the screen. 0, 1, and 2 are fine for most users; greater numbers are useful for debugging.

---

cdrecord

`cdrecord [`*general-options*`] dev=`*device* `[`*track-options*`]` *track1* *track2* `...`

Record data or audio compact discs or DVDs. This program normally requires privileged user access, and has a large number of options and settings. A number of useful examples can be found in the manpage, which is quite extensive.

General Options

General options go directly after the `cdrecord` command name. Options affecting the track arguments are placed after the device argument and before the track arguments themselves. Options have two forms: traditional options that start with a hyphen, and "variable" assignments, of the form *`variable=value`*. Long named options start with only a single hyphen. The general options are:

`-abort`
: Attempt to send an abort sequence to the drive. May be needed if other software has left the drive in an unusable state. `cdrecord -reset` may be necessary as well.

`-atip`
: Display the ATIP (Absolute Time In Pregroove) information for a disc. Only some drives allow you to read this information.

`blank=`*`type`*
: Erase data from a CD-RW in one of the following ways:

`all`	Erase all information on the disc. May take a long time.
`fast`	Perform a quick erase of the disc, erasing only the PMA, TOC, and pregap.
`help`	Display a possible list of blanking methods.
`session`	Blank the last session.
`track`	Blank a track.
`trtail`	Blank the tail of a track only.
`unclose`	Unclose the last session.
`unreserve`	Unreserve a track previously marked as reserved.

`-checkdrive`
: Check to see if there are valid drivers for the current drive. Returns 0 if the drive is valid.

`cuefile=`*`file`*
: Obtain all recording information from *file*, which is a CDRWIN-compliant CUE sheet file. This option disallows specifying individual track files, and also requires the use of `-dao`.

`-dao, -sao`
: Disk-at-once mode. Works only with MMC drives that support non-raw session-at-once modes.

`debug=`*`n`*`, -d`
: Set the debug level to an integer (greater numbers are more verbose), or use multiple `-d` flags as with the `-v` and `-V` flags.

`defpregap=`*`n`*
: Set the default pre-gap size for all tracks except the first to *n*. Useful only with TEAC drives for creating TAO disks without

the two-second silence between tracks. This option may be removed in future versions.

dev=*target*
: Set the device used for writing CD or DVD media. See the section "The device Argument" later in this entry.

driver=*name*
: Lets you specify a driver for your system. Suggested for experts only. The special drivers `cdr_simul` and `dvd_simul` are used for simulation and profiling tests.

driveropts=*optlist*
: Specify a comma-separated list of driver options. To get a list of valid options, use `driveropts=help` and `-checkdrive`.

-dummy
: Perform a dry run, doing all the steps of recording with the laser turned off. This will let you know whether the process is going to work.

-eject
: Eject disc after recording. Some hardware may need to eject a disc after a dummy recording and before the actual recording.

-fix
: Close ("fixate") the session, preventing future multisession recordings and allowing the disc to be played in standard audio CD players (some can also play a disc that has not been closed).

-force
: Override errors if possible. May allow you to blank an otherwise broken CD-RW.

-format
: Format CD-RW/DVD-RW/DVD+RW media. Currently only implemented for DVD+RW media, which must be formatted before the first use. However, `cdrecord` detects such media and automatically formats it in this case. This option is thus mainly useful to reformat a DVD+RW disc.

fs=*n*
: Set the FIFO buffer size to *n*, in bytes. You may use `k`, `m`, `s`, or `f` to specify kilobytes, megabytes, or units of 2048 and 2352 bytes, respectively. The default is 4MB.

gracetime=*n*
: Set the grace time before writing to *n* seconds. A value less than two seconds is ignored.

-ignsize
: Ignores the known size of the medium. Debugging option, use with extreme care. Implies `-overburn`.

-immed
: Experimental feature that sets the SCSI `IMMED` flag for certain commands. Useful on some systems where the CD/DVD writer and ATAPI hard disc are on the same bus or on SCSI systems that don't use disconnect/reconnect. Use with caution.

`-inq`
: Do a drive inquiry, print the resulting information, and exit.

`kdebug=`*n*, `kd=`*n*
: Set the kernel's debug notification value to *n* during SCSI command execution. Works through the scg-driver.

`-load`
: Load media and exit. Works with tray-loading mechanisms only.

`-lock`
: Load media, lock door, and exit. Works with tray-loading mechanisms only. Possibly useful with the Kodak disc transporter.

`mcn=`*n*
: Set the Media Catalog Number to *n*.

`minbuf=`*n*
: Experimental feature. Sets the minimum drive buffer fill ratio to *n*, which is a number between 25 and 95 for 25% to 95% minimum drive buffer fill ratio.

`-msinfo`
: Get multisession information from the CD. Used only with multisession discs onto which you can still record more sessions.

`-multi`
: Set to record in multisession mode. Must be present on all sessions but the last one for a multisession disc.

`-noclose`
: Experimental feature: do not close the current track. Useful only in packet-writing mode.

`-nofix`
: Do not close the disc after writing.

`-overburn`
: Allow writing of more data than the official size of a medium. Not guaranteed to work on any specific drive.

`-packet`
: Experimental feature: use packet-writing mode.

`pktsize=`*n*
: Experimental feature: set the packet size to *n*. Forces fixed packet mode.

`-prcap`
: Print the drive capabilities for SCSI-3/MMC-compliant drives. Values marked `kB` use 1000 bytes, while values marked `KB` use 1024 bytes.

`-raw`, `-raw96r`
: Use RAW writing mode with 2352 byte sectors plus 96 bytes of raw P-W subchannel data. This results in a sector size of 2448 bytes. Useful for drives with bad firmware where TAO and SAO mode don't work. This option does require more CPU time, thus it may cause buffer underruns on slow CPUs.

Note: for this to work, `cdrecord` must know the size each track in advance. See the manpage for more information.

`-raw16`
: Similar to `-raw96r`, but with a 2352 byte sector and 16 bytes of P-Q subchannel data. Does not allow writing CD-Text or CD+Graphics. Don't use if `-raw96r` does work on your drive.

`-raw96p`
: Similar to `-raw96r` but not as widely supported. Don't use if `-raw96r` or `-raw16` do work on your drive.

`-reset`
: Attempt to reset the SCSI bus. Does not work on all systems.

`-s, -silent`
: Silent mode. Do not print any SCSI error commands.

`-scanbus`
: Scan for SCSI devices. Use this to find out which drives you have and to get the correct numbers for the `dev=` option.

`-setdropts`
: Set the driver options list as provided by `driveropts=` and the dummy flag, and then exit. Useful to set parameters without burning or reading media.

`speed=`*n*
: Set the speed to *n*, a multiple of the audio speed. Normally, `cdrecord` will get this from the CDR_SPEED environment variable. If your drive has trouble with higher numbers, try 0 as the value.

`-tao`
: Use Track At Once (TAO) mode. Required for multi-session recording. This was the default writing mode in previous versions.

`-text`
: Write CD-Text information. The information comes from either `.inf` files or from a CUE sheet file. Use with the `-useinfo` or `cuefile=` options.

`textfile=`*file*
: Obtain CD-Text information from *file*, which must be in the binary file format defined in the Red Book. This is the best way to copy CD-Text data obtained from existing CDs.

`timeout=`*n*
: Set the timeout to *n* seconds. Defaults to 40.

`-toc`
: Display the table of contents for the CD currently in the drive. Works for CD-ROM as well as CD-R and CD-RW media.

`ts=`*n*
: Set the maximum transfer size for a single SCSI command to *n*. The syntax for *n* is the same as for the `fs=` option. The default transfer size is 63 kB.

`-useinfo`
: Use `.inf` files to override audio options set elsewhere.

-v
: Verbose mode. Use one v for each level of verbosity: -vv would be very verbose, and -vvv would be even more so.

-V
: As with the -v, a verbose mode counter. However, this applies only to SCSI transport messages. This will slow down the application.

-waiti
: Wait for input to become available on standard input before opening the SCSI driver. This is necessary for multi-session recording, where mkisofs has to read the old session from the current disc before writing the new session, and mkisofs won't be able to open the device if cdrecord has already opened it.

The device Argument

The device argument is one of the more difficult parts of cdrecord. It consists of an optional transport specification, followed by a comma-separated list of integers representing the bus, target, and logical unit of the drive. The default transport is for a SCSI device. You can use cdrecord dev=help to see a list of supported transports. On some systems, you can use a device name followed by :@ to use that device; for example, on GNU/Linux, dev=/dev/scd0:@ for an external USB-connected DVD writer. For an IDE-connected CD writer, on GNU/Linux, you might use ATA:1,0,0.

Track Options and Arguments

Track options may be mixed with track arguments, and normally apply to the track immediately after them or to all tracks after them. The track arguments themselves should be the files that you will be writing to the CD or DVD. Options are:

-audio
: Write all tracks after this track in digital audio format (playable by standard CD players). If you do not use this flag or the -data flag, cdrecord assumes that .au and .wav files are to be recorded as raw audio and that all other files are data.

-cdi
: Write subsequent tracks in CDI format.

-copy
: For subsequent audio tracks, indicate in the TOC that the audio data has permission to be copied without limit.

-data
: Record subsequent tracks as CD-ROM data. If you do not use this flag or the -audio flag, all files except for those ending in .wav or .au are assumed to be data.

index=*a,b,c*
: Set the index list for the next track. The values should be increasing comma-separated integers, starting with index 1 and counting in sectors (75ths of a second). For example, you could set three indices in a track with index=0,750,7500 and they would occur at the beginning of the track, after 10 seconds, and after 100 seconds.

`-isosize`
: The size of the next track should match the size of the ISO-9660 filesystem. This is used when duplicating CDs or copying from raw-data filesystems.

`isrc=`*n*
: Set the International Standard Recording Number for the track following this argument.

`-mode2`
: Write all subsequent tracks in CD-ROM mode 2 format. Data size is a multipe of 2336 bytes.

`-nocopy`
: For subsequent audio tracks, indicate in the TOC that the audio data has permission to be copied only once for personal use. This is the default.

`-nopad`
: Do not insert blank data between data tracks following this flag. This is the default behavior.

`-nopreemp`
: For subsequent audio tracks, indicate in the TOC that audio data was mastered with linear data. This is the default.

`-noshorttrack`
: Require subsequent tracks to be at least four seconds in length. See `-shorttrack`.

`-pad`
: Insert 15 sectors of blank data padding between data tracks. Applies to all subsequent tracks or until you use the `-nopad` argument, and is overridden by the `padsize=`*n* argument.

`padsize=`*n*
: Insert *n* sectors of blank data padding after the next track. Applies only to the track immediately after it.

`-preemp`
: For subsequent audio tracks, indicate in the TOC that audio data was sampled with 50/15 microsecond pre-emphasis.

`pregap=`*n*
: Set the pre-gap size for the next track to *n*. Useful only with TEAC drives for creating TAO disks without the two-second silence between tracks. This option may be removed in future versions.

`-scms`
: For subsequent audio tracks, indicate in the TOC that the audio data has no permission to be copied.

`-shorttrack`
: Allow subsequent tracks to be less than four seconds in length, violating the Red Book standard. Useful only in SAO or RAW mode. Does not work with all drives.

`-swab`
: Declare that your data is in byte-swapped (little-endian) byte order. This is not normally necessary.

`tsize=n`
: Set the size of the next track. Useful only if you are recording from a raw disk for which `cdrecord` cannot determine the file size. If you are recording from an ISO 9660 filesystem, use the `-isosize` flag instead.

`-xa`
: Write subsequent tracks in CD-ROM XA mode 2 form 1 format, with 2048-byte sectors.

`-xa1`
: Write subsequent tracks in CD-ROM XA mode 2 form 1 format, with 2056-byte sectors.

`-xa2`
: Write subsequent tracks in CD-ROM XA mode 2 form 2 format, with 2324-byte sectors.

`-xamix`
: Write subsequent tracks in a way that allows mixing XA mode 2 forms 1 and 2. See the manpage.

dir

`dir [options] [file]`

List directory contents. `dir` is equivalent to the command `ls -C -b` (list files in columns, sorted vertically, special characters escaped) and it takes the same arguments as `ls`. This is an alternate invocation of the `ls` command and is provided for the convenience of those converting from Microsoft Windows and the DOS shell.

dircolors

`dircolors [options] [file]`

Set the color options for `ls` by changing the LS_COLORS environment variable. If you specify a file, `dircolors` reads it to determine which colors to use. Otherwise, it uses a default set of colors.

Options

`-b, --sh, --bourne-shell`
: Use the Bourne shell syntax when setting the LS_COLORS variable.

`-c, --csh, --c-shell`
: Use csh (C shell) syntax when setting the LS_COLORS variable.

`-p, --print-database`
: Display the default colors. You can copy this information into a file and change it to suit your preferences, and then run the program with the file as its argument to set the colors to your new values.

Example

In your `.profile`, you might have this:

```
eval `dircolors`
```

dvdrecord

```
dvdrecord options files ...
```

Record DVDs. In earlier systems, dvdrecord was a modified version of cdrecord. In Fedora Core 3, the DVD functionality is part of cdrecord, and dvdrecord is a shell script that prints an informational message to this effect and then does an exec of cdrecord. See also **cdrecord**.

gawk

```
gawk [options] 'script' [var=value ...] [files ...]
gawk [options] -f scriptfile [var=value ...] [files ...]
```

The GNU Project's implementation of the awk programming language. This is the standard version of awk on GNU/Linux systems. For more information see **awk** in the earlier section "Alphabetical Summary of Common Commands," and Chapter 11.

gettextize

```
gettextize [options] [directory]
```

Install GNU gettext infrastructure into a source package. This command copies files and directories into a source package so that a program can use GNU gettext for managing translations. The files are placed in *directory* if given, otherwise in the current directory. If the package already uses gettext, the infrastructure is upgraded to the current version.

Full documentation for GNU gettext is available in its manual. See *http://www.gnu.org/software/gettext/* for more information and a pointer to the documentation.

Options

`-c, --copy`
: Copy files instead of making symbolic links. (Recommended.)

`-f, --force`
: Force creation of files, even if old ones exist. Useful for upgrading.

`--intl`
: Create and install the `libintl` subdirectory, which holds a private copy of the gettext library.

`-n, --dry-run`
: Print the changes that would be made, but don't actually do them.

`--no-changelog`
: Do not create or update `ChangeLog` files.

igawk

```
igawk gawk-options files ...
```

A shell script that allows the use of file inclusion with awk programs. Distributed with GNU Awk (gawk). For more information, see Chapter 11.

ispell

`ispell [options] [files]`

Compare the words of one or more named *files* with the system dictionary. Display unrecognized words at the top of the screen, accompanied by possible correct spellings, and allow editing via a series of commands. See also **aspell** and **spell** in the earlier section "Alphabetical Summary of Common Commands."

URL: *http://www.gnu.org/software/ispell.*

Options

The `-c`, `-D`, and `-e1`, `-e2`, `-e3`, and `-e4` options are specialized (for use by the `munchlist` helper program) and are not covered here.

`-a`
: Function in back-end mode, printing a one-line version identification and then one line of output for each input word. See the manpage.

`-A`
: Like `-A`, but read files named on lines beginning with `&Include_File&`. Includes may be nested up to five levels deep.

`-b`
: Back up original file in *filename*`.bak`.

`-B`
: Search for missing blanks (resulting in concatenated words) in addition to ordinary misspellings.

`-C`
: Do not produce error messages in response to concatenated words.

`-d` *file*
: Search *file* instead of the standard dictionary file.

`-f` *outfile*
: Write output to *outfile* instead of to standard output. Must be used with `-a` or `-A`.

`-F` *program*
: Use *program* to remove formatting markup.

`-H`
: Input is in SGML/HTML format.

`-k`*setname list*
: Add the keywords in *list* to the predefined set of keywords *setname*. See the manpage for details.

`-l`
: Generate a list of misspelled words (batch mode).

`-L` *number*
: Show *number* lines of context.

`-m`
: Suggest different root/affix combinations.

`-M`
: List interactive commands at bottom of screen.

`-n`
: Expect `nroff` or `troff` input file.

`-N`
: Suppress printing of interactive commands.

`-p` *file*
: Search *file* instead of personal dictionary file.

`-P`
: Do not attempt to suggest more root/affix combinations.

`-S`
: Sort suggested replacements by likelihood that they are correct.

`-t`
: Expect TeX or LaTeX input file.

-T *type*
: Expect all files to be formatted by *type*.

-v, -vv
: With plain -v, print version information and exit. With -vv, also print compilation options.

-V
: Use hat notation (^L) to display control characters, and M- to display characters with the high bit set.

-w *chars*
: Consider *chars* to be legal, in addition to a–z and A–Z.

-W *n*
: Never consider words that are *n* characters or fewer to be misspelled.

-x
: Do not back up the original file.

Interactive commands

?
: Display help screen.

space
: Accept the word in this instance.

number
: Replace with suggested word that corresponds to *number*.

!*command*
: Invoke shell and execute *command* in it. Prompt before exiting.

a
: Accept word as correctly spelled, but do not add it to personal dictionary.

i
: Accept word and add it (with any current capitalization) to personal dictionary.

l
: Search system dictionary for words.

q
: Exit without saving.

r
: Replace word.

u
: Accept word and add lowercase version of it to personal dictionary.

x
: Skip to the next file, saving changes.

^L
: Redraw screen.

^Z
: Suspend ispell.

ltrace

`ltrace [options] command [arguments]`

Trace the dynamic library calls for *command* and *arguments*. ltrace can also trace and print the system calls. It is very similar to strace (see also **strace**).

Options

-a *n*
: Align the return values in column *n*.

-c
: Count all calls and signals and create a summary report when the program has ended.

`-C, --demangle`
: Demangle C++ encoded names.

`-d, --debug`
: Debug mode. Print debugging information for `ltrace` on standard error.

`-e [`*keyword*`=][!]`*values*
: Pass an expression to `ltrace` to limit the types of calls or signals that are traced or to change how they are displayed. See **strace** for the full list.

`-f`
: Trace forked processes.

`-h, --help`
: Print help and exit.

`-i`
: Print instruction pointer with each system call.

`-l` *file*`, --library` *file*
: Print only the symbols from library *file*. Up to 20 files may be specified.

`-L`
: Do not display library calls. Use together with `-S`.

`-n` *count*`, --indent` *count*
: Indent trace output by *count* spaces for each new nested function call.

`-o` *filename*`, --output` *filename*
: Write output to *filename* instead of standard error. If *filename* starts with the pipe symbol |, treat the rest of the name as a command to which output should be piped.

`-p` *pid*
: Attach to the given process ID and begin tracking. `ltrace` can track more than one process if more than one `-p` option is given. Type CTRL-C to end the trace.

`-r`
: Relative timestamp. Print time in microseconds between system calls.

`-s` *n*
: Print only the first *n* characters of a string. Default value is 32.

`-S`
: Display system calls and library calls.

`-t`
: Print time of day on each line of output.

`-tt`
: Print time of day with microseconds on each line of output.

`-ttt`
: Print timestamp on each line as number of seconds since the Epoch.

`-T`
: Print time spent in each system call.

`-u` *username*
: Run command as *username*. Needed when tracing `setuid` and `setgid` programs.

`-V`
: Print version and exit.

lynx lynx [*options*] [*path* | *URL*]

lynx is a "text mode" browser, for use on ASCII terminals or terminal emulators. It is particularly valuable for taking a quick look at a web page when you don't want to wait for a graphical browser to start up on a heavily loaded system, and for use in scripts. It has an astonishing number of options.

URL: *http://lynx.isc.org/*.

Primary Options

`-`
: Read arguments from standard input. Useful for long command lines and to avoid having sensitive arguments being visible with ps.

`-base`
: For use with `-source`, prepend a request URL and BASE tag to text or HTML outputs.

`-case`
: Make string searching case-sensitive.

`-color`
: For use with the *slang* terminal library. Enable a default set of color control sequences that work on many terminals if the terminal description does not provide color control information.

`-crawl`
: When used with `-traversal`, output each page to a separate file. When used with `-dump`, output is formatted as for `-traversal` but sent to standard output.

`-dump`
: Send the formatted output to standard output. Useful for converting web pages to text files.

`-editor=`*program*
: Use *program* as the external editor.

`-emacskeys`
: Enable Emacs-style motion commands.

`-ftp`
: Disallow FTP access.

`-justify`
: Do text justification.

`-source`
: Like `-dump`, but outputs HTML source, not formatted text.

`-telnet`
: Do not allow telnet commands.

`-term=`*termtype*
: Specify that the terminal is of type *termtype*. Especially useful for remote connections.

`-traversal`
: Traverse all the HTTP links derived from the starting file or URL.

`-use_mouse`
: Enable mouse actions if the underlying library supports the mouse. The left mouse button traverses a link and the right button pops back. Clicking on the top and bottom lines scroll up and down. For the *ncurses* library, the middle button pops up a simple menu.

`-vikeys`
: Enable vi-style motion commands.

`-width=`*count*
: Use *count* columns for formatting dumps. The default is 80.

`-with_backspaces`
: For `-dump` and `-crawl`, place backspaces in the output (similar to the `man` command).

See the manpage for a description of the other options.

---

mac2unix

`mac2unix [`*options*`] [-n `*infile outfile*`]`

Convert files from Macintosh OS 9 format to Unix format. On GNU/Linux, the `dos2unix` and `unix2dos` commands accept the same options as `mac2unix`. See **dos2unix** in the earlier section "Alphabetical Summary of Common Commands" for the option list.

---

md5sum

`md5sum [`*options*`] [`*file* ...`]`
`md5sum [`*options*`]` *--check* `[`*file*`]`

Compute or check the MD5 algorithm checksum for one or more files. The checksum is computed using the algorithm in RFC 1321. Use the saved output of the program as input when checking. See also **sha1sum**.

Options

`-b, --binary`
: Use binary mode to read files. This is the default on non-Unix systems.

`-c, --check`
: Check MD5 sums against the given list.

`--status`
: Do not print anything. Instead, use the exit code to indicate success.

`-t, --text`
: Read files in "text" mode. This is the default on Unix systems.

`-w, --warn`
: Warn about checksum lines that are not formatted correctly.

Examples

```
$ md5sum bash-3.0.tar.gz > MD5SUM          Compute and save checksum
$ cat MD5SUM                               Show it
26c4d642e29b3533d8d754995bc277b3  bash-3.0.tar.gz
$ md5sum --check < MD5SUM                  Verify it
bash-3.0.tar.gz: OK
```

mount

```
mount [options] [[device] directory]
```

System administration command. Mount a file structure. The file structure on *device* is mounted on *directory*. If no *device* is specified, `mount` looks for an entry in `/etc/fstab` to find what device is associated with the given directory. The directory, which must already exist and should be empty, becomes the name of the root of the newly mounted file structure. If `mount` is invoked with no arguments, it displays the name of each mounted device, the directory on which it is mounted, its filesystem type, and any mount options associated with the device.

Options

`-a` Mount all filesystems listed in `/etc/fstab`. Use `-t` to limit this to all filesystems of a particular type.

`-f` Fake mount. Go through the motions of checking the device and directory, but do not actually mount the filesystem.

`-F` When used with `-a`, fork a new process to mount each filesystem.

`-h` Print help message, then exit.

`-i` For a filesystem type *fs*, don't run the helper program `/sbin/mount.`*fs*.

`-l` When reporting on mounted filesystems, show filesystem labels for filesystems that have them.

`-L` *label*
Mount filesystem with the specified label.

`-n` Do not record the mount in `/etc/mtab`.

`-o` *option*
Qualify the mount with a mount option. Many filesystem types have their own options. The following are common to most filesystems:

`async`
Do input and output to the device asynchronously.

`atime`, `noatime`
Update inode access time for each access. This is the default behavior. `noatime` does not update the access time.

`auto`, `noauto`
Allow (do not allow) mounting with the `-a` option.

`defaults`
Use all options' default values (`async`, `auto`, `dev`, `exec`, `nouser`, `rw`, `suid`).

`dev`, `nodev`
The `dev` option allows the system to interpret any special devices that exist on the filesystem as device files. The `nodev` option disallows it; device files are ignored.

`dirsync`
: All directory updates on the filesystem should be done synchronously.

`exec`, `noexec`
: The exec option allows the system to execute binary files on the filesystem. The `noexec` option disallows it.

`_netdev`
: Filesystem is a network device requiring network access.

`remount`
: Expect the filesystem to have already been mounted, and remount it.

`ro`
: Allow read-only access to the filesystem.

`rw`
: Allow read/write access to the filesystem.

`suid`, `nosuid`
: Acknowledge (do not acknowledge) setuid and setgid bits.

`user`, `nouser`
: Allow (do not allow) unprivileged users to mount or unmount the filesystem. The defaults on such a filesystem will be `nodev`, `noexec`, and `nosuid`, unless otherwise specified.

`users`
: Allow any user to mount or unmount the filesystem. The defaults on such a filesystem will be `nodev`, `noexec`, and `nosuid`, unless otherwise specified.

`-O` *option*
: Limit systems mounted with `-a` by its filesystem options. (As used with `-o`.) Use a comma-separated list to specify more than one option, and prefix an option with `no` to exclude filesystems with that option. Options `-t` and `-O` are cumulative.

`-p` *fd*
: For an encrypted filesystem, read the passphrase from file descriptor number *fd*.

`-r`
: Mount filesystem read-only.

`-s`
: Where possible, ignore mount options specified by `-o` that are not supported by the filesystem.

`-t` *type*
: Specify the filesystem type. Possible values include `adfs`, `affs`, `autofs`, `coda`, `cramfs`, `devpts`, `efs`, `ext2`, `ext3`, `hfs`, `hpfs`, `iso9660`, `jfs`, `msdos`, `ncpfs`, `nfs`, `nfs4` `ntfs`, `proc`, `qnx4`, `ramfs`, `reiserfs`, `romfs`, `smbfs`, `sysv`, `tmpfs`, `udf`, `ufs`, `umsdos`, `usbfs`, `vfat`, and `xfs`. The default type is `iso9660`. The type `auto` may also be used to have `mount` autodetect the filesystem. When used with `-a`, this option can limit the types mounted. Use a comma-separated list to specify more than one type to mount, and prefix a type with `no` to exclude that type.

-U *uuid*
: Mount filesystem with the specified *uuid*.

-v
: Display mount information verbosely.

-V
: Print version, then exit.

-w
: Mount filesystem read/write. This is the default.

Files

/etc/fstab
: List of filesystems to be mounted and options to use when mounting them.

/etc/mtab
: List of filesystems currently mounted and the options with which they were mounted.

/proc/partitions
: Used to find filesystems by label and UUID.

---

mutt

mutt [*reading-options*]
mutt [*sending-options*] *address* ...

mutt is a screen-oriented Mail User Agent (MUA) program, for reading and sending mail. Its design is derived from that of several earlier MUA programs, including Berkeley Mail, ELM, and MUSH: hence the name.

URL: *http://www.mutt.org/*.

Options

-a *file*
: Attach *file* to the message using MIME.

-b *address*
: Send a blind carbon copy (BCC) to *address*.

-c *address*
: Send a carbon copy (CC) to *address*.

-e *command*
: Run *command* after reading the configuration files.

-f *file*
: Use *file* as the mailbox to read messages from.

-F *muttrcfile*
: Read *muttrcfile* for initialization, instead of $HOME/.muttrc.

-h
: Print an option summary and exit.

-H *draftfile*
: Read an initial message header and body from *draftfile* when sending a message.

-i *file*
: Include the contents of *file* into a message.

`-m` *type*
: Use mailbox type *type*. Possible values are `mbox`, `MMDF`, `MH`, and `Maildir`.

`-n` Do not read the sytsem configuration file `/etc/Muttrc`.

`-p` Continue a postponed message.

`-R` Process a mailbox in read-only mode.

`-s` *text*
: Use *text* as the subject of the message.

`-v` Print version and compile-time option information, and exit.

`-x` Emulate the `mailx` compose mode.

`-y` At startup, list all mailboxes specified with the `mailboxes` command.

`-z` When used with `-f`, do not start if the mailbox is empty.

`-Z` Process the first mailbox specified with the `mailboxes` command that contains new mail. If there are none, exit immediately.

---

ooffice

`ooffice [`*files*`]`

The Open Office office productivity suite. A set of commands that provides compatibility with other widely used office productivity programs.

URL: *http://www.openoffice.org/*.

Tools

Calc
: A "feature-packed" spreadsheet program with built-in charting tools.

Database tools
: Tools for doing database work in spreadsheet-like form. The tools support dBASE databases for simple applications, or OODBC or JDBC compliant databases for "industrial strength" work.

Draw
: A program for producing illustrations.

Impress
: A program for creating multimedia presentations.

Math
: A component for use with Writer in creating equations and formulae, it may also be used standalone.

Writer
: A word processor for documents, reports, newsletters, brochures, etc.

pdksh

`pdksh [options] [arguments ...]`

The Public Domain Korn Shell. pdksh is a fairly complete although not exact clone of the 1988 Korn shell. Full details are available in the online manpage and at the web site. For more information about the Korn shell, see Chapter 4.

URL: *http://web.cs.mun.ca/~michael/pdksh/*.

ps

`ps [options]`

Report on active processes. ps has three types of options. GNU long options start with two dashes, which are required. BSD options may be grouped and do not start with a dash, while Unix98 options may be grouped and require an initial dash. The meaning of the short options can vary depending on whether or not there is a dash. In options, *list* arguments should either be separated by commas or put in double quotes. In comparing the amount of output produced, note that e prints more than a and l prints more than f for each entry.

Options

nums, p *nums*, -p *nums*, --pid=*nums*
: Include only specified processes, which are given in a space-delimited list.

--*nums*, --sid=*nums*
: Include only specified session IDs, which are given in a space-delimited list.

[-]a
: As a, list all processes on a terminal. As -a, list all processes on a terminal except session leaders.

[-]c
: As c, show the true command name. As -c, show different scheduler information with -l.

-C *cmds*
: Select by command name.

--cols=*cols*, --columns=*cols*, --width=*cols*
: Set the output width (the number of columns to display).

-d
: Select all processes except session leaders.

-e, -A
: Select all processes.

e
: Include environment information after the command.

[-]f, -F, --forest
: As -f, display full listing. As f or --forest, display "forest" family tree format, with ASCII art showing the relationships.

-g *list*, -G *list*, --group=*groups*, --Group=*groups*
: For -g, select by session leader if *list* contains numbers, or by group if it contains group names. For -G, select by the group IDs in *list*. --group selects by effective group and --Group

selects by real group, where *groups* can be either group names or group IDs.

`h, --no-headers`
: Suppress header. If you select a BSD personality by setting the environment variable PS_PERSONALITY to `bsd`, then `h` prints a header on each page.

`H, -H`
: As `H`, display threads as if they were processes. As `-H`, display "forest" family tree format, without ASCII art.

`--headers`
: Repeat headers.

`--info`
: Print debugging information.

`[-]j`
: Jobs format. `j` prints more information than `-j`.

`[-]l`
: Produce a long listing. `-l` prints more information than `l`.

`L, -L`
: As `L`, print list of field specifiers that can be used for output formatting or for sorting. As `-L`, show threads, possibly with LWP and NLWP columns.

`--lines=`*`num`*`, --rows=`*`num`*
: Set the screen height to *num* lines. If `--headers` is also set, the headers repeat every *num* lines.

`[-]m`
: Show threads.

`-M` Add security data for SELinux.

`n` Print user IDs and `WCHAN` numerically.

`-n`*`file`*`, N`*`file`*
: Specify the system map file for `ps` to use as a namelist file. The map file must correspond to the Linux kernel; e.g., `/boot/System.map-2.6.9-1.667`.

`-N, --deselect`
: Negate the selection.

`[-]o` *`fields`*`, --format=`*`fields`*
: As `-o`, `o`, or `--format`, specify user-defined format with a list of fields to display.

`[-]O` *`fields`*
: As `-O`, is like `-o`, but some common fields are predefined. As `O`, can be either the same as `-O` in specifying fields to display, or can specify single-letter fields for sorting. For sorting, each field specified as a key can optionally have a leading `+` (return to default sort direction on key) or `-` (reverse the default direction).

`--ppid` *`pids`*
: Include only processes whose parent process IDs are in *pids*.

`r` Show only processes that are currently running.

`s` Display signal format.

`-s` *`sessions`*
: Show processes belonging to the specified sessions.

`S, --cumulative`
: As `S`, sum up certain information, such as CPU usage from dead children. Otherwise, include some dead child process data in parent total.

`--sort` *`sort-spec`*
: Like `O` for sorting.

`[-]t[`*`ttys`*`], --tty=`*`ttys`*
: Display processes running on the specified terminals. As `t`, *ttys* may be missing, which specifies the current terminal.

`T`
: Display all processes on this terminal.

`[-]u [`*`users`*`], --user=`*`users`*
: As `u` with no argument, display user-oriented output . As `-u` or `--users`, display by effective user ID (and also support names), showing results for *users*. With no argument, `-u` displays results for the current user.

`[-]U` *`users`*`, --User=`*`users`*
: As `U`, display processes for the specified users. As `-U` or `--User`, display processes for *users* by real user ID (and also support names).

`v`
: Display virtual memory format.

`[-]V, --version`
: Display version information and then exit.

`[-]w`
: Wide format. Don't truncate long lines.

`x`
: Display processes without an associated terminal.

`X`
: Use old Linux i386 register format.

`-y`
: Do not show flags; show `rss` instead of `addr`.

`[-]Z, --context`
: As `Z`, add security data for SELinux. As `-Z`, display the security context format, also for SELinux.

Sort keys

`c, cmd`	Name of executable.
`C, pcpu`	CPU utilization.
`f, flags`	Flags.
`g, pgrp`	Group ID of process.
`G, tpgid`	Group ID of associated tty.
`j, cutime`	Cumulative user time.
`J, cstime`	Cumulative system time.
`k, utime`	User time.
`m, min_flt`	Number of minor page faults.
`M, maj_flt`	Number of major page faults.
`n, cmin_flt`	Total minor page faults.
`N, cmaj_flt`	Total major page faults.
`o, session`	Session ID.

`p, pid`	Process ID.
`P, ppid`	Parent's process ID.
`r, rss`	Resident set size.
`R, resident`	Resident pages.
`s, size`	Kilobytes of memory used.
`S, share`	Number of shared pages.
`t, tty`	Terminal.
`T, start_time`	Process's start time.
`u, user`	User's name.
`U, uid`	User ID.
`v, vsize`	Bytes of virtual memory used.
`y, priority`	Kernel's scheduling priority.

Fields

`%CPU`	Percent of CPU time used recently.
`%MEM`	Percent of memory used.
`ADDR`	Address of the process.
`BLOCKED`	Mask of blocked signals.
`C`	CPU utilization percentage.
`CAUGHT`	Mask of caught signals.
`CLS, POL`	Process scheduling class.
`CMD, COMMAND`	The command the process is running.
`CP`	Per-mill CPU usage.
`EGID, GID`	Effective group ID as a decimal integer.
`EGROUP, GROUP`	Effective group ID as a name if available, otherwise as a number.
`EIP`	Instruction pointer.
`ELAPSED`	Elapsed time since the start of the process.
`ESP`	Stack pointer.
`EUID, UID`	Effective user ID as a decimal integer.
`EUSER, USER`	Effective user ID as a name if available, otherwise as a number.
`F`	Process flags: `001` Print alignment warning messages. `002` Being created. `004` Being shut down. `010` `ptrace(0)` has been called. `020` Tracing system calls. `040` Forked but didn't exec. `100` Used superuser privileges. `200` Dumped core. `400` Killed by a signal.
`FGID`	Filesystem access group ID as a decimal integer.
`FGROUP`	Filesystem access group ID as a name if available, otherwise as a number.
`FUID`	Filesystem access user ID as a decimal integer.
`FUSER`	Filesystem access user ID as a name if available, otherwise as a number.
`IGNORED`	Mask of ignored signals.
`LABEL`	SELinux security label for Mandatory Access Control.

LWP, SPID, TID	Lightweight process (thread) ID.
NI	The nice value of the process. A higher number indicates less CPU priority.
NLWP, THCNT	Number of lightweight processes (threads) in the process.
PENDING	Mask of pending signals.
PGID, PGRP	Process group ID.
PID	Process ID.
PPID	Parent process ID.
PRI	Process's scheduling priority. A higher number indicates lower priority.
P, PSR	Processor that the process is assigned to.
RGID	Real group ID as a decimal integer.
RGROUP	Real group ID as a name if available, otherwise as a number.
RSS, RSZ	Resident set size (the amount of physical memory), in kilobytes.
RTPRIO	Realtime priority.
RUID	Real user ID as a decimal integer.
RUSER	Real user ID as a name if available, otherwise as a number.
S	One-character state display.
SCH	Process's scheduling policy.
SESS, SID	Process's session ID.
SGID, SVGID	Saved group ID as a decimal integer.
SGROUP	Saved group ID as a name if available, otherwise as a number.
SHARE	Shared memory.
SIZE	Size of virtual image.
STACKP	Address of the bottom (start) of the process's stack.
START	Process start time in HH:MM format.
STARTED	Process start time in HH:MM:SS format.
STAT	Status: D Asleep and not interruptible. N Positive nice value (third field). R Runnable. S Asleep. T Stopped. W No resident pages (second field). Z Zombie.
SUID, SVUID	Saved user ID as a decimal integer.
SUSER	Saved user ID as a name if available, otherwise as a number.
SWAP	Amount of swap used, in kilobytes.
SZ	Approximate amount of swap needed to write out entire process.
TIME	Cumulative CPU time.
TPGID	Foreground process group ID for terminal.
TRS	Size of resident text.
TT, TTY	Associated terminal.
VSZ	Virtual memory size, in kilobytes.
WCHAN	Kernel function in which process resides.

rename

rename *from to files* ...

Rename *files* by replacing the first occurrence of *from* in each filename with *to*.

Example

Rename files that start with `test` so they start with `mytest`:

```
rename test mytest test*
```

seq

seq [*options*] [*first* [*increment*]] *last*

Print the numbers from *first* through *last* by *increment*. The default is to print one number per line to standard output. Both *first* and *increment* can be omitted and default to 1, but if *first* is omitted then *increment* must also be omitted. In other words, if only two numbers are specified, they are taken to be the first and last numbers. The numbers are treated as floating point.

Options

-f *format*, --format=*format*
: Write the output using the specified `printf` floating-point format, which can be one of `%e`, `%f`, or `%g` (the default).

-s *string*, --separator=*string*
: Use *string* to separate numbers in the output. Default is newline.

-w, --equal-width
: Equalize the width of the numbers by padding with leading zeros. (Use `-f` for other types of padding.)

sha1sum

sha1sum [*options*] [*file* ...]
sha1sum [*options*] --check [*file*]

Compute or check SHA1 160-bit checksums for one or more files. The checksum is computed using the algorithm in FIPS-180-1. Use the saved output of the program as input when checking. See also **md5sum**.

Options

-b, --binary
: Use binary mode to read files. This is the default on non-Unix systems.

-c, --check
: Check SHA1 sums against the given list.

--status
: Do not print anything. Instead, use the exit code to indicate success.

-t, --text
: Read files in "text" mode. This is the default on Unix systems.

-w, --warn
: Warn about checksum lines that are not formatted correctly.

Examples

```
$ sha1sum bash-3.0.tar.gz > SHA1SUM        Compute and save checksum
$ cat SHA1SUM                              Show it
3acf1ff4910d4bc863620c7533cbf4858370017b  bash-3.0.tar.gz
$ sha1sum --check < SHA1SUM                Verify it
bash-3.0.tar.gz: OK
```


shred

shred [*options*] *files*

Overwrite a file to make the contents unrecoverable, and delete the file afterwards if requested.

Options

\-
: Shred standard output.

-*num*, --iterations=*num*
: Overwrite files *num* times (default is 25).

-f, --force
: Force permissions to allow writing to *files*.

-s *num*, --size=*num*
: Shred *num* bytes. *num* can be expressed with suffixes (e.g., K, M, or G).

-u, --remove
: Remove file after overwriting. shred does not remove the file unless this option is specified.

-v, --verbose
: Verbose mode.

-x, --exact
: Shred the exact file size; do not round up to the next full block.

-z, --zero
: On the final pass, overwrite with zeros to hide the shredding.

skill

skill [*signal*] [*options*] *processes*
snice [*priority*] [*options*] *processes*

Send a signal to *processes* or reset the priority. The default signal for skill is TERM, and the default priority for snice is +4 but can be in the range +20 (slowest) to –20 (fastest). The selection options -c, -p, -t, and -u are not required, but can be specified to insure that *processes* are interpreted correctly.

Options

-c
: The next argument is a command.

-i
: Use interactive mode.

-l, -L
: List available signals.

-n
: Display the process ID, but take no other action.

-p
: The next argument is a process ID.

-t
: The next argument is a tty or pty.

-u
: The next argument is a username.

-v
: Verbose mode.

-w
: Enable warnings.

---

slocate

`slocate [`*options*`] [`*search-string*`]`

Security Enhanced version of GNU `locate`. This command searches a database listing every file on the system; it is intended as a faster replacement for `find / -name` *pattern* .... (See **locate** in the "Alphabetical Summary of Common Commands" section earlier in this chapter). This version stores file permissions and ownership, in order to prevent unauthorized access to files.

URL: *http://www.geekreview.org/slocate/*.

Options

-c
: Read `/etc/updatedb.conf` when updating the database.

-d *file*, --database=*file*
: Use *file* as the database to search.

-e *dir1*[,*dir2*...]
: Exclude the given directories from the database.

-f *fstype1*[,*fstype2*...]
: Exclude files on filesystems of the given types (e.g., NFS).

-h, --help
: Print an option summary and exit.

-i
: Ignore case when searching.

-l *level*
: Security level. If *level* is `0`, no security checks are done, providing faster searches. The default is `1`, which turns on security checking.

-n *count*
: Do not print more than *count* results.

-o *file*, --output=*file*
: Use *file* as the database to create.

-q
: Do not print error messages (quiet mode).

-r *regex*, --regexp=*regex*
: Use the Basic Regular Expression *regex* to search the database.

-u
: Create the database starting at `/`.

-U *dir*
: Create the database starting at *dir*.

`-v, --verbose`
: Display filenames when creating the database.

`-V, --version`
: Print version information and exit.

splint

`splint [options] files ...`

Secure Programming Lint. A freely available version of the original Unix `lint` command, `splint` performs static checking of C programs. By adding annotations in the form of special comments to your source files, `splint` can perform many additional, stronger checks than would otherwise be possible.

`splint` has a very large number of options. They are broken down here into separate sections based on task. `splint` allows the use of a leading + and a leading minus to indicate an option. In many cases they do the same thing; in others one enables a feature while the other disables it.

URL: *http://www.splint.org/*.

Initialization Options

`-f` *`file`*
: Read options from *file* instead of from `$HOME/.splintrc`.

`-I`*`dir`*
: Add *dir* to the list of directories searched for C include files. As with the C compiler, there is no space separating the `-I` from the directory name.

`-nof`
: Do not read either of the default option files `./.splintrc` and `$HOME/.splintrc`.

`-S` *`dir`*
: Add *dir* to the list of directories searched for `.lcl` specification files.

`-tmpdir` *`directory`*
: Use *directory* for temporary files. The default is `/tmp`.

`-systemdirs` *`dirlist`*
: Set the list of system directories to search for include files. The default is `/usr/include`. To include multiple directories, separate them with a colon.

`-systemdirerrors`
: Do not report errors for files in system directories.

Preprocessor Options

`-D` *`macro-definition`*
: Define a macro. This option is passed on to the C preprocessor.

`-U` *`macroname`*
: Undefine a macro. This option is passed on to the C preprocessor.

Library Options

`-1-lib`
: Use the Unix version of the standard library.

`-1-strict-lib`
: Use the "strict" version of the Unix standard library.

`-ansi-lib`
: Use the ANSI standard library. This is the default.

`-dump` *file*
: Save `splint`'s state in *file*. The default file extension is `.lcd`.

`-load` *file*
: Load state from *file*, created previously with `-dump`. See the online documentation for more information.

`-nolib`
: Do not load information about any library. This also prevents loading information about the standard C library.

`-posix-lib`
: Use the POSIX version of the standard library.

`-posix-strict-lib`
: Use the "strict" version of the POSIX standard library.

`-strict-lib`
: Use the "strict" version of the ANSI standard library.

Output Options

Use a leading minus to disable these options, and a leading + to enable them. By default they are all disabled.

`-limit` *count*
: Do not report more than *count* similar errors consecutively. Instead, show a count of suppressed errors.

`-quiet`
: Do not print version information or the error count summary.

`-showalluses`
: Print a list of external identifiers and their uses, sorted by the number of times each one is used.

`-showscan`
: Print each filename as it's processed.

`-showsummary`
: Print a summary of reported and suppressed errors. The count of suppressed errors may not be completely correct.

`-stats`
: Print the number of lines processed and the time it took to check them.

`-timedist`
: Print a distribution showing where the checking time was spent.

`-usestderr`
: Send error messages to standard error instead of to standard output.

`-whichlib`
: Print the filename and creation info for the standard library.

Expected Errors Option

`-expect` *count*
: Expect *count* errors. Exit with a failure status if exactly that number of errors are not detected. Useful for use with `make`.

Message Format Options

For most of these options, a leading + turns on the behavior, whereas a leading minus turns it off. You may use either one for the `-limit` and `-linelen` options.

`-forcehints`
: Similar to `-hints`, but provide hints for all errors in a class, not just the first one. Default is off.

`-hints`
: Give hints describing the error and how to suppress it for the first error in each error class. Default is on.

`-linelen` *count*
: Set the maximum line length for a message line to *count*. Default is 80.

`-paren-file-format`
: Use messages of the form `file(line)`.

`-showallconj`
: Print all possible alternate types. See the online documentation for more information. Default is off.

`-showcolumn`
: Print the column number of the error. Default is on.

`-showfunc`
: Print the name of the macro or function containing the error. Function names are only printed once. Default is on.

Mode Options

The mode flags enable a coarse-grain grouping of different classes of checking. For more detail, use `splint -help modes`. From weakest to strongest, the options are `-weak`, `-standard`, `-checks`, and `-strict`.

`-checks`
: Strict checking. It does the same checking as `-standard`, plus must modification checking, rep exposure, return alias, memory management, and complete interfaces.

`-standard`
: This is the default. It does the same checking as `-weak`, plus modifies checking, global alias checking, use all parameters, using released storage, ignored return values of any type, macro checking, unreachable code, infinite loops, and fall-through cases. Old style declarations are reported. The types `bool`, `int`, and `char` are treated as being distinct.

`-strict`
: "Absurdly strict checking." Does the same checking as `-checks`, plus modifications and global variables used in unspecified functions, strict standard library, and strict typing of C operators. The manpage states "A special reward will be presented

to the first person to produce a real program that produces no errors with strict checking."

`-weak`
: Checking intended for unannotated C code. In particular, `splint` does *not* do modifies checking, macro checking, rep exposure, or clean interface checking. It is allowed to ignore `int` return values. Old style declarations are not reported. The types `bool`, `int`, `char`, and `enum` are treated as being the same.

---

strace

`strace [`*`options`*`]`*`command`*`[`*`arguments`*`]`

Trace the system calls and signals for *command* and *arguments*. `strace` shows you how data is passed between the program and the system kernel. With no options, `strace` prints a line to standard error for each system call. It shows the call name, arguments given, return value, and any error messages generated. A signal is printed with both its signal symbol and a descriptive string.

Options

`-a` *n* Align the return values in column *n*.

`-c` Count all calls and signals and create a summary report when the program has ended.

`-d` Debug mode. Print debugging information for `strace` on standard error.

`-e [`*`keyword`*`=][!]`*`values`*
: Pass an expression to `strace` to limit the types of calls or signals that are traced or to change how they are displayed. If no *keyword* is given, `trace` is assumed. The *values* can be given as a comma-separated list. Preceding the list with an exclamation mark (!) negates the list. The special *values* `all` and `none` are valid, as are the *values* listed with the following *keywords*.

  `abbrev=`*`names`*
  : Abbreviate output from large structures for system calls listed in *names*.

  `read=`*`descriptors`*
  : Print all data read from the given file *descriptors*.

  `signal=`*`symbols`*
  : Trace the listed signal *symbols* (for example, `signal=SIGIO,SIGHUP`).

  `trace=`*`sets`*
  : *sets* may be a list of system call names or one of the following:

`file`	Calls that take a filename as an argument
`ipc`	Interprocess communication
`network`	Network-related
`process`	Process management
`signal`	Signal-related

`raw=`*`names`*
: Print arguments for the given system calls in hexadecimal.

`verbose=`*`names`*
: Unabbreviate structures for the given system calls. Default is `none`.

`write=`*`descriptors`*
: Print all data written to the given file *descriptors*.

`-E` *`var`*`[=`*`val`*`]`
: With no *val*, remove *var* from the environment before running *command*. Otherwise, run *command* with environment variable *var* defined to *val* in the environment.

`-f` Trace forked processes.

`-ff` Write system calls for forked processes to separate files named *filename.pid* when using the `-o` option.

`-h` Print help and exit.

`-i` Print instruction pointer with each system call.

`-o` *`filename`*
: Write output to *filename* instead of standard error. If *filename* starts with the pipe symbol |, treat the rest of the name as a command to which output should be piped.

`-O` *`n`* Override `strace`'s built-in timing estimates, and just subtract *n* microseconds from the timing of each system call to adjust for the time it takes to measure the call.

`-p` *`pid`*
: Attach to the given process ID and begin tracing. `strace` can trace more than one process if more than one `-p` option is given. Type CTRL-C to end the trace.

`-q` Quiet mode. Suppress attach and detach messages.

`-r` Relative timestamp. Print time in microseconds between system calls.

`-s` *`n`* Print only the first *n* characters of a string. Default value is 32.

`-S` *`value`*
: Sort output of `-c` option by the given *value*. *value* may be `calls`, `name`, `time`, or `nothing`. Default is `time`.

`-t` Print time of day on each line of output.

`-tt` Print time of day with microseconds on each line of output.

`-ttt`
: Print timestamp on each line as number of seconds since the Epoch.

`-T` Print time spent in each system call.

`-u` *`username`*
: Run command as *username*. Needed when tracing setuid and setgid programs.

`-v` Verbose. Do not abbreviate structure information.

`-V` Print version and exit.

-x Print all non-ASCII strings in hexadecimal.

-xx Print all strings in hexadecimal.

umount

`umount [options] [directory | special-device]`

System administration command. Unmount a filesystem. `umount` announces to the system that the removable file structure previously mounted on the specified directory is to be removed. `umount` also accepts the *special-device* to indicate the filesystem to be unmounted; however, this usage is obsolete and will fail if the device is mounted on more than one directory. Any pending I/O for the filesystem is completed, and the file structure is flagged as clean. A busy filesystem (one with open files or with a directory that is some process's current directory) cannot be unmounted.

Options

`-a` Unmount all filesystems that are listed in `/etc/mtab`.

`-d` If the unmounted device was a loop device, free the loop device too. See also *losetup*(8).

`-f` Force the unmount.

`-h` Print help message and exit.

`-l` Lazy unmount. Detach the filesystem from the hierarchy immediately, but don't clean up references until it is no longer busy. Requires kernel 2.4.11 or later.

`-n` Unmount, but do not record changes in `/etc/mtab`.

`-O` *options*
: Unmount only filesystems with the specified options in `/etc/fstab`. Specify multiple options as a comma-separated list. Add `no` as a prefix to an option to indicate filesystems that should not be unmounted.

`-r` If unmounting fails, try to remount read-only.

`-t` *type*
: Unmount only filesystems of type *type*. Multiple types can be specified as a comma-separated list, and any type can be prefixed with `no` to specify that filesystems of that type should not be unmounted.

`-v` Verbose mode.

`-V` Print version information and exit.

watch

`watch [options] command [cmd_options]`

Run the specified command repeatedly (by default, every 2 seconds) and display the output so you can watch it change over time. The command and any options are passed to `sh -c`, so you may need to use quotes to get correct results.

Options

`-d, --differences[=cumulative]`
: Highlight changes between iterations. If `cumulative` is specified, the highlighting remains on the screen throughout, giving a cumulative picture of the changes.

`-h, --help`
: Display help message and exit.

`-n` *`secs`*`, --interval=`*`secs`*
: Run the command every *secs* seconds.

`-t, --no-title`
: Do not print a header line.

`-v, --version`
: Print version information and exit.

---

wget

`wget [`*`options`*`] [`*`URL`*` ...]`

`wget` retrieves files from the Internet, most often using FTP or HTTP. It is capable of following links embedded in retrieved files, making it possible to mirror entire web sites. It has a plethora of options, making it difficult to use easily. See also **curl** in the earlier section "Alphabetical Summary of Common Commands."

URL: *http://www.gnu.org/software/wget/*.

Primary Options

`-a` *`file`*`, --append-output=`*`file`*
: The same as `-o`, but output is appended to the file, instead of overwriting it.

`-b, --background`
: Start off in the background. If no log file is specified with `-o`, use `wget-log`.

`-c, --continue`
: Continue retrieving a file that was partially downloaded. Very useful if a previous download was interrupted. See the manpage for some version-dependent caveats.

`-d, --debug`
: Enable debugging output.

`-h, --help`
: Print a help message summarizing the options and exit.

`--http-passwd=`*`password`*
: Use *password* as the password when an HTTP server prompts for a user and password. See the manpage for a discussion of security issues.

`--http-user=`*`user`*
: Use *user* as the user when an HTTP server prompts for a user and password. See the manpage for a discussion of security issues.

`-I` *dirlist*, `--include-directories=`*dirlist*
When downloading, follow the directories in the comma-separated list *dirlist*. Elements in *dirlist* may contain wildcards.

`-l` *depth*, `--level=`*depth*
Set the maximum recursion level to *depth*. The default is five.

`-m, --mirror`
Enable options needed for mirroring. Equivalent to `-r -N -l inf --no-remove-listing`.

`--no-glob`
Turn off FTP globbing (wildcard expansion). Globbing is automatically enabled if a URL contains shell wildcard characters. URLs with such characters should be quoted to protect them from the shell.

`-nv, --non-verbose`
More verbose than `-q` but less verbose than `-v`. Only errors and basic information are printed.

`-o` *file*, `--output-file=`*file*
Log all messages to *file*, instead of to standard error.

`-P` *prefix*, `--directory-prefix=`*prefix*
Use *prefix* for the directory prefix, i.e., the directory under which all retrieved files are saved. The default is `.` (dot), i.e., the current directory.

`--passive-ftp`
Use passive FTP to retrieve files. Often needed for clients residing behind a firewall.

`--progress=`*type*
Set the progress indicator. Valid values are `dot` and `bar`, the default is `bar`.

`--proxy-passwd=`*password*
Use *password* as the password for authentication on a proxy server. See the manpage for a discussion of security issues.

`--proxy-user=`*user*
Use *user* as the user for authentication on a proxy server. See the manpage for a discussion of security issues.

`-q, --quiet`
Be quiet, printing no output.

`-r, --recursive`
Enable recursive retrieval.

`-t` *count*, `--tries=`*count*
Retry no more than *count* times. Use `0` or `inf` to retry infinitely. The default is to retry 20 times.

`-v, --verbose`
Be verbose. This is the default.

`-V, --version`
Print a version message and exit.

`-X dirlist, --exclude-directories=dirlist`
When downloading, exclude the directories in the comma-separated list *dirlist* from consideration. Elements in *dirlist* may contain wildcards.

`-Y val, --proxy=val`
Enable/disable proxy support. Use one of `on` or `off` for *val*.

See the manpage for a description of the other options.

xmlto

`xmlto [options] format file`

Convert a DocBook/XML file into a formatted file. The *format* is typically something like `pdf` or `html`. The *file* should be a text file containing DocBook/XML markup. `xmlto` applies a stylesheet to convert the document to the appropriate format, possibly formatting it in the process.

Available Formats

`dvi`	TeX DVI file.
`fo`	XSL-FO formatting objects.
`html`	Hypertext Markup Language.
`html-nochunks`	HTML, in one large file.
`htmlhelp`	HTML Help files.
`javahelp`	Java Help files.
`man`	Unix-style manpages.
`pdf`	Adobe's Portable Document Format (PDF) files.
`ps`	PostScript files.
`txt`	Plain text files.
`xhtml`	XHTML (XML-derived HTML) files.
`xhtml-nochunks`	XHTML, in one large file.

Options

`--extensions`
Enable stylesheet extensions for the toolchain in use.

`-m XSL-file`
Use the XSL in *XSL-file* to modify the stylesheet.

`-o dir`
Place output files in the directory *dir* instead of in the current directory.

`-p options`
Pass the *options* on to the post-processing program. Repeat `-p` to pass options on to the second stage post-processor. (This currently applies only to the `ps` format, which uses TeX to produce DVI and `dvips` to produce PostScript.)

`--searchpath path`
Add the directories in the colon-separated *path* to the search path for files to include.

--skip-validation
: Skip the normal validation check.

-x *stylesheet*
: Use *stylesheet* instead of picking one automatically.

Examples

Produce a PDF file from DocBook/XML input:

```
xmlto pdf brochure.xml
```

Generate HTML in a separate directory:

```
xmlto -o /share/webserver/brochure html brochure.xml
```

Alphabetical Summary of Mac OS X Commands

apply

`apply [options] command argument ...`

Apply *command* to one or more of the following *arguments* in turn. *command* may contain a % followed by a digit from 1 to 9. Such text is replaced with the corresponding following unused argument.

Options

-*N* Use arguments in groups of *N*. For example, -2 uses two arguments for each invocation of *command*. Occurrences of %*N* in *command* override this option.

-a *char*
: Use *char* instead of % as the special character to represent arguments.

-d Display the commands that would be executed, but don't actually execute them.

Example

Run awk against multiple test programs and data. The example uses brace expansion as in Bash and tcsh:

```
apply -2 'awk -f' test1.{awk,in} test2.{awk,in} test3.{awk,in}
```

chflags

`chflags [-R [-H | -L | -P]] flags file ...`

Change the file flags associated with *files*. The flags are additional control bits that can be displayed by using ls -lo.

Options

-H With -R, follow symbolic links on the command line. Symbolic links found during file traversal normally are not followed.

-L With -R, follow all symbolic links.

-P With -R, don't follow any symbolic links. This is the default.

-R Recursive. For each *file* that is a directory, change the flags in the entire contained directory hierarchy. Otherwise, just changes the flags for each named *file*.

Flags

`arch, archived`
: The archived flag (privileged user only)

`nodump`
: The nodump flag (owner or privileged user only)

`opaque`
: The opaque flag (owner or privileged user only)

`sappnd, sappend`
: The system append-only flag (privileged user only)

`schg, schange, simmutable`
: The system immutable flag (privileged user only)

`sunlnk, sunlink`
: The system undeletable flag (privileged user only)

`uappnd, uappend`
: The user append-only flag (owner or privileged user only)

`uchg, uchange, uimmutable`
: The user immutable flag (owner or privileged user only)

`uunlnk, uunlink`
: The user undeletable flag (owner or privileged user only)

Put the letters no in front of a flag name to clear the given flag. Symbolic links don't have flags, thus the operation always succeeds but makes no change.

---

chfn

`chfn [options] [user]`

Identical to chpass. See **chpass** for more information.

---

chpass

`chpass [options] [user]`

Change information in the user database. If supplied, the information for *user* is changed; otherwise, the current user's information is updated. Only a privileged user may change information for a different user, and several options are restricted to privileged users. chpass places the information into a temporary file and invokes an editor. Once the new values are filled in and the information is verified, the program updates the system's user database, /etc/master.passwd.

On Mac OS X, you are probably better off using the graphical system administration tools for user management.

Options

`-a` *list*
: Use the literal user database entry *list* directly. It is a colon-separated list of items as found in each line of `/etc/master.passwd`. Privileged users only.

`-e` *time*
: Set the account's expire time to *time*. Privileged users only.

`-p` *pass*
: Use *pass* as the encrypted password. See *getpwent*(3) for the implications of this option. Privileged users only.

`-s` *shell*
: Use *shell* as the user's shell. Valid shells are listed in `/etc/shells`.

---

chsh

`chsh [`*options*`] [`*user*`]`

Identical to `chpass`. See **chpass** for more information.

---

defaults

`defaults [`*options*`]` *command* `[`*arguments*`]`

Access or update the application defaults database. Most Mac OS X applications maintain a set of application defaults in a per-user database. The database provides storage for these defaults for when the application is not running. The `defaults` command provides access to this database from the Unix shell. Besides the per-user database, there is also a system-wide, global database of default values.

Applications are specified either by name with the `-app` option, or via a Java-style domain name, such as `com.apple.TextEdit`. Defaults are stored as key/value pairs. Keys are always strings, but values may be complicated structures such as arrays and dictionaries, or strings or binary data. They are stored as XML property lists.

It is inadvisable to change the defaults for an application that is running. The application will not see the change, and could potentially overwrite the new values when it exits.

Options

`-app` *appname*
: Access the defaults for application *appname*.

`-array`
: The value for a preference key is an array. The array values are given as separate arguments in a list. The new value overwrites any previous value for the key.

`-array-add`
: Like `-array`, but the new elements are appended to an existing array of values.

`-bool[ean]`
: The value for a preference key is a boolean. The value must be one of `TRUE`, `FALSE`, `YES`, or `NO`.

`-currentHost`
: Preference operations may be performed only on the current host.

`-data`
: The value for a preference key consists of raw data bytes. The data must be provided in hexadecimal.

`-date`
: The value for a preference key is a date.

`-dict`
: The value for a preference key is a dictionary. Dictionaries consist of key/value pairs. They are provided as separate arguments in key-pair, key-pair order. Any existing value for the key is replaced with the dictionary.

`-dict-add`
: Like `-dict`, but the key/value pairs are appended to an existing dictionary.

`-float`
: The value for a preference key is a floating point number.

`-g, -globalDomain, NSGlobalDomain`
: Access the global system defaults in the Global Domain. Note that `NSGlobalDomain` is a domain name, not really an option.

`-host` *`hostname`*
: Preference operations may be performed only on the host named *hostname*.

`-int[eger]`
: The value for a preference key is an integer.

`-string`
: The value for a preference key is a string.

Commands

`delete` *`domain`* `[`*`key`*`]`
: With a *key*, remove the given key from *domain*'s defaults. Without *key*, remove all the information for *domain*.

`domains`
: Print the names of all domains in the user's default system.

`find` *`string`*
: Look for *string* in the user's domain names, keys, and values, and print a list of found matches.

`help`
: Print a help message showing command formats.

`read [`*`domain`* `[`*`key`*`]]`
: With no *domain* or *key*, read all of the current user's defaults, for every domain. With just a *domain*, read all of the current user's defaults for that domain. With both a *domain* and a *key*, read the current user's default for the given key in the given domain. In all cases, the retrieved data are printed to standard output.

`read-type` *`domain key`*
Print the property list type for the key *key* in the domain *domain*.

`write` *`domain key value`*
Store *value* as the value for the key *key* in the application domain *domain*. Quote *value* if it contains whitespace or shell metacharacters.

`write` *`domain proplist`*
Store the property list *proplist* as the defaults for the application domain *domain*. The *proplist* must be a property list representation of a dictionary, and must be quoted so that it is a single argument.

developer

`/Developer/Tools/*`

The `/Developer/Tools` directory contains a number of programs primarily for use by developers. The following three programs are useful for general users as well; see their manpages for more information:

`CpMac`	Copy files, keeping multiple resource forks and HFS attributes intact
`MvMac`	Move or rename files while preserving resource forks and HFS metadata
`SplitForks`	Copy the resource fork and HFS attributes from `file` into `._file`.

The rest of the programs are:

`agvtool`	`firewire`	`pbprojectdump`	`SetFile`
`BuildStrings`	`GetFileInfo`	`PPCExplain`	`uninstall-dev`
`cvs-unwrap`	`MergePef`	`ResMerger`	`UnRezWack`
`cvs-wrap`	`packagemaker`	`Rez`	`WSMakeStubs`
`DeRez`	`pbhelpindexer`	`RezWack`	

ditto

`ditto [`*`options`*`]` *`files directory`*
`ditto [`*`options`*`]` *`directory1 directory2`*

Copies files and directories while preserving most file information, including resource fork and HFS metadata information when desired. `ditto` preserves the permissions, ownership, and timestamp of the source files in the copies. `ditto` overwrites identically named files in the target directory without prompting for confirmation.

`ditto` works like `cp` in the first synopsis form. However, the second form differs in that `cp -r` copies the entire *directory1* into an existing *directory2*, while `ditto` copies the contents of *directory1* into *directory2*, creating *directory2* if it doesn't already exist.

Options

`-arch` *arch*
: When copying fat binary files, copy only the code for CPU type *arch*. Fat binary files contain different code for different CPU architectures. The `-arch` flag allows you to "thin" the binary by copying only the code for the specified architecture. Possible values for *arch* include `ppc`, `m68k`, `i386`, `hppa`, and `sparc`.

`-bom` *pathname*
: When copying a directory, include in the copy only those items listed in BOM (Bill of Materials) file *pathname*. See *mkbom*(8), *lsbom*(8), and *bom*(5) for more information on BOM files.

`-c`
: Create a `cpio` archive at *directory2*.

`--extattr`
: Preserve POSIX extended attributes. This is the default.

`-h`, `--help`
: Print a usage message.

`-k`
: Specify that archives are PKZip format.

`--keepParent`
: Embed *directory1*'s parent directory in *directory2*.

`--nocache`
: Do not use the Mac OS X Unified Buffer Cache when copying files.

`--noextattr`
: Do not preserve POSIX extended attributes. Use with `--rsrc` to copy only resource forks and HFS metadata, without copying other extended attributes.

`--norsrc`
: When copying files, do not preserve any resource forks or HFS metadata information.

`--rsrc`
: When copying files, do include any resource fork and HFS metadata information.

`--sequesterRsrc`
: For PKZip archives, preserve resource forks and HFS metadata in the subdirectory `__MACOSX`. The resources will be found automatically when doing a PKZip extraction.

`-v`
: Be verbose; report each directory copied.

`-V`
: Be very verbose; report each file, symbolic link and device copied.

`-x`
: Treat *directory1* as a source archive and extract it. The assumed format is `cpio`, unless `-k` is used. Compressed `cpio` format is automatically recognized and handled.

`-X`
: Don't descend into directories on another device.

`-z`
: Create or read compressed `cpio` archives.

Example

Duplicate an entire home directory, copying the contents of `/Users/arnold` into the directory `/Volumes/Bigdisk/Users/arnold` and preserving resource forks and HFS metadata:

```
ditto --rsrc /Users/arnold "/Volumes/Big Disk/Users/arnold"
```

lam

`lam [`*options*`]` *file* ...

Laminate files. Lines are read from the given *files* and pasted together side by side. In other words, line 1 of the output is the concatenation of line 1 from each input file, line 2 is the concatenation of line 2 from each input file, and so on. Use `-` to mean standard input.

Options

`-f` *min.max*
: Use *min* as the minimum field width for the following *file*'s lines, and *max* as the maximum field width. *min* may start with a zero, in which case padding is done with zeros. It may also start with a `-`, in which case the output is left-adjusted.

`-F` *min.max*
: Like `-f`, but apply the field width specification to all following input files, until another `-f` is encountered.

`-p` *min.max*
: Like `-f`, but pad this file's field in the output if end-of-file is encountered on it while the other files still have data.

`-P` *min.max*
: Like `-p`, but apply the field width specification to all following input files, until another `-p` is encountered.

`-s` *sep*
: Print *sep* after the following file's line, before the line from the next file. Normally, the lines are joined without any intervening separator.

`-S` *sep*
: Like `-S`, but apply the separator specification to all following input files, until another `-s` is encountered.

`-t` *char*
: Input lines are terminated by the character *char*, instead of newline.

`-T` *char*
: Like `-t`, but apply the input line terminator specification to all following input files, until another `-t` is encountered.

leave

`leave [[+]`*hhmm*`]`

Remind you when you have to leave. The time given, *hhmm*, may be in 12 or 24-hour format. *hh* represents hours and *mm* represents minutes. The time is converted to the corresponding wall clock time in the upcoming 12 hours. *leave* prompts you to leave five minutes before, one minute before, and at the given time, and then every minute thereafter. With a leading +, the time is taken as an offset from the current time. With no argument, `leave` prompts you for a time; this is useful from a shell start-up file, such as `~/.profile` or `~/.login`. Logout, or kill it with `kill` in order to terminate it.

mount

`mount [`*options*`] [[`*device*`]` *directory*`]`

System administration command. Mount a filesystem. The filesystem on *device* is mounted on *directory*. If no *device* is specified, `mount` looks for an entry in `/etc/fstab` to find what device is associated with the given directory. The directory, which must already exist and should be empty, becomes the name of the root of the newly mounted filesystem. If `mount` is invoked with no arguments, it displays the name of each mounted device, the directory on which it is mounted, its filesystem type, and any mount options associated with the device. See also **umount**.

Note: despite the references in the Mac OS X *mount*(8) manpage to `/etc/fstab`, that file is not used. On Mac OS X 10.4, the file `/etc/fstab.hd` (note the slightly different name) has these contents:

```
$ cat /etc/fstab.hd
IGNORE THIS FILE.
This file does nothing, contains no useful data, and might
go away in future releases.  Do not depend on this file or
its contents.
```

Options

`-a` Mount all filesystems that are available for mounting. Use `-t` to limit this to all filesystems of a particular type. Filesystems marked `noauto` are not mounted.

`-d` Debugging; does everything but actually make the system call. Useful with `-v`.

`-f` Force removal of write status; used for changing a mount from read-write to read-only.

`-o` *option*
: Qualify the mount with a mount option. Filesystem specific options may be passed as a comma separated list in the argument to `-o`, and different filesystems may have additional options. The following general options are available:

`auto, noauto`
: Filesystems marked `auto` are mounted automatically with the `-a` option. Those marked `noauto` are not.

`async, noasync`
: The `async` option uses asynchronous I/O to the device. This can improve throughput at a potential cost in reliability. `noasync` disables this.

dev, nodev
: The dev option allows the system to interpret any special devices that exist on the filesystem as device files. The nodev option disallows it; device files are ignored.

exec, noexec
: The exec option allows the system to execute binary files on the filesystem. The noexec option disallows it.

force
: Identical to -f, removes write access from a mount.

nosuid
: Do not acknowledge any setuid or setgid bits.

rdonly
: Same as -r; the filesystem is mounted read-only.

sync
: All I/O is done synchronously.

union
: Merge the mounted filesystem's root and the contents of the directory upon which its mounted. Lookup operations are done in the mounted filesystem first, and then in the underlying directory. New files are created in the mounted filesystem.

update
: Same as -u, changes the status of an already mounted filesystem.

-r
: Mount the filesystem read-only.

-t *type*
: Specify the filesystem type. Possible values include afp, autofs, cd9660, cddafs, devfs, fdesc, ftp, hfs, ldf, msdos, nfs, ntfs, smbfs, synthfs, udf, ufs, volfs, and webdav. The default type is ufs. Use a comma-separated list to specify more than one type to mount, and prefix a type with no to exclude that type.

-u
: Update (change) the status of an already mounted filesystem. E.g., from read-only to read-write.

-v
: Display mount information verbosely.

-w
: Mount filesystem read/write. This is the default.

nano

nano [+*line*] [*options*] [*file*]

Replacement program for the non-free Pico editor supplied with the Pine email reader. Mac OS X provides pico as a symbolic link to nano.

URL: *http://www.nano-editor.org/*.

Options

The options -a, -b, -e, -f, -g, and -j are accepted but ignored for compatibility with pico.

+*line*
: Go to line number *line* at startup.

-B, --backup
: Upon saving a file, keep the previous version in a file with the same name and a ~ character at the end.

`-c, --const`
: Always (constantly) show the cursor position.

`-D, --dos`
: Write files in MS-DOS format (CR-LF line terminators).

`-F, --multibuffer`
: Use multiple file buffers.

`-h, --help`
: Print a command-line option summary.

`-H, --historylog`
: If support for startup files is configured, log search and replace stings in `~/.nano_history`.

`-i, --autoindent`
: Enable auto-indentation. Useful for source code.

`-I, --ignorercfiles`
: If support for startup files is configured, do not read the `$SYSCONFDIR/nanorc` or `~/.nanorc` files.

`-k, --cut`
: Enable cut from cursor to end of line with `^K`.

`-K, --keypad`
: Use the *ncurses* `keypad()` function only if necessary. Try this option if the arrow keys on the numeric keypad do not work for you.

`-l, --nofollow`
: If editing a symbolic link, replace the link with a regular file, instead of following the link.

`-m, --mouse`
: Enable mouse support.

`-M --mac`
: Write files in Macintosh (presumably Mac OS 9) format (CR line terminators).

`-N --noconvert`
: Disable the automatic conversion of files from MS-DOS or Macintosh formats.

`-o` *`dir`*`, --operatingdir=`*`dir`*
: Use *dir* as the operating directory. The manual page says "Makes `nano` set up something similar to a `chroot`."

`-p, --preserve`
: Allow the terminal to use XON and XOFF (`^Q` and `^S`).

`-Q` *`str`*`, --quote=`*`str`*
: Use *str* as the quoting string for justifying. If regular expression support is available, the default is "`^([ \t]*[|>:}#])+`"; otherwise, it's "`> `".

`-r` *`cols`*`, --fill=`*`cols`*
: Upon reaching column *cols*, wrap the line.

`-R, --regexp`
: If regular expression support is available, enable regular expression matching for all search strings, and the use of *\n* in replacement strings. (See Chapter 7.)

`-s` *`prog`*`, --speller=`*`prog`*
: Use *prog* to check spelling.

`-S, --smooth`
: Enable smooth, line-by-line scrolling.

`-t, --tempfile`
: Always save the changed buffer without prompting for confirmation.

`-T` *`num`*`, --tabsize=`*`num`*
: Set the width of a tab to *num* characters.

`-v, --view`
: View the file. (Read-only mode.)

`-V, --version`
: Show the version number and author.

`-w, --nowrap`
: Don't wrap long lines.

`-x, --nohelp`
: Disable the help screen at the bottom of the editor.

`-Y` *`name`*`, --syntax=`*`name`*
: Use *name* as the kind of syntax highlighting to use.

`-z, --suspend`
: Enable suspension of the editor.

open-x11

`open-x11` *`program`* `...`

Run *program* so that it can connect to the current X server. Needed for X11 applications under Mac OS X, since Aqua is not an X server.

pbcopy

`pbcopy [-help] [-pboard` *`pasteboard`*`]`

Copy standard input into one of the system pasteboards. The `general` pasteboard is used by default. The data are stored as ASCII, unless they begin with an EPS (encapsulated PostScript) or RTF (Rich Text Format) header, in which case those formats are used. See also **pbpaste**.

Options

`-help`
: Print a help message.

`-pboard` *`pasteboard`*
: Use the *pasteboard* pasteboard. Possible values are `general`, `ruler`, `find`, or `font`.

pbpaste

`pbpaste [-help] [-pboard pasteboard] [-Prefer type]`

Retrieve the data from the given *pasteboard* and print them to standard output. The `general` pasteboard is used by default. See also **pbcopy**.

Options

`-help`
: Print a help message.

`-pboard pasteboard`
: Use the *pasteboard* pasteboard. Possible values are `general`, `ruler`, `find`, or `font`.

`-Prefer type`
: Try to retrieve data of the given *type* first. Possible values are `ascii`, `rtf`, or `ps`. If data of the given type are not found, `pbpaste` retrieves whatever data are there.

pico

`pico [+line] [options] [file]`

Small simple editor. This is actually the "Nano" Free Software editor. See **nano** for more information.

ps

`ps [options]`

Report on active processes. Following the BSD tradition, a minus sign is allowed but not required in front of options. In options, *list* arguments should either be separated by commas or put in double quotes.

Options

`-a` List other users' processes, as well as your own.

`-A` List other users' processes, including those without a controlling terminal.

`-c` In the `command` column, print just the command name, instead of the full command line.

`-C` Use a different algorithm for calculating CPU percentage which ignores resident time.

`-e` Include environment information after the command.

`-h` Print a header on each page of output.

`-j` Jobs format. Print the information for the `command`, `jobc`, `pgid`, `pid`, `ppid`, `sess`, `state`, `time` `tt`, and `user` keywords.

`-l` Produce a long listing. Print the information for the `command`, `cpu`, `nice`, `pid`, `ppid`, `pri`, `rss`, `state`, `time` `tt`, `uid`, `vsz`, and `wchan` keywords.

`-L` Print list of keywords (field specifiers) that can be used for output formatting or for sorting.

`-m` Sort by memory usage, not by process ID.

-M Show threads.

-N, --deselect
: Negate the selection.

-o *list*
: Like -O, but use only the keywords in *list*.

-O *list*
: Append the keywords in *list* after the PID. The title of each keyword may be changed by using an = sign after the keyword (*keyword=newtitle*).

-p *nums*
: Include only specified processes, which are given in a space-delimited list.

-r Sort by CPU usage instead of by process ID number.

-S Include dead child process data in parent's total.

-t*ttys*
: Display processes running on the specified terminals.

-T List information about processes using the current standard input.

-u Give information for the keywords command, %cpu, %mem, pid, rss, start, state, time tt, user, and vsz. This option implies -r.

-U *user*
: Display processes for the specified user.

-v Display virtual memory format. This includes the keywords command, %cpu, lim, %mem, pagein, pid, re, rss, sl, state, time, tsiz, and vsz. This option implies -m.

-w Wide format. By default, use 132 columns. Repeating this option causes ps to never truncate lines.

-x Display processes without an associated controlling terminal.

Keywords

Aliases for keywords are listed second, next to the keyword.

%cpu, pcpu	Percentage of CPU used.
%mem, pmem	Percentage of memory used.
acflag, acflg	Accounting flag.
command	Command and arguments.
cpu	Short-term factor of CPU used.
flags, f	Hexadecimal representation of process flags.
inblk, inblock	Total amount of blocks read.
jobc	Count for job control.
ktrace	Tracing flags.
ktracep	Tracing vnode.
lim	Limit of memory usage.
logname	Username of the user that started the command.
lstart	Start time.
majflt	Page fault totals.
minflt	Page reclaim totals.
msgrcv	Messages received total.

`msgsnd`	Messages sent total.
`nice, ni`	Nice value.
`nivcsw`	Involuntary context switches total.
`nsigs, nsignals`	Signals taken total.
`nswap`	Swaps in/out total.
`nvcsw`	Voluntary context switches total.
`nwchan`	Wait channel (as number).
`oublk, oublock`	Blocks written total.
`p_ru`	Resource usage (valid only for zombie).
`paddr`	Swap address.
`pagein`	Pageins (same as `majflt`).
`pgid`	Process group number.
`pid`	Process ID number.
`poip`	Number of pageouts in progress.
`ppid`	Parent process ID.
`pri`	Scheduling priority.
`re`	Core residency time.
`rgid`	Real GID.
`rlink`	Reverse link on run queue.
`rss`	Resident set size.
`rsz, rssize`	Resident set size + (text size/text use count).
`rtprio`	Realtime priority (`101` = not a realtime process).
`ruid`	Real UID.
`ruser`	Username (from `ruid`).
`sess`	Session pointer.
`sig, pending`	Signals that are pending.
`sigcatch, caught`	Signals that have been caught.
`sigignore, ignored`	Signals that are ignored.
`sigmask, blocked`	Signals that are blocked.
`sl`	Sleep time.
`start`	Start time.
`state, stat`	Symbolic process state.
`svgid`	Saved GID from a setgid executable.
`svuid`	Saved UID from a setuid executable.
`tdev`	Device number of the controlling terminal.
`time, cputime`	Total of user and system CPU time.
`tpgid`	Process group ID of the controlling terminal.
`tsess`	Session pointer for the controlling terminal.
`tsiz`	Text size (in kilobytes).
`tt`	Name of controlling terminal.
`tty`	Controlling terminal's full name.
`uprocp`	Process pointer.
`ucomm`	Command name used for accounting.
`uid`	Effective UID.
`upr, usrpri`	Scheduling priority after a system call has been made.
`user`	Username (from `uid`).
`vsz, vsize`	Virtual size (in kilobytes).
`wchan`	Wait channel (as symbolic name).
`xstat`	Exit or stop status (only for stopped or zombie processes).

pstopdf

`pstopdf [inputfile] [-o outfile] [options]`

Convert a PostScript input file to a PDF file. The PDF file is always written to a file, whose name is either derived from the input filename, or which must be supplied via `-o` if the input data is read from standard input.

Options

`-i` Read PostScript from standard input instead of from *inputfile*.

`-l` Write messages to a log file instead of to standard output. The log file name is the same as the output filename, with a `.log` extension added to it.

`-p` Print a progress message at the end of each page. The messages always go to standard output, even with `-l`.

`-o file`
Place the output in *file*. By default, for an input PostScript file `whizprogdoc.ps`, the PDF file will be named `whizprogdoc.pdf`.

pythonw

`pythonw python-args ...`

Run a `python` program that has a GUI (Graphical User Interface).

URL: *http://www.python.org*.

say

`say [options] string | -f file`

Text to speech synthesizer. The text is converted to sound and played through the system's speakers, or saved to a file.

Options

`-f file`
Read the text in *file*.

`-o file.aiff`
Save the sound in the given output file.

`-v voice`
Use the given *voice* for producing speech. Both masculine and feminine voices are available. The default voice is selected in the `System Preferences`.

Example

Add voice prompts to your shell scripts with the following shell function:

```
prompt () {
    say "$*" &              Play prompt in background
    echo -n "$*"": "        Traditional shell prompting
}
```

shar

```
shar file ...
```

Produce a **Sh**ell **ar**chive. The output is a shell script, which when run with a Bourne-compatible shell, will extract the original files and directories. It is useful for distributing files via electronic mail or `ftp`. All directories should be named on the command line before regular files so that they will be re-created correctly.

This version of `shar` is very simple. It cannot handle binary data files, and may not be robust in the face of unusual filenames either.

shlock

```
shlock -f lockfile [-p PID] [-u] [-v]
```

Create or verify a lockfile that can be used from shell scripts. `shlock` uses the *rename*(2) system call for making the final lock file; its operation is atomic.

When creating a lock, use `-p` to place the process ID into the file, so that a later invocation can verify the existence of the original creating process.

When verifying a lock, do not use the `-p` option. `shlock` then uses the `kill` command to verify that the process recorded in the file is still alive. If not, `shlock` exits with a value of 1.

Options

`-f` *lockfile*
: Use *lockfile* as the name of the file to create or check. This option must be provided.

`-p` *PID*
: Write *PID* into *lockfile*.

`-u`
: UUCP-compatible locking. `shlock` writes the *pid* number as a binary value.

`-v`
: Be verbose.

Example

Create and use a lock file:

```
lockf=/tmp/whizprog.lock

if shlock -f $lockf -p $$
then
    do whatever is needed with the file locked
    rm -f $lockf
else
    echo "$0: Process ID $(cat $lockf) holds the lock" 1>&2
    exit 1
fi
```

srm

```
srm [options] file ...
```

Securely remove files. `srm` overwrites the data in each *file* before unlinking it. This prevents recovery of file data by examination of the raw disk blocks. The options are purposely similar to those of the standard `rm` command.

URL: *http://srm.sourceforge.net*.

Options

`-d, --directory`
: Ignored. For compatibility with `rm`.

`-f, --force`
: Ignore nonexistent files. This prevents `srm` from prompting.

`--help`
: Display an option summary and then exit.

`-i, --interactive`
: Interactive. Prompt before removing files.

`-m, --medium`
: Use seven US DOD compliant passes (`0xF6`, `0x00`, `0xFF`, random, `0x00`, `0xFF`, and random).

`-n, --nounlink`
: Overwrite the file, but do not unlink or rename it.

`-r, -R, --recursive`
: Recursively remove the contents of directories.

`-s, --simple`
: Overwrite files with just a single pass of random data.

`-v, --verbose`
: Be verbose.

`--version`
: Print version information and then exit.

`-z, --zero`
: Zero the blocks used by the file after overwriting them.

umount

```
umount [-fv] device | remotespec
umount -a|-A [-fv] [-h host] [-t type]
```

System administration command. Unmount a mounted filesystem. *device* is a device name or other string indicating what is mounted. A *remotespec* is a string of the form `host:directory` indicating a remote host and filesystem (typically mounted via NFS). See also **mount**.

Options

`-a`
: Unmount all filesystems listed in `/etc/fstab` or Open Directory. (See **mount** for information about Mac OS X and `/etc/fstab`.)

`-A`
: Unmount all currently mounted filesystems, except for the root filesystem (mounted at `/`).

`-f` Force the unmount. Open device files continue to work. Other file accesses fail.

`-h` *host*
: Unmount all filesystems from the server *host*.

`-t` *type*
: Unmount filesystems of only the specified type.

`-v` Be verbose.

Alphabetical Summary of Java Commands

appletviewer

`appletviewer [options] urls`

Connect to the specified *urls* and run any Java applets they specify in their own windows, outside the context of a web browser.

Options

`-debug`
: Run the applet viewer from within the Java debugger, `jdb`.

`-encoding` *name*
: Specify the input HTML file encoding.

`-J` *java-option*
: Pass *java-option* on to the `java` program. Useful for changing the execution environment or memory usage. *java-option* should not contain spaces; use multiple `-J` options if necessary.

apt

`apt [options] [files ...] [@file ...]`

Annotation processing tool. The `apt` command uses reflective APIs from `com.sun.mirror` to annotate source code in order to provide a view of a program's structure. The APIs model the Java language's type structure, including generics.

Operands

files
: Zero or more Java source files.

@file
: One or more files listing the names of Java source files, or other options.

Options

`-A[key[=val]]`
: Options passed on to specific annotation processes, not interpreted directly by apt itself.

`-cp` *path*, `-classpath` *path*
: Look in *path* for class files and annotation processor factories. With `-factorypath`, the classpath is not searched for factories.

`-d` *dir*
: Place processor and compiled class files in *dir*.

`-factory` *classname*
: Use *classname* as the annotation process factory. This bypasses apt's default discovery process.

`-factorypath` *path*
: Find annotation processor factories in *path*. This option disables searching the classpath for factories.

`-nocompile`
: Disable compilation of source files into class files.

`-print`
: Print a textual version of the types; do not do any annotation processing or compilation.

`-s` *dir*
: Use *dir* as the root directory in which to place generated source files. Files are placed in subdirectories based on the package namespace.

---

jar

`jar [`*options*`] [`*manifest*`]` *dest files*

Java archive tool. All the named objects and directory trees (if directories are given) are combined into a single Java archive, presumably for downloading. `jar` is based on the ZIP and ZLIB compression formats; `zip` and `unzip` can process `.jar` files with no trouble. If a *manifest* is not provided, `jar` creates one automatically. The manifest becomes the first entry in the archive, and it contains any needed metadata about the archive.

Usage is similar to `tar`, in that the leading `-` may be omitted from the options. `jar` is an excellent tool for creating and for opening ZIP format files; its usage is much more intuitive for the long-time Unix user already familiar with `tar`.

Options

`-0` Do not use ZIP compression when creating the archive.

`-c` Create a new or empty archive to standard output.

`-C` *directory*
: Change to *directory* before processing the filenames that follow. Multiple `-C` options are allowed.

`-f` The second argument, *dest*, is the archive to process.

`-i` Create index information for the `.jar` file and the ones it depends upon. Include a file named `INDEX.LIST` in the archive which lists location information for each package in the `.jar` file and all the `.jar` files in the `Class-Path` attribute of the file.

`-J` *java-option*
: Pass *java-option* on to the `java` program. Useful for changing the execution environment or memory usage. *java-option* should not contain spaces; use multiple `-J` options if necessary.

`-m` Use specified *manifest* instead of creating a manifest file.

`-M` Don't create a manifest file.

`-o` Don't compress the files with ZIP compression.

`-t` Print a table of contents for the archive on standard output.

`-u` Update an existing `.jar` file by adding to it the files and directories specified on the command line.

`-v` Produce verbose output to standard error.

`-x[`*file*`]`
: Extract named *file*, or all files if no *file* given.

jarsigner

```
jarsigner [options] jarfile alias
jarsigner -verify [options] jarfile
```

Sign or verify `.jar` files. Adding a digital signature to a `.jar` file improves its security, since changing the contents causes the signature to become invalid. *jarfile* is the original file to be signed; *alias* is a recognized alias for the identity of the signer. By default `jarsigner` replaces the original file with the signed one. This can be changed with the `-signedjar` option.

The generated signed `.jar` file is identical to the input one, with the addition of two new files: a `.SF` signature file, and a `.DSA` signature block file. The default names of these files are taken from the first eight characters of *alias*, but this may be overridden with the `-sigfile` option.

The `-keypass`, `-keystore`, `-sigfile`, `-signedjar`, and `-storepass` options are only for signing a file.

Whenever `jarsigner` accepts a password for an option, if not provided on the command line, the program prompts for a password. Such options should not be used in scripts or on the command line, since they allow passwords to be seen. Similarly, `jarsigner` does *not* turn off echoing when prompting for a password, so make sure no one else can see your screen when using such options! See also **keytool**.

Options

`-certs`
: Together with `-verify` and `-verbose`, provide certificate information for each signer of the `.jar` file.

`-internalsf`
: Revert to earlier behavior, whereby the `.DSA` file also contains a copy of the `.SF` file. Useful mainly for testing.

`-J` *java-option*
: Pass *java-option* on to the `java` program. Useful for changing the execution environment or memory usage. *java-option* should not contain spaces; use multiple `-J` options if necessary.

`-keypass` *password*
: Use *password* to protect *alias*'s private key in the keystore. This password must be used when signing a `.jar` file.

`-keystore` *file* | *url*
: Provide the location of the keystore (database file) holding the signer's keys. The default is the `.keystore` file in the user's home directory, as specified by the `user.home` system property. This defaults to the user's home directory. The location may be specified as either a filename or a URL.

`-provider` *class_name*
: Use *class_name* as the master class file for the cryptographic service provider when such is not listed in the security properties file.

`-sectionsonly`
: Prevent `jarsigner` from including a header in the `.SF` file with a hash of the entire manifest file. This prevents a useful optimization, and should only be used for testing.

`-sigfile` *name*
: Use *name* as the base part of the filename for the signature and signature block files added to the `.jar` file.

`-signedjar` *file*
: Use *file* as the signed file.

`-storepass` *password*
: Use *password* as the password to access the keystore.

`-storetype` *type*
: Use *type* as the type of keystore to instantiate.

`-verbose`
: Provide extra information about progress during signing or about the verification.

`-verify`
: Verify a `.jar` file instead of signing one. `jarsigner` can also verify a file signed with the JDK 1.1 `javakey` program.

Examples

Sign a `.jar` file by multiple users:

```
jp$ jarsigner whizprog.jar jp            User jp signs it
boss$ jarsigner whizprog.jar boss        User boss signs it
```

Verify the signatures:

```
customer$ jarsigner -verify whizprog.jar Customer checks it out
jar verified
```

java

```
java [options] classname [args]
java [options] -jar jarfile [args]
```

Load and execute Java bytecode class files. By default, `java` uses the "Just In Time" (JIT) compiler for the current system. *args* are passed on to the Java program's `main( )` method.

Options

`-agentlib:lib[=options]`
: Load the native agent library *lib*, optionally passing *options* to it.

`-agentpath:path[=options]`
: Use *path* to load a native agent library by full path.

`-client`
: Use the Java HotSpot Client VM.

`-cp path, -classpath path`
: Use the colon-separated list of directories in *path* instead of $CLASSPATH to find class files. It is usually a good idea to have the current directory (".") on the search path.

`-d32, -d64`
: Specify a 32- or 64-bit environment, respectively. On 64-bit systems, 64 bits is the default. Otherwise, the 32-bit environment is used.

`-dsa, -disablesystemassertions`
: Disable assertions in all system classes.

`-Dprop=val`
: Redefine the value of *prop* to be *val*. This option may be used any number of times.

`-esa, -enablesystemassertions`
: Enable assertions in all system classes.

`-jar jarfile`
: Invoke the `main( )` method of the class listed in the `Main-Class` manifest header in *jarfile*.

`-javaagent:jarpath[=options]`
: Use *jarpath* to load a Java agent.

`-server`
: Use the Java HotSpot Server VM.

`-showversion`
: Display version information and continue running.

`-verbose[:item]`
: With *item*, display information about that item. Possible values for *item* are `class`, to print a message to standard output each time a class file is loaded; `gc`, to report each garbage collection event; and `jni`, for information about native methods. Plain `-verbose` is the same as `-verbose:class`.

`-version`
: Display version information for `java`.

`-X` Print information about nonstandard options, such as for debugging, control of garbage collection, interpreted mode only, and so on. The Solaris *java*(1) manpage says: "The -X options are nonstandard and subject to change without notice."

-?, -help
: Print a usage message.

javac

javac [*options*] *files*

Compile Java source code into Java bytecode, for execution with java. Java source files must have a .java suffix and must be named for the class whose code they contain. The generated bytecode files have a .class suffix. By default, class files are created in the same directory as the corresponding source files. Use the CLASSPATH variable to list directories and/or ZIP files that javac will search to find your classes.

In the case that there are too many files to list on the command line, you may list the source and class files in a separate file, and indicate the contents of the file to javac by prepending an @ to the filename.

Options

-bootclasspath *path*
: Use the colon-separated list of directories in *path* for the boot classes, instead of the boot classes used by the java command itself.

-classpath *path*
: Use the colon-separated list of directories in *path* instead of $CLASSPATH to find class files. It is usually a good idea to have the current directory (".") on the search path.

-cldc1.0
: For compiling CLDC programs. This causes the compiler to generate stack maps, which obviates the need for the preverifier.

-d *dir*
: Specify where to create generated class files.

-deprecation
: Warn about every use or override of a deprecated member or class, instead of warning at the end.

-Djava.ext.dirs=*dirs*
: Use *dirs* as the location for installed extensions.

-Djava.endorsed.dirs=*dirs*
: Use *dirs* as the endorsed standards path.

-encoding *encoding*
: The source file is encoded using *encoding*. Without this option, the system's default converter is used.

-extdirs *dirs*
: For cross-compilation, use the specified *dirs* as the extension directories.

-g
: Generate all debugging information, including local variables.

-g:*type*
Generate only the debugging information specified by *type*. Possible values are:

lines	Line number debugging information.
none	No debugging information.
source	Source file debugging information.
vars	Local variable debugging information.

-help
Print a usage message.

-J *java-option*
Pass *java-option* on to the java program. Useful for changing the execution environment or memory usage. *java-option* should not contain spaces; use multiple -J options if necessary.

-nowarn
Disable all warnings.

-O Perform optimizations that may produce faster but larger class files. It may also slow down compilation. This option should be used with discretion.

-source *version*
Accept Java language source as specified by *version*. Acceptable values are 1.5 and 5 for JDK 1.5 features, such as generics, 1.4 for JDK 1.4 features (assertions), or 1.3 for only JDK 1.3 language features.

-sourcepath *path*
Use *path* to search for class and interface definitions. Classes found through the classpath may be recompiled if their source files are found.

-target *version*
Compile for the JVM matching *version*. Values for *version* are 1.1, 1.2, 1.3, 1.4, 1.5, and 5 (a synonym for 1.5). The default is 1.2, although -source 1.4 or lower changes the default JVM to 1.4.

-verbose
Print messages as files are compiled and loaded.

-X Print information about nonstandard options and exit.

javadoc

javadoc [*options*] *files* | *classes*

Process declaration and documentation comments in Java source files and produce HTML pages describing the public and protected classes, interfaces, constructors, methods, and fields.

In the case that there are too many files to list on the command line, you may list the source and class files in a separate file, and indicate the contents of the file to javadoc by prepending an @ to the filename.

`javadoc` uses "doclets" to format the source code. You can supply your own doclet with the `-doclet` option. The standard doclet produces HTML. The following section lists the union of the `javadoc` options and those of the standard doclet.

Options

Options are case-insensitive, although option arguments may not be.

`-1.1`
: Create documentation matching that of `javadoc` 1.1. No longer available; use `javadoc` 1.2 or 1.3 if you need it.

`-author`
: Include `@author` tags.

`-bootclasspath` *path*
: Use the colon-separated list of directories in *path* for the boot classes, instead of the boot classes used by the `java` command itself.

`-bottom` *text*
: Place *text* at the bottom of each output file. *text* may contain HTML tags and whitespace, but must be quoted if it does.

`-breakiterator`
: Use internationalized sentence boundary of `java.text.BreakIterator` for English for the first sentence, which is copied to the index. The default is to use a locale-specific algorithm for English.

`-charset` *charset*
: Use *charset* as the HTML character set for the document.

`-classpath` *path*
: Use the colon-separated list of directories in *path* instead of $CLASSPATH to find class files. It is usually a good idea to have the current directory (".") on the search path. It is better to use `-sourcepath` instead of `-classpath`.

`-d` *dir*
: Create the generated HTML files in *dir*.

`-docencoding` *encoding*
: Use *encoding* for the generated HTML file.

`-docfilessubdirs`
: Enable deep copying of directories for document files.

`-doclet` *class*
: Use *class* as the doclet to produce documentation.

`-docletpath` *pathlist*
: Use *pathlist* to find the doclet class file(s).

`-doctitle` *title*
: Use *title* as the title of the document, which is placed near the top of the overview summary file.

`-encoding` *encoding*
: The Java source file is encoded using *encoding*.

`-exclude` *packages*
: Unconditionally exclude *packages*, even if they would otherwise be included.

`-excludedocfilessubdir` *names*
: Exclude the subdirectories *names*. Useful to avoid copying source code control directories.

`-extdirs` *directories*
: Search for extensions in *directories*.

`-footer` *text*
: Place *text* at the bottom of each output file.

`-group` *groupheading package-list*
: Group the packages in *package-list* into a group labeled *groupheading*. Each group gets its own table on the overview page.

`-header` *text*
: Place *text* at the top of each output file.

`-help`
: Print a short help message.

`-helpfile` *file*
: Use *file* as the help file, instead of the automatically-generated `helpdoc.html` file.

`-J` *java-option*
: Pass *java-option* on to the `java` program. Useful for changing the execution environment or memory usage. *java-option* should not contain spaces; use multiple `-J` options if necessary.

`-keywords`
: Place HTML `meta` keyword tags into the file.

`-link` *URL*
: Add a link to the `javadoc`-generated document specified by *URL*. It must specify a directory, not a file, and may be either a relative or absolute URL.

`-linkoffline` *URL packagelistfile*
: Use instead of `-link` when `javadoc` is not able to access the *URL* over the Web. The list of packages is provided in *packagelistfile*, which is usually a local file.

`-linksource`
: Create an HTML version of the source code that is linked-to by the HTML documentation.

`-locale` *locale-spec*
: Generate documentation using the language described by *locale-spec*. This option must come before any options provided by any doclet, or else all the navigation bars will be in English.

`-nocomment`
: Suppress the comment body, generating only declarations.

`-nodeprecated`
: Exclude paragraphs marked with `@deprecated`.

`-nodeprecatedlist`
: Do not generate the `deprecated-list.html` file or the link to it from the navigation bar. Useful if you use no deprecated APIs to make the documentation cleaner.

`-nohelp`
: Do not generate the `HELP` link.

`-noindex`
: Do not generate the package index.

`-nonavbar`
: Do not generate the navigation bar, header, or footer. Useful if all you need is the documentation itself.

`-noqualifier all | *package-list*`
: Omit package qualifiers from the packages in *package-list*, or from all packages if `all` is used.

`-nosince`
: Do not generate the "since" sections from `@since` tags.

`-notimestamp`
: Suppress the hidden timestamp in each file. Useful for comparing two versions of the documentation.

`-notree`
: Do not generate the class and interface hierarchy.

`-overview *file*`
: Use *file* for the overview documentation in the overview page, `overview-summary.html`.

`-package`
: Include only package, protected, and public classes and members.

`-private`
: Include all classes and members.

`-protected`
: Include only protected and public classes and members. This is the default.

`-public`
: Include only public classes and members.

`-quiet`
: Do not include the version number of the standard doclet in the generated output.

`-serialwarn`
: Warn about missing `@serial` tags.

`-sourcepath *path*`
: Use *path* as the search path for class source files. *path* is a colon-separated list of directories. If not specified, it defaults to the current `-classpath` directory. Running `javadoc` in the directory with the sources allows you to omit this option.

`-splitindex`
: Split the index into multiple files, one per letter of the alphabet.

`-stylesheetfile` *file*
: Use *file* as the HTML stylesheet file. The default is to create a stylesheet file, `stylesheet.css`.

`-subpackages` *package-list*
: Document the packages and recursively their subpackages for the packages listed in *package-list*.

`-tag` *tagname*`:`*placement*`:`*text*
: Inform `javadoc` about a custom tag named *tagname*. *text* is the text placed into the documentation in bold. *placement* describes where to use the tag, as follows:

`a`	Use the tag in all places.
`c`	Use the tag for constructors.
`f`	Use the tag for fields.
`m`	Use the tag for methods.
`o`	Use the tag in overviews.
`p`	Use the tag in packages.
`t`	Use the tag for types (classes and interfaces).
`X`	Tag is disabled, don't generate it.

`-taglet` *class*
: Use *class* as the taglet for generating custom output. The taglet is used for tags specified after it with the `-tag` option.

`-tagletpath` *path*
: Search *path* to find taglets.

`-title`
: This option no longer exists; use `-doctitle`.

`-use`
: Create a "Use" page for each class, listing the classes that use the page's class.

`-verbose`
: Print additional messages about time spent parsing source files.

`-version`
: Include `@version` tags.

`-windowtitle` *title*
: Place *title* in the HTML `<title>` tag.

---

javah

`javah [`*options*`]` *classes* `|` *files*

Generate C header and/or source files for implementing `native` methods. The generated `.h` file defines a structure whose members parallel those of the corresponding Java class.

The header filename is derived from the corresponding Java class. If the class is inside a package, the package name is prepended to the filename and the structure name, separated by an underscore.

Note: the Java Native Interface (JNI) does not require header or stub files. Use the `-jni` option to create function prototypes for JNI native methods.

Options

`-bootclasspath` *path*
: Use the colon-separated list of directories in *path* for the boot classes, instead of the boot classes used by the `java` command itself.

`-classpath` *path*
: Use the colon-separated list of directories in *path* instead of $CLASSPATH to find class files. It is usually a good idea to have the current directory (".") on the search path.

`-d` *dir*
: Place generated files in *dir*.

`-force`
: Always write output files.

`-help`
: Print a help message.

`-J` *java-option*
: Pass *java-option* on to the `java` program. Useful for changing the execution environment or memory usage. *java-option* should not contain spaces; use multiple `-J` options if necessary.

`-jni`
: Produce JNI native method function prototypes.

`-o` *file*
: Concatenate all generated header or source files for all the classes and write them to *file*.

`-old`
: Produce JDK 1.0-style headers.

`-stubs`
: Generate C declarations, not headers.

`-trace`
: Add tracing information to the generated stubs.

`-verbose`
: Verbose.

`-version`
: Print the version of `javah`.

---

javap

`javap [`*options*`]` *classfiles*

Disassemble Java class files and print the results. By default, `javap` prints the public fields and methods of the named classes.

Options

`-b` Ignored. For backward compatibility with the JDK 1.1 `javap`.

`-bootclasspath` *`path`*
: Use the colon-separated list of directories in *path* for the boot classes, instead of the boot classes used by the `java` command itself.

`-c` Print out the disassembled byte-codes for each method in the given classes.

`-classpath` *`path`*
: Use the colon-separated list of directories in *path* instead of $CLASSPATH to find class files. It is usually a good idea to have the current directory (".") on the search path.

`-extdirs` *`dirs`*
: For cross-compilation, use the specified *dirs* as the extension directories.

`-h` Generate code that can be used in a C header file.

`-help`
: Print a usage message.

`-J` *`java-option`*
: Pass *java-option* on to the `java` program. Useful for changing the execution environment or memory usage. *java-option* should not contain spaces; use multiple `-J` options if necessary.

`-l` Display line number and local variable information.

`-package`
: Only disassemble package, protected, and public classes and members. This is the default.

`-private`
: Disassemble all classes and members.

`-protected`
: Only disassemble protected and public classes and members.

`-public`
: Only disassemble public classes and members.

`-s` Display the internal type signatures.

`-verbose`
: For each method, print the stack size, number of arguments, and number of local variables.

---

jdb

`jdb [`*`options`*`] [`*`class`*`] [`*`args`*`]`

`jdb` is the Java **Deb**ugger. It is a line-oriented debugger, similar to traditional Unix debuggers, providing inspection and debugging of local or remote Java interpreters.

`jdb` can be used in place of `java`, in which case the program to be run is already started in the debugger. Or, it may be used to attach to an already running `java` session. In the latter case, `java` must have been started with the option `-agentlib:jdwp=transport=dt_socket,server=y,suspend=n,address=`*`PORT`*. You then attach to the running JVM with `jdb -attach` *PORT*, where *PORT* is the same numeric port number used to run `java`.

Options

`jdb` forwards the `-v`, `-D`, `-classpath`, and `-X` options to the JVM running the program to be debugged. See **java**.

`-attach` *address*
: Attach to an already running JVM at port *address*.

`-connect` *connector*:*name*=*value*...
: Connect to the JVM using the specified connector.

`-J` *java-option*
: Pass *java-option* on to the `java` program. Useful for changing the execution environment or memory usage. *java-option* should not contain spaces; use multiple `-J` options if necessary.

`-launch`
: Start the application immediately, stopping before the initial application class is loaded. This saves having to use the `run` command from within `jdb`.

`-listconnectors`
: List the connectors available in this JVM.

`-listen` *address*
: Wait for a JVM to connect to the debugger at *address*.

`-listenany`
: Wait for a JVM to connect to the debugger at any address.

`-sourcepath` *path*
: Use *path* to search for class and interface definitions.

`-tclient`
: Use the HotSpot Client Performance Engine to run the application.

`-tserver`
: Use the HotSpot Server Performance Engine to run the application.

keytool

`keytool [`*subcommands*`]`

Key and certificate management utility. Together with `jarsigner`, replaces the JDK 1.1 `javakey` utility. Keys and certificates are maintained in a *keystore*. `keytool` manages the keystore, and `jarsigner` uses the information in it for signing `.jar` files. If you need to work with keys and keystores, read the *keytool*(1) manpage carefully first!

The command-line arguments to `keytool` are subcommands, each of which begins with a hyphen. Each subcommand, in turn, accepts suboptions.

Whenever `keytool` accepts a password for an option, if a password is not provided on the command line, the program prompts for one. Such options should not be used in scripts or on the command line, since they allow passwords to be seen. Similarly, `keytool` does *not* turn off echoing when prompting for a password, so make sure no one else can see your screen when using such options! See also **jarsigner**.

Subcommands

`-certreq` *`suboptions`*
: Generate a Certificate Signing Request.

`-delete` *`suboptions`*
: Delete the entry for the alias given with `-alias` from the keystore. With no `-alias` option, prompt for the alias name.

`-export` *`suboptions`*
: From the keystore, export the certificate belonging to the user specified with `-alias`, storing it in the file specified with `-file`.

`-genkey` *`suboptions`*
: Add a new public/private key pair to the keystore.

`-help`
: Print a command usage summary.

`-identitydb` *`suboptions`*
: Import information from the JDK 1.1 style identity database specified with `-file`. If no such option is used, read from standard input. Create the keystore if it doesn't exist.

`-import` *`suboptions`*
: Import a certificate or certificate chain from the file specified by the `-file` suboption. The certificates must be in either binary encoding or in RFC 1421 Base64 printable encoding.

`-keyclone` *`suboptions`*
: Create a new keystore entry with the same private key and certificate chain as the original. Specify the source with `-alias` and the new password for the copy with `-new`.

`-keypasswd` *`suboptions`*
: Change the password protecting a private key. Specify whose key with `-alias`, the original password with `-keypass`, and the new one with `-new`.

`-list` *`suboptions`*
: Print the contents of the keystore for the user specified with `-alias` to standard output. With no `-alias`, print the entire keystore.

`-printcert` *`suboptions`*
: Read a certificate from the file specified with `-file` or from standard input and print the contents in a human-readable format. The original certificate may be binary-encoded or RFC 1421 encoded.

`-selfcert` *`suboptions`*
: Generate an X.509 v1 self-signed certificate. Use `-alias` to provide the alias of the user signing the certificate. Use `-dname` to provide an X.500 Distinguished Name if you don't wish to use the Distinguished Name associated with the user's alias.

`-storepasswd` *suboptions*
: Change the password that protects the entire keystore. Use `-new` to provide the new password, which must be at least six characters long.

Suboptions for Subcommands

Following is the list of suboptions and their meanings. The entry for each suboption lists the subcommands with which it may be used.

`-alias` *name*
: Use *name* as the user or alias name in order to specify which key pair and/or certificates to use. May be used with: `-certreq`, `-delete`, `-export`, `-genkey`, `-import`, `-keyclone`, `-keypasswd`, and `-selfcert`.

`-dest` *alias*
: Use *alias* as the new user alias. May be used with: `-keyclone`.

`-dname` *name*
: Use *name* as the X.500 Distinguished Name. May be used with: `-genkey` and `-selfcert`.

`-file` *filename*
: Use *filename* as the source or sink of data, depending on the subcommand in use. May be used with: `-certreq`, `-export`, `-import`, and `-printcert`.

`-keyalg` *algorithm*
: Use *algorithm* for producing keys. May be used with: `-genkey`.

`-keypass` *password*
: Use *password* as the password for the given private key. Used with: `-certreq`, `-genkey`, `-import`, `-keyclone`, `-keypasswd`, and `-selfcert`.

`-keysize` *size*
: Use *size* as the size in bits of the key. For DSA key pairs, *size* must be in the range from 512 to 1024, and it must be a multiple of 64. May be used with: `-genkey`.

`-keystore` *filename*
: Use *filename* as the keystore. May be used with: `-certreq`, `-delete`, `-export`, `-genkey`, `-import`, `-keyclone`, `-keypasswd`, `-list`, `-selfcert`, and `-storepasswd`.

`-new` *newpasswd*
: Use *newpasswd* as new password. May be used with: `-keyclone`, `-keypasswd`, and `-storepasswd`.

`-noprompt`
: Do not interact with the user. May be used with: `-import`.

`-provider` *provider_class*
: Use *provider_class* as the name of the cryptographic service provider's master class file if the security properties file does not list a service provider. May be used with: `-certreq`, `-delete`, `-export`, `-genkey`, `-import`, `-keyclone`, `-keypasswd`, `-list`, `-selfcert`, and `-storepasswd`.

`-rfc`
Use the RFC 1421 (Base64) printable encoding for output. May be used with: `-export` and `-list`.

`-sigalg` *algorithm*
Use *algorithm* for producing signatures. Used with: `-certreq`, `-genkey`, and `-selfcert`.

`-storepass` *password*
Use *password* as the password that protects the entire keystore. Must be at least six characters long and must be provided for all commands that access the keystore's contents. If this password isn't provided on the command line, the user is prompted for it. May be used with: `-certreq`, `-delete`, `-export`, `-genkey`, `-import`, `-keyclone`, `-keypasswd`, `-list`, `-selfcert`, and `-storepasswd`.

`-storetype` *type*
Use *type* as the type of the keystore. This an esoteric option; see the manpage for more details. May be used with: `-certreq`, `-delete`, `-export`, `-genkey`, `-import`, `-keyclone`, `-keypasswd`, `-list`, `-selfcert`, and `-storepasswd`.

`-trustcacerts`
Use certificates in the "cacerts" (Certificate Authority certificates) file, in addition to those in the keystore. May be used with: `-import`.

`-validity` *days*
Signature is valid for *days* days. May be used with: `-genkey` and `-selfcert`.

The following table shows default values for several of the most frequently used suboptions.

Suboption	Purpose	Default value
`-alias`	User name	`mykey`
`-file`	Data source / sink	Standard input if reading, standard output if writing
`-keyalg`	Signature Algorithm	`DSA`
`-keysize`	Encryption key size	`1024`
`-keystore`	Location of keystore	`$HOME/.keystore`
`-validity`	Days signature is valid for	`90`

rmic

`rmic [`*options*`]` *classes*

Remote Method Invocation compiler for Java. `rmic` takes the fully package-qualified class names and generates skeleton and stub class files to provide remote method invocation. The classes must have previously been successfully compiled with `java`.

For a method `WhizImpl` in class `whiz`, `rmic` creates two files, `WhizImpl_Skel.class` and `WhizImpl_Stub.class`. The "skeleton" file implements the server side of the RMI; the "stub" file implements the client side.

Options

`-always, -alwaysgenerate`
: Always generate code, even if the existing IDL files are newer than the input class. Use with `-idl` or `-iiop` only.

`-bootclasspath` *path*
: Use the colon-separated list of directories in *path* for the boot classes, instead of the boot classes used by the `java` command itself.

`-classpath` *path*
: Use the colon-separated list of directories in *path* instead of $CLASSPATH to find class files. It is usually a good idea to have the current directory (".") on the search path.

`-d` *dir*
: Place the generated files in *dir*.

`-extdirs` *dirs*
: For cross-compilation, use the specified *dirs* as the extension directories.

`-factory`
: Use the `factory` keyword in the IDL. Use with `-idl` only.

`-g` Generate all debugging information, instead of just line numbers.

`-idl` Generate OMG IDL for the specified classes.

`-idlFile` *package*`[.class]` *file*
: Provide an IDLEntity file mapping from Java package *package* to IDL module *file*. Use with `-idl` only.

`-idlModule` *package*`[.class]` *module*
: Provide an IDLEntity package mapping from Java package *package* to IDL module *module*. Use with `-idl` only.

`-iiop`
: Generate IIOP stub and tie classes, instead of the default JRMP stub and skeleton classes.

`-J` *java-option*
: Pass *java-option* on to the `java` program. Useful for changing the execution environment or memory usage. *java-option* should not contain spaces; use multiple `-J` options if necessary.

`-keepg, -keepgenerated`
: Keep the generated `.java` source files for the skeletons and the stubs.

`-nolocalstubs`
: Do not create stubs optimized for clients and servers that will run in the same process. Use with `-iiop` only.

`-noValueMethods`
: Do not use valuetype methods and initializers in the generated IDL. Use with `-idl` only.

`-nowarn`
: Disable all warnings.

`-poa`
: Use the Portable Object Adapter. In other words, use `org.omg.PortableServer.Servant` instead of `org.omg.CORBA_2_3.portable.ObjectImpl`. Use with `-idl` only.

`-sourcepath` *path*
: Use *path* to search for class and interface definitions. Classes found through the classpath may be recompiled if their source files are found.

`-v`*VERS*
: Generate code compatible with version *VERS* of the JRMP protocol. *VERS* is one of `1.1`, for the JDK 1.1 protocol, `1.2`, for the JDK 1.2 protocol, or `compat` for code compatible with both versions.

`-verbose`
: Print messages as files are compiled and loaded.

---

rmid

`rmid [`*options*`]`

RMI activation system daemon. This daemon must be started before activatable objects can be registered or activated.

Options

`-C`*child-option*
: Pass *child-option* on to each child process. Useful, for example, for specifying a property's default value.

`-J` *java-option*
: Pass *java-option* on to the `java` program. Useful for changing the execution environment or memory usage. *java-option* should not contain spaces; use multiple `-J` options if necessary.

`-J-Dsun.rmi.activation.execPolicy=`*policy*
: Specify the policy for checking commands and command-line options. Specific to Sun's JVM. See the *rmid*(1) manpage for the details.

`-log` *directory*
: Use *directory* as the directory in which to place the database and other information. The default is `./log`.

`-port` *port*
: Use *port* as the port for the `rmid` registry.

`-stop`
: Stop the invocation of `rmid` that is using the port specified with `-port`. If no `-port` is given, stop the `rmid` running on port `1098`.

rmiregistry

`rmiregistry [port] [-Jjava-option]`

Create and start a remote object registry on the specified *port*. The default *port* is 1099. The registry provides naming services for RMI (Remote Method Invocation) servers and clients.

Option

`-J` *java-option*
: Pass *java-option* on to the `java` program. Useful for changing the execution environment or memory usage. *java-option* should not contain spaces; use multiple `-J` options if necessary.

3
The Unix Shell: An Overview

For novice users, this chapter presents basic concepts about the Unix shell. For advanced users, this chapter also summarizes the major similarities and differences between the Bash, Korn, and "Tenex" C shells. Details on the three shells are provided in Chapters 4 and 5.

The following topics are presented:

- Introduction to the shell
- Purpose of the shell
- Shell flavors
- Shell source code
- Common features
- Differing features

Introduction to the Shell

Today's microwave ovens, and many other household appliances (ovens, washing machines, dishwashers), let you use simple push-buttons to instruct them what to do. They provide a simple user interface to a possibly complicated internal system.

The shell is the user interface to Unix, and by the same token, several shells are available in Unix. Most systems provide more than one for you to choose from. Each shell has different features, but all of them affect how commands will be interpreted and provide tools to create your Unix environment.

The original shells were developed before the time of Graphical User Interfaces (GUIs), and at first glance, appear harder to use than GUI interfaces. The truth, though, is that they aren't harder to use, they are harder to *learn*. However, once you've mastered them, you'll find that you can accomplish an infinite variety of tasks that just cannot be managed with a GUI.

The shell is simply a program that allows the system to understand your commands. (That's why the shell is often called a *command interpreter*.) For many users, the shell works invisibly—"behind the scenes." Your only concern is that the system does what you tell it to do; you don't care about the inner workings. In our microwave analogy, this is comparable to pressing the START button. Most of us don't care whether the user interface communicates with an embedded microcomputer, or drives analog electronics, as long as the popcorn is ready in time for the movie, and doesn't burn.

Purpose of the Shell

There are three uses for the shell:

- Interactive use
- Customization of your Unix session
- Programming

Interactive Use

When the shell is used interactively, the system waits for you to type a command at the Unix prompt. Your commands can include special symbols that let you abbreviate filenames or redirect input and output.

Customization of Your Unix Session

A Unix shell defines variables to control the behavior of your Unix session. Setting these variables tells the system, for example, which directory to use as your home directory, or the file in which you store your mail. Some variables are preset by the system; you can define others in startup files that are read when you log in. Startup files can also contain Unix commands or special shell commands. These are executed every time you log in. Many shells also support special variables and internal commands that let you tailor the behavior of the shell itself.

Programming

Unix shells provide a set of special (or built-in) commands that let you create programs called *shell scripts*. In fact, many built-in commands can be used interactively like Unix commands, and Unix commands are frequently used in shell scripts. Scripts are useful for executing a series of individual commands. This is similar to BATCH files in MS-DOS and Windows. Scripts can also execute commands repeatedly (in a loop) or conditionally (`if-else`), as in many high-level programming languages.

Shell Flavors

Many different Unix shells are available. This quick reference describes the three most popular shells:

- The GNU Project's Bash (Bourne-Again SHell), arguably the most popular shell in use today. It is a superset of the original Bourne shell, including command-line editing and many features first implemented in the Korn shell.
- The Korn shell, a superset of the original Bourne shell that lets you edit the command line. There are two commonly available versions of the Korn shell, distinguished by the year they were released, and referred to in this book as `ksh88` and `ksh93` respectively.
- The "Tenex" C shell, an enhanced version of the original BSD C shell, which uses C-like syntax and is more convenient for the interactive user than the original Bourne shell.

The original Bourne shell is available as `/bin/sh` on commercial Unix systems, and if invoked as `sh`, Bash will do its best to emulate the original Bourne shell's behavior. However, it is rare today to find the original Bourne shell being used interactively as a login shell; other shells that provide better interactive features and the Bourne shell's programming language, such as Bash and `ksh`, are more popular. However, when writing shell scripts, most people are careful to restrict themselves to just those features of the Bourne shell.

The `/etc/passwd` file determines which shell takes effect during your interactive Unix session. When you log in, the system checks your entry in `/etc/passwd`. The last field of each entry names a program to run as the default shell.* For example:

If the program name is:	Your shell is the:
`/bin/sh`	Bourne shell
`/bin/bash`	The Bash shell
`/bin/ksh`	Korn shell
`/usr/dt/bin/dtksh`	The Desktop Korn shell, a version of `ksh93` (Solaris only)
`/bin/csh`	C shell or Tenex C shell (system dependent)
`/bin/tcsh`	Tenex C shell

You can change to another shell by typing the program name at the command line. For example, to change from the Bourne shell to the Korn shell, type:

```
$ exec ksh
```

Which Shell Do I Want?

If you are new to Unix, picking a shell may be a bewildering question. Before `ksh` was commonly available, the general advice was to use `csh` for interactive use

* On Solaris or other networked Unix systems, this information may come from NIS or NIS+. Usually, your system administrator will handle this for you; just don't be surprised if your login name doesn't appear in `/etc/passwd`.

(because it supported job control and had other features that made it a better interactive shell than the Bourne shell), but to use the Bourne shell for scripting (because it is a more powerful programming language, and more universally available).

Today, a wide variety of Bourne-compatible shells are available that all support job control and some sort of command history and command-line editing. Of these, Bash is arguably the most popular, and it is a good choice. If Bash is not available but the Korn shell is, you should use the Korn shell. In any case, source code for both shells (as well as others) are easily available from the Internet.

Shell Source Code URLs

Here is a list of URLs for the source code for different shells.

Shell	Location
Bash	*ftp://ftp.gnu.org/gnu/bash*
Bash source code patches	*ftp://ftp.gnu.org/gnu/bash/bash-3.0-patches*
Ksh93	*http://www.research.att.com/sw/download/*
The Z Shell	*http://www.zsh.org*
The Public Domain Korn Shell	*http://web.cs.mun.ca/~michael/pdksh/*
Tcsh	*http://www.tcsh.org*

The Public Domain Korn shell is mostly compatible with `ksh88`, and is usually the version of `ksh` shipped with GNU/Linux systems. The Z shell (`zsh`) has many features of the Bourne shell, Bash, and the Korn shell, and a plethora of features unique to it.

Common Features

The following table displays features that are common to the Bash, Korn, and C shells. Note that both the Korn shell and Bash are enhanced versions of the Bourne shell; therefore, they include all features of the Bourne shell, plus some others.

Symbol/command	Meaning/action
`>`	Redirect output.
`>>`	Append to file.
`<`	Redirect input.
`<<`	"Here" document (redirect input).
`|`	Pipe output.
`&`	Run process in background.
`;`	Separate commands on same line.
`~`	Home directory symbol.
`*`	Match any character(s) in filename.
`?`	Match single character in filename.
`[ ]`	Match any characters enclosed.

Symbol/command	Meaning/action
`( )`	Execute in subshell.
`{ }`	Expand elements in list.[a]
`` ` ` ``	Substitute output of enclosed command.
`" "`	Partial quote (allows variable and command expansion).
`' '`	Full quote (no expansion).
`\`	Quote following character.
`$`*`var`*	Use value for variable.
`$$`	Process ID.
`$0`	Command name.
`$`*`n`*	*n*th argument ($0 \leq n \leq 9$).
`$*`	All arguments as simple words.
`#`	Begin comment.
`bg`	Background execution.
`break`	Break from loop statements.
`cd`	Change directory.
`continue`	Resume a program loop.
`echo`	Display output.
`eval`	Evaluate arguments.
`exec`	Execute a new shell.
`fg`	Foreground execution.
`history`	List previous commands.
`jobs`	Show active jobs.
`kill`	Terminate running jobs.
`shift`	Shift positional parameters.
`suspend`	Suspend a foreground job (such as a shell created by `su`).
`time`	Time a command.
`umask`	Set default file permissions for new files.
`unset`	Erase variable or function definitions.
`wait`	Wait for a background job to finish.

[a] Brace expansion is a compile-time feature in the Korn shell. Usually commercial versions don't have it, but if you compile from source code, you do get it by default.

Differing Features

The following table displays features that are different among the three shells.

<table>
<tr><th>bash</th><th>ksh</th><th>tcsh</th><th>Meaning/action</th></tr>
<tr><td><code>$</code></td><td><code>$</code></td><td><code>%</code></td><td>Prompt.</td></tr>
<tr><td><code>>|</code></td><td><code>>|</code></td><td><code>>!</code></td><td>Force redirection.</td></tr>
<tr><td></td><td></td><td><code>>>!</code></td><td>Force append.</td></tr>
<tr><td><code>> file 2>&1</code></td><td><code>> file 2>&1</code></td><td><code>>& file</code></td><td>Combine stdout and stderr.</td></tr>
<tr><td><code>>& file</code></td><td></td><td><code>>& file</code></td><td>Combine stdout and stderr.</td></tr>
</table>

bash	ksh	tcsh	Meaning/action
` `	` `	` `	Substitute output of enclosed command.
$( )	$( )		Substitute output of enclosed command. (Preferred form.)
$HOME	$HOME	$home	Home directory.
var=value	*var=value*	set *var=value*	Variable assignment.
export *var=val*	export *var=val*	setenv *var val*	Set environment variable.
${*nn*}	${*nn*}		More than nine args can be referenced.
"$@"	"$@"		All args as separate words.
$#	$#	$#argv	Number of arguments.
$?	$?	$status	Exit status.
$!	$!		Last background Process ID.
$-	$-		Current options.
. *file*	. *file*	source *file*	Read commands in *file*.
alias *x=y*	alias *x=y*	alias *x y*	Name *x* stands for *y*.
case	case	switch/case	Choose alternatives.
cd ~-	cd ~-	popd/pushd	Switch directories.
popd/pushd		popd/pushd	Switch directories.
done	done	end	End a loop statement.
esac	esac	endsw	End case or switch.
exit [*n*]	exit [*n*]	exit [(*expr*)]	Exit with a status.
for/do	for/do	foreach	Loop through values.
echo -E	print -r	glob	Ignore echo escapes.
hash	alias -t	hashstat	Display hashed commands (tracked aliases).
hash *cmds*	alias -t *cmds*	rehash	Remember command locations.
hash -r	PATH=$PATH	unhash	Forget command locations.
history	history	history	List previous commands.
fc -s	r	!!	Redo previous command.
fc -s *str*	r *str*	!*str*	Redo command that starts with *str*.
fc -s *x=y* [*cmd*]	r *x=y* [*cmd*]	!*cmd*:s/*x*/*y*/	Edit command, then execute.
if ((i==5))	if ((i==5))	if ($i==5)	Sample if statement.
fi	fi	endif	End if statement.
ulimit	ulimit	limit	Set resource limits.
pwd	pwd	dirs	Print working directory.
read	read	$<	Read from standard input.
trap INTR	trap INTR	onintr	Ignore interrupts.
unalias	unalias	unalias	Remove aliases.
until/do	until/do		Begin until loop.
while/do	while/do	while	Begin while loop.

4
The Bash and Korn Shells

The original Bourne shell distributed with V7 Unix in 1979 became the standard shell for writing shell scripts. The Bourne shell is still to be found in `/bin/sh` on many commercial Unix systems. The Bourne shell itself has not changed that much since its initial release, although it has seen modest enhancements over the years. The most notable new features were the CDPATH variable and a built-in test command with System III (circa 1980), command hashing and shell functions for System V Release 2 (circa 1984), and the addition of job control features for System V Release 4 (1989).

Because the Berkeley C shell (`csh`) offered features that were more pleasant for interactive use, such as command history and job control, for a long time the standard practice in the Unix world was to use the Bourne shell for programming and the C shell for daily use. David Korn at Bell Labs was the first developer to enhance the Bourne shell by adding `csh`-like features to it: history, job control, and additional programmability. Eventually, the Korn shell's feature set surpassed both the Bourne shell and the C shell, while remaining compatible with the Bourne shell for shell programming. Today, the POSIX standard defines the "standard shell" language and behavior based on the System V Bourne shell, with a selected subset of features from the Korn shell.

On most commercial Unix systems, including Solaris, `/bin/ksh` is `ksh88`. On Mac OS X (10.4 and newer), however, it's a recent version of `ksh93` from AT&T Research.

The Free Software Foundation, in keeping with its goal to produce a complete Unix work-alike system, developed a clone of the Bourne shell, written from scratch, named "Bash," the Bourne-Again SHell. Over time, Bash has become a POSIX-compliant version of the shell, with many additional features. A large part of these additional features overlap the features of the Korn shell, but Bash is not an exact Korn shell clone.

This chapter covers Bash, which is the primary shell for GNU/Linux and Mac OS X. Because `ksh88` is still commonly found, and because the source code for `ksh93` is available, this chapter also covers the two main versions of the Korn shell, `ksh88` and `ksh93`. It presents the following topics:

- Overview of features
- Invoking the shell
- Syntax
- Functions
- Variables
- Arithmetic expressions
- Command history
- Job control
- Command execution
- Restricted shells
- Built-in commands

http://www.gnu.org/software/bash/bash.html provides information about the Bash shell. Another page is *http://cnswww.cns.cwru.edu/~chet/bash/bashtop.html*. *http://www.kornshell.com* provides considerable information about the Korn shell. The section "Shell Source Code URLs" in Chapter 3 provides Internet URLs for source code download. See also *Classic Shell Scripting*, *Learning the Korn Shell*, and *Learning the bash Shell*, which are listed in the Bibliography.

All references in this chapter to the Bash shell are for Bash version 3. Many of the features listed for `ksh93` are found only in the version available from AT&T Research. Practically speaking, `ksh93` binaries on commercial Unix systems tend to be very early versions of `ksh93`; you should download the source and build your own executable version if you wish to use `ksh93` for production work.

Overview of Features

The Bash and Korn shells provide the following features:

- Input/output redirection
- Wildcard characters (metacharacters) for filename abbreviation
- Shell variables and options for customizing your environment
- A built-in command set for writing shell programs
- Shell functions, for modularizing tasks within a shell program
- Job control
- Command-line editing (using the command syntax of either `vi` or Emacs)
- Access to previous commands (command history)
- Integer arithmetic
- Arrays and arithmetic expressions
- Command-name abbreviation (aliasing)

ksh93 and Bash (but not ksh88) have the following capabilities:

- Upwards compliance with POSIX
- Internationalization facilities
- An arithmetic for loop
- More ways to substitute variables

ksh93 adds the following capabilities:

- Floating-point arithmetic and built-in arithmetic functions
- Structured variable names and indirect variable references
- Associative arrays
- More ways to match patterns

Invoking the Shell

The command interpreter for the Bash shell (bash) or the Korn shell (ksh) can be invoked as follows:

```
bash  [options]  [arguments]
ksh   [options]  [arguments]
```

ksh and Bash can execute commands from a terminal, from a file (when the first *argument* is an executable script), or from standard input (if no arguments remain or if -s is specified). Both shells automatically print prompts if standard input is a terminal, or if -i is given on the command line.

On many systems, /bin/sh is a link to Bash. When invoked as sh, Bash acts more like the traditional Bourne shell: login shells read /etc/profile and ~/.profile, and regular shells read $ENV, if it's set. Full details are available in the *bash*(1) manpage.

Bash and Korn

Options

Common options

-c *str*
: Read commands from string *str*.

-D
: Print all $"..." strings in the program. Not ksh88.

-i
: Create an interactive shell (prompt for input).

-p
: Start up as a privileged user. Bash: don't read $ENV or $BASH_ENV, don't import functions from the environment, and ignore the value of $SHELLOPTS. Korn shell: don't process $HOME/.profile, read /etc/suid_profile instead of $ENV.

-r
: Create a restricted shell.

-s
: Read commands from standard input. Output from built-in commands goes to file descriptor 1; all other shell output goes to file descriptor 2.

-, --
: End option processing.

Bash options

`-O` *option*
: Enable `shopt` option *option*.

`--debugger`
: Read the debugging profile at start-up, turn on the `extdebug` option to `shopt`, and enable function tracing. For use by the Bash debugger.

`--dump-po-strings`
: Same as `-D`, but output in GNU `gettext` format.

`--dump-strings`
: Same as `-D`.

`--help`
: Print a usage message and exit successfully.

`--init-file` *file*, `--rcfile` *file*
: Use *file* as the start-up file instead of `~/.bashrc` for interactive shells.

`--login`
: Shell is a login shell.

`--noediting`
: Do not use the *readline* library for input, even in an interactive shell.

`--noprofile`
: Do not read `/etc/profile` or any of the personal start-up files.

`--norc`
: Do not read `~/.bashrc`. Enabled automatically when invoked as `sh`.

`--posix`
: Turn on POSIX mode.

`--restricted`
: Same as `-r`.

`--verbose`
: Same as `set -v`; the shell prints lines as it reads them.

`--version`
: Print a version message and exit.

The remaining options to Bash and `ksh` are listed under the `set` built-in command.

Arguments

Arguments are assigned in order to the positional parameters `$1`, `$2`, etc. If the first argument is an executable script, commands are read from it, and the remaining arguments are assigned to `$1`, `$2`, etc. The name of the script is available as `$0`.

Syntax

This section describes the many symbols peculiar to the Bash and Korn shells. The topics are arranged as follows:

- Special files
- Filename metacharacters

- Quoting
- Command forms
- Redirection forms
- Coprocesses (Korn shell only)

Special Files

Both shells read one or more start-up files. Some of the files are read only when a shell is a login shell.

The Korn shell reads these files:

1. `/etc/profile`. Executed automatically at login, first.
2. `~/.profile`. Executed automatically at login, second.
3. $ENV. Specifies the name of a file to read when a new Korn shell is created. (`ksh88`: all shells. `ksh93`: interactive shells only.) The value is variable (`ksh93`: and command and arithmetic) substituted in order to determine the actual file name. Login shells read $ENV after processing the files `/etc/profile` and `$HOME/.profile`.

Bash reads these files:

1. `/etc/profile`. Executed automatically at login, first.
2. The first file found from this list: `~/.bash_profile`, `~/.bash_login`, or `~/.profile`. Executed automatically at login, second.
3. `~/.bashrc` is read by every shell, after the login files. However, if invoked as `sh`, Bash instead reads $ENV, just as the Korn shell does.

For both shells, the `getpwnam()` and `getpwuid()` functions are the sources of home directories for ~*name* abbreviations. (On single-user systems, the user database is stored in `/etc/passwd`. However on networked systems, this information may come from NIS, NIS+, or LDAP, not your workstation password file.)

Filename Metacharacters

`*`	Match any string of zero or more characters.
`?`	Match any single character.
[*abc*...]	Match any one of the enclosed characters; a hyphen can specify a range (e.g., `a-z`, `A-Z`, `0-9`).
[!*abc*...]	Match any character *not* enclosed as above.
`~`	Home directory of the current user.
~*name*	Home directory of user *name*.
`~+`	Current working directory ($PWD).
`~-`	Previous working directory ($OLDPWD).

In the Korn shell, or Bash with the `extglob` option on:

?(*pattern*)	Match zero or one instance of *pattern*.
*(*pattern*)	Match zero or more instances of *pattern*.
+(*pattern*)	Match one or more instances of *pattern*.

`@(pattern)`	Match exactly one instance of *pattern*.
`!(pattern)`	Match any strings that don't match *pattern*.
`\n`	Match the text matched by the *n*'th subpattern in `(...)`. `ksh93` only.

This *pattern* can be a sequence of patterns separated by `|`, meaning that the match applies to any of the patterns. This extended syntax resembles that available in `egrep` and `awk`. In the Korn shell, but not in Bash, if `&` is used instead of `|`, all the patterns must match. `&` has higher precedence than `|`.

`ksh93` and Bash support the POSIX `[[=c=]]` notation for matching characters that have the same weight, and `[[.c.]]` for specifying collating sequences. In addition, character classes, of the form `[[:class:]]`, allow you to match the following classes of characters.

Class	Characters matched	Class	Characters matched
`alnum`	Alphanumeric characters	`graph`	Nonspace characters
`alpha`	Alphabetic characters	`print`	Printable characters
`blank`	Space or tab	`punct`	Punctuation characters
`cntrl`	Control characters	`space`	Whitespace characters
`digit`	Decimal digits	`upper`	Uppercase characters
`lower`	Lowercase characters	`xdigit`	Hexadecimal digits

Bash and `ksh93` also accept the `[:word:]` character class, which is not in POSIX. `[[:word:]]` is equivalent to `[[:alnum:]_]`.

Examples

```
$ ls new*                  List new and new.1
$ cat ch?                  Match ch9 but not ch10
$ vi [D-R]*                Match files that begin with uppercase D through R
$ pr !(*.o|core) | lp      Print files that are not object files or core dumps
```

On modern systems, ranges such as `[D-R]` are not portable; the system's locale may include more than just the uppercase letters from `D` to `R` in the range.

Quoting

Quoting disables a character's special meaning and allows it to be used literally, as itself. The following table displays characters that have special meaning to the Bash and Korn shells.

Character	Meaning
`;`	Command separator
`&`	Background execution
`( )`	Command grouping
`|`	Pipe
`< > &`	Redirection symbols

Character	Meaning
`* ? [ ] ~ + - @ !`	Filename metacharacters
`" ' \`	Used in quoting other characters
`` ` ``	Command substitution
`$`	Variable substitution (or command or arithmetic substitution)
`space tab newline`	Word separators

These characters can be used for quoting:

`" "`
: Everything between " and " is taken literally, except for the following characters that keep their special meaning:

    `$` Variable (or command and arithmetic) substitution will occur.

    `` ` `` Command substitution will occur.

    `"` This marks the end of the double quote.

`' '`
: Everything between ' and ' is taken literally except for another '. You cannot embed another ' within such a quoted string.

`\`
: The character following a \ is taken literally. Use within " " to escape ", $, and `. Often used to escape itself, spaces, or newlines.

`$" "`
: Not ksh88. Just like "", except that locale translation is done.

`$' '`
: Not ksh88. Similar to '', but the quoted text is processed for the following escape sequences:

Sequence	Value	Sequence	Value
\a	Alert	\t	Tab
\b	Backspace	\v	Vertical tab
\c*X*	Control character *X*	*nnn*	Octal value *nnn*
\e	Escape	\x*nn*	Hexadecimal value *nn*
\E	Escape	\'	Single quote
\f	Form feed	\"	Double quote
\n	Newline	\\	Backslash
\r	Carriage return		

Examples

```
$ echo 'Single quotes "protect" double quotes'
Single quotes "protect" double quotes
$ echo "Well, isn't that \"special\"?"
Well, isn't that "special"?
$ echo "You have `ls | wc -l` files in `pwd`"
You have       43 files in /home/bob
$ echo "The value of \$x is $x"
The value of $x is 100
```

Command Forms

cmd &	Execute *cmd* in background.
cmd1 ; *cmd2*	Command sequence; execute multiple *cmd*s on the same line.
{ *cmd1* ; *cmd2* ; }	Execute commands as a group in the current shell.
(*cmd1* ; *cmd2*)	Execute commands as a group in a subshell.
cmd1 | *cmd2*	Pipe; use output from *cmd1* as input to *cmd2*.
cmd1 `` `cmd2` ``	Command substitution; use *cmd2* output as arguments to *cmd1*.
cmd1 $(*cmd2*)	POSIX shell command substitution; nesting is allowed.
cmd $((*expression*))	POSIX shell arithmetic substitution. Use the result of *expression* as argument to *cmd*.
cmd1 && *cmd2*	AND; execute *cmd1* and then (if *cmd1* succeeds) *cmd2*. This is a "short-circuit" operation; *cmd2* is never executed if *cmd1* fails.
cmd1 || *cmd2*	OR; execute either *cmd1* or (if *cmd1* fails) *cmd2*. This is a "short-circuit" operation; *cmd2* is never executed if *cmd1* succeeds.
! *cmd*	NOT; execute *cmd*, and produce a zero exit status if *cmd* exits with a nonzero status. Otherwise, produce a nonzero status when *cmd* exits with a zero status. Not ksh88.

Examples

```
$ nroff file > file.txt &                 Format in the background
$ cd; ls                                  Execute sequentially
$ (date; who; pwd) > logfile              All output is redirected
$ sort file | pr -3 | lp                  Sort file, page output, then print
$ vi `grep -l ifdef *.c`                  Edit files found by grep
$ egrep '(yes|no)' `cat list`             Specify a list of files to search
$ egrep '(yes|no)' $(cat list)            POSIX version of previous
$ egrep '(yes|no)' $(< list)              Faster, not in POSIX
$ grep XX file && lp file                 Print file if it contains the pattern;
$ grep XX file || echo "XX not found"     otherwise, echo an error message
```

Redirection Forms

File descriptor	Name	Common abbreviation	Typical default
0	Standard input	stdin	Keyboard
1	Standard output	stdout	Screen
2	Standard error	stderr	Screen

The usual input source or output destination can be changed, as seen in the following sections.

Simple redirection

cmd > *file*
: Send output of *cmd* to *file* (overwrite).

cmd >> *file*
: Send output of *cmd* to *file* (append).

cmd < *file*
: Take input for *cmd* from *file*.

cmd << *text*

The contents of the shell script up to a line identical to *text* become the standard input for *cmd* (*text* can be stored in a shell variable). This command form is sometimes called a *Here document*. Input is usually typed at the keyboard or in the shell program. Commands that typically use this syntax include cat, ex, and sed. (If <<- is used, leading tabs are stripped from the contents of the here document, and the tabs are ignored when comparing input with the end-of-input *text* marker.) If any part of *text* is quoted, the input is passed through verbatim. Otherwise, the contents are processed for variable, command, and arithmetic substitutions.

cmd <<< *word*

Supply text of *word*, with trailing newline, as input to *cmd*. (This is known as a *here string*, from the free version of the rc shell.) Not ksh88.

cmd <> *file*

Open *file* for reading *and* writing on the standard input. The contents are not destroyed.*

cmd >| *file*

Send output of *cmd* to *file* (overwrite), even if the shell's noclobber option is set.

Redirection using file descriptors

cmd >&*n*	Send *cmd* output to file descriptor *n*.
cmd *m*>&*n*	Same, except that output that would normally go to file descriptor *m* is sent to file descriptor *n* instead.
cmd >&-	Close standard output.
cmd <&*n*	Take input for *cmd* from file descriptor *n*.
cmd *m*<&*n*	Same, except that input that would normally come from file descriptor *m* comes from file descriptor *n* instead.
cmd <&-	Close standard input.
cmd <&*n*-	Move input file descriptor *n* instead of duplicating it. Not ksh88.
cmd >&*n*-	Move output file descriptor *n* instead of duplicating it. Not ksh88.

Multiple redirection

cmd 2>*file*	Send standard error to *file*; standard output remains the same (e.g., the screen).
cmd > *file* 2>&1	Send both standard error and standard output to *file*.
cmd &> *file*	Same. Bash only, preferred form.
cmd >& *file*	Same. Bash only.
cmd > *f1* 2>*f2*	Send standard output to file *f1*, standard error to file *f2*.
cmd | tee *files*	Send output of *cmd* to standard output (usually the terminal) and to *files*. (See the Example in Chapter 2, under **tee**.)
cmd 2>&1 | tee *files*	Send standard output and error output of *cmd* to standard output (usually the terminal) and to *files*.

* With <, the file is opened read-only, and writes on the file descriptor will fail. With <>, the file is opened read-write; it is up to the application to actually take advantage of this.

No space should appear between file descriptors and a redirection symbol; spacing is optional in the other cases.

Bash allows multidigit file descriptor numbers. The other shells do not.

Examples

```
$ cat part1 > book
$ cat part2 part3 >> book
$ mail tim < report
$ sed 's/^/XX /g' << END_ARCHIVE
> This is often how a shell archive is "wrapped",
> bundling text for distribution.  You would normally
> run sed from a shell program, not from the command line.
> END_ARCHIVE
XX This is often how a shell archive is "wrapped",
XX bundling text for distribution.  You would normally
XX run sed from a shell program, not from the command line.
```

To redirect standard output to standard error:

```
$ echo "Usage error: see administrator" 1>&2
```

The following command sends output (files found) to `filelist` and error messages (inaccessible files) to file `no_access`:

```
$ find / -print > filelist 2>no_access
```

Coprocesses

Coprocesses are a feature of the Korn shell only.

cmd1 | *cmd2* |&	Coprocess; execute the pipeline in the background. The shell sets up a two-way pipe, allowing redirection of both standard input and standard output.
`read -p` *var*	Read coprocess output into variable *var*.
`print -p` *string*	Write *string* to the coprocess.
cmd <&p	Take input for *cmd* from the coprocess.
cmd >&p	Send output of *cmd* to the coprocess.
exec *n*<&p	Move input from coprocess to file descriptor *n*.
exec *n*>&p	Move output for coprocess to file descriptor *n*.

Moving the coprocess input and output file descriptors to standard file descriptors allows you to open multiple coprocesses.

Examples

```
$ ed - memo |&              Start coprocess
$ print -p /word/           Send ed command to coprocess
$ read -p search            Read output of ed command into variable search
$ print "$search"           Show the line on standard output
A word to the wise.
```

Functions

A shell *function* is a grouping of commands within a shell script. Shell functions let you modularize your program by dividing it up into separate tasks. This way the code for each task need not be repeated every time you need to perform the task. The POSIX shell syntax for defining a function follows the Bourne shell:

```
name () {
    function body's code come here
}
```

Functions are invoked just as are regular shell built-in commands or external commands. The command line parameters `$1`, `$2`, and so on receive the function's arguments, temporarily hiding the global values of `$1`, etc. For example:

```
# fatal --- print an error message and die:

fatal () {
    echo "$0: fatal error:" "$@" >&2      # messages to standard error
    exit 1
}
...
if [ $# = 0 ]     # not enough arguments
then
    fatal not enough arguments
fi
```

A function may use the `return` command to return an exit value to the calling shell program. Be careful *not* to use `exit` from within a function unless you really wish to terminate the entire program.

Bash and the Korn shell allow you to define functions using an additional keyword, `function`, as follows:

```
function fatal {
    echo "$0: fatal error:" "$@" >&2      # messages to standard error
    exit 1
}
```

When working with the different shells and defining functions, there are semantic differences that should be kept in mind:

- In Bash, all functions share traps with the "parent" shell (except the `DEBUG` trap, if function tracing has been turned on). With the `errtrace` option enabled (either `set -E` or `set -o errtrace`), functions also inherit the `ERR` trap. If function tracing has been enabled, functions inherit the `RETURN` trap. Functions may have local variables, and they may be recursive. The syntax used to define a function is irrelevant.
- In `ksh88`, all functions have their own traps and local variables, and may be recursive.
- In `ksh93`, *name* `()` functions share traps with the "parent" shell and may not be recursive.
- In `ksh93`, `function` functions have their own traps and local variables, and may be recursive. Using the `.` command with a `function` function gives it POSIX shell semantics (i.e., shared traps and variables).

Variables

This section describes the following:

- Variable substitution
- Built-in shell variables
- Other shell variables
- Arrays
- Discipline functions (`ksh93` only)
- Special prompt strings

Variable Substitution

`ksh93` provides structured variables, such as `pos.x` and `pos.y`. To create either one, `pos` must already exist, and braces must be used to retrieve their values. Names beginning with `.sh` are reserved for use by `ksh`.

No spaces should be used in the following expressions. The colon (:) is optional; if it's included, *var* must be nonnull as well as set.

var=*value* ...	Set each variable *var* to a *value*.
${*var*}	Use value of *var*; braces are optional if *var* is separated from the following text. They are required for array variables, and in `ksh93` if a variable name contains periods.
${*var*:-*value*}	Use *var* if set; otherwise, use *value*.
${*var*:=*value*}	Use *var* if set; otherwise, use *value* and assign *value* to *var*.
${*var*:?*value*}	Use *var* if set; otherwise, print *value* and exit (if not interactive). If *value* isn't supplied, print the phrase "parameter null or not set."
${*var*:+*value*}	Use *value* if *var* is set; otherwise, use nothing.
${#*var*}	Use the length of *var*.
${#*}	Use the number of positional parameters.
${#@}	Same.
${*var*#*pattern*}	Use value of *var* after removing *pattern* from the left. Remove the shortest matching piece.
${*var*##*pattern*}	Same as #*pattern*, but remove the longest matching piece.
${*var*%*pattern*}	Use value of *var* after removing *pattern* from the right. Remove the shortest matching piece.
${*var*%%*pattern*}	Same as %*pattern*, but remove the longest matching piece.

In `ksh93` and Bash:

${!*prefix**}, ${!*prefix*@}	List of variables whose names begin with *prefix*.
${*var*:*pos*}, ${*var*:*pos*:*len*}	Starting at position *pos* (0-based) in variable *var*, extract *len* characters, or rest of string if no *len*. *pos* and *len* may be arithmetic expressions.
${*var*/*pat*/*repl*}	Use value of *var*, with first match of *pat* replaced with *repl*.
${*var*/*pat*}	Use value of *var*, with first match of *pat* deleted.
${*var*//*pat*/*repl*}	Use value of *var*, with every match of *pat* replaced with *repl*.
${*var*/#*pat*/*repl*}	Use value of *var*, with match of *pat* replaced with *repl*. Match must occur at beginning of the value.
${*var*/%*pat*/*repl*}	Use value of *var*, with match of *pat* replaced with *repl*. Match must occur at end of the value.

In ksh93, indirect variables allow you to "alias" one variable name to affect the value of another. This is accomplished using typeset -n:

```
$ greet="hello, world"                    Create initial variable
$ typeset -n friendly_message=greet       Set up alias
$ echo $friendly_message                  Access old value through new name
hello, world
$ friendly_message="don't panic"          Change the value
$ echo $greet                             Old variable is changed
don't panic
```

Bash has a similar mechanism for indirect variable referencing:

```
$ greet="hello, world"                    Create initial variable
$ friendly_message=greet                  Aliasing variable
$ echo ${!friendly_message}               Use the alias
hello, world
```

Examples

```
$ u=up d=down blank=             Assign values to three variables (last is null)
$ echo ${u}root                  Braces are needed here
uproot
$ echo ${u-$d}                   Display value of u or d; since u is set, it's printed
up
$ echo ${tmp-`date`}             If tmp is not set, the date command is executed
Mon Aug 30 11:15:23 EDT 2004
$ echo ${blank="no data"}        blank is set, so it is printed (a blank line)
$ echo ${blank:="no data"}       blank is set but null, so the string is printed
no data
$ echo $blank                    blank now has a new value
no data
$ tail=${PWD##*/}                Take the current directory name and remove the
                                 longest character string ending with /, which
                                 removes the leading pathname and leaves the tail
```

Built-in Shell Variables

Built-in variables are automatically set by the shell and are typically used inside shell scripts. Built-in variables can make use of the variable substitution patterns shown previously. Note that the $ is not actually part of the variable name, although the variable is always referenced this way. The following are available in any Bourne-compatible shell:

`$#`	Number of command-line arguments.
`$-`	Options currently in effect (arguments supplied on command line or to set).
`$?`	Exit value of last executed command.
`$$`	Process number of current process.
`$!`	Process number of last background command.
`$0`	First word; that is, command name. This will have the full pathname if it was found via a PATH search.
`$n`	Individual arguments on command line (positional parameters). The Bourne shell allows only nine parameters to be referenced directly (*n* = 1–9); Bash and the Korn shell allow *n* to be greater than 9 if specified as ${*n*}.

`$*`, `$@`	All arguments on command line (`$1 $2` ...).
`"$*"`	All arguments on command line as one string (`"$1 $2..."`). The values are separated by the first character in IFS.
`"$@"`	All arguments on command line, individually quoted (`"$1" "$2"` ...).

Bash and the Korn shell automatically set these additional variables:

`$_`	Temporary variable; initialized to pathname of script or program being executed. Later, stores the last argument of previous command. Also stores name of matching MAIL file during mail checks.
`HISTCMD`	The history number of the current command.
`LINENO`	Current line number within the script or function.
`OLDPWD`	Previous working directory (set by `cd`).
`OPTARG`	Name of last option processed by `getopts`.
`OPTIND`	Numerical index of OPTARG.
`PPID`	Process number of this shell's parent.
`PWD`	Current working directory (set by `cd`).
`RANDOM[=`*n*`]`	Generate a new random number with each reference; start with integer *n*, if given.
`REPLY`	Default reply, used by `select` and `read`.
`SECONDS[=`*n*`]`	Number of seconds since the shell was started, or, if *n* is given, number of seconds + *n* since the shell started.

`ksh93` automatically sets these additional variables. Variables whose names contain "." must be enclosed in braces when referenced, e.g., `${.sh.edchar}`.

`.sh.edchar`	The character(s) entered when processing a `KEYBD` trap. Changing it replaces the characters that caused the trap.
`.sh.edcol`	The position of the cursor in the most recent `KEYBD` trap.
`.sh.edmode`	Will be equal to ESCAPE if in a `KEYBD` trap in `vi` mode, otherwise empty.
`.sh.edtext`	The characters in the input buffer during a `KEYBD` trap.
`.sh.file`	The pathename of the current script.
`.sh.fun`	The name of the current function.
`.sh.match`	Array variable containing text matched during a variable substitution. Index `0` is the entire value; the others correspond to parenthesized subexpressions.
`.sh.name`	The name of the variable running a discipline function.
`.sh.subscript`	The subscript of the variable running a discipline function.
`.sh.value`	The value of the variable inside the `set` and `get` discipline functions.
`.sh.version`	The version of `ksh93`.

Bash automatically sets these additional variables. Many of these variables are for use by the Bash Debugger (see *http://bashdb.sourceforge.net*) or for providing programmable completion (see the section "Programmable Completion (Bash Only)," later in this chapter).

`BASH`	The full pathname used to invoke this instance of Bash.
`BASH_ARGC`	Array variable. Each element holds the number of arguments for the corresponding function or dot-script invocation. Set only in extended debug mode, with `shopt -s extdebug`.

BASH_ARGV	An array variable similar to BASH_ARGC. Each element is one of the arguments passed to a function or dot-script. It functions as a stack, with values being pushed on at each call. Thus, the last element is the last argument to the most recent function or script invocation. Set only in extended debug mode, with `shopt -s extdebug`.
BASH_COMMAND	The command currently executing or about to be executed. Inside a trap handler, it is the command running when the trap was invoked.
BASH_EXECUTION_STRING	The string argument passed to the `-c` option.
BASH_LINENO	Array variable, corresponding to BASH_SOURCE and FUNCNAME. For any given function number *i* (starting at 0), `${FUNCNAME[i]}` was invoked in file `${BASH_SOURCE[i]}` on line `${BASH_LINENO[i]}`. The information is stored with the most recent function invocation first.
BASH_REMATCH	Array variable, assigned by the `=~` operator of the `[[ ]]` construct. Index 0 is the text that matched the entire pattern. The other indices are the text matched by parenthesized subexpressions. This variable is read-only.
BASH_SOURCE	Array variable, containing source filenames. Each element corresponds to those in FUNCNAME and BASH_LINENO.
BASH_SUBSHELL	This variable is incremented by one each time a subshell or subshell environment is created.
BASH_VERSINFO[0]	The major version number, or release, of Bash.
BASH_VERSINFO[1]	The minor version number, or version, of Bash.
BASH_VERSINFO[2]	The patch level.
BASH_VERSINFO[3]	The build version.
BASH_VERSINFO[4]	The release status.
BASH_VERSINFO[5]	The machine type, same value as in MACHTYPE.
BASH_VERSION	A string describing the version of Bash.
COMP_CWORD	For programmable completion. Index into COMP_WORDS, indicating the current cursor position.
COMP_LINE	For programmable completion. The current command line.
COMP_POINT	For programmable completion. The position of the cursor as a character index in COMP_LINE.
COMP_WORDBREAKS	For programmable completion. The characters that the *readline* library treats as word separators when doing word completion.
COMP_WORDS	For programmable completion. Array variable containing the individual words on the command line.
DIRSTACK	Array variable, containing the contents of the directory stack as displayed by `dirs`. Changing existing elements modifies the stack, but only pushd and popd can add or remove elements from the stack.
EUID	Read-only variable with the numeric effective UID of the current user.
FUNCNAME	Array variable, containing function names. Each element corresponds to those in BASH_SOURCE and BASH_LINENO.
GROUPS	Array variable containing the list of numeric group IDs in which the current user is a member.
HISTCMD	The history number of the current command.
HOSTNAME	The name of the current host.
HOSTTYPE	A string that describes the host system.
MACHTYPE	A string that describes the host system in the GNU *cpu–company–system* format.
OSTYPE	A string that describes the operating system.

`PIPESTATUS`	An array variable containing the exit statuses of the commands in the most recent foreground pipeline.
`SHELLOPTS`	A colon-separated list of shell options (for `set -o`). If set in the environment at start-up, Bash enables each option present in the list.
`SHLVL`	Incremented by one every time a new Bash starts up.
`UID`	Read-only variable with the numeric real UID of the current user.

Other Shell Variables

The following variables are not automatically set by the shell, although many of them can influence the shell's behavior. They are typically used in your `.profile` file, where you can define them to suit your needs. Variables can be assigned values by issuing commands of the form:

```
variable=value
```

This list includes the type of value expected when defining these variables. Those that are specific to the Bash shell are marked as (B). Those that are specific to the Korn shell are marked as (K). Those that are specific to `ksh93` are marked (K93).

`CDPATH=`*`dirs`*	Directories searched by `cd`; allows shortcuts in changing directories; unset by default.
`COLUMNS=`*`n`*	Screen's column width; used in line edit modes and `select` lists.
`COMPREPLY=(`*`words`*` ...)`	(B) Array variable from which Bash reads the possible completions generated by a completion function.
`EDITOR=`*`file`*	(K) Pathname of line edit mode to turn on (can end in `emacs` or `vi`); used when VISUAL is not set.
`EMACS`	(B) If the value starts with `t`, Bash assumes it's running in an Emacs buffer and disables line editing.
`ENV=`*`file`*	Name of script that gets executed at start-up; useful for storing alias and function definitions. For example, `ENV=$HOME/.kshrc`.
`FCEDIT=`*`file`*	Editor used by `fc` command (default is `/bin/ed`). Obsoleted in `ksh93` by HISTEDIT.
`FIGNORE=`*`pattern`*	(K93) Pattern describing the set of filenames to ignore during pattern matching. (B) Similar: colon-separated list of patterns describing filenames to ignore when doing filename completion.
`FPATH=`*`dirs`*	(K) Directories to search for function definitions; undefined functions are set via `typeset -fu`; FPATH is searched when these functions are first referenced. (`ksh93` also searches PATH.)
`GLOBIGNORE=`*`patlist`*	(B) Colon-separated list of patterns describing the set of filenames to ignore during pattern matching.
`HISTCONTROL=`*`list`*	(B) Colon-separated list of values controlling how commands are saved in the history file. Recognized values are: `ignoredups`, `ignorespace`, `ignoreboth`, and `erasedups`.
`HISTEDIT=`*`file`*	(K93) Editor used by `hist` command, if set. Overrides the setting of FCEDIT.
`HISTFILE=`*`file`*	File in which to store command history. For `ksh`, it must be set before `ksh` is started, and the default is `$HOME/.sh_history`. If you use both Bash and `ksh`, be sure to have different files for this value, as the format of the saved history file is *not* compatible between the two shells.

`HISTFILESIZE=`*n*
: (B) Number of lines to be kept in the history file. This may be different than the number of commands.

`HISTIGNORE=`*list*
: (B) A colon-separated list of patterns that must match the entire command line. Matching lines are *not* saved in the history file. An unescaped `&` in a pattern matches the previous history line.

`HISTSIZE=`*n*
: Number of history commands to be kept in the history file.

`HISTTIMEFORMAT=`*string*
: (B) A format string for *strftime*(3) to use for printing timestamps along with commands from the `history` command. If set (even if null), Bash saves timestamps in the history file along with the commands.

`HOME=`*dir*
: Home directory; set by `login` (from `/etc/passwd` file).

`HOSTFILE=`*file*
: (B) Name of a file in the same format as `/etc/hosts` that Bash should use to find hostnames for hostname completion.

`IFS='`*chars*`'`
: Input field separators; default is space, tab, and newline.

`IGNOREEOF=`*n*
: (B) Numeric value indicating how many successive EOF characters must be typed before Bash exits. If null or nonnumeric value, default is 10.

`INPUTRC=`*file*
: (B) Initialization file for the *readline* library. This overrides the default value of `~/.inputrc`.

`LANG=`*dir*
: Default value for locale, used if no LC_* variables are set.

`LC_ALL=`*locale*
: (B, K93) Current locale; overrides LANG and the other LC_* variables.

`LC_COLLATE=`*locale*
: (B, K93) Locale to use for character collation (sorting order).

`LC_CTYPE=`*locale*
: (B, K93) Locale to use for character class functions. (See the earlier section "Filename Metacharacters.")

`LC_MESSAGES=`*locale*
: (B) Locale to use for translating `$"..."` strings.

`LC_NUMERIC=`*locale*
: (B, K93) Locale to use for the decimal-point character.

`LINES=`*n*
: Screen's height; used for `select` lists.

`MAIL=`*file*
: Default file to check for incoming mail; set by `login`.

`MAILCHECK=`*n*
: Number of seconds between mail checks; default is 600 (10 minutes).

`MAILPATH=`*files*
: One or more files, delimited by a colon, to check for incoming mail. Along with each file, you may supply an optional message that the shell prints when the file increases in size. Messages are separated from the filename by a ? character, and the default message is `You have mail in $_`. `$_` is replaced with the name of the file. For example, you might have:

```
MAILPATH="$MAIL? Candygram!:/etc/motd?New Login Message"
```

`OPTERR=`*n*
: (B) When set to 1 (the default value), Bash prints error messages from the built-in `getopts` command.

`PATH=`*dirlist*
: One or more pathnames, delimited by colons, in which to search for commands to execute. Default for many systems is `/bin:/usr/bin`. On Solaris, the default is `/usr/bin:`. However, the standard start-up scripts change it to:

```
/usr/bin:/usr/ucb:/etc:.
```

`ksh93`: PATH is also searched for function definitions for undefined functions.

`POSIXLY_CORRECT=`*string*
: (B) When set at start-up or while running, Bash enters POSIX mode, disabling behavior and modifying features that conflict with the POSIX standard.

`PROMPT_COMMAND=`*command*
: (B) If set, Bash executes this command each time before printing the primary prompt.

`PS1=`*string*
: Primary prompt string; default is $.

PS2=*string*	Secondary prompt (used in multiline commands); default is >.
PS3=*string*	Prompt string in `select` loops; default is `#?`.
PS4=*string*	Prompt string for execution trace (`ksh -x`, `bash -x`, or `set -x`); default is +.
SHELL=*file*	Name of default shell (e.g., `/bin/sh`). Bash sets this if it's not in the environment at start-up.
TERM=*string*	Terminal type.
TIMEFORMAT=*string*	(B) A format string for the output for the `time` keyword.
TMOUT=*n*	If no command is typed after *n* seconds, exit the shell. Also affects the `read` command and the `select` loop.
VISUAL=*path*	(K) Same as EDITOR, but VISUAL is checked first.
auto_resume=*list*	(B) Enables the use of simple strings for resuming stopped jobs. With a value of `exact`, the string must match a command name exactly. With a value of `substring`, it can match a substring of the command name.
histchars=*chars*	(B) Two or three characters that control Bash's `csh`-style history expansion. The first character signals a history event. The second is the "quick substitution" character; the third indicates the start of a comment. The default value is `!^#`.

Arrays

Both shells support one-dimensional arrays. The first element is numbered 0. Bash has no limit on the number of elements. `ksh88` allowed up 1024 elements, early versions of `ksh93` allowed at least 4096 elements, and modern versions allow up to 65,536 elements. Arrays are initialized with a special form of assignment:

```
message=(hi there how are you today)          Bash and ksh93
```

where the specified values become elements of the array. The Korn shell has an additional syntax:

```
set -A message hi there how are you today     Ksh88 and ksh93
```

Individual elements may also be assigned to:

```
message[0]=hi                                 This is the hard way
message[1]=there
message[2]=how
message[3]=are
message[4]=you
message[5]=today
```

Declaring arrays is not required. Any valid reference to a subscripted variable can create an array.

When referencing arrays, use the `${ ... }` syntax. This isn't needed when referencing arrays inside `(( ))` (the form of `let` that does automatic quoting). Note that [and] are typed literally (i.e., they don't stand for optional syntax).

${*name*[*i*]}	Use element *i* of array *name*. *i* can be any arithmetic expression as described under `let`.
${*name*}	Use element 0 of array *name*.
${*name*[*]}	Use all elements of array *name*.
${*name*[@]}	Same.
${#*name*[*]}	Use the number of elements in array *name*.
${#*name*[@]}	Same.

ksh93 provides associative arrays, where the indices are strings instead of numbers (as in awk). In this case, [and] act like double quotes. Associative arrays are created with typeset -A. A special syntax allows assigning to multiple elements at once:

```
data=([joe]=30 [mary]=25)
```

The values would be retrieved as ${data[joe]} and ${data[mary]}.

Discipline Functions (ksh93 Only)

Along with structured variables, ksh93 introduces *discipline functions*. These are special functions that are called whenever a variable's value is accessed or changed. For a shell variable named x, you can define the following functions:

x.get	Called when x's value is retrieved ($x).
x.set	Called when x's value is changed (x=2).
x.unset	Called when x is unset (unset x).

Within the discipline functions, special variables provide information about the variable being changed:

.sh.name	The name of the variable being changed.
.sh.subscript	The subscript of the array element being changed.
.sh.value	The value of the variable being assigned or returned. Changing it within the discipline function changes the value that is actually assigned or returned.

Special Prompt Strings

Both shells process the value of PS1 for special strings. The Korn shell expands a single ! into the current command number. Use !! to get a literal !. For example:

```
PS1='cmd !> '
```

Bash processes the values of PS1, PS2, and PS4 for the following special escape sequences.

\a	An ASCII BEL character (octal 07).
\A	The current time in 24-hour HH:MM format.
\d	The date in "weekday month day" format.
\D{*format*}	The date as specified by the *strftime*(3) format *format*. The braces are required.
\e	An ASCII Escape character (octal 033).
\h	The hostname, up to the first period.
\H	The full hostname.
\j	The current number of jobs.
\l	The basename of the shell's terminal device.
\n	A newline character.
\r	A carriage return character.
\s	The name of the shell (basename of $0).
\t	The current time in 24-hour HH:MM:SS format.
\T	The current time in 12-hour HH:MM:SS format.
\u	The current user's username.

`\v`	The version of Bash.
`\V`	The release (version plus patchlevel) of Bash.
`\w`	The current directory, with $HOME abbreviated as ~.
`\W`	The basename of the current directory, with $HOME abbreviated as ~.
`\!`	The history number of this command.
`\#`	The command number of this command.
`\$`	If the effective UID is 0, a #, otherwise a $.
`\@`	The current time in 12-hour a.m./p.m. format.
`\nnn`	The character represented by octal value *nnn*.
`\\`	A literal backslash.
`\[`	Start a sequence of nonprinting characters, such as for highlighting or changing colors on a terminal.
`\]`	End a sequence of nonprinting characters.

In addition, some or all of the PS1–PS4 variables undergo different substitutions, as outlined in the following table:

Substitution	ksh88	ksh93	Bash
! for command number	PS1	PS1	
Escape sequences			PS1, PS2, PS4
Variable substitution	PS1	PS1	PS1, PS2, PS4
Command substitution		PS1	PS1, PS2, PS4
Arithmetic substitution		PS1	PS1, PS2, PS4

In Bash, the escape sequences are processed first, and then, if the `promptvars` shell option is enabled via the `shopt` command (the default), the substitutions are performed.

Arithmetic Expressions

The `let` command performs arithmetic. `ksh88` and Bash are restricted to integer arithmetic. `ksh93` can do floating-point arithmetic as well. Both shells provide a way to substitute arithmetic values (for use as command arguments or in variables); base conversion is also possible:

`$(( expr ))`	Use the value of the enclosed arithmetic expression.
B`#`*n*	Interpret integer *n* in numeric base *B*. For example, `8#100` specifies the octal equivalent of decimal 64.

Operators

The shells use arithmetic operators from the C programming language, in decreasing order of precedence. `ksh88` does not support the ++, --, unary +, ?:, comma, or ** operators. Early versions of `ksh93` do not have **.

Operator	Description
`++ --`	Auto-increment and auto-decrement, both prefix and postfix.
`+ - ! ~`	Unary plus and minus, logical negation and binary inversion (one's complement).

Operator	Description
`**`	Exponentiation.[a]
`* / %`	Multiplication; division; modulus (remainder).
`+ -`	Addition; subtraction.
`<< >>`	Bitwise left shift; bitwise right shift.
`< <= > >=`	Less than; less than or equal to; greater than; greater than or equal to.
`== !=`	Equality; inequality (both evaluated left to right).
`&`	Bitwise AND.
`^`	Bitwise exclusive OR.
`|`	Bitwise OR.
`&&`	Logical AND (short-circuit).
`||`	Logical OR (short-circuit).
`?:`	Inline conditional evaluation.

`= += -=`
`*= /= %=`
`<<= >>=`
`&= ^= |=`
	Assignment.

`,`	Sequential expression evaluation.

[a] In ksh93, the ** operator is right-associative. In bash versions prior to 3.1, it is left-associative. It will be changed to right-associative starting with version 3.1.

Built-in Mathematical Functions (ksh93 Only)

ksh93 provides access to the standard set of mathematical functions. They are called using C function call syntax.

Name	Function	Name	Function
abs	Absolute value	hypot	Euclidean distance
acos	Arc cosine	int	Integer part of floating-point number
asin	Arc sine	log	Natural logarithm
atan	Arc tangent	pow	Exponentiation (x^y)
atan2	Arc tangent of two values	sin	Sine
cos	Cosine	sinh	Hyperbolic sine
cosh	Hyperbolic cosine	sqrt	Square root
exp	Exponential (e^x)	tan	Tangent
fmod	Floating-point remainder	tanh	Hyperbolic tangent

Examples

```
let "count=0" "i = i + 1"                Assign i and count
let "num % 2"                            Test for an even number
(( percent >= 0 && percent <= 100 ))     Test the range of a value
```

See the **let** entry in the later section "Built-in Commands (Bash and Korn Shells)" for more information and examples.

Command History

Both shells let you display or modify previous commands. Commands in the history list can be modified using:

- Line-edit mode
- The `fc` and `hist` commands

Bash also supports a command history mechanism very similar to that of the C shell. Because the interactive line-editing features are considerably superior, and because Bash's command history is almost identical to that of the C shell, we have chosen not to cover those features here. See Chapter 5 and the Bash manpage for more information.

Line-Edit Mode

Line-edit mode emulates many features of the `vi` and `emacs` editors. The history list is treated like a file. When the editor is invoked, you type editing keystrokes to move to the command line you want to execute. You can also change the line before executing it. When you're ready to issue the command, press the ENTER key.

In `ksh`, line-edit mode can be started in several ways. For example, these are equivalent:

```
$ VISUAL=vi
$ EDITOR=vi
$ set -o vi          Overrides value of VISUAL or EDITOR
```

For Bash, you must use either `set -o vi` or `set -o emacs`; assignment to the VISUAL or EDITOR variables has no effect.

Note that `vi` starts in input mode; to type a `vi` command, press the Escape key first.

Common editing keystrokes

vi	emacs	Result
`k`	`CTRL-p`	Get previous command.
`j`	`CTRL-n`	Get next command.
`/`*`string`*	`CTRL-r` *`string`*	Get previous command containing *string*.
`h`	`CTRL-b`	Move back one character.
`l`	`CTRL-f`	Move forward one character.
`b`	`ESC-b`	Move back one word.
`w`	`ESC-f`	Move forward one word.
`X`	`DEL`	Delete previous character.
`x`	`CTRL-d`	Delete character under cursor.
`dw`	`ESC-d`	Delete word forward.
`db`	`ESC-h`	Delete word backward.
`xp`	`CTRL-t`	Transpose two characters.

The fc and hist Commands

"fc" stands for either "find command" or "fix command," since it does both jobs. Use `fc -l` to list history commands and `fc -e` to edit them. See the **fc** entry in the later section "Built-in Commands (Bash and Korn Shells)," for more information.

In `ksh93`, the `fc` command has been renamed `hist`, and `alias fc=hist` is predefined.

Examples

`$ history`	*List the last 16 commands*
`$ fc -l 20 30`	*List commands 20 through 30*
`$ fc -l -5`	*List the last 5 commands*
`$ fc -l cat`	*List all commands since the last command beginning with cat*
`$ fc -l 50`	*List all commands since command 50*
`$ fc -ln 5 > doit`	*Save command 5 to file doit*
`$ fc -e vi 5 20`	*Edit commands 5 through 20 using vi*
`$ fc -e emacs`	*Edit previous command using emacs*

The following only work in the Korn shell, which predefines the `r` alias:

`$ r`	*Reexecute previous command*
`$ r cat`	*Reexecute last cat command*
`$ r doc=Doc`	*Substitute, then reexecute last command*
`$ r chap=doc c`	*Reexecute last command that begins with c, but change string chap to doc*

For both shells, the interactive line-editing is easier to use than `fc`, since you can move up and down in the saved command history using your favorite editor commands (as long as your favorite editor is either `vi` or Emacs!). Current versions of both shells also let you use the Up and Down arrow keys to traverse the command history.

Programmable Completion (Bash Only)

Bash and the *readline* library provide *completion* facilities, whereby you can type part of a command name, hit the TAB key, and have Bash fill in part or all of the rest of the command or filename. *Programmable completion* lets you, as a shell programmer, write code to customize the list of possible completions that Bash will present for a particular, partially entered word. This is accomplished through the combination of several facilities.

- The `complete` command allows you provide a completion specification, or *compspec*, for individual commands. You specify, via various options, how to tailor the list of possible completions for the particular command. This is simple, but adequate for many needs. (See the **complete** entry in the section "Built-in Commands (Bash and Korn Shells)," later in this chapter.)
- For more flexibility, you may use `complete -F` *`funcname command`*. This tells Bash to call *funcname* to provide the list of completions for *command*. You write the *funcname* function.
- Within the code for a `-F` function, the COMP* shell variables provide information about the current command line. COMPREPLY is an array into which the function places the final list of completion results.

- Also within the code for a `-F` function, you may use the `compgen` command to generate a list of results, such as "usernames that begin with `a`" or "all set variables." The intent is that such results would be used with an array assignment:

  ```
  ...
  COMPREPLY=( $( compgen options arguments ) )
  ...
  ```

Compspecs may be associated with either a full pathname for a command, or more commonly, with an unadorned command name (`/usr/bin/man` versus plain `man`). Completions are attempted in the following order, based on the options provided to the `complete` command.

1. Bash first identifies the command. If a pathname is used, Bash looks to see if a compspec exists for the full pathname. Otherwise, it sets the command name to the last component of the pathname, and searches for a compspec for the command name.
2. If a compspec exists, Bash uses it. If not, Bash falls back to the default built-in completions.
3. Bash performs the action indicated by the compspec to generate a list of possible matches. Of this list, only those that have the word being completed as a prefix are used for the list of possible completions. For the `-d` and `-f` options, the variable FIGNORE is used to filter out undesirable matches.
4. Bash generates filenames as specified by the `-G` option. GLOBIGNORE is not used to filter the results, but FIGNORE is.
5. Bash processes the argument string provided to `-W`. The string is split using the characters in $IFS. The resulting list provides the candidates for completion. This is often used to provide a list of options that a command accepts.
6. Bash runs functions and commands as specified by the `-F` and `-C` options. For both, Bash sets COMP_LINE and COMP_POINT as described previously. For a shell function, COMP_WORDS and COMP_CWORD are also set.

   Also for both, `$1` is the name of the command whose arguments are being completed, `$2` is the word being completed, and `$3` is the word in front of the word being completed. Bash does *not* filter the results of the command or function.

   a. Functions named with `-F` are run first. The function should set the COMPREPLY array to the list of possible completions. Bash retrieves the list from there.

   b. Commands provided with `-C` are run next, in an environment equivalent to command substitution. The command should print the list of possible completions, one per line. An embedded newline should be escaped with a backslash.
7. Once the list is generated, Bash filters the results according to the `-X` option. The argument to `-X` is a pattern specifying files to exclude. By prefixing the pattern with a `!`, the sense is reversed, and the pattern instead specifies that only matching files should be retained in the list.

   An `&` in the pattern is replaced with the text of the word being completed. Use `\&` to produce a literal `&`.

8. Finally, Bash prepends or appends any prefixes or suffixes supplied with the -P or -S options.
9. In the case that no matches were generated, if -o dirnames was used, Bash attempts directory name completion.
10. On the other hand, if -o plusdirs was provided, Bash *adds* the result of directory completion to the previously generated list.
11. Normally, when a compspec is provided, Bash's default completions are not attempted, nor are the *readline* library's default filename completions.
    a. If the compspec produces no results and -o bashdefault was provided, then Bash attempts its default completions.
    b. If neither the compspec nor the Bash default completions with -o bashdefault produced any results, and -o default was provided, then Bash has the *readline* library attempt its filename completions.

Ian Macdonald has collected a large set of useful compspecs, often distributed as the file /etc/bash_completion. If your system does not have it, one location for downloading it is *http://www.dreamind.de/files/bash-stuff/bash_completion*. It is worth retrieving and reviewing.

Bash and Korn

Examples

Restrict files for the C compiler to C, C++ and assembler source files, and relocatable object files:

```
complete -f -X '!*.[Ccos]' gcc cc
```

For the man command, restrict expansions to things that have manpages:

```
# Simple example of programmable completion for manual pages.
# A more elaborate example appears in the bash_completion file.
# Assumes   man [num] command   command syntax.

shopt -s extglob                                   Enable extended pattern
                                                   matching

_man () {
    local dir mandir=/usr/share/man                Local variables

    COMPREPLY=( )                                  Clear reply list
    if [[ ${COMP_WORDS[1]} = +([0-9]) ]]           Section number provided
    then
        # section provided: man 3 foo
        dir=$mandir/man${COMP_WORDS[COMP_CWORD-1]}  Look in that directory
    else
        # no section, default to commands
        dir=$mandir/'man[18]'                      Look in command
                                                   directories
    fi
    COMPREPLY=( $( find $dir -type f |             Generate raw file list
            sed 's;..*/;;' |                       Remove leading directories
            sed 's/\.[0-9].*$//' |                 Remove trailing suffixes
            grep "^${COMP_WORDS[$COMP_CWORD]}" |   Keep those that match
                                                   given prefix
```

```
            sort                                    Sort final list
            ) )
    }
    complete -F _man man                            Associate function with
                                                    command
```

Job Control

Job control lets you place foreground jobs in the background, bring background jobs to the foreground, or suspend (temporarily stop) running jobs. All modern Unix systems, including Linux and BSD systems, support job control; thus, the job control features are automatically enabled. Many job control commands take a *jobID* as an argument. This argument can be specified as follows:

%*n* Job number *n*.

%*s* Job whose command line starts with string *s*.

%?*s* Job whose command line contains string *s*.

%% Current job.

%+ Current job (same as above).

%- Previous job.

Both shells provide the following job control commands. For more information on these commands, see the section "Built-in Commands (Bash and Korn Shells)" later in this chapter.

`bg` Put a job in the background.

`fg` Put a job in the foreground.

`jobs`
: List active jobs.

`kill`
: Terminate a job.

`stty tostop`
: Stop background jobs if they try to send output to the terminal. (Note that `stty` is not a built-in command.)

`suspend`
: Suspend a job-control shell (such as one created by `su`).

`wait`
: Wait for background jobs to finish.

`CTRL-Z`
: Suspend a foreground job. Then use `bg` or `fg`. (Your terminal may use something other than `CTRL-Z` as the suspend character.)

Command Execution

When you type a command to Bash or `ksh93`, they look in the following places until they find a match:

1. Keywords such as if and for.
2. Aliases. You can't define an alias whose name is a shell keyword, but you can define an alias that expands to a keyword, e.g., alias aslongas=while. (Bash, when not in POSIX mode, does allow you to define an alias for a shell keyword.)
3. Special built-ins like break and continue. The list of POSIX special built-ins is . (dot), :, break, continue, eval, exec, exit, export, readonly, return, set, shift, times, trap, and unset. The Korn shell adds alias, login, typeset, and unalias, while Bash adds source.
4. Functions. When not in POSIX mode, Bash finds functions before built-in commands.
5. Nonspecial built-ins like cd and test.
6. Scripts and executable programs, for which the shell searches in the directories listed in the PATH environment variable.

The distinction between "special" built-in commands and nonspecial ones comes from POSIX. This distinction, combined with the command command, makes it possible to write functions that override shell built-ins, such as cd. For example:

```
cd () {                      Shell function; found before built-in cd
    command cd "$@"          Use real cd to change directory
    echo now in $PWD         Other stuff we want to do
}
```

Bash and Korn

In ksh88, the search order is different, all built-ins are found before shell functions. Thus you have to do more work to override a built-in command with a function. You do so using a combination of functions and aliases:

```
_cd () {                     Shell function; note leading underscore
    cd "$@"                  Use real cd to change directory
    echo now in $PWD         Other stuff we want to do
}
alias cd=_cd                 Alias found first
```

Restricted Shells

A *restricted shell* is one that disallows certain actions, such as changing directory, setting PATH, or running commands whose names contain a / character.

The original V7 Bourne shell had an undocumented restricted mode. Later versions of the Bourne shell clarified the code and documented the facility. Today, Bash and the Korn shell both supply a restricted mode, but with differing sets of items that get restricted. (See the respective manual pages for the details.)

Shell scripts can still be run, since in that case the restricted shell calls the unrestricted version of the shell to run the script. This includes the /etc/profile, $HOME/.profile, and other start-up files.

Restricted shells are not used much in practice, as they are difficult to set up correctly.

Built-in Commands (Bash and Korn Shells)

Examples to be entered as a command line are shown with the $ prompt. Otherwise, examples should be treated as code fragments that might be included in a shell script. For convenience, some of the reserved words used by multiline commands are also included.

!

`! pipeline`

Not ksh88. Negate the sense of a pipeline. Returns an exit status of 0 if the pipeline exited nonzero, and an exit status of 1 if the pipeline exited zero. Typically used in `if` and `while` statements.

Example

This code prints a message if user `jane` is not logged on:

```
if ! who | grep jane > /dev/null
then
        echo jane is not currently logged on
fi
```

#

`#`

Ignore all text that follows on the same line. `#` is used in shell scripts as the comment character and is not really a command.

#!shell

`#!shell [option]`

Used as the first line of a script to invoke the named *shell*. Anything given on the rest of the line is passed *as a single argument* to the named *shell*. This feature is typically implemented by the kernel, but may not be supported on some older systems. Some systems have a limit of around 32 characters on the maximum length of *shell*. For example:

```
#!/bin/sh
```

:

`:`

Null command. Returns an exit status of 0. See this Example and the ones under **case**. The line is still processed for side effects, such as variable and command substitutions, or I/O redirection.

Example

Check whether someone is logged in:

```
if who | grep $1 > /dev/null
then :   # Do nothing if user is found
else echo "User $1 is not logged in"
fi
```

.

`. file [arguments]`

Read and execute lines in *file*. *file* does not have to be executable but must reside in a directory searched by PATH. The *arguments* are stored in the positional parameters. If Bash is not in POSIX mode and *file* is not found in PATH, Bash will look in the current directory for *file*.

[[ ]]

`[[ expression ]]`

Same as `test` *expression* or [*expression*], except that `[[ ]]` allows additional operators. Word splitting and filename expansion are disabled. Note that the brackets ([ ]) are typed literally, and that they must be surrounded by whitespace.

Additional Operators

`&&`	Logical AND of test expressions (short circuit).
`||`	Logical OR of test expressions (short circuit).
`<`	First string is lexically "less than" the second.
`>`	First string is lexically "greater than" the second.

name()

`name () { commands; }`

Define *name* as a function. POSIX syntax. The function definition can be written on one line or across many. Bash and the Korn shell provide the `function` keyword, alternate forms that work similarly. See the earlier section "Functions."

Example

```
$ count () {
> ls | wc -l
> }
```

When issued at the command line, `count` now displays the number of files in the current directory.

alias

`alias [options] [name[='cmd']]`

Assign a shorthand *name* as a synonym for *cmd*. If `='cmd'` is omitted, print the alias for *name*; if *name* is also omitted, print all aliases. If the alias value contains a trailing space, the next word on the command line also becomes a candidate for alias expansion. See also **unalias**.

These aliases are built into `ksh88`. Some use names of existing Bourne shell or C shell commands.

```
autoload='typeset -fu'
false='let 0'
functions='typeset -f'
hash='alias -t'
```

```
history='fc -l'
integer='typeset -i'
nohup='nohup '
r='fc -e -'
true=':'
type='whence -v'
```

The following aliases are built into ksh93:

```
autoload='typeset -fu'
command='command '
fc='hist'
float='typeset -E'
functions='typeset -f'
hash='alias -t --'
history='hist -l'
integer='typeset -i'
nameref='typeset -n'
nohup='nohup '
r='hist -s'
redirect='command exec'
stop='kill -s STOP'
times='{ {time;} 2>&1;}'
type='whence -v'
```

Options

-p
: Print the word alias before each alias. Not ksh88.

-t
: Create a tracked alias for a Unix command *name*. The Korn shell remembers the full pathname of the command, allowing it to be found more quickly and to be issued from any directory. If no name is supplied, current tracked aliases are listed. Tracked aliases are the similar to hashed commands in Bash. Korn shell only. ksh93 always does alias tracking.

-x
: Export the alias; it can now be used in shell scripts and other subshells. If no name is supplied, current exported aliases are listed. Korn shell only. ksh93 accepts this option but ignores it.

Example

```
alias dir='echo ${PWD##*/}'
```

autoload

autoload [*functions*]

Korn shell alias for typeset -fu. Load (define) the *functions* only when they are first used.

bind

bind [-m *map*] [*options*]
bind [-m *map*] [-q *function*] [-r *sequence*] [-u *function*]
bind [-m *map*] -f *file*
bind [-m *map*] -x *sequence*:*command*
bind [-m *map*] *sequence*:*function*
bind *readline-command*

Bash only. Manage the *readline* library. Non-option arguments have the same form as in a .inputrc file.

Options

-f *file*
: Read key bindings from *file*.

-l
: List the names of all the *readline* functions.

-m *map*
: Use *map* as the keymap. Available keymaps are: `emacs`, `emacs-standard`, `emacs-meta`, `emacs-ctlx`, `vi`, `vi-move`, `vi-command`, and `vi-insert`. `vi` is the same as `vi-command` and `emacs` is the same `emacs-standard`.

-p
: Print the current *readline* bindings such that they can be reread from a `.inputrc` file.

-P
: Print the current *readline* bindings.

-q *function*
: Query which keys invoke the *readline* function *function*.

-r *sequence*
: Remove the binding for key sequence *sequence*.

-s
: Print the current *readline* key sequence and macro bindings such that they can be reread from a `.inputrc` file.

-S
: Print the current *readline* key sequence and macro bindings.

-u *function*
: Unbind all keys that invoke the *readline* function *function*.

-v
: Print the current *readline* variables such that they can be reread from a `.inputrc` file.

-V
: Print the current *readline* variables.

-x *sequence*:*command*
: Execute the shell command *command* whenever *sequence* is entered.

---

bg

`bg [`*jobIDs*`]`

Put current job or *jobIDs* in the background. See the earlier section "Job Control."

---

break

`break [`*n*`]`

Exit from a `for`, `while`, `select`, or `until` loop (or break out of *n* loops).

---

builtin

`builtin` *command* `[` *arguments* `... ]`

Bash version. Run the shell built-in command *command* with the given arguments. This allows you to bypass any functions that redefine a built-in command's name. The `command` command is more portable.

Example

This function lets you do your own tasks when you change directory:

```
cd () {
    builtin cd "$@"                Actually change directory
    pwd                            Report location
}
```

builtin

`builtin [ -ds ] [ -f library ] [ name ... ]`

ksh93 version. This command allows you to load new built-in commands into the shell at runtime from shared library files.

If no arguments are given, `builtin` prints all the built-in command names. With arguments, `builtin` adds each *name* as a new built-in command (like `cd` or `pwd`). If the *name* contains a slash, the newly-added built-in version is used only if a path search would otherwise have found a command of the same name. (This allows replacement of system commands with faster, built-in versions.) Otherwise, the built-in command is always found.

Options

`-d` Delete the built-in command *name*.

`-f` Load new built-in command from *library*.

`-s` Only print "special" built-ins (those designated as special by POSIX).

caller

`caller [expression]`

Bash only. Print the line number and source filename of the current function call or dot file. With nonzero *expression*, prints that element from the call stack. The most recent is zero. This command is for use by the Bash debugger.

case

```
case value in
 pattern1) cmds1;;
 pattern2) cmds2;;
 .
 .
 .
esac
```

Execute the first set of commands (*cmds1*) if *value* matches *pattern1*, execute the second set of commands (*cmds2*) if *value* matches *pattern2*, etc. Be sure the last command in each set ends with `;;`. *value* is typically a positional parameter or other shell variable. *cmds* are typically Unix commands, shell programming commands, or variable assignments. Patterns can use file-generation metacharacters. Multiple patterns (separated by |) can be specified on the same line; in this case, the associated *cmds* are executed whenever *value* matches any of these patterns. See the Examples here and under **eval**.

The shells allow *pattern* to be preceded by an optional open parenthesis, as in (*pattern*). In Bash and ksh88, it's necessary for balancing parentheses inside a $( ) construct.

The Korn shell allows a case to end with ;& instead of ;;. In such cases control "falls through" to the group of statements for the next *pattern*.

Examples

Check first command-line argument and take appropriate action:

```
case $1 in        # Match the first arg
    no|yes) response=1;;
    -[tT])  table=TRUE;;
    *)      echo "unknown option"; exit 1;;
esac
```

Read user-supplied lines until user exits:

```
while :           # Null command; always true
do
   printf "Type . to finish ==> "
   read line
   case "$line" in
      .) echo "Message done"
         break ;;
      *) echo "$line" >> $message ;;
   esac
done
```


---

cd

```
cd [-LP] [dir]
cd [-LP] [-]
cd [-LP] [old new]
```

With no arguments, change to home directory of user. Otherwise, change working directory to *dir*. If *dir* is a relative pathname but is not in the current directory, the CDPATH variable is searched. A directory of - stands for the previous directory. The last syntax is specific to the Korn shell. It modifies the current directory name by replacing string *old* with *new* and then switches to the resulting directory.

Options

-L
: Use the logical path (what the user typed, including any symbolic links) for cd .. and the value of PWD. This is the default.

-P
: Use the actual filesystem physical path for cd .. and the value of PWD.

Example

```
$ pwd
/var/spool/cron
$ cd cron uucp    Ksh: cd prints the new directory
/var/spool/uucp
```

command

`command [-pvV] name [arg ...]`

Not ksh88. Without `-v` or `-V`, execute *name* with given arguments. This command bypasses any aliases or functions that may be defined for *name*. When used with a special built-in, prevents the built-in from exiting the script if it fails.

Options

`-p` Use a predefined, default search path, not the current value of PATH.

`-v` Print a description of how the shell interprets *name*.

`-V` Print a more verbose description of how the shell interprets *name*.

Example

Create an alias for `rm` that will get the system's version, and run it with the `-i` option:

```
$ alias 'rm=command -p rm -i'
```

compgen

`compgen [options] [string]`

Bash only. Generate possible completions for *string* according to the options. Options are those accepted by `complete`, except for `-p` and `-r`. For more information, see the entry for **complete**.

complete

`complete [options] command ...`

Bash only. Specifies the way to complete arguments for each *command*. This is discussed in the section "Programmable Completion (Bash Only)," earlier in the chapter.

Options

`-a` Same as `-A alias`.

`-A` *type*
Use *type* to specify a list of possible completions. The *type* may be one of the following.

`alias`	Alias names.
`arrayvar`	Array variable names.
`binding`	Bindings from the *readline* library.
`builtin`	Shell built-in command names.
`command`	Command names.
`directory`	Directory names.
`disabled`	Names of disabled shell built-in commands.
`enabled`	Names of enabled shell built-in commands.
`export`	Exported variables.
`file`	Filenames.
`function`	Names of shell functions.
`group`	Group names.

`helptopic`	Help topics as allowed by the `help` built-in command.
`hostname`	Hostnames, as found in the file named by $HOSTFILE.
`job`	Job names.
`keyword`	Shell reserved keywords.
`running`	Names of running jobs.
`service`	Service names (from `/etc/services`).
`setopt`	Valid arguments for `set -o`.
`shopt`	Valid option names for the `shopt` built-in command.
`signal`	Signal names.
`stopped`	Names of stopped jobs.
`user`	Usernames.
`variable`	Shell variable names.

`-b` Same as `-A builtin`.

`-c` Same as `-A command`.

`-C` *`command`*
: Run *command* in a subshell and use its output as the list of completions.

`-d` Same as `-A directory`.

`-e` Same as `-A export`.

`-f` Same as `-A file`.

`-F` *`function`*
: Run shell function *function* in the current shell. Upon its return, retrieve the list of completions from the COMPREPLY array.

`-g` Same as `-A group`.

`-G` *`pattern`*
: Expand *pattern* to generate completions.

`-j` Same as `-A job`.

`-k` Same as `-A keyword`.

`-o` *`option`*
: Control the behavior of the completion specification. The value for *option* is one of the following.

`bashdefault`	Fall back to the normal Bash completions if no matches are produced.
`default`	Use the default *readline* completions if no matches are produced.
`dirnames`	Do directory name completion if no matches are produced.
`filenames`	Inform the *readline* library that the intended output is filenames, so the library can do any filename-specific processing, such as adding a trailing slash for directories, or removing trailing spaces.

Bash and Korn

nospace	Inform the *readline* library that it should not append a space to words completed at the end of a line.
plusdirs	Attempt directory completion and add any results to the list of completions already generated.

-p With no commands, print all completion settings in a way that can be reread.

-P *prefix*
: The *prefix* is added to each resulting string as a prefix after all the other options have been applied.

-r Remove the completion settings for the given commands, or all settings if no commands.

-s Save as -A service.

-S *suffix*
: The *suffix* is added to each resulting string as a suffix after all the other options have been applied.

-u Same as -A user.

-v Same as -A variable.

-W *wordlist*
: Split *wordlist* (a single shell word) using $IFS. The generated list contains the members of the split list that matched the word being completed. Each member is expanded using brace expansion, tilde expansion, parameter and variable expansion, command substitution, and arithmetic expansion. Shell quoting is respected.

-X *pattern*
: Exclude filenames matching *pattern* from the filename completion list. With a leading !, the sense is reversed, and only filenames matching *pattern* are retained.

continue

continue [*n*]

Skip remaining commands in a for, while, select, or until loop, resuming with the next iteration of the loop (or skipping *n* loops).

declare

declare [*options*] [*name*[=*value*]]

Bash only. Declare variables and manage their attributes. In function bodies, variables are local, as if declared with the local command.

Options

-a Each *name* is an array.

-f Each *name* is a function.

-F For functions, print just the functions' name and attributes, not the function definition (body).

- `-i` Each variable is an integer; in an assignment, the value is evaluated as an arithmetic expression.
- `-p` With no *names*, print all variables and their values. With *names*, print the names, attributes, and values of the given variables. This option causes all other options to be ignored.
- `-r` Mark *names* as read-only. Subsequent assignments will fail.
- `-t` Apply the *trace* attribute to each name. Traced functions inherit the `DEBUG` trap. This attribute has no meaning for variables.
- `-x` Mark *names* for export into the environment of child processes.

With a `+` instead of a `-`, the given attribute is disabled. With no variable names, all variables having the given attribute(s) are printed in a form that can be reread as input to the shell.

Examples

```
$ declare -i val                    Make val an integer
$ val=4+7                           Evaluate value
$ echo $val                         Show result
11

$ declare -r z=42                   Make z readonly
$ z=31                              Try to assign to it
bash: z: readonly variable          Assignment fails
$ echo $z
42

$ declare -p val z                  Show attributes and values
declare -i val="11"
declare -r z="42"
```

Bash and Korn

dirs

`dirs [-clpv] [+n] [-n]`

Bash only. Print the directory stack, which is managed with `pushd` and `popd`.

Options

- `+n` Print the *n*th entry from the left; first entry is zero.
- `-n` Print the *n*th entry from the right; first entry is zero.
- `-c` Remove all entries from (clear) the directory stack.
- `-l` Produce a longer listing, one that does not replace $HOME with ~.
- `-p` Print the directory stack, one entry per line.
- `-v` Print the directory stack, one entry per line, with each entry preceded by its index in the stack.

disown

`disown [-ahr] [job ...]`

Bash version. Removes *jobs* from the list of jobs managed by Bash.

Options

-a Remove all jobs. With -h, mark all jobs.

-h Instead of removing jobs from the list of known jobs, mark them to *not* receive SIGHUP when Bash exits.

-r With no jobs, remove (or mark) only running jobs.

---

disown

`disown [job ...]`

ksh93 version. When a login shell exits, do not send a SIGHUP to the given jobs. If no jobs are listed, no background jobs will receive SIGHUP.

---

do

`do`

Reserved word that precedes the command sequence in a for, while, until, or select statement.

---

done

`done`

Reserved word that ends a for, while, until, or select statement.

---

echo

`echo [-eEn] [string]`

Bash version, built-in to the shell. Write *string* to standard output. (See also **echo** in Chapter 2.)

Options

-e Enable interpretation of the following escape sequences, which must be quoted (or escaped with a \) to prevent interpretation by the shell:

\a Alert (ASCII BEL).

\b Backspace.

\c Suppress the terminating newline (same as -n).

\e ASCII Escape character.

\f Formfeed.

\n Newline.

\r Carriage return.

\t Tab character.

\v Vertical-tab character.

\\ Backslash.

\0*nnn*
ASCII character represented by octal number *nnn*, where *nnn* is zero, one, two, or three digits and is preceded by a 0.

\nnn
: ASCII character represented by octal number *nnn*, where *nnn* is one, two, or three digits.

\xHH
: ASCII character represented by hexadecimal number *HH*, where *HH* is one or two hexadecimal digits.

-E
: Do not interpret escape sequences, even on systems where the default behavior of the built-in echo is to interpret them.

-n
: Do not print the terminating newline.

Examples

```
$ echo "testing printer" | lp
$ echo "Warning: ringing bell \a"
```

---

echo

`echo [-n] [string]`

Korn shell version. Write *string* to standard output; if -n is specified, the output is not terminated by a newline. If no *string* is supplied, echo a newline.

The Korn shell's echo, even though it is built-in to the shell, emulates the system's version of echo. Thus, if the version found by a path search supports -n, the built-in version does too. Similarly, if the external version supports the escape sequences described below, the built-in version does too; otherwise it does not.* (See also **echo** in Chapter 2.) echo understands special escape characters, which must be quoted (or escaped with a \) to prevent interpretation by the shell:

\a
: Alert (ASCII BEL).

\b
: Backspace.

\c
: Suppress the terminating newline (same as -n).

\f
: Formfeed.

\n
: Newline.

\r
: Carriage return.

\t
: Tab character.

\v
: Vertical-tab character.

\\
: Backslash.

\0nnn
: ASCII character represented by octal number *nnn*, where *nnn* is one, two, or three digits and is preceded by a 0.

* The situation with echo is a mess; consider using printf instead.

enable

`enable [-adnps] [-f file] [command ...]`

Bash only. Enable or disable shell built-in commands. Disabling a built-in lets you use an external version of a command that would otherwise use a built-in version, such as echo or test.

Options

-a For use with -p; print information about all built-in commands, disabled and enabled.

-d Remove (delete) a built-in previously loaded with -f.

-f *file*
Load a new built-in command *command* from the shared library file *file*.

-n Disable the named built-in commands.

-p Print a list of enabled built-in commands.

-s Print only the POSIX special built-in commands. When combined with -f, the new built-in command becomes a POSIX special built-in.

esac

`esac`

Reserved word that ends a case statement.

eval

`eval args`

Typically, eval is used in shell scripts, and *args* is a line of code that contains shell variables. eval forces variable expansion to happen first and then runs the resulting command. This "double-scanning" is useful any time shell variables contain input/output redirection symbols, aliases, or other shell variables. (For example, redirection normally happens before variable expansion, so a variable containing redirection symbols must be expanded first using eval; otherwise, the redirection symbols remain uninterpreted.) See the C shell **eval** entry (Chapter 5) for another example.

Example

This fragment of a shell script shows how eval constructs a command that is interpreted in the right order:

```
for option
do
   case "$option" in     Define where output goes
      save) out=' > $newfile' ;;
      show) out=' | more' ;;
   esac
done

eval sort $file $out
```

exec

```
exec [command args ...]
exec [-a name] [-cl] [command args ... ]
```

Execute *command* in place of the current process (instead of creating a new process). exec is also useful for opening, closing, or copying file descriptors. The second form is for ksh93 and Bash.

Options

-a
: Use *name* for the value of argv[0].

-c
: Clear the environment before executing the program.

-l
: Place a minus sign at the front of argv[0], just as *login*(1) does. Bash only.

Examples

`trap 'exec 2>&-' 0`	*Close standard error when shell script exits (signal 0)*
`$ exec /bin/csh`	*Replace shell with C shell*
`$ exec < infile`	*Reassign standard input to infile*

exit

```
exit [n]
```

Exit a shell script with status *n* (e.g., exit 1). *n* can be 0 (success) or nonzero (failure). If *n* is not given, the shell's exit status is that of the most recent command. exit can be issued at the command line to close a window (log out). Exit statuses can range in value from 0 to 255.

Example

```
if [ $# -eq 0 ]
then
   echo "Usage: $0 [-c] [-d] file(s)" 1>&2
   exit 1                    # Error status
fi
```

export

```
export [variables]
export [name=[value] ...]
export -p
export [-fn] [name=[value] ...]
```

Pass (export) the value of one or more shell *variables*, giving global meaning to the variables (which are local by default). For example, a variable defined in one shell script must be exported if its value is used in other programs called by the script. If no *variables* are given, export lists the variables exported by the current shell. The second form is the POSIX version, which is similar to the first form except that you can set a variable *name* to a *value* before exporting it. The third form is not available in ksh88. The fourth form is specific to Bash.

Options

-f
: Names refer to functions; the functions are exported in the environment. Bash only.

-n
: Remove the named variables or functions from the environment. Bash only.

-p
: Print export before printing the names and values of exported variables. This allows saving a list of exported variables for rereading later.

Examples

In the original Bourne shell, you would type:

```
TERM=vt100
export TERM
```

In Bash and the Korn shell, you could type this instead:

```
export TERM=vt100
```

---

false

`false`

`ksh88` alias for `let 0`. Built-in command in Bash and `ksh93` that exits with a false return value.

---

fc

`fc [`*`options`*`] [`*`first`*` [`*`last`*`]]`
`fc -e - [`*`old=new`*`] [`*`command`*`]`
`fc -s [`*`old=new`*`] [`*`command`*`]`

`ksh88` and Bash. Display or edit commands in the history list. (Use only one of `-e`, `-l` or `-s`.) *first* and *last* are numbers or strings specifying the range of commands to display or edit. If *last* is omitted, `fc` applies to a single command (specified by *first*). If both *first* and *last* are omitted, `fc` edits the previous command or lists the last 16. The second form of `fc` takes a history *command*, replaces *old* with *new*, and executes the modified command. If no strings are specified, *command* is just reexecuted. If no *command* is given either, the previous command is reexecuted. *command* is a number or string like *first*. See the examples in the earlier section "Command History." The third form, available in Bash and `ksh93`, is equivalent to the second form.

Options

-e [*editor*]
: Invoke *editor* to edit the specified history commands. The default *editor* is set by the shell variable FCEDIT. If that variable is not set, the default is `/bin/ed`. (Bash defaults to `vi`; version 3.1 and newer will default to `/bin/ed` when in POSIX mode.) Bash tries FCEDIT, then EDITOR, and then `/bin/ed`.

-e -
: Execute (or redo) a history command; refer to second syntax line above.

-l List the specified command or range of commands, or list the last 16.

-n Suppress command numbering from the -l listing.

-r Reverse the order of the -l listing.

-s Equivalent to -e -. Not in ksh88.

fc

```
fc
```

ksh93 alias for hist.

fg

```
fg [jobIDs]
```

Bring current job or *jobIDs* to the foreground. See the earlier section "Job Control."

fi

```
fi
```

Reserved word that ends an if statement. (Don't forget to use it!)

for

```
for x [in list]
do
 commands
done
```

For variable *x* (in optional *list* of values) do *commands*. If in *list* is omitted, "$@" (the positional parameters) is assumed.

Examples

Paginate files specified on the command line; save each result:

```
for file; do
    pr $file > $file.tmp
done
```

Same, but put entire loop into the background:

```
for file; do
    pr $file > $file.tmp
done &
```

Search chapters for a list of words (like fgrep -f):

```
for item in `cat program_list`
do
    echo "Checking chapters for"
    echo "references to program $item..."
    grep -c "$item.[co]" chap*
done
```

Extract a one-word title from each file and use as new filename:

```
for file
do
    name=`sed -n 's/NAME: //p' $file`
    mv $file $name
done
```

for

```
for ((init; cond; incr))
do
 commands
done
```

Bash and ksh93. Arithmetic for loop, similar to C's. Evaluate *init*. While *cond* is true, execute the body of the loop. Evaluate *incr* before retesting *cond*. Any one of the expressions may be omitted; a missing *cond* is treated as being true.

Example

Search for a phrase in each odd chapter:

```
for ((x=1; x <= 20; x += 2))
do
        grep $1 chap$x
done
```

function

```
function name { commands; }
function name ( ) { commands; }
```

Define *name* as a shell function. See the description of semantic issues in the earlier section "Functions." The first form is for the Korn shell, although it may also be used with Bash. The second form is specific to Bash. Bash does not give different semantics to functions declared differently; all Bash functions behave the same way.

Example

Define a function to count files.

```
$ function fcount {
>    ls | wc -l
> }
```

functions

```
functions
```

Korn shell alias for typeset -f. (Note the "s" in the name; function is a Korn shell keyword.) See **typeset** later in this listing.

getconf

```
getconf [name [path]]
```

ksh93 only. Retrieve the values for parameters that can vary across systems. *name* is the parameter to retrieve; *path* is a filename to test for parameters that can vary on different filesystem types.

The parameters are defined by the POSIX 1003.1 standard. See the entry for **getconf** in Chapter 2.

Example

Print the maximum value that can be held in a C int.

```
$ getconf INT_MAX
2147483647
```

getopts

`getopts [-a name] string name [args]`

Process command-line arguments (or *args*, if specified) and check for legal options. getopts is used in shell script loops and is intended to ensure standard syntax for command-line options. Standard syntax dictates that command-line options begin with a -. Options can be stacked; i.e., consecutive letters can follow a single -. End processing of options by specifying -- on the command line. *string* contains the option letters to be recognized by getopts when running the shell script. Valid options are processed in turn and stored in the shell variable *name*. If an option is followed by a colon, the option must be followed by one or more arguments. (Multiple arguments must be given to the command as one shell *word*. This is done by quoting the arguments or separating them with commas. The application must be written to expect multiple arguments in this format.) getopts uses the shell variables OPTARG and OPTIND. The Bash version also uses OPTERR.

Option

-a Use *name* in error messages about invalid options. ksh93 only.

Bash and Korn

hash

`hash [-dlrt] [-p file] [commands]`

Bash version. As the shell finds commands along the search path ($PATH), it remembers the found location in an internal hash table. The next time you enter a command, the shell uses the value stored in its hash table.

With no arguments, hash lists the current hashed commands. The display shows *hits* (the number of times the command has been called by the shell) and the command name.

With *commands*, the shell adds those commands to the hash table.

Options

-d Remove (delete) just the specified commands from the hash table.

-l Produce output in a format that can be reread to rebuild the hash table.

-p *file*
Associate *file* with *command* in the hash table.

-r Remove all commands from the hash table.

-t With one name, print the full pathname of the command. With more than one name, print the name and the full path, in two columns.

Besides the -r option, the hash table is also cleared when PATH is assigned. Use PATH=$PATH to clear the hash table without affecting your search path. This is most useful if you have installed a new version of a command in a directory that is earlier in $PATH than the current version of the command.

hash

```
hash
```

Korn shell alias for `alias -t` (`alias -t --` in `ksh93`). Approximates the Bourne shell's `hash`.

help

`help [-s] [`*pattern*`]`

Bash only. Print usage information on standard output for each command that matches *pattern*. The information includes descriptions of each command's options. With the `-s` option, print only brief usage information.

Examples

```
$ help -s cd            Short help
cd: cd [-L|-P] [dir]

$ help true             Full help
true: true
    Return a successful result.
```

hist

`hist [`*options*`] [`*first* `[`*last*`]]`
`hist -s [`*old=new*`] [`*command*`]`

`ksh93` only. Display or edit commands in the history list. (Use only one of `-l` or `-s`.) *first* and *last* are numbers or strings specifying the range of commands to display or edit. If *last* is omitted, `hist` applies to a single command (specified by *first*). If both *first* and *last* are omitted, `hist` edits the previous command or lists the last 16. The second form of `hist` takes a history *command*, replaces *old* with *new*, and executes the modified command. If no strings are specified, *command* is just reexecuted. If no *command* is given either, the previous command is reexecuted. *command* is a number or string like *first*. See the examples in the earlier section "Command History."

Options

`-e [`*editor*`]`
: Invoke *editor* to edit the specified history commands. The default *editor* is set by the shell variable HISTEDIT. If that variable is not set, FCEDIT is used. If neither is set, the default is `/bin/ed`.

`-l`
: List the specified command or range of commands, or list the last 16.

`-n`
: Suppress command numbering from the `-l` listing.

`-N` *n*
: Start with the command *n* commands before the current one.

`-r`
: Reverse the order of the `-l` listing.

`-s`
: Execute (or redo) a history command; refer to second syntax line above.

history

```
history [count]
history [options]
```

Bash version. Print commands in the history list or manage the history file. With no options or arguments, display the history list with command numbers. With a *count* argument, print only that many of the most recent commands.

Options

`-a` Append new history lines (those executed since the beginning of the session) to the history file.

`-c` Clear the history list (remove all entries).

`-d` *position*
Delete the history item at position *position*.

`-n` Read unread history lines from the history file into the history list.

`-p` *argument ...*
Perform csh-style history expansion on each *argument*, printing the results to standard output. The results are not saved in the history list.

`-r` Read the history file and replace the history list with its contents.

`-s` *argument ...*
Store the *arguments* in the history list, as a single entry.

`-w` Write the current history list to the history file, overwriting it entirely.

history

```
history
```

ksh88 alias for `fc -l`. ksh93 alias for `hist -l`. Show the last 16 commands.

if

```
if condition1
then commands1
[ elif condition2
 then commands2 ]
 .
 .
 .
[ else commands3 ]
fi
```

If *condition1* is met, do *commands1*; otherwise, if *condition2* is met, do *commands2*; if neither is met, do *commands3*. Conditions are often specified with the test and [[ ]] commands. See **test** and [[ ]] for a full list of conditions, and see additional Examples under : and **exit**.

Bash and Korn

Examples

Insert a 0 before numbers less than 10:

```
if [ $counter -lt 10 ]
then number=0$counter
else number=$counter
fi
```

Make a directory if it doesn't exist:

```
if [ ! -d $dir ]; then
   mkdir $dir
   chmod 775 $dir
fi
```

---

integer

`integer`

Korn shell alias for `typeset -i`. Specify integer variables.

---

jobs

`jobs [options] [jobIDs]`

List all running or stopped jobs, or list those specified by *jobIDs*. For example, you can check whether a long compilation or text format is still running. Also useful before logging out. See the earlier section "Job Control."

Options

`-l` List job IDs and process group IDs.

`-n` List only jobs whose status changed since last notification.

`-p` List process group IDs only.

`-r` List running jobs only. Bash only.

`-x` *cmd*
Replace each job ID found in *cmd* with the associated process ID and then execute *cmd*. Bash only.

---

kill

`kill [options] IDs`

Terminate each specified process *ID* or job *ID*. You must own the process or be a privileged user. This built-in is similar to the external `kill` command described in Chapter 2 but also allows symbolic job names. See the **kill** entry in Chapter 2 for a list of commonly available signals and for the header files where the corresponding signal numbers may be found. Stubborn processes can be killed using signal 9. See the earlier section "Job Control."

Options

`-l` List the signal names. (Used by itself.)

`-n` *num*
Send the given signal number. Not `ksh88`.

-s *name*
Send the given signal name. Not ksh88.

-*signal*
The signal number (from <signal.h>) or name (from kill -l). With a signal number of 9, the kill is absolute.

let

let *expressions*
or
((*expressions*))

Perform arithmetic as specified by one or more *expressions*. *expressions* consist of numbers, operators, and shell variables (which don't need a preceding $). Expressions must be quoted if they contain spaces or other special characters. The (( )) form does the quoting for you. For more information and examples, see the section "Arithmetic Expressions," earlier in this chapter. See also **expr** in Chapter 2.

Examples

Each of these examples adds 1 to variable i:

```
i=`expr $i + 1`          All Bourne shells
let i=i+1                Bash, ksh
let "i = i + 1"
(( i = i + 1 ))
(( i += 1 ))
(( i++ ))                Bash, ksh93
```

local

local [*options*] [*name*[=*value*]]

Bash only. Declares local variables for use inside functions. The *options* are the same as those accepted by declare; see **declare** for the full list. It is an error to use local outside a function body.

login

login [*user*]

Korn shell only. The shell does an *execve*(2) of the standard login program, allowing you to replace one login session with another, without having to logout first.

logout

logout

Bash only. Exit a login shell. The command fails if the current shell is not a login shell.

nameref

nameref *newvar*=*oldvar* ...

ksh93 alias for typeset -n. See the discussion of indirect variables in the section "Variables," earlier in this chapter.

nohup

`nohup command [arguments] &`

Don't terminate a command after logout. nohup is a Korn shell alias:

```
nohup='nohup '
```

The embedded space at the end lets the shell interpret the following command as an alias, if needed.

popd

`popd [-n] [+count] [-count]`

Bash only. Pop the top directory off the directory stack (as shown by the dirs command), and change to the new top directory, or manage the directory stack.

Options

-n
: Don't change to the new top directory, just manipulate the stack.

+*count*
: Remove the item *count* entries from the left, as shown by dirs. Counting starts at zero. No directory change occurs.

-*count*
: Remove the item *count* entries from the right, as shown by dirs. Counting starts at zero. No directory change occurs.

print

`print [options] [string ...]`

Korn shell only. Display *string* (on standard output by default). print includes the functions of echo and can be used in its place on most Unix systems.

Options

-
: Ignore all subsequent options.

--
: Same as -.

-e
: Interpret escape sequences in argument strings. (This is the default, anyway.) Use it to undo an earlier -r in the same command line. ksh93 only.

-f *format*
: Print like printf, using *format* as the format string. Ignores the -n, -r, and -R options. ksh93 only.

-n
: Don't end output with a newline.

-p
: Send *string* to the process created by |&, instead of to standard output.

-r
: Ignore the escape sequences often used with echo.

-R
: Same as -r and ignore subsequent options (except -n).

-s
: Send *string* to the history file.

-u[*n*]
: Send *string* to file descriptor *n* (default is 1).

printf

`printf format [val ...]`

Not ksh88. Formatted printing, like the ANSI C `printf` function.

Additional Format Letters

Both Bash and ksh93 accept additional format letters. Bash only provides `%b` and `%q`, while ksh93 provides all those in the following list.

`%b` Expand escape sequences in strings (e.g., `\t` to tab, and so on).

`%B` The corresponding argument is a variable name (typically created via `typeset -b`); its value is retrieved and printed.

`%d` An additional period and the output base can follow the precision (e.g., `%5.3.6d` to produce output in base 6).

`%H` Output strings in HTML/XML format. (Spaces become ` ` and < and > become `<` and `>`.)

`%n` Place the number of characters printed so far into the named variable.

`%P` Translate egrep extended regular expression into ksh pattern.

`%q` Print a quoted string that can be reread later on.

`%R` Reverse of `%P`: translate ksh pattern into egrep extended regular expression.

`%(format)T`
: Print a string representing a date and time according to the *strftime*(3) format *format*. The parentheses are entered literally. See the Examples.

`%Z` Print an ASCII NUL (8 zero bits).

Examples

```
$ date                                            Reformat date/time
Tue Sep 7 15:39:42 EDT 2004
$ printf "%(It is now %m/%d/%Y %H:%M:%S)T\n" "$(date)"
It is now 09/07/2004 15:40:10

$ printf "%H\n" "Here is a <string>"              Convert to HTML
Here is a &lt;string&gt;
```

pwd

`pwd [-LP]`

Print your present working directory on standard output.

Options

Options give control over the use of logical versus physical treatment of the printed path. See also the entry for **cd**, earlier in this section.

`-L` Use logical path (what the user typed, including any symbolic links) and the value of PWD for the current directory. This is the default.

`-P` Use the actual filesystem physical path for the current directory.

pushd

```
pushd [-n] [directory]
pushd [-n] [+count] [-count]
```

Bash only. Add *directory* to the directory stack, or rotate the directory stack. With no arguments, swap the top two entries on the stack, and change to the new top entry.

Options

`-n` Don't change to the new top directory, just manipulate the stack.

`+count`
: Rotate the stack so that the *count*'th item from the left, as shown by `dirs`, is the new top of the stack. Counting starts at zero. The new top becomes the current directory.

`-count`
: Rotate the stack so that the *count*'th item from the left, as shown by `dirs`, is the new top of the stack. Counting starts at zero. The new top becomes the current directory.

r

```
r
```

`ksh88` alias for `fc -e -`. `ksh93` alias for `hist -s`. Reexecute previous command.

read

```
read [options] [variable1[?string]] [variable2 ...]
```

Read one line of standard input and assign each word to the corresponding *variable*, with all leftover words assigned to the last variable. If only one variable is specified, the entire line is assigned to that variable. See the Examples here and under **case**. The return status is 0 unless *EOF* is reached. Both Bash and the Korn shell support options, as shown below. If no variables are given, input is stored in the REPLY variable.

Additionally, the Korn shell version supports the ? syntax for prompting. If the first variable is followed by `?string`, *string* is displayed as a user prompt.

Options

`-a array`
: Read into indexed array *array*. Bash only.

`-A array`
: Read into indexed array *array*. `ksh93` only.

`-d delim`
: Read up to first occurrence of *delim*, instead of newline. Not `ksh88`.

`-e` Use the *readline* library if reading from a terminal. Bash only.

`-n count`
: Read at most *count* bytes. Not `ksh88`.

-p *prompt*
: Bash: print *prompt* before reading input.

-p
: Korn shell: read from the output of a |& coprocess.

-r
: Raw mode; ignore \ as a line-continuation character.

-s
: Bash: read silently; characters are not echoed.

-s
: Korn shell: save input as a command in the history file.

-t *timeout*
: When reading from a terminal or pipe, if no data is entered after *timeout* seconds, return 1. This prevents an application from hanging forever, waiting for user input. Not ksh88.

-u[*n*]
: Read input from file descriptor *n* (default is 0).

Examples

Read three variables:

```
$ read first last address
Sarah Caldwell 123 Main Street

$ echo "$last, $first\n$address"
Caldwell, Sarah
123 Main Street
```

Prompt yourself to enter two temperatures, Korn shell version:

```
$ read n1?"High low: " n2
High low: 65 33
```


readonly

readonly [-afp] [*variable*[=*value*] ...]

Prevent the specified shell variables from being assigned new values. An initial value may be supplied using the assignment syntax, but that value may not be changed subsequently.

Options

ksh88 does not accept options for this command.

-a
: Each *variable* must refer to an array. Bash only.

-f
: Each *variable* must refer to an function. Bash only.

-p
: Print readonly before printing the names and values of read-only variables. This allows saving a list of read-only variables for rereading later.

redirect

redirect *i/o-redirection* ...

ksh93 alias for command exec.

Example

Change the shell's standard error to the console:

```
$ redirect 2>/dev/console
```

return

```
return [n]
```

Use inside a function definition. Exit the function with status *n* or with the exit status of the previously executed command.

select

```
select x [in list]
do
  commands
done
```

Display a list of menu items on standard error, numbered in the order they are specified in *list*. If no `in` *list* is given, items are taken from the command line (via `"$@"`). Following the menu is a prompt string (set by PS3). At the PS3 prompt, users select a menu item by typing its number, or they redisplay the menu by pressing the ENTER key. User input is stored in the shell variable REPLY. If a valid item number is typed, *commands* are executed. Typing *EOF* terminates the loop.

Example

```
PS3="Select the item number: "
select event in Format Page View Exit
do
   case "$event" in
     Format) nroff $file | lp;;
     Page)   pr $file | lp;;
     View)   more $file;;
     Exit)   exit 0;;
     *   )   echo "Invalid selection";;
   esac
done
```

The output of this script looks like this:

```
1. Format
2. Page
3. View
4. Exit
Select the item number:
```

set

```
set [options arg1 arg2 ...]
```

With no arguments, set prints the values of all variables known to the current shell. Options can be enabled (*-option*) or disabled (*+option*). Options can also be set when the shell is invoked. (See the earlier section "Invoking the Shell.") Arguments are assigned in order to `$1`, `$2`, etc.

Options

There is a large set of overlapping options amongst `ksh88`, `ksh93`, and Bash. To minimize confusion, the following list includes every option. The table provided after the list summarizes which options are available in which shells.

-a
: From now on automatically mark variables for export after defining or changing them.

+A *name*
: Assign remaining arguments as elements of array *name*. Korn shell only.

-A *name*
: Same as +A, but unset *name* before making assignments. Korn shell only.

-b
: Print job completion messages as soon as jobs terminate; don't wait until the next prompt. Not ksh88.

-B
: Enable brace expansion. On by default. Bash only.

-C
: Prevent overwriting via > redirection; use >| to overwrite files. Not ksh88.

-e
: Exit if a command yields a nonzero exit status. The ERR trap executes before the shell exits.

-E
: Cause shell functions, command substitutions, and subshells to inherit the ERR trap. Bash only.

-f
: Ignore filename metacharacters (e.g., * ? [ ]).

-G
: Cause ** to also match subdirectories during filename expansion. ksh93 only.

-h
: Locate commands as they are defined. The Korn shell creates tracked aliases, whereas Bash hashes command names. On by default. See **hash**.

-H
: Enable csh-style history substitution. On by default. Bash only.

-k
: Assignment of environment variables (*var=value*) takes effect regardless of where they appear on the command line. Normally, assignments must precede the command name.

-m
: Enable job control; background jobs execute in a separate process group. -m is usually set automatically.

-n
: Read commands but don't execute; useful for checking syntax. Both shells ignore this option if interactive.

+o [*mode*]
: With *mode*, disable the given shell option. Plain set +o prints the settings of all the current options. For Bash and ksh93, this is in a form that can be reread by the shell later.

-o [*mode*]
: List shell modes, or turn on mode *mode*. Many modes can be set by other options. Modes are:

allexport	Same as -a.
bgnice	Run background jobs at lower priority. Korn shell only.
braceexpand	Same as -B. Bash only.
emacs	Set command-line editor to emacs.

Bash and Korn

`errexit`	Same as `-e`.
`errtrace`	Same as `-E`. Bash only.
`functrace`	Same as `-T`. Bash only.
`globstar`	Same as `-G`. `ksh93` only.
`gmacs`	Set command-line editor to `gmacs` (like GNU Emacs). Korn shell only.
`hashall`	Same as `-h`. Bash only.
`histexpand`	Same as `-H`. Bash only.
`history`	Enable command history. On by default. Bash only.
`ignoreeof`	Don't process *EOF* signals. To exit the shell, type `exit`.
`keyword`	Same as `-k`.
`markdirs`	Append `/` to directory names. Korn shell only.
`monitor`	Same as `-m`.
`noclobber`	Same as `-C`.
`noexec`	Same as `-n`.
`noglob`	Same as `-f`.
`nolog`	Omit function definitions from history file. Accepted but ignored by Bash.
`notify`	Same as `-b`.
`nounset`	Same as `-u`.
`onecmd`	Same as `-t`. Bash only.
`physical`	Same as `-P`. Bash only.
`pipefail`	Change pipeline exit status to be that of the rightmost command that failed, or zero if all exited successfully. Not `ksh88`.
`posix`	Change to POSIX mode. Bash only.
`privileged`	Same as `-p`.
`trackall`	Same as `-h`. Korn shell only.
`verbose`	Same as `-v`.
`vi`	Set command-line editor to `vi`.
`viraw`	Same as `vi`, but process each character when it's typed. Korn shell only.
`xtrace`	Same as `-x`.

`+p` Reset effective UID to real UID.

`-p` Start up as a privileged user. Bash: don't read $ENV or $BASH_ENV, don't import functions from the environment, and ignore the value of $SHELLOPTS. Korn shell: don't process `$HOME/.profile`; read `/etc/suid_profile` instead of $ENV.

`-P` Always use physical paths for `cd` and `pwd`. Bash only.

`-s` Sort the positional parameters. Korn shell only.

`-t` Exit after one command is executed.

`-T` Cause shell functions, command substitutions, and subshells to inherit the `DEBUG` trap. Bash only.

`-u` In substitutions, treat unset variables as errors.

`-v` Show each shell command line when read.

-x Show commands and arguments when executed, preceded by the value of PS4. This provides step-by-step tracing of shell scripts.

\- Turn off -v and -x, and turn off option processing. Included for compatibility with older versions of the Bourne shell.

-- Used as the last option; -- turns off option processing so that arguments beginning with - are not misinterpreted as options. (For example, you can set $1 to –1.) If no arguments are given after --, unset the positional parameters.

Option Availability Summary

Option	Same as	ksh88	ksh93	Bash
-a	-o allexport	•	•	•
-A		•	•	
-b	-o notify		•	•
-B	-o braceexpand			•
-C	-o noclobber		•	•
-e	-o errexit	•	•	•
-E	-o errtrace			•
-f	-o noglob	•	•	•
-G	-o globstar		•	
-h	-o hashall			•
-h	-o trackall	•	•	
-H	-o histexpand			•
-k	-o keyword	•	•	•
-m	-o monitor	•	•	•
-n	-o noexec	•	•	•
-o allexport	-a	•	•	•
-o bgnice		•	•	
-o braceexpand	-B			•
-o emacs		•	•	•
-o errexit	-e	•	•	•
-o errtrace	-E			•
-o functrace	-T			•
-o globstar	-G		•	
-o gmacs		•	•	
-o hashall	-h			•
-o history				•
-o histexpand	-H			•
-o ignoreeof		•	•	•
-o keyword	-k	•	•	•
-o markdirs		•	•	
-o monitor	-m	•	•	•
-o noclobber	-C	•	•	•

Option	Same as	ksh88	ksh93	Bash
-o noexec	-n	•	•	•
-o noglob	-f	•	•	•
-o nolog		•	•	•
-o notify	-b		•	•
-o nounset	-u			•
-o onecmd	-t			•
-o physical	-P			•
-o pipefail			•	•
-o posix				•
-o privileged	-p	•	•	•
-o trackall	-h	•	•	
-o verbose	-v	•	•	•
-o vi		•	•	•
-o viraw		•	•	
-o xtrace	-x	•	•	•
-p	-o privileged	•	•	•
-P	-o physical			•
-s		•	•	
-t	-o onecmd	•	•	•
-T	-o functrace			•
-u	-o nonunset	•	•	•
-v	-o verbose	•	•	•
-x	-o xtrace	•	•	•

Examples

`set -- "$num" -20 -30`	*Set $1 to $num, $2 to –20, $3 to –30*
`set -vx`	*Read each command line; show it; execute it; show it again (with arguments)*
`set +x`	*Stop command tracing*
`set -o noclobber`	*Prevent file overwriting*
`set +o noclobber`	*Allow file overwriting again*

shopt

`shopt [-opqsu] [`*`option`*`]`

Bash only. Sets or unsets shell options. With no options or just `-p`, prints the names and settings of the options.

Options

`-o` Each *option* must be one of the shell option names for `set -o`, instead of the options listed in the next section.

`-p` Print the option settings as `shopt` commands that can be reread later.

-q Quiet mode. The exit status is zero if the given option is set, nonzero otherwise. With multiple options, all of them must be set for a zero exit status.

-s Set the given *options*. With no *options*, prints only those that are set.

-u Unset the given *options*. With no *options*, prints only those that are unset.

Settable Shell Options

The following descriptions describe the behavior when set. Options marked with a dagger (†) are enabled by default.

`cdable_vars`
: Treat a nondirectory argument to `cd` as a variable whose value is the directory to go to.

`cdspell`
: Attempt spelling correction on each directory component of an argument to `cd`. Allowed in interactive shells only.

`checkhash`
: Check that commands found in the hash table still exist before attempting to use them. If not, perform a normal PATH search.

`checkwinsize`
: Check the window size after each command and update LINES and COLUMNS if the size has changed.

`cmdhist` †
: Save all lines of a multiline command in one history entry. This permits easy re-editing of multiline commands.

`dotglob`
: Include filenames starting with a period in the results of filename expansion.

`execfail`
: Do not exit a noninteractive shell if the command given to exec cannot be executed. Interactive shells do not exit in such a case, no matter the setting of this option.

`expand_aliases` †
: Expand aliases created with `alias`. Disabled in noninteractive shells.

`extdebug`
: Enable behavior needed for debuggers:

- `declare -F` displays the source filename and line number for each function name argument.
- When a command run by the `DEBUG` trap fails, the next command is skipped.
- When a command run by the `DEBUG` trap inside a shell function or script sourced with `.` (dot) or `source` returns with an exit status of 2, the shell simulates a call to `return`.

Bash and Korn

- BASH_ARGC and BASH_ARGV are set as described earlier.
- Function tracing is enabled. Command substitutions, shell functions, and subshells invoked via (...) inherit the `DEBUG` and `RETURN` traps.
- Error tracing is enabled. Command substitutions, shell functions and subshells invoked via (...) inherit the `ERROR` trap.

`extglob`
: Enable extended pattern matching facilities such as `+(...)`. (These were not in the Bourne shell and are not in POSIX; thus Bash requires you to enable them if you want them.)

`extquote` †
: Allow `$'...'` and `$"..."` within `${`*`variable`*`}` expansions inside double quotes.

`failglob`
: Cause patterns that do not match filenames to produce an error.

`force_fignore` †
: When doing completion, ignore words matching the list of suffixes in FIGNORE, even if such words are the only possible completions.

`gnu_errfmt`
: Print error messages in the standard GNU format.

`histappend`
: Append the history list to the file named by HISTFILE upon exit, instead of overwriting the file.

`histreedit`
: Allow a user to re-edit a failed `csh`-style history substitution with the *readline* library.

`histverify`
: Place the results of `csh`-style history substitution into the *readline* library's editing buffer, in case the user wishes to modify it further, instead of executing it directly.

`hostcomplete` †
: If using *readline*, attempt hostname completion when a word containing an `@` is being completed.

`huponexit`
: Send a `SIGHUP` to all running jobs upon exiting an interactive shell.

`interactive_comments` †
: Allow words beginning with # to start a comment in an interactive shell.

`lithist`
: If `cmdhist` is also set, save mutliline commands to the history file with newlines instead of semicolons.

`login_shell`
: Set by the shell when it is a login shell. This is a read-only option.

`mailwarn`
: Print the message `The mail in` *`mailfile`* `has been read` when a file being checked for mail has been accessed since the last time Bash checked it.

`no_empty_cmd_completion`
: If using *readline*, do *not* search $PATH when a completion is attempted on an empty line.

`nocaseglob`
: Ignore letter case when doing filename matching.

`nullglob`
: Expand patterns that do not match any files to the null string, instead of using the literal pattern as an argument.

`progcomp` †
: Enable programmable completion.

`promptvars` †
: Perform variable, command, and arithmetic substitution on the values of PS1, PS2 and PS4.

`restricted_shell`
: Set by the shell when it is a restricted shell. This is a read-only option.

`shift_verbose`
: Causes `shift` to print an error message when the shift count is greater than the number of positional parameters.

`sourcepath` †
: Causes the `.` (dot) and `source` commands to search $PATH in order to find the file to read and execute.

`xpg_echo`
: Causes echo to expand escape sequences, even without the `-e` or `-E` options.

---

shift

`shift [`*`n`*`]`

Shift positional arguments (e.g., `$2` becomes `$1`). If *n* is given, shift to the left *n* places. Used in `while` loops to iterate through command-line arguments. In the Korn shell, *n* can be an integer expression.

Examples

`shift $1+$6` *Korn shell: use expression result as shift count*

`shift $(($1 + $6))` *Same, portable to any POSIX shell*

---

sleep

`sleep [`*`n`*`]`

`ksh93` only. Sleep for *n* seconds. *n* can have a fractional part.

source

`source file [arguments]`

Bash only. Identical to the . (dot) command; see that entry.

stop

`stop [jobIDs]`

ksh88 alias for kill -STOP. ksh93 alias for kill -s STOP. Suspend the background job specified by *jobIDs*; this is the complement of CTRL-Z or suspend. See the earlier section "Job Control."

suspend

`suspend [-f]`

Suspend the current shell. Often used to stop an su command. In ksh88, suspend is an alias for kill -STOP $$. In ksh93, it is an alias for kill -s STOP $$. In Bash, it is a built-in command.

Option

-f
Force the suspension, even if the shell is a login shell. Bash only.

test

`test condition`
or
`[ condition ]`
or
`[[ condition ]]`

Evaluate a *condition* and, if its value is true, return a zero exit status; otherwise, return a nonzero exit status. An alternate form of the command uses [ ] rather than the word test. An additional alternate form uses [[ ]], in which case word splitting and pathname expansion are not done. (See the [[ ]] entry.) *condition* is constructed using the following expressions. Conditions are true if the description holds true. Features that are specific to Bash are marked with a (B). Features that are specific to the Korn shell are marked with a (K). Features that are specific to ksh93 are marked with a (K93).

File Conditions

-a *file*	*file* exists.
-b *file*	*file* exists and is a block special file.
-c *file*	*file* exists and is a character special file.
-C *file*	(K) *file* exists and is a contiguous file. This facility is not available on most Unix systems.
-d *file*	*file* exists and is a directory.
-f *file*	*file* exists and is a regular file.
-g *file*	*file* exists, and its set-group-id bit is set.
-G *file*	*file* exists, and its group is the effective group ID.
-h *file*	*file* exists and is a symbolic link.
-k *file*	*file* exists, and its sticky bit is set.

-L *file*	*file* exists and is a symbolic link.
-N *file*	(B) *file* exists and was modified after it was last read.
-O *file*	*file* exists, and its owner is the effective user ID.
-p *file*	*file* exists and is a named pipe (FIFO).
-r *file*	*file* exists and is readable.
-s *file*	*file* exists and has a size greater than zero.
-S *file*	*file* exists and is a socket.
-t [*n*]	The open file descriptor *n* is associated with a terminal device; default *n* is 1.
-u *file*	*file* exists, and its set-user-id bit is set.
-w *file*	*file* exists and is writable.
-x *file*	*file* exists and is executable.
f1 -ef *f2*	Files *f1* and *f2* are linked (refer to same file).
f1 -nt *f2*	File *f1* is newer than *f2*.
f1 -ot *f2*	File *f1* is older than *f2*.

String Conditions

string	*string* is not null.
-n *s1*	String *s1* has nonzero length.
-z *s1*	String *s1* has zero length.
s1 = *s2*	(K) Strings *s1* and *s2* are identical. *s2* can be a wildcard pattern. Quote *s2* to treat it literally. (See the section "Filename Metacharacters" earlier in this chapter.)
s1 == *s2*	(B, K93) Strings *s1* and *s2* are identical. *s2* can be a wildcard pattern. Quote *s2* to treat it literally. Preferred over =.
s1 != *s2*	Strings *s1* and *s2* are *not* identical. *s2* can be a wildcard pattern. Quote *s2* to treat it literally.
s1 =~ *s2*	(B) String *s1* matches extended regular expression *s2*. Quote *s2* to keep the shell from expanding embedded shell metacharacters. Strings matched by parenthesized subexpressions are placed into elements of the BASH_REMATCH array. See the description of BASH_REMATCH in the "Built-in Shell Variables" section earlier in this chapter.
s1 < *s2*	ASCII value of *s1* precedes that of *s2*. (Valid only within [[ ]] construct.)
s1 > *s2*	ASCII value of *s1* follows that of *s2*. (Valid only within [[ ]] construct.)

Internal Shell Conditions

-o *opt*	Option *opt* for set -o is on.

Integer Comparisons

n1 -eq *n2*	*n1* equals *n2*.
n1 -ge *n2*	*n1* is greater than or equal to *n2*.
n1 -gt *n2*	*n1* is greater than *n2*.
n1 -le *n2*	*n1* is less than or equal to *n2*.
n1 -lt *n2*	*n1* is less than *n2*.
n1 -ne *n2*	*n1* does not equal *n2*.

Bash and Korn

Combined Forms

(condition)
: True if *condition* is true (used for grouping). For test and [ ], the ( )s should be quoted by a \. The form using [[ ]] doesn't require quoting the parentheses.

! *condition*
: True if *condition* is false.

condition1 -a *condition2*
: True if both conditions are true.

condition1 && *condition2*
: True if both conditions are true. (Valid only within [[ ]] construct.)

condition1 -o *condition2*
: True if either condition is true.

condition1 || *condition2*
: True if either condition is true. (Valid only within [[ ]] construct.)

Examples

The following examples show the first line of various statements that might use a test condition:

`while test $# -gt 0`	*While there are arguments...*
`while [ -n "$1" ]`	*While there are nonempty arguments...*
`if [ $count -lt 10 ]`	*If $count is less than 10...*
`if [ -d RCS ]`	*If the RCS directory exists...*
`if [ "$answer" != "y" ]`	*If the answer is not y...*
`if [ ! -r "$1" -o ! -f "$1" ]`	*If the first argument is not a readable file or a regular file...*

---

time

time *command*
time [*command*]

Execute *command* and print the total elapsed time, user time, and system time (in seconds). Same as the Unix command time (see Chapter 2), except that the built-in version can also time other built-in commands as well as all commands in a pipeline.

The second form applies to ksh93; with no *command*, the total user and system times for the shell, and all children are printed.

---

times

times

Print accumulated process times for user and system.

---

times

times

ksh93 alias for { {time;} 2>&1;}. See also **time**.

trap

```
trap [ [commands] signals]
trap -p
trap -l
```

Execute *commands* if any *signals* are received. The second form is specific to Bash and ksh93; it prints the current trap settings in a form suitable for rereading later. The third form is specific to Bash; it lists all signals and their numbers, like `kill -l`.

Common signals include `EXIT` (0), `HUP` (1), `INT` (2), and `TERM` (15). Multiple commands must be quoted as a group and separated by semicolons internally. If *commands* is the null string (i.e., `trap "" signals`), *signals* are ignored by the shell. If *commands* are omitted entirely, reset processing of specified signals to the default action. Bash and ksh93: if *commands* is "–", reset *signals* to their initial defaults.

If both *commands* and *signals* are omitted, list current trap assignments. See the Examples here and in **exec**.

Signals

A list of signal names, numbers, and meanings were given earlier, in the **kill** entry in Chapter 2. The shells allow you to use either the signal number, or the signal name (without the `SIG` prefix). In addition, the shells support "pseudo-signals," signal names or numbers that aren't real operating system signals but which direct the shell to perform a specific action. These signals are:

`DEBUG`	Execution of any command.
`ERR`	Nonzero exit status.
`EXIT`	Exit from shell (usually when shell script finishes).
`0`	Same as `EXIT`, for historical compatibility with the Bourne shell.
`KEYBD`	A key has been read in `emacs`, `gmacs`, or `vi` editing mode. ksh93 only.
`RETURN`	A `return` is executed, or a script run with `.` (dot) or `source` finishes. Bash only.

Examples

```
trap "" INT      Ignore interrupts (signal 2)
trap INT         Obey interrupts again
```

Remove a `$tmp` file when the shell program exits, or if the user logs out, presses `CTRL-C`, or does a `kill`:

```
trap "rm -f $tmp; exit" EXIT HUP INT TERM     POSIX style
trap "rm -f $tmp; exit" 0 1 2 15   Pre-POSIX Bourne shell style
```

Print a "clean up" message when the shell program receives signals `SIGHUP`, `SIGINT`, or `SIGTERM`:

```
trap 'echo Interrupt!  Cleaning up...' HUP INT TERM
```

true

`true`

ksh88 alias for :. Bash and ksh93 built-in command that exits with a true return value.

type

`type [-afpPt] commands`

Bash version. Show whether each command name is a Unix command, a built-in command, an alias, a shell keyword, or a defined shell function.

Options

-a Print all locations in $PATH that include *command*, including aliases and functions. Use -p together with -a to suppress aliases and functions.

-f Suppress function lookup, as with command.

-p If type -t would print file for a given *command*, this option prints the full pathname for the executable files. Otherwise, it prints nothing.

-P Like -p, but force a PATH search, even if type -t would not print file.

-t Print a word describing each *command*. The word is one of alias, builtin, file, function, or keyword, depending upon the type of each *command*.

Example

```
$ type mv read if
mv is /bin/mv
read is a shell builtin
if is a shell keyword
```

type

`type commands`

Korn shell alias for whence -v.

typeset

```
typeset [options] [variable[=value ...]]
typeset -p
```

In Bash, identical to declare. See **declare**.

In the Korn shell, assign a type to each variable (along with an optional initial *value*), or, if no variables are supplied, display all variables of a particular type (as determined by the options). When variables are specified, *-option* enables the type and *+option* disables it. With no variables, *-option* prints variable names and values; *+option* prints only the names.

The second form shown is specific to ksh93.

Options

`-A` *arr*
: *arr* is an associative array. `ksh93` only.

`-b` The variable can hold any data, including binary data. References retrieve the value printed in base-64 notation; The `%B` format with `printf` may be used to print the value. `ksh93` only.

`-E` *d* *variable* is a floating-point number. *d* is the number of decimal places. The value is printed using `printf %g` format. `ksh93` only.

`-f[`*c*`]`
: The named variable is a function; no assignment is allowed. If no variable is given, list current function names. Flag *c* can be `t`, `u`, or `x`. `t` turns on tracing (same as `set -x`). `u` marks the function as undefined, which causes autoloading of the function (i.e., a search of FPATH locates the function when it's first used. `ksh93` also searches PATH). In `ksh88`, `x` exports the function. In `ksh93`, `x` is accepted but does nothing. Note the aliases **autoload** and **functions**.

`-F` *d* *variable* is a floating-point number. *d* is the number of decimal places. The value is printed using `printf %f` format. `ksh93` only.

`-H` On non-Unix systems, map Unix filenames to host filenames.

`-i[`*n*`]`
: Define variables as integers of base *n*. `integer` is an alias for `typeset -i`.

`-L[`*n*`]`
: Define variables as left-justified strings, *n* characters long (truncate or pad with blanks on the right as needed). Leading blanks are stripped; leading zeroes are stripped if `-Z` is also specified. If no *n* is supplied, field width is that of the variable's first assigned value.

`-l` Convert uppercase to lowercase.

`-n` *variable* is an indirect reference to another variable (a *nameref*). `ksh93` only. (See the section "Variables," earlier in this chapter.)

`-p` Print `typeset` commands to re-create the types of all the current variables. `ksh93` only.

`-R[`*n*`]`
: Define variables as right-justified strings, *n* characters long (truncate or pad with blanks on the left as needed). Trailing blanks are stripped. If no *n* is supplied, field width is that of the variable's first assigned value.

`-r` Mark variables as read-only. See also **readonly**.

`-t` Mark variables with a user-definable tag.

`-u` Convert lowercase to uppercase.

`-ui[`*n*`]`
: Define variables as unsigned integers of base *n*. `ksh93` only.

`-x` Mark variables for automatic export.

`-Z[`*n*`]`
: When used with `-L`, strip leading zeroes. When used alone, it's similar to `-R` except that `-Z` pads numeric values with zeroes and pads text values with blanks.

Examples

`typeset`	*List name, value, and type of all set variables*
`typeset -x`	*List names and values of exported variables*
`typeset +r PWD`	*End read-only status of PWD*
`typeset -i n1 n2 n3`	*Three variables are integers*
`typeset -R5 zipcode`	*zipcode is flush right, five characters wide*

ulimit

`ulimit [options] [n]`

Print the value of one or more resource limits, or, if *n* is specified, set a resource limit to *n*. Resource limits can be either hard (`-H`) or soft (`-S`). By default, `ulimit` sets both limits or prints the soft limit. The options determine which resource is acted on.

Options

`-H` Hard limit. Anyone can lower a hard limit; only privileged users can raise it.

`-S` Soft limit. Must be less than or equal to the hard limit.

`-a` Print all limits.

`-b` Size of socket buffers. `ksh93` only.

`-c` Maximum size of core files.

`-d` Maximum kilobytes of data segment or heap.

`-f` Maximum size of files (the default option).

`-l` Maximum size of address space that can be locked in memory. Not `ksh88`.

`-L` Maximum number of file locks. `ksh93` only.

`-m` Maximum kilobytes of physical memory. (Not effective on all Unix systems.)

`-M` Maximum size of the address space. `ksh93` only.

`-n` Maximum number of file descriptors.

`-p` Size of pipe buffers. (Not effective on all Unix systems.)

`-s` Maximum kilobytes of stack segment.

`-t` Maximum CPU seconds.

`-T` Maximum number of threads. `ksh93` only.

`-u` Maximum number of processes a single user can have.

`-v` Maximum kilobytes of virtual memory.

umask

```
umask [nnn]
umask [-pS] [mask]
```

Display file creation mask or set file creation mask to octal value *nnn*. The file creation mask determines which permission bits are turned off (e.g., `umask 002` produces `rw-rw-r--`). See the entry in Chapter 2 for examples.

The second form is not in `ksh88`. A symbolic mask is permissions to keep.

Options

`-p` Output is in a form that can be reread later by the shell. Bash only.

`-S` Print the current mask using symbolic notation. Not ksh88.

---

unalias

```
unalias names
unalias -a
```

Remove *names* from the alias list. See also **alias**.

Option

`-a` Remove all aliases. Not ksh88.

---

unset

```
unset [options] names
```

Erase definitions of functions or variables listed in *names*.

Options

`-f` Unset functions *names*.

`-n` Unset indirect variable (nameref) *name*, not the variable the nameref refers to. ksh93 only.

`-v` Unset variables *names* (default). Not ksh88.

---

until

```
until condition
do
 commands
done
```

Until *condition* is met, do *commands*. *condition* is often specified with the test command. See the Examples under **case** and **test**.

---

wait

```
wait [ID]
```

Pause in execution until all background jobs complete (exit status 0 is returned), or pause until the specified background process *ID* or job *ID* completes (exit status of *ID* is returned). Note that the shell variable $! contains the process ID of the most recent background process.

Example

```
wait $!    Wait for most recent background process to finish
```

---

whence

```
whence [options] commands
```

Korn shell only. Show whether each command name is a Unix command, a built-in command, a defined shell function, or an alias.

Options

-a Print all interpretations of *commands*. ksh93 only.

-f Skip the search for shell functions. ksh93 only.

-p Search for the pathname of *commands*.

-v Verbose output.

---

while

```
while condition
do
 commands
done
```

While *condition* is met, do *commands*. *condition* is often specified with the test commands. See the Examples under **case** and **test**.

---

filename

```
filename
```

Read and execute commands from executable file *filename*, or execute a binary object file.

5

tcsh: An Extended C Shell

This chapter describes tcsh, an enhanced version of the C shell. On many systems, tcsh is also the regular C shell (/bin/csh); in that case, the tcsh features described in this chapter work even when you run csh. The C shell was so named because many of its programming constructs and symbols resemble those of the C programming language. The following topics are presented:

- Overview of features
- Invoking the shell
- Syntax
- Variables
- Expressions
- Command history
- Command-line manipulation
- Job control
- Built-in commands

For more information on tcsh, see *Using csh & tcsh*, which is listed in the Bibliography. The web site for tcsh is *http://www.tcsh.org*.

Overview of Features

Features of tcsh include:

- Input/output redirection
- Wildcard characters (metacharacters) for filename abbreviation
- Shell variables for customizing your environment
- Integer arithmetic
- Access to previous commands (command history)

- Command-name abbreviation (aliasing)
- A built-in command language for writing shell programs
- Job control
- Command-line editing and editor commands
- Word completion (tab completion)
- Spellchecking
- Scheduled events, such as logout or terminal locking after a set idle period and delayed commands
- Read-only variables

Invoking the Shell

The `tcsh` shell can be invoked as follows:

```
tcsh [options] [arguments]
```

`tcsh` executes commands from a terminal or a file. The options `-n`, `-v`, and `-x` are useful when debugging scripts.

Options

`-b` Allow the remaining command-line options to be interpreted as options to a specified command rather than as options to `tcsh` itself.

`-c` Read and execute commands specified by the argument that follows and place any remaining arguments in the `argv` shell variable.

`-d` Load directory stack from `~/.cshdirs` even if not a login shell.

`-e` Exit if a command produces errors.

`-f` Fast startup; start without executing `.tcshrc` or `.login`.

`-i` Invoke interactive shell (prompt for input) even if not on a terminal.

`-l` Login shell (must be the only option specified).

`-m` Load `~/.tcshrc` even if effective user is not the owner of the file.

`-n` Parse commands, but do not execute.

`-q` Accept `SIGQUIT` when used under a debugger. Disables job control.

`-s` Read commands from the standard input.

`-t` Exit after executing one line of input (which may be continued with a `\` to escape the newline).

`-v` Display commands before executing them; expand history substitutions, but not other substitutions (e.g., filename, variable, and command). Same as setting `verbose`.

`-V` Same as `-v`, but also display `.tcshrc`.

`-x` Display commands before executing them, but expand all substitutions. Same as setting the `echo` shell variable. `-x` is often combined with `-v`.

`-X` Same as `-x`, but also display `.tcshrc`.

Arguments

Arguments are assigned, in order, to the positional parameters $1, $2, and so on. If the first argument is an executable file, commands are read from it, and the remaining arguments are assigned to $1, $2, and so forth. The positional parameters are also available in the argv shell variable.

Syntax

This section describes the syntax used by tcsh. The topics are arranged as follows:

- Special files
- Filename metacharacters
- Quoting
- Command forms
- Redirection forms

Special Files

Filename	Description
/etc/csh.cshrc	Read by any shell before reading per-user initialization files.
~/.tcshrc or ~/.cshrc	Executed at each instance of shell startup. If no ~/.tcshrc is found, tcsh tries ~/.cshrc.
/etc/csh.login	Read by login shell before reading per-user initialization files.
~/.login	Executed by login shell after .tcshrc.
~/.cshdirs	Used to reload the directory stack after executing ~/.login. (See the savedirs variable.)
~/.history	History list saved from previous login.
/etc/csh.logout	Executed by login shell at logout, before ~/.logout.
~/.logout	Executed by login shell at logout.
/etc/passwd	Source of home directories for ~*name* abbreviations. (May come from NIS or NIS+ instead.)

Example startup files are available from *http://tcshrc.sourceforge.net*.

Filename Metacharacters

Metacharacters	Meaning
*	Match any string of zero or more characters.
?	Match any single character.
[*abc*...]	Match any one of the enclosed characters; a hyphen can be used to specify a range (e.g., a–z, A–Z, 0–9).
[^*abc*...]	Match any character *not* enclosed as above.

Metacharacters	Meaning
{abc,xxx,...}	Expand each comma-separated string inside braces. The strings need not match actual filenames.
~	Home directory for the current user.
~name	Home directory of user *name*.
=n	The *n*th entry in the directory stack, counting from zero.
=-	The last entry in the directory stack.
^pattern	Matches anything that *pattern* does not match. To work correctly, *pattern* must contain ?, *, or [...], and should not contain {...} or ~.

Examples

`% ls new*`	*Match new and new.1*
`% cat ch?`	*Match ch9 but not ch10*
`% vi [D-R]*`	*Match files that begin with uppercase D through R*
`% ls {ch,app}?`	*Expand, then match ch1, ch2, app1, app2*
`% mv info{,.old}`	*Expands to mv info info.old*
`% cd ~tom`	*Change to tom's home directory*
`% touch aa bb cc`	*Create some files*
`% ls ^a*`	*List nonmatching filenames*
`bb  cc`	

On modern systems, ranges such as `[D-R]` are not portable; the system's locale may include more than just the uppercase letters from `D` to `R` in the range.

Quoting

Quoting disables a character's special meaning and allows it to be used literally, as itself. The characters in the following table have special meaning to `tcsh`.

Characters	Description
;	Command separator
&	Background execution
( )	Command grouping
|	Pipe
* ? [ ] ~ ^	Filename metacharacters
{ }	String expansion characters (usually don't require quoting)
< > & !	Redirection symbols
! ^	History substitution, quick substitution
" ' \	Used in quoting other characters
`	Command substitution
$	Variable substitution
space tab newline	Word separators

The characters that follow can be used for quoting:

" " Everything between " and " is taken literally except for the following characters, which keep their special meaning:

- `$` Variable substitution will occur.
- `` ` `` Command substitution will occur.
- `"` The end of the double quote.
- `\` Escape next character.
- `!` The history character.
- `newline` The newline character.

' ' Everything between ' and ' is taken literally except for ! (history), another ', and newline.

\ The character following a \ is taken literally. Use within " " to escape ", $, `, and newline. Use within ' ' to escape newlines. Often used to escape itself, spaces, or newlines. Always needed to escape a history character (usually !).

Examples

```
% echo 'Single quotes "protect" double quotes'
Single quotes "protect" double quotes

% echo "Don't double quotes protect single quotes too?"
Don't double quotes protect single quotes too?

% echo "You have `ls|wc -l` files in `pwd`"
You have       43 files in /home/bob

% echo The value of \$x is $x
The value of $x is 100
```

tcsh

Command Forms

Command	Action
cmd &	Execute *cmd* in the background.
cmd1 ; *cmd2*	Command sequence; execute multiple *cmds* on the same line.
(*cmd1* ; *cmd2*)	Subshell; treat *cmd1* and *cmd2* as a command group.
cmd1 | *cmd2*	Pipe; use output from *cmd1* as input to *cmd2*.
cmd1 \`*cmd2*\`	Command substitution; run *cmd2* first and use its output as arguments to *cmd1*.
cmd1 && *cmd2*	AND; execute *cmd1* and then (if *cmd1* succeeds) *cmd2*. This is a "short-circuit" operation; *cmd2* is never executed if *cmd1* fails.
cmd1 || *cmd2*	OR; execute either *cmd1* or (if *cmd1* fails) *cmd2*. This is a "short-circuit" operation; *cmd2* is never executed if *cmd1* succeeds.

Examples

`% nroff file > file.out &`	*Format in the background*
`% cd; ls`	*Execute sequentially*
`% (date; who; pwd) > logfile`	*All output is redirected*
`% sort file | pr -3 | lp`	*Sort file, page output, then print*
``% vi `grep -l ifdef *.c` ``	*Edit files found by grep*
``% egrep '(yes|no)' `cat list` ``	*Specify a list of files to search*
`% grep XX file && lp file`	*Print file if it contains the pattern,*
`% grep XX file || echo XX not found`	*otherwise, echo an error message*

Redirection Forms

File descriptor	Name	Common abbreviation	Typical default
0	Standard input	stdin	Keyboard
1	Standard output	stdout	Screen
2	Standard error	stderr	Screen

The usual input source or output destination can be changed with the redirection commands listed in the following sections.

Simple redirection

Command	Action
cmd > *file*	Send output of *cmd* to *file* (overwrite).
cmd >! *file*	Same as preceding, even if `noclobber` is set.
cmd >> *file*	Send output of *cmd* to *file* (append).
cmd >>! *file*	Same as preceding, even if `noclobber` is set.
cmd < *file*	Take input for *cmd* from *file*.
cmd << *text*	Read standard input up to a line identical to *text* (*text* can be stored in a shell variable). Input usually is typed at the keyboard or in the shell program. Commands that typically use this syntax include `cat`, `echo`, `ex`, and `sed`. If *text* is quoted (using any of the shell's quoting mechanisms), the input is passed through verbatim. Otherwise, the shell performs variable and command substitutions on the input. When quoting *text*, the ending delimiter must be quoted identically.

Multiple redirection

Command	Action
cmd >& *file*	Send both standard output and standard error to *file*.
cmd >&! *file*	Same as preceding, even if `noclobber` is set.
cmd >>& *file*	Append standard output and standard error to end of *file*.
cmd >>&! *file*	Same as preceding, even if `noclobber` is set.
cmd1 |& *cmd2*	Pipe standard error together with standard output.
(*cmd* > *f1*) >& *f2*	Send standard output to file *f1* and standard error to file *f2*.
cmd | tee *files*	Send output of *cmd* to standard output (usually the screen) and to *files*. (See the Example in Chapter 2 under **tee**.)

Examples

```
% cat part1 > book                          Copy part1 to book
% cat part2 part3 >> book                   Append parts 2 and 3 to same file as part1
% mail tim < report                         Take input to message from report
% cc calc.c >& error_out                    Store all messages, including errors
% cc newcalc.c >&! error_out                Overwrite old file
% grep Unix ch* |& pr                       Pipe all messages, including errors
% (find / -print > filelist) >& no_access   Separate error messages from list of files
% sed 's/^/XX /' << "END_ARCHIVE"           Supply text right after command
? This is often how a shell archive is "wrapped",
? bundling text for distribution. You would normally
? run sed from a shell program, not from the command line.
? "END_ARCHIVE"
XX This is often how a shell archive is "wrapped",
XX bundling text for distribution.  You would normally
XX run sed from a shell program, not from the command line.
```

Variables

This subsection describes the following:

- Variable substitution
- Variable modifiers
- Predefined shell variables
- Formatting in the prompt variable
- Sample .tcshrc file
- Environment variables

tcsh

Variable Substitution

In the following substitutions, braces ({ }) are optional, except when needed to separate a variable name from following characters that would otherwise be considered part of the name.

Variable	Description
${*var*}	The value of variable *var*.
${*var*[*i*]}	Select word or words in position *i* of *var*. *i* can be a single number, a range *m–n*, a range *-n* (missing *m* implies 1), a range *m-* (missing *n* implies all remaining words), or * (select all words). *i* also can be a variable that expands to one of these values.
${#*var*}	The number of words in *var*.
${#argv}	The number of arguments.
$#	Same as ${#argv}.
${%*var*}	The number of characters in *var*.
${%*n*}	The number of characters in $argv[*n*].
$0	Name of the program.
${argv[*n*]}	Individual arguments on command line (positional parameters); 1 ≤ *n* ≤ 9.
${*n*}	Same as ${argv[*n*]}.

Variable	Description
`${argv[*]}`	All arguments on command line.
`$*`	Same as `{$argv[*]}`.
`$argv[$#argv]`	The last argument.
`${?`*`var`*`}`	Return 1 if *var* is set; 0 if *var* is not set.
`$?0`	Return 1 if input filename is known, 0 if not.
`$$`	Process number of current shell; useful as part of a filename for creating temporary files with unique names.
`$?`	Same as `$status`.
`$!`	Process ID number of last background process started by the shell.
`$_`	Text of the command line of the last command executed.
`$<`	Read a line from standard input.

Examples

Sort the third through last arguments and save the output in a file whose name is unique to this process:

```
sort $argv[3-] > tmp.$$
```

In a `.tcshrc` file, process commands only if the shell is interactive (i.e., if the `prompt` variable is set):

```
if ($?prompt) then
    set commands,
    alias commands,
    etc.
endif
```

Variable Modifiers

Except for `$?`*`var`*, `$?0`, `$#`*`var`*, `$%`*`var`*, `$#`, `$$`, `$?`, `$!`, `$_`, and `$<`, the variable substitutions in the preceding section may be followed by one of these modifiers (when braces are used, the modifier goes inside them):

- `:r` Return the variable's root (the portion before the last dot).
- `:e` Return the variable's extension.
- `:h` Return the variable's header (the directory portion).
- `:t` Return the variable's tail (the portion after the last slash).
- `:gr` Return all roots.
- `:ge` Return all extensions.
- `:gh` Return all headers.
- `:gt` Return all tails.
- `:q` Quote a wordlist variable, keeping the items separate. Prevents further substitution. Useful when the variable contains filename metacharacters that should not be expanded.
- `:x` Quote a pattern, expanding it into a wordlist.

Examples using pathname modifiers

The following table shows the effect of pathname modifiers if the aa variable is set as follows:

```
set aa=(/progs/num.c /book/chap.ps)
```

Variable portion	Specification	Output result
Normal variable	echo $aa	/progs/num.c /book/chap.ps
Second root	echo $aa[2]:r	/book/chap
Second header	echo $aa[2]:h	/book
Second tail	echo $aa[2]:t	chap.ps
Second extension	echo $aa[2]:e	ps
Root	echo $aa:r	/progs/num /book/chap.ps
Global root	echo $aa:gr	/progs/num /book/chap
Header	echo $aa:h	/progs /book/chap.ps
Global header	echo $aa:gh	/progs /book
Tail	echo $aa:t	num.c /book/chap.ps
Global tail	echo $aa:gt	num.c chap.ps
Extension	echo $aa:e	c /book/chap.ps
Global extension	echo $aa:ge	c ps

Examples using quoting modifiers

Unless quoted, the shell expands variables to represent files in the current directory:

```
% set a="[a-z]*" A="[A-Z]*"
% echo "$a" "$A"
[a-z]* [A-Z]*

% echo $a $A
at cc m4 Book Doc

% echo $a:x $A
[a-z]* Book Doc

% set d=($a:q $A:q)
% echo $d
at cc m4 Book Doc

% echo $d:q
[a-z]* [A-Z]*

% echo $d[1] +++ $d[2]
at cc m4 +++ Book Doc

% echo $d[1]:q
[a-z]*
```

tcsh

Predefined Shell Variables

Variables can be set in one of two ways; by assigning a value:

```
set var=value
```

or by simply turning the variable on:

```
set var
```

The latter case is useful for simple "Is the variable set?" kinds of tests.

In the following list, variables that accept values are shown with the equals sign followed by the type of value they accept; the value is then described. (Note, however, that variables such as `argv`, `cwd`, and `status` are never explicitly assigned.) For variables that are turned on or off, the list describes what they do when set. `tcsh` automatically sets (and, in some cases, updates) the variables `addsuffix`, `argv`, `autologout`, `command`, `csubstnonl`, `cwd`, `dirstack`, `echo-style`, `edit`, `gid`, `home`, `loginsh`, `logout`, `owd`, `path`, `prompt`, `prompt2`, `prompt3`, `shell`, `shlvl`, `status`, `tcsh`, `term`, `tty`, `uid`, `user`, and `version`.

`addsuffix`
: Append `/` to directories and a space to files during tab completion to indicate a precise match.

`afsuser`
: Set value to be used instead of the local username for Kerberos authentication with the `autologout` locking feature.

`ampm`
: Display all times in 12-hour format.

`argv=(`*`args`*`)`
: List of arguments passed to current command; default is `( )`.

`autocorrect`
: Check spelling before attempting to complete commands.

`autoexpand`
: Expand history (such as `!` references) during command completion.

`autolist[=ambiguous]`
: Print possible completions when correct one is ambiguous. If `ambiguous` is specified, print possible completions only when completion adds no new characters.

`autologout=(`*`logout-minutes`* `[`*`locking-minutes`*`])`
: Log out after *logout-minutes* of idle time. Lock the terminal after *locking-minutes* of idle time, requiring a password before continuing. Not used if the `DISPLAY` environment variable is set.

`backslash_quote`
: Always allow backslashes to quote `\`, `'`, and `"`.

`catalog`
: Use `tcsh.${catalog}` as the filename of the message catalog. The default is `tcsh`.

`cdpath=(dirs)`
: List of alternate directories to search when locating arguments for `cd`, `popd`, or `pushd`.

`color`
: Turn on color for `ls-F`, `ls`, or both. Setting to nothing is equivalent to setting for both.

`colorcat`
: Enable color escape sequence for Native Language System (NLS) support and display NLS messages in color.

`command`
: If set, holds the command passed to the shell with the `-c` option.

`complete=enhance`
: If set to `enhance`, ignore case in completion, treat ., -, and _ as word separators, and consider _ and - to be the same.

`continue=(cmdlist)`
: *cmdlist* is a list of command names. If a stopped job consists of one of the named commands, restart that job when the user enters the corresponding command name, instead of starting a new job.

`continue_args=(cmdlist)`
: Like `continue`, but execute the following:

```
echo `pwd` $argv > ~/.cmd_pause; %cmd
```

`correct={cmd|complete|all}`
: When `cmd`, spellcheck commands. When `complete`, complete commands. When `all`, spellcheck whole command line.

`csubstnonl`
: Newlines and carriage returns in command substitution output are replaced by spaces. Set by default.

`cwd=dir`
: Full pathname of current directory.

`dextract`
: When set, the `pushd` command extracts the desired directory and puts it at the top of the stack instead of rotating the stack.

`dirsfile=file`
: History file consulted by `dirs -S` and `dirs -L`. Default is `~/.cshdirs`.

`dirstack`
: Directory stack, in array format. `dirstack[1]` is always equivalent to `cwd`. The other elements can be artificially changed.

`dspmbyte=code`
: Enable use of multibyte code; for use with Kanji. See the `tcsh` manpage for details.

`dunique`
: Make sure that each directory exists only once in the stack.

`echo`
: Redisplay each command line before execution; same as `tcsh -x`.

echo_style={bsd|sysv|both|none}
: Don't echo a newline with the -n option (bsd), parse escaped characters (sysv), do both, or do neither.

edit
: Enable command-line editor. Set by default for interactive shells.

ellipsis
: For use with prompt variable. Use ... to represent skipped directories.

fignore=(*suffs*)
: List of filename suffixes to ignore during filename completion.

filec
: This variable exists for compatibility with the 4.3 BSD csh. By default, it is ignored in tcsh. However, if edit has been unset, then if filec is set a filename that is partially typed on the command line can be expanded to its full name when the Escape key is pressed. If more than one filename matches, type CTRL-D (EOF) to list possible completions.

gid
: User's group ID.

group
: User's group name.

histchars=*ab*
: A two-character string that sets the characters to use in history-substitution and quick-substitution (default is !^).

histdup={all|prev|erase}
: Maintain a record only of unique history events (all), do not enter a new event when it is the same as the previous one (prev), or remove an old event that is the same as the new one (erase).

histfile=*file*
: History file consulted by history -S and history -L. Default is ~/.history.

histlit
: Do not expand history lines when recalling them.

history=(*n format*)
: The first word indicates the number of commands to save in the history list. The second indicates the format with which to display that list. See the section "Formatting for the Prompt Variable" later in this chapter for possible formats.

home=*dir*
: Home directory of user, initialized from the environment variable HOME. The ~ character is shorthand for this value.

ignoreeof
: Ignore an end-of-file (EOF) from terminals; prevents accidental logout.

implicitcd[=verbose]
: If a directory name is entered as a command, cd to that directory. Can be set to verbose to echo the cd to standard output.

inputmode={insert|overwrite}
: Control editor's mode.

killdup={all|prev|erase}
: Enter only unique strings in the kill ring (all), do not enter a new string when it is the same as the current killed string (prev), or erase from the kill ring an old string that is the same as the current string (erase).

killring=*num*
: Set the number of killed strings to keep in memory to *num*. The default is 30. If unset or set to a number less than two, keep only the most recently killed string.

listflags=(*flags* [*path*])
: One or more of the a, A, or x options for the ls-F built-in command. The second word can be set to the path for the ls command.

listjobs[=long]
: When a job is suspended, list all jobs (in long format, if specified).

listlinks
: In the ls-F command, include the type of file to which links point (directory, nonexistent file, nondirectory).

listmax=*num*
: Do not allow the list-choices editor command to print more than *num* choices before prompting.

listmaxrows=*num*
: Do not allow the list-choices editor command to print more than *num* rows of choices before prompting.

loginsh
: Set if shell is a login shell.

logout
: Indicates status of an imminent logout (normal, automatic, or hangup). Useful in a ~/.logout file.

mail=(*n files*)
: One or more files checked for new mail every five minutes or (if *n* is supplied) every *n* seconds.

matchbeep={never|nomatch|ambiguous|notunique}
: Specifies circumstances under which completion should beep: never, if no match exists, if multiple matches exist, or if multiple matches exist and one is exact. If unset, ambiguous is used.

nobeep
: Disable beeping, such as for ambiguous file completion.

noclobber
: Don't redirect output to an existing file; prevents accidental destruction of files.

noding
: Don't print DING! in prompt time specifiers when the hour changes.

noglob
: Turn off filename expansion; useful in shell scripts.

nokanji
: Disable Kanji (if supported).

nonomatch
: Treat filename metacharacters as literal characters if no match exists (e.g., `vi ch*` creates new file `ch*` instead of printing "No match").

nostat=(*directory-list*)
: Do not stat *directory-list* during completion.

notify
: Notify user of completed jobs right away, instead of waiting for the next prompt.

owd
: Old working directory.

path=(*dirs*)
: List of pathnames in which to search for commands to execute. Initialized from `PATH`; the default is `. /usr/ucb /bin /usr/bin`. However, standard start-up scripts may change it.

printexitvalue
: Print all nonzero exit values.

prompt='*str*'
: String that prompts for interactive input; default is `%#` in interactive shells. See the section "Formatting for the Prompt Variable" later in this chapter for formatting information.

prompt2='*str*'
: String that prompts for interactive input in `foreach` and `while` loops and continued lines (those with escaped newlines). See the section "Formatting for the Prompt Variable" for formatting information.

prompt3='*str*'
: String that prompts for interactive input in automatic spelling correction. See the section "Formatting for the Prompt Variable" for formatting information.

promptchars=*cc*
: Use the two characters specified as *cc* with the `%# prompt` sequence to indicate normal users and the superuser, respectively.

pushdsilent
: Do not print directory stack when `pushd` and `popd` are invoked.

pushdtohome
: Change to home directory when `pushd` is invoked without arguments.

recexact
: Consider completion to be concluded on first exact match.

recognize_only_executables
: When command completion is invoked, show only executable files.

rmstar
: Prompt before executing the command `rm *`.

`rprompt=string`
: The string to print on the right side of the screen while the prompt is displayed on the left. The *string* may have the same special contents as for the `prompt` variable.

`savedirs`
: Execute `dirs -S` before exiting.

`savehist=(max [merge])`
: Execute `history -S` before exiting. Save no more than *max* lines of history. If `merge` specified, merge those lines with previous history saves, and sort by time.

`sched=string`
: Format for `sched`'s printing of events. See the section "Formatting for the Prompt Variable" for formatting information.

`shell=file`
: Pathname of the shell program.

`shlvl`
: Number of nested shells.

`status=n`
: Exit status of last command. Built-in commands return 0 (success) or 1 (failure).

`symlinks={chase|ignore|expand}`
: Specify manner in which to deal with symbolic links. Expand them to real directory name in `cwd` (`chase`), treat them as real directories (`ignore`), or expand arguments that resemble pathnames (`expand`).

`tcsh`
: Version of `tcsh`.

`term`
: Terminal type.

`time='n %c'`
: If command execution takes more than *n* CPU seconds, report user time, system time, elapsed time, and CPU percentage. Supply optional `%c` flags to show other data. See the `tcsh` manpage for the details.

`tperiod`
: Number of minutes between executions of the `periodic` alias (described later in this chapter).

`tty`
: Name of tty, if applicable.

`uid`
: User ID.

`user`
: Login name of user, initialized from `USER`.

`verbose`
: Display a command after history substitution; same as `tcsh -v`.

`version`
: Shell's version and additional information, including options set at compile time.

`visiblebell`
: Flash screen instead of beeping.

`watch=([n] user terminal...)`
: Watch for *user* logging in at *terminal*, where *terminal* can be a device name or `any`. Check every *n* minutes, or 10 by default.

`who=string`
: Specify information to be printed by `watch`. See the `tcsh` manpage for the details.

`wordchars=chars`
: List of all nonalphanumeric characters that may be part of a word. Default is `*?_-.[]~=`.

Formatting for the Prompt Variable

`tcsh` provides a list of substitutions that can be used in formatting the prompt. The list of available substitutions includes:

`%%`	Literal `%`.
`%/`	The present working directory.
`%~`	The present working directory, in ~ notation.
`%#`	# for the superuser, > for others.
`%?`	Previous command's exit status.
`%$var`	The value of the shell or environment variable *var*.
`%{string%}`	Include *string* as a literal escape sequence to change terminal attributes (but should not move the cursor location); cannot be the last sequence in the prompt.
`\c`, `^c`	Parse *c* as in the `bindkey` built-in command.
`%b`	End boldfacing.
`%B`	Begin boldfacing.
`%c[[0]n]`, `%.[[0]n]`	The last *n* (default 1) components of the present working directory; if a leading `0` is specified, replace removed components with `/<skipped>`.
`%C`	Similar to `%c`, but use full pathnames instead of ~ notation.
`%d`	Day of the week (e.g., `Mon`, `Tue`).
`%D`	Day of month (e.g., 09, 10).
`%h`, `%!`, `!`	Number of current history event.
`%j`	The number of jobs.
`%l`	Current tty.
`%L`	Clear from the end of the prompt to the end of the display or the line.
`%m`	First component of hostname.
`%M`	Fully qualified hostname.
`%n`	Username.
`%p`	Current time, with seconds (12-hour mode).
`%P`	Current time, with seconds (24-hour format).
`%R`	In `prompt2`, the parser status; in `prompt3`, the corrected string; and in `history`, the history string.
`%s`	End standout mode (reverse video).
`%S`	Begin standout mode (reverse video).

%t, %@	Current time (12-hour format).
%T	Current time (24-hour format).
%u	End underlining.
%U	Begin underlining.
%w	Month name (e.g., Jan, Feb).
%W	Month number (e.g., 09, 10).
%y	Year, two digits (e.g., 06, 07).
%Y	Year, four digits (e.g., 2006, 2007).

Sample .tcshrc File

```
# PREDEFINED VARIABLES

set path=(~ ~/bin /usr/ucb /bin /usr/bin)
set mail=(/var/mail/tom)

if ($?prompt) then                    # settings for interactive use
  set echo
  set noclobber ignoreeof

  set cdpath=(/usr/lib /var/spool/uucp)
# Now I can type cd macros
# instead of cd /usr/lib/macros

  set history=100
  set prompt='tom \!% '               # includes history number
  set time=3

# MY VARIABLES

  set man1="/usr/share/man/man1"      # lets me do   cd $man1, ls $man1
  set a="[a-z]*"                      # lets me do   vi $a
  set A="[A-Z]*"                      # or           grep string $A

# ALIASES

  alias c "clear; dirs"               # use quotes to protect ; or |
  alias h "history|more"
  alias j jobs -l
  alias ls ls -sFC                    # redefine ls command
  alias del 'mv \!* ~/tmp_dir'        # a safe alternative to rm
endif
```

Environment Variables

tcsh maintains a set of *environment variables*, which are distinct from shell variables and aren't really part of the shell. Shell variables are meaningful only within the currently running shell, but environment variables are exported automatically, making them available to other programs run by the shell. For example, shell variables are accessible only to the particular script in which they're defined, whereas environment variables can be used by any shell scripts, mail utilities, or editors you might invoke.

Environment variables are assigned as follows:

```
setenv VAR value
```

By convention, environment variable names are all uppercase. You can create your own environment variables, or you can use the predefined environment variables that follow.

The following environment variables have corresponding `tcsh` shell variables. When either one changes, the value is copied to the other.

`AFSUSER`	Alternative to local user for Kerberos authentication with `autologout` locking; same as `afsuser`.
`GROUP`	User's group name; same as `group`.
`HOME`	Home directory; same as `home`.
`PATH`	Search path for commands; same as `path`.
`SHLVL`	Number of nested shell levels; same as `shlvl`.
`TERM`	Terminal type; same as `term`.
`USER`	User's login name; same as `user`.

Other environment variables, which do not have corresponding shell variables, include the following:

`COLUMNS`	Number of columns on terminal.
`DISPLAY`	Identifies user's display for the X Window System. If set, the shell doesn't set `autologout`.
`EDITOR`	Pathname to default editor. See also `VISUAL`.
`EXINIT`	A string of ex commands similar to those found in the startup `.exrc` file (e.g., `set ai`). Used by `vi` and `ex`. See also Chapter 9.
`HOST`	Name of machine.
`HOSTTYPE`	Type of machine. Obsolete; will be removed eventually.
`HPATH`	Colon-separated list of directories to search for documentation for the `run-help` editor command.
`LANG`	Preferred language. Used for native language support.
`LC_CTYPE`	The locale, as it affects character handling. Used for native language support.
`LINES`	Number of lines on the screen.
`LOGNAME`	Another name for the `USER` variable.
`LS_COLORS`	Colors for use with the `ls` command. See the `tcsh` manpage for detailed information.
`MACHTYPE`	Type of machine.
`MAIL`	The file that holds mail. Used by mail programs. This is not the same as the shell variable `mail`, which only checks for new mail.
`NOREBIND`	Printable characters not rebound. Used for native language support.
`OSTYPE`	Operating system.
`PWD`	The current directory; the value is copied from `cwd`, but only after a directory change.
`REMOTEHOST`	Machine name of remote host from which the user logged in.
`SHELL`	Undefined by default; once initialized to `shell`, the two are identical.
`TERMCAP`	The file that holds the cursor-positioning codes for your terminal type. Default is `/etc/termcap`.
`VENDOR`	System vendor.
`VISUAL`	Pathname to default full-screen editor. See also `EDITOR`.

Expressions

Expressions are used in `@` (the C shell math operator), `if`, and `while` statements to perform arithmetic, string comparisons, file testing, and so on. `exit` and `set` also specify expressions, as can the `tcsh` built-in command `filetest`. Expressions are formed by combining variables and constants with operators that resemble those in the C programming language. Operator precedence is the same as in C. It is easiest to just remember the following precedence rules:

- `* / %`
- `+ -`
- Group all other expressions inside `()`s; parentheses are required if the expression contains <, >, &, or |

Operators

Operators can be one of the following types.

Assignment operators

<table>
<tr><th>Operator</th><th>Description</th></tr>
<tr><td>=</td><td>Assign value.</td></tr>
<tr><td>+=   -=</td><td>Reassign after addition/subtraction.</td></tr>
<tr><td>*=   /=   %=</td><td>Reassign after multiplication/division/remainder.</td></tr>
<tr><td>&=   ^= |=</td><td>Reassign after bitwise AND/XOR/OR.</td></tr>
<tr><td>++</td><td>Increment.</td></tr>
<tr><td>--</td><td>Decrement.</td></tr>
</table>

Arithmetic operators

Operator	Description
`* / %`	Multiplication; integer division; modulus (remainder).
`+ -`	Addition; subtraction.

Bitwise and logical operators

<table>
<tr><th>Operator</th><th>Description</th></tr>
<tr><td>~</td><td>Binary inversion (one's complement).</td></tr>
<tr><td>!</td><td>Logical negation.</td></tr>
<tr><td><<   >></td><td>Bitwise left shift; bitwise right shift.</td></tr>
<tr><td>&</td><td>Bitwise AND.</td></tr>
<tr><td>^</td><td>Bitwise exclusive OR.</td></tr>
<tr><td>|</td><td>Bitwise OR.</td></tr>
<tr><td>&&</td><td>Logical AND (short-circuit).</td></tr>
<tr><td>||</td><td>Logical OR (short-circuit).</td></tr>
<tr><td>{ command }</td><td>Return 1 if command is successful, 0 otherwise. Note that this is the opposite of command's normal return code. The <code>$status</code> variable may be more practical.</td></tr>
</table>

Comparison operators

Operator	Description
`==` `!=`	Equality; inequality.
`<=` `>=`	Less than or equal to; greater than or equal to.
`<` `>`	Less than; greater than.
`=~`	String on left matches a filename pattern on right containing *, ?, or [...].
`!~`	String on left does not match a filename pattern on right containing *, ?, or [...].

File inquiry operators

Command substitution and filename expansion are performed on *file* before the test is performed. Operators can be combined (e.g., `-ef`). The following is a list of the valid file inquiry operators.

Operator	Description
`-b` *file*	The file is a block special file.
`-c` *file*	The file is a character special file.
`-d` *file*	The file is a directory.
`-e` *file*	The file exists.
`-f` *file*	The file is a plain file.
`-g` *file*	The file's set-group-ID bit is set.
`-k` *file*	The file's sticky bit is set.
`-l` *file*	The file is a symbolic link.
`-L` *file*	Apply any remaining operators to symbolic link, not the file it points to.
`-o` *file*	The current user owns the file.
`-p` *file*	The file is a named pipe (FIFO).
`-r` *file*	The current user has read permission.
`-s` *file*	The file has nonzero size.
`-S` *file*	The file is a socket special file.
`-t` *file*	*file* is a digit and is an open file descriptor for a terminal device.
`-u` *file*	The file's set-user-ID bit is set.
`-w` *file*	The current user has write permission.
`-x` *file*	The current user has execute permission.
`-X` *file*	The file is executable and is in the path, or is a shell built-in.
`-z` *file*	The file has zero size.
`!`	Reverse the sense of any following inquiry, which may be any of the tests in this table.

Finally, `tcsh` provides the following operators, which return other kinds of information.

Operator	Description
-A[:] *file*	Last time file was accessed, as the number of seconds since the epoch. With a colon (:), the result is in timestamp format.
-C[:] *file*	Last time inode was modified. With a colon (:), the result is in timestamp format.
-D *file*	Device number.
-F *file*	Composite file identifier, in the form *device:inode*.
-G[:] *file*	Numeric group ID for the file. With a colon (:), the result is the group name if known, otherwise the numeric group ID.
-I *file*	Inode number.
-L *file*	The name of the file pointed to by symbolic link *file*.
-M[:] *file*	Last time file was modified. With a colon (:), the result is in timestamp format.
-N *file*	Number of hard links.
-P[:] *file*	Permissions in octal, without leading 0. With a colon (:), the result includes a leading 0.
-P*mode*[:] *file*	Equivalent to -P *file* ANDed with *mode*. With a colon (:), the result includes a leading 0.
-U[:] *file*	Numeric user ID of the file's owner. With a colon (:), the result is the username if known, otherwise the numeric user ID.
-Z *file*	The file's size, in bytes.

These operators may only be used in multioperator tests, and they must be the last operator in such tests.

tcsh

Examples

The following examples show @ commands and assume n = 4.

Expression	Value of $x
`@ x = ($n > 10 || $n < 5)`	1
`@ x = ($n >= 0 && $n < 3)`	0
`@ x = ($n << 2)`	16
`@ x = ($n >> 2)`	1
`@ x = $n % 2`	0
`@ x = $n % 3`	1

The following examples show the first line of `if` or `while` statements.

Expression	Meaning
`while ($#argv != 0)`	While there are arguments ...
`if ($today[1] == "Fri")`	If the first word is "Fri" ...
`if ($file !~ *.[zZ])`	If the file doesn't end with .z or .Z ...
`if ($argv[1] =~ chap?)`	If the first argument is chap followed by a single character ...
`if (-f $argv[1])`	If the first argument is a plain file ...
`if (! -d $tmpdir)`	If `tmpdir` is not a directory ...

Command History

Previously executed commands are stored in a history list. You can access this list to verify commands, repeat them, or execute modified versions of them. The `history` built-in command displays the history list; the predefined variables `histchars`, `history`, and `savehist` also affect the history mechanism. There are a number of ways to use the history list:

- Rerun a previous command
- Edit a previous command
- Make command substitutions
- Make argument substitutions (replace specific words in a command)
- Extract or replace parts of a command or word

The easiest way to take advantage of the command history is to use the arrow keys to move around in the history, select the command you want, and then rerun it or use the editing features described in the section "Command-Line Editing," later in this chapter, to modify the command. The arrow keys are:

Key	Description
Up arrow (↑)	Previous command.
Down arrow (↓)	Next command.
Left arrow (←)	Move left in command line.
Right arrow (→)	Move right in command line.

The next sections describe some tools for editing and rerunning commands. With the C shell, which does not have the command-line editing features of `tcsh`, these features are important for rerunning commands. With `tcsh`, they are less often used, but they still work.

Command Substitution

Command	Description
`!`	Begin a history substitution.
`!!`	Previous command.
`!N`	Command number *N* in history list.
`!-N`	*N*th command back from current command.
`!string`	Most recent command that starts with *string*.
`!?string?`	Most recent command that contains *string*.
`!?string?%`	Most recent command argument that contains *string*.
`!$`	Last argument of previous command.
`!!string`	Previous command, then append *string*.
`!N string`	Command *N*, then append *string*.
`!{s1}s2`	Most recent command starting with string *s1*, then append string *s2*.
`^old^new^`	Quick substitution; change string *old* to *new* in previous command, and execute modified command.

Command Substitution Examples

The following command is assumed:

```
3% vi cprogs/01.c ch002 ch03
```

Event number	Command typed	Command executed
4	`^00^0`	`vi cprogs/01.c ch02 ch03`
5	`nroff !*`	`nroff cprogs/01.c ch02 ch03`
6	`nroff !$`	`nroff ch03`
7	`!vi`	`vi cprogs/01.c ch02 ch03`
8	`!6`	`nroff ch03`
9	`!?01`	`vi cprogs/01.c ch02 ch03`
10	`!{nr}.new`	`nroff ch03.new`
11	`!!|lp`	`nroff ch03.new | lp`
12	`more !?pr?%`	`more cprogs/01.c`

Word Substitution

Word specifiers allow you to retrieve individual words from previous command lines. Colons may precede any word specifier. After an event number, colons are optional unless shown here.

Specifier	Description
`:0`	Command name.
`:n`	Argument number *n*.
`^`	First argument.
`$`	Last argument.
`%`	Argument matched by a `!?string?` search.
`:n-m`	Arguments *n* through *m*.
`-m`	Words 0 through *m*; same as `:0-m`.
`:n-`	Arguments *n* through next-to-last.
`:n*`	Arguments *n* through last; same as `n-$`.
`*`	All arguments; same as `^-$` or `1-$`.
`#`	Current command line up to this point; fairly useless.

Word Substitution Examples

The following command is assumed:

```
13% cat ch01 ch02 ch03 biblio back
```

Event number	Command typed	Command executed
14	`ls !13^`	`ls ch01`
15	`sort !13:*`	`sort ch01 ch02 ch03 biblio back`
16	`lp !cat:3*`	`lp ch03 biblio back`
17	`!cat:0-3`	`cat ch01 ch02 ch03`
18	`vi !-5:4`	`vi biblio`

tcsh

History Modifiers

Command and word substitutions can be modified by one or more of the following modifiers.

Printing, substitution, and quoting

Modifier	Description
`:p`	Display command, but don't execute.
`:s/`*old*`/`*new*	Substitute string *new* for *old*, first instance only.
`:gs/`*old*`/`*new*	Substitute string *new* for *old*, all instances.
`:&`	Repeat previous substitution (`:s` or `^` command), first instance only.
`:g&`	Repeat previous substitution, all instances.
`:q`	Quote a word list.
`:x`	Quote separate words.

Truncation

Modifier	Description
`:r`	Extract the first available pathname root (the portion before the last period).
`:gr`	Extract all pathname roots.
`:e`	Extract the first available pathname extension (the portion after the last period).
`:ge`	Extract all pathname extensions.
`:h`	Extract the first available pathname header (the portion before the last slash).
`:gh`	Extract all pathname headers.
`:t`	Extract the first available pathname tail (the portion after the last slash).
`:gt`	Extract all pathname tails.
`:u`	Make first lowercase letter uppercase.
`:l`	Make first uppercase letter lowercase.
`:a`	Apply modifier(s) following `a` as many times as possible to a word. If used with `g`, `a` is applied to all words.

History Modifier Examples

From the table in the section "Word Substitution Examples," command number 17 is:

```
17% cat ch01 ch02 ch03
```

Event number	Command typed	Command executed
19	`!17:s/ch/CH/`	`cat CH01 ch02 ch03`
20	`!17:g&`	`cat CH01 CH02 CH03`
21	`!more:p`	`more cprogs/01.c` *(displayed only)*
22	`cd !$:h`	`cd cprogs`
23	`vi !mo:$:t`	`vi 01.c`

Event number	Command typed	Command executed
24	`grep stdio !$`	`grep stdio 01.c`
25	`^stdio^include stdio^:q`	`grep "include stdio" 01.c` *(quotes not shown in* `tcsh` output)
26	`nroff !21:t:p`	`nroff 01.c` *(is that what I wanted?)*
27	`!!`	`nroff 01.c` *(execute it)*

Special Aliases

Certain special aliases can be set in `tcsh`. The aliases are initially undefined. Once set, the commands they specify are executed when specific events occur. The following is a list of the special aliases and when they are executed:

`beepcmd`
: At beep.

`cwdcmd`
: When the current working directory changes.

`jobcmd`
: Before running a command or before its state changes. Like `postcmd`, but does not print built-ins.

`helpcommand`
: Invoked by the `run-help` editor command. See the `tcsh` manpage for details.

`periodic`
: Every few minutes. The exact amount of time is set by the `tperiod` shell variable.

`precmd`
: Before printing a new prompt.

`postcmd`
: Before running a command.

`shell` *program*
: If a script does not specify a shell, interpret it with *program*, which should be a full pathname.

Examples

Demonstrate the `cwdcmd` alias:

```
[arnold@mybox ~]$ alias cwdcmd 'echo now in $PWD'       Set alias
[arnold@mybox ~]$ cd /tmp                               Change directory
now in /tmp                                             Output from alias
[arnold@mybox /tmp]$ cd                                 Change back home
now in /home/arnold                                     Output from alias
```

Demonstrate the `postcmd` alias:

```
[arnold@mybox ~]$ alias postcmd 'echo now starting\!'   Set alias
[arnold@mybox ~]$ ls -FC *.txt                          Run a command
now starting!                                           Output from alias
adr.gdb.backcover.txt  gdb.backcover.txt  sol-d1-2.txt  Output from command
awkhomepage.txt        sol-d1-1.txt
```

tcsh

Command-Line Manipulation

tcsh provides functionality for manipulating the command line, including word or command completion and the ability to edit a command line.

Completion

The shell automatically completes words and commands when you press the Tab key, and notifies you when a completion is finished by appending a space to complete filenames or commands and a / to complete directories.

In addition, tcsh recognizes ~ notation for home directories; it assumes that words at the beginning of a line and following |, &, ;, ||, or && are commands, and modifies the search path appropriately. Completion can be done midword; only the letters to the left of the cursor are checked for completion.

Related Shell Variables

- autolist
- fignore
- filec
- listmax
- listmaxrows

Related Command-Line Editor Commands

- complete-word-back
- complete-word-forward
- expand-glob
- list-glob

See the tcsh manpage for a discussion of the built-in command-line editor and its commands.

Related Shell Built-ins

- complete
- uncomplete

Command-Line Editing

tcsh lets you move your cursor around in the command line, editing the line as you type. There are two main modes for editing the command line, based on the two most common text editors: Emacs and vi. Emacs mode is the default; you can switch between the modes with:

```
% bindkey -e      Select Emacs bindings
% bindkey -v      Select vi bindings
```

The main difference between the Emacs and vi bindings is that the Emacs bindings are modeless (i.e., they always work). With the vi bindings, you must switch between input and command modes; different commands are useful in each mode. Additionally:

- Emacs mode is simpler; vi mode allows finer control.
- Emacs mode allows you to yank cut text and set a mark; vi mode does not.
- The command-history searching capabilities differ.

Emacs mode

The various editing keystrokes available in Emacs mode are described in Tables 5-1 through 5-3.

Table 5-1. Cursor positioning (Emacs mode)

Command	Description
CTRL-B	Move cursor back (left) one character.
CTRL-F	Move cursor forward (right) one character.
M-b	Move cursor back one word.
M-f	Move cursor forward one word.
CTRL-A	Move cursor to beginning of line.
CTRL-E	Move cursor to end of line.

Table 5-2. Text deletion (Emacs mode)

Command	Description
DEL or CTRL-H	Delete character to left of cursor.
CTRL-D	Delete character under cursor.
M-d	Delete word.
M-DEL or M-CTRL-H	Delete word backward.
CTRL-K	Delete from cursor to end-of-line.
CTRL-U	Delete entire line.

Table 5-3. Command history (Emacs mode)

Command	Description
CTRL-P	Previous command.
CTRL-N	Next command.
Up arrow	Previous command.
Down arrow	Next command.
cmd-fragment M-p	Search history for *cmd-fragment*, which must be the beginning of a command.
cmd-fragment M-n	Like M-p, but search forward.
M-*num*	Repeat next command *num* times.
CTRL-Y	Yank previously deleted string.

vi mode

vi mode has two submodes, input mode and command mode. The default mode is input. You can toggle modes by pressing Esc; alternatively, in command mode, typing a (append) or i (insert) will return you to input mode.

The editing keystrokes available in vi mode are described in Tables 5-4 through 5-10.

Table 5-4. Command history (vi input and command modes)

Command	Description
CTRL-P	Previous command.
CTRL-N	Next command.
Up arrow	Previous command.
Down arrow	Next command.
Esc	Toggle mode.

Table 5-5. Editing (vi input mode)

Command	Description
CTRL-B	Move cursor back (left) one character.
CTRL-F	Move cursor forward (right) one character.
CTRL-A	Move cursor to beginning of line.
CTRL-E	Move cursor to end-of-line.
DEL or CTRL-H	Delete character to left of cursor.
CTRL-W	Delete word backward.
CTRL-U	Delete from beginning of line to cursor.
CTRL-K	Delete from cursor to end-of-line.

Table 5-6. Cursor positioning (vi command mode)

Command	Description
h or CTRL-H	Move cursor back (left) one character.
l or SPACE	Move cursor forward (right) one character.
w	Move cursor forward one word.
b	Move cursor back one word.
e	Move cursor to next word ending.
W, B, E	Like w, b, and e, but treat only whitespace as word separator instead of any nonalphanumeric character.
^ or CTRL-A	Move cursor to beginning of line (first nonwhitespace character).
0	Move cursor to beginning of line.
$ or CTRL-E	Move cursor to end-of-line.

Table 5-7. Text insertion (vi command mode)

Command	Description
a	Append new text after cursor until Esc.
i	Insert new text before cursor until Esc.
A	Append new text after end of line until Esc.
I	Insert new text before beginning of line until Esc.

Table 5-8. Text deletion (vi command mode)

Command	Description
x	Delete character under cursor.
X or DEL	Delete character to left of cursor.
d*m*	Delete from cursor to end of motion command *m*.
D	Same as d$.
CTRL-W	Delete word backward.
CTRL-U	Delete from beginning of line to cursor.
CTRL-K	Delete from cursor to end of line.

Table 5-9. Text replacement (vi command mode)

Command	Description
c*m*	Change characters from cursor to end of motion command *m* until Esc.
C	Same as c$.
r*c*	Replace character under cursor with character *c*.
R	Replace multiple characters until Esc.
s	Substitute character under cursor with characters typed until Esc.

Table 5-10. Character-seeking motion (vi command mode)

Command	Description
f*c*	Move cursor to next instance of *c* in line.
F*c*	Move cursor to previous instance of *c* in line.
t*c*	Move cursor to just before next instance of *c* in line.
T*c*	Move cursor to just after previous instance of *c* in line.
;	Repeat previous f or F command.
,	Repeat previous f or F command in opposite direction.

Job Control

Job control lets you place foreground jobs in the background, bring background jobs to the foreground, or suspend (temporarily stop) running jobs. The shell provides the following commands for job control. For more information on these commands, see the following section, "Built-in Commands."

`bg`	Put a job in the background.
`fg`	Put a job in the foreground.
`jobs`	List active jobs.
`kill`	Terminate a job.
`notify`	Notify when a background job finishes.
`stop`	Suspend a background job.
CTRL-Z	Suspend the foreground job.

Many job-control commands take a *jobID* as an argument. This argument can be specified as follows:

`%n`	Job number *n*.
`%s`	Job whose command line starts with string *s*.
`%?s`	Job whose command line contains string *s*.
`%%`	Current job.
`%`	Current job (same as preceding).
`%+`	Current job (same as preceding).
`%-`	Previous job.

Built-in Commands

@

```
@ variable = expression
@ variable[n] = expression
@
```

Assign the value of the arithmetic *expression* to *variable*, or to the *n*th element of *variable* if the index *n* is specified. With no *variable* or *expression* specified, print the values of all shell variables (same as set). Expression operators as well as examples are listed under the section "Expressions," earlier in this chapter. Two special forms are also valid:

`@ variable++`
`@ variable[n]++`
Increment *variable* or element by 1.

`@ variable--`
`@ variable[n]--`
Decrement *variable* or element by 1.

#

```
#
```

Ignore all text that follows on the same line. # is used in shell scripts as the comment character and is not really a command. In addition, a file that has # as its first character is sometimes interpreted by older systems as a C shell script.

#!

```
#! shell
```

Used as the first line of a script to invoke the named *shell*. Anything given on the rest of the line is passed *as a single argument* to the named *shell*. This feature is typically implemented by the kernel, but may not be supported on some older systems. Some systems have a limit of around 32 characters on the maximum length of *shell*. Any program that interprets input may be used for *shell*, such as awk or Perl. For example:

```
#! /bin/tcsh -f
```

:

```
:
```

Null command. Returns an exit status of 0. The colon command is often put as the first character of a Bourne or Korn shell script to act as a place-holder to keep a # (hash) from accidentally becoming the first character.

alias

alias [*name* [*command*]]

Assign *name* as the shorthand name, or *alias*, for *command*. If *command* is omitted, print the alias for *name*; if *name* also is omitted, print all aliases. Aliases can be defined on the command line, but more often they are stored in .tcshrc so that they take effect upon logging in. (See the section "Sample .tcshrc File" earlier in this chapter.) Alias definitions can reference command-line arguments, much like the history list. Use \!* to refer to all command-line arguments, \!^ for the first argument, \!\!:2 for the second, \!$ for the last, and so on. An alias *name* can also be any valid Unix command except alias or unalias; however, you lose the original command's meaning unless you type *name*. See also **unalias** and the earlier section "Special Aliases."

Examples

Set the size for xterm windows under the X Window System:

```
alias R 'set noglob; eval `resize`; unset noglob'
```

Show aliases that contain the string "ls":

```
alias | grep ls
```

Run nroff on all command-line arguments:

```
alias ms 'nroff -ms \!*'
```

Copy the file that is named as the first argument:

```
alias back 'cp \!^ \!^.old'
```

Use the regular ls, not its alias:

```
% \ls
```

alloc

```
alloc
```

Print total amount of used and free memory.

tcsh

bg

`bg [jobIDs]`

Put the current job or the *jobIDs* in the background. See the earlier section "Job Control."

Example

To place a time-consuming process in the background, you might begin with:

```
4% nroff -ms report | col > report.txt
CTRL-Z
```

and then issue any one of the following:

```
5% bg
5% bg %          Current job
5% bg %1         Job number 1
5% bg %nr        Match initial string nroff
5% % &
```

bindkey

`bindkey [options] [key] [command]`

Display all key bindings, or bind a key to an editor command.

Options

-a
List standard and alternate key bindings.

-b *key*
Expect *key* to be one of the following: a control character (in hat notation, e.g., ^B, or C notation, e.g., C-B); a metacharacter (e.g., M-B); a function key (e.g., F-*string*); or an extended prefix key (e.g., X-B).

-c *command*
Interpret *command* as a shell command, not as an editor command.

-d *key*
Bind key to its original binding.

-e
Bind to standard Emacs bindings.

-k *key*
Expect *key* to refer to an arrow (left, right, up, or down).

-l
List and describe all editor commands.

-r *key*
Completely unbind *key*.

-s
Interpret *command* as a literal string and treat as terminal input.

-u
Print usage message.

-v
Bind to standard vi bindings.

--
End option processing. The following item is treated as a *key*, even if it looks like an option.

break

`break`

Resume execution following the `end` command of the nearest enclosing `while` or `foreach`.

breaksw

`breaksw`

Break from a `switch`; continue execution after the `endsw`.

built-ins

`built-ins`

Print all built-in shell commands.

bye

`bye`

Same as `logout`. Must have been compiled into the shell; see the `version` variable.

case

`case` *`pattern`*`:`

Identify a *pattern* in a `switch`.

cd

`cd [`*`options`*`] [`*`dir`*`]`

Change working directory to *dir*; default is home directory of user. If *dir* is a relative pathname but is not in the current directory, the `cdpath` variable is searched. See the section "Sample .tcshrc File" earlier in this chapter.

Options

- `-` Change to previous directory. (Compare to `popd`, which manipulates the directory stack.)
- `-l` Explicitly expand ~ notation; implies `-p`.
- `-n` Wrap entries before end-of-line; implies `-p`.
- `-p` Print directory stack.
- `-v` Print entries one per line; implies `-p`.

chdir

`chdir [`*`dir`*`]`

Same as `cd`. Useful if you are redefining `cd` as an alias.

complete

`complete [`*`string`*` [`*`word/pattern/list`*`[:`*`select`*`]/[`*`suffix`*`]]]`

List all completions, or, if specified, all completions for *string* (which may be a pattern). Further options can be specified.

tcsh

Options for word

`c`	Complete current word only, without referring to *pattern*.
`C`	Complete current word only, referring to *pattern*.
`n`	Complete previous word.
`N`	Complete word before previous word.
`p`	Expect *pattern* to be a range of numbers. Perform completion within that range.

Options for list

Various *lists* of strings can be searched for possible completions. Some *list* options include:

`(`*`string`*`)`	Members of the list *string*.
`$`*`variable`*	Words from *variable*.
`` ` ``*`command`*`` ` ``	Output from *command*.
`a`	Aliases.
`b`	Bindings.
`c`	Commands.
`C`	External (not built-in) commands.
`d`	Directories.
`D`	Directories whose names begin with *string*.
`e`	Environment variables.
`f`	Filenames.
`F`	Filenames that begin with *string*.
`g`	Groups.
`j`	Jobs.
`l`	Limits.
`n`	Nothing.
`s`	Shell variables.
`S`	Signals.
`t`	Text files.
`T`	Text files whose names begin with *string*.
`u`	Users.
`v`	Any variables.
`x`	Like `n`, but prints *select* as an explanation with the editor command `list-choices`.
`X`	Completions.

select

select should be a glob pattern. Completions are limited to words that match this pattern. *suffix* is appended to all completions.

---

continue

```
continue
```

Resume execution of nearest enclosing `while` or `foreach`.

default

`default:`

Label the default case (typically last) in a `switch`.

dirs

`dirs [options]`

Print the directory stack, showing the current directory first. See also **popd** and **pushd**.

Options

`-c` Clear the directory stack.

`-l` Expand the home directory symbol (~) to the actual directory name.

`-L` *file*
: Recreate stack from *file*, which should have been created by `dirs -S` *file*.

`-n` Wrap output.

`-S` *file*
: Print to *file* a series of `pushd` and `popd` commands that can be invoked to replicate the stack.

`-v` Print one directory per line.

echo

`echo [-n] string`

Write *string* to standard output; if `-n` is specified, the output is not terminated by a newline. Set the `echo_style` shell variable to emulate BSD and/or System V `echo` flags and escape sequences. See also **echo** in Chapter 2 and Chapter 4.

echotc

`echotc [options] arguments`

Display terminal capabilities or move cursor on screen, depending on the argument.

Options

`-s` Return empty string, not error, if capability doesn't exist.

`-v` Display verbose messages.

Arguments

`baud`	Display current baud rate.
`cols`	Display current column.
`cm` *column row*	Move cursor to specified coordinates.
`home`	Move cursor to home position.
`lines`	Print number of lines per screen.
`meta`	Does this terminal have meta capacity (usually the Alt key)?
`tabs`	Does this terminal have tab capacity?

tcsh

else

`else`

Reserved word for interior of `if` ... `endif` statement.

end

`end`

Reserved word that ends a `foreach` or `while` statement.

endif

`endif`

Reserved word that ends an `if` statement.

endsw

`endsw`

Reserved word that ends a `switch` statement.

eval

`eval` *`args`*

Typically, `eval` is used in shell scripts, and *args* is a line of code that may contain shell variables. `eval` forces variable expansion to happen first and then runs the resulting command. This "double scanning" is useful any time shell variables contain input/output redirection symbols, aliases, or other shell variables. (For example, redirection normally happens before variable expansion, so a variable containing redirection symbols must be expanded first using `eval`; otherwise, the redirection symbols remain uninterpreted.) A Bourne shell example can be found under **eval** in Chapter 4. A `tcsh` example of `eval` can be found under **alias**. Other uses of `eval` are shown next.

Examples

The following lines can be placed in the `.login` file to set up terminal characteristics:

```
set noglob
eval `tset -s xterm`
unset noglob
```

The following commands show the effect of `eval`:

```
% set b='$a'
% set a=hello
% echo $b              Read the command line once
$a
% eval echo $b         Read the command line twice
hello
```

exec

`exec` *`command`* `[`*`args`* `...]`

Execute *command* in place of current shell. This terminates the current shell, rather than creating a new process under it.

exit

```
exit [expr]
```

Exit a shell script with the status given by *expr*. A status of zero means success; nonzero means failure. If *expr* is not specified, the exit value is that of the status variable. exit can be issued at the command line to close a window (log out).

fg

```
fg [jobIDs]
```

Bring the current job or the *jobIDs* to the foreground. *jobID* can be *%job-number*. See also the section "Job Control" earlier in this chapter.

Example

If you suspend a vi editing session (by pressing CTRL-Z), you might resume vi using any of these commands:

```
% %
% fg
% fg %
% fg %vi        Match initial string
```

filetest

```
filetest -op files
```

Apply *op* file-test operator to *files*. Print results in a list. See the section "File inquiry operators" earlier in this chapter for the list of file-test operators.

foreach

```
foreach name (wordlist)
 commands
end
```

Assign variable *name* to each value in *wordlist* and execute *commands* between foreach and end. You can use foreach as a multiline command issued at the shell prompt (first of the following examples), or you can use it in a shell script (second example).

Examples

Rename all files that begin with a capital letter:

```
% foreach i ([A-Z]*)
foreach? mv $i $i.old
foreach? end
```

Check whether each command-line argument is an option or not:

```
foreach arg ($argv)
   # does it begin with - ?
   if ("$arg" =~ -*) then
      echo "Argument is an option"
   else
      echo "Argument is a filename"
   endif
end
```


tcsh

glob

`glob wordlist`

Do filename, variable, and history substitutions on *wordlist*. This expands it much like `echo`, except that no \ escapes are recognized, and words are delimited by null characters. `glob` is typically used in shell scripts to "hardcode" a value so that it remains the same for the rest of the script.

goto

`goto string`

Skip to a line whose first nonblank word is *string* followed by a colon, and continue execution below that line. On the `goto` line, *string* can be a variable or filename pattern, but the label branched to must be a literal, expanded value and must not occur within a `foreach` or `while`.

hashstat

`hashstat`

Display statistics that show the hash table's level of success at locating commands via the `path` variable.

history

`history [options]`

Display the list of history events. (History syntax is discussed earlier in the section "Command History.")

Note: multiline compound commands such as `foreach ... end` are *not* saved in the history list. In general, the interactive command-line editing facilities are preferable to those of `history` and history substitution with the `!` character.

Options

n
: Display only the last *n* history commands, instead of the number set by the `history` shell variable.

`-c`
: Clear history list.

`-h`
: Print history list without event numbers.

`-L` *file*
: Append the list of saved history commands in *file* to the history list.

`-M` *file*
: Merge the current history list and the history list in *file*, sorted by time.

`-r`
: Print in reverse order; show oldest commands last.

`-S` *file*
: Save the history list to *file*. See also the `savehist` variable.

`-T`
: Print with timestamp.

Example

To save and execute the last five commands:

```
history -h 5 > do_it
source do_it
```

hup

hup [*command*]

Start *command* but make it exit when sent a hangup signal, which is sent when shell exits. With no arguments, set the shell to exit on hangup signal. This latter form is allowed only in scripts.

if

if

Begin a conditional statement. The simple format is:

```
if (expr) cmd
```

There are three other possible formats, shown side by side:

```
if (expr) then     if (expr) then     if (expr) then
   cmds               cmds1              cmds1
endif              else               else if (expr) then
                      cmds2              cmds2
                   endif              else
                                         cmds3
                                      endif
```

In the simplest form, execute *cmds* if *expr* is true, otherwise do nothing. (Even if *expr* is false, any redirection in *cmd* still occurs; this is a bug.) In the other forms, execute one or more commands. If *expr* is true, continue with the commands after then; if *expr* is false, branch to the commands after else or else if and continue checking. For more examples, see the section "Expressions" earlier in this chapter, or the **shift** or **while** commands.

Example

Take a default action if no command-line arguments are given:

```
if ($#argv == 0) then
   echo "No filename given. Sending to Report."
   set outfile = Report
else
   set outfile = $argv[1]
endif
```

jobs

jobs [-l]

List all running or stopped jobs; -l includes process IDs. For example, you can check whether a long compilation or text format is still running. Also useful before logging out.

kill

`kill [options] IDs`

Terminate each specified process *ID* or job *ID*. You must own the process or be a privileged user. This built-in is similar to the external `kill` command described in Chapter 2 but also allows symbolic job names. See the **kill** entry in Chapter 2 for a list of commonly available signals and for the header files where the corresponding signal numbers may be found. Stubborn processes can be killed using signal 9. See also the earlier section "Job Control."

Options

`-l` List the signal names. (Used by itself.)

`-signal`, `-s signal`
Send the given signal to the jobs specified by *IDs*. The *signal* is either a signal number, or a signal name without the `SIG` prefix (e.g., `HUP`, not `SIGHUP`).

Examples

If you've issued the following command:

```
44% nroff -ms report > report.txt &
[1] 19536                    tcsh prints job and process IDs
```

you can terminate it in any of the following ways:

```
45% kill 19536               Process ID
45% kill %                   Current job
45% kill %1                  Job number 1
45% kill %nr                 Initial string
45% kill %?report            Matching string
```

limit

`limit [-h] [resource [limit]]`

Display limits or set a *limit* on resources used by the current process and by each process it creates. If no *limit* is given, the current limit is printed for *resource*. If *resource* also is omitted, all limits are printed. By default, the current soft limits are shown or set; with `-h`, hard limits are used. A soft limit may be increased or decreased without requiring special privileges. A hard limit imposes an absolute limit that can't be exceeded. Only a privileged user may raise it. See also **unlimit**.

Option

`-h` Use hard, not soft, limits.

Resources

`concurrency`	Maximum number of per-process threads. Not available on all systems.
`coredumpsize`	Maximum size of a core dump file.
`cputime`	Maximum number of seconds the CPU can spend; can be abbreviated as cpu.
`datasize`	Maximum size of data (including stack).

`descriptors`	Maximum number of open files.
`filesize`	Maximum size of any one file.
`maxproc`	Maximum number of processes.
`memorylocked`	Maximum size a process can lock into memory.
`memoryuse`	Maximum amount of physical memory that can be allocated to a process.
`sbsize`	Maximum size of a socket buffer. Not available on all systems.
`stacksize`	Maximum size of stack.
`vmemoryuse`	Maximum amount of virtual memory that can be allocated to a process.

Limit

A number followed by an optional character (a unit specifier).

For `cputime`:	*n*`h` (for *n* hours)
	n`m` (for *n* minutes)
	mm`:`*ss* (minutes and seconds)
For others:	*n*`k` (for *n* kilobytes, the default)
	n`m` (for *n* megabytes)

---

log

`log`

Consult the `watch` variable for list of users being watched. Print list of those who are presently logged in.

---

login

`login [options] [user]`

Replace a login shell with `/bin/login`. See the entry for **login** in Chapter 2 and your system's `login` manpage.

---

logout

`logout`

Terminate the login shell.

---

ls-F

`ls-F [options] [files]`

Faster alternative to `ls -F`. If given any options, invokes `ls`. See also the `listlinks` variable.

---

newgrp

`newgrp [-] [group]`

Change user's group ID to specified group ID or, if none is specified, to original group ID. If `-` is entered as an option, reset environment as if user had logged in with new group. Must have been compiled into the shell; see the `version` variable.

nice

`nice [±n] command`

Change the execution priority for *command* or, if none is given, change priority for the current shell. (See also **nice** in Chapter 2.) The priority range is –20 to 19, with a default of 4. The range is backwards from what you might expect: –20 gives the highest priority (fastest execution); 19 gives the lowest. Only a privileged user may specify a negative number.

+n Add *n* to the priority value (lower job priority).

-n Subtract *n* from the priority value (raise job priority). Privileged users only.

nohup

`nohup [command]`

"No hangup signals." Do not terminate *command* after terminal line is closed (i.e., when you hang up from a phone or log out). Use without *command* in shell scripts to keep script from being terminated. (See also **nohup** in Chapter 2.)

notify

`notify [jobID]`

Report immediately when a background job finishes (instead of waiting for you to exit a long editing session, for example). If no *jobID* is given, the current background job is assumed.

onintr

```
onintr label
onintr -
onintr
```

"On interrupt." Used in shell scripts to handle interrupt signals (similar to the `trap 2` and `trap "" 2` commands in the Bourne shell). The first form is like a `goto` *label*. The script will branch to *label*: if it catches an interrupt signal (e.g., CTRL-C). The second form lets the script ignore interrupts. This is useful at the beginning of a script or before any code segment that needs to run unhindered (e.g., when moving files). The third form restores interrupt handling previously disabled with `onintr -`.

Example

```
onintr cleanup        Go to "cleanup" on interrupt
  .
  .                   Shell script commands
  .
cleanup:              Label for interrupts
  onintr -            Ignore additional interrupts
  rm -f $tmpfiles     Remove any files created
  exit 2              Exit with an error status
```

popd

`popd [options]`

Remove the current entry from the directory stack or remove the *n*th entry from the stack. The current entry has number zero and appears on the left. See also **dirs** and **pushd**.

Options

`+n` Specify *n*th entry.

`-l` Expand ~ notation.

`-n` Wrap long lines.

`-p` Override the `pushdsilent` shell variable, which otherwise prevents the printing of the final stack.

`-v` Print precisely one directory per line.

printenv

`printenv [variable]`

Print all (or one specified) environment variables and their values.

pushd

```
pushd [options] name
pushd [options] +n
pushd
```

The first form changes the working directory to *name* and adds it to the directory stack. The second form rotates the *n*th entry to the beginning, making it the working directory. (Entry numbers begin at zero.) With no arguments, `pushd` switches the first two entries and changes to the new current directory.

The `-l`, `-n`, and `-v` options behave the same as in `popd`. See also **dirs** and **popd**.

Examples

```
% dirs
/home/bob /usr
% pushd /etc                Add /etc to directory stack
/etc /home/bob /usr
% pushd +2                  Switch to third directory
/usr /etc /home/bob
% pushd                     Switch top two directories
/etc /usr /home/bob
% popd                      Discard current entry; go to next
/usr /home/bob
```

rehash

`rehash`

Recompute the internal hash table for the `path` variable. Use `rehash` whenever a new command is created during the current session. This allows the `path` variable to locate and execute the command. (If the new command resides in a directory not listed in `path`, add the directory to `path` before rehashing.) See also **unhash**.

tcsh

repeat

```
repeat n command
```

Execute *n* instances of *command*.

Examples

Generate a test file for a program by saving 25 copies of `/usr/dict/words` in a file:

```
% repeat 25 cat /usr/dict/words > test_file
```

Read 10 lines from the terminal and store in `item_list`:

```
% repeat 10 line > item_list
```

Append 50 boilerplate files to report:

```
% repeat 50 cat template >> report
```

sched

```
sched [options]
sched time command
```

Without options, print all scheduled events. The second form schedules an event. *time* should be specified in *hh:mm* form (e.g., 13:00).

Options

+hh:mm
: Schedule event to take place *hh:mm* from now.

-n
: Remove *n*th item from schedule.

set

```
set [-r] variable = value
set [-r] variable[n] = value
set [-f | -l] variable=(list)
set [-r] variable
set [-r]
```

Set *variable* to *value* or, if multiple values are specified, set the variable to the list of words in the value list. If an index *n* is specified, set the *n*th word in the variable to *value*. (The variable must already contain at least that number of words.) If only *variable* is specified, set the variable to null. With no arguments, display the names and values of all set variables. See also the section "Predefined Shell Variables," earlier in this chapter. Only one of `-f` or `-l` can be given.

Options

`-f` When setting a variable to a list, remove duplicate words from the list, keeping only the first occurrence of a duplicate.

`-l` When setting a variable to a list, remove duplicate words from the list, keeping only the last occurrence of a duplicate.

`-r` List only read-only variables, or set specified variable to read-only.

Examples

`% set list=(yes no maybe)`	*Assign a wordlist*
`% set list[3]=maybe`	*Assign an item in existing wordlist*
`% set quote="Make my day"`	*Assign a variable*
`% set x=5 y=10 history=100`	*Assign several variables*
`% set blank`	*Assign a null value to blank*

setenv

setenv [*name* [*value*]]

Assign a *value* to an environment variable *name*. By convention, *name* should be uppercase. *value* can be a single word or a quoted string. If no *value* is given, the null value is assigned. With no arguments, display the names and values of all environment variables. A number of environment variables are automatically exported from the corresponding shell variables; see the earlier section "Environment Variables."

settc

settc *capability value*

Set terminal *capability* to *value*.

setty

setty [*options*] [±*mode*]

Do not allow shell to change specified tty modes. There are three sets of modes, *edit*, *quote*, and *execute*. By default, act on the execute set.

Options

+mode
: Without arguments, list all modes in specified set that are on. Otherwise, turn on specified mode.

-mode
: Without arguments, list all modes in specified set that are off. Otherwise, turn off specified mode.

-a
: List all modes in specified set.

-d
: Act on the edit set of modes (used when editing commands).

-q
: Act on the quote set of modes (used when entering characters verbatim).

-x
: Act on the execute set of modes (used when executing commands). This is the default.

shift

shift [*variable*]

If *variable* is given, shift the words in a word list variable; e.g., assuming a wordlist variable named `offices`, `offices[2]` becomes `offices[1]`. With no argument, shift the positional parameters (command-line arguments); i.e., `$2` becomes `$1`. `shift` is typically used in a `while` loop. See additional example under **while**.

Example

```
while ($#argv)          While there are arguments
    if (-f $argv[1])
        wc -l $argv[1]
    else
        echo "$argv[1] is not a regular file"
    endif
    shift               Get the next argument
end
```

---

source

`source [-h] *script* [*args*]`

Read and execute commands from a shell script. With `-h`, the commands are added to the history list but aren't executed. Arguments can be passed to the script and are put in `argv`.

Example

```
% source ~/.tcshrc
```

---

stop

`stop *jobIDs*`

Stop the background jobs specified by *jobIDs*; this is the complement of CTRL-Z or `suspend`.

---

suspend

`suspend`

Suspend the current foreground job; similar to CTRL-Z. Often used to stop an `su` command.

---

switch

`switch`

Process commands depending on a string value. When you need to handle more than three choices, `switch` is a useful alternative to an `if-then-else` statement. If the *string* matches *pattern1*, the first set of *commands* executes; if *string* matches *pattern2*, the second set of *commands* executes; and so on. If no patterns match, the set of *commands* under the `default` case executes. *string* can be specified using command substitution, variable substitution, or filename expansion. Patterns can be specified using the pattern-matching symbols *, ?, [, and]. `breaksw` exits the `switch` after *commands* are executed. If `breaksw` is omitted (which is rarely done), the `switch` continues to execute another set of commands until it reaches a `breaksw` or `endsw`. Here is the general syntax of `switch`, side-by-side with an example that processes the first command-line argument.

```
switch (string)           switch ($argv[1])
  case pattern1:            case -[nN]:
      commands                  nroff $file | lp
      breaksw                   breaksw
  case pattern2:            case -[Pp]:
      commands                  pr $file | lp
```

```
        breaksw                 breaksw
    case pattern3:          case -[Mm]:
        commands                more $file
        breaksw                 breaksw
        .                   case -[Ss]:
        .                       sort $file
        .                       breaksw
    default:                default:
        commands                echo "Error--no such option"
                                exit 1
        breaksw                 breaksw
endsw                   endsw
```

telltc

`telltc`

Print all terminal capabilities and their values.

termname

`termname [`*`termtype`*`]`

Check the termcap or terminfo database to see if *termtype* exists. With no argument, use the current value of the `TERM` variable. This command prints the *termtype* to standard output and returns zero if the terminal type is found in the database, one otherwise.

time

`time [`*`command`*`]`

Execute a *command* and show how much time it uses. With no argument, `time` can be used in a shell script to time the script.

umask

`umask [`*`nnn`*`]`

Display file-creation mask or set file-creation mask to octal *nnn*. The file-creation mask determines which permission bits are turned off. With no *nnn*, print the current mask. See the **umask** entry in Chapter 2 for examples.

unalias

`unalias` *`pattern`*

Remove all aliases whose names match *pattern* from the alias list. See **alias** for more information.

uncomplete

`uncomplete` *`pattern`*

Remove completions (specified by `complete`) whose names match *pattern*.

unhash

`unhash`

Stop using the internal hash table. The shell stops using hashed values and searches the `path` directories to locate a command. See also **rehash**.

unlimit

`unlimit [-h] [`*`resource`*`]`

Remove the allocation limits on *resource*. If *resource* is not specified, remove limits for all resources. See **limit** for more information. With `-h`, remove hard limits. Removing hard limits can be done only by a privileged user.

unset

`unset` *`variables`*

Remove one or more *variables*. Variable names may be specified as a pattern, using filename metacharacters. Does not remove read-only variables. See **set**.

unsetenv

`unsetenv` *`variables`*

Remove one or more environment variables. Variable names may be specified as a pattern, using filename metacharacters. See **setenv**.

wait

`wait`

Pause in execution until all child processes complete, or until an interrupt signal is received.

watchlog

`watchlog`

Same as `log`. Must have been compiled into the shell; see the `version` shell variable.

where

`where` *`command`*

Display all aliases, built-in commands, and executables named *command* found in the path.

which

`which` *`command`*

Report which version of *command* will be executed. Same as the external executable `which`, but faster, and checks `tcsh` built-ins.

while

```
while (expression)
 commands
end
```

As long as *expression* is true (evaluates to nonzero), evaluate *commands* between `while` and `end`. `break` and `continue` can be used to terminate or continue the loop. See also the example under **shift**.

Example

```
set user = (alice bob carol ted)
while ($argv[1] != $user[1])
    Cycle through each user, checking for a match
    shift user
    If we cycled through with no match...
    if ($#user == 0) then
      echo "$argv[1] is not on the list of users"
      exit 1
    endif
end
```

tcsh

6

Package Management

Package management systems automate the installation, removal and upgrade of software. Different systems do things in similar but not identical ways. GNU/Linux systems have the most highly developed package management systems. This chapter describes the facilities available for Linux, Solaris, and Mac OS X. It presents the following topics:

- Linux package management
- The Red Hat package manager
- Yum: Yellowdog Updater Modified
- up2date: Red Hat update agent
- The Debian package manager
- Mac OS X package management
- Solaris package management

Linux Package Management

This chapter describes the two major Linux packaging systems: the Red Hat Package Manager (RPM) and the Debian GNU/Linux Package Manager. It also describes the major frontend applications designed to simplify and automate package management: `yum` and `up2date` for RPM-based systems, `aptitude` and `synaptic` for Debian-based systems, and `apt`, which is a Debian package management tool that is now also available for RPM-based systems.

When you install applications on your Linux system, most often you'll find a binary or a source package containing the application you want, instead of (or in addition to) a `.tar.gz` file. A *package* is a file containing the files necessary to install an application. However, while the package contains the files you need for installation, the application might require the presence of other files or packages that are not included, such as particular libraries (and even specific versions of the libraries), to actually be able to run. Such requirements are known as *dependencies*.

Package management systems offer many benefits. As a user, you may want to query the package database to find out what packages are installed on the system and their versions. As a system administrator, you need tools to install and manage the packages on your system. And if you are a developer, you need to know how to build a package for distribution.

Among other things, package managers do the following:

- Provide tools for installing, updating, removing, and managing the software on your system.
- Allow you to install new or upgraded software directly across a network.
- Tell you what software package a particular file belongs to or what files a package contains.
- Maintain a database of packages on the system and their status, so that you can determine what packages or versions are installed on your system.
- Provide dependency checking, so that you don't mess up your system with incompatible software.
- Provide GPG, PGP, MD5, or other signature verification tools.
- Provide tools for building packages.

Any user can list or query packages. However, installing, upgrading, or removing packages generally requires `root` privileges. This is because the packages normally are installed in system-wide directories that are writable only by `root`. Sometimes you can specify an alternate directory to install a package into your home directory or into a project directory where you have write permission, if you aren't running as `root`.

Signature verification is an important feature of package management systems that helps maintain the security of your system. An MD5 checksum is used to check the integrity of a package, making sure, for example, that it was downloaded correctly and that it has not been tampered with by a malicious user. GPG (and PGP) encrypt a digital signature into the package, which is used to verify the authenticity of the package creator.

Most often you'll install a binary package, where the source code has been compiled and the software is ready to run once it is installed. You may also want or need to install source packages, which provide the source code and instructions for compiling and installing the program. Source code packages do not contain executable files. Packages follow certain naming conventions, and you can tell from the name whether it is a binary or source package. RPM and Debian package names contain the same information, but they are expressed slightly differently. An RPM package has the form:

```
package-version-release.architecture.rpm
```

A Debian package has the form:

```
package_version-revision_architecture.deb
```

In both cases, *package* is the name of the package, *version* is the version number of the software, *release* (RPM) and *revision* (Debian) indicate the revision number of the package for that version, and *architecture* shows what system architecture the software was packaged for (e.g., `i386` or `m68k`). The value of *architecture* may also be `noarch` for a package that is not hardware-specific or `src` for an RPM source package (Debian source packages come as tarred, gzipped files).

All the package managers check for dependencies when you install a package. In the case of RPM, if there are missing dependencies, it prints an error and terminates without installing the package. To proceed, you need to first install the missing package (or packages). This can become an involved process if the missing package has its own dependencies. A major advantage of the high-level package managers described in this chapter (i.e., `apt`, `yum`, `up2date`, `synaptic`, and `aptitude`) is that they automatically resolve dependencies and install missing packages for you. Another advantage is that they locate and download the package automatically, based on information in configuration files specifying where to look for packages. With RPM, you first have to locate the package, then download it, and only then can you run `rpm` to do the install. On the other hand, if you already have the package file on your system or on a CD, `rpm` is quick and easy to run.

Both RPM and the `apt` system back up old files before installing an updated package. Not only does this let you go back if there is a problem, but it also ensures that you don't lose your changes (to configuration files, for example).

The following list shows the package management programs described in the rest of this chapter. Which program to use is very much a matter of personal preference, and you can use more than one at different times. However, it's best to pick the program you prefer and use it consistently, so that all your packages are maintained in a single database that you can query.

The Advanced Package Tool (APT)
: APT is a modern, user-friendly package management tool that consists of a number of commands. The most frequently used of these commands is `apt-get`, which is used to download and install a Debian package. `apt-get` can be run from the command line or selected as a method from `dselect`. One of the features of `apt-get` is that you can use it to get and install packages across the Internet by specifying an FTP or HTTP URL. You can also use it to upgrade all packages currently installed on your system in a single operation.

  Note that there are versions of the `apt` commands that can be used on an RPM-based system. If you plan to do that, it's best to install the version of `apt` that comes with your Linux distribution.

`aptitude`
: High-level text-based interface to APT. Runs either from the command line or in a visual mode inside a terminal window such as an `xterm`.

`dpkg`
: The original Debian packaging tool. Used to install or uninstall packages or as a frontend to `dpkg-deb`. Getting and installing packages is usually done with `apt-get`, but `dpkg` is still commonly used to install a package that is already on your system. In fact, `apt-get` calls `dpkg` to do the installation once it's gotten the package.

`dpkg-deb`
: Lower-level packaging tool. Used to create and manage the Debian package archives. Accepts and executes commands from `dpkg` or can be called directly.

`dselect`
: An interactive frontend to `dpkg`. With the advent of the newer tools and the increased number of packages, the use of `dselect` is deprecated.

RPM
: The original command-line system for installing and managing RPM packages. RPM has two commands, `rpm` for installing and managing packages, and `rpmbuild` for creating packages.

`synaptic`
: A graphical frontend to APT.

`up2date`
: A graphical frontend to RPM.

`yum`
: A frontend to RPM that runs from the command line.

If you want to update your system daily, to keep it current and to be sure you have the latest security fixes, you can set up a command that you can reissue every day, or you can set it up as a `cron` job to run overnight. (See the description of the `crontab` command in Chapter 2 for more information on setting up a `cron` job.)

For example, with `apt-get`, you can set up the command:

```
apt-get update && apt-get -u dist-upgrade
```

This command runs `apt-get` twice; first to update the local package lists and then to actually do the upgrade. The `dist-upgrade` command handles all dependencies when it does the upgrade, and the `-u` option prints a list of the packages being upgraded.

`yum`, on the other hand, comes with a `cron` job that can be run daily. This job first updates `yum` itself, then updates all the remaining packages:

```
#!/bin/sh
if [ -f /var/lock/subsys/yum ]; then
        /usr/bin/yum -R 10 -e 0 -d 0 -y update yum
        /usr/bin/yum -R 120 -e 0 -d 0 -y update
fi
```

The `-R` option sets a maximum time, in minutes, for `yum` to wait before running the command, `-e` sets the error level to 0 to print only critical errors, `-d` specifies a debug level of 0 to print no debugging messages, and `-y` assumes "yes" as the answer to any questions.

The Red Hat Package Manager

The Red Hat Package Manager (RPM) is a freely available packaging system for software distribution and installation. In addition to the Red Hat Enterprise Linux and Fedora Core distributions, both SuSE and Mandrake are among the Linux distributions that use RPM.

Using RPM is straightforward. A single command, `rpm`, has options to perform all package management functions except building packages.* For example, to find out if the Emacs editor is installed on your system, you could say:

```
$ rpm -q emacs
emacs-21.3-17
```

This command prints the full package name, confirming its presence.

You use the `rpmbuild` command to build both binary and source packages.

RPM Package Concepts

This section provides an overview of some of the parts of an RPM package. Much of the information is of primary use to developers, but because some of the terms are referenced in the RPM command descriptions, they are explained briefly here.

An RPM package has three primary components. The *header* contains all the information about the package, such as its name and version, a description, a list of included files, the copyright terms, and where the source file can be found. The *signature* contains information used to verify the integrity and authenticity of the package. The *archive* contains the actual files that make up the package.

When a package is being built, one of the requirements for the developers is to create a *spec* file. If you download the source RPM for a package, you can look at the spec file; it has a filename of *package*`.spec` (e.g., `yum.spec` for the `yum` spec file). The spec file contains all the information required for building a package, including a description of the software, instructions telling the `rpmbuild` command how to build the package, and a list of the files included and where they get installed. Some other features of spec files include the following:

Macros
: Macros are sequences of commands stored together and executed by invoking the macro name. The RPM build process provides two standard macros, `%setup` to unpack the original sources and `%patch` to apply patches. Other macros appear later in this chapter in the command descriptions and are described there.

Scripts
: Scripts are used to control the build process. Some of the scripts RPM uses include `%prep` to begin the build process, `%build` primarily to run `make` and perhaps do some configuration, `%install` to do a `make install` and `%clean` to clean up afterwards. Four additional scripts may be created to run when a package is actually installed on a system. These scripts are `%pre` for scripts run before package installation, `%post` for scripts run after package installation, `%preun` for scripts run before a package is uninstalled, and `%postun` for scripts run after a package is uninstalled.

Package Management

* In older versions of RPM, the build options were part of the `rpm` command.

Trigger scriptlets
: Trigger scriptlets are extensions of the normal install and uninstall scripts. They provide for interaction between packages. A trigger scriptlet provided with one package will be triggered to run by the installation or removal of some other package. For example, a newly installed RPM package may cause an existing application to run or restart once installation is complete. In many cases, a newly installed package requires services to be restarted.

The rpm Command

RPM packages are installed and queried with the `rpm` command. RPM package filenames usually end with a `.rpm` extension. `rpm` has a set of modes, each with its own options. The format of the `rpm` command is:

```
rpm [options] [packages]
```

With a few exceptions, as noted in the lists of options that follow, the first option specifies the `rpm` mode (install, query, update, etc.), and any remaining options affect that mode.

Options that refer to packages are sometimes specified as *package-name* and sometimes as *package-file*. The package name is the name of the program or application, such as `xpdf`. The package file is the name of the RPM file, such as `xpdf-3.00-10.1.i386.rpm`.

RPM provides a configuration file for specifying frequently used options. The default global configuration file is usually `/usr/lib/rpm/rpmrc`, the local system configuration file is `/etc/rpmrc`, and users can set up their own `$HOME/.rpmrc` files. You can use the `--showrc` option to show the values RPM will use by default for all the options that may be set in an `rpmrc` file:

```
rpm --showrc
```

The `rpm` command includes FTP and HTTP clients, so you can specify an `ftp://` or `http://` URL to install or query a package across the Internet. You can use an FTP or HTTP URL wherever *package-file* is specified in the commands presented here. Be careful, however, when downloading packages from the Internet. Always verify package contents by checking MD5 checksums and signatures. Whenever possible, install from trusted media.

Any user can query the RPM database. Most of the other functions, such as installing and removing packages, require superuser privileges.

General options

The following options can be used with all modes:

`--dbpath` *path*
: Use *path* as the path to the RPM database instead of the default `/var/lib/rpm`.

`-?, --help`
: Print a long usage message (running `rpm` with no options gives a shorter usage message).

`--quiet`
: Display only error messages.

`--rcfile` *`filelist`*
: Get configuration from the files in the colon-separated *filelist*. If `--rcfile` is specified, there must be at least one file in the list and the file must exist. *filelist* defaults to `/usr/lib/rpm/rpmrc:/usr/lib/rpm/redhat/rpmrc:/etc/rpmrc:~/.rpmrc`. Use with `--showrc` to see what options will be used if alternate configuration files are specified.

`--root` *`dir`*
: Perform all operations within the directory tree rooted at *dir*.

`-v`
: Verbose. Print progress messages.

`--version`
: Print the version number of `rpm`.

`-vv`
: Print debugging information. Each additional `v` character makes `rpm` be more verbose.

Install, upgrade, and freshen options

Use the *install* command to install or upgrade an RPM package. Upgrading with *install* leaves any existing versions on the system. The *install* syntax is:

```
rpm -i [install-options] package_file ...
rpm --install [install-options] package_file ...
```

To install a new version of a package and remove an existing version at the same time, use the *upgrade* option instead:

```
rpm -U [install-options] package_file ...
rpm --upgrade [install-options] package_file ...
```

If the package doesn't already exist on the system, `-U` acts like `-i` and installs it. To prevent that behavior, you can *freshen* a package instead; in that case, `rpm` upgrades the package only if an earlier version is already installed. The *freshen* syntax is:

```
rpm -F [install-options] package_file ...
rpm --freshen [install-options] package_file ...
```

For all forms, *package-file* can be specified as an FTP or HTTP URL to download the file before installing it. See the section "FTP/HTTP options," later in this chapter.

The installation and upgrade options are:

`--aid`
: If `rpm` suggests additional packages, add them to the list of package files.

`--allfiles`
: Install or upgrade all files.

`--badreloc`
: Used with `--relocate` to force relocation even if the package is not relocatable.

`--excludedocs`
: Don't install any documentation files.

`--excludepath` *path*
: Don't install any file whose filename begins with *path*.

`--force`
: Force the installation. Equivalent to `--replacepkgs --replacefiles --oldpackage`.

`-h, --hash`
: Print 50 hash marks as the package archive is unpacked. Can be used with `-v` or `--verbose` for a nicer display.

`--ignorearch`
: Install even if the binary package is intended for a different architecture.

`--ignoreos`
: Install binary package even if the operating systems don't match.

`--ignoresize`
: Don't check disk space availability before installing.

`--includedocs`
: Install documentation files. This is needed only if `excludedocs: 1` is specified in an `rpmrc` file.

`--justdb`
: Update the database only; don't change any files.

`--nodeps`
: Don't check whether this package depends on the presence of other packages.

`--nodigest`
: Don't verify package or header digests.

`--noorder`
: Don't reorder packages to satisfy dependencies before installing.

`--nopost`
: Don't execute any post-install script.

`--nopostun`
: Don't execute any post-uninstall script.

`--nopre`
: Don't execute any pre-install script.

`--nopreun`
: Don't execute any pre-uninstall script.

`--noscripts`
: Don't execute any pre-install or post-install scripts. Equivalent to `--nopre --nopost --nopreun --nopostun`.

`--nosignature`
: Don't verify package or header signatures.

`--nosuggest`
: Don't suggest packages that provide a missing dependency.

`--notriggerin`
: Don't execute any install trigger scriptlet.

`--notriggerun`
: Don't execute any uninstall trigger scriptlet.

`--notriggerpostun`
: Don't execute any post-uninstall trigger scriptlet.

`--notriggers`
: Don't execute any scripts triggered by package installation. Equivalent to `--notriggerin --notriggerun --notriggerpostun`.

`--oldpackage`
: Allow an upgrade to replace a newer package with an older one.

`--percent`
: Print percent-completion messages as files are unpacked. Useful for running `rpm` from other tools.

`--prefix` *path*
: Set the installation prefix to *path* for relocatable binary packages.

`--relocate` *oldpath=newpath*
: For relocatable binary files, change all file paths from *oldpath* to *newpath*. Can be specified more than once to relocate multiple paths.

`--repackage`
: Repackage the package files before erasing an older version, to save the package in case a transaction rollback is necessary. Rename the package as specified by the macro `%_repackage_name_fmt` and save it in the directory specified by the macro `%_repackage_dir` (by default `/var/spool/repackage`). The repackaged file is not identical to the original package.

`--replacefiles`
: Install the packages even if they replace files from other installed packages.

`--replacepkgs`
: Install the packages even if some of them are already installed.

`--test`
: Go through the installation to see what it would do, but don't actually install the package. This option lets you test for problems before doing the installation.

Query options

The syntax for the *query* option is:

```
rpm -q [package-options] [information-options]
rpm --query [package-options] [information-options]
```

There are two subsets of query options. *Package selection* options determine what packages to query, and *information selection* options determine what information to provide.

Here are the package selection options:

package_name
: Query the installed package *package_name*.

`-a, --all`
: Query all installed packages.

Package Management

`-f` *file*, `--file` *file*
: Find out what package owns *file*.

`--fileid` *md5*
: Query package with the specified MD5 checksum.

`-g` *group*, `--group` *group*
: Find out what packages have group *group*.

`--hdrid` *sha1*
: Query package with the specified SHA1 digest in the package header.

`-p` *package_file*, `--package` *package_file*
: Query the uninstalled package *package_file*, which can be a URL. If *package_file* is not a binary package, it is treated as a text file containing a package manifest, with each line of the manifest containing a path or one or more whitespace-separated glob expressions to be expanded to paths. These paths are then used instead of *package_file* as the query arguments. The manifest can contain comments that begin with a hash mark (#).

`--pkgid` *md5*
: Query the package with a package identifier that is the given MD5 checksum of the combined header and contents.

`--querybynumber` *num*
: Query the *num*th database entry. Useful for debugging.

`-qf` *string*, `--queryformat` *string*
: Specify the format for displaying the query output, using tags to represent different types of data (e.g., NAME, FILENAME, DISTRIBUTION). The format specification is a variation of the standard `printf` formatting, with the type specifier omitted and replaced by the name of the header tag inclosed in curly braces ({...}). For example:

```
%{NAME}
```

The tag names are case-insensitive. Use `--querytags` (see the later section "Miscellaneous options") to view a list of available tags. The tag can be followed by *:type* to get a different output format type. The possible types are:

`:armor`
: Wrap a public key in ASCII armor.

`:base64`
: Encode binary data as base64.

`:date`
: Use `"%c"` format as in *strftime*(3) to display the preferred date and time format for this locale.

`:day`
: Use `"%a %b %d %Y"` format as in the function *strftime*(3). This format displays the day of the week, the day of the month, the month as a decimal number, and the four-digit year.

`:depflags`
: Format dependency flags.

`:fflags`
: Format file flags.

`:hex`
: Use hexadecimal format.

`:octal`
: Use octal format.

`:perms`
: Format file permissions.

`:shescape`
: Escape single quotes for use in a script.

`:triggertype`
: Display trigger suffix (i.e., `in`, `un`, or `postun`, indicating whether it's an install, uninstall, or post-uninstall trigger).

`--specfile` *specfile*
: Query *specfile* as if it were a package. Useful for extracting information from a spec file.

`--tid` *tid*
: List packages with the specified transaction identifier (*tid*). The tid is a Unix timestamp. All packages installed or erased in a single transaction have the same tid.

`--triggeredby` *pkg*
: List packages containing triggers that are run when the installation status of package *pkg* changes. For example:

```
$ rpm -q --triggeredby glibc
redhat-lsb-1.3-4
```

In this example, the package `redhat-lsb-1.3.4` contains a `triggerpostun` scriptlet that runs after `glibc` is uninstalled.

`--whatrequires` *capability*
: List packages that require the given capability to function. For example:

```
$ rpm -q --whatrequires popt
rpm-4.3.2-21
gstreamer-0.8.7-3
librsvg2-2.8.1-1
planner-0.12.1-1
```

`--whatprovides` *capability*
: List packages that provide the given capability. For example:

```
$ rpm -q --whatprovides popt
popt-1.9.1-21
```

Here are the information selection options:

`-c`, `--configfiles`
: List configuration files in the package. Implies `-l`.

`--changelog`
: Display the log of change information for the package.

-d, --docfiles
: List documentation files in the package. Implies -l.

--dump
: Dump information for each file in the package. This option must be used with at least one of -l, -c, or -d. The output includes the following information in this order:

```
path size mtime md5sum mode owner group isconfig isdoc rdev symlink
```

--filesbypkg
: List all files in each package.

-i, --info
: Display package information, including the name, version, and description. Formats the results according to --queryformat if specified.

-l, --list
: List all files in the package.

--last
: List packages by install time, with the latest packages listed first.

--provides
: List the capabilities this package provides.

-R, --requires
: List any packages this package depends on.

-s, --state
: List each file in the package and its state. The possible states are normal, not installed, or replaced. Implies -l.

--scripts
: List any package-specific shell scripts used during installation and uninstallation of the package.

--triggers, --triggerscript
: Display any trigger scripts in the package.

Uninstall options

The syntax for the *erase* (uninstall) option is:

```
rpm -e [uninstall-options] package_name ...
rpm --erase [uninstall-options] package_name ...
```

The uninstall options are:

--allmatches
: Remove all versions of the package. Only one package should be specified; otherwise, an error results.

--nodeps
: Don't check dependencies before uninstalling the package.

--nopostun
: Don't run any post-uninstall scripts.

`--nopreun`
: Don't run any pre-uninstall scripts.

`--noscripts`
: Don't execute any pre-uninstall or post-uninstall scripts. Equivalent to `--nopreun --nopostun`.

`--notriggerpostun`
: Don't execute any post-uninstall scripts triggered by the removal of this package.

`--notriggers`
: Don't execute any scripts triggered by the removal of this package. Equivalent to `--notriggerun --notriggerpostun`.

`--notriggerun`
: Don't execute any uninstall scripts triggered by the removal of this package.

`--repackage`
: Repackage the files before uninstalling them, to save the package in case a transaction rollback is necessary. Rename the package as specified by the macro `%_repackage_name_fmt` and save it in the directory specified by the macro `%_repackage_dir` (by default `/var/spool/repackage`). The repackaged file is not identical to the original package file.

`--test`
: Don't really uninstall anything; just go through the motions. Use with `-vv` for debugging.

Verify options

The syntax for the *verify* option is:

```
rpm -V [package-selection-options] [verify-options]
rpm --verify [package-selection-options] [verify-options]
```

Verify mode compares information about the installed files in a package with information about the files that came in the original package, and displays any discrepancies. The information compared includes the size, MD5 checksum, permissions, type, owner, and group of each file. Uninstalled files are ignored.

The package selection options include those available for query mode. In addition, the following *verify* options are available:

`--nodeps`
: Ignore package dependencies.

`--nodigest`
: Ignore package or header digests.

`--nofiles`
: Ignore attributes of package files.

`--nogroup`
: Ignore group ownership errors.

`--nolinkto`
: Ignore symbolic link errors.

`--nomd5`
: Ignore MD5 checksum errors.

`--nomode`
: Ignore file mode (permissions) errors.

`--nordev`
: Ignore major and minor device number errors.

`--nomtime`
: Ignore modification time errors.

`--noscripts`
: Ignore any verify script.

`--nosignature`
: Ignore package or header signatures.

`--nosize`
: Ignore file size errors.

`--nouser`
: Ignore user ownership errors.

The output is formatted as an eight-character string, possibly followed by an attribute marker, and then the filename. Each of the eight characters in the string represents the result of comparing one file attribute to the value of that attribute from the RPM database. A period (.) indicates that the file passed that test. The following characters indicate failure of the corresponding test:

`5`	MD5 checksum
`D`	Device
`G`	Group
`L`	Symlink
`M`	Mode (includes permissions and file type)
`S`	File size
`T`	Modification time
`U`	User

The possible attribute markers are:

`c`	Configuration file
`d`	Documentation file
`g`	Ghost file (contents not included in package)
`l`	License file
`r`	Readme file

Database rebuild options

The syntax of the command to rebuild the RPM database is:

```
rpm --rebuilddb [options]
```

You also can build a new database:

```
rpm --initdb [options]
```

The options available with the database rebuild mode are the `--dbpath`, `--root`, and -v options described in the earlier section "General options."

Signature check options

RPM packages may have a GPG signature built into them. There are three types of digital signature options: you can check signatures, add signatures to packages, and import signatures.

The syntax of the signature check mode is:

```
rpm --checksig [options] package_file ...
rpm -K [options] package_file ...
```

The signature-checking options `-K` and `--checksig` check the digests and signatures contained in the specified packages to insure the integrity and origin of the packages. Note that RPM now automatically checks the signature of any package when it is read; this option is still useful, however, for checking all headers and signatures associated with a package.

The `--nosignature` and `--nodigest` options described in the earlier section "Install, upgrade, and freshen options," are available for use with signature check mode.

The syntax for adding signatures to binary packages is:

```
rpm --addsign binary-pkgfile ...
rpm --resign binary-pkgfile ...
```

Both `--addsign` and `--resign` generate and insert new signatures, replacing any that already exist in the specified binary packages.*

The syntax for importing signatures is:

```
rpm --import public-key
```

The `--import` option is used to import an ASCII public key to the RPM database so that digital signatures for packages using that key can be verified. Imported public keys are carried in headers, and keys are kept in a ring, which can be queried and managed like any package file.

Miscellaneous options

Several additional `rpm` options are available:

`--querytags`
: Print the tags available for use with the `--queryformat` option in query mode.

`--setperms` *packages*
: Set file permissions of the specified packages to those in the database.

`--setugids` *packages*
: Set file owner and group of the specified packages to those in the database.

`--showrc`
: Show the values `rpm` will use for all options that can be set in an `rpmrc` file.

* In older versions of RPM, `--addsign` was used to add new signatures without replacing existing ones, but currently both options work the same way and replace any existing signatures.

FTP/HTTP options

The following options are available for use with FTP and HTTP URLs in install, update, and query modes.

`--ftpport` *port*
: Use *port* for making an FTP connection on the proxy FTP server instead of the default port. Same as specifying the macro `%_ftpport`.

`--ftpproxy` *host*
: Use *host* as the proxy server for FTP transfers through a firewall that uses a proxy. Same as specifying the macro `%_ftpproxy`.

`--httpport` *port*
: Use *port* for making an HTTP connection on the proxy HTTP server instead of the default port. Same as specifying the macro `%_httpport`.

`--httpproxy` *host*
: Use *host* as the proxy server for HTTP transfers. Same as specifying the macro `%_httpproxy`.

RPM Examples

Query the RPM database to find Emacs-related packages:

```
rpm -q -a | grep emacs
```

Query an uninstalled package, printing information about the package and listing the files it contains:

```
rpm -qpil ~/downloads/bash2-doc-2.03-8.i386.rpm
```

Install a package (assumes superuser privileges):

```
rpm -i sudo-1.6.7p5-30.1.i386.rpm
```

Do the same thing, but report on the progress of the installation:

```
rpm -ivh sudo-1.6.7p5-30.1.i386.rpm
```

The rpmbuild Command

The `rpmbuild` command is used to build RPM packages. The syntax for `rpmbuild` is:

```
rpmbuild -bstage [build-options] spec-file ...
rpmbuild -tstage [build-options] spec-file ...
```

Specify `-b` to build a package directly from a spec file, or `-t` to open a tarred, gzipped file and use its spec file.

Both forms take the following single-character *stage* arguments, which specify the stages, or steps, required to build a package. The stages are listed in the order they would be performed:

`p`
: Perform the prep stage, unpacking source files and applying patches.

`l`
: Do a list check, expanding macros in the files section of the spec file and verifying that each file exists.

`c`
: Perform the prep and build stages; generally equivalent to running `make`.

i
: Perform the prep, build, and install stages; generally equivalent to running `make install`.

b
: Perform the prep, build, and install stages, then build a binary package.

s
: Build a source package.

a
: Perform the prep, build, and install stages, then build both binary and source packages.

The difference between the build stage, which is one of the early steps, and building a binary package in `b` or `a` is the difference between building a working binary for the software and putting all the pieces together into a final `rpm` package.

rpmbuild options

The general `rpm` options described in the earlier section "General options" can be used with `rpmbuild`. The following additional options can also be used when building an RPM file with `rpmbuild`:

`--buildroot` *dir*
: Override the `BuildRoot` tag with *dir* when building the package.

`--clean`
: Clean up (remove) the build files after the package has been made.

`--nobuild`
: Go through the motions, but don't execute any build stages. Used for testing spec files.

`--rmsource`
: Remove the source files when the build is done. Can be used as a standalone option with `rpmbuild` to clean up files separately from creating the packages.

`--rmspec`
: Remove the spec file when the build is done. Like `--rmsource`, `--rmspec` can be used as a standalone option with `rpmbuild`.

`--short-circuit`
: Can be used with `-bc` and `-bi` to skip previous stages that already ran successfully. With `--short-circuit`, `-bc` starts directly at the build stage and `-bi` starts with the install stage.

`--sign`
: Add a GPG signature to the package for verifying its integrity and origin.

`--target` *platform*
: When building the package, set the `%_target`, `%_target_arch`, and `%_target_os` macros to the value indicated by *platform*.

Two other options can be used standalone with `rpmbuild` to recompile or rebuild a package:

`--rebuild` *source-pkgfile ...*
: Like `--recompile`, but also build a new binary package. Remove the build directory, the source files, and the spec file once the build is complete.

`--recompile` *source-pkgfile ...*
: Install the named source package, and prep, compile, and install the package.

Finally, the `--showrc` option shows the current `rpmbuild` configuration:

```
rpmbuild --showrc
```

This option shows the values that will be used for all options that can be set in an `rpmrc` file.

Yum: Yellowdog Updater Modified

Yum is a system for managing RPM packages, including installing, updating, removing, and maintaining packages; it automatically handles dependencies between packages. Yum is derived from `yup`, an updating system written for Yellow Dog Linux, an RPM-based Macintosh distribution. Yum downloads the information in the package headers to a directory on your system, which it then uses to make decisions about what it needs to do. Yum obtains both the headers and the RPMs themselves from a collection of packages on a server, known as a *repository*.

A repository consists of a set of RPM packages and the package headers on a server that can be accessed via FTP or HTTP, from an NFS server, or from a local filesystem. A single server can contain multiple repositories, repositories are often mirrored on many servers, and you can configure `yum` to use multiple repositories. When they are downloaded to your system, the header and package files are maintained in `/var/cache/yum`.

The configuration file, `/etc/yum.conf`, is where you customize `yum`. It consists of two section types. The first section, `[main]`, sets configuration defaults for `yum` operation. This section is followed by `[`*`server`*`]` sections, where each server is named according to the repository it specifies. For example, for Fedora Core, you might have `[base]` for the base Fedora Core repository and `[development]` for the development repository.

The server sections can also be stored, one to a file, in `/etc/yum.repos.d`. `yum` comes with a default `yum.conf` file, which you can use as-is or as a starting point from which to add additional repositories.

The yum Command

The `yum` command is an automated system for updating `rpm`-based packages, particularly on Fedora Core and Red Hat Enterprise Linux. Yum can automatically install, upgrade, and remove packages. In addition to individual packages or a list of packages, `yum` can operate on an entire group of packages at a time.

When you run `yum`, it first updates the cache (unless you tell it not to with the `-C` option), then it proceeds to perform the requested operation.

The format of the `yum` command is:

```
yum [options] [command] [package ...]
```

Any general options are specified first, followed by a command telling `yum` what you want it to do, usually followed by a list of one or more packages. The *command* is always required, except with the `--help`, `-h`, and `--version` options.

Package names can be specified in various combinations of name, architecture, version, and release. For example, you could refer to the bash package as bash, bash.i386, bash-3.0, bash-3.0-17, or bash-3.0-17.i386.

General options

The following general options can be set on the command line. For those that can also be set in the [main] section of the yum.conf configuration file, the name of the configuration option is given.

-c *config-file*
: Specify the location of the yum configuration file. The file can be specified as a path to a local file or as an HTTP or FTP URL. The default is /etc/yum.conf.

-C
: Run entirely from the local cache. Don't download or update headers unless required to complete the requested action.

-d *num*
: Set the debug level to *num*, which is generally a number between 0 and 10, to specify how much debugging information to print. The configuration option is debuglevel.

--disablerepo=*repoid*
: Disable the repository specified by *repoid* so yum won't use it for this operation. The configuration option is enabled.

-e *num*
: Set the error level to *num*, where *num* is a number, generally between 0 and 10. If the value is 0, print only critical errors. If it is 1, print all errors. Values greater than 1 mean print more errors, if there are any.

--enablerepo=*repoid*
: Enable the specified repository that is marked as disabled (enable=0) in the configuration file. This allows the repository to be used for this operation. The configuration option is enabled.

--exclude=*package*
: Exclude the specified package from updates on all repositories. *package* can be given as a name or a glob. The configuration option is exclude.

-h, --help
: Display a help message and exit.

--installroot=*root*
: Specify an alternative root for package installation. All packages will be installed relative to *root*. The configuration option is installroot.

--obsoletes
: Enable obsoletes processing logic, taking into consideration packages that are obsoleted by other packages in the repository. Only meaningful with the yum update command. The configuration option is obsoletes.

-R *min*
: Set the maximum amount of time in minutes that yum will wait before performing a command.

`--rss-filename=`*`filename`*
: Use *`filename`* as the output file for the `generate-rss` command. The configuration option is `rss-filename`.

`-t, --tolerant`
: Keep going (be tolerant) if there are package errors on the command line. This allows `yum` to continue processing other packages even if there is a problem with one package (e.g., trying to install a package that is already installed). The configuration option is `tolerant`.

`-y`
: Assume that the answer to any question is yes. The configuration option is `assumeyes`.

Yum Command Summary

The individual `yum` commands are listed here.

---

check-update

`check-update`

Determine if updates are available, without running `yum` interactively. If any package updates are available, return an exit value of 100 and a list of packages. If there are no updates, return 0.

---

clean

`clean [`*`options`*`]`

Clean up the `yum` cache directory.

Options

`all`
: Clean everything: headers, packages, metadata, and the cache.

`cache`
: Clean up the cache.

`headers`
: Remove all header files, forcing `yum` to download new headers the next time it runs.

`metadata`
: Remove the metadata files, which maintain information about the packages such as package name, file size, description, dependencies, etc.

`packages`
: Remove cached packages.

---

generate-rss

`generate-rss [updates]`

Create an `rss` file that lists changelogs for all packages in the enabled repositories. If `updates` is specified, the `rss` file lists only updates that apply to your system.

groupinfo

`groupinfo` *`groups`*

Like `info`, but operates on package groups instead of individual packages.

groupinstall

`groupinstall` *`groups`*

Like `install`, but operates on package groups instead of individual packages.

grouplist

`grouplist`

Generate a list of installed and available groups to standard output. You can use these groups as input parameters to the other `group` commands, with their names in quotes ("...").

groupremove

`groupremove` *`groups`*

Like `remove`, but operates on package groups instead of individual packages.

groupupdate

`groupupdate` *`groups`*

Like update, but operates on package groups instead of individual packages.

info

`info [`*`options`*`] [`*`packages`*`]`

Display version information, a summary, and a description for each package, or for all packages if none is specified. See **list** for a description of the options.

install

`install` *`packages`*

Install the latest version of a package or packages, ensuring that all dependencies are met. If no package matches the name as specified, the name is treated as a shell glob and any matches are installed.

list

`list [`*`options`*`] [`*`packages`*`]`

Display a list of packages that match the *packages* specification and that are installed or available for installation.

Options

`all` List all installed or available packages.

`available`
List packages on the repository that are available for installation.

Package Management

`extras`
: List packages on the system that are not available on any repository in the configuration file.

`installed`
: List installed packages.

`obsoletes`
: List installed packages that are made obsolete by any packages in any repository in the configuration file.

`updates`
: List packages that have updates available for installation.

---

localinstall

`localinstall` *`packages`*

Install the specified packages, which reside on the local system, rather than downloading them from a repository.

---

localupdate

`localupdate` *`packages`*

Update the specified packages, which reside on the local system, rather than downloading them from a repository.

---

makecache

`makecache`

Download and cache the metadata files from the repository. Once the cache has been built, you can use the `-C` option to run the commands that use the metadata (`check-update`, `info`, `list`, `provides`, and `search`) directly from the cache.

---

provides

`provides` *`feature1`* `[`*`feature2`* `...]`

List packages that are available or installed that provide the specified features. The features can be specified as a name or as a wildcard in file-glob syntax format, and Perl or Python regular expressions can be used.

---

remove

`remove` *`package1`* `[`*`package2`* `...]`
`erase` *`package1`* `[`*`package2`* `...]`

Remove the specified packages from the system. Also remove any packages that depend on the specified packages.

---

search

`search` *`string1`* `[`*`string2`* `...]`

Find packages matching the specified string or strings in the description, summary, packager, or package name fields. Perl or Python regular expressions can be used for the strings. Useful for finding a package if you don't know the name.

update

`update [packages]`

With no packages specified, update all installed packages. Otherwise, update the specified packages. In either case, `yum` makes sure that all dependencies are satisfied. If no package matches, the names specified are assumed to be shell globs and any matches are installed.

With the `--obsoletes` option, `yum` includes obsolete processing logic in its calculations.

upgrade

`upgrade [packages]`

Equivalent to `update --obsoletes`.

whatprovides

`whatprovides feature1 [feature2 ...]`

Same as `provides`. See **provides** for more information.

up2date: Red Hat Update Agent

The Red Hat Update Agent, `up2date`, installs and updates packages on RPM-based systems, primarily on Red Hat and Fedora Core Linux systems. Originally, `up2date` was intended for use with Red Hat Enterprise Linux and the Red Hat Network, but it has since been updated to work with `yum` and `apt` repositories as well. `up2date` operates on groupings of packages known as *channels*, based on the system architecture and Fedora Core or Red Hat Enterprise release. For example, a channel might be `fedora-core-3`, containing packages for that distribution; this type of channel is a *base channel*. *Child channels* are associated with a base channel and contain extra packages, such as for an application or a set of applications. Entries for the channels are found in `/etc/sysconfig/rhn/sources`. This file contains an entry for each channel that associates the repository type (e.g., `up2date`, `yum`, or `apt`) with a channel name and a URL in the case of a `yum` repository. For an `apt` repository, the URL is separated by spaces into parts: *service:server*, *path*, and *repository name*. You can also include entries for a local directory of packages, known as a `dir` repository.

`up2date` has both a command-line and a graphical interface; it is primarily the command-line interface that we describe in this section. If you are running GNOME or KDE and have the `rhn-applet` installed, clicking on the icon in the panel brings up the graphical `up2date` interface. The `rhn-applet` is the Red Hat Network Notification Tool, which runs in your desktop panel and notifies you when package updates are available. The panel icon is red with a blinking exclamation point if updates are available, and blue with a check mark if your system is up-to-date.

The format of the up2date command is:

```
up2date [options] [packages]
```

There are two additional commands:

```
up2date-nox [options] [packages]
up2date-config
```

Running up2date-nox is equivalent to running up2date with the --nox option; it runs without X (without the graphical interface). up2date-config runs a graphical tool for configuring up2date. You can also configure the program by editing the configuration file, /etc/sysconfig/rhn/up2date, directly. These versions of the up2date command are not described further here.

Running up2date with no packages specified brings up the graphical interface. With packages, up2date updates or installs those packages, resolving dependencies as needed. Specify packages by name; up2date determines the appropriate version, release, and distribution.

Options

--arch=*arch*
: Install the package for the specified architecture. Not valid with -u, --list, or --dry-run.

--configure
: Configure the Update Agent. Puts up a graphical window that lets you configure proxy and authentication information, retrieval options, and packages and files to skip.

--channel *channels*
: Specify the channels to use.

-d, --download
: Download the specified package, but do not install it.

--dbpath *path*
: Specify the path to an alternate RPM database. The default path is /var/lib/rpm.

--dry-run
: Go through the motions, but don't actually download and install any packages.

--exclude *packages*
: Exclude packages in the comma-separated list *packages* from being installed or updated.

-f, --force
: Force package installation. Overrides file, package, and configuration skip lists.

--get
: Download the packages, but don't resolve any dependencies.

--get-source
: Download the source package. Don't resolve any dependencies.

--gpg-flags
: List the flags that will be used when GPG is invoked. Useful for scripts that want to invoke GPG the way up2date does.

-h, --help
: Print a help message and exit.

-i, --install
: Download and install the package. Overrides configuration option. Cannot be used with --download.

--installall
: Install all available packages on the channel specified by --channel.

--justdb
: Add packages to the database, but do not install them to the filesystem.

-k, --packagedir *dirs*
: Use the colon-separated list of directories to search for packages.

-l, --list
: List packages available for update. Also shows packages marked to be skipped.

--list-rollbacks
: Display a list of all RPM rollbacks available. A rollback lets you return to an earlier state, from before you installed a package.

--nodownload
: Do not download any packages. Used for testing.

--nosig
: Do not use GPG to check package signatures. If specified, overrides configuration option.

--nosrc
: Do not download source packages. If specified, overrides configuration option.

--nox
: Do not display the graphical interface.

--proxy *proxy*
: Specify an HTTP proxy to use.

--proxyUser=*username*
: Specify the username to use with an authenticated HTTP proxy.

--proxyPassword=*password*
: Specify a password to use with an authenticated HTTP proxy.

--register
: Register or re-register the system.

--showall
: Display a list of all packages available for download, including both packages that are already installed and those that are not.

--show-available
: Display a list of all packages available for download and not currently installed.

`--show-channels`
: Show the channels associated with a package. If used alone, show the currently subscribed channels.

`--show-groups`
: Display a list of package groups that are available for download.

`--show-orphans`
: List any installed packages that are not in any of the subscribed-to channels.

`--show-package-dialog`
: When running in GUI mode, show the package installation dialog.

`--solve-deps=`*`dependencies`*
: Download and install packages needed to resolve the specified dependencies. The dependencies are given in a comma-separated list.

`--src`
: Download source, as well as binary, RPMs.

`--serverUrl=`*`url`*
: Specify the URL of the server to use.

`--tmpdir=`*`directory`*
: Specify a temporary storage directory for files and packages, overriding the configured value.

`-u, --update`
: Do a complete system update, downloading and installing all relevant packages.

`--undo`
: Undo the last package set update.

`--upgrade-to-release=`*`release-version`*
: Upgrade to the specified release, where *release-version* indicates the channel for that release.

`-v, --verbose`
: Display additional output.

`--version`
: Print version information and exit.

`--what-provides=`*`dependencies`*
: List packages that solve the comma-separated list of dependencies.

The Debian Package Manager

Debian GNU/Linux provides several package management tools, primarily intended to facilitate the building, installation, and management of binary packages. In addition to Debian GNU/Linux, the tools described here also work on other Debian-based systems such as Xandros, Knoppix, Ubuntu, and numerous others.

Debian package names generally end in `.deb`. The Debian package management tools described here include `apt`, `aptitude`, `dpkg`, `dpkg-deb`, `dselect`, and `synaptic`.

Each of these tools is described in detail in the section "Debian Package Manager Command Summary," later in this chapter.

Files

Some important files used by the Debian package management tools are described briefly here:

`control`
: Comes with each package. Documents dependencies; contains the name and version of the package, a description, maintainer, installed size, the package priority, etc.

`conffiles`
: Comes with each package. Contains a list of the configuration files associated with the package.

`preinst`, `postinst`, `prerm`, `postrm`
: Scripts that developers can include in a package to be run before installation, after installation, before removal, or after removal of the package.

`/var/lib/dpkg/available`
: Contains information about packages available on the system.

`/var/lib/dpkg/status`
: Contains information about the status of packages available on the system.

`/etc/apt/sources.list`
: A list for APT of package sources, used to locate packages. The sources are listed one per line, in order of preference.

`/etc/apt/apt.conf`
: The main APT configuration file.

`/etc/apt/apt_preferences`
: A preferences file that controls various aspects of APT, such as letting a user select the version or release of a package to install.

`/etc/dpkg/dpkg.cfg`
: A configuration file containing default options for `dpkg`.

For a user, the important file is `/etc/apt/sources.list`. This file is where you set up the paths to the package archives, telling `apt` where to go to find packages. `apt` is installed with a default file. You aren't required to modify the sources in the file, but you'll probably want to change some sources, or add additional ones at some point. You might also want to change some of the options in the configuration files `apt.conf`, `apt_preferences`, and `dpkg.config` if you aren't satisfied with the defaults. The `control`, `conffiles`, and the pre- and post- install and removal script files are created by the package developers and used internally by the package management system.

Package Priorities

Every Debian package has a priority associated with it, indicating how important the package is to the system. The priorities are:

`required`
: The package is essential to the proper functioning of the system.

`important`
: The package provides important functionality that enables the system to run well.

`standard`
: The package is included in a standard system installation.

`optional`
: The package is one that you might want to install, but you can omit it if you are short on disk space, for example.

`extra`
: The package either conflicts with other packages that have a higher priority, has specialized requirements, or is one that you would want to install only if you need it.

The control file for `dpkg`, for example, shows that `dpkg` itself has a priority of `required`, while `dpkg-dev` (which provides tools for building Debian packages) has a priority of `standard`, and `dpkg-doc` is `optional`.

Package and Selection States

The possible states that a package can be in are:

`config-files`
: Only the configuration files for the package are present on the system.

`half-configured`
: The package is unpacked and configuration was started but not completed.

`half-installed`
: Installation was started but not completed.

`installed`
: The package is unpacked and configured.

`not-installed`
: The package is not installed.

`unpacked`
: The package is unpacked but not configured.

The possible package selection states are:

`deinstall`
: The package has been selected for deinstallation (i.e., for removal of everything but the configuration files).

`install`
: The package has been selected for installation.

`purge`
: The package has been selected to be purged (i.e., for removal of everything including the configuration files).

Package Flags

Two possible package flags can be set for a package:

`hold`
: The package shouldn't be handled by `dpkg` unless forced with the `--force-hold` option. Holding a package keeps it at the current version, preventing it from being updated. You might hold a package, for example, if the latest

version is broken and you want to stay with the version you have until a newer one is released.

`reinst-required`
: The package is broken and needs to be reinstalled. Such a package cannot be removed unless forced with the `--force-reinstreq` option.

Scripts

In addition to the commands described in the next section, a number of shell and Perl scripts are included with the package manager for use in managing and building packages:

`apt-file`
: Search for packages, specifying an action and a pattern to search for. (Perl script)

`apt-rdepends`
: Recursively list dependencies. (Perl script)

`apt-setup`
: An interactive script for adding download sources to the `sources.list` file. (Shell script)

`dpkg-architecture`
: Determine and set the build and host architecture for package building. (Perl script)

`dpkg-checkbuilddeps`
: Check installed packages against the build dependencies and build conflicts listed in the control file. (Perl script)

`dpkg-buildpackage`
: A control script to help automate package building. (Shell script)

`dpkg-distaddfile`
: Add an entry for a file to `debian/files`. (Perl script)

`dpkg-divert`
: Create and manage the list of diversions, used to override the default location for installing files. (Perl script)

`dpkg-genchanges`
: Generate an upload control file from the information in an unpacked built source tree and the files it has generated. (Perl script)

`dpkg-gencontrol`
: Read information from an unpacked source tree, generate a binary package control file (by default, `debian/tmp/DEBIAN/control`), and add an entry for the binary file to `debian/files`. (Perl script)

`dpkg-name`
: Rename Debian packages to their full package names. (Shell script)

`dpkg-parsechangelog`
: Read and parse the changelog from an unpacked source tree and write the information to standard output in machine-readable form. (Perl script)

`dpkg-preconfigure`
: Let packages ask questions prior to installation. (Perl script)

`dpkg-reconfigure`
: Reconfigure a package that is already installed. (Perl script)

`dpkg-scanpackages`
: Create a `Packages` file from a tree of binary packages. The `Packages` file is used by `dselect` to provide a list of packages available for installation. (Perl script)

`dpkg-shlibdeps`
: Calculate shared library dependencies for named executables. (Perl script)

`dpkg-source`
: Pack and unpack Debian source archives. (Perl script)

`dpkg-statoverride`
: Manage the list of stat overrides, which let `dpkg` override file ownership and mode when a package is installed. (Perl script)

Debian Package Manager Command Summary

For the `apt-` commands, options can be specified on the command line or set in the configuration file. Boolean options set in the configuration file can be overridden on the command line in a number of different ways, such as `--no-`*`opt`* and -*`opt`*`=no`, where *opt* is the single-character or full name of the option.

Many of these commands accept the following the common options:

`-c` *`file`*, `--config-file=`*`file`*
: Specify a configuration file to be read after the default configuration file.

`-h, --help`
: Print usage information and exit.

`-o, --option`
: Set a configuration option. Syntax is `-o` *`group`*`::`*`tool`*`=`*`option`*.

`-v, --version`
: Print version information and exit.

---

apt-cache

`apt-cache [`*`options`*`]` *`command`*

Perform low-level operations on the APT binary cache, including the ability to perform searches and produce output reports from package metadata.

Commands

`add` *`files`*
: Add the specified package index files to the source cache.

`depends` *`pkgs`*
: For each specified package, show a list of dependencies and packages that can fulfill them.

`dotty` *pkgs*
: Graph the relationships between the specified packages. The default is to trace out all dependent packages; turn this behavior off by setting the `APT::Cache::GivenOnly` configuration option.

`dump`
: List every package in the cache. Used for debugging.

`dumpavail`
: Print a list of available packages to standard output, suitable for use with `dpkg`.

`gencaches`
: Build source and package caches from the sources in the file `sources.list` and from `/var/lib/dpkg/status`. Equivalent to running `apt-get check`.

`madison` [*pkgs*]
: Display a table showing the available versions of each specified package. Similar to `madison`, a Debian tool that checks for package versions and reports their status. This option works locally and doesn't require access to the Debian project's internal archive.

`pkgnames` [*prefix*]
: Print a list of packages in the system. If *prefix* is specified, print only packages whose names begin with that prefix. Most useful with the `--generate` option.

`policy` [*pkgs*]
: Print detailed information about the priority selection of each specified package. With no arguments, print the priorities of all sources. Useful for debugging issues related to the `preferences` file.

`rdepends` [*pkgs*]
: Show a list of reverse dependencies for each specified package; i.e., list any packages that depend on the specified packages.

`search` *regex*
: Search package names and descriptions of all available package files for the specified regular expression and print the name and short description of each matching package. With `--full`, the output is identical to that from the `show` command. With `--names-only`, only the package name is searched. Multiple regular expressions can be specified. Useful for finding packages when you don't know the actual package name.

`show` *pkgs*
: Display the package records for each specified package. See the `-a` option for more details.

`showpkg` *pkgs*
: Display information about the specified packages. For each package, the output includes the available versions, packages that depend on this package, and packages that this package depends on. Useful for debugging.

`showsrc` *pkgs*
: Display source package records for each specified package.

`stats`
: Display statistics about the cache.

`unmet`
: Display the unmet dependencies in the package cache.

Options

The common options listed earlier are also accepted.

`-a, --all-versions`
: Print full records for all available versions. For use with the `show` command. The default is to show all versions; turn it off with `--no-all-versions` to display only the version that would be installed. The configuration option is `APT::Cache::AllVersions`.

`--all-names`
: Cause `pkgnames` to print all names, including virtual packages and missing dependencies. The configuration option is `APT::Cache::AllNames`.

`-f, --full`
: Print full package records when searching. The configuration option is `APT::Cache::ShowFull`.

`-g, --generate`
: Automatically regenerate the package cache rather than using the current cache. The default is to regenerate; you can turn it off with `--no-generate`. The configuration option is `APT::Cache::Generate`.

`-i, --important`
: Print only important dependencies (Depends and Pre-Depends relations). For use with `unmet`. The configuration option is `APT::Cache::Important`.

`--installed`
: Only produce output for currently installed packages. For use with `depends` and `rdepends`. The configuration option is `APT::Cache::Installed`.

`-n, --names-only`
: Search only on package names, not long descriptions. The configuration option is `APT::Cache::NamesOnly`.

`-p` *file*, `--pkg-cache=`*file*
: Use the specified file for the package cache, which is the primary cache used by all operations. The configuration option is `Dir::Cache::pkgcache`.

`-q, --quiet`
: Operate quietly, producing output for logging but no progress indicators. Use `-qq` for even quieter operation. The configuration option is `quiet`.

`--recurse`
: Run `depends` or `rdepends` recursively, so that all specified packages are printed once. The configuration option is `APT::Cache::RecurseDepends`.

`-s` *file*, `--src-cache=`*file*
: Specify the source cache file used by `gencaches`. The configuration option is `Dir::Cache::srcpkgcache`.

---

apt-cdrom

apt-cdrom [*options*] *command*

Add a new CD-ROM to APT's list of available sources. The database of CD-ROM IDs that APT maintains is `/var/lib/apt/cdroms.list`.

Commands

`add` Add a CD-ROM to the source list.

`ident`
: Print the identity of the current CD-ROM and the stored filename. Used for debugging.

Options

The common options listed earlier are also accepted.

`-a`, `--thorough`
: Do a thorough package scan. May be needed with some old Debian CD-ROMs.

`-d` *mount-point*, `--cdrom=`*mount-point*
: Specify the CD-ROM mount point, which must be listed in `/etc/fstab`. The configuration option is `Acquire::cdrom::mount`.

`-f`, `--fast`
: Do a fast copy, assuming the files are valid and don't all need checking. Specify this only if the disk has been run before without error. The configuration option is `APT::CDROM::Fast`.

`-m`, `--no-mount`
: Don't mount or unmount the mount point. The configuration option is `APT::CDROM::NoMount`.

`-n`, `--just-print`, `--recon`, `--no-act`
: Check everything, but don't actually make any changes. The configuration option is `APT::CDROM::NoAct`.

`-r`, `--rename`
: Prompt for a new label and rename the disk to the new value. The configuration option is `APT::CDROM::Rename`.

---

apt-config

```
apt-config [options] shell args
apt-config [options] dump
```

An internal program for querying configuration information.

Commands

`dump`
: Display the contents of the configuration space.

`shell`
: Access the configuration information from a shell script. The arguments are in pairs, specifying the name of a shell variable and a configuration value to query. The value may be postfixed with `/x`, where *x* is one of the following letters:

  `b` Return true or false.

  `d` Return directories.

  `f` Return filenames.

  `i` Return an integer.

Options

The common options listed earlier are accepted.

---

apt-extracttemplates

`apt-extracttemplates [options] files`

Extract configuration scripts and templates from the specified Debian package files. For each specified file, a line of output is generated with the following information:

`package version template-file config-script`

and the template files and configuration scripts are written to the directory specified with `-t` or `--temp-dir` or by the configuration option `APT::ExtractTemplates::TempDir`. The filenames are in the form `package.template.xxxx` and `package.config.xxxx`.

Options

The common options listed earlier are also accepted.

`-t dir, --tempdir=dir`
: Write the extracted template files and configuration scripts to the specified directory. The configuration option is `APT::ExtractTemplates::TempDir`.

---

apt-ftparchive

`apt-ftparchive [options] command`

Generate package and other index files used to access a distribution source. The files should be generated on the source's origin site.

Commands

`clean config-file`
: Clean the databases used by the specified configuration file by removing obsolete records.

`contents path`
: Search the specified directory tree recursively. For each `.deb` file found, read the file list, sort the files by package, and write the results to standard output. Use with `--db` to specify a binary caching database.

generate *config-file sections*
: Build indexes according to the specified configuration file.

packages *path* [*override* [*pathprefix*]]
: Generate a package file from the specified directory tree. The optional override file contains information describing how the package fits into the distribution, and the optional path prefix is a string prepended to the filename fields. Similar to `dpkg-scanpackages`. Use with `--db` to specify a binary caching database.

release *path*
: Generate a release file from the specified directory tree.

sources *paths* [*override* [*pathprefix*]]
: Generate a source index file from the specified directory tree. The optional override file contains information used to set priorities in the index file and to modify maintainer information. The optional path prefix is a string prepended to the directory field in the generated source index. Use `--source-override` to specify a different source override file. Similar to `dpkg-scansources`.

Options

The common options listed earlier are also accepted.

`--contents`
: Perform contents generation. If set, and package indexes are being generated with a cache database, the file listing is extracted and stored in the database. If used with `generate`, allows the creation of any contents files. The default is on. The configuration option is `APT::FTPArchive::Contents`.

`-d, --db`
: Use a binary caching database. This option has no effect on `generate`. The configuration option is `APT::FTPArchive::DB`.

`--delink`
: Enable delinking of files when used with the `External-Links` setting. The default is on; turn off with `--no-delink`. The configuration option is `APT::FTPArchive::DeLinkAct`.

`--md5`
: Generate MD5 checksums for the index files. The default is on. The configuration option is `APT::FTPArchive::MD5`.

`-q, --quiet`
: Run quietly, producing logging information but no progress indicators. Use `-qq` for quieter operation. The configuration option is `quiet`.

`--read-only`
: Make the caching databases read-only. The configuration option is `APT::FTPArchive::ReadOnlyDB`.

`-s` *file*, `--source-override=`*file*
: Specify a source override file. For use with the `sources` command. See **sources** description for more information. The configuration option is `APT::FTPArchive::SourceOverride`.

Package Management

apt-get

`apt-get [options] command [package ...]`

A command-line tool for handling packages. Also serves as a backend to other APT tools such as `dselect`, `synaptic`, and `aptitude` (all described later in this section). As described earlier in this chapter, the following command can be run every day to keep your system updated:

```
apt-get update && apt-get -u dist-upgrade
```

Commands

`autoclean`
: Like `clean`, but remove only package files that can no longer be downloaded. Set the configuration option `APT::Clean-Installed` to off to prevent installed packages from being erased.

`build-dep`
: Install or remove packages to satisfy the build dependencies for a source package.

`clean`
: Clear the local repository of retrieved package files. Useful for freeing up disk space.

`check`
: Update the package cache and check for broken packages.

`dist-upgrade`
: Like `upgrade`, but also handle dependencies intelligently. See the `-f` option for more information.

`dselect-upgrade`
: Used with `dselect`. Track the changes made by `dselect` to the `Status` field of available packages and take actions necessary to realize that status.

`install` *packages*
: Install one or more packages. Specify the package name, not the full filename. Other required packages are also retrieved and installed. With a hyphen appended to the package name, the package is removed if it is already installed. Select a version to install by appending an equals sign and the version.

`remove` *packages*
: Remove one or more packages. Specify the package name, not the full filename. With a plus sign appended to the name, the package is installed.

`source` *packages*
: Find source packages and download them into the current directory. If specified with `--compile`, the source packages are compiled into binary packages. With `--download-only`, the source packages are not unpacked. Select a specific version by appending an equals sign and the version.

`update`
: Resynchronize the package overview files from their sources. Must be done before an `upgrade` or `dist-upgrade`.

`upgrade`
: Install the latest versions of all packages currently installed. Remember to run `update` first.

Options

The common options listed earlier are also accepted.

`--arch-only`
: Process only architecture-dependent build dependencies. Configuration option is `APT::Get::Arch-Only`.

`-b, --build, --compile`
: Compile source packages after download. The configuration option is `APT::Get::Compile`.

`-d, --download-only`
: Retrieve package files, but don't unpack or install them. The configuration option is `APT::Get::Download-only`.

`--diff-only`
: Download only the diff file from a source archive. The configuration option is `APT::Get::Diff-Only`.

`-f, --fix-broken`
: Try to fix a system with broken dependencies. Can be used alone or with a command. Run with the `install` command if you have problems installing packages. You can run the sequence:

```
apt-get -f install
apt-get dist-upgrade
```

several times to clean up interlocking dependency problems. The configuration option is `APT::Get::Fix-Broken`.

`--force-yes`
: Force yes. Causes APT to continue without prompting if it is doing something that could damage your system. Use with great caution and only if absolutely necessary. The configuration option is `APT::Get::force-yes`.

`--ignore-hold`
: Ignore a hold placed on a package, which normally prevents the package from being upgraded. Use with `dist-upgrade` to override many undesired holds. The configuration option is `APT::Get::Ignore-Hold`.

`--list-cleanup`
: Erase obsolete files from `/var/lib/apt/lists`. The default is on; use `--no-list-cleanup` to turn it off, which you would normally do only if you frequently modify your list of sources. The configuration option is `APT::Get::List-Cleanup`.

`-m, --ignore-missing, --fix-missing`
: Ignore missing or corrupted packages or packages that cannot be retrieved. Can cause problems when used with `-f`. The configuration option is `APT::Get::Fix-Missing`.

`--no-download`
: Disable package downloading; use with `--ignore-missing` to force APT to use only the packages that have already been downloaded. The configuration option is `APT::Get::Download`.

`--no-remove`
: Do not remove any packages; instead, abort without prompting. The configuration option is `APT::Get::Remove`.

`--no-upgrade`
: Do not upgrade packages. Use with `install` to prevent upgrade of packages that are already installed. The configuration option is `APT::Get::Upgrade`.

`--only-source`
: Do not map the names specified with the `source` or `build-dep` commands through the binary table. With this option, only source package names can be specified. The configuration option is `APT::Get::Only-Source`.

`--print-uris`
: Print Uniform Resource Indicators (URIs) of files instead of fetching them. Print path, destination filename, size, and expected MD5 checksum. The configuration option is `APT::Get::Print-URIs`.

`--purge`
: Tell `dpkg` to do a purge instead of a remove for items that would be removed. Purging removes packages completely, including any configuration files. The configuration option is `APT::Get::Purge`.

`-q`, `--quiet`
: Quiet mode. Omit progress indicators and produce only logging output. Use `-qq` to make even quieter. The configuration option is `quiet`.

`--reinstall`
: Reinstall packages that are already installed, upgrading them to the latest version. The configuration option is `APT::Get::ReInstall`.

`-s`, `--simulate`, `--just-print`, `--dry-run`, `--recon`, `--no-act`
: Go through the motions, but don't actually make any changes to the system. The configuration option is `APT::Get::Simulate`.

`-t` *`rel`*, `--target-release=`*`rel`*, `--default-release=`*`rel`*
: Retrieve packages only from the specified release. The value of *rel* can be a release number or a value such as `unstable`. The configuration option is `APT::Default-Release`.

`--tar-only`
: Download only the tar file from a source archive. The configuration option is `APT::Get::Tar-Only`.

`--trivial-only`
: Perform only operations that are considered trivial; i.e., ones that won't harm your system, by, say, removing needed files. Unlike `--assume-yes`, which always answers "yes" to any

prompts, `--trivial-only` always answers "no." The configuration option is `APT::Get::Trivial-Only`.

`-u, --show-upgraded`
Print a list of all packages to be upgraded. The configuration option is `APT::Get::Show-Upgraded`.

`-V, --verbose-versions`
Show full versions for upgraded and installed packages. The configuration option is `APT::Get::Show-Versions`.

`-y, --yes, --assume-yes`
Automatically reply "yes" to prompts and run noninteractively. Abort if there is an error. The configuration option is `APT::Get::Assume-Yes`.

---

apt-sortpkgs

`apt-sortpkgs [`*`options`*`]` *`indexfiles`*

Sort the records in a source or package index file by package name and write the results to standard output. `apt-sortpkgs` also sorts the internal fields of each record.

Options

The common options listed earlier are also accepted.

`-s, --source`
Order by source index field. The configuration option is `APT::SortPkgs::Source`.

---

aptitude

`aptitude [`*`options`*`] [`*`action`*` [`*`arguments`*`]]`

A text-based frontend to `apt`, which can be run either directly from the command line or from a visual mode that runs in a terminal window.

Actions

The following actions are supported. Running `aptitude` with no action invokes the visual mode. Package names can be entered individually or as search patterns. A search pattern consists of terms starting with a tilde (~), followed by a character indicating the type of term, followed by the text to be searched for. The most common usage is to use `~n` to search for a package name (e.g., `~nemacs`, to search for packages that have `emacs` in their name). You can find the full list of term types in the *Aptitude User's Manual*. The manual can be found in `/usr/share/doc/README` on a Debian system. On an RPM-based system with `aptitude` installed, the `README` file may be in `/usr/share/aptitude` or `/usr/share/doc/aptitude`.

`autoclean`
Clean out the cache by removing only packages that can no longer be downloaded.

`clean`
Clean out the cache by removing all previously downloaded `.deb` files.

Package Management

`dist-upgrade`
: Upgrade as many installed packages as possible, installing and removing packages as needed to satisfy dependencies.

`download` *packages*
: Download the `.deb` file for each specified package to the current directory.

`forbid-version` *package*[=*version*] ...
: Don't allow `aptitude` to upgrade the package to a particular version. If no version is specified, it is assumed to be the version that would normally be used.

`forget-new`
: Remove internal information about what packages are "new."

`help`
: Display help information and exit.

`hold` *packages*
: Place a hold on each specified package.

`install` [*package*[=*version*] ...]
: Install the specified packages. With a version, install that version. With no arguments, install any stored or pending actions. You can also use `install` to perform different actions on multiple packages with a single command. Append - to the package name to `remove`, + to `install`, _ to `purge`, or = to `hold` a package.

`markauto` *packages*
: Mark the specified packages as automatically installed.

`purge` [*package*[=*version*] ...]
: Remove the specified packages and their configuration files.

`remove` [*package*[=*version*] ...]
: Remove the specified packages.

`search` *patterns*
: Search for packages matching each of the specified patterns and display a list of matches. The full list of search terms can be found in the *Aptitude User's Manual*.

`show` *patterns*
: Search for packages matching each of the specified patterns and display detailed information for every match it finds.

`unhold` *packages*
: Remove the hold on each specified package.

`unmarkauto` *packages*
: Mark the specified packages as manually installed.

`update`
: Update the list of available packages by downloading the names of new and upgradeable packages.

`upgrade`
: Upgrade as many packages as possible; if a package has dependency problems, avoid upgrading that package (but don't remove it).

Options

Most of the aptitude options have corresponding configuration options that can be set in the configuration file.

-d, --download-only
: Download packages to the cache but do not install them. Configuration option is Aptitude::CmdLine::Download-Only.

-D, --show-deps
: Show summaries of why packages will be automatically installed or removed. Aptitude::CmdLine::Show-Deps is the configuration option.

-f
: Attempt to fix dependencies of broken packages. Configuration option is Aptitude::CmdLine::Fix-Broken.

-F *format*, --display-format *format*
: Specify the output format for search. See the *Aptitude User's Manual* for details on specifying the format. Configuration option is Aptitude::CmdLine::Package-Display-Format.

-h, --help
: Print help message and exit.

-O *order*, --sort *order*
: Specify the sort order for search output. See the *Aptitude User's Manual* for details.

-P, --prompt
: Always display a prompt, even for actions that were explicitly requested. Configuration option is Aptitude::CmdLine::Always-Prompt.

-r, --with-recommends
: Treat recommendations as dependencies when installing new packages. Aptitude::CmdLine::Recommends-Important is the configuration option.

-R, --without-recommends
: Do not treat recommendations as dependencies when installing new packages. The configuration option is Aptitude::CmdLine::Recommends-Important.

-s, --simulate
: Go through the motions, but do not actually perform the actions. Print the actions that would be performed. The configuration option is Aptitude::CmdLine::Simulate.

-t *release*, --target-release *release*
: Specify the release to use for installing packages. The configuration option is Aptitude::CmdLine::Default-Release.

-v, --verbose
: Operate verbosely, displaying additional information. Specify multiple times to get even more information displayed. Configuration option is Aptitude::CmdLine::Verbose.

-V, --show-versions
: Display the version for packages being installed. The configuration option is Aptitude::CmdLine::Show-Versions.

`--version`
: Display the version information for `aptitude` and exit.

`--visual-preview`
: Start the visual interface and display the preview screen.

`-w` *`width`*, `--width` *`width`*
: Specify the output display width for `search`. The default is the terminal width. `Aptitude::CmdLine::Package-Display-Width` is the configuration option.

`-y`, `--assume-yes`
: Assume a "yes" response to a yes/no prompt and don't display the prompt. Prompts for dangerous actions are still shown. This option overrides `-P`. The configuration option is `Aptitude::CmdLine::Assume-Yes`.

`-Z`
: Display the disk space that will be used or freed by the packages being acted upon. The configuration option is `Aptitude::CmdLine::Show-Size-Changes`.

Internal options

The following options are used internally for `aptitude`'s visual mode. You shouldn't need to issue them directly.

`-i`
: Display a download preview when the program starts. Cannot be used with `-u`.

`-S` *`filename`*
: Load extended state information from the specified file, not the default state file.

`-u`
: Begin updating the package lists as soon as the program starts. Cannot be used with `-i`.

dpkg

`dpkg [`*`options`*`]` *`action`*

A tool for installing, managing, and building packages. Also serves as a frontend to `dpkg-deb` and `dpkg-query`.

dpkg actions

These actions are carried out by `dpkg` itself:

`-A` *`pkgfile`*, `--record-avail` *`pkgfile`*
: Update the record of available files kept in `/var/lib/dpkg/available` with information from *pkgfile*. This information is used by `dpkg` and `dselect` to determine what packages are available. With `-R` or `--recursive`, *pkgfile* must be a directory.

`-C`, `--audit`
: Search for partially installed packages and suggest how to get them working.

`--clear-avail`
: Remove existing information about what packages are available.

`--command-fd` *n*
: Accept commands passed on the file descriptor given by *n*. Note that any additional options set through this file descriptor or on the command line are not reset, but remain for other commands issued during the same session.

`--compare-versions` *ver1 op ver2*
: Perform a binary comparison of two version numbers. The operators `lt`, `le`, `eq`, `ne`, `ge`, and `gt` treat a missing version as earlier. The operators `lt-nl`, `le-nl`, `ge-nl`, and `gt-nl` treat a missing version as later (where `nl` is "not later"). A third set of operators (`< << <= = >= >> >`) is provided for compatibility with control-file syntax. `dpkg` returns zero for success (i.e., the condition is satisfied) and nonzero otherwise.

`--configure [`*packages*`|-a|--pending]`
: Reconfigure one or more unpacked *packages*. If `-a` or `--pending` is given instead of *packages*, configure all packages that are unpacked but not configured. Configuring a package involves unpacking the configuration files, backing up the old configuration files, and running the `postinst` script if one is present.

`-Dh, --debug=help`
: Print debugging help message and exit.

`--force-help`
: Print help message about the `--force-`*list* options and exit. See the `--force-`*list* option description later in this entry for the possible values of *list*.

`--forget-old-unavail`
: Forget about uninstalled, unavailable packages.

`--get-selections [`*pattern*`]`
: Get list of package selections and write to standard output. With *pattern* specified, write selections that match the pattern.

`--help`
: Print help message and exit.

`-i` *pkgfile*, `--install` *pkgfile*
: Install the package specified as *pkgfile*. With `-R` or `--recursive`, *pkgfile* must be a directory.

`--license, --licence`
: Print `dpkg` license information and exit.

`--merge-avail` *pkgs-file*
: Update the record of available files kept in `/var/lib/dpkg/available`. This information is used by `dpkg` and `dselect` to determine what packages are available. Merging combines the information from *pkgs-file* (distributed as `Packages`) with the existing information.

`--print-architecture`
: Print the target architecture.

`--print-gnu-build-architecture`
: Print the GNU version of the target architecture.

`--print-installation-architecture`
: Print the host architecture for installation.

`--purge [`*packages*`|-a|--pending]`
`-r, --remove [`*packages*`|-a|--pending]`
: Purge or remove one or more installed `packages`. Removal gets rid of everything except the configuration files listed in `debian/conffiles`; purging also removes the configuration files. If `-a` or `--pending` is given instead of *packages*, `dpkg` removes or purges all packages that are unpacked and marked (in `/var/lib/dpkg/status`) for removing or purging.

`--set-selections`
: Set package selections based on input file read from standard input.

`--unpack` *pkgfile*
: Unpack the package, but do not configure it. With `-R` or `--recursive`, *pkgfile* must be a directory.

`--update-avail` *pkgs-file*
: Like `--merge-avail`, but replaces the information with the contents of the *pkgs-file*.

`--version`
: Print `dpkg` version information and exit.

`--yet-to-unpack`
: Search for uninstalled packages that have been selected for installation.

dpkg-deb actions

The following actions can be specified for `dpkg` and are passed to `dpkg-deb` for execution. Also see **dpkg-deb**.

`-b` *dir* [*archive*], `--build` *dir* [*archive*]
: Build a package.

`-c` *archive*, `--contents` *archive*
: List the contents of a package.

`-e` *archive* [*dir*], `--control` *archive* [*dir*]
: Extract control information from a package.

`-f` *archive* [*control-fields*], `--field` *archive* [*control-fields*]
: Display the control field or fields of a package.

`-I` *archive* [*control-files*], `--info` *archive* [*control-files*]
: Show information about a package.

`--fsys-tarfile` *archive*
: Write the filesystem tree contained in *archive* to standard output in `tar` format.

`-x` *archive dir*, `--extract` *archive dir*
: Extract the files from a package.

`-X` *archive dir*, `--vextract` *archive dir*
: Extract the files and display the filenames from a package.

dpkg-query actions

The following actions can be specified for dpkg and are passed to dpkg-query for execution. Also see **dpkg-query**.

-l, --list [*pkg-name-pattern*]
: List all packages whose names match the specified pattern. With no pattern, list all packages in /var/lib/dpkg/available. The pattern can include standard shell wildcard characters and may have to be quoted to prevent the shell from doing filename expansion.

-L *packages*, --listfiles *packages*
: List installed files that came from the specified package or packages.

-p, --print-avail *package*
: Print the details about *package* from /var/lib/dpkg/available.

-s *packages*, --status *packages*
: Report the status of one or more *packages* by displaying the entry in the status database /var/lib/dpkg/status.

-S *filename-pattern*, --search *filename-pattern*
: Search installed packages for a filename. The pattern can include standard shell wildcard characters and may have to be quoted to prevent the shell from doing filename expansion.

Options

dpkg options can be specified on the command line or set in the configuration file. Each line in the configuration file contains a single option, specified without the leading dash (-).

--abort-after=*num*
: Abort processing after *num* errors. Default is 50.

--admindir=*adir*, --instdir=*idir*, --root=*rdir*
: Change default directories. *adir* contains administrative files with status and other information about packages; it defaults to /var/lib/dpkg. *idir* is the directory into which packages are installed; it defaults to /. Changing the root directory to *rdir* automatically changes *idir* to *rdir* and *adir* to /*rdir*/var/lib/dpkg.

-B, --auto-deconfigure
: When a package is removed, automatically deconfigure any other package that depended on it.

-D*octal*, --debug=*octal*
: Turn on debugging, with the *octal* value specifying the desired level of debugging information. Use -Dh or --debug=help to display the possible values. You can OR the values to get the desired output.

-E, --skip-same-version
: Don't install the package if this version is already installed.

--force-*list*, --no-force-*list*, --refuse-*list*
: Force or refuse to force an operation. *list* is specified as a comma-separated list of options. With --force, a warning is printed, but processing continues. --refuse and --no-force

cause processing to stop with an error. Use `--force-help` to display a message describing the options. The force/refuse options are:

`all` Turn all force options on or off.

`architecture`
: Process even if intended for a different architecture.

`auto-select`
: Select or deselect packages to install or remove them. Forced by default.

`bad-path`
: Some programs are missing from the path.

`bad-verify`
: Install package even if it fails to verify.

`confdef`
: Always choose the default action for modified configuration files. If there is no default and `confnew` or `confold` is also specified, use that to decide; otherwise, ask the user.

`configure-any`
: Configure any unconfigured package that the package depends on.

`conflicts`
: Permit installation of conflicting packages. Can result in problems from files being overwritten.

`confmiss`
: Always install a missing configuration file. Be careful using this option, since it means overriding the removal of the file.

`confnew`
: Always install the new version of a modified configuration file unless `confdef` is also specified. In that case, use the default action if there is one.

`confold`
: Keep the old version of a modified configuration file unless `confdef` is also specified. In that case, use the default action if there is one.

`depends`
: Turn dependency problems into warnings.

`depends-version`
: Warn of version problems when checking dependencies, but otherwise ignore.

`downgrade`
: Install even if a newer version is already installed. Forced by default.

`hold`
: Process packages even if they are marked to be held.

`not-root`
: Try to install or remove even when not logged on as `root`.

`overwrite`
: Overwrite a file from one package with the same file from another package.

`overwrite-dir`
: Overwrite one package's directory with a file from another package.

`overwrite-diverted`
: Overwrite a diverted file with an undiverted version.

`remove-essential`
: Remove a package even if it is essential. Note that this can cause your system to stop working.

`remove-reinstreq`
: Remove a package even if it is broken and is marked to require reinstallation.

`-G` Don't install a package if a newer version is already installed. Same as `--refuse-downgrade`.

`--ignore-depends=`*`pkglist`*
: Dependency problems result only in a warning for the packages in *pkglist*.

`--new`
: New binary package format. This is a `dpkg-deb` option.

`--no-act`, `--dry-run`, `--simulate`
: Go through the motions, but don't actually write any changes. Used for testing. Be sure to specify before the action; otherwise, changes might be written.

`--nocheck`
: Ignore the contents of the control file when building a package. This is a `dpkg-deb` option.

`-O`, `--selected-only`
: Process only packages that are marked as selected for installation.

`--old`
: Old binary package format. This is a `dpkg-deb` option.

`-R`, `--recursive`
: Recursively handle `.deb` files found in the directories and their subdirectories specified with `-A`, `-i`, `--install`, `--unpack`, and `--avail`.

`--status-fd` *n*
: Send the package status information to the specified file descriptor. Can be given more than once.

Package Management

---

dpkg-deb

`dpkg-deb` *`action`* `[`*`options`*`]`

Backend command for building and managing Debian package archives. Also see **dpkg**; you'll often want to use `dpkg` to pass commands through to `dpkg-deb`, rather than call `dpkg-deb` directly.

Actions

`-b` *`dir`* [*`archive`*], `--build` *`dir`* [*`archive`*]
: Create an *archive* from the filesystem tree starting with directory *dir*. The directory must have a `DEBIAN` subdirectory containing the control file and any other control information. If *archive* is specified and is a filename, the package is written to that file; if no *archive* is specified, the package is written to *`dir`*`.deb`. If the archive already exists, it is replaced. If *archive* is the name of a directory, `dpkg-deb` looks in the control file for the information it needs to generate the package name. (Note that for this reason, you cannot use `--nocheck` with a directory name.)

`-c` *`archive`*, `--contents` *`archive`*
: List the filesystem-tree portion of *archive*.

`-e` *`archive`* [*`dir`*], `--control` *`archive`* [*`dir`*]
: Extract control information from *archive* into the directory *dir*, which is created if it doesn't exist. If *dir* is omitted, a `DEBIAN` subdirectory in the current directory is used.

`-f` *`archive`* [*`control-fields`*], `--field` *`archive`* [*`control-fields`*]
: Extract information about one or more fields in the control file for *archive*. If no fields are provided, print the entire control file.

`-h`, `--help`
: Print help information and exit.

`-I` *`archive`* [*`control-files`*], `--info` *`archive`* [*`control-files`*]
: Write information about binary package *archive* to standard output. If no control files are provided, print a summary of the package contents; otherwise, print the control files in the order they were specified. An error message is printed to standard error for any missing components.

`--fsys-tarfile` *`archive`*
: Extract the filesystem tree from *archive*, and send it to standard output in `tar` format. Can be used with `tar` to extract individual files from an archive.

`--license`, `--licence`
: Print the license information and exit.

`--version`
: Print the version number and exit.

`-W` *`archive`*, `--showarchive` *`archive`*
: Show information about the specified archive. The output can be customized with the `--showformat` option.

`-x` *`archive dir`*, `--extract` *`archive dir`*
`-X` *`archive dir`*, `--vextract` *`archive dir`*
: Extract the filesystem tree from *archive* into the specified directory, creating *dir* if it doesn't already exist. `-x` (`--extract`) works silently, while `-X` (`--vextract`) lists the files as it extracts them. Do not use this action to install packages; use `dpkg` instead.

Options

-D, --debug
: Turn on debugging.

--new
: Build a new-style archive format (this is the default).

--nocheck
: Don't check the control file before building an archive. This lets you build a broken archive.

--old
: Build an old-style archive format.

--showformat=*format*
: Specify the output format for -W/--show. The format can include the standard escape sequences \n (newline), \r (carriage return), or \\ (backslash). Specify package fields with the syntax ${*var*[;*width*]}. Fields are right-aligned by default, or left-aligned if *width* is negative.

-z# Set the compression level to the value specified by #.

-Z *type*
: Set the type of compression to use when building an archive. Possible values are: gzip, bzip2, and none.

---

dpkg-query

dpkg-query [*option*] *command*

Display information about packages listed in the dpkg database. You can also use dpkg-query as a backend for dpkg, instead of calling dpkg-query directly.

Commands

--help
: Print help information and exit.

-l [*patterns*], --list [*patterns*]
: List packages whose names match any of the specified patterns. With no pattern specified, list all packages in /var/lib/dpkg/available. The pattern may need to be in quotes to avoid expansion by the shell.

-L *packages*, --listfiles *packages*
: List files installed on your system from each of the specified packages. This command does not list files created by package-specific installation scripts.

--license, --licence
: Print the license information and exit.

-p *package*, --print-avail *package*
: Display details for the specified package, as found in /var/lib/dpkg/available.

-s *package*, --status *package*
: Report on the status of the specified package.

`-S` *patterns*, `--search` *patterns*
: Search the installed packages for filenames matching one of the specified patterns. At least one pattern must be specified.

`-W [`*patterns*`]`, `--show [`*patterns*`]`
: Similar to `-l`; however, the output can be customized with the `--showformat` option.

`--version`
: Print version information and exit.

Options

`--admindir=`*dir*
: Use *dir* as the location of the `dpkg` database. The default is `/var/lib/dpkg`.

`--showformat=`*format*
: Specify the output format for `-W`/`--show`. The format can include the standard escape sequences `\n` (newline), `\r` (carriage return), or `\\` (backslash). Specify package fields with the syntax `${`*var*`[;`*width*`]}`. Fields are right-aligned by default, or left-aligned if *width* is negative.

---

dpkg-split

`dpkg-split [`*action*`] [`*options*`]`

Split a binary package into smaller pieces and reassemble the pieces, either manually or in automatic mode. The automatic mode maintains a queue of parts for reassembling. Useful for transferring to and from floppy disks on older systems.

Actions

`-a -o` *output part*, `--auto -o` *output part*
: Add *part* to the queue for automatic reassembly, and if all the parts are available, reassemble the package as *output*. Requires the use of the `-o` (or `--output`) option, as shown.

`-d [`*packages*`]`, `--discard [`*packages*`]`
: Discard parts from the automatic-assembly queue. If any *packages* are specified, discard only parts from those packages. Otherwise, empty the queue.

`-I` *parts*, `--info` *parts*
: Print information about the part file or files specified to standard output.

`-j` *parts*, `--join` *parts*
: Join the parts of a package file together from the *parts* specified. The default output file is *package-version*`.deb`.

`-l`, `--listq`
: List the contents of the queue of parts waiting for reassembly, giving the package name, the parts that are on the queue, and the number of bytes.

-s *full-package* [*prefix*], --split *full-package* [*prefix*]
: Split the package *full-package* into parts, named *prefixNofM*.deb. The prefix defaults to the *full-package* name without the .deb extension.

-h, --help
: Print help message and exit.

--license, --licence
: Print license information and exit.

--version
: Print version information and exit.

Options

--depotdir *dir*
: Specify an alternate directory *dir* for the queue of parts waiting for reassembly. Default is /var/lib/dpkg.

--msdos
: Force --split output filenames to be MS-DOS-compatible.

-o *output*, --output *output*
: Use *output* as the filename for a reassembled package.

-Q, --npquiet
: Do not print an error message for a part that doesn't belong to a binary package when doing automatic queuing or reassembly.

-S *num*, --partsize *num*
: When splitting, specify the maximum part size (*num*) in kilobytes. Default is 450 KB.

dselect

dselect [*options*] [*action*]

A screen-oriented user frontend to dpkg. One of the primary user interfaces for installing and managing packages. See **dpkg** and **dpkg-deb** for information on building packages.

Actions

If dselect is run with no action specified on the command line, it displays the following menu:

```
* 0. [A]ccess   Choose the access method to use.
  1. [U]pdate   Update list of available packages, if
                possible.
  2. [S]elect   Request which packages you want on your
                system.
  3. [I]nstall  Install and upgrade wanted packages.
  4. [C]onfig   Configure any packages that are
                unconfigured.
  5. [R]emove   Remove unwanted software.
  6. [Q]uit     Quit dselect.
```

The asterisk (on the first line) shows the currently selected option. Any of the menu items can be specified directly on the command line as an action (`access`, `update`, `select`, `install`, `config`, `remove`, `quit`) to go directly to the desired activity. For example:

```
dselect access
```

If you enter `quit` on the command line, `dselect` exits immediately without doing anything. An additional command-line action is `menu`, which displays the menu and is equivalent to running `dselect` with no action.

Options

Options can be specified both on the command line and in the `dselect` configuration file, `/etc/dpkg/dselect.cfg`.

`--admindir` *dir*
: Change the directory that holds internal data files to *dir*. Default is `/var/lib/dpkg`.

`--color` *colorspec*, `--colour` *colorspec*
: Set colors for different parts of the screen, as specified by *colorspec* as follows:

```
screenpart:[fgcolor],[bgcolor][:attr[+attr+ ...]]
```

This option can be specified multiple times, to override the default colors for different screen parts. Rather than having to specify the colors on the command line each time you run `dselect`, you might prefer to set them in the configuration file. The possible screen parts (going from the top of the screen to the bottom) are:

`title`
: The screen title.

`listhead`
: The header line above the package list.

`list`
: The scrolling list of packages and some help text.

`listsel`
: The selected item in the list.

`pkgstate`
: The text showing the current state of each package.

`pkgstatesel`
: The text showing the current state of the selected package.

`infohead`
: The header line showing the state of the selected package.

`infodesc`
: The short description of the package.

`info`
: The text that displays information such as the package description.

`infofoot`
: The last line of the screen when selecting packages.

`query`
: Query lines.

`helpscreen`
: The color of help screens.

Either the foreground color, the background color, or both can be specified for each screen part. The colors are given as the standard *curses* colors. After the color specification, you can specify a list of attributes separated by plus signs (+). The possible attributes are `normal`, `standout`, `underline`, `reverse`, `blink`, `bright`, `dim`, and `bold`. Not all attributes work on all terminals.

`--expert`
: Run in expert mode; don't print help messages.

`-D` [*file*], `--debug` [*file*]
: Turn on debugging. Send output to *file* if specified.

`--help`
: Print help message and exit.

`--license`, `licence`
: Print license information and exit.

`--version`
: Print version information and exit.

---

synaptic

`synaptic [options]`

Graphical frontend for APT. Use in place of `apt-get` to install, upgrade, or remove packages from your system. With `synaptic`, you can view a list of all available packages, or you can break the list down in various ways to make it more manageable. From the `synaptic` window, you can select from a list of categories. The categories are section (e.g., view only development-related packages), package status, alphabetic (e.g., view only packages whose name starts with the letter A), search history, or filter.

If you choose to display by filter, there are a set of predefined filters, or you can define your own. The predefined filters include ones to display all packages, packages marked for a status change, packages that can be configured with `debconf` (Debian systems only), packages with broken dependencies, and packages that can be upgraded to a later version. You can edit the existing filters or define your own, by selecting Preferences → Filters from the Edit menu.

Once you've used the selection criteria to find the list of packages, you can select a single package, or you can select multiple packages by holding down the SHIFT or CTRL key. Like `apt-get`, first do an `update` to update the package lists, then you can do an `install` or `upgrade`.

To start synaptic from Gnome, select System tools → Synaptic Package Manager from the Application menu. From the KDE menu, select Settings → Extra → Synaptic Package Manager. You can also start the graphical interface from the command line, with the command:

```
synaptic [options]
```

Options

In addition to the following options, synaptic accepts the standard GTK+ toolkit command-line options.

-f *filename*, --filter-file=*filename*
: Use the specified file as an alternative filter settings file.

-h, --help
: Print help message and exit.

-i *num*, --initial-filter=*num*
: Start up with the filter numbered *num* as the initial filter.

--non-interactive
: Run without prompting for user input.

-o *option*, --option=*option*
: Set an internal option. Don't use this option unless you are sure you know what you are doing.

-r
: Open with the file repository window displayed. This window lists the repositories and shows which are active.

Mac OS X Package Management

There are two freely available package management systems for Mac OS X.

Fink and Fink Commander

The Fink project's goal is to port important Open Source and Free Software to Darwin and Mac OS X. To that end, the project provides the Fink package management system, which makes it easy to install, upgrade, and uninstall Open Source software.

Fink is based on the Debian tools dpkg, dselect, and apt-get (described earlier in this chapter). It uses these tools to manage downloading, building, and installation of available packages. The current default location for installation is the /sw directory; this name does not conflict with any of the other standard Unix or Mac OS X installation directories, which keeps package management simple.

The Fink project is based at *http://fink.sourceforge.net*. From there you can download the fink command-line program and other tools and start downloading the packages that are available.

Fink Commander provides an Aqua-based GUI interface to Fink. The web starting point is *http://finkcommander.sourceforge.net*. A binary version of Fink Commander is included when you download Fink, so you don't have to build Fink Commander yourself.

For more information, including screenshots of Fink Commander, see the two web sites just cited.

The GNU Mac OS X Public Archive

The GNU Mac OS X Public Archive (OSXGNU) at *http://www.osxgnu.org* provides an alternative to Fink. It provides a package management system that extends the rudimentary facilities already available in Mac OS X (i.e., the standard Mac OS X installer facilities).

The advantage to the OSXGNU project is that you don't have to use a terminal to install packages; you just launch them. The OSXGNU project provides the OS X Package Manager, which is an Aqua-based GUI interface to the Mac OS X package management system. It lets you manage all the packages installed on your system, not just those downloaded from the OSXGNU site.

A disadvantage to the OSXGNU system is that it doesn't track different versions of packages or automatically download new software for you. You have to do that yourself manually, whereas Fink's Debian-based tools are considerably more Internet-aware.

Building from Source

Of course, you can always build software from source code as well. Open a `Terminal` window and download whatever package you wish to build using a program such as `curl` or `ftp`. Be sure you have the development tools installed, and then follow the standard recipe as presented in Chapter 1.

Package Management

Solaris Package Management

Solaris uses an enhanced version of the System V Release 4 package management system. These tools are used for installation of Sun's software and for software available from *http://www.sunfreeware.com*. The tools are different from those of GNU/Linux, since they do not manage automatic updating of installed packages. (`pkgadd` can, however, download and install packages provided with `http://` URLs.)

If you need to create Solaris packages, you should read Sun's *Application Packaging Developer's Guide*. The Solaris 9 version of this document is currently available at *http://docs.sun.com/app/docs/doc/806-7008/*.

Solaris Package Management Command Summary

Adding and removing packages are straightforward operations: use the pkgadd and pkgrm commands. The pkginfo command provides information about installed packages. The pkgadm command provides rudimentary control over installed packages.

Creating packages is more involved, requiring the use of pkgproto to build a *prototype*(4) file and then pkgmk to actually create the package.

The installf and removef commands are useful when writing scripts to be run by pkgadd and pkgrm.

---

installf

```
/usr/sbin/installf [options] pkginst pathname
                   [ftype [major minor] [mode owner group]]
/usr/sbin/installf [options] pkginst -
/usr/sbin/installf -f [options] pkginst
```

installf adds a file to the system installation database that isn't listed in the pkgmap file. It's used for files created dynamically (such as device files in /dev) during package installation. All invocations supply the package name and instance, *pkginst*, associated with the new file. This command should be run before any files are changed.

The first synatx supplies the file type, its *major* and *minor* device numbers if the file is a device file, and the protection *mode*, *owner*, and *group* on the command line.

The second syntax is similar to the first, but reads the information from standard input, one file's information per line. The third syntax is used after the files are all in place: it finalizes the information in the installation database.

Options

-c *class*
: The class with which the objects should be associated. The default is none.

-f
: Indicate that installation is complete (final).

-M
: Do not use $root_path/etc/vfstab for determining a client's mount points. Rather, assume that the mount points are correct on the server.

-R *root-path*
: Install all files under *root-path*. This is used on server systems when installing packages for clients.

-V *vfstab-file*
: Use *vfstab-file* instead of $root_path/etc/vfstab when installing files. This is primarily useful on a server installing software for a client, where the client's /etc/vfstab file is not available or is incorrect.

ftype

The *ftype* value is a single character indicating the type of the file. The allowed values are:

b   A block-special device file.

c   A character-special device file.

d   A directory.

e   A file that will be edited on installation or removal.

f   A regular file (executable or data).

l   A linked file.

p   A named-pipe or FIFO.

s   A symbolic link.

v   A *volatile* file; one whose contents are expected to change over time.

x   An exclusive directory.

---

pkgadd

```
/usr/sbin/pkgadd [options] [source-loc] [pkg-name]
/usr/sbin/pkgadd -s [source-loc] [pkg-name]
```

Install a package. By default, `pkgadd` looks in `/var/spool/pkg` for installable package files; this can be changed with the `-d` option. The `-s` option may be used to write a package from installation media to the spool directory instead of installing it.

Options

`-a` *adminfile*
: Use *adminfile* as the installation administration file, instead of the system default file (`/var/sadm/install/admin/default`). This file specifies policies for installation in terms of user interaction, how many instances of a package may be installed, and so on.

`-d` *device*
: Use *device* as the source for the package to be installed or copied.

`-G`
: Install the package only in the current zone. If installed in the global zone, the package is not propogated to any nonglobal zones.

`-k` *keystore*
: Use *keystore* as the source for trusted certificate authority certificates.

`-M`
: Do not use `$root_path/etc/vfstab` for determining a client's mount points. Rather, assume that the mount points are correct on the server.

`-n`
: Do a noninteractive installation. This suppresses the output list of installed files.

`-P` *password*
: Use *password* to decrypt the *keystore* provided with `-k`.

`-r` *response-file*
: The full pathname *response-file* provides the output of `pkgask`. Use the contents to provide the responses to questions that `pkgadd` would otherwise ask interactively. See **pkgask**.

`-R` *root-path*
: Install all files under *root-path*. This is used on server systems when installing packages for clients.

`-s` *spooldir*
: Write the package to *spooldir* instead of installing it.

`-v`
: Verbose: trace execution of all scripts run by `pkgadd`.

`-V` *vfstab-file*
: Use *vfstab-file* instead of `$root_path/etc/vfstab` when installing packages. This is primarily useful on a server installing software for a client, where the client's `/etc/vfstab` file is not available or is incorrect.

`-x` *host*`:`*port*
: Use an HTTP or HTTPS proxy on host *host* at port number *port*.

Sources

The *sources* parameter is either the name of a package, in which case `pkgadd` searches for the package in `/var/spool/pkg`, or a device (such as a floppy disk or CD-ROM) specified with the `-d` option.

Instances

The *instances* parameter specifies which instances of the named packages should be installed, as follows:

`all`
: Install all packages on the given source media.

pkg-name, *pkg-name*`.*`
: Install just the named package. With the suffix `.*`, all instances of the named package are installed.

`-Y` *category*`[,`*category* ...`]`
: Install packages whose `CATEGORY` parameter in the package's `pkginfo` file matches one of the given categories.

---

pkgadm

```
pkgadm addcert [options] certfile
pkgadm removecert -n name [options]
pkgadm listcert -n name [options]
pkgadm dbstatus [-R rootpath]
pkgadm -V | -?
```

The `pkgadm` command manages the Solaris packaging system. The first argument is a command indicating what it should do, with options controlling the behavior. The *certfile* is a file containing the certificate and optionally, the private key for adding to the database.

Commands

`addcert`
: Import a certificate into the database. Optionally, specify the trust of the certificate.

`dbstatus`
: Print the type of internal database used for managing packages. The current version always prints `text`, but this could change in future Solaris releases.

`listcert`
: Print the details of one or more certificates in the keystore.

`removecert`
: Remove either a certificate/private key pair, or a trusted certificate authority certificate from the keystore. Once removed, they cannot be used.

Options

`-a` *`application`*
: Use the keystore for *application* instead of the global keystore.

`-e` *`keyfile`*
: Obtain the private key for a non-trusted certificate/key combination from *keyfile* instead of from the file containing the certificate.

`-f` *`format`*
: Use *format* for reading or printing keys. Allowed values for input and output are `pem` for PEM encoding and `der` for DER encoding. Output also allows `text` format for human-readable output.

`-k` *`keystore`*
: Use *keystore* as the keystore instead of the system default keystore.

`-n` *`name`*
: Specify the name of the entity in the keystore on which the operation is being performed (key removed, deleted, etc.). When printing, if this option isn't supplied, all keystore entities are printed.

`-o` *`file`*
: Send output to *file* instead of to standard output. Used when printing certificates.

`-p` *`method`*
: Use the password retrieval method *method* for decrypting the certificate or private key. The *method* is one of those listed in *pkgadd*(1); the default is `console`.

`-P` *`method`*
: Like `-p` but for decrypting the keystore.

`-R` *`rootpath`*
: Use *`rootpath`*`/var/sadm/security` to store keys and certificates instead of the default `$HOME/.pkg`. You must have sufficient permissions to access this directory.

-t The certificate being imported is a trusted CA certificate. pkgadm asks you to verify the details in the certificate; this step can be skipped with -y.

-V Print version information for the package management programs.

-y Do not bother verifying the details in a certificate being imported as a trusted certificate with -t.

-? Print a help message.

pkgask

`/usr/sbin/pkgask [-d device] [-R root-path] -r response pkginst ...`

This command creates response files for use with pkgadd. By producing "canned" responses for otherwise interactive installations, it's possible to install packages without requiring any interaction.

Options

-d *device*
: Use *device* as the source for the package to be installed or copied.

-r *response-file*
: The full pathname *response-file* for the output of pkgask. The argument may be a directory, in which case the response files for multiple packages are placed there, each one named according to the corresponding package.

-R *root-path*
: Install all files under *root-path*. This is used on server systems when installing packages for clients.

pkgchk

`/usr/sbin/pkgchk [-d device] [options] pkginst`

pkgchk checks the integrity of installed packages by comparing the information in the package file to what is actually on the system. With the -d option, it checks the packages on a particular device but cannot check the file attributes of the packages therein. The *pkginst* is a package name, possibly followed by .* to indicate all instances of the package.

Options

-a Check file attributes only, do not check file contents.

-c Check file contents only, do not check file attributes.

-d *device*
: Use *device* as the source for the package to be checked.

-e *file*
: Resolve parameters in the given package map file using information in the environment file *file*.

-f Correct file attributes. With -x, remove hidden files.

-i *file*
: Read pathnames from *file* and compare the list against the installation database or against the given package map file.

-l
: List information on the files that make up a package. May not be used with -a, -c, -f, -g, or -v.

-m *pkg-map-file*
: Check the package against *pkg-map-file* which is a package map file (see *pkgmap*(4)).

-M
: Do not use $root_path/etc/vfstab for determining a client's mount points. Rather, assume that the mount points are correct on the server.

-n
: Do not check files that are editable or are likely to change during normal operation. Intended for post-installation checking.

-p *path*
: Check only the *path* listed. You can check multiple paths by separating pathnames with a comma, or quoting the list and separating them with spaces.

-P *partial-path*
: Like -p, but checks the *partial-path* (a portion of a path, such as a file or directory name) instead of requiring a full path. It matches any pathname containing the *partial-path*.

-q
: Quiet mode. Do not print messages about missing files.

-R *root-path*
: Check all files under *root-path*. This is used on server systems when checking packages for clients.

-v
: Verbose: list files as they are processed.

-V *vfstab-file*
: Use *vfstab-file* instead of $root_path/etc/vfstab when checking packages. This is primarily useful on a server checking software for a client, where the client's /etc/vfstab file is not available or is incorrect.

-x
: Search exclusive directories, looking for files which exist but are not in the database of installed packages or in the package map file.

-Y *category*[,*category* ...]
: Check packages whose CATEGORY parameter in the package's pkginfo file matches one of the given categories.

---

pkginfo

pkginfo [*options*] [*pkginst* ...]

With no options, display the primary category, package instance and names of all installed packages. With -d, provide information about the packages on the given device. With one or more *pkginsts*, print information about the named packages.

The *pkginst* may be a package name, optionally followed by a period and a version number to restrict it to a particular instance. Use `.*` to specify all instances.

Options

Options `-l`, `-q` and `-x` are mutually exclusive, and `-p` and `-i` have no meaning if used with `-d`.

`-a` *arch*
: Use *arch* for the package's architecture.

`-c` *category*[,*category* ...]
: Provide information about packages whose `CATEGORY` parameter in the package's `pkginfo` file matches one of the given categories.

`-d` *device*
: Use *device* as the source for the package(s) to be described.

`-i` Display information only about fully installed packages.

`-l` Use long format output, which prints all available information.

`-p` Display information only about partially installed packages.

`-q` Quiet mode: do not display any information. Useful for scripts which need to check if a package has been installed.

`-r` Print the installation base for relocatable packages.

`-R` *root-path*
: Print information about all files under *root-path*. This is used on server systems when working with packages for clients.

`-v` *version*
: Use *version* as the package version (corresponding to the `VERSION` parameter in the `pkginfo` file). All compatible versions can be requested by prefixing *version* with a ~ character.

`-x` Print an "extracted" listing, giving the package abbreviation, the name, the architecture (if available), and the version (if available).

pkgmk

`pkgmk [`*options*`] [`*variable=value ...*`] [`*package-name*`]`

`pkgmk` reads a package prototype file (see *prototype*(4)) and creates a package installable with `pkgadd`. It also creates the corresponding package map file (see *pkgmap*(4)). Prototype files are most easily created with `pkgproto` (see **pkgproto**).

variable=value places *variable* in the packaging environment with the given *value*. See *prototype*(4) for more information.

The *package-name* is a package name, optionally followed by a period and a version number to restrict it to a particular instance. Use `.*` to specify all instances.

`pkgmk` uses an elaborate algorithm for finding files to put in the package: see the *pkgmk*(1) manpage for the details.

Options

-a *arch*
: Use *arch* as the architecture, overriding what's provided in the pkginfo file.

-b *base-dir*
: Search under *base-dir* for objects named in the prototype file.

-d *device*
: Use *device* as the destination for the package being built.

-f *file*
: Use *file* as the prototype file. The default is to use a file named Prototype or prototype.

-l *max*
: Use *max* as the maximum size of the output device. The value is in units of 512-byte blocks. Normally pkgmk uses df to determine if enough space is available.

-o
: Overwrite the same instance of the package if it already exists.

-p *stamp*
: Use *stamp* instead of the stamp definition in the pkginfo file.

-r *root-path*
: Find files to be included in the package under *root-path*.

-v *version*
: Use *version* as the version instead of what's in the pkginfo file.

pkgparam

```
pkgparam [options] pkginst [param ...]
pkgparam -f filename [-v] [param ...]
```

pkgparam prints the values of the given parameters for the named packages. With no parameters, it prints the values of all parameters. By default it looks in the pkginfo file for the package, but the -f option restricts pkgparam to looking in the named file. *pkginst* is the package for which information should be printed.

Options

-d *device*
: Use *device* as the source for the package to be processed.

-f *file*
: Read parameter values from *file* instead of from the pkginfo file.

-R *root-path*
: Process all files under *root-path*. This is used on server systems when working with packages for clients.

-v
: Verbose mode. Display the parameter name and value, instead of just the value.

pkgproto

```
pkgproto [-i] [-c class] [path1[=path2] ...]
```

pkgproto builds the prototype file for use with pkgmk. With no directories on the command line, it reads a list of pathnames from standard input to process. Otherwise, it processes the directories named on the command line. *path1* is where objects are located on the system building the package. *path2* indicates where the file should be placed on systems where the package is installed, if that location is different.

Options

-c *class*
: Map the class of all objects to *class*.

-i
: Follow symbolic links, recording them as regular files (ftype=f), instead of as links (ftype=s).

pkgrm

```
/usr/sbin/pkgrm [options] [instances]
/usr/sbin/pkgrm -s spool [instances]
```

pkgrm removes installed packages. If some other package depends upon a package being removed, the action taken will be what's defined in the admin file.

Options

-a *adminfile*
: Use *adminfile* as the removal administration file, instead of the system default file (/var/sadm/install/admin/default). This file specifies policies for installation and removal in terms of user interaction, how many instances of a package may be installed, and so on.

-A
: Absolutely remove the package's files from the client's filesystem. However, if the file is shared with other packages, the default is not to remove it.

-M
: Do not use $root_path/etc/vfstab for determining a client's mount points. Rather, assume that the mount points are correct on the server.

-n
: Do a non-interactive removal. If a need for interaction arises, pkgrm exits.

-R *root-path*
: Remove files from under *root-path*. This is used on server systems when removing packages for clients.

-s *spooldir*
: Remove the package from *spooldir* instead of from the system.

-v
: Verbose: trace execution of all scripts run by pkgrm.

-V *vfstab-file*
: Use *vfstab-file* instead of $root_path/etc/vfstab when removing packages. This is primarily useful on a server removing software for a client, where the client's /etc/vfstab file is not available or is incorrect.

Instances

The *instances* parameter specifies which instances of the named packages should be installed.

pkg-name, pkg-name`.*`
: Remove just the named package. With the suffix `.*`, all instances of the named package are removed.

`-Y` *category*`[,`*category* ...`]`
: Remove packages whose `CATEGORY` parameter in the packages `pkginfo` file matches one of the given categories.

---

removef

`/usr/sbin/removef [`*options*`]` *pkginst path* ...
`/usr/sbin/removef [`*options*`] -f` *pkginst*

`removef` updates the installation database with a list of pathnames that are about to be removed. The resulting output is a list of files that may be safely removed (i.e., for which there are no dependencies from other packages). This command is useful in scripts that are run when packages are removed; for example, removing device files created upon package installation.

Like `installf`, this command should be invoked twice; the first time before removing any files, and the second time, with the `-f` option, to indicate that the removal has indeed taken place. See also **installf**.

Options

`-f`
: Indicate that removal is complete (final).

`-M`
: Do not use `$root_path/etc/vfstab` for determining a client's mount points. Rather, assume that the mount points are correct on the server.

`-R` *root-path*
: Remove files from under *root-path*. This is used on server systems when installing packages for clients.

`-V` *vfstab-file*
: Use *vfstab-file* instead of `$root_path/etc/vfstab` when installing files. This is primarily useful on a server removing software for a client, where the client's `/etc/vfstab` file is not available or is incorrect.

Text Editing and Processing

Part II summarizes the command set for the text editors and related utilities in Unix. Chapter 7 reviews pattern matching, an important aspect of text editing.

II

Text Editing and Processing

Part II summarizes the command set for the text editors and related utilities in Unix. Chapter 7 reviews pattern matching, an important aspect of text editing.

- Chapter 7, Pattern Matching
- Chapter 8, The Emacs Editor
- Chapter 9, The vi, ex, and vim Editors
- Chapter 10, The sed Editor
- Chapter 11, The awk Programming Language

7

Pattern Matching

A number of Unix text-processing utilities let you search for, and in some cases change, text patterns rather than fixed strings. These utilities include the editing programs `ed`, `ex`, `vi`, and `sed`, the `awk` programming language, and the commands `grep` and `egrep`. Text patterns (called *regular expressions* in the computer science literature) contain normal characters mixed with special characters (called *metacharacters*).

This chapter presents the following topics:

- Filenames versus patterns
- Description of metacharacters
- List of metacharacters available to each program
- Examples

For more information on regular expressions, see *Mastering Regular Expressions*, listed in the Bibliography.

Filenames Versus Patterns

Metacharacters used in pattern matching are different from metacharacters used for filename expansion (see Chapter 4 and Chapter 5). However, several metacharacters have meaning for both regular expressions and for filename expansion. This can lead to a problem: the shell sees the command line first, and can potentially interpret an unquoted regular expression metacharacter as a filename expansion. For example, the command:

```
$ grep [A-Z]* chap[12]
```

could be transformed by the shell into:

```
$ grep Array.c Bug.c Comp.c chap1 chap2
```

and grep would then try to find the pattern Array.c in files Bug.c, Comp.c, chap1, and chap2. To bypass the shell and pass the special characters to grep, use quotes as follows:

```
$ grep "[A-Z]*" chap[12]
```

Double quotes suffice in most cases, but single quotes are the safest bet, since the shell does absolutely no expansions on single-quoted text.

Note also that in pattern matching, ? matches zero or one instance of a regular expression; in filename expansion, ? matches a single character.

Metacharacters

Different metacharacters have different meanings, depending upon where they are used. In particular, regular expressions used for searching through text (matching) have one set of metacharacters, while the metacharacters used when processing replacement text (such as in a text editor) have a different set. These sets also vary somewhat per program. This section covers the metacharacters used for searching and replacing, with descriptions of the variants in the different utilities.

Search Patterns

The characters in the following table have special meaning only in search patterns.

Character	Pattern
.	Match any *single* character except newline. Can match newline in awk.
*	Match any number (or none) of the single character that immediately precedes it. The preceding character can also be a regular expression. For example, since . (dot) means any character, .* means "match any number of any character."
^	Match the following regular expression at the beginning of the line or string.
$	Match the preceding regular expression at the end of the line or string.
[ ]	Match any *one* of the enclosed characters: a hyphen (-) indicates a range of consecutive characters. A circumflex (^) as the first character in the brackets reverses the sense: it matches any one character *not* in the list. A hyphen or close bracket (]) as the first character is treated as a member of the list. All other metacharacters are treated as members of the list (i.e., literally).
{*n*,*m*}	Match a range of occurrences of the single character that immediately precedes it. The preceding character can also be a regular expression. {*n*} matches exactly *n* occurrences, {*n*,} matches at least *n* occurrences, and {*n*,*m*} matches any number of occurrences between *n* and *m*. *n* and *m* must be between 0 and 255, inclusive. (GNU programs allow a range of 0 to 32,767.)
\{*n*,*m*\}	Just like {*n*,*m*}, earlier, but with backslashes in front of the braces. (Historically, different utilities used different syntaxes for the same thing.)
\	Turn off the special meaning of the following character.
\(\)	Save the subpattern enclosed between \(and \) into a special holding space. Up to nine subpatterns can be saved on a single line. The text matched by the subpatterns can be "replayed" in substitutions by the escape sequences \1 to \9.
n	Replay the *n*th subpattern enclosed in \(and \) into the pattern at this point. *n* is a number from 1 to 9, with 1 starting on the left. See the following Examples.
\< \>	Match characters at beginning (\<) or end (\>) of a word.

Character	Pattern
+	Match one or more instances of preceding regular expression.
?	Match zero or one instances of preceding regular expression.
|	Match the regular expression specified before or after the vertical bar (alternation).
( )	Apply a match to the enclosed group of regular expressions.

Many Unix systems allow the use of POSIX "character classes" within the square brackets that enclose a group of characters. They are typed enclosed in [: and :]. For example, [[:alnum:]] matches a single alphanumeric character.

Class	Characters matched	Class	Characters matched
alnum	Alphanumeric characters	lower	Lowercase characters
alpha	Alphabetic characters	print	Printable characters
blank	Space or TAB	punct	Punctuation characters
cntrl	Control characters	space	Whitespace characters
digit	Decimal digits	upper	Uppercase characters
graph	Non-space characters	xdigit	Hexadecimal digits

Finally, the GNU versions of the standard utilities accept additional escape sequences that act like metacharacters. (Because \b can also be interpreted as the sequence for the ASCII Backspace character, different utilities treat it differently. Check each utility's documentation.)

Sequence	Meaning
\b	Word boundary, either beginning or end of a word, as for the \< and \> metacharacters described earlier.
\B	Interword match; matches between two word-constituent characters.
\w	Matches any word-constituent character; equivalent to [[:alnum:]_].
\W	Matches any non-word-constituent character; equivalent to [^[:alnum:]_].
\`	Beginning of an Emacs buffer. Used by most other GNU utilities to mean unambiguously "beginning of string."
\'	End of an Emacs buffer. Used by most other GNU utilities to mean unambiguously "end of string."

Replacement Patterns

The characters in the following table have special meaning only in replacement patterns.

Character	Pattern
\	Turn off the special meaning of the following character.
\n	Reuse the text matched by the *n*th subpattern previously saved by \(and \) as part of the replacement pattern. *n* is a number from 1 to 9, with 1 starting on the left.
&	Reuse the text matched by the search pattern as part of the replacement pattern.

Character	Pattern
~	Reuse the previous replacement pattern in the current replacement pattern. Must be the only character in the replacement pattern (ex and vi).
%	Reuse the previous replacement pattern in the current replacement pattern. Must be the only character in the replacement pattern (ed).
\u	Convert first character of replacement pattern to uppercase.
\U	Convert entire replacement pattern to uppercase.
\l	Convert first character of replacement pattern to lowercase.
\L	Convert entire replacement pattern to lowercase.
\e	Turn off previous \u or \l.
\E	Turn off previous \U or \L.

Metacharacters, Listed by Unix Program

Some metacharacters are valid for one program but not for another. Those that are available are marked by a bullet (•) in Table 7-1. (This table is correct for most commercial Unix systems, including Solaris.) Items marked with a "P" are specified by POSIX; double-check your system's version. (On Solaris, the versions in `/usr/xpg4/bin` and `/usr/xpg6/bin` accept these items.) Full descriptions were provided in the previous section.

Table 7-1. Unix metacharacters

Symbol	ed	ex	vi	sed	awk	grep	egrep	Action
.	•	•	•	•	•	•	•	Match any character.
*	•	•	•	•	•	•	•	Match zero or more preceding.
^	•	•	•	•	•	•	•	Match beginning of line/string.
$	•	•	•	•	•	•	•	Match end of line/string.
\	•	•	•	•	•	•	•	Escape following character.
[ ]	•	•	•	•	•	•	•	Match one from a set.
\(\)	•	•	•	•		•		Store pattern for later replay.[a]
\n	•	•	•	•		•		Replay subpattern in match.
{ }					• P		• P	Match a range of instances.
\{ \}	•			•		•		Match a range of instances.
\< \>	•	•	•					Match word's beginning or end.
+					•		•	Match one or more preceding.
?					•		•	Match zero or one preceding.
|					•		•	Separate choices to match.
( )					•		•	Group expressions to match.

[a] Stored subpatterns can be "replayed" during matching. See Table 7-2.

Note that in ed, ex, vi, and sed, you specify both a search pattern (on the left) and a replacement pattern (on the right). The metacharacters in Table 7-1 are meaningful only in a search pattern.

In ed, ex, vi, and sed, the metacharacters in Table 7-2 are valid only in a replacement pattern.

Table 7-2. Metacharacters in replacement patterns

Symbol	ex	vi	sed	ed	Action
\	•	•	•	•	Escape following character.
\n	•	•	•	•	Text matching pattern stored in \(\).
&	•	•	•	•	Text matching search pattern.
~	•	•			Reuse previous replacement pattern.
%				•	Reuse previous replacement pattern.
\u \U	•	•			Change character(s) to uppercase.
\l \L	•	•			Change character(s) to lowercase.
\e	•	•			Turn off previous \u or \l.
\E	•	•			Turn off previous \U or \L.

Examples of Searching

When used with grep or egrep, regular expressions should be surrounded by quotes. (If the pattern contains a $, you must use single quotes; e.g., '*pattern*'.) When used with ed, ex, sed, and awk, regular expressions are usually surrounded by /, although (except for awk) any delimiter works. The following tables show some example patterns.

Pattern	What does it match?
bag	The string *bag*.
^bag	*bag* at the beginning of the line.
bag$	*bag* at the end of the line.
^bag$	*bag* as the only word on the line.
[Bb]ag	*Bag* or *bag*.
b[aeiou]g	Second letter is a vowel.
b[^aeiou]g	Second letter is a consonant (or uppercase or symbol).
b.g	Second letter is any character.
^...$	Any line containing exactly three characters.
^\.	Any line that begins with a dot.
^\.[a-z][a-z]	Same, followed by two lowercase letters (e.g., troff requests).
^\.[a-z]\{2\}	Same as previous, ed, grep, and sed only.
^[^.]	Any line that doesn't begin with a dot.
bugs*	*bug*, *bugs*, *bugss*, etc.
"word"	A word in quotes.
"*word"*	A word, with or without quotes.
[A-Z][A-Z]*	One or more uppercase letters.
[A-Z]+	Same; egrep or awk only.

Pattern	What does it match?
`[[:upper:]]+`	Same as previous, POSIX `egrep` or `awk`.
`[A-Z].*`	An uppercase letter, followed by zero or more characters.
`[A-Z]*`	Zero or more uppercase letters.
`[a-zA-Z]`	Any letter, either lower- or uppercase.
`[^0-9A-Za-z]`	Any symbol or space (not a letter or a number).
`[^[:alnum:]]`	Same, using POSIX character class.

<table>
<tr><th>egrep or awk pattern</th><th>What does it match?</th></tr>
<tr><td><code>[567]</code></td><td>One of the numbers 5, 6, or 7.</td></tr>
<tr><td><code>five|six|seven</code></td><td>One of the words five, six, or seven.</td></tr>
<tr><td><code>80[2-4]?86</code></td><td>8086, 80286, 80386, or 80486.</td></tr>
<tr><td><code>80[2-4]?86|(Pentium(-III?)?)</code></td><td>8086, 80286, 80386, 80486, Pentium, Pentium-II, or Pentium-III.</td></tr>
<tr><td><code>compan(y|ies)</code></td><td>company or companies.</td></tr>
</table>

ex or vi pattern	What does it match?
`\<the`	Words like *theater* or *the*.
`the\>`	Words like *breathe* or *the*.
`\<the\>`	The word *the*.

ed, sed, or grep pattern	What does it match?
`0\{5,\}`	Five or more zeros in a row.
`[0-9]\{3\}-[0-9]\{2\}-[0-9]\{4\}`	U.S. Social Security number (*nnn-nn-nnnn*).
`\(why\).*\1`	A line with two occurrences of *why*.
`\([[:alpha:]_][[:alnum:]_.]*\) = \1;`	C/C++ simple assignment statements.

Examples of Searching and Replacing

The examples in Table 7-3 show the metacharacters available to `sed` or `ex`. Note that `ex` commands begin with a colon. A space is marked by a ❑; a TAB is marked by a ➔.

Table 7-3. Searching and replacing

Command	Result
`s/.*/( & )/`	Redo the entire line, but add spaces and parentheses.
`s/.*/mv & &.old/`	Change a wordlist (one word per line) into `mv` commands.
`/^$/d`	Delete blank lines.
`:g/^$/d`	Same as previous, in ex editor.
`/^[❑➔]*$/d`	Delete blank lines, plus lines containing only spaces or TABs.
`:g/^[❑➔]*$/d`	Same as previous, in ex editor.

Table 7-3. Searching and replacing (continued)

Command	Result
`s/❑❑*/❑/g`	Turn one or more spaces into one space.
`:%s/❑❑*/❑/g`	Same as previous, in ex editor.
`:s/[0-9]/Item &:/`	Turn a number into an item label (on the current line).
`:s`	Repeat the substitution on the first occurrence.
`:&`	Same as previous.
`:sg`	Same as previous, but for all occurrences on the line.
`:&g`	Same as previous.
`:%&g`	Repeat the substitution globally (i.e., on all lines).
`:.,$s/Fortran/\U&/g`	On current line to last line, change word to uppercase.
`:.,$s/\(F\)\(ORTRAN\)/\1\L\2/g`	On current line to last line, change spelling of "FORTRAN" to correct, modern usage.
`:%s/.*/\L&/`	Lowercase entire file.
`:s/\<./\u&/g`	Uppercase first letter of each word on current line. (Useful for titles.)
`:%s/yes/No/g`	Globally change a word to *No*.
`:%s/Yes/~/g`	Globally change a different word to *No* (previous replacement).

Finally, here are some sed examples for transposing words. A simple transposition of two words might look like this:

`s/die or do/do or die/` *Transpose words*

The real trick is to use hold buffers to transpose variable patterns. For example:

`s/\([Dd]ie\) or \([Dd]o\)/\2 or \1/` *Transpose, using hold buffers*

8
The Emacs Editor

Although most commercial operating systems do not come with Emacs, it is available for all versions of Unix, including Mac OS X, and MS-Windows. (GNU/Linux systems usually do supply it.) On all these systems, there are often multiple versions: one for character terminals, another for X11, and possibly yet another for the native windowing system. This text editor is a popular alternative to `vi`. This chapter documents GNU Emacs (Version 21.3), which is available from the Free Software Foundation (*http://www.gnu.org/software/emacs*).

This chapter presents the following topics:

- Conceptual overview
- Command-line syntax
- Summary of `emacs` commands by group
- Summary of `emacs` commands by key
- Summary of `emacs` commands by name

For more information about `emacs`, see *Learning GNU Emacs*, listed in the Bibliography.

Conceptual Overview

This section describes some Emacs terminology that may be unfamiliar if you haven't used Emacs before.

Modes

One of the features that makes Emacs popular is its editing modes. The modes set up an environment designed for the type of editing you are doing, with features like having appropriate key bindings available, and automatically indenting according to standard conventions for a particular type of document. There are two types of modes, major and minor. The major modes include modes for various programming languages like C or Java, for text processing (e.g., SGML or even straight text), and many more. One particularly useful major mode is Dired (Directory Editor), which has commands that let you manage directories. Minor modes set or unset features that are independent of the major mode, such as auto-fill (which controls line wrapping), insert versus overwrite, and auto-save. For a full discussion of modes, see *Learning GNU Emacs* or the Emacs Info documentation system (`C-h i`).

Buffer and Window

When you open a file in Emacs, the file is put into a *buffer* so you can edit it. If you open another file, that file goes into another buffer. The view of the buffer contents that you have at any point in time is called a *window*. For a small file, the window might show the entire file; for a large file, it shows only a portion of a file. Emacs allows multiple windows to be open at the same time, to display the contents of different buffers or different portions of a single buffer.

Point and Mark

When you are editing in Emacs, the position of the cursor is known as *point*. You can set a *mark* at another place in the text to operate on the region between point and mark. This is a very useful feature for such operations as deleting or moving an area of text.

Kill and Yank

Emacs uses the terms *kill* and *yank* for the concepts more commonly known today as *cut* and *paste*. You cut text in Emacs by killing it, and paste it by yanking it back. If you do multiple kills in a row, you can yank them back all at once.

Emacs can store any number of deleted chunks up to a user-settable maximum. In addition, it has powerful Undo and Redo facilities, letting you undo all the changes back to the last time your file was saved.

Notes on the Tables

Emacs commands use the Control key and the Meta key (Meta is usually the Alt key or the Escape key). In this chapter, the notation `C-` indicates that the Control key is pressed at the same time as the character that follows. Similarly, `M-` indicates the use of the Meta key. When using Escape for Meta, press and release the Escape key, then type the next key. If you use Alt (or Option on the Macintosh) for Meta, it is just like Control or Shift, and you should press it simultaneously with the other key(s).

In the command tables that follow, the first column lists the keystroke and the last column describes it. When there is a middle column, it lists the command name. If there are no keystrokes for a given command, you'll see `(none)` in the first column. Access these commands by typing M-x followed by the command name. If you're unsure of the name, you can type a tab or a carriage return, and Emacs lists possible completions of what you've typed so far.

Because Emacs is such a comprehensive editor, containing literally thousands of commands, some commands must be omitted for the sake of preserving a "quick" reference. You can browse the command set by typing C-h (for help) or M-x Tab (for command names).

Absolutely Essential Commands

If you're just getting started with Emacs, here's a short list of the most important commands:

Keystrokes	Description
C-h	Enter the online help system.
C-x C-s	Save the file.
C-x C-c	Exit emacs.
C-_	Undo last edit (can be repeated).
C-g	Get out of current command operation.
C-p C-n C-f C-b	Up/down/forward/back by line or character.
C-v M-v	Forward/backward by one screen.
C-s C-r	Search forward/backward for characters.
C-d Del	Delete next/previous character.

Command-Line Syntax

To start an Emacs editing session, type:

```
emacs [file]
```

Emacs

Summary of Commands by Group

Reminder: `C-` indicates the Control key; `M-` indicates the Meta key.

File-Handling Commands

Keystrokes	Command name	Description
C-x C-f	find-file	Find file and read it.
C-x C-v	find-alternate-file	Read another file; replace the one read with C-x C-f.
C-x i	insert-file	Insert file at cursor position.
C-x C-s	save-buffer	Save file (may hang terminal; use C-q to restart).
C-x C-w	write-file	Write buffer contents to file.
C-x C-c	save-buffers-kill-emacs	Exit `emacs`.
C-z	suspend-emacs	Suspend `emacs` (use `exit` or `fg` to restart).

Cursor-Movement Commands

Keystrokes	Command name	Description
C-f	forward-char	Move *forward* one character (right).
C-b	backward-char	Move *backward* one character (left).
C-p	previous-line	Move to *previous* line (up).
C-n	next-line	Move to *next* line (down).
M-f	forward-word	Move one word *forward*.
M-b	backward-word	Move one word *backward*.
C-a	beginning-of-line	Move to beginning of line.
C-e	end-of-line	Move to *end* of line.
M-a	backward-sentence	Move backward one sentence.
M-e	forward-sentence	Move forward one sentence.
M-{	backward-paragraph	Move backward one paragraph.
M-}	forward-paragraph	Move forward one paragraph.
C-v	scroll-up	Move forward one screen.
M-v	scroll-down	Move backward one screen.
C-x [	backward-page	Move backward one page.
C-x]	forward-page	Move forward one page.
M->	end-of-buffer	Move to end of file.
M-<	beginning-of-buffer	Move to beginning of file.
(none)	goto-line	Go to line *n* of file.
(none)	goto-char	Go to character *n* of file.
C-l	recenter	Redraw screen with current line in the center.
M-*n*	digit-argument	Repeat the next command *n* times.
C-u *n*	universal-argument	Repeat the next command *n* times.

Deletion Commands

Keystrokes	Command name	Description
Del	backward-delete-char	Delete previous character.
C-d	delete-char	Delete character under cursor.
M-Del	backward-kill-word	Delete from point to beginning of word.
M-d	kill-word	Delete from point to end of word.
C-k	kill-line	Delete from cursor to end of line.
M-k	kill-sentence	Delete from point to end of sentence.
C-x Del	backward-kill-sentence	Delete from point to beginning of sentence.
C-y	yank	Restore what you've deleted.
C-w	kill-region	Delete a marked region (see next section).
(none)	backward-kill-paragraph	Delete previous paragraph.
(none)	kill-paragraph	Delete from the cursor to the end of the paragraph.

Paragraphs and Regions

Keystrokes	Command name	Description
C-@	set-mark-command	Mark the beginning (or end) of a region.
C-Space	(same as above)	
C-x C-p	mark-page	Mark page.
C-x C-x	exchange-point-and-mark	Exchange location of cursor and mark.
C-x h	mark-whole-buffer	Mark buffer.
M-q	fill-paragraph	Reformat paragraph.
(none)	fill-region	Reformat individual paragraphs within a region.
M-h	mark-paragraph	Mark paragraph.

Stopping and Undoing Commands

Keystrokes	Command name	Description
C-g	keyboard-quit	Abort current command.
C-_	advertised-undo	Undo last edit (can be done repeatedly).
(none)	revert-buffer	Restore buffer to the state it was in when the file was last saved (or auto-saved).

Transposition Commands

Keystrokes	Command name	Description
C-t	transpose-chars	Transpose two letters.
M-t	transpose-words	Transpose two words.
C-x C-t	transpose-lines	Transpose two lines.

Keystrokes	Command name	Description
(none)	transpose-sentences	Transpose two sentences.
(none)	transpose-paragraphs	Transpose two paragraphs.

Search Commands

Keystrokes	Command name	Description
C-s	isearch-forward	Incremental search forward.
C-r	isearch-backward	Incremental search backward
M-%	query-replace	Search and replace.
C-M-s Enter	re-search-forward	Regular expression search forward.
C-M-r Enter	re-search-backward	Regular expression search backward

Capitalization Commands

Keystrokes	Command name	Description
M-c	capitalize-word	Capitalize first letter of word.
M-u	upcase-word	Uppercase word.
M-l	downcase-word	Lowercase word.
M-– M-c	negative-argument; capitalize-word	Capitalize previous word.
M-– M-u	negative-argument; upcase-word	Uppercase previous word.
M-– M-l	negative-argument; downcase-word	Lowercase previous word.
(none)	capitalize-region	Capitalize region.
C-x C-u	upcase-region	Uppercase region
C-x C-l	downcase-region	Lowercase region.

Word-Abbreviation Commands

Keystrokes	Command name	Description
(none)	abbrev-mode	Enter (or exit) word abbreviation mode.
M-/	dabbrev-expand	Expand to the most recent preceding word.
C-x a i g	inverse-add-global-abbrev	Type global abbreviation, then definition.
C-x a i l	inverse-add-local-abbrev	Type local abbreviation, then definition.
(none)	unexpand-abbrev	Undo the last word abbreviation.
(none)	write-abbrev-file	Write the word abbreviation file.
(none)	edit-abbrevs	Edit the word abbreviations.
(none)	list-abbrevs	View the word abbreviations.
(none)	kill-all-abbrevs	Kill abbreviations for this session.

Buffer-Manipulation Commands

Keystrokes	Command name	Description
C-x b	switch-to-buffer	Move to specified buffer.
C-x C-b	list-buffers	Display buffer list.
C-x k	kill-buffer	Delete specified buffer.
(none)	kill-some-buffers	Ask about deleting each buffer.
(none)	rename-buffer	Change buffer name to specified name.
C-x s	save-some-buffers	Ask whether to save each modified buffer.

Window Commands

Keystrokes	Command name	Description
C-x 2	split-window-vertically	Divide the current window into two, one on top of the other.
C-x 3	split-window-horizontally	Divide the current window into two, side by side.
C-x >	scroll-right	Scroll the window right.
C-x <	scroll-left	Scroll the window left.
C-x o	other-window	Move to the other window.
C-x 0	delete-window	Delete current window.
C-x 1	delete-other-windows	Delete all windows but this one.
(none)	delete-windows-on	Delete all windows on a given buffer.
C-x ^	enlarge-window	Make window taller.
(none)	shrink-window	Make window shorter.
C-x }	enlarge-window-horizontally	Make window wider.
C-x {	shrink-window-horizontally	Make window narrower.
C-M-v	scroll-other-window	Scroll other window.
C-x 4 f	find-file-other-window	Find a file in the other window.
C-x 4 b	switch-to-buffer-other-window	Select a buffer in the other window.
C-x 5 f	find-file-other-frame	Find a file in a new frame.
C-x 5 b	switch-to-buffer-other-frame	Select a buffer in another frame.
(none)	compare-windows	Compare two buffers; show first difference.

Special Shell Characters

Keystrokes	Command name	Description
(none)	shell	Start a shell buffer.
C-c C-c	comint-interrupt-subjob	Terminate the current job.
C-c C-d	comint-send-eof	End of file character.

Keystrokes	Command name	Description
C-c C-u	comint-kill-inputw	Erase current line.
C-c C-w	backward-kill-word	Erase the previous word.
C-c C-z	comint-stop-subjob	Suspend the current job.

Indentation Commands

Keystrokes	Command name	Description
C-x .	set-fill-prefix	Use characters from the beginning of the line up to the cursor column as the "fill prefix." This prefix is prepended to each line in the paragraph. Cancel the prefix by typing this command in column 1.
(none)	indented-text-mode	Major mode: each tab defines a new indent for subsequent lines.
(none)	text-mode	Exit indented text mode; return to text mode.
C-M-\	indent-region	Indent a region to match first line in region.
M-m	back-to-indentation	Move cursor to first character on line.
C-M-o	split-line	Split line at cursor; indent to column of cursor.
(none)	fill-individual-paragraphs	Reformat indented paragraphs, keeping indentation.

Centering Commands

Keystrokes	Command name	Description
M-s	center-line	Center line that cursor is on.
(none)	center-paragraph	Center paragraph that cursor is on.
(none)	center-region	Center currently defined region.

Macro Commands

Keystrokes	Command name	Description
C-x (	start-kbd-macro	Start macro definition.
C-x)	end-kbd-macro	End macro definition.
C-x e	call-last-kbd-macro	Execute last macro defined.
M-*n* C-x e	digit-argument and call-last-kbd-macro	Execute last macro defined *n* times.
C-u C-x (	universal-argument and start-kbd-macro	Execute last macro defined, then add keystrokes.
(none)	name-last-kbd-macro	Name last macro you created (before saving it).
(none)	insert-keyboard-macro	Insert the macro you named into a file.
(none)	load-file	Load macro files you've saved and loaded.
(none)	*macroname*	Execute a keyboard macro you've saved.

Keystrokes	Command name	Description
C-x q	kbd-macro-query	Insert a query in a macro definition.
C-u C-x q	(none)	Insert a recursive edit in a macro definition.
C-M-c	exit-recursive-edit	Exit a recursive edit.

Basic Indentation Commands

Keystrokes	Command name	Description
C-M-\	indent-region	Indent a region to match first line in region.
M-m	back-to-indentation	Move to first nonblank character on line.
M-^	delete-indentation	Join this line to the previous one.

Detail Information Help Commands

Keystrokes	Command name	Description
C-h a	command-apropos	What commands involve this concept?
(none)	apropos	What functions and variables involve this concept?
C-h c	describe-key-briefly	What command does this keystroke sequence run?
C-h b	describe-bindings	What are all the key bindings for this buffer?
C-h k	describe-key	What command does this keystroke sequence run, and what does it do?
C-h l	view-lossage	What are the last 100 characters I typed?
C-h w	where-is	What is the key binding for this command?
C-h f	describe-function	What does this function do?
C-h v	describe-variable	What does this variable mean, and what is its value?
C-h m	describe-mode	Tell me about the mode the current buffer is in.
C-h s	describe-syntax	What is the syntax table for this buffer?

Help Commands

Keystrokes	Command name	Description
C-h t	help-with-tutorial	Run the `emacs` tutorial.
C-h i	info	Start the Info documentation reader.
C-h n	view-emacs-news	View news about updates to `emacs`.
C-h C-c	describe-copying	View the `emacs` General Public License.
C-h C-d	describe-distribution	View information on ordering `emacs` from the FSF.
C-h C-w	describe-no-warranty	View the (non)warranty for `emacs`.

Summary of Commands by Key

Emacs commands are presented below in two alphabetical lists. Reminder: C-indicates the Control key; M- indicates the Meta key.

Control-Key Sequences

Keystrokes	Command name	Description
C-@	set-mark-command	Mark the beginning (or end) of a region.
C-Space	(same as previous)	
C-]	(none)	Exit recursive edit and exit query-replace.
C-a	beginning-of-line	Move to beginning of line.
C-b	backward-char	Move *backward* one character (left).
C-c C-c	comint-interrupt-subjob	Terminate the current job.
C-c C-d	comint-send-eof	End-of-file character.
C-c C-u	comint-kill-input	Erase current line.
C-c C-w	backward-kill-word	Erase the previous word.
C-c C-z	comint-stop-subjob	Suspend the current job.
C-d	delete-char	Delete character under cursor.
C-e	end-of-line	Move to *end* of line.
C-f	forward-char	Move *forward* one character (right).
C-g	keyboard-quit	Abort current command.
C-h	help-command	Enter the online help system.
C-h a	command-apropos	What commands involve this concept?
C-h b	describe-bindings	What are all the key bindings for this buffer?
C-h C-c	describe-copying	View the emacs General Public License.
C-h C-d	describe-distribution	View information on ordering emacs from FSF.
C-h C-w	describe-no-warranty	View the (non-)warranty for emacs.
C-h c	describe-key-briefly	What command does this keystroke sequence run?
C-h f	describe-function	What does this function do?
C-h i	info	Start the Info documentation reader.
C-h k	describe-key	What command does this keystroke sequence run, and what does it do?
C-h l	view-lossage	What are the last 100 characters I typed?
C-h m	describe-mode	Tell me about the mode the current buffer is in.
C-h n	view-emacs-news	View news about updates to emacs.
C-h s	describe-syntax	What is the syntax table for this buffer?
C-h t	help-with-tutorial	Run the emacs tutorial.
C-h v	describe-variable	What does this variable mean, and what is its value?
C-h w	where-is	What is the key binding for this command?
C-k	kill-line	Delete from cursor to end of line.

Keystrokes	Command name	Description
C-l	recenter	Redraw screen with current line in the center.
C-M-\	indent-region	Indent a region to match first line in region.
C-M-c	exit-recursive-edit	Exit a recursive edit.
C-M-o	split-line	Split line at cursor; indent to column of cursor.
C-M-v	scroll-other-window	Scroll other window.
C-n	next-line	Move to *next* line (down).
C-p	previous-line	Move to *previous* line (up).
C-r	isearch-backward	Start incremental search backward.
C-s	isearch-forward	Start incremental search forward.
C-t	transpose-chars	Transpose two letters.
C-u *n*	universal-argument	Repeat the next command *n* times.
C-u C-x (	universal-argument and start-kbd-macro	Execute last macro defined, then add keystrokes.
C-u C-x q	(none)	Insert recursive edit in a macro definition.
C-v	scroll-up	Move forward one screen.
C-w	kill-region	Delete a marked region.
C-x (	start-kbd-macro	Start macro definition.
C-x)	end-kbd-macro	End macro definition.
C-x [	backward-page	Move backward one page.
C-x]	forward-page	Move forward one page.
C-x ^	enlarge-window	Make window taller.
C-x {	shrink-window-horizontally	Make window narrower.
C-x }	enlarge-window-horizontally	Make window wider.
C-x <	scroll-left	Scroll the window left.
C-x >	scroll-right	Scroll the window right.
C-x .	set-fill-prefix	Use characters from the beginning of the line up to the cursor column as the "fill prefix." This prefix is prepended to each line in the paragraph. Cancel the prefix by typing this command in column 1.
C-x 0	delete-window	Delete current window.
C-x 1	delete-other-windows	Delete all windows but this one.
C-x 2	split-window-vertically	Divide the current window into two, one on top of the other.
C-x 3	split-window-horizontally	Divide the current window into two, side by side.
C-x 4 b	switch-to-buffer-other-window	Select a buffer in the other window.
C-x 4 f	find-file-other-window	Find a file in the other window.
C-x 5 b	switch-to-buffer-other-frame	Select a buffer in another frame.
C-x 5 f	find-file-other-frame	Find a file in a new frame.
C-x C-b	list-buffers	Display the buffer list.

Keystrokes	Command name	Description
C-x C-c	save-buffers-kill-emacs	Exit `emacs`.
C-x C-f	find-file	Find file and read it.
C-x C-l	downcase-region	Lowercase region.
C-x C-p	mark-page	Mark page.
C-x C-q	(none)	Toggle read-only status of buffer.
C-x C-s	save-buffer	Save file (may hang terminal; use C-q to restart).
C-x C-t	transpose-lines	Transpose two lines.
C-x C-u	upcase-region	Uppercase region
C-x C-v	find-alternate-file	Read an alternate file, replacing the one read with C-x C-f.
C-x C-w	write-file	Write buffer contents to file.
C-x C-x	exchange-point-and-mark	Exchange location of cursor and mark.
C-x DEL	backward-kill-sentence	Delete previous sentence.
C-x a i g	inverse-add-global-abbrev	Type global abbreviation, then definition.
C-x a i l	inverse-add-local-abbrev	Type local abbreviation, then definition.
C-x b	switch-to-buffer	Move to the buffer specified.
C-x e	call-last-kbd-macro	Execute last macro defined.
C-x h	mark-whole-buffer	Mark buffer.
C-x i	insert-file	Insert file at cursor position.
C-x k	kill-buffer	Delete the buffer specified.
C-x o	other-window	Move to the other window.
C-x q	kbd-macro-query	Insert a query in a macro definition.
C-x s	save-some-buffers	Ask whether to save each modified buffer.
C-_	advertised-undo	Undo last edit (can be done repeatedly).
C-y	yank	Restore what you've deleted.
C-z	suspend-emacs	Suspend `emacs` (use `exit` or `fg` to restart).

Meta-Key Sequences

Keystrokes	Command name	Description
Meta	(none)	Exit a query-replace or successful search.
M-– M-c	negative-argument; capitalize-word	Capitalize previous word.
M-– M-l	negative-argument; downcase-word	Lowercase previous word.
M-– M-u	negative-argument; upcase-word	Uppercase previous word.
M-$	spell-word	Check spelling of word after cursor.
M-<	beginning-of-buffer	Move to beginning of file.
M->	end-of-buffer	Move to end of file.
M-{	backward-paragraph	Move backward one paragraph.
M-}	forward-paragraph	Move forward one paragraph.

Keystrokes	Command name	Description
M-^	delete-indentation	Join this line to the previous one.
M-/	dabbrev-expand	Expand to the most recent preceding word.
M-*n*	digit-argument	Repeat the next command *n* times.
M-*n* C-x e	digit-argument and call-last-kbd-macro	Execute the last defined macro, *n* times.
M-a	backward-sentence	Move backward one sentence.
M-b	backward-word	Move one word *backward*.
M-c	capitalize-word	Capitalize first letter of word.
M-d	kill-word	Delete word that cursor is on.
M-DEL	backward-kill-word	Delete previous word.
M-e	forward-sentence	Move forward one sentence.
M-f	forward-word	Move one word *forward*.
(none)	fill-region	Reformat individual paragraphs within a region.
M-h	mark-paragraph	Mark paragraph.
M-k	kill-sentence	Delete sentence the cursor is on.
M-l	downcase-word	Lowercase word.
M-m	back-to-indentation	Move cursor to first nonblank character on line.
M-q	fill-paragraph	Reformat paragraph.
M-s	center-line	Center line that cursor is on.
M-t	transpose-words	Transpose two words.
M-u	upcase-word	Uppercase word.
M-v	scroll-down	Move backward one screen.
M-x	(none)	Access command by command name.

Summary of Commands by Name

The emacs commands below are presented alphabetically by command name. Use M-x to access the command name. Reminder: C- indicates the Control key; M- indicates the Meta key.

Command name	Keystrokes	Description
macroname	(none)	Execute a keyboard macro you've saved.
abbrev-mode	(none)	Enter (or exit) word abbreviation mode.
advertised-undo	C-_	Undo last edit (can be done repeatedly).
apropos	(none)	What functions and variables involve this concept?
back-to-indentation	M-m	Move cursor to first nonblank character on line.
backward-char	C-b	Move *backward* one character (left).
backward-delete-char	Del	Delete previous character.
backward-kill-paragraph	(none)	Delete previous paragraph.
backward-kill-sentence	C-x Del	Delete previous sentence.
backward-kill-word	C-c C-w	Erase previous word.

Command name	Keystrokes	Description
backward-kill-word	M-Del	Delete previous word.
backward-page	C-x [	Move backward one page.
backward-paragraph	M-{	Move backward one paragraph.
backward-sentence	M-a	Move backward one sentence.
backward-word	M-b	Move backward one word.
beginning-of-buffer	M-<	Move to beginning of file.
beginning-of-line	C-a	Move to beginning of line.
call-last-kbd-macro	C-x e	Execute last macro defined.
capitalize-region	(none)	Capitalize region.
capitalize-word	M-c	Capitalize first letter of word.
center-line	M-s	Center line that cursor is on.
center-paragraph	(none)	Center paragraph that cursor is on.
center-region	(none)	Center currently defined region.
comint-interrupt-subjob	C-c C-c	Terminate the current job.
comint-kill-input	C-c C-u	Erase current line.
comint-send-eof	C-c C-d	End of file character.
comint-stop-subjob	C-c C-z	Suspend current job.
command-apropos	C-h a	What commands involve this concept?
compare-windows	(none)	Compare two buffers; show first difference.
dabbrev-expand	M-/	Expand to the most recent preceding word.
M-^	delete-indentation	Join this line to the previous one.
delete-char	C-d	Delete character under cursor.
delete-indentation	M-^	Join this line to previous one.
delete-other-windows	C-x 1	Delete all windows but this one.
delete-window	C-x 0	Delete current window.
delete-windows-on	(none)	Delete all windows on a given buffer.
describe-bindings	C-h b	What are all the key bindings for in this buffer?
describe-copying	C-h C-c	View the emacs General Public License.
describe-distribution	C-h C-d	View information on ordering emacs from the FSF.
describe-function	C-h f	What does this function do?
describe-key	C-h k	What command does this keystroke sequence run, and what does it do?
describe-key-briefly	C-h c	What command does this keystroke sequence run?
describe-mode	C-h m	Tell me about the mode the current buffer is in.
describe-no-warranty	C-h C-w	View the (non)warranty for emacs.
describe-syntax	C-h s	What is the syntax table for this buffer?
describe-variable	C-h v	What does this variable mean, and what is its value?
digit-argument and call-last-kbd-macro	M-*n* C-x e	Execute the last defined macro, *n* times.

Command name	Keystrokes	Description
digit-argument	M-*n*	Repeat next command, *n* times.
downcase-region	C-x C-l	Lowercase region.
downcase-word	M-l	Lowercase word.
edit-abbrevs	(none)	Edit word abbreviations.
end-kbd-macro	C-x)	End macro definition.
end-of-buffer	M->	Move to end of file.
end-of-line	C-e	Move to end of line.
enlarge-window	C-x ^	Make window taller.
enlarge-window-horizontally	C-x }	Make window wider.
exchange-point-and-mark	C-x C-x	Exchange location of cursor and mark.
exit-recursive-edit	C-M-c	Exit a recursive edit.
fill-individual-paragraphs	(none)	Reformat indented paragraphs, keeping indentation.
fill-paragraph	M-q	Reformat paragraph.
fill-region	(none)	Reformat individual paragraphs within a region.
find-alternate-file	C-x C-v	Read an alternate file, replacing the one read with C-x C-f.
find-file	C-x C-f	Find file and read it.
find-file-other-frame	C-x 5 f	Find a file in a new frame.
find-file-other-window	C-x 4 f	Find a file in the other window.
forward-char	C-f	Move *forward* one character (right).
forward-page	C-x]	Move forward one page.
forward-paragraph	M-}	Move forward one paragraph.
forward-sentence	M-e	Move forward one sentence.
forward-word	M-f	Move forward one word.
goto-char	(none)	Go to character *n* of file.
goto-line	(none)	Go to line *n* of file.
help-command	C-h	Enter the online help system.
help-with-tutorial	C-h t	Run the `emacs` tutorial.
indent-region	C-M-\	Indent a region to match first line in region.
indented-text-mode	(none)	Major mode: each tab defines a new indent for subsequent lines.
info	C-h i	Start the Info documentation reader.
insert-file	C-x i	Insert file at cursor position.
insert-keyboard-macro	(none)	Insert the macro you named into a file.
inverse-add-global-abbrev	C-x a i g	Type global abbreviation, then definition.
inverse-add-local-abbrev	C-x a i l	Type local abbreviation, then definition.
isearch-backward	C-r	Start incremental search backward.
isearch-backward-regexp	C-r	Same, but search for regular expression.
isearch-forward	C-s	Start incremental search forward.
isearch-forward-regexp	C-r	Same, but search for regular expression.

Command name	Keystrokes	Description
kbd-macro-query	C-x q	Insert a query in a macro definition.
keyboard-quit	C-g	Abort current command.
kill-all-abbrevs	(none)	Kill abbreviations for this session.
kill-buffer	C-x k	Delete the buffer specified.
kill-line	C-k	Delete from cursor to end of line.
kill-paragraph	(none)	Delete from cursor to end of paragraph.
kill-region	C-w	Delete a marked region.
kill-sentence	M-k	Delete sentence the cursor is on.
kill-some-buffers	(none)	Ask about deleting each buffer.
kill-word	M-d	Delete word the cursor is on.
list-abbrevs	(none)	View word abbreviations.
list-buffers	C-x C-b	Display buffer list.
load-file	(none)	Load macro files you've saved.
mark-page	C-x C-p	Mark page.
mark-paragraph	M-h	Mark paragraph.
mark-whole-buffer	C-x h	Mark buffer.
name-last-kbd-macro	(none)	Name last macro you created (before saving it).
negative-argument; capitalize-word	M-- M-c	Capitalize previous word.
negative-argument; downcase-word	M-- M-l	Lowercase previous word.
negative-argument; upcase-word	M-- M-u	Uppercase previous word.
next-line	C-n	Move to *next* line (down).
other-window	C-x o	Move to the other window.
previous-line	C-p	Move to *previous* line (up).
query-replace-regexp	C-M-%	Query-replace a regular expression.
recenter	C-l	Redraw screen, with current line in center.
rename-buffer	(none)	Change buffer name to specified name.
replace-regexp	(none)	Replace a regular expression unconditionally.
re-search-backward	(none)	Simple regular expression search backward.
re-search-forward	(none)	Simple regular expression search forward.
revert-buffer	(none)	Restore buffer to the state it was in when the file was last saved (or auto-saved).
save-buffer	C-x C-s	Save file (may hang terminal; use C-q to restart).
save-buffers-kill-emacs	C-x C-c	Exit `emacs`.
save-some-buffers	C-x s	Ask whether to save each modified buffer.
scroll-down	M-v	Move backward one screen.
scroll-left	C-x <	Scroll the window left.
scroll-other-window	C-M-v	Scroll other window.
scroll-right	C-x >	Scroll the window right.
scroll-up	C-v	Move forward one screen.

Command name	Keystrokes	Description
set-fill-prefix	C-x .	Use characters from the beginning of the line up to the cursor column as the "fill prefix." This prefix is prepended to each line in the paragraph. Cancel the prefix by typing this command in column 1.
set-mark-command	C-@ or C-Space	Mark the beginning (or end) of a region.
shell	(none)	Start a shell buffer.
shrink-window	(none)	Make window shorter.
shrink-window-horizontally	C-x {	Make window narrower.
spell-buffer	(none)	Check spelling of current buffer.
spell-region	(none)	Check spelling of current region.
spell-string	(none)	Check spelling of string typed in minibuffer.
spell-word	M-$	Check spelling of word after cursor.
split-line	C-M-o	Split line at cursor; indent to column of cursor.
split-window-vertically	C-x 2	Divide the current window into two, one on top of the other.
split-window-horizontally	C-x 3	Divide the current window into two, side by side.
start-kbd-macro	C-x (	Start macro definition.
suspend-emacs	C-z	Suspend `emacs` (use `exit` or `fg` to restart).
switch-to-buffer	C-x b	Move to the buffer specified.
switch-to-buffer-other-frame	C-x 5 b	Select a buffer in another frame.
switch-to-buffer-other-window	C-x 4 b	Select a buffer in the other window.
text-mode	(none)	Exit indented text mode; return to text mode.
transpose-chars	C-t	Transpose two letters.
transpose-lines	C-x C-t	Transpose two lines.
transpose-paragraphs	(none)	Transpose two paragraphs.
transpose-sentences	(none)	Transpose two sentences.
transpose-words	M-t	Transpose two words.
unexpand-abbrev	(none)	Undo the last word abbreviation.
universal-argument	C-u *n*	Repeat the next command *n* times.
universal-argument and start-kbd-macro	C-u C-x (	Execute last macro defined, then add keystrokes to it.
upcase-region	C-x C-u	Uppercase region.
upcase-word	M-u	Uppercase word.
view-emacs-news	C-h n	View news about updates to `emacs`.
view-lossage	C-h l	What are the last 100 characters I typed?
where-is	C-h w	What is the key binding for this command?
write-abbrev-file	(none)	Write the word abbreviation file.
write-file	C-x C-w	Write buffer contents to file.
yank	C-y	Restore what you've deleted.

9 The vi, ex, and vim Editors

The vi and ex editors are the "standard" editors on Unix systems. You can count on there being some version of them, no matter what Unix flavor you are using. The two editors are in fact the same program; based on how the editor was invoked, it enters full-screen mode or line mode. vim is a popular extended version of vi.

This chapter presents the following topics:

- Conceptual overview
- Command-line syntax
- Review of vi operations
- Alphabetical list of keys in command mode
- vi commands
- vi configuration
- ex basics
- Alphabetical summary of ex commands

vi is pronounced "vee eye."

Besides the original Unix vi, there are a number of freely available vi clones (including vim). Both the original vi and the clones are covered in *Learning the vi Editor*, listed in the Bibliography. The Internet starting point for vim is *http://www.vim.org*.

Conceptual Overview

vi is the classic screen-editing program for Unix. A number of enhanced versions exist, including nvi, vim, vile, and elvis. On GNU/Linux systems, the vi command is usually one of these programs (either a copy or a link). The Emacs editor, covered in Chapter 8, has several vi modes that allow you to use many of the same commands covered in this chapter.

The vi editor operates in two modes, command mode and insert mode. The dual mode makes vi an attractive editor for users who separate text entry from editing. For users who edit as they type, the modeless editing of emacs can be more comfortable. However, vim supports both ways of editing, through the insertmode option and the evim command for invoking vim.

vi is based on an older line editor called ex. (ex, in turn, was developed by Bill Joy at the University of California, Berkeley, from the primordial Unix line editor, ed.) A user can invoke powerful editing capabilities within vi by typing a colon (:), entering an ex command, and pressing the ENTER key. Furthermore, you can place ex commands in a startup file called ~/.exrc, which vi reads at the beginning of your editing session. Because ex commands are such an important part of vi, they are also described in this chapter.

One of the most common versions of vi found on GNU/Linux systems is Bram Moolenaar's Vi IMproved, or vim. On some GNU/Linux distributions, vim is the default version of vi and runs when you invoke vi. vim offers many extra features, and optionally changes some of the basic features of vi, most notoriously changing the undo command to support multiple levels of undo.

Fully documenting vim is beyond the scope of this chapter, but we do cover some of its most commonly used options and features. Beyond what we cover here, vim offers enhanced support to programmers through an integrated build and debugging process, syntax highlighting, extended ctags support, and support for Perl and Python, as well as GUI fonts and menus, function key mapping, independent mapping for each mode, and more. Fortunately, vim comes with a powerful internal help system that you can use to learn more about the things that we just couldn't fit into this chapter. See *http://www.vim.org/* for more information.

Command-Line Syntax

The three most common ways of starting a vi session are:

```
vi [options] file
vi [options] +num file
vi [options] +/pattern file
```

You can open *file* for editing, optionally at line *num* or at the first line matching *pattern*. If no *file* is specified, vi opens with an empty buffer.

Command-Line Options

Because vi and ex are the same program, they share the same options. However, some options only make sense for one version of the program. Options specific to vim are so marked.

+[*num*]
: Start editing at line number *num*, or the last line of the file if *num* is omitted.

+/*pattern*
: Start editing at the first line matching *pattern*. (For ex, this fails if nowrapscan is set in your .exrc startup file, since ex starts editing at the last line of a file.)

-b
: Edit the file in binary mode. {vim}

`-c` *command*
: Run the given `ex` command upon startup. Only one `-c` option is permitted for `vi`; `vim` accepts up to 10. An older form of this option, `+`*command*, is still supported.

`--cmd` *command*
: Like `-c`, but execute the command before any resource files are read. {vim}

`-C`
: Solaris `vi`: Same as `-x`, but assume the file is encrypted already.

  `vim`: Start the editor in `vi`-compatible mode.

`-d`
: Run in diff mode. Works like `vimdiff`. (See **vimdiff** in Chapter 2.) {vim}

`-D`
: Debugging mode for use with scripts. {vim}

`-e`
: Run as `ex` (line editing rather than full-screen mode).

`-h`
: Print help message, then exit. {vim}

`-i` *file*
: Use the specified *file* instead of the default (`~/.viminfo`) to save or restore `vim`'s state. {vim}

`-l`
: Enter Lisp mode for running Lisp programs (not supported in all versions).

`-L`
: List files that were saved due to an aborted editor session or system crash (not supported in all versions). For `vim`, this option is the same as `-r`.

`-m`
: Start the editor with the `write` option turned off so that the user cannot write to files. {vim}

`-M`
: Do not allow text in files to be modified. {vim}

`-n`
: Do not use a swap file; record changes in memory only. {vim}

`--noplugin`
: Do not load any plug-ins. {vim}

`-N`
: Run `vim` in a non-`vi`-compatible mode. {vim}

`-o[`*num*`]`
: Start `vim` with *num* open windows. The default is to open one window for each file. {vim}

`-O[`*num*`]`
: Start `vim` with *num* open windows arranged horizontally (split vertically) on the screen. {vim}

`-r [`*file*`]`
: Recovery mode; recover and resume editing on *file* after an aborted editor session or system crash. Without *file*, list files available for recovery.

`-R`
: Edit files read-only.

`-s`
: Silent; do not display prompts. Useful when running a script. This behavior also can be set through the older `-` option. For `vim`, only applies when used together with `-e`.

`-s` *scriptfile*
: Read and execute commands given in the specified *scriptfile* as if they were typed in from the keyboard. {vim}

`-S` *`commandfile`*
: Read and execute commands given in *commandfile* after loading any files for editing specified on the command line. Shorthand for `vim -c 'source` *`commandfile`*`'`. {vim}

`-t` *`tag`*
: Edit the file containing *tag* and position the cursor at its definition. (See **ctags** in Chapter 2 for more information.)

`-T` *`type`*
: Set the terminal type. This value overrides the $TERM environment variable. {vim}

`-u` *`file`*
: Read configuration information from the specified resource file instead of default `.vimrc` resource file. If the *file* argument is `NONE`, `vim` will read no resource files, load no plug-ins, and run in compatible mode. If the argument is `NORC`, it will read no resource files but it will load plug-ins. {vim}

`-v`
: Run in full-screen mode (default for `vi`).

`--version`
: Print version information, then exit. {vim}

`-V[`*`num`*`]`
: Verbose mode; print messages about what options are being set and what files are being read or written. You can set a level of verbosity to increase or decrease the number of messages received. The default value is 10 for high verbosity. {vim}

`-w` *`rows`*
: Set the window size so *rows* lines at a time are displayed; useful when editing over a slow dial-up line (or long distance Internet connection). Older versions of `vi` do not permit a space between the option and its argument. `vim` does not support this option.

`-W` *`scriptfile`*
: Write all typed commands from the current session to the specified *scriptfile*. The file created can be used with the `-s` command. {vim}

`-x`
: Prompt for a key that will be used to try to encrypt or decrypt a file using `crypt` (not supported in all versions).*

`-y`
: Modeless `vi`; run `vim` in insert mode only, without a command mode. This is the same as invoking `vim` as `evim`. (See **evim** in Chapter 2.) {vim}

`-Z`
: Start `vim` in restricted mode. Do not allow shell commands or suspension of the editor. {vim}

While most people know `ex` commands only by their use within `vi`, the editor also exists as a separate program and can be invoked from the shell (for instance, to edit files as part of a script). Within `ex`, you can enter the `vi` or `visual` command to start `vi`. Similarly, within `vi`, you can enter `Q` to quit the `vi` editor and enter `ex`.

* The `crypt` command's encryption is weak. Don't use it for serious secrets.

You can exit ex in several ways:

`:x`	Exit (save changes and quit).
`:q!`	Quit without saving changes.
`:vi`	Enter the vi editor.

Review of vi Operations

This section provides a review of the following:

- vi modes
- Syntax of vi commands
- Status-line commands

Command Mode

Once the file is opened, you are in command mode. From command mode, you can:

- Invoke insert mode
- Issue editing commands
- Move the cursor to a different position in the file
- Invoke ex commands
- Invoke a Unix shell
- Save the current version of the file
- Exit vi

Insert Mode

In insert mode, you can enter new text in the file. You normally enter insert mode with the `i` command. Press the ESCAPE key to exit insert mode and return to command mode. The full list of commands that enter insert mode is provided later, in the section "Insert Commands."

Syntax of vi Commands

In vi, editing commands have the following general form:

```
[n] operator [m] motion
```

The basic editing *operators* are:

`c`	Begin a change.
`d`	Begin a deletion.
`y`	Begin a yank (or copy).

If the current line is the object of the operation, the *motion* is the same as the operator: `cc`, `dd`, `yy`. Otherwise, the editing operators act on objects specified by cursor-movement commands or pattern-matching commands. (For example, `cf.` changes up to the next period.) *n* and *m* are the number of times the operation is performed, or the number of objects the operation is performed on. If both *n* and *m* are specified, the effect is $n \times m$.

An object of operation can be any of the following text blocks:

word	Includes characters up to a whitespace character (space or tab) or punctuation mark. A capitalized object is a variant form that recognizes only whitespace.
sentence	Up to `.`, `!`, or `?`, followed by two spaces.
paragraph	Up to the next blank line or paragraph macro defined by the `para=` option.
section	Up to the next `nroff/troff` section heading defined by the `sect=` option.
motion	Up to the character or other text object as specified by a motion specifier, including pattern searches.

Examples

`2cw`	Change the next two words.
`d}`	Delete up to next paragraph.
`d^`	Delete back to beginning of line.
`5yy`	Copy the next five lines.
`y]]`	Copy up to the next section.
`cG`	Change to the end of the edit buffer.

More commands and examples may be found in the section "Changing and deleting text," later in this chapter.

Visual mode (vim only)

`vim` provides an additional facility, "visual mode." This allows you to highlight blocks of text which then become the object of edit commands such as deletion or saving (yanking). Graphical versions of `vim` allow you to use the mouse to highlight text in a similar fashion. See the `vim` help file `visual.txt` for the full story.

`v`	Select text in visual mode one character at a time.
`V`	Select text in visual mode one line at a time.
`CTRL-V`	Select text in visual mode in blocks.

Status-Line Commands

Most commands are not echoed on the screen as you input them. However, the status line at the bottom of the screen is used to edit these commands:

`/`	Search forward for a pattern.
`?`	Search backward for a pattern.
`:`	Invoke an ex command.
`!`	Invoke a Unix command that takes as its input an object in the buffer and replaces it with output from the command. You type a motion command after the `!` to describe what should passed to the Unix command. The command itself is entered on the status line.

Commands that are entered on the status line must be entered by pressing the ENTER key. In addition, error messages and output from the CTRL-G command are displayed on the status line.

vi Commands

vi supplies a large set of single-key commands when in command mode. vim supplies additional multikey commands.

Movement Commands

Some versions of vi do not recognize extended keyboard keys (e.g., arrow keys, Page Up, Page Down, Home, Insert, and Delete); some do. All, however, recognize the keys in this section. Many users of vi prefer to use these keys, as it helps them keep their fingers on the home row of the keyboard. A number preceding a command repeats the movement. Movement commands are also used after an operator. The operator works on the text that is moved.

Character

h, j, k, l	Left, down, up, right (←, ↓, ↑, →).
Spacebar	Right.
BACKSPACE	Left.
CTRL-H	Left.

Text

w, b	Forward, backward by "word" (letters, numbers, and underscore make up words).
W, B	Forward, backward by "WORD" (only whitespace separates items).
e	End of word.
E	End of WORD.
ge	End of previous word. {vim}
gE	End of previous WORD. {vim}
), (	Beginning of next, current sentence.
}, {	Beginning of next, current paragraph.
]], [[	Beginning of next, current section.
][, []	End of next, current section. {vim}

Lines

Long lines in a file may show up on the screen as multiple lines. (They *wrap* around from one screen line to the next.) While most commands work on the lines as defined in the file, a few commands work on lines as they appear on the screen. The vim option wrap allows you to control how long lines are displayed.

0, $	First, last position of current line.
^, _	First nonblank character of current line.
+, -	First nonblank character of next, previous line.
ENTER	First nonblank character of next line.
num|	Column *num* of current line.
g0, g$	First, last position of screen line. {vim}
g^	First nonblank character of screen line. {vim}
gm	Middle of screen line. {vim}
gk, gj	Move up, down one screen line. {vim}

H	Top line of screen (Home position).
M	Middle line of screen.
L	Last line of screen.
*num*H	*num* lines after top line.
*num*L	*num* lines before last line.

Screens

CTRL-F, CTRL-B	Scroll forward, backward one screen.
CTRL-D, CTRL-U	Scroll down, up one-half screen.
CTRL-E, CTRL-Y	Show one more line at bottom, top of screen.
z ENTER	Reposition line with cursor to top of screen.
z.	Reposition line with cursor to middle of screen.
z-	Reposition line with cursor to bottom of screen.
CTRL-L	Redraw screen (without scrolling).
CTRL-R	vi: Redraw screen (without scrolling). vim: Redo last undone change.

Searches

/*pattern*	Search forward for *pattern*. End with ENTER.
/*pattern*/+*num*	Go to line *num* after *pattern*.
?*pattern*	Search backward for *pattern*. End with ENTER.
?*pattern*?-*num*	Go to line *num* before *pattern*.
:noh	Suspend search highlighting until next search. {vim}.
n	Repeat previous search.
N	Repeat search in opposite direction.
/	Repeat previous search forward.
?	Repeat previous search backward.
*	Search forward for word under cursor. Matches only exact words. {vim}
#	Search backward for word under cursor. Matches only exact words. {vim}
g*	Search backward for word under cursor. Matches the characters of this word when embedded in a longer word. {vim}
g#	Search backward for word under cursor. Matches the characters of this word when embedded in a longer word. {vim}
%	Find match of current parenthesis, brace, or bracket.
f*x*	Move cursor forward to *x* on current line.
F*x*	Move cursor backward to *x* on current line.
t*x*	Move cursor forward to character before *x* in current line.
T*x*	Move cursor backward to character after *x* in current line.
,	Reverse search direction of last f, F, t, or T.
;	Repeat last f, F, t, or T.

Line numbering

CTRL-G	Display current line number.
gg	Move to first line in file. {vim}
*num*G	Move to line number *num*.
G	Move to last line in file.
:*num*	Move to line number *num*.

Marks

`mx`	Place mark *x* at current position.
`` `x ``	(backquote) Move cursor to mark *x*.
`'x`	(apostrophe) Move to start of line containing *x*.
` `` `	(backquotes) Return to position before most recent jump.
`''`	(apostrophes) Like preceding, but return to start of line.
`'"`	(apostrophe quote) Move to position when last editing the file. {vim}
`` `[, `] ``	(backquote bracket) Move to beginning/end of previous text operation. {vim}
`'[, ']`	(apostrophe bracket) Like preceding, but return to start of line where operation occurred. {vim}
`` `. ``	(backquote period) Move to last change in file. {vim}
`'.`	(apostrophe period) Like preceding, but return to start of line. {vim}
`` `0 ``	Position where you last exited `vim`. {vim}
`:marks`	List active marks. {vim}

Insert Commands

`a`	Append after cursor.
`A`	Append to end of line.
`c`	Begin change operation.
`C`	Change to end of line.
`gI`	Insert at beginning of line. {vim}
`i`	Insert before cursor.
`I`	Insert at beginning of line.
`o`	Open a line below cursor.
`O`	Open a line above cursor.
`R`	Begin overwriting text.
`s`	Substitute a character.
`S`	Substitute entire line.
`ESC`	Terminate insert mode.

The following commands work in insert mode.

BACKSPACE	Delete previous character.
DELETE	Delete current character.
TAB	Insert a tab.
CTRL-A	Repeat last insertion. {vim}
CTRL-D	Shift line left to previous shift width. {vim}
CTRL-E	Insert character found just below cursor. {vim}
CTRL-H	Delete previous character (same as Backspace).
CTRL-I	Insert a tab.
CTRL-K	Begin insertion of multi-keystroke character.
CTRL-N	Insert next completion of the pattern to the left of the cursor. {vim}
CTRL-P	Insert previous completion of the pattern to the left of the cursor. {vim}
CTRL-T	Shift line right to next shift width. {vim}
CTRL-U	Delete current line.
CTRL-V	Insert next character verbatim.
CTRL-W	Delete previous word.
CTRL-Y	Insert character found just above cursor. {vim}
CTRL-[	(ESCAPE) Terminate insert mode.

Some of the control characters listed in the previous table are set by stty. Your terminal settings may differ.

Edit Commands

Recall that c, d, and y are the basic editing operators.

Changing and deleting text

The following table is not exhaustive, but illustrates the most common operations.

cw	Change word.
cc	Change line.
c$	Change text from current position to end-of-line.
C	Same as c$.
dd	Delete current line.
*num*dd	Delete *num* lines.
d$	Delete text from current position to end-of-line.
D	Same as d$.
dw	Delete a word.
d}	Delete up to next paragraph.
d^	Delete back to beginning of line.
d/*pat*	Delete up to first occurrence of pattern.
dn	Delete up to next occurrence of pattern.
df*x*	Delete up to and including *x* on current line.
dt*x*	Delete up to (but not including) *x* on current line.
dL	Delete up to last line on screen.
dG	Delete to end of file.
gqap	Reformat current paragraph to textwidth. {vim}
g~w	Switch case of word. {vim}
guw	Change word to lowercase. {vim}
gUw	Change word to uppercase. {vim}
p	Insert last deleted or yanked text after cursor.
gp	Same as p, but leave cursor at end of inserted text. {vim}
]p	Same as p, but match current indention. {vim}
[p	Same as P, but match current indention. {vim}
P	Insert last deleted or yanked text before cursor.
gP	Same as P, but leave cursor at end of inserted text. {vim}
r*x*	Replace character with *x*.
R*text*	Replace with new *text* (overwrite), beginning at cursor. ESCAPE ends replace mode.
s	Substitute character.
4s	Substitute four characters.
S	Substitute entire line.
u	Undo last change.
CTRL-R	Redo last change. {vim}
U	Restore current line.
x	Delete current cursor position.
X	Delete back one character.
5X	Delete previous five characters.
.	Repeat last change.

~	Reverse case and move cursor right.
CTRL-A	Increment number under cursor. {vim}
CTRL-X	Decrement number under cursor. {vim}

Copying and moving

Register names are the letters a–z. Uppercase names append text to the corresponding register.

Y	Copy current line.
yy	Copy current line.
"xyy	Copy current line to register *x*.
ye	Copy text to end of word.
yw	Like ye, but include the whitespace after the word.
y$	Copy rest of line.
"xdd	Delete current line into register *x*.
"xd	Delete into register *x*.
"xp	Put contents of register *x*.
y]]	Copy up to next section heading.
J	Join current line to next line.
gJ	Same as J, but without inserting a space. {vim}
:j	Same as J.
:j!	Same as gJ.

Saving and Exiting

Writing a file means overwriting the file with the current text.

ZZ	Quit vi, writing the file only if changes were made.
:x	Same as ZZ.
:wq	Write file and quit.
:w	Write file.
:w *file*	Save copy to *file*.
:*n*,*m*w *file*	Write lines *n* to *m* to new *file*.
:*n*,*m*w >> *file*	Append lines *n* to *m* to existing *file*.
:w!	Write file (overriding protection).
:w! *file*	Overwrite *file* with current text.
:w %.*new*	Write current buffer named *file* as *file*.new.
:q	Quit vi (fails if changes were made).
:q!	Quit vi (discarding edits).
Q	Quit vi and invoke ex.
:vi	Return to vi after Q command.
%	Replaced with current filename in editing commands.
#	Replaced with alternate filename in editing commands.

Accessing Multiple Files

:e *file*	Edit another *file*; current file becomes alternate.
:e!	Return to version of current file at time of last write.
:e + *file*	Begin editing at end of *file*.

`:e +`*num file*	Open *file* at line *num*.
`:e #`	Open to previous position in alternate file.
`:ta` *tag*	Edit file at location *tag*.
`:n`	Edit next file in the list of files.
`:n!`	Force next file.
`:n` *files*	Specify new list of *files*.
`:rewind`	Edit first file in the list.
`CTRL-G`	Show current file and line number.
`:args`	Display list of files to be edited.
`:prev`	Edit previous file in the list of files.

Window Commands (vim)

The following table lists common commands for controlling windows in `vim`. See also the **split**, **vsplit**, and **resize** commands in the later section "Alphabetical Summary of ex Commands." For brevity, control characters are marked in the following list by ^.

`:new`	Open a new window.
`:new` *file*	Open *file* in a new window.
`:sp` [*file*]	Split the current window. With *file*, edit that file in the new window.
`:sv` [*file*]	Same as `:sp`, but make new window read-only.
`:sn` [*file*]	Edit next file in file list in new window.
`:vsp` [*file*]	Like `:sp`, but split vertically instead of horizontally.
`:clo`	Close current window.
`:hid`	Hide current window, unless it is the only visible window.
`:on`	Make current window the only visible one.
`:res` *num*	Resize window to *num* lines.
`:wa`	Write all changed buffers to their files.
`:qa`	Close all buffers and exit.
`^W s`	Same as `:sp`.
`^W n`	Same as `:new`.
`^W ^`	Open new window with alternate (previously edited) file.
`^W c`	Same as `:clo`.
`^W o`	Same as `:only`.
`^W j`, `^W k`	Move cursor to next/previous window.
`^W p`	Move cursor to previous window.
`^W h`, `^W l`	Move cursor to window on left/right.
`^W t`, `^W b`	Move cursor to window on top/bottom of screen.
`^W K`, `^W B`	Move current window to top/bottom of screen.
`^W H`, `^W L`	Move current window to far left/right of screen.
`^W r`, `^W R`	Rotate windows down/up.
`^W +`, `^W -`	Increase/decrease current window size.
`^W =`	Make all windows same height.

Interacting with the System

`:r` *file*	Read in contents of *file* after cursor.
`:r !`*command*	Read in output from *command* after current line.
`:`*num*`r !`*command*	Like above, but place after line *num* (0 for top of file).

`:!command`	Run *command*, then return.
`!motion command`	Send the text covered by *motion* to Unix *command*; replace with output.
`:n,m! command`	Send lines *n–m* to *command*; replace with output.
`num!!command`	Send *num* lines to Unix *command*; replace with output.
`:!!`	Repeat last system command.
`:sh`	Create subshell; return to editor with *EOF*.
`CTRL-Z`	Suspend editor, resume with `fg`.
`:so file`	Read and execute `ex` commands from *file*.

Macros

`:ab in out`	Use *in* as abbreviation for *out* in insert mode.
`:unab in`	Remove abbreviation for *in*.
`:ab`	List abbreviations.
`:map string sequence`	Map characters *string* as *sequence* of commands. Use `#1`, `#2`, etc., for the function keys.
`:unmap string`	Remove map for characters *string*.
`:map`	List character strings that are mapped.
`:map! string sequence`	Map characters *string* to input mode *sequence*.
`:unmap! string`	Remove input mode map (you may need to quote the characters with `CTRL-V`).
`:map!`	List character strings that are mapped for input mode.
`qx`	Record typed characters into register specified by letter *x*. If letter is uppercase, append to register. {vim}
`q`	Stop recording. {vim}
`@x`	Execute the register specified by letter *x*. Use `@@` to repeat the last `@` command.

In `vi`, the following characters are unused in command mode and can be mapped as user-defined commands:

Letters
`g K q V v`

Control keys
`^A ^K ^O ^W ^X ^_ ^\`

Symbols
`_ * \ = #`

The `=` is used by `vi` if Lisp mode is set. Different versions of `vi` may use some of these characters, so test them before using.

`vim` does not use `^K`, `^_`, `_`, or `\`.

Miscellaneous Commands

`<`	Shift text described by following motion command left by one shiftwidth. {vim}
`>`	Shift text described by following motion command right by one shiftwidth. {vim}
`<<`	Shift line left one shift width (default is eight spaces).

`>>`	Shift line right one shift width (default is eight spaces).
`>}`	Shift right to end of paragraph.
`<%`	Shift left until matching parenthesis, brace, or bracket. (Cursor must be on the matching symbol.)
`==`	Indent line in C-style, or using program specified in `equalprg` option. {vim}
`g`	Start many multiple character commands in `vim`.
`K`	Look up word under cursor in manpages (or program defined in `keywordprg`). {vim}
`^O`	Return to previous jump. {vim}
`q`	Record keystrokes. {vim}
`^Q`	Same as `^V`. {vim} (On some terminals, resume data flow.)
`^T`	Return to the previous location in the tag stack. (Solaris `vi` and `vim`)
`^]`	Perform a tag lookup on the text under the cursor.
`^\`	Enter `ex` line-editing mode.
`^^`	(Caret key with CTRL key pressed) Return to previously edited file.

vi Configuration

This section describes the following:

- The `:set` command
- Options available with `:set`
- Example `.exrc` file

The :set Command

The `:set` command allows you to specify options that change characteristics of your editing environment. Options may be put in the `~/.exrc` file or set during a `vi` session.

The colon does not need to be typed if the command is put in `.exrc`:

`:set` *x*	Enable boolean option *x*, show value of other options.
`:set no`*x*	Disable option *x*.
`:set` *x*=*value*	Give *value* to option *x*.
`:set`	Show changed options.
`:set all`	Show all options.
`:set` *x*?	Show value of option *x*.

Options Used by :set

Table 9-1 contains brief descriptions of the important set command options. In the first column, options are listed in alphabetical order; if the option can be abbreviated, that abbreviation is shown in parentheses. The second column shows the default setting. The last column describes what the option does, when enabled.

This table lists set options for the Solaris version of `vi`, with the addition of important `vim` options. Other versions of `vi` may have more or fewer or different options. See your local documentation, or use `:set all` to see the full list. Options that receive a value are marked with an `=`.

Table 9-1. :set options

Option	Default	Description
`autoindent (ai)`	`noai`	In insert mode, indent each line to the same level as the line above or below. Use with the `shiftwidth` option.
`autoprint (ap)`	`ap`	Display changes after each editor command. (For global replacement, display last replacement.)
`autowrite (aw)`	`noaw`	Automatically write (save) the file if changed before opening another file with a command such as `:n` or before giving a Unix command with `:!`.
`background (bg)`		Describe the background so the editor can choose appropriate highlighting colors. Default value of `dark` or `light` depends on the environment in which the editor is invoked. {vim}
`backup (bk)`	`nobackup`	Create a backup file when overwriting an existing file. {vim}
`backupdir= (bdir)`	`.,~/tmp/,~/`	Name directories in which to store backup files if possible. The list of directories is comma-separated and in order of preference. {vim}
`beautify (bf)`	`nobf`	Ignore all control characters during input (except tab, newline, or formfeed).
`backupext= (bex)`	`~`	String to append to filenames for backup files. {vim}
`cindent (cin)`	`nocindent`	In insert mode, indents each line relative to the one above it, as is appropriate for C or C++ code. {vim}
`compatible (cp)`	`cp`	Make `vim` behave more like `vi`. Default is `nocp` when a `~/.vimrc` file is found. {vim}
`directory (dir)`	`/tmp`	Name of directory in which `ex`/`vi` stores buffer files. (Directory must be writable.) This can be a comma-separated list for `vim`.
`edcompatible`	`noedcompatible`	Remember the flags used with the most recent substitute command (global, confirming) and use them for the next substitute command. Despite the name, no version of `ed` actually does this.
`equalprg= (ep)`		Use the specified program for the `=` command. When the option is blank (the default), the key invokes the internal C indenting function or the value of the `indentexpr` option. {vim}
`errorbells (eb)`	`errorbells`	Sound bell when an error occurs.
`exrc (ex)`	`noexrc`	Allow the execution of `.exrc` files that reside outside the user's home directory.
`flash (fp)`		Flash the screen instead of ringing the bell.
`formatprg= (fp)`		The `gq` command invokes the named external program to format text. It calls internal formatting functions when this option is empty (the default). {vim}

Table 9-1. :set options (continued)

Option	Default	Description
gdefault (gd)	nogdefault	Set the g flag on for substitutions by default. {vim}
hardtabs= (ht)	8	Define boundaries for terminal hardware tabs.
hidden (hid)	nohidden	Hide buffers rather than unload them when they are abandoned. {vim}
hlsearch (hls)	hlsearch	Highlight all matches of most recent search pattern. Use :nohlsearch to remove highlighting. {vim}
history= (hi)	20	Number of ex commands to store in the history table. {vim}
ignorecase (ic)	noic	Disregard case during a search.
incsearch (is)	noincsearch	Highlight matches to a search pattern as it is typed. {vim}
lisp	nolisp	Insert indents in appropriate Lisp format. (,), {, }, [[, and]] are modified to have meaning for Lisp.
list	nolist	Print tabs as ^I; mark ends of lines with $. (Use list to tell if end character is a tab or a space.)
magic	magic	Wildcard characters . (dot), * (asterisk), and [] (brackets) have special meaning in patterns.
mesg	mesg	Permit system messages to display on terminal while editing in vi.
mousehide (mh)	mousehide	When characters are typed, hide the mouse pointer. {vim}
novice	nonovice	Require the use of long ex command names, such as copy or read.
number (nu)	nonu	Display line numbers on left of screen during editing session.
open	open	Allow entry to *open* or *visual* mode from ex. Although not in Solaris vi or vim, this option has traditionally been in vi, and may be in your version of vi.
optimize (opt)	noopt	Abolish carriage returns at the end of lines when printing multiple lines; speed output on dumb terminals when printing lines with leading whitespace (spaces or tabs).
paragraphs (para)	IPLPPPQPP LIpplpipnpbplpipbp	Define paragraph delimiters for movement by { or }. The pairs of characters in the value are the names of troff macros that begin paragraphs.
paste	nopaste	Change the defaults of various options to make pasting text into a terminal window work better. All options are returned to their original value when the paste option is reset. {vim}
prompt	prompt	Display the ex prompt (:) when vi's Q command is given.
readonly (ro)	noro	Any writes (saves) of a file fail unless you use ! after the write (works with w, ZZ, or autowrite).

Table 9-1. :set options (continued)

Option	Default	Description
redraw (re)		vi redraws the screen whenever edits are made. noredraw is useful at slow speeds on a dumb terminal: the screen isn't fully updated until you press ESCAPE. Default depends on line speed and terminal type.
remap	remap	Allow nested map sequences.
report=	5	Display a message on the status line whenever you make an edit that affects at least a certain number of lines. For example, 6dd reports the message "6 lines deleted."
ruler (ru)	ruler	Show line and column numbers for the current cursor position. {vim}
scroll=	[½ window]	Number of lines to scroll with ^D and ^U commands.
sections= (sect)	NHSHH HUuhsh+c	Define section delimiters for [[and]] movement. The pairs of characters in the value are the names of troff macros that begin sections.
shell= (sh)	/bin/sh	Pathname of shell used for shell escape (:!) and shell command (:sh). Default value is derived from shell environment, which varies on different systems.
shiftwidth= (sw)	8	Define number of spaces used when the indent is increased or decreased.
showmatch (sm)	nosm	In vi, when) or } is entered, cursor moves briefly to matching (or {. (If no match, rings the error message bell.) Very useful for programming.
showmode	noshowmode	In insert mode, display a message on the prompt line indicating the type of insert you are making. For example, "OPEN MODE" or "APPEND MODE."
slowopen (slow)		Hold off display during insert. Default depends on line speed and terminal type.
smartcase (scs)	nosmartcase	Override the ignorecase option when a search pattern contains uppercase characters. {vim}
tabstop= (ts)	8	Define number of spaces a tab indents during editing session. (Printer still uses system tab of 8.)
taglength= (tl)	0	Define number of characters that are significant for tags. Default (zero) means that all characters are significant.
tags=	tags /usr/lib/tags	Define pathname of files containing tags. (See the Unix ctags command.) (By default, vi searches the file tags in the current directory and /usr/lib/tags.)
tagstack	tagstack	Enable stacking of tag locations on a stack. (Solaris vi and vim.)
term=		Set terminal type.
terse	noterse	Display shorter error messages.
textwidth= (tw)	0	The maximum width of text to be inserted; longer lines are broken after whitespace. Default (zero) disables this feature, in which case wrapmargin is used. {vim}

Table 9-1. :set options (continued)

Option	Default	Description
`timeout (to)`	`timeout`	Keyboard maps time out after 1 second.[a]
`timeoutlen= (tm)`	`1000`	Number of milliseconds after which keyboard maps time out. Default value of 1000 provides traditional `vi` behavior. {vim}
`ttytype=`		Set terminal type. This is just another name for `term`.
`undolevels= (ul)`	`1000`	Number of changes that can be undone. {vim}
`warn`	`warn`	Display the warning message, "No write since last change."
`window (w)`		Show a certain number of lines of the file on the screen. Default depends on line speed and terminal type.
`wrap`	`wrap`	When on, long lines wrap on the screen. When off, only the first part of the line is displayed. {vim}
`wrapmargin (wm)`	`0`	Define right margin. If greater than zero, `vi` automatically inserts carriage returns to break lines.
`wrapscan (ws)`	`ws`	Searches wrap around either end of file.
`writeany (wa)`	`nowa`	Allow saving to any file.
`writebackup (wb)`	`wb`	Back up files before attempting to overwrite them. Remove the backup when the file has been successfully written, unless the `backup` option is set. {vim}

[a] When you have mappings of several keys (for example, `:map zzz 3dw`), you probably want to use `notimeout`. Otherwise, you need to type `zzz` within one second. When you have an insert mode mapping for a cursor key (for example, `:map! ^[OB ^[ja`), you should use `timeout`. Otherwise, `vi` won't react to ESCAPE until you type another key.

Example .exrc File

In an ex script file, comments start with the double-quote character. The following lines of code are an example of a customized `.exrc` file:

```
set nowrapscan                  " Searches don't wrap at end of file
set wrapmargin=7                " Wrap text at 7 columns from right margin
set sections=SeAhBhChDh nomesg  " Set troff macros, disallow message
map q :w^M:n^M                  " Alias to move to next file
map v dwElp                     " Move a word
ab ORA O'Reilly Media, Inc.     " Input shortcut
```

The `q` alias isn't needed for `vim`, which has the `:wn` command. The `v` alias would hide the `vim` command `v`, which enters character-at-a-time visual mode operation.

ex Basics

The ex line editor serves as the foundation for the screen editor vi. Commands in ex work on the current line or on a range of lines in a file. Most often, you use ex from within vi. In vi, ex commands are preceded by a colon and entered by pressing ENTER.

You can also invoke ex on its own—from the command line—just as you would invoke vi. (You could execute an ex script this way.) Or you can use the vi command Q to quit the vi editor and enter ex.

Syntax of ex Commands

To enter an ex command from vi, type:

```
:[address] command [options]
```

An initial : indicates an ex command. As you type the command, it is echoed on the status line. Execute the command by pressing the ENTER key. *address* is the line number or range of lines that are the object of *command*. *options* and *addresses* are described below. ex commands are described in the section "Alphabetical Summary of ex Commands."

You can exit ex in several ways:

`:x`	Exit (save changes and quit).
`:q!`	Quit without saving changes.
`:vi`	Switch to the vi editor on the current file.

Addresses

If no address is given, the current line is the object of the command. If the address specifies a range of lines, the format is:

```
x,y
```

where *x* and *y* are the first and last addressed lines (*x* must precede *y* in the buffer). *x* and *y* may each be a line number or a symbol. Using ; instead of , sets the current line to *x* before interpreting *y*. The notation `1,$` addresses all lines in the file, as does `%`.

Address Symbols

`1,$`	All lines in the file.
x,*y*	Lines *x* through *y*.
x;*y*	Lines *x* through *y*, with current line reset to *x*.
`0`	Top of file.
`.`	Current line.
num	Absolute line number *num*.
`$`	Last line.
`%`	All lines; same as `1,$`.
x-*n*	*n* lines before *x*.

x+*n*	*n* lines after *x*.
-[*num*]	One or *num* lines previous.
+[*num*]	One or *num* lines ahead.
'*x*	Line marked with *x*.
''	Previous mark.
/*pattern*/	Forward to line matching *pattern*.
?*pattern*?	Backward to line matching *pattern*.

See Chapter 7 for more information on using patterns.

Options

! Indicates a variant form of the command, overriding the normal behavior. The ! must come immediately after the command.

count
The number of times the command is to be repeated. Unlike in vi commands, *count* cannot precede the command, because a number preceding an ex command is treated as a line address. For example, d3 deletes three lines beginning with the current line; 3d deletes line 3.

file
The name of a file that is affected by the command. % stands for the current file; # stands for the previous file.

Alphabetical Summary of ex Commands

ex commands can be entered by specifying any unique abbreviation. In this listing, the full name appears in the margin, and the shortest possible abbreviation is used in the syntax line. Examples are assumed to be typed from vi, so they include the : prompt.

abbreviate

```
ab [string text]
```

Define *string* when typed to be translated into *text*. If *string* and *text* are not specified, list all current abbreviations.

Examples

Note: ^M appears when you type ^V followed by ENTER.

```
:ab ora O'Reilly Media, Inc.
:ab id Name:^MRank:^MPhone:
```

append

```
[address] a[!]
text
.
```

Append new *text* at specified *address*, or at present address if none is specified. Add a ! to toggle the autoindent setting that is used during input. That is, if autoindent was enabled, ! disables it. Enter new text after entering the command. Terminate input of new text by entering a line consisting of just a period.

Example

```
:a                          Begin appending to current line
Append this line
and this line too.
.                           Terminate input of text to append
```

---

args

```
ar
args file ...
```

Print the members of the argument list (files named on the command line), with the current argument printed in brackets ([ ]).

The second syntax is for `vim`, which allows you to reset the list of files to be edited.

---

bdelete

```
[num] bd[!] [num]
```

Unload buffer *num* and remove it from the buffer list. Add a `!` to force removal of an unsaved buffer. The buffer may also be specified by filename. If no buffer is specified, remove the current buffer. {vim}

---

buffer

```
[num] b[!] [num]
```

Begin editing buffer *num* in the buffer list. Add a `!` to force a switch from an unsaved buffer. The buffer may also be specified by filename. If no buffer is specified, continue editing the current buffer. {vim}

---

buffers

```
buffers[!]
```

Print the members of the buffer list. Some buffers (e.g., deleted buffers) will not be listed. Add `!` to show unlisted buffers. `ls` is another abbreviation for this command. {vim}

---

cd

```
cd dir
chdir dir
```

Change current directory within the editor to *dir*.

---

center

```
[address] ce [width]
```

Center line within the specified *width*. If *width* is not specified, use `textwidth`. {vim}

---

change

```
[address] c[!]
text
.
```

Replace the specified lines with *text*. Add a `!` to switch the `autoindent` setting during input of *text*. Terminate input by entering a line consisting of just a period.

close

`clo[!]`

Close current window unless it is the last window. If buffer in window is not open in another window, unload it from memory. This command will not close a buffer with unsaved changes, but you may add `!` to hide it instead. {vim}

copy

`[address] co destination`

Copy the lines included in *address* to the specified *destination* address. The command `t` (short for "to") is a synonym for `copy`.

Example

`:1,10 co 50`	*Copy first 10 lines to just after line 50*

delete

`[address] d [register]`

Delete the lines included in *address*. If *register* is specified, save or append the text to the named register. Register names are the lowercase letters `a`–`z`. Uppercase names append text to the corresponding register.

Examples

`:/Part I/,/Part II/-1d`	*Delete to line above "Part II"*
`:/main/+d`	*Delete line below "main"*
`:.,$d x`	*Delete from this line to last line into register x*

edit

`e[!] [+num] [filename]`

Begin editing on *filename*. If no *filename* is given, start over with a copy of the current file. Add a `!` to edit the new file even if the current file has not been saved since the last change. With the *+num* argument, begin editing on line *num*. Or *num* may be a pattern, of the form `/`*pattern*.

Examples

`:e file`	*Edit file in current editing buffer*
`:e +/^Index #`	*Edit alternate file at pattern match*
`:e!`	*Start over again on current file*

file

`f [filename]`

Change the filename for the current buffer to *filename*. The next time the buffer is written, it will be written to file *filename*. When the name is changed, the buffer's "not edited" flag is set, to indicate you are not editing an existing file. If the new filename is the same as a file that already exists on the disk, you will need to use `:w!` to overwrite the existing file. When specifying a filename, the `%`

character can be used to indicate the current filename. A # can be used to indicate the alternate filename. If no *filename* is specified, print the current name and status of the buffer.

Example

```
:f %.new
```

---

fold

`address fo`

Fold the lines specified by *address*. A fold collapses several lines on the screen into one line, which can later be unfolded. It doesn't affect the text of the file. {vim}

---

foldclose

`[address] foldc[!]`

Close folds in specified *address*, or at present address if none is specified. Add a ! to close more than one level of folds. {vim}

---

foldopen

`[address] foldo[!]`

Open folds in specified *address*, or at present address if none is specified. Add a ! to open more than one level of folds. {vim}

---

global

`[address] g[!]/pattern/[commands]`

Execute *commands* on all lines that contain *pattern* or, if *address* is specified, on all lines within that range. If *commands* are not specified, print all such lines. Add a ! to execute *commands* on all lines *not* containing *pattern*. See also **v**.

Examples

`:g/Unix/p`	*Print all lines containing "Unix"*
`:g/Name:/s/tom/Tom/`	*Change "tom" to "Tom" on all lines containing "Name:"*

---

hide

`hid`

Close current window unless it is the last window, but do not remove the buffer from memory. This is a safe command to use on an unsaved buffer. {vim}

---

insert

```
[address] i[!]
text
.
```

Insert *text* at line before the specified *address*, or at present address if none is specified. Add a ! to switch the `autoindent` setting during input of *text*. Terminate input of new text by entering a line consisting of just a period.

join

[*address*] j[!] [*count*]

Place the text in the specified range on one line, with whitespace adjusted to provide two space characters after a period (.), no space characters before a), and one space character otherwise. Add a ! to prevent whitespace adjustment.

Example

```
:1,5j!                Join first five lines, preserving whitespace
```

jumps

ju

Print jump list used with CTRL-I and CTRL-O commands. The jump list is a record of most movement commands that skip over multiple lines. It records the position of the cursor before each jump. {vim}

k

[*address*] k *char*

Same as mark; see **mark**, later in this list.

left

[*address*] le [*count*]

Left-align lines specified by *address*, or current line if no address is specified. Indent lines by *count* spaces. {vim}

list

[*address*] l [*count*]

Print the specified lines so that tabs display as ^I, and the ends of lines display as $. l is like a temporary version of :set list.

map

map[!] [*string commands*]

Define a keyboard macro named *string* as the specified sequence of *commands*. *string* is usually a single character, or the sequence #*num*, representing a function key on the keyboard. Use a ! to create a macro for input mode. With no arguments, list the currently defined macros.

Examples

```
:map K dwwP          Transpose two words
:map q :w^M:n^M      Write current file; go to next
:map! + ^[bi(^[ea)   Enclose previous word in parentheses
```

vim has K and q commands, which the above aliases would hide.

mark

[address] `ma` *char*

Mark the specified line with *char*, a single lowercase letter. Return later to the line with `'x` (where *x* is the same as *char*). `vim` also uses uppercase and numeric characters for marks. Lowercase letters work the same as in `vi`. Uppercase letters are associated with filenames and can be used between multiple files. Numbered marks, however, are maintained in a special `viminfo` file and cannot be set using this command. Same as `k`.

marks

`marks` *[chars]*

Print list of marks specified by *chars*, or all current marks if no chars specified. {vim}

Example

`:marks abc`	*Print marks a, b, and c*

mkexrc

`mk[!]` *file*

Create an `.exrc` file containing `set` commands for changed `ex` options and key mappings. This saves the current option settings, allowing you to restore them later.

move

[address] `m` *destination*

Move the lines specified by *address* to the *destination* address.

Example

`:.,/Note/m /END/`	*Move text block to after line containing "END"*

new

[count] `new`

Create a new window *count* lines high with an empty buffer. {vim}

next

`n[!] [[`*+num*`]` *filelist*`]`

Edit the next file from the command-line argument list. Use `args` to list these files. If *filelist* is provided, replace the current argument list with *filelist* and begin editing on the first file. With the *+num* argument, begin editing on line *num*. Or *num* may be a pattern, of the form */pattern*.

Example

`:n chap*`	*Start editing all "chapter" files*

nohlsearch

noh

Temporarily stop highlighting all matches to a search when using the hlsearch option. Highlighting is resumed with the next search. {vim}

number

[*address*] nu [*count*]

Print each line specified by *address*, preceded by its buffer line number. Use # as an alternate abbreviation for number. *count* specifies the number of lines to show, starting with *address*.

only

on [!]

Make the current window be the only one on the screen. Windows open on modified buffers are not removed from the screen (hidden), unless you also use the ! character. {vim}

open

[*address*] o [*/pattern/*]

Enter open mode (vi) at the lines specified by *address*, or at the lines matching *pattern*. Exit open mode with Q. Open mode lets you use the regular vi commands, but only one line at a time. It can be useful on slow dialup lines (or on very distant Internet ssh connections).

preserve

pre

Save the current editor buffer as though the system were about to crash.

previous

prev[!]

Edit the previous file from the command-line argument list. {vim}

print

[*address*] p [*count*]

Print the lines specified by *address*. *count* specifies the number of lines to print, starting with *address*. P is another abbreviation.

Example

:100;+5p	*Show line 100 and the next 5 lines*

put

[*address*] pu [*char*]

Place previously deleted or yanked lines from named register specified by *char*, to the line specified by *address*. If *char* is not specified, the last deleted or yanked text is restored.

qall

`qa[!]`

Close all windows and terminate current editing session. Use ! to discard changes made since the last save. {vim}

quit

`q[!]`

Terminate current editing session. Use ! to discard changes made since the last save. If the editing session includes additional files in the argument list that were never accessed, quit by typing `q!` or by typing `q` twice. `vim` only closes the editing window if there are still other windows open on the screen.

read

[*address*] r *filename*

Copy the text of *filename* after the line specified by *address*. If *filename* is not specified, the current filename is used.

Example

`:0r $HOME/data` — *Read file in at top of current file*

read

[*address*] r !*command*

Read the output of shell *command* into the text after the line specified by *address*.

Example

`:$r !spell %` — *Place results of spell checking at end of file*

recover

rec [*file*]

Recover *file* from the system save area.

redo

`red`

Restore last undone change. Same as `CTRL-R`. {vim}

resize

res [[±]*num*]

Resize current window to be *num* lines high. If + or - is specified, increase or decrease the current window height by *num* lines. {vim}

rewind

`rew[!]`

Rewind argument list and begin editing the first file in the list. Add a ! to rewind even if the current file has not been saved since the last change.

right

`[address] ri [width]`

Right-align lines specified by *address*, or current line if no address is specified, to column *width*. Use `textwidth` option if no *width* is specified. {vim}

sbnext

`[count] sbn [count]`

Split the current window and begin editing the *count* next buffer from the buffer list. If no count is specified, edit the next buffer in the buffer list. {vim}

sbuffer

`[num] sb [num]`

Split the current window and begin editing buffer *num* from the buffer list in the new window. The buffer to be edited may also be specified by filename. If no buffer is specified, open the current buffer in the new window. {vim}

set

`se parameter1 parameter2 ...`

Set a value to an option with each *parameter*, or, if no *parameter* is supplied, print all options that have been changed from their defaults. For boolean options, each *parameter* can be phrased as *option* or no*option*; other options can be assigned with the syntax *option=value*. Specify `all` to list current settings. The form set *option*? displays the value of *option*. See the list of set options in the section "The :set Command," earlier in this chapter.

Examples

```
:set nows wm=10
:set all
```

shell

`sh`

Create a new shell. Resume editing when the shell terminates.

snext

`[count] sn [[+num] filelist]`

Split the current window and begin editing the next file from the command-line argument list. If *count* is provided, edit the *count* next file. If *filelist* is provided, replace the current argument list with *filelist* and begin editing the first file. With the +*n* argument, begin editing on line *num*. Alternately, *num* may be a pattern of the form /*pattern*. {vim}

source

`so file`

Read (source) and execute ex commands from *file*.

Example

```
:so $HOME/.exrc
```

split

`[count] sp [+num] [filename]`

Split the current window and load *filename* in the new window, or the same buffer in both windows if no file is specified. Make the new window *count* lines high, or if *count* is not specified, split the window into equal parts. With the +*n* argument, begin editing on line *num*. *num* may also be a pattern of the form /*pattern*. {vim}

sprevious

`[count] spr [+num]`

Split the current window and begin editing the previous file from the command-line argument list in the new window. If *count* is specified, edit the *count* previous file. With the +*num* argument, begin editing on line *num*. *num* may also be a pattern of the form /*pattern*. {vim}

stop

`st`

Suspend the editing session. Same as CTRL-Z. Use the shell `fg` command to resume the session.

substitute

`[address] s [/pattern/replacement/] [options] [count]`

Replace the first instance of *pattern* on each of the specified lines with *replacement*. If *pattern* and *replacement* are omitted, repeat last substitution. *count* specifies the number of lines on which to substitute, starting with *address*. See additional examples in Chapter 7. (Spelling out the command name does not work in Solaris `vi`.)

Options

`c`	Prompt for confirmation before each change.
`g`	Substitute all instances of *pattern* on each line (global).
`p`	Print the last line on which a substitution was made.

Examples

`:1,10s/yes/no/g`	*Substitute on first 10 lines*
`:%s/[Hh]ello/Hi/gc`	*Confirm global substitutions*
`:s/Fortran/\U&/ 3`	*Uppercase "Fortran" on next three lines*
`:g/^[0-9][0-9]*/s//Line &:/`	*For every line beginning with one or more digits, add "Line" and a colon*

suspend

`su`

Suspend the editing session. Same as CTRL-Z. Use the shell `fg` command to resume the session.

sview

`[`*count*`] sv [+`*num*`] [`*filename*`]`

Same as the `split` command, but set the `readonly` option for the new buffer. {vim}

t

`[`*address*`] t` *destination*

Copy the lines included in *address* to the specified *destination* address. `t` is equivalent to `copy`.

Example

`:%t$` *Copy the file and add it to the end*

tag

`[`*address*`] ta` *tag*

In the tags file, locate the file and line matching *tag* and start editing there.

Example

Run `ctags`, then switch to the file containing *myfunction*:

```
:!ctags *.c
:tag myfunction
```

tags

`tags`

Print list of tags in the tag stack. {vim}

unabbreviate

`una` *word*

Remove *word* from the list of abbreviations.

undo

`u`

Reverse the changes made by the last editing command. In `vi` the undo command will undo itself, redoing what you undid. `vim` supports multiple levels of undo. Use `redo` to redo an undone change in `vim`.

unhide

`[`*count*`] unh`

Split screen to show one window for each active buffer in the buffer list. If specified, limit the number of windows to *count*. {vim}

unmap

`unm[!] string`

Remove *string* from the list of keyboard macros. Use ! to remove a macro for input mode.

v

`[address] v/pattern/[command]`

Execute *command* on all lines *not* containing *pattern*. If *command* is not specified, print all such lines. v is equivalent to g!. See **global**.

Example

`:v/#include/d`	*Delete all lines except "#include" lines*

version

`ve`

Print the editor's current version number and date of last change.

view

`vie[[+num] filename]`

Same as edit, but set file to readonly. When executed in ex mode, return to normal or visual mode. {vim}

visual

`[address] vi [type] [count]`

Enter visual mode (vi) at the line specified by *address*. Return to ex mode with Q. *type* can be one of -, ^, or . (see the z command). *count* specifies an initial window size.

visual

`vi [+ num] file`

Begin editing *file* in visual mode (vi), optionally at line *num*.

vsplit

`[count] vs [+num] [filename]`

Same as the split command, but split the screen vertically. The *count* argument can be used to specify a width for the new window. {vim}

wall

`wa[!]`

Write all changed buffers with filenames. Add ! to force writing of any buffers marked readonly. {vim}

wnext

`[count] wn[!] [[+num] filename]`

Write current buffer and open next file in argument list, or the *count* next file if specified. If *filename* is specified, edit it next. With the *+num* argument, begin editing on line *num*. *num* may also be a pattern of the form */pattern*. {vim}

write

`[address] w[!] [[>>] file]`

Write lines specified by *address* to *file*, or write full contents of buffer if *address* is not specified. If *file* is also omitted, save the contents of the buffer to the current filename. If >> *file* is used, append lines to the end of the specified *file*. Add a ! to force the editor to write over any current contents of *file*.

Examples

```
:1,10w name_list           Copy first 10 lines to file name_list
:50w >> name_list          Now append line 50
```

write

`[address] w !command`

Write lines specified by *address* to *command*.

Example

```
:1,66w !pr -h myfile | lp        Print first page of file
```

wq

`wq[!]`

Write and quit the file in one action. The file is always written. The ! flag forces the editor to write over any current contents of *file*.

wqall

`wqa[!]`

Write all changed buffers and quit the editor. Add ! to force writing of any buffers marked `readonly`. `xall` is another alias for this command. {vim}

X

`X`

Prompt for an encryption key. This can be preferable to `:set key` as typing the key is not echoed to the console. To remove an encryption key, just reset the key option to an empty value. {vim}

xit

`x`

Write the file if it was changed since the last write; then quit.

yank

`[address] y [char] [count]`

Place lines specified by *address* in named register *char*. Register names are the lowercase letters a–z. Uppercase names append text to the corresponding register. If no *char* is given, place lines in the general register. *count* specifies the number of lines to yank, starting with *address*.

Example

```
:101,200 ya a        Copy lines 100–200 to register "a"
```

---

z

[*address*] z [*type*] [*count*]

Print a window of text with the line specified by *address* at the top. *count* specifies the number of lines to be displayed.

Type

+ Place specified line at the top of the window (default).
- Place specified line at the bottom of the window.
. Place specified line in the center of the window.
^ Print the previous window.
= Place specified line in the center of the window and leave the current line at this line.

&

[*address*] & [*options*] [*count*]

Repeat the previous substitute (s) command. *count* specifies the number of lines on which to substitute, starting with *address*. *options* are the same as for the substitute command.

Examples

```
:s/Overdue/Paid/       Substitute once on current line
:g/Status/&            Redo substitution on all "Status" lines
```

@

[*address*] @ [*char*]

Execute contents of register specified by *char*. If *address* is given, move cursor to the specified address first. If *char* is @, repeat the last @ command.

=

[*address*] =

Print the line number of the line indicated by *address*. Default is line number of the last line.

!

[*address*] !*command*

Execute Unix *command* in a shell. If *address* is specified, use the lines contained in *address* as standard input to *command*, and replace the lines with the output and error output. (This is called *filtering* the text through the *command*.)

Examples

`:!ls`	*List files in the current directory*
`:11,20!sort -f`	*Sort lines 11–20 of current file*

<>

[address] < *[count]*
or
[address] > *[count]*

Shift lines specified by *address* either left (<) or right (>). Only leading spaces and tabs are added or removed when shifting lines. *count* specifies the number of lines to shift, starting with *address*. The `shiftwidth` option controls the number of columns that are shifted. Repeating the < or > increases the shift amount. For example, :>>> shifts three times as much as :>.

~

[address] ~ *[count]*

Replace the last used regular expression (even if from a search, and not from an `s` command) with the replacement pattern from the most recent `s` (substitute) command. This is rather obscure; see Chapter 6 of *Learning the vi Editor* for details.

---

address

address

Print the lines specified in *address*.

ENTER

Print the next line in the file. (For ex only, not from the : prompt in `vi`.)

10
The sed Editor

The sed "stream editor" is one of the most prominent Unix text processing tools. It is most often used for performing simple substitutions on data streams going through pipelines, but sed scripts can be written to do much more.

This chapter presents the following topics:

- Conceptual overview of sed
- Command-line syntax
- Syntax of sed commands
- Group summary of sed commands
- Alphabetical summary of sed commands

Source code for GNU sed is available from *ftp://ftp.gnu.org/gnu/sed/*. The Free Software Foundation's home page for sed is *http://www.gnu.org/software/sed/sed.html*. For more information on sed, see *sed & awk*, listed in the Bibliography.

Conceptual Overview

The stream editor, sed, is a noninteractive editor. It interprets a script and performs the actions in the script. sed is stream-oriented because, like many Unix programs, input flows through the program and is directed to standard output. For example, sort is stream-oriented; vi is not. sed's input typically comes from a file or pipe but it can also be taken from the keyboard. Output goes to the screen by default but can be captured in a file or sent through a pipe instead. GNU sed can edit files that use multibyte character sets.

Typical Uses of sed

- Editing one or more files automatically.
- Simplifying repetitive edits to multiple files.
- Writing conversion programs.

sed Operation

sed operates as follows:

- Each line of input is copied into a "pattern space," an internal buffer where editing operations are performed.
- All editing commands in a sed script are applied, in order, to each line of input.
- Editing commands are applied to all lines (globally) unless line addressing restricts the lines affected.
- If a command changes the input, subsequent commands and address tests are applied to the current line in the pattern space, not the original input line.
- The original input file is unchanged because the editing commands modify an in-memory copy of each original input line. The copy is sent to standard output (but can be redirected to a file).
- sed also maintains the "hold space," a separate buffer that can be used to save data for later retrieval.

Command-Line Syntax

The syntax for invoking sed has two forms:

```
sed [-n] [-e] 'command' file(s)
sed [-n]  -f  scriptfile file(s)
```

The first form allows you to specify an editing command on the command line, surrounded by single quotes. The second form allows you to specify a *scriptfile*, a file containing sed commands. Both forms may be used together, and they may be used multiple times. If no *file(s)* is specified, sed reads from standard input.

Standard Options

The following options are recognized:

-n
: Suppress the default output; sed displays only those lines specified with the p command or with the p flag of the s command.

-e *cmd*
: Next argument is an editing command. Necessary if multiple scripts or commands are specified.

-f *file*
: Next argument is a file containing editing commands.

If the first line of the script is `#n`, `sed` behaves as if `-n` had been specified.

Multiple `-e` and `-f` options may be provided, and they may be mixed. The final script consists of the concatenation of all the *script* and *file* arguments.

GNU sed Options

GNU `sed` accepts a number of additional command-line options, as well as long-option equivalents for the standard options. The GNU `sed` options are:

`-e` *cmd*, `--expression` *cmd*
: Use *cmd* as editing commands.

`-f` *file*, `--file` *file*
: Obtain editing commands from *file*.

`--help`
: Print a usage message and exit.

`-i[`*suffix*`]`, `--in-place[=`*suffix*`]`
: Edit files in place, overwriting the original file. If optional *suffix* is supplied, use it for renaming the original file as a backup file. See the GNU `sed` online Info documentation for the details.

`-l` *len*, `--line-length` *len*
: Set the line length for the `l` command to *len* characters.

`-n`, `--quiet`, `--silent`
: Suppress the default output; `sed` displays only those lines specified with the `p` command or with the `p` flag of the `s` command.

`--posix`
: Disable *all* GNU extensions. Setting POSIXLY_CORRECT in the environment merely disables those extensions that are incompatible with the POSIX standard.

`-r`, `--regex-extended`
: Use Extended Regular Expressions instead of Basic Regular Expressions. See Chapter 7 for more information.

`-s`, `--separate`
: Instead of considering the input to be one long stream consisting of the concatenation of all the input files, treat each file separately. Line numbers start over with each file; the address `$` refers to the last line of each file; files read by the `R` command are rewound; and range addresses (`/x/,/y/`) may not cross file boundaries.

`-u`, `--unbuffered`
: Buffer input and output as little as possible. Useful for editing the output of `tail -f` when you don't want to wait for the output.

`--version`
: Print the version of GNU `sed` and a copyright notice, and then exit.

Syntax of sed Commands

sed commands have the general form:

    [address[,address]][!]command [arguments]

commands consist of a single letter or symbol; they are described later, by group and alphabetically. *arguments* include the label supplied to b or t, the filename supplied to r or w, and the substitution flags for s. *addresses* are described below.

Pattern Addressing

A sed command can specify zero, one, or two addresses. In POSIX sed, an address has one of the forms in the following table. Regular expressions are described in Chapter 7. Additionally, \n can be used to match any newline in the pattern space (resulting from the N command), but not the newline at the end of the pattern space.

Address	Meaning
/pattern/	Lines that match *pattern*.
\;*pattern*;	Like previous, but use semicolon as the delimiter instead of slash. Any character may be used. This is useful if *pattern* contains multiple slash characters.
N	Line number *N*.
$	The last input line.

If the command specifies:	Then the command is applied to:
No address	Each input line.
One address	Any line matching the address. Some commands accept only one address: a, i, r, q, and =.
Two comma-separated addresses	First matching line and all succeeding lines up to and including a line matching the second address.
An address followed by !	All lines that do *not* match the address.

GNU sed allows additional address forms:

Address	Meaning
*/pattern/*i	Match pattern, ignoring case. I may be used instead of i.
*/pattern/*m	Match pattern, allowing ^ and $ to match around an embedded newline. M may be used instead of m.
0,*/pattern/*	Similar to 1,*/pattern/*, but if line 1 matches *pattern*, it will end the range.
address,+*N*	Matches line matching *address*, and the *N* following lines.
address~*incr*	Matches line matching *address*, and every *incr* lines after it. For example, 42~3 matches 42, 45, 48, and so on.

Examples

Command	Action performed
`s/xx/yy/g`	Substitute on all lines (all occurrences).
`/BSD/d`	Delete lines containing BSD.
`/^BEGIN/,/^END/p`	Print between BEGIN and END, inclusive.
`/SAVE/!d`	Delete any line that doesn't contain SAVE.
`/BEGIN/,/END/!s/xx/yy/g`	Substitute on all lines, except between BEGIN and END.

Braces ({}) are used in sed to nest one address inside another or to apply multiple commands at a single matched address.

```
[/pattern/[,/pattern/]]{
command1
command2
}
```

The opening curly brace must end its line, and the closing curly brace must be on a line by itself. Be sure there are no spaces after the braces.

GNU sed Regular Expression Extensions

With the -r option, GNU sed uses Extended Regular Expressions instead of Basic Regular Expressions. (See Chapter 7 for more information.) However, even without -r, you can use additional escape sequences for more powerful text matching. The following escape sequences are valid only in regular expressions:

`\b`
: Matches on a word boundary, where of the two surrounding characters (*x*\b*y*) one is a word-constituent character and the other is not.

`\B`
: Matches on a nonword boundary, where both of the two surrounding characters (*x*\B*y*) are either word-constituent or not word-constituent.

`\w`
: Matches any word-constituent character (i.e., a letter, digit, or underscore).

`\W`
: Matches any non-word-constituent character (i.e., anything that is *not* a letter, digit, or underscore).

`` \` ``
: Matches the beginning of the pattern space. This is different from ^ when the m modifier is used for a pattern or the s command.

`\'`
: Matches the end of the pattern space. This is different from $ when the m modifier is used for a pattern or the s command.

The following escape sequences may be used anywhere.

`\a`
: The ASCII BEL character.

`\f`
: The ASCII formfeed character.

`\n`
: The ASCII newline character.

`\r`
: The ASCII carriage return character.

`\v`
: The ASCII vertical tab character.

`\d`*NN*
: The character whose ASCII decimal value is *NN* (version 4.0 and later).

`\o`*NN*
: The character whose ASCII octal value is *NN* (version 4.0 and later).

`\x`*NN*
: The character whose ASCII hexadecimal value is *NN* (version 4.0 and later).

Group Summary of sed Commands

In the lists that follow, the sed commands are grouped by function and are described tersely. Full descriptions, including syntax and examples, can be found in the following section, "Alphabetical Summary." Commands marked with a † are specific to GNU sed.

Basic Editing

`a\`	Append text after a line.
`c\`	Replace text (usually a text block).
`i\`	Insert text before a line.
`d`	Delete lines.
`s`	Make substitutions.
`y`	Translate characters (like Unix `tr`).

Line Information

`=`	Display line number of a line.
`l`	Display control characters in ASCII.
`p`	Display the line.

Input/Output Processing

`e`†	Execute commands.
`n`	Skip current line and go to the next line.
`r`	Read another file's contents into the output stream.
`R`†	Read one line from a file into the output.
`w`	Write input lines to another file.
`W`†	Write first line in pattern space to another file.
`q`	Quit the sed script (no further output).
`Q`†	Quit without printing the pattern space.
`v`†	Require a specific version of GNU sed to run the script.

Yanking and Putting

`h`	Copy into hold space; wipe out what's there.
`H`	Copy into hold space; append to what's there.
`g`	Get the hold space back; wipe out the destination line.
`G`	Get the hold space back; append to the pattern space.
`x`	Exchange contents of the hold and pattern spaces.

Branching Commands

`b`	Branch to *label* or to end of script.
`t`	Same as `b`, but branch only after substitution.

T†	Same as t, but branch only if no successful substitutions.
:*label*	Label branched to by t or b.

Multiline Input Processing

N	Read another line of input (creates embedded newline).
D	Delete up to the embedded newline.
P	Print up to the embedded newline.

Alphabetical Summary of sed Commands

GNU sed lets you use the filenames /dev/stdin, /dev/stdout, and /dev/stderr to refer to standard input, output, and error respectively for the r, R, w, and W commands and the w flag to the s command.

GNU-specific commands or extensions are noted with {G} in the command synopsis. When the GNU version allows a command to have two addresses, the command is performed for each input line within the range.

#

#

Begin a comment in a sed script. Valid only as the first character of the first line. (Some versions, including GNU sed, allow comments anywhere, but it is better not to rely on this.) If the first line of the script is #n, sed behaves as if -n had been specified.

:

:*label*

Label a line in the script for the transfer of control by b or t. According to POSIX, sed must support labels that are unique in the first eight characters. GNU sed has no limit, but some older versions only support up to seven characters.

=

[/*pattern*/]=
[*address1*[,*address2*]]= {G}

Write to standard output the line number of each line addressed by *pattern*.

---

a

[*address*]a\
text
[*address1*[,*address2*]]a \ {G}
text

Append *text* following each line matched by *address*. If *text* goes over more than one line, newlines must be "hidden" by preceding them with a backslash. The *text* is terminated by the first newline that is not hidden in this way. The *text* is not available in the pattern space, and subsequent commands cannot be applied to it. The results of this command are sent to standard output when the list of editing commands is finished, regardless of what happens to the current line in the pattern space.

The GNU version accepts two addresses, and allows you to put the first line of *text* on the same line as the a command.

Example

```
$a\
This goes after the last line in the file\
(marked by $).  This text is escaped at the\
end of each line, except for the last one.
```

---

b

`[`*`address1`*`[,`*`address2`*`]]b[`*`label`*`]`

Unconditionally transfer control to `:`*`label`* elsewhere in script. That is, the command following the *label* is the next command applied to the current line. If no *label* is specified, control falls through to the end of the script, so no more commands are applied to the current line.

Example

```
# Ignore HTML tables; resume script after </table>:
/<table/,/<\/table>/b
```

---

c

`[`*`address1`*`[,`*`address2`*`]]c\`
`text`

Replace (change) the lines selected by the address(es) with *text*. (See **a** for details on *text*.) When a range of lines is specified, all lines are replaced as a group by a single copy of *text*. The contents of the pattern space are, in effect, deleted and no subsequent editing commands can be applied to the pattern space (or to *text*).

Example

```
# Replace first 100 lines in a file:
1,100c\
\
<First 100 names to be supplied>
```

---

d

`[`*`address1`*`[,`*`address2`*`]]d`

Delete the addressed line (or lines) from the pattern space. Thus, the line is not passed to standard output. A new line of input is read, and editing resumes with the first command in the script.

Example

```
# Delete all empty lines, including lines with just whitespace:
/^[□→]*$/d
```

D

*[address1[,address2]]*D

Delete the first part (up to embedded newline) of a multiline pattern space created by the N command and resume editing with the first command in the script. If this command empties the pattern space, then a new line of input is read, as if the d command had been executed.

Example

```
# Strip multiple blank lines, leaving only one:
/^$/{
N
/^\n$/D
}
```

e

*[address1[,address2]]*e *[command]* {G}

With *command*, execute the command and send the result to standard output. Without *command*, execute the contents of the pattern space as a command, and replace the pattern space with the results.

g

*[address1[,address2]]*g

Paste the contents of the hold space (see **h** and **H**) back into the pattern space, wiping out the previous contents of the pattern space. The Example shows a simple way to copy lines.

Example

This script collects all lines containing the word *Item*: and copies them to a place marker later in the file. The place marker is overwritten:

```
/Item:/H
/<Replace this line with the item list>/g
```

G

*[address1[,address2]]*G

Same as g, except that a newline and the hold space are pasted to the end of the pattern space instead of overwriting it. The Example shows a simple way to "cut and paste" lines.

Example

This script collects all lines containing the word *Item*: and moves them after a place marker later in the file. The original *Item*: lines are deleted.

```
/Item:/{
H
d
}
/Summary of items:/G
```

h

[*address1*[,*address2*]]h

Copy the pattern space into the hold space, a special temporary buffer. The previous contents of the hold space are obliterated. You can use h to save a line before editing it.

Example

```
# Edit a line; print the change; replay the original
/Unix/{
h
s/.* Unix \(.*\) .*/\1:/
p
x
}
```

Sample input:

```
This describes the Unix ls command.
This describes the Unix cp command.
```

Sample output:

```
ls:
This describes the Unix ls command.
cp:
This describes the Unix cp command.
```

H

[*address1*[,*address2*]]H

Append a newline and then the contents of the pattern space to the contents of the hold space. Even if the hold space is empty, H still appends a newline. H is like an incremental copy. See the Examples under **g** and **G**.

i

[*address*]i\
text
[*address1*[,*address2*]]i \ {G}
text

Insert *text* before each line matched by *address*. (See **a** for details on *text*.)

The GNU version accepts two addresses, and allows you to put the first line of *text* on the same line as the i command.

Example

```
/Item 1/i\
The five items are listed below:
```

l

[*address1*[,*address2*]]l
[*address1*[,*address2*]]l [*len*] {G}

List the contents of the pattern space, showing nonprinting characters as ASCII codes. Long lines are wrapped. With GNU sed, *len* is the character position at which to wrap long lines. A value of 0 means to never break lines.

n

[*address1*[,*address2*]]n

Read the next line of input into pattern space. The current line is sent to standard output, and the next line becomes the current line. Control passes to the command following n instead of resuming at the top of the script.

Example

In DocBook/XML, titles follow section tags. Suppose you are using a convention where each opening section tag is on a line by itself, with the title on the following line. To print all the section titles, invoke this script with sed -n:

```
/<sect[1-4]/{
n
p
}
```

N

[*address1*[,*address2*]]N

Append the next input line to contents of pattern space; the new line is separated from the previous contents of the pattern space by a newline. (This command is designed to allow pattern matches across two lines.) By using \n to match the embedded newline, you can match patterns across multiple lines. See the Example under **D**.

Examples

Like the Example in **n**, but print the section tag line as well as header title:

```
/<sect[1-4]/{
N
p
}
```

Join two lines (replace newline with space):

```
/<sect[1-4]/{
N
s/\n/ /
p
}
```

p

*[address1[,address2]]*p

Print the addressed line(s). Note that this can result in duplicate output unless default output is suppressed by using `#n` or the `-n` command-line option. Typically used before commands that change control flow (`d`, `n`, `b`), which might prevent the current line from being output. See the Examples under **h**, **n**, and **N**.

P

*[address1[,address2]]*P

Print first part (up to embedded newline) of multiline pattern space created by `N` command. Same as `p` if `N` has not been applied to a line.

Example

Suppose you have function references in two formats:

```
function(arg1, arg2)
function(arg1,
         arg2)
```

The following script changes argument `arg2`, regardless of whether it appears on the same line as the function name:

```
s/function(arg1, arg2)/function(arg1, XX)/
/function(/{
N
s/arg2/XX/
P
D
}
```

q

*[address]*q
*[address]*q *[value]* {G}

Quit when *address* is encountered. The addressed line is first written to the output (if default output is not suppressed), along with any text appended to it by previous `a` or `r` commands. GNU sed allows you to provide *value*, which is used as the exit status.

Examples

Delete everything after the addressed line:

```
/Garbled text follows:/q
```

Print only the first 50 lines of a file:

```
50q
```

Q

*[address]*Q *[value]* {G}

Quits processing, but without printing the pattern space. If *value* is provided, it is used as sed's exit status.

r

*[address]*r *file*
*[address1[,address2]]*r *file* {G}

Read contents of *file* and append to the output after the contents of the pattern space. There must be exactly one space between the r and the filename. The GNU version accepts two addresses.

Example

```
/The list of items follows:/r item_file
```

R

*[address1[,address2]]*R *file* {G}

Read one line of *file* and append to the output after the contents of the pattern space. Successive R commands read successive lines from *file*.

s

*[address1[,address2]]*s/*pattern*/*replacement*/*[flags]*

Substitute *replacement* for *pattern* on each addressed line. If pattern addresses are used, the pattern // represents the last pattern address specified. Any delimiter may be used. Use \ within *pattern* or *replacement* to escape the delimiter. The following flags can be specified (those marked with a † are specific to GNU sed):

n
: Replace *n*th instance of *pattern* on each addressed line. *n* is any number in the range 1 to 512, and the default is 1.

e†
: If the substitution was made, execute the contents of the pattern space as a shell command and replace the pattern space with the results.

g
: Replace all instances of *pattern* on each addressed line, not just the first instance.

i *or* I†
: Do a case-insensitive regular expression match.

m *or* M†
: Allow ^ and $ to match around a newline embedded in the pattern space.

p
: Print the line if the substitution is successful. If several successive substitutions are successful, sed prints multiple copies of the line.

w *file*
: Write the line to *file* if a replacement was done. In Unix sed, a maximum of 10 different *files* can be opened.

  GNU sed allows you to use the special filenames /dev/stdout and /dev/stderr to write to standard output or standard error, respectively.

Within the *replacement*, GNU sed accepts special escape sequences, with the following meanings:

`\L`	Lowercase the replacement text until a terminating `\E` or `\U`.
`\l`	Lowercase the following character only.
`\U`	Uppercase the replacement text until a terminating `\E` or `\L`.
`\u`	Uppercase the following character only.
`\E`	Terminate case conversion from `\L` or `\U`.

Examples

Here are some short, commented scripts:

```
# Change third and fourth quote to ( and ):
/function/{
s/"/)/4
s/"/(/3
}

# Remove all quotes on a given line:
/Title/s/"//g

# Remove first colon and all quotes; print resulting
lines:
s/://p
s/"//gp

# Change first "if" but leave "ifdef" alone:
/ifdef/!s/if/   if/
```

---

t

`[address1[,address2]]t [label]`

Test if successful substitutions have been made on addressed lines, and if so, branch to the line marked by `:label`. (See **b** and **:**.) If *label* is not specified, control branches to the bottom of the script. The `t` command is like a case statement in the C programming language or the various shell programming languages. You test each case; when it's true, you exit the construct.

Example

Suppose you want to fill empty fields of a database. You have this:

```
ID: 1   Name: greg   Rate: 45
ID: 2   Name: dale
ID: 3
```

You want this:

```
ID: 1   Name: greg   Rate: 45   Phone: ??
ID: 2   Name: dale   Rate: ??   Phone: ??
ID: 3   Name: ????   Rate: ??   Phone: ??
```

You need to test the number of fields already there. Here's the script (fields are tab-separated):

```
#n
/ID/{
s/ID: .* Name: .* Rate: .*/&	Phone: ??/p
t
s/ID: .* Name: .*/&	Rate: ??	Phone: ??/p
t
s/ID: .*/&	Name: ????	Rate: ??	Phone: ??/p
}
```

T

[*address1*[,*address2*]]T [*label*] **{G}**

Like t, but only branches to *label* if there were *not* any successful substitutions. (See **b**, **t**, and **:**.) If *label* is not specified, control branches to the bottom of the script.

---

v

[*address1*[,*address2*]]v [*version*] **{G}**

This command doesn't do anything. You use it to require GNU sed for your script. This works, since non-GNU versions of sed don't implement the command at all, and will therefore fail. If you supply a specific *version*, then GNU sed fails if the required version is newer than the one executing the script.

---

w

[*address1*[,*address2*]]w *file*

Append contents of pattern space to *file*. This action occurs when the command is encountered rather than when the pattern space is output. Exactly one space must separate the w and the filename. This command creates the file if it does not exist; if the file exists, its contents are overwritten each time the script is executed. Multiple write commands that direct output to the same file append to the end of the file.

Most Unix versions of sed allow a maximum of only 10 different files to be opened in a script. The GNU version does not have this limit.

GNU sed allows you to use the special filenames /dev/stdout and /dev/stderr to write to standard output or standard error, respectively.

Example

```
# Store HTML tables in  a file
/<table/,/<\/table>/w tables.html
```

W

[*address1*[,*address2*]]W *file*

Like w, but only write the contents of the first line in the pattern space to the file.

x

[*address1*[,*address2*]]x

Exchange the contents of the pattern space with the contents of the hold space. See **h** for an example.

y

[*address1*[,*address2*]]y/*abc*/*xyz*/

Translate characters. Change every instance of *a* to *x*, *b* to *y*, *c* to *z*, etc.

Example

```
# Change item 1, 2, 3 to Item A, B, C ...
/^item [1-9]/y/i123456789/IABCDEFGHI/
```

11 The awk Programming Language

The awk programming language is often used for text and string manipulation within shell scripts, particularly when input data can be viewed as records and fields. However, it is also an elegant and capable programming language that allows you to accomplish a lot with very little work.

This chapter presents the following topics:

- Conceptual overview
- Command-line syntax
- Patterns and actions
- Built-in variables
- Operators
- Variables and array assignment
- User-defined functions
- gawk-specific facilities
- Implementation limits
- Group listing of awk functions and commands
- Alphabetical summary of awk functions and commands
- Source code

For more information, see *sed & awk* and *Effective awk Programming*, listed in the Bibliography.

Conceptual Overview

awk is a pattern-matching program for processing files, especially when each line has a simple field-oriented layout. The new version of awk, called nawk, provides additional capabilities.* Every modern Unix system comes with a version of new awk, and its use is recommended over old awk. The GNU version of awk, called gawk, implements new awk and provides a number of additional features.

Different systems vary in what new and old awk are called. Some have oawk and awk, for the old and new versions, respectively. Others have awk and nawk. Still others only have awk, which is the new version. This example shows what happens if your awk is the old one:

```
$ awk 1 /dev/null
awk: syntax error near line 1
awk: bailing out near line 1
```

awk will exit silently if it is the new version.

The POSIX standard for awk is based on new awk, and the standard uses the simple designation awk for that language. Thus, we do also. If your system's awk is the old one, find the new one, and use it for your programs.

Solaris is the only modern Unix system that persists in having old awk as the default version. You should be sure to put /usr/xpg4/bin in your shell's search path *before* /usr/bin, so that you will get a POSIX-compliant version of awk. Alternatively, just install the GNU version.

Items described here as "common extensions" are often available in different versions of new awk, as well as in gawk, but should not be used if strict portability of your programs is important to you.

The freely available versions of awk described in the section "Source Code," later in this chapter, all implement new awk.

With awk, you can:

- Think of a text file as made up of records and fields in a textual database.
- Perform arithmetic and string operations.
- Use programming constructs such as loops and conditionals.
- Produce formatted reports.
- Define your own functions.
- Execute Unix commands from a script.
- Process the results of Unix commands.
- Process command-line arguments gracefully.
- Work easily with multiple input streams.
- Flush open output files and pipes (with the latest Bell Laboratories version of awk).

In addition, with GNU awk (gawk), you can:

- Use regular expressions to separate records, as well as fields.
- Skip to the start of the next file, not just the next record.

* It really isn't so new. The additional features were added in 1984, and it was first shipped with System V Release 3.1 in 1987.

- Perform more powerful string substitutions.
- Sort arrays.
- Retrieve and format system time values.
- Use octal and hexadecimal constants in your program.
- Do bit manipulation.
- Internationalize your awk programs, allowing strings to be translated into a local language at runtime.
- Perform two-way I/O to a coprocess.
- Open a two-way TCP/IP connection to a socket.
- Dynamically add built-in functions.
- Profile your awk programs.

Command-Line Syntax

The syntax for invoking awk has two forms:

```
awk [options] 'script' var=value file(s)
awk [options] -f scriptfile var=value file(s)
```

You can specify a *script* directly on the command line, or you can store a script in a *scriptfile* and specify it with -f. POSIX awk allows multiple -f scripts. Variables can be assigned a value on the command line. The value can be a string or numeric constant, a shell variable ($*name*), or a command substitution (`*cmd*`), but the value is available only after the BEGIN statement is executed.

awk operates on one or more *files*. If none are specified (or if - is specified), awk reads from the standard input.

Standard Options

The standard options are:

-F*fs*
: Set the field separator to *fs*. This is the same as setting the built-in variable FS. POSIX awk allows *fs* to be a regular expression. Each input line, or *record*, is divided into fields by white space (spaces or TABs) or by some other user-definable field separator. Fields are referred to by the variables $1, $2,..., $*n*. $0 refers to the entire record.

-v *var*=*value*
: Assign a *value* to variable *var*. This allows assignment before the script begins execution.

For example, to print the first three (colon-separated) fields of each record on separate lines:

```
awk -F: '{ print $1; print $2; print $3 }' /etc/passwd
```

Many examples are shown later in the section "Simple Pattern-Action Examples."

Important gawk Options

Besides the standard command-line options, `gawk` has a large number of additional options. This section lists those that are of most value in day-to-day use. Any unique abbreviation of these options is acceptable.

`--dump-variables[=`*`file`*`]`
: When the program has finished running, print a sorted list of global variables and their types and final values to *file*. The default file is `awkvars.out`.

`--gen-po`
: Read the `awk` program and print all strings marked as translatable to standard output in the form of a GNU `gettext` Portable Object file. See the later section "Internationalization," for more information.

`--help`
: Print a usage message to standard error and exit.

`--lint[=fatal]`
: Enable checking of nonportable or dubious constructs, both when the program is read, and as it runs. With an argument of `fatal`, lint warnings become fatal errors.

`--non-decimal-data`
: Allow octal and hexadecimal data in the input to be recognized as such. This option is not recommended; use `strtonum()` in your program, instead.

`--profile[=`*`file`*`]`
: With `gawk`, put a "prettyprinted" version of the program in *file*. Default is `awkprof.out`. With `pgawk` (see the "Profiling" section later in this chapter), put the profiled listing of the program in *file*.

`--posix`
: Turn on strict POSIX compatibility, in which all common and `gawk`-specific extensions are disabled.

`--source='`*`program text`*`'`
: Use *program text* as the `awk` source code. Use this option with `-f` to mix command line programs with `awk` library files.

`--traditional`
: Disable all `gawk`-specific extensions, but allow common extensions (e.g., the ** operator for exponentiation).

`--version`
: Print the version of `gawk` on standard error and exit.

Patterns and Procedures

`awk` scripts consist of patterns and actions:

```
pattern  { action }
```

Both are optional. If *pattern* is missing, { *action* } is applied to all lines. If { *action* } is missing, the matched line is printed.

Patterns

A pattern can be any of the following:

```
general expression
/regular expression/
relational expression
pattern-matching expression
BEGIN
END
```

- General expressions can be composed of quoted strings, numbers, operators, function calls, user-defined variables, or any of the predefined variables described later in the section "Built-in Variables."
- Regular expressions use the extended set of metacharacters as described in Chapter 7.
- The `^` and `$` metacharacters refer to the beginning and end of a string (such as the fields), respectively, rather than the beginning and end of a line. In particular, these metacharacters will *not* match at a newline embedded in the middle of a string.
- Relational expressions use the relational operators listed in the section "Operators," later in this chapter. For example, `$2 > $1` selects lines for which the second field is greater than the first. Comparisons can be either string or numeric. Thus, depending upon the types of data in `$1` and `$2`, `awk` will do either a numeric or a string comparison. This can change from one record to the next.
- Pattern-matching expressions use the operators `~` (matches) and `!~` (doesn't match). See the section "Operators" later in this chapter.
- The `BEGIN` pattern lets you specify actions that take place *before* the first input line is processed. (Generally, you process the command line and set global variables here.)
- The `END` pattern lets you specify actions that take place *after* the last input record is read.
- `BEGIN` and `END` patterns may appear multiple times. The actions are merged as if there had been one large action.

Except for `BEGIN` and `END`, patterns can be combined with the Boolean operators `||` (or), `&&` (and), and `!` (not). An inclusive range of lines can also be specified using comma-separated patterns:

```
pattern,pattern
```

Procedures

Procedures consist of one or more commands, function calls, or variable assignments, separated by newlines or semicolons, and are contained within curly braces. Commands fall into five groups:

- Variable or array assignments
- Input/output commands
- Built-in functions

- Control-flow commands
- User-defined functions

Simple Pattern-Action Examples

- Print first field of each line:

```
{ print $1 }
```

- Print all lines that contain *pattern*:

```
/pattern/
```

- Print first field of lines that contain *pattern*:

```
/pattern/ { print $1 }
```

- Select records containing more than two fields:

```
NF > 2
```

- Interpret input records as a group of lines up to a blank line. Each line is a single field:

```
BEGIN { FS = "\n"; RS = "" }
```

- Print fields 2 and 3 in switched order, but only on lines whose first field matches the string `URGENT`:

```
$1 ~ /URGENT/ { print $3, $2 }
```

- Count and print the number of lines matching *pattern*:

```
/pattern/ { ++x }
END { print x }
```

- Add numbers in second column and print the total:

```
{ total += $2 }
END { print "column total is", total}
```

- Print lines that contain fewer than 20 characters:

```
length($0) < 20
```

- Print each line that begins with `Name:` and that contains exactly 7 fields:

```
NF == 7 && /^Name:/
```

- Print the fields of each record in reverse order, one per line:

```
{
        for (i = NF; i >= 1; i--)
                print $i
}
```

Built-in Variables

All `awk` variables are included in `gawk`.

Version	Variable	Description
awk	ARGC	Number of arguments on the command line.
	ARGV	An array containing the command-line arguments, indexed from 0 to ARGC - 1.
	CONVFMT	String conversion format for numbers ("%.6g"). (POSIX)
	ENVIRON	An associative array of environment variables.
	FILENAME	Current filename.
	FNR	Like NR, but relative to the current file.
	FS	Field separator (a space).
	NF	Number of fields in current record.
	NR	Number of the current record.
	OFMT	Output format for numbers ("%.6g"). (Pre-POSIX awk used this for string conversion also.)
	OFS	Output field separator (a space).
	ORS	Output record separator (a newline).
	RLENGTH	Length of the string matched by match( ) function.
	RS	Record separator (a newline).
	RSTART	First position in the string matched by match( ) function.
	SUBSEP	Separator character for array subscripts ("\034").
	$0	Entire input record.
	$*n*	*n*th field in current record; fields are separated by FS.
gawk	ARGIND	Index in ARGV of current input file.
	BINMODE	Controls binary I/O for input and output files. Use values of 1, 2, or 3 for input, output, or both kinds of files, respectively. Set it on the command line to affect standard input, standard output and standard error.
	ERRNO	A string indicating the error when a redirection fails for getline or if close( ) fails.
	FIELDWIDTHS	A space-separated list of field widths to use for splitting up the record, instead of FS.
	IGNORECASE	When true, all regular expression matches, string comparisons and index( ) ignore case.
	LINT	Dynamically controls production of "lint" warnings. With a value of "fatal", lint warnings become fatal errors.
	PROCINFO	An array containing information about the process, such as real and effective UID numbers, process ID number, and so on.
	RT	The text matched by RS, which can be a regular expression in gawk.
	TEXTDOMAIN	The text domain (application name) for internationalized messages ("messages").

Operators

The following table lists the operators, in order of increasing precedence, that are available in awk.

Symbol	Meaning
`= += -= *= /= %= ^= **=`	Assignment
`?:`	C conditional expression
`||`	Logical OR (short-circuit)
`&&`	Logical AND (short-circuit)
`in`	Array membership
`~ !~`	Match regular expression and negation
`< <= > >= != ==`	Relational operators
(blank)	Concatenation
`+ -`	Addition, subtraction
`* / %`	Multiplication, division, and modulus (remainder)
`+ - !`	Unary plus and minus, and logical negation
`^ **`	Exponentiation
`++ --`	Increment and decrement, either prefix or postfix
`$`	Field reference

While `**` and `**=` are common extensions, they are not part of POSIX `awk`.

Variable and Array Assignment

Variables can be assigned a value with an `=` sign. For example:

```
FS = ","
```

Expressions using the operators `+`, `-`, `/`, and `%` (modulo) can be assigned to variables.

Arrays can be created with the `split()` function (described later), or they can simply be named in an assignment statement. Array elements can be subscripted with numbers (*array*`[1]`, ..., *array*`[`*n*`]`) or with strings. Arrays subscripted by strings are called *associative arrays*.* For example, to count the number of widgets you have, you could use the following script:

```
/widget/ { count["widget"]++ }        Count widgets
END      { print count["widget"] }    Print the count
```

You can use the special `for` loop to read all the elements of an associative array:

```
for (item in array)
        process array[item]
```

The index of the array is available as `item`, while the value of an element of the array can be referenced as `array[item]`.

* In fact, all arrays in `awk` are associative; numeric subscripts are converted to strings before using them as array subscripts. Associative arrays are one of `awk`'s most powerful features.

You can use the in operator to test that an element exists by testing to see if its index exists. For example:

```
if (index in array)
        ...
```

tests that array[index] exists, but you cannot use it to test the value of the element referenced by array[index].

You can also delete individual elements of the array using the delete statement. (See also the **delete** entry in the section "Alphabetical Summary of awk Functions and Commands," later in this chapter.)

awk

Escape Sequences

Within string and regular expression constants, the following escape sequences may be used.

Sequence	Meaning	Sequence	Meaning
\a	Alert (bell)	\v	Vertical tab
\b	Backspace	\\	Literal backslash
\f	Form feed	*nnn*	Octal value *nnn*
\n	Newline	\x*nn*	Hexadecimal value *nn*
\r	Carriage return	\"	Literal double quote (in strings)
\t	TAB	\/	Literal slash (in regular expressions)

The \x escape sequence is a common extension; it is not part of POSIX awk.

Octal and Hexadecimal Constants in gawk

gawk allows you to use octal and hexadecimal constants in your program source code. The form is as in C: octal constants start with a leading 0, and hexadecimal constants with a leading 0x or 0X. The hexadecimal digits a–f may be in either upper- or lowercase.

```
$ gawk 'BEGIN { print 042, 42, 0x42 }'
34 42 66
```

Use the strtonum() function to convert octal or hexadecimal input data into numerical values.

User-Defined Functions

POSIX awk allows you to define your own functions. This makes it easy to encapsulate sequences of steps that need to be repeated into a single place, and reuse the code from anywhere in your program.

The following function capitalizes each word in a string. It has one parameter, named input, and five local variables that are written as extra parameters:

```
# capitalize each word in a string
function capitalize(input,    result, words, n, i, w)
{
   result = ""
   n = split(input, words, " ")
   for (i = 1; i <= n; i++) {
        w = words[i]
        w = toupper(substr(w, 1, 1)) substr(w, 2)
        if (i > 1)
                result = result " "
        result = result w
   }
   return result
}

# main program, for testing
{ print capitalize($0) }
```

With this input data:

```
A test line with words and numbers like 12 on it.
```

This program produces:

```
A Test Line With Words And Numbers Like 12 On It.
```

For user-defined functions, no space is allowed between the function name and the left parenthesis when the function is called.

Gawk-Specific Features

This section describes features unique to gawk.

Coprocesses and Sockets

gawk allows you to open a two-way pipe to another process, called a *coprocess*. This is done with the |& operator used with getline and print or printf.

```
print database command |& "db_server"
"db_server" |& getline response
```

If the *command* used with |& is a filename beginning with /inet/, gawk opens a TCP/IP connection. The filename should be of the following form:

```
/inet/protocol/lport/hostname/rport
```

The parts of the filename are:

protocol
: One of tcp, udp, or raw, for TCP, UDP, or raw IP sockets, respectively. Note: raw is currently reserved but unsupported.

lport
: The local TCP or UPD port number to use. Use 0 to let the operating system pick a port.

hostname
: The name or IP address of the remote host to connect to.

rport
: The port (application) on the remote host to connect to. A service name (e.g., tftp) is looked up using the C getservbyname( ) function.

awk

Profiling

When gawk is built and installed, a separate program named pgawk (*profiling* gawk) is built and installed with it. The two programs behave identically; however, pgawk runs more slowly since it keeps execution counts for each statement as it runs. When it is done, it automatically places an execution profile of your program in a file named awkprof.out. (You can change the filename with the --profile option.)

The execution profile is a "prettyprinted" version of your program with execution counts listed in the left margin. For example, after running this program:

```
$ pgawk '/bash$/ { nusers++ }
> END { print nusers, "users use Bash." }' /etc/passwd
16 users use Bash.
```

The execution profile looks like this:

```
        # gawk profile, created Mon Nov  1 14:34:38 2004

        # Rule(s)

    35  /bash$/ { # 16
    16          nusers++
        }

        # END block(s)

        END {
     1          print nusers, "users use Bash."
        }
```

If sent SIGUSR1, pgawk prints the profile and an awk function call stack trace, and then keeps going. Multiple SIGUSR1 signals may be sent; the profile and trace will be printed each time. This facility is useful if your awk program appears to be looping, and you want to see if something unexpected is being executed.

If sent SIGHUP, pgawk prints the profile and stack trace, and then exits.

File Inclusion

The igawk program provides a file inclusion facility for gawk. You invoke it the same way you do gawk: it passes all command-line arguments on to gawk. However, igawk processes source files and command-line programs for special statements of the form:

```
@include file.awk
```

Such files are searched for along the list of directories specified by the AWKPATH environment variable. When found, the @include line is replaced with the text of the corresponding file. Included files may themselves include other files with @include.

The combination of the AWKPATH environment variable and igawk makes it easy to have and use libraries of awk functions.

Internationalization

You can *internationalize* your programs if you use gawk. This consists of choosing a text domain for your program, marking strings that are to be translated, and if necessary, using the bindtextdomain( ), dcgettext( ), and dcngettext( ) functions.

Localizing your program consists of extracting the marked strings, creating translations, and compiling and installing the translations in the proper place. Full details are given in *Effective awk Programming*, cited in the Bibliography.

The internationalization features in gawk use GNU gettext. You may need to install the GNU gettext tools to create translations if your system doesn't already have them. Here is a very brief outline of the steps involved.

1. Set TEXTDOMAIN to your text domain in a BEGIN block:

   ```
   BEGIN { TEXTDOMAIN = "whizprog" }
   ```

2. Mark all strings to be translated by prepending a leading underscore:

   ```
   printf(_"whizprog: can't open /dev/telepath (%s)\n",
                               dcgettext(ERRNO)) > "/dev/stderr"
   ```

3. Extract the strings with the --gen-po option:

   ```
   $ gawk --gen-po -f whizprog.awk > whizprog.pot
   ```

4. Copy the file for translating, and make the translations:

   ```
   $ cp whizprog.pot esperanto.po
   $ ed esperanto.po
   ```

5. Use the msgfmt program from GNU gettext to compile the translations. The binary format allows fast lookup of the translations at runtime. The default output is a file named messages:

   ```
   $ msgfmt esperanto.po
   $ mv messages esperanto.mo
   ```

6. Install the file in the standard location. This is usually done at program installation. The location can vary from system to system.

That's it! gawk will automatically find and use the translated messages, if they exist.

Implementation Limits

Many versions of awk have various implementation limits, on things such as:

- Number of fields per record
- Number of characters per input record
- Number of characters per output record
- Number of characters per field
- Number of characters per printf string
- Number of characters in literal string
- Number of characters in character class

- Number of files open
- Number of pipes open
- The ability to handle 8-bit characters and characters that are all zero (ASCII NUL)

gawk does not have limits on any of the above items, other than those imposed by the machine architecture and/or the operating system.

awk

Group Listing of awk Functions and Commands

The following table classifies awk functions and commands.

Function type	Functions or commands				
Arithmetic	atan2	cos	exp	int	log
	rand	sin	sqrt	srand	
String	asort[a]	asorti[a]	gensub[a]	gsub	index
	length	match	split	sprintf	strtonum[a]
	sub	substr	tolower	toupper	
Control Flow	break	continue	do/while	exit	for
	if/else	return	while		
I/O	close	fflush[b]	getline	next	nextfile[b]
	print	printf			
Programming	extension[b]	delete	function	system	

[a] Available in gawk.
[b] Available in Bell Labs awk and gawk.

The following functions are specific to gawk.

Function type	Functions or commands				
Bit Manipulation	and	compl	lshift	or	rshift
	xor				
Time	mktime	strftime	systime		
Translation	bindtextdomain	dcgettext	dcngettext		

Alphabetical Summary of awk Functions and Commands

The following alphabetical list of keywords and functions includes all that are available in POSIX awk and gawk. Extensions that aren't part of POSIX awk but that are in both gawk and the Bell Laboratories awk are marked as **{E}**. Cases where gawk has extensions are marked as **{G}**. Items that aren't marked with a symbol are available in all versions.

`#`

Ignore all text that follows on the same line. # is used in awk scripts as the comment character and is not really a command.

and `and(`*expr1*`,` *expr2*`)` {G}

Return the bitwise AND of *expr1* and *expr2*, which should be values that fit in a C `unsigned long`.

asort `asort(`*src* `[,`*dest*`])` {G}

Sort the array *src* based on the element values, destructively replacing the indices with values from one to the number of elements in the array. If *dest* is supplied, copy *src* to *dest* and sort *dest*, leaving *src* unchanged. Returns the number of elements in *src*.

asorti `asorti(`*src* `[,`*dest*`])` {G}

Like `asort()`, but the sorting is done based on the indices in the array, not based on the element values. For gawk 3.1.2 and later.

atan2 `atan2(`*y*`,` *x*`)`

Return the arctangent of *y/x* in radians.

bindtextdomain `bindtextdomain(`*dir* `[,`*domain*`])` {G}

Look in directory *dir* for message translation files for text domain *domain* (default: value of `TEXTDOMAIN`). Returns the directory where *domain* is bound.

break `break`

Exit from a `while`, `for`, or `do` loop.

close `close(`*expr*`)`
`close(`*expr*`,` *how*`)` {G}

In most implementations of awk, you can only have up to 10 files open simultaneously and one pipe. Therefore, POSIX awk provides a `close()` function that allows you to close a file or a pipe. It takes the same expression that opened the pipe or file as an argument. This expression must be identical, character by character, to the one that opened the file or pipe—even whitespace is significant.

In the second form, close one end of either a TCP/IP socket or a two-way pipe to a coprocess. *how* is a string, either `"from"` or `"to"`. Case does not matter.

compl

`compl(expr) {G}`

Return the bitwise complement of *expr*, which should be a value that fits in a C `unsigned long`.

continue

`continue`

Begin next iteration of `while`, `for`, or `do` loop.

cos

`cos(x)`

Return the cosine of *x*, an angle in radians.

dcgettext

`dcgettext(str [, dom [, cat]]) {G}`

Return the translation of *str* for the text domain *dom* in message category *cat*. Default text domain is value of `TEXTDOMAIN`. Default category is `"LC_MESSAGES"`.

dcngettext

`dcngettext(str1, str2, num [, dom [, cat]]) {G}`

If *num* is one, return the translation of *str1* for the text domain *dom* in message category *cat*. Otherwise return the translation of *str2*. Default text domain is value of `TEXTDOMAIN`. Default category is `"LC_MESSAGES"`. For `gawk` 3.1.1 and later.

delete

```
delete array[element]
delete array {E}
```

Delete *element* from *array*. The brackets are typed literally. The second form is a common extension, which deletes *all* elements of the array in one shot.

do

```
do
 statement
while (expr)
```

Looping statement. Execute *statement*, then evaluate *expr* and if true, execute *statement* again. A series of statements must be put within braces.

exit

`exit [expr]`

Exit from script, reading no new input. The `END` action, if it exists, will be executed. An optional *expr* becomes `awk`'s return value.

exp

```
exp(x)
```

Return exponential of *x* (e^x).

extension

```
extension(lib, init) {G}
```

Dynamically load the shared object file *lib*, calling the function *init* to initialize it. Return the value returned by the *init* function. This function allows you to add new built-in functions to gawk. See *Effective awk Programming* for the details.

fflush

```
fflush([output-expr]) {E}
```

Flush any buffers associated with open output file or pipe *output-expr*.

gawk extends this function. If no *output-expr* is supplied, it flushes standard output. If *output-expr* is the null string (""), it flushes all open files and pipes.

for

```
for (init-expr; test-expr; incr-expr)
 statement
```

C-style looping construct. *init-expr* assigns the initial value of a counter variable. *test-expr* is a relational expression that is evaluated each time before executing the *statement*. When *test-expr* is false, the loop is exited. *incr-expr* is used to increment the counter variable after each pass. All of the expressions are optional. A missing *test-expr* is considered to be true. A series of statements must be put within braces.

for

```
for (item in array)
 statement
```

Special loop designed for reading associative arrays. For each element of the array, the *statement* is executed; the element can be referenced by *array*[*item*]. A series of statements must be put within braces.

function

```
function name(parameter-list) {
 statements
}
```

Create *name* as a user-defined function consisting of awk *statements* that apply to the specified list of parameters. No space is allowed between *name* and the left parenthesis when the function is called.

gensub

```
gensub(regex, str, how [, target]) {G}
```

General substitution function. Substitute *str* for matches of the regular expression *regex* in the string *target*. If *how* is a number, replace the *how*th match. If it is "g" or "G", substitute globally. If *target* is not supplied, `$0` is used. Return the new string value. The original *target* is *not* modified. (Compare with **gsub** and **sub**.) Use `&` in the replacement string to stand for the text matched by the pattern.

getline

```
getline
getline [var] [< file]
command | getline [var]
command |& getline [var] {G}
```

Read next line of input.

The second form reads input from *file* and the third form reads the output of *command*. All forms read one record at a time, and each time the statement is executed it gets the next record of input. The record is assigned to `$0` and is parsed into fields, setting `NF`, `NR`, and `FNR`. If *var* is specified, the result is assigned to *var* and `$0` and `NF` are not changed. Thus, if the result is assigned to a variable, the current record does not change. `getline` is actually a function and it returns 1 if it reads a record successfully, 0 if end-of-file is encountered, and –1 if for some reason it is otherwise unsuccessful.

The fourth form reads the output from coprocess *command*. See the earlier section "Coprocesses and Sockets" for more information.

gsub

```
gsub(regex, str [, target])
```

Globally substitute *str* for each match of the regular expression *regex* in the string *target*. If *target* is not supplied, default to `$0`. Return the number of substitutions. Use `&` in the replacement string to stand for the text matched by the pattern.

if

```
if (condition)
 statement1
[else
 statement2]
```

If *condition* is true, do *statement1*; otherwise, do *statement2* in optional `else` clause. The *condition* can be an expression using any of the relational operators `<`, `<=`, `==`, `!=`, `>=`, or `>`, as well as the array membership operator `in`, and the pattern-matching operators `~` and `!~` (e.g., `if ($1 ~ /[Aa].*/)`). A series of statements must be put within braces. Another `if` can directly follow an `else` in order to produce a chain of tests or decisions.

index

`index(`*`str, substr`*`)`

Return the position (starting at 1) of *substr* in *str*, or zero if *substr* is not present in *str*.

int

`int(`*`x`*`)`

Return integer value of *x* by truncating any fractional part.

length

`length([`*`arg`*`])`

Return length of *arg*, or the length of `$0` if no argument.

log

`log(`*`x`*`)`

Return the natural logarithm (base *e*) of *x*.

lshift

`lshift(`*`expr, count`*`)` {G}

Return the result of shifting *expr* left by *count* bits. Both *expr* and *count* should be values that fit in a C `unsigned long`.

match

`match(`*`str, regex`*`)`
`match(`*`str, regex`*` [, `*`array`*`])` {G}

Function that matches the pattern, specified by the regular expression *regex*, in the string *str*, and returns either the position in *str* where the match begins, or 0 if no occurrences are found. Sets the values of `RSTART` and `RLENGTH` to the start and length of the match, respectively.

If *array* is provided, gawk puts the text that matched the entire regular expression in *array*`[0]`, the text that matched the first parenthesized subexpression in *array*`[1]`, the second in *array*`[2]`, and so on.

mktime

`mktime(`*`timespec`*`)` {G}

Turns *timespec* (a string of the form `"`*`YYYY MM DD HH MM SS [DST]`*`"` representing a local time) into a time-of-day value in seconds since Midnight, January 1, 1970, UTC.

next

`next`

Read next input line and start new cycle through pattern/actions statements.

nextfile `nextfile` {E}

Stop processing the current input file and start new cycle through pattern/actions statements, beginning with the first record of the next file.

or `or(`*expr1*`,` *expr2*`)` {G}

Return the bitwise OR of *expr1* and *expr2*, which should be values that fit in a C `unsigned long`.

print `print [` *output-expr*`[, ...]] [` *dest-expr* `]`

Evaluate the *output-expr* and direct it to standard output followed by the value of `ORS`. Each comma-separated *output-expr* is separated in the output by the value of `OFS`. With no *output-expr*, print `$0`. The output may be redirected to a file or pipe via the *dest-expr*, which is described in the section "Output Redirections," later in this chapter.

printf `printf(`*format* `[,` *expr-list* `]) [` *dest-expr* `]`

An alternative output statement borrowed from the C language. It has the ability to produce formatted output. It can also be used to output data without automatically producing a newline. *format* is a string of format specifications and constants. *expr-list* is a list of arguments corresponding to format specifiers. As for `print`, output may be redirected to a file or pipe. See the section "printf Formats," later in the chapter, for a description of allowed format specifiers.

Like any string, *format* can also contain embedded escape sequences: `\n` (newline) or `\t` (tab) being the most common. Spaces and literal text can be placed in the *format* argument by quoting the entire argument. If there are multiple expressions to be printed, there should be multiple format specifiers.

Example

Using the script:

```
{ printf("The sum on line %d is %.0f.\n", NR, $1+$2) }
```

The following input line:

```
5   5
```

produces this output, followed by a newline:

```
The sum on line 1 is 10.
```

rand `rand( )`

Generate a random number between 0 and 1. This function returns the same series of numbers each time the script is executed, unless the random number generator is seeded using `srand( )`.

return

`return [expr]`

Used within a user-defined function to exit the function, returning the value of *expr*. The return value of a function is undefined if *expr* is not provided.

rshift

`rshift(expr, count)` {G}

Return the result of shifting *expr* right by *count* bits. Both *expr* and *count* should be values that fit in a C `unsigned long`.

sin

`sin(x)`

Return the sine of *x*, an angle in radians.

split

`split(string, array [, sep])`

Split *string* into elements of array *array*`[1]`,...,*array*`[n]`. Return the number of array elements created. The string is split at each occurrence of separator *sep*. If *sep* is not specified, `FS` is used.

sprintf

`sprintf(format [, expressions])`

Return the formatted value of one or more *expressions*, using the specified *format*. Data is formatted but not printed. See the section "printf Formats," later in the chapter, for a description of allowed format specifiers.

sqrt

`sqrt(arg)`

Return the square root of *arg*.

srand

`srand([expr])`

Use optional *expr* to set a new seed for the random number generator. Default is the time of day. Return value is the old seed.

strftime

`strftime([format [,timestamp]])` {G}

Format *timestamp* according to *format*. Return the formatted string. The *timestamp* is a time-of-day value in seconds since Midnight, January 1, 1970, UTC. The *format* string is similar to that of `sprintf`, in that it is a mixture of literal text and format specifiers. If *timestamp* is omitted, it defaults to the current time. If *format* is omitted, it defaults to a value that produces output similar to that of the Unix `date` command. See the **date** entry in Chapter 2 for a list.

strtonum

`strtonum(`*`expr`*`)` {G}

Return the numeric value of *expr*, which is a string representing an octal, decimal, or hexadecimal number in the usual C notations. Use this function for processing nondecimal input data.

sub

`sub(`*`regex, str`*` [, `*`target`*`])`

Substitute *str* for first match of the regular expression *regex* in the string *target*. If *target* is not supplied, default to `$0`. Return 1 if successful; 0 otherwise. Use `&` in the replacement string to stand for the text matched by the pattern.

substr

`substr(`*`string, beg`*` [, `*`len`*`])`

Return substring of *string* at beginning position *beg* (counting from 1), and the characters that follow to maximum specified length *len*. If no length is given, use the rest of the string.

system

`system(`*`command`*`)`

Function that executes the specified *command* and returns its exit status. The status of the executed command typically indicates success or failure. A value of 0 means that the command executed successfully. A nonzero value indicates a failure of some sort. The documentation for the command that you're running will give you the details.

`awk` does *not* make the output of the command available for processing within the `awk` script. Use *command* `| getline` to read the output of a command into the script.

systime

`systime( )` {G}

Return a time-of-day value in seconds since Midnight, January 1, 1970, UTC.

Example

Log the start and end times of a data-processing program:

```
BEGIN {
        now = systime( )
        mesg = strftime("Started at %Y-%m-%d %H:%M:%S", now)
        print mesg
}
process data ...
END {
        now = systime( )
        mesg = strftime("Ended at %Y-%m-%d %H:%M:%S", now)
        print mesg
}
```

tolower

`tolower(str)`

Translate all uppercase characters in *str* to lowercase and return the new string.*

toupper

`toupper(str)`

Translate all lowercase characters in *str* to uppercase and return the new string.

while

```
while (condition)
 statement
```

Do *statement* while *condition* is true (see **if** for a description of allowable conditions). A series of statements must be put within braces.

xor

`xor(expr1, expr2)` {G}

Return the bitwise XOR of *expr1* and *expr2*, which should be values that fit in a C `unsigned long`.

Output Redirections

For `print` and `printf`, *dest-expr* is an optional expression that directs the output to a file or pipe.

> *file*
: Directs the output to a file, overwriting its previous contents.

>> *file*
: Appends the output to a file, preserving its previous contents. In both of these cases, the file will be created if it does not already exist.

| *command*
: Directs the output as the input to a system command.

|& *command*
: Directs the output as the input to a coprocess. gawk only.

Be careful not to mix > and >> for the same file. Once a file has been opened with >, subsequent output statements continue to append to the file until it is closed.

Remember to call `close()` when you have finished with a file, pipe, or coprocess. If you don't, eventually you will hit the system limit on the number of simultaneously open files.

* Very early versions of nawk don't support `tolower()` and `toupper()`. However, they are now part of the POSIX specification for awk.

printf Formats

Format specifiers for printf and sprintf have the following form:

```
%[posn$][flag][width][.precision]letter
```

The control letter is required. The format conversion control letters are given in the following table.

Character	Description
c	ASCII character.
d	Decimal integer.
i	Decimal integer. (Added in POSIX)
e	Floating-point format ([-]*d.precision*e[+-]*dd*).
E	Floating-point format ([-]*d.precision*E[+-]*dd*).
f	Floating-point format ([-]*ddd.precision*).
g	e or f conversion, whichever is shortest, with trailing zeros removed.
G	E or f conversion, whichever is shortest, with trailing zeros removed.
o	Unsigned octal value.
s	String.
u	Unsigned decimal value.
x	Unsigned hexadecimal number. Uses a–f for 10 to 15.
X	Unsigned hexadecimal number. Uses A–F for 10 to 15.
%	Literal %.

gawk allows you to provide a *positional specifier* after the % (*posn*$). A positional specifier is an integer count followed by a $. The count indicates which argument to use at that point. Counts start at one, and don't include the format string. This feature is primarily for use in producing translations of format strings. For example:

```
$ gawk 'BEGIN { printf "%2$s, %1$s\n", "world", "hello" }'
hello, world
```

The optional *flag* is one of the following:

Character	Description
-	Left-justify the formatted value within the field.
space	Prefix positive values with a space and negative values with a minus.
+	Always prefix numeric values with a sign, even if the value is positive.
#	Use an alternate form: %o has a preceding 0; %x and %X are prefixed with 0x and 0X, respectively; %e, %E, and %f always have a decimal point in the result; and %g and %G do not have trailing zeros removed.
0	Pad output with zeros, not spaces. This only happens when the field width is wider than the converted result. This flag applies to all output formats, even nonnumeric ones. (Unfortunately, not all awk implementations do this correctly.)
'	gawk 3.1.4 and later only. For numeric formats, in locales that support it, supply a thousands-separator character.

The optional *width* is the minimum number of characters to output. The result will be padded to this size if it is smaller. The `0` flag causes padding with zeros; otherwise, padding is with spaces.

The *precision* is optional. Its meaning varies by control letter, as shown in this table:

Conversion	Precision means
%d, %i, %o, %u, %x, %X	The minimum number of digits to print.
%e, %E, %f	The number of digits to the right of the decimal point.
%g, %G	The maximum number of significant digits.
%s	The maximum number of characters to print.

Source Code

The following URLs indicate where to get source code for four freely available versions of awk, and for GNU gettext.

http://cm.bell-labs.com/~bwk
: Brian Kernighan's home page, with links to the source code for the latest version of awk from Bell Laboratories.

ftp://ftp.whidbey.net/pub/brennan/mawk1.3.3.tar.gz
: Michael Brennan's mawk. A very fast, very robust version of awk.

ftp://ftp.gnu.org/gnu/gawk/
: The Free Software Foundation's version of awk, called gawk.

http://www.gnu.org/software/gawk/gawk.html
: The Free Software Foundation's home page for gawk.

http://awka.sourceforge.net
: The home page for awka, a translator that turns awk programs into C, compiles the generated C, and then links the object code with a library that performs the core awk functions.

ftp://ftp.gnu.org/gnu/gettext/
: The source code for GNU gettext. Get this if you need to produce translations for your awk programs that use gawk.

Software Development

Part III describes important tools for software development. The Unix operating system earned its reputation by providing an unexcelled environment for software development. RCS, CVS, Subversion, `make`, and GDB are major contributors to the efficiency of this environment.

RCS allows multiple versions of a source file to be stored in a single archival file. CVS goes further, enabling easy multideveloper access to a group of shared source files. Subversion is a new version control system intended to "build a better CVS." `make` automatically updates a group of interrelated programs. The GDB debugger lets you examine the state of your program as it runs in order to find and fix problems.

Finally, an important part of software development is program documentation. Unix programs traditionally come with a "man page," a file that documents the program's usage, for use with the `man` command. Manual pages are written using the venerable `troff` text formatting program. `troff` is no longer used for much else, though. Therefore, we have provided enough information to enable you to write a manual page.

III

Software Development

12 Source Code Management: An Overview

The following chapters describe three popular source code management systems for Unix. This chapter introduces the major concepts involved with using these systems for users who may never have used one. If you're already familiar with source code management, feel free to skip ahead to the particular software suite that interests you. See also the related books in the Bibliography.

This chapter covers the following topics:

- Introduction and terminology
- Usage models
- Unix source code management systems
- Other source code management systems

Introduction and Terminology

Source code management systems let you store and retrieve multiple versions of a file. While originally designed for program source code, they can be used for any kind of file: source code, documentation, configuration files, and so on. Modern systems allow you to store binary files as well, such as image or audio data.

Source code management systems let you compare different versions of a file, as well as do "parallel development." In other words, you can work on two different versions of a file at the same time, with the source code management system storing both versions. You can then merge changes from two versions into a third version. This will become more clear shortly. We'll start by defining some terms.

Repository
: A *repository* is where the source code management system stores its copy of your file. Usually one Unix file is used to hold all the different versions of a source file. Each source code management system uses its own format to

allow it to retrieve different versions easily, and to track who made what changes, and when.

Sandbox
: A *sandbox* is your personal, so-called "working copy" of the program or set of documents under development. You edit your private copy of the file in your own sandbox, returning changes to the source code management system when you're satisfied with the new version.

Check in, check out
: You "check out" files from the repository, edit them, and then "check them in" when you're satisfied with your changes. Other developers working against the same repository will not see your changes until after you check them back in. Another term used for check-in is *commit*.

Log message
: Every time you check in a file, you are prompted for a message describing the changes you made. You should do so in a concise fashion. If your software development practices include the use of a bug tracking system, you might also wish to include the bug number or problem report (PR) number which your change resolves.

Keyword substitutions
: When you check out a file, the source code management system can replace special *keywords* with values representing such things as the file's version number, the name of the user who made the most recent change, the date and time the file was last changed, the file's name, and so on. Each of the systems described in this book uses an overlapping set of keywords. Some systems always do keyword substitution, while others require that you explicitly enable the feature for each file.

Branch
: A *branch* is a separate development path. For example, once you've released version 1.0 of `whizprog`, you will wish to proceed with the development for version 2.0. The main line of development is often called the *trunk*.

  Now consider what happens when you wish to make a bug-fix release to `whizprog` 1.0, to be named version 1.1. You create a separate branch, based on the original 1.0 code, in a new sandbox. You perform all your development *there*, without disturbing the development being done for the 2.0 release.

Tag
: A *tag* is a name you give to a whole group of files at once, at whatever version each individual file may be, in order to identify those files as part of a particular group. For example, you might create tags `WHIZPROG-1_0-ALPHA`, `WHIZPROG-1_0-BETA`, `WHIZPROG-1_0-RELEASE`, and so on. This is a powerful facility which should be used well, since it allows you to retrieve a "snapshot" of your entire development tree as it existed at different points in time.

Merging
: Most typically, when development along a branch is completed, it becomes necessary to *merge* the changes from that branch back into the main line of development. In our hypothetical example, all the bugs fixed in `whizprog` 1.0 to

create version 1.1 should also be fixed in the ongoing 2.0 development. Source code management systems can help you automate the process of merging.

Conflict
: A *conflict* occurs when two developers make inconsistent changes to the same part of a source file. Modern source code management systems detect the conflict, usually marking the conflicting parts of the file in your working copy using special markers. You first discuss the conflict with the other developer, in order to arrive at a correct resolution of the conflict. Once that's done, you then resolve the conflict manually (by making the appropriate changes), and then you check in the new version of the file.

Client/server
: As with other "client/server" networking models, the idea here is that the repository is stored on one machine, the *server*, and that different developers may access the repository from multiple *client* systems. This powerful feature facilitates distributed development, allowing developers to work easily on their local systems, with the repository kept in a central place where it can be easily accessed and administered.

Usage Models

Different systems have different conceptual "models" as to how they're used.

Older systems such as SCCS and RCS use a "check out with locking" model. These systems were developed before client/server computing, when software development was done on centralized minicomputers and mainframes. In this model, the repository is a central directory on the same machine where the developers work, and each developer checks out a private copy into their own sandbox. In order to avoid two developers making conflicting changes to a file, the file must be *locked* when it's checked out. Only one user may lock a particular version of a file at a time. When that user has checked in their changes, they *unlock* the file so that the next user can check in changes. If necessary, the second user may "break" the first user's lock, in which case the first user is notified via electronic mail.

This model works well for small projects where developers are co-located and can communicate easily. As long as one developer locks a file when she checks it out, another developer wishing to work with the file will know that he can't until the first one is done. The drawback is that such locking can slow down development significantly.

Newer systems, such as CVS and Subversion, use a "copy, modify, merge" model. In practice, when two developers wish to work on the same file, they usually end up changing different, unrelated parts of the file. Most of the time each developer can make changes without adversely affecting the other. Thus, files are not locked upon checkout into a sandbox. Instead, the source code management system detects conflicts and disallows a check-in when conflicts exist.

For example, consider two developers, `dangermouse` and `penfold`, who are both working on `whizprog.c`. They each start with version 1.4 of the file. `dangermouse` commits his changes, creating version 1.5. Before `penfold` can commit his changes, the source code management system notices that the file has changed in the repository. `penfold` must first merge `dangermouse`'s changes into his working copy. If there are no conflicts, he can then commit his changes, creating version 1.6. On the other hand, if there are conflicts, he must first resolve them (they'll be marked in the working copy), and only then may he commit his version.

The combination of the "copy, modify, merge" model with a networked client/server facility creates a powerful environment for doing distributed development. Developers no longer have to worry about file locks. Because the source code management system enforces serialization (making sure that new changes are based on the latest version in the repository), development can move more smoothly, with little danger of miscommunication or that successive changes will be lost.

Unix Source Code Management Systems

There are several source code management systems for Unix.

Source Code Control System (SCCS)
: SCCS is the original Unix source code management system. It was developed in the late 1970s for the Programmer's Workbench (PWB) Unix systems within Bell Labs. It is still in use at a few large long-time Unix sites. However, for a long time it was not available as a standard part of most commercial or BSD Unix systems, and it did not achieve the wide-spread popularity of other, later systems. (It is still available with Solaris.) SCCS uses a file storage format that allows it to retrieve any version of a source file in constant time.

Revision Control System (RCS)
: RCS was developed in the early 1980s at Purdue University by Walter F. Tichy. It became popular in the Unix world when it was shipped with 4.2 BSD in 1983. At the time, Berkeley Unix was the most widely-used Unix variant, even though to get it a site had to have a Unix license from AT&T.

: RCS is easier to use than SCCS. Although it has a number of related commands, only three or four are needed for day-to-day use, and they are quickly mastered. A central repository is easy to use: you first create a directory for the sandbox. In the sandbox, you make a symbolic link to the repository named `RCS`, and then all the developers can share the repository. RCS uses a file format that is optimized for retrieving the most recent version of a file.

Concurrent Versions System (CVS)
: CVS was initially built as a series of shell scripts sitting atop RCS. Later it was rewritten in C for robustness, although still using RCS commands to manage the storage of files. However, for quite some time, CVS has had the RCS functionality built into it, and no longer requires that RCS be available. The file format continues to be the same. CVS was the first distributed source code management system, and is currently the standard one for Unix systems, and in particular for collaborative, distributed, Free, and Open Source development projects.

The repository is named when you create a sandbox, and is then stored in the files in the sandbox, so that it need not be provided every time you run a CVS command. Unlike SCCS and RCS, which provide multiple commands, CVS has one main command (named cvs), which you use for just about every operation.

Subversion
With increasing use, it became clear that CVS lacked some fundamental capabilities. The Subversion project was started by several long-time CVS users and developers with the explicit goal to "build a better CVS," not necessarily to explore uncharted territory in source code management systems. Subversion is thus intentionally easy to learn for CVS users. Subversion uses its own format for data storage, based on the Berkeley DB in-process data library. Distributed use was designed in from day one, providing useful facilities that leverage the capabilities of the well-known Apache HTTP server.

RCS, CVS, and Subversion represent a progression, each one building on the features of its predecessors. For example, all three share a large subset of the same keyword substitutions, and command names are similar or identical in all three. They also demonstrate the progression from centralized, locking-based development to distributed, conflict-resolution–based development.

Other Source Code Management Systems

Besides the source code management systems covered in this book, several other systems are worth knowing about. The following list, though, is by no means exhaustive.

Arch
GNU Arch is a distributed source code management system similar to CVS and Subversion. One of its significant strengths is that you can do off-line development with it, working on multiple versions even on systems that are not connected to the Internet and that cannot communicate with the central repository. For more information, see *http://www.gnu.org/software/gnu-arch/*.

Codeville
Codeville is a distributed version control system in the early stages of development. It is written in Python, is easy to set up and use, and shows a lot of promise. For more information, see *http://codeville.org/*.

CSSC
CSSC is a free clone of SCCS. It intends to provide full compatibility with SCCS, including file format, command names and options, and "bug for bug" compatible behavior. If you have an existing SCCS repository, you should be able to drop CSSC into your environment, in place of SCCS. CSSC can be used to migrate from a commercial Unix system to a freely available clone, such as GNU/Linux or a BSD system. For more information, see *http://directory.fsf.org/GNU/CSSC.html*.

Monotone

The web page for `monotone` describes it well:

> `monotone` is a free distributed version control system. It provides a simple, single-file transactional version store, with fully disconnected operation and an efficient peer-to-peer synchronization protocol. It understands history-sensitive merging, lightweight branches, integrated code review, and third party testing. It uses cryptographic version naming and client-side RSA certificates. It has good internationalization support, has no external dependencies, runs on Linux, Solaris, Mac OS X, NetBSD, and Windows, and is licensed under the GNU GPL.

For more information, see *http://www.venge.net/monotone/*.

13
The Revision Control System

The Revision Control System (RCS) provides a series of commands for maintaining multiple versions of files. It can manage both textual and binary data. While primarily used for software development, RCS can manage other files as well: documentation, textual databases, and so on.

This chapter presents the following topics:

- Overview of commands
- Basic operation
- General RCS specifications
- Alphabetical summary of commands

The Revision Control System (RCS) is designed to keep track of multiple file revisions, thereby reducing the amount of storage space needed. With RCS you can automatically store and retrieve revisions, merge or compare revisions, keep a complete history (or log) of changes, and identify revisions using symbolic keywords. RCS preserves execute permission on the files it manages, and you can store binary data in RCS files.

RCS is not a standard part of Solaris. It can be obtained from the Free Software Foundation (see *http://www.gnu.org/software/rcs/*). It typically does come with GNU/Linux and Mac OS X. The Official RCS Homepage may be found at *http://www.cs.purdue.edu/homes/trinkle/RCS/*. This chapter describes RCS Version 5.7.

For more information, see *Applying RCS and SCCS*, listed in the Bibliography.

Overview of Commands

The three most important RCS commands are:

`ci`	Check in revisions (put a file under RCS control).
`co`	Check out revisions.
`rcs`	Set up or change attributes of RCS files.

Two commands provide information about RCS files:

`ident`	Extract keyword values from an RCS file.
`rlog`	Display a summary (log) about the revisions in an RCS file.

You can compare RCS files with these commands:

`merge`	Incorporate changes from two files into a third file.
`rcsdiff`	Report differences between revisions.
`rcsmerge`	Incorporate changes from two RCS files into a third RCS file.

The following commands help with configuration management. However, they are considered optional, so they are not always installed:

`rcsclean`	Remove working files that have not been changed.
`rcsfreeze`	Label the files that make up a configuration.

Basic Operation

Normally, you maintain RCS files in a subdirectory called `RCS`, so the first step in using RCS should be:

```
mkdir RCS
```

Next, you place an existing file (or files) under RCS control by running the check-in command:

```
ci file
```

This creates a file called *file*`,v` in the `RCS` directory. *file*`,v` is called an RCS file, and it stores all future revisions of *file*. When you run `ci` on a file for the first time, you are prompted to describe the contents. `ci` then deposits *file* into the RCS file as revision 1.1.

To edit a new revision, check out a copy:

```
co -l file
```

This causes RCS to extract a copy of *file* from the RCS file. You must lock the file with `-l` to make it writable by you. This copy is called a *working file*. When you're done editing, you can record the changes by checking the working file back in again:

```
ci file
```

This time, you are prompted to enter a log of the changes made, and the file is deposited as revision 1.2. Note that a check-in normally removes the working file. To retrieve a read-only copy, do a check-out without a lock:

```
co file
```

This is useful when you need to keep a copy on hand for compiling or searching. As a shortcut to the previous `ci`/`co`, you could type:

```
ci -u file
```

This checks in the file but immediately checks out a read-only ("unlocked") copy. In practice, you would probably make a "checkpoint" of your working version and then keep going, like this:

```
ci -l file
```

This checks in the file, and then checks it back out again, locked, for continued work. To compare changes between a working file and its latest revision, you can type:

```
rcsdiff file
```

Another useful command is `rlog`, which shows a summary of log messages. System administrators can use the `rcs` command to set up the default behavior of RCS.

General RCS Specifications

This section discusses:

- Keyword substitution
- Keywords
- Example values
- Revision numbering
- Specifying the date
- Specifying states
- Standard options and environment variables

RCS

Keyword Substitution

RCS lets you place keyword variables in your working files. These variables are later expanded into revision notes. You can then use the notes either as embedded comments in the input file or as text strings that appear when the output is printed. To create revision notes via keyword substitution, follow this procedure:

1. In your working file, type any of the keywords listed below.
2. Check the file in.
3. Check the file out again. Upon checkout, the `co` command expands each keyword to include its value. That is, `co` replaces instances of:

   ```
   $keyword$
   ```

   with:

   ```
   $keyword:value $.
   ```

4. Subsequent check-in and check-out of a file updates any existing keyword values. Unless otherwise noted below, existing values are replaced by new values.

Many commands have a `-k` option that provides considerable flexibility during keyword substitution.

Keywords

`$Author$`	Username of person who checked in the revision.
`$Date$`	Date and time of check-in.
`$Header$`	A title that includes the RCS file's full pathname, revision number, date, author, state, and (if locked) the person who locked the file.
`$Id$`	Same as `$Header$`, but exclude the full pathname of the RCS file.
`$Locker$`	Username of person who locked the revision. If the file isn't locked, this value is empty.
`$Log$`	The message that was typed during check-in to describe the file, preceded by the RCS filename, revision number, author, and date. Log messages accumulate rather than being overwritten. RCS uses the "comment leader" of the `$Log$` line for the log messages left in the file. The comment leader stored in the RCS file is useful only for exchanging files with older versions of RCS.
`$Name$`	The symbolic name used to check in the revision, if any.
`$RCSfile$`	The RCS filename, without its pathname.
`$Revision$`	The assigned revision number.
`$Source$`	The RCS filename, including its pathname.
`$State$`	The state assigned by the `-s` option of `ci` or `rcs`.

Example Values

Let's assume that the file `/projects/new/mydata` has been checked in and out by a user named `arnold`. Here's what keyword substitution produces for each keyword, for the second revision of the file:

```
$Author: arnold $

$Date: 2004/08/05 10:32:27 $

$Header: /projects/new/RCS/mydata,v 1.2 2004/08/05 10:32:27 arnold Exp arnold $

$ID$

$Locker: arnold $

$Log: mydata,v
Revision 1.2  2004/08/05 10:32:27  arnold
Added more important information.

Revision 1.1  2004/08/05 10:31:44  arnold
Initial revision


$Name:  $

$RCSfile: mydata,v $

$Revision: 1.2 $

$Source: /projects/new/RCS/mydata,v $

$State: Exp $
```

```
Test data file.
This second line is very important.
```

Revision Numbering

Unless told otherwise, RCS commands typically operate on the latest revision. Some commands have a -r option that specifies a revision number. In addition, many options accept a revision number as an optional argument. (In the command summary, this argument is shown as [*R*].) Revision numbers consist of up to four fields: release, level, branch, and sequence, but most revisions consist of only the release and level. For example, you can check out revision 1.4 as follows:

```
co -l -r1.4 ch01
```

When you check it in again, the new revision will be marked as 1.5. Now suppose the edited copy needs to be checked in as the next release. You would type:

```
ci -r2 ch01
```

This creates revision 2.1. (Revision numbers always start at one, not at zero.) You can also create a branch from an earlier revision. The following command creates revision 1.4.1.1:

```
ci -r1.4.1 ch01
```

Numbers that begin with a period are considered to be relative to the default branch of the RCS file. Normally, this is the "trunk" of the revision tree.

Numbers are not the only way to specify revisions, though. You can assign a text label as a revision name, using the -n option of ci or rcs. You can also specify this name in any option that accepts a revision number for an argument. For example, you could check in each of your C files, using the same label regardless of the current revision number:

```
ci -u -nPrototype *.c
```

In addition, you may specify a $, which means the revision number extracted from the keywords of a working file. For example:

```
rcsdiff -r$ ch01
```

compares ch01 to the revision that is checked in. You can also combine names and symbols. The command:

```
rcs -nDraft:$ ch*
```

assigns a name to the revision numbers associated with several chapter files. (These last two examples require that the file contain a ID line.)

Specifying the Date

Revisions are timestamped by time and date of check-in. Several keyword strings include the date in their values. Dates can be supplied in options to ci, co, and rlog. RCS uses the following date format as its default:

```
2000/01/10 02:00:00        Year/month/day time
```

The default time zone is Greenwich Mean Time (GMT), which is also referred to as Coordinated Universal Time (UTC). Dates can be supplied in free format. This

RCS

lets you specify many different styles. Here are some of the more common ones, which show the same time as in the previous example:

```
6:00 pm lt                    Assuming today is Jan. 10, 2000
2:00 AM, Jan. 10, 2000
Mon Jan 10 18:00:00 2000 LT
Mon Jan 10 18:00:00 PST 2000
```

The uppercase or lowercase "lt" indicates local time (here, Pacific Standard Time). The third line shows `ctime` format (plus the "LT"); the fourth line is the `date` command format.

Specifying States

In some situations, particularly programming environments, you want to know the status of a set of revisions. RCS files are marked by a text string that describes their *state*. The default state is `Exp` (experimental). Other common choices include `Stab` (stable) or `Rel` (released). These words are user-defined and have no special internal meaning. Several keyword strings include the state in their values. In addition, states can be supplied in options to `ci`, `co`, `rcs`, and `rlog`.

Standard Options and Environment Variables

RCS defines an environment variable, RCSINIT, which sets up default options for RCS commands. If you set RCSINIT to a space-separated list of options, they will be prepended to the command-line options that you supply to any RCS command.

Six options are useful to include in RCSINIT: `-q`, `-V`, `-Vn`, `-T`, `-x`, and `-z`. They can be thought of as standard options because most RCS commands accept them.

`-q[R]`
: Quiet mode; don't show diagnostic output. *R* specifies a file revision.

`-T`
: If the file with the new revision has a later modification time than that of the RCS file, update the RCS file's modification time. Otherwise, preserve the RCS file's modification time. This option should be used with care; see the discussion in the `ci` manpage for more detail.

`-V`
: Print the RCS version number.

`-Vn`
: Emulate version *n* of RCS; useful when trading files between systems that run different versions. *n* can be 3, 4, or 5.

`-xsuffixes`
: Specify an alternate list of *suffixes* for RCS files. Each suffix is separated by a `/`. On Unix systems, RCS files normally end with the characters `,v`. The `-x` option provides a workaround for systems that don't allow a comma character in filenames.

`-ztimezone`
: *timezone* controls the output format for dates in keyword substitution. *timezone* should have one of the following values:

Value	Effect
empty	Default format: UTC with no time zone and slashes separating the parts of the date.
`LT`	The local time and date, in ISO-8601 format, with time-zone indication (*YYYY-MM-DD HH*:*MM*:*SS-ZZ*).
`±hh:mm`	With a numeric offset from UTC, the output is in ISO-8601 format.

For example, when depositing a working file into an RCS file, the command:

```
ci -x,v/ ch01     Second suffix is blank
```

searches in order for the RCS filenames:

```
RCS/ch01,v
ch01,v
RCS/ch01
```

RCS allows you to specify a location for temporary files. It checks the environment variables TMPDIR, TMP, and TEMP, in that order. If none of those exist, it uses a default location, such as `/tmp`.

Alphabetical Summary of Commands

For details on the syntax of keywords, revision numbers, dates, states, and standard options, refer to the previous discussions.

RCS

ci

`ci [options] files`

Check in revisions. `ci` stores the contents of the specified working *files* into their corresponding RCS files. Normally, `ci` deletes the working file after storing it. If no RCS file exists, the working file is an initial revision. In this case, the RCS file is created, and you are prompted to enter a description of the file. If an RCS file exists, `ci` increments the revision number and prompts you to enter a message that logs the changes made. If a working file is checked in without changes, the file reverts to the previous revision.

The two mutually exclusive options `-u` and `-l`, along with `-r`, are the most common. Use `-u` to keep a read-only copy of the working file (for example, so the file can be compiled or searched). Use `-l` to update a revision and then immediately check it out again with a lock. This allows you to save intermediate changes but continue editing (for example, during a long editing session). Use `-r` to check in a file with a different release number. `ci` accepts the standard options `-q`, `-V`, `-V`*n*, `-T`, `-x`, and `-z`.

Options

`-d[`*date*`]`
: Check the file in with a timestamp of *date* or, if no date is specified, with the time of last modification.

`-f[`*R*`]`
: Force a check-in even if there are no differences.

`-i[`*R*`]`
: Initial check-in, report an error if the RCS file already exists.

`-I[`*R*`]`
: Interactive mode; prompt user even when standard input is not a terminal (e.g., when `ci` is part of a command pipeline).

-j[*R*]
: Just check in and do not initialize. Report an error if the RCS file does not already exist.

-k[*R*]
: Assign a revision number, creation date, state, and author from keyword values that were placed in the working file, instead of computing the revision information from the local environment. -k is useful for software distribution: the preset keywords serve as a timestamp shared by all distribution sites.

-l[*R*]
: Do a co -l after checking in. This leaves a locked copy of the next revision.

-m*msg*
: Use the *msg* string as the log message for all files checked in. When checking in multiple files, ci normally prompts whether to reuse the log message of the previous file. -m bypasses this prompting.

-M[*R*]
: Set the working file's modification time to that of the retrieved version. Use of -M can confuse make and should be used with care.

-n*name*
: Associate a text *name* with the new revision number.

-N*name*
: Same as -n, but override a previous *name*.

-r*R* Check the file in as revision *R*.

-r Without a revision number, -r restores the default behavior of releasing a lock and removing the working file. It is intended to override any default -l or -u set up by aliases or scripts. The behavior of -r in ci is different from most other RCS commands.

-s*state*
: Set the *state* of the checked-in revision.

-t*file*
: Replace RCS file description with contents of *file*. This works only for initial check-in.

-t-*string*
: Replace RCS file description with *string*. This works only for initial check-in.

-u[*R*]
: Do a co -u after checking in. This leaves a read-only copy.

-w*user*
: Set the author field to *user* in the checked-in revision.

Examples

Check in chapter files using the same log message:

```
ci -m'First round edits' chap*
```

Check in edits to prog.c, leaving a read-only copy:

```
ci -u prog.c
```

Start revision level 2; refer to revision 2.1 as "Prototype":

```
ci -r2 -nPrototype prog.c
```

co

`co [options] files`

Retrieve (check out) a previously checked-in revision and place it in the corresponding working file (or print to standard output if `-p` is specified). If you intend to edit the working file and check it in again, specify `-l` to lock the file. `co` accepts the standard options `-q`, `-V`, `-Vn`, `-T`, `-x`, and `-z`.

Options

`-ddate`
: Retrieve latest revision whose check-in timestamp is on or before *date*.

`-f[R]`
: Force the working file to be overwritten.

`-I[R]`
: Interactive mode; prompt user even when standard input is not a terminal.

`-jR2:R3[,...]`
: This works like `rcsmerge`. *R2* and *R3* specify two revisions whose changes are merged into a third file: either the corresponding working file or a third revision (any *R* specified by other `co` options). Multiple comma-separated pairs may be provided; the output of the first join becomes the input of the next. See the `co` manpage for more details.

`-kc` Expand keyword symbols according to flag *c*. *c* can be:

`b`	Like `-ko`, but uses binary I/O. This is most useful on non-Unix systems.
`kv`	Expand symbols to keyword and value (the default). Insert the locker's name only during a `ci -l` or `co -l`.
`kvl`	Like `kv`, but always insert the locker's name.
`k`	Expand symbols to keywords only (no values). This is useful for ignoring trivial differences during file comparison.
`o`	Expand symbols to keyword and value present in previous revision. This is useful for binary files that don't allow substring changes.
`v`	Expand symbols to values only (no keywords). This prevents further keyword substitution and is not recommended.

`-l[R]`
: Same as `-r`, but also lock the retrieved revision.

`-M[R]`
: Set the working file's modification time to that of the retrieved version. Use of `-M` can confuse `make` and should be used with care.

`-p[R]`
: Send retrieved revision to standard output instead of to a working file. Useful for output redirection or filtering.

`-r[R]`
: Retrieve the latest revision or, if *R* is given, retrieve the latest revision that is equal to or lower than *R*. If *R* is `$`, retrieve the version specified by the keywords in the working file.

-s*state*
: Retrieve the latest revision having the given *state*.

-u[*R*]
: Same as -r, but also unlock the retrieved revision if you locked it previously.

-w[*user*]
: Retrieve the latest revision that was checked in either by the invoking user or by the specified *user*.

Examples

Sort the latest stored version of *file*:

```
co -p file | sort
```

Check out (and lock) all files whose names start with an uppercase letter for editing:

```
co -l [A-Z]*
```

Note that filename expansion fails unless a working copy resides in the current directory. Therefore, this example works only if the files were previously checked in via `ci -u`. Finally, here are some different ways to extract the working files for a set of RCS files (in the current directory):

`co -r3 *,v`	*Latest revisions of release 3*
`co -r3 -wjim *,v`	*Same, but only if checked in by jim*
`co -rPrototype *,v`	*Latest revisions named Prototype*
`co -d'May 5, 2 pm LT' *,v`	*Latest revisions that were modified on or before the date*

ident

`ident [options] [files]`

Extract keyword/value symbols from *files*. *files* can be text files, object files, or dumps. `ident` accepts the standard option `-V`.

Options

-q
: Suppress warning message when no keyword patterns are found.

-V
: Print the version number of `ident`.

Examples

If file `prog.c` is compiled, and it contains this line of code:

```
char rcsID[ ] = "$Author: arnold $";
```

the following output is produced:

```
$ ident prog.c prog.o
prog.c:
     $Author: arnold $
prog.o:
     $Author: arnold $
```

Show keywords for all RCS files (suppress warnings):

```
co -p RCS/*,v | ident -q
```

merge

`merge [options] [diff3 options] file1 file2 file3`

Perform a three-way merge of files (via `diff3`) and place changes in *file1*. *file2* is the original file. *file1* is the "good" modification of *file2*. *file3* is another, conflicting modification of *file2*. `merge` finds the differences between *file2* and *file3*, and then incorporates those changes into *file1*. If both *file1* and *file3* have changes to common lines, `merge` warns about overlapping lines and inserts both choices in *file1*. The insertion appears as follows:

```
<<<<<<< file1
lines from file1
========
lines from file3
>>>>>>> file3
```

You'll need to edit *file1* by deleting one of the choices. `merge` exits with a status of 0 (no overlaps), 1 (some overlaps), or 2 (unknown problem). See also **rcsmerge**.

`merge` accepts the `-A`, `-e`, and `-E` options for `diff3`, and simply passes them on, causing `diff3` to perform the corresponding kind of merge. See the entry for **diff3** in Chapter 2 for details. (The `-A` option is for the GNU version of `diff3`.)

RCS

Options

`-L label`
: This option may be provided up to three times, supplying different labels in place of the filenames *file1*, *file2*, and *file3*, respectively.

`-p` Send merged version to standard output instead of to *file1*.

`-q` Produce overlap insertions but don't warn about them.

rcs

`rcs [options] files`

An administrative command for setting up or changing the default attributes of RCS files. `rcs` requires you to supply at least one option. (This is for "future expansion.")

Among other things, `rcs` lets you set strict locking (`-L`), delete revisions (`-o`), and override locks set by `co` (`-l` and `-u`). RCS files have an access list (created via `-a`); anyone whose username is on the list can run `rcs`. The access list is often empty, meaning that `rcs` is available to everyone. In addition, you can always invoke `rcs` if you own the file, if you're a privileged user, or if you run `rcs` with `-i`. `rcs` accepts the standard options `-q`, `-V`, `-Vn`, `-T`, `-x`, and `-z`.

Options

`-ausers`
: Append the comma-separated list of *users* to the access list.

`-Aotherfile`
: Append *otherfile*'s access list to the access lists of *files*.

`-b[R]`
: Set the default branch to *R* or, if *R* is omitted, to the highest branch on the trunk.

`-c's'`
: The comment leader for `$Log$` keyword is set to string *s*. You could, for example, set *s* to .\" for `troff` files or set *s* to * for C programs. (You would need to manually insert an enclosing /* and */ before and after `$Log$`.)

  `-c` is obsolescent; RCS uses the character(s) preceding `$Log$` in the file as the comment leader for log messages. You may wish to set this, though, if you are accessing the RCS file with older versions of RCS.

`-e[users]`
: Erase everyone (or only the specified *users*) from the access list.

`-i` Create (initialize) an RCS file, but don't deposit a revision.

`-I` Interactive mode; prompt user even when standard input is not a terminal.

`-kc` Use *c* as the default style for keyword substitution. (See **co** for values of *c*.) `-kkv` restores the default substitution style.

`-l[R]`
: Lock revision *R* or the latest revision. `-l` "retroactively locks" a file and is useful if you checked out a file incorrectly by typing `co` instead of `co -l`. `rcs` will ask you if it should break the lock if someone else has the file locked.

`-L` Turn on strict locking (the default). This means that everyone, including the owner of the RCS file, must use `co -l` to edit files. Strict locking is recommended when files are to be shared. (See `-U`.)

`-mR:msg`
: Use the *msg* string to replace the log message of revision *R*.

`-M` Do not send mail when breaking a lock. This is intended for use by RCS frontends, not for direct use by users!

`-nflags`
: Add or delete an association between a revision and a name. *flags* can be:

name:*R*	Associate *name* with revision *R*.
name:	Associate *name* with latest revision.
name	Remove association of *name*.

`-Nflags`
: Same as `-n`, but overwrite existing *names*.

`-oR_list`
: Delete (outdate) revisions listed in *R_list*. *R_list* can be specified as: *R1*, *R1*:*R2*, *R1*:, or :*R2*. When a branch is given, `-o` deletes only the latest revision on it. The - range separator character from RCS versions prior to 5.6 is still valid.

`-sstate[:R]`
: Set the state of revision *R* (or the latest revision) to the word *state*.

`-t[file]`
: Replace RCS file description with contents of *file* or, if no file is given, with standard input.

`-t-string`
: Replace RCS file description with *string*.

`-u[R]`
: The complement of `-l`: unlock a revision that was previously checked out via `co -l`. If someone else did the check-out, you are prompted to state the reason for breaking the lock. This message is mailed to the original locker.

`-U`
: Turn on nonstrict locking. Everyone except the file owner must use `co -l` to edit files. (See `-L`.)

Examples

Associate the label *To_customer* with the latest revision of all RCS files:

```
rcs -nTo_customer: RCS/*
```

Add three users to the access list of file `beatle_deals`:

```
rcs -ageorge,paul,ringo beatle_deals
```

Delete revisions 1.2 through 1.5:

```
rcs -o1.2:1.5 doc
```

Replace an RCS file description with the contents of a variable:

```
echo "$description" | rcs -t file
```

---

rcsclean

`rcsclean [options] [files]`

Although included with RCS, this command is optional and might not be installed on your system. `rcsclean` compares checked-out files against the corresponding latest revision or revision *R* (as given by the options). If no differences are found, the working file is removed. (Use `rcsdiff` to find differences.) `rcsclean` is useful in makefiles; for example, you could specify a "clean-up" target to update your directories. `rcsclean` is also useful prior to running `rcsfreeze`. `rcsclean` accepts the standard options `-q`, `-V`, `-Vn`, `-T`, `-x`, and `-z`.

Options

`-kc`
: When comparing revisions, expand keywords using style *c*. (See **co** for values of *c*.)

`-n[R]`
: Show what would happen but don't actually execute.

`-r[R]`
: Compare against revision *R*. *R* can be supplied as arguments to other options, so `-r` is redundant.

`-u[R]`
: Unlock the revision if it's the same as the working file.

Example

Remove unchanged copies of program and header files:

```
rcsclean *.c *.h
```

rcsdiff

`rcsdiff [options] [diff_options] files`

Compare revisions via `diff`. Specify revisions using `-r` as follows:

# of revisions	Comparison made
None	Working file against latest revision.
One	Working file against specified revision.
Two	One revision against the other.

`rcsdiff` accepts the standard options `-q`, `-V`, `-V`*n*, `-T`, `-x`, and `-z`, as well as *diff_options*, which can be any valid `diff` option. `rcsdiff` exits with a status of 0 (no differences), 1 (some differences), or 2 (unknown problem). The `-c` and `-u` options to `diff` can be very useful with `rcsdiff`.

`rcsdiff` prints "retrieving revision ..." messages to standard error, as well as a line of equals signs for separating multiple files. It is often useful to redirect standard error and standard output to the same file.

Options

`-k`*c* When comparing revisions, expand keywords using style *c*. (See **co** for values of *c*.)

`-r`*R1*
: Use revision *R1* in the comparison.

`-r`*R2*
: Use revision *R2* in the comparison. (`-r`*R1* must also be specified.)

Examples

Compare the current working file against the last checked-in version:

```
rcsdiff -c ch19.sgm 2>&1 | more
```

Compare the current working file against the very first version:

```
rcsdiff -c -r1.1 ch19.sgm 2>&1 | more
```

Compare two earlier versions of a file against each other:

```
rcsdiff -c -r1.3 -r1.4 ch19.sgm 2>&1 | more
```

rcsfreeze

`rcsfreeze [name]`

Although included with RCS, this shell script is optional and might not be installed on your system. `rcsfreeze` assigns a name to an entire set of RCS files, which must already be checked in. This is useful for marking a group of files as a single configuration. The default *name* is `C_`*n*, where *n* is incremented each time you run `rcsfreeze`.

rcsmerge

`rcsmerge [options] [diff3 options] file`

Perform a three-way merge of file revisions, taking two differing versions and incorporating the changes into the working *file*. You must provide either one or two revisions to merge (typically with `-r`). Overlaps are handled the same as with `merge`, by placing warnings in the resulting file. `rcsmerge` accepts the standard options `-q`, `-V`, `-Vn`, `-T`, `-x`, and `-z`. `rcsmerge` exits with a status of 0 (no overlaps), 1 (some overlaps), or 2 (unknown problem).

`rcsmerge` accepts the `-A`, `-e`, and `-E` options for `diff3` and simply passes them on, causing `diff3` to perform the corresponding kind of merge. See **merge**, and also see the entry for **diff3** in Chapter 2 for details. (The `-A` option is for the GNU version of `diff3`.)

Options

`-kc` When comparing revisions, expand keywords using style *c*. (See **co** for values of *c*.)

`-p[R]`
: Send merged version to standard output instead of overwriting *file*.

`-r[R]`
: Merge revision *R* or, if no *R* is given, merge the latest revision.

Examples

Suppose you need to add updates to an old revision (1.3) of `prog.c`, but the current file is already at revision 1.6. To incorporate the changes:

```
$ co -l prog.c        Get latest revision
(Edit latest revision by adding updates for revision 1.3, then:)
$ rcsmerge -p -r1.3 -r1.6 prog.c > prog.updated.c
```

Undo changes between revisions 3.5 and 3.2, and overwrite the working file:

```
rcsmerge -r3.5 -r3.2 chap08
```

rlog

`rlog [options] files`

Display identification information for RCS *files*, including the log message associated with each revision, the number of lines added or removed, date of last check-in, etc. With no options, `rlog` displays all information. Use options to display specific items. `rlog` accepts the standard options `-q`, `-V`, `-Vn`, `-T`, `-x`, and `-z`.

Options

`-b` Prune the display; print information only about the default branch.

`-ddates`
: Display information for revisions whose check-in timestamp falls in the range of *dates* (a list separated by semicolons). Be sure to use quotes. Each date can be specified as:

`d1 < d2`
: Select revisions between date *d1* and *d2*, inclusive.

`d1 <`
: Select revisions made on or after *date1*.

`d1 >`
: Select revisions made on or before *date1*.

Timestamp comparisons are strict. If two files have exactly the same time, `<` and `>` won't work. Use `<=` and `>=` instead.

`-h` Display the beginning of the normal `rlog` listing.

`-l[users]`
: Display information only about locked revisions or, if *users* is specified, only about revisions locked by the list of *users*.

`-L` Skip files that aren't locked.

`-N` Don't print symbolic names.

`-r[list]`
: Display information for revisions in the comma-separated *list* of revision numbers. If no *list* is given, the latest revision is used. Items can be specified as:

R1	Select revision *R1*. If *R1* is a branch, select all revisions on it.
R1.	If *R1* is a branch, select its latest revision.
R1:*R2*	Select revisions *R1* through *R2*.
:*R1*	Select revisions from beginning of branch through *R1*.
R1:	Select revisions from *R1* through end of branch.

The - range separator character from RCS versions prior to 5.6 is still valid.

`-R` Display only the name of the RCS file.

`-sstates`
: Display information for revisions whose state matches one from the comma-separated list of *states*.

`-t` Same as `-h`, but also display the file's description.

`-w[users]`
: Display information for revisions checked in by anyone in the comma-separated list of *users*. If no *users* are supplied, assume the name of the invoking user.

Examples

Display the revision histories of all your RCS files:

```
rlog RCS/*,v | more
```

Display names of RCS files that are locked by user `arnold`:

```
rlog -R -L -larnold RCS/*
```

Display the "title" portion (no revision history) of a working file:

```
rlog -t calc.c
```

14 The Concurrent Versions System

This chapter is a comprehensive reference of all CVS commands, with a brief summary of what each does. It is intended to be useful as a quick reference, not as a tutorial.

This chapter covers the following topics:

- Conceptual overview
- Command-line syntax and options
- CVS dot files
- Environment variables
- Keywords and keyword modes
- Dates
- CVSROOT variables
- Alphabetical summary of commands

Most of the material in this chapter is adapted from *Essential CVS*, which is cited in the Bibliography. See that book for much more information on CVS. The Internet starting point for CVS is *http://www.cvshome.org/*.

Conceptual Overview

The basic concepts for source code management systems were presented earlier in Chapter 12. As described there, CVS is a distributed source code management system based on the "copy, modify, merge" model. It uses RCS format files for storing data in its repository and is currently the most popular source code management suite for Unix and Unix-like systems.

Table 14-1 is a quick-start guide to using CVS. You would use the commands in the order shown to create and start using a CVS repository. (The basic steps for the Subversion source code management system are shown in more detail in the section "Using Subversion: A Quick Tour" in Chapter 15. Using CVS is similar.)

Table 14-1. CVS commands quick-start guide

Command	Purpose
`mkdir /path/to/repos`	Make the repository directory.
`cvs init /path/to/repos`	Initialize the repository.
`cvs import ...`	Import the initial version of a project into the repository.
`cvs checkout ...`	Create a sandbox.
`cvs diff ...`	Compare the sandbox to the repository, or different versions in the repository.
`cvs status`	Check if files have changed in the sandbox or the repository.
`cvs update`	Download changes from the repository to the sandbox.
`cvs commit`	Upload changes from the sandbox to the repository.

CVS Wrappers

When resolving conflicts, the usual method CVS uses is `MERGE`, which means that CVS puts both versions of the conflicting group of lines into the file, surrounded by special markers. However, this method doesn't work for binary files. Thus the second conflict-resolution method is `COPY`, which presents both versions of the file to the user for manual resolution.

You can manually specify the conflict resolution method and keyword expansion method when a file is added to a repository, as well as later, after the file is already there. However, doing so manually for lots of files is painful and error-prone. *Wrappers* allow you to specify the conflict resolution method and keyword expansion method for groups of files, based on filename patterns. You may do this on the command line, or more conveniently, by placing the wrappers into a `.cvswrappers` file. Each line has the following format:

```
wildcard option 'value' [option 'value' ...]
```

The *wildcard* is a shell-style wildcard pattern. If *option* is `-m`, it indicates the conflict resolution method. In this case, *value* should be either `MERGE` or `COPY`. If *option* is `-k`, then *value* is one of the keyword resolution modes (`b`, `k`, `o`, etc.).

Stickiness

When some aspect of the persistent state of a file in a sandbox is different from that of the file in the repository, that aspect is said to be *sticky*. For example, when a file is retrieved based on a specific date, tag, or revision, those attributes are sticky. Similarly, when a file in a sandbox belongs to a branch, the branch is said to be sticky, and if the keyword expansion mode is set on a file, that mode is also sticky. Entire directories may be marked as sticky, not just individual files.

These attributes are termed "sticky" because the state of the file becomes persistent. In particular, a `cvs update` does *not* update such files to the latest revision in the repository. Similarly, you cannot use `cvs commit` to make such a file become the head of a branch or the trunk in the repository. Finally, when a file is on a sticky branch, it can only be committed on that branch. `cvs status` shows the stickiness of various attributes.

This all makes sense: work on a branch should be done only on that branch. When work on the branch is finished, the branch's changes should be merged into the files on the trunk, instead of checking the files into the head of the trunk directly.

Stickiness is created or changed using the `-D`, `-k` or `-r` options to `cvs checkout` and `cvs update`. Use `cvs update -A` to remove stickiness. You must use this command on a sticky directory directly; applying it just to all the contained files in the directory is not enough.

See Chapter 4 in *Essential CVS* for more details.

Command-Line Syntax and Options

CVS supports a number of command-line options that you can use to control various aspects of CVS behavior. Each CVS subcommand has its own options, as well.

The syntax of any CVS command is as follows:

```
cvs [cvs-options] [command] [command-options-and-arguments]
```

The *cvs-options* modify the behavior of the main CVS code, rather than the code for a specific command.

CVS

cvs Options

Options to the cvs command are supplied *before* the particular subcommand to be executed. This section focuses on options that you pass to the cvs executable itself, not to any specific CVS command. The following options are valid:

`-a`
: Authenticate all network traffic. Without this option, the initial connection for the command is authenticated, but later traffic along the same data stream is assumed to be from the same source.

  This option is available only with GSS-API connections, but if you use `ssh` as your `rsh` replacement in the `ext` connection mode, `ssh` authenticates the data stream.

  This option is supported if it is listed in `cvs --help-options`. The command-line client can be compiled to support it by using the `--enable-client` option to the `configure` script.

`--allow-root=`*`directory`*
: Used as part of the `inetd` command string for the `server`, `kserver`, and `pserver` connection methods. The *directory* is the repository root directory that the server allows connections to. Using `--allow-root` more than once in a command allows users to connect to any of the specified repositories.

`-d` *repository_path*
: Use *repository_path* as the path to the repository root directory. This option overrides both the CVSROOT environment variable and the contents of the `Root` file in the sandbox's `CVS` subdirectory. It also overrides the contents of the `.cvsrc` file.

  The syntax for the repository path is:

  ```
  [:method:][[[user][:password]@]hostname[:[port]]]/path
  ```

  See *Essential CVS* for a full explanation of each element of the repository path.

`-e` *editor*
: Use the specified *editor* when CVS calls an editor for log information during the `commit` or `import` process. This option overrides the EDITOR, CVSEDITOR, and VISUAL environment variables and the contents of the `.cvsrc` file.

`-f`
: Prevent CVS from reading the `~/.cvsrc` file and using the options in it.

`-H, --help`
: If called as `cvs -H` or `cvs --help`, CVS displays a general CVS help message.

  If called as `cvs -H` *command* or `cvs --help` *command*, CVS displays the available options and help information for the specified *command*.

`--help-commands`
: List the available CVS commands with brief descriptions of their purposes.

`--help-options`
: List the available *cvs-options* with brief descriptions of their purposes.

`--help-synonyms`
: List the valid synonyms (short names) for the CVS commands.

`-l`
: Do not log the current command to the `history` file in the repository's `CVSROOT` directory. The command will not show in subsequent `cvs history` output.

`-n`
: Execute only commands that do not change the repository. Using this option with `cvs update` can provide a status report on the current sandbox.

`-q`
: Run in *quiet mode*. This option causes CVS to display only some of the informational messages.

`-Q`
: Run in *very quiet mode*. This option causes CVS to display only the most critical information.

`-r`
: Set files checked out to the sandbox as read-only. This option only sets newly checked-out files. If a file is being watched with `cvs watch`, read-only is the default. This option overrides settings in the `.cvsrc` file.

`-s` *variable=value*
: Set a user variable for use with one of the scripting files in `CVSROOT`. The user variables are explained in the later section "CVSROOT Variables."

`-t`
: Display messages that trace the execution of the command. This option can be used with `-n` to determine precisely what a command does.

`-T directory`
: Use the named *directory* to store temporary files. This option overrides environment variables or settings in the `.cvsrc` file.

`-v, --version`
: Display CVS version and copyright information.

`-w`
: Set files checked out to the sandbox as readable and writable. This option only sets the permissions of newly checked-out files. This option overrides the CVSREAD environment variable and it overrides settings in the `.cvsrc` file.

`-x`
: Encrypt all data that travels across the network between the client and the server. This option is currently available in GSS-API or Kerberos mode only, but if you use `ssh` as your `rsh` replacement in the `ext` connection mode, `ssh` encrypts the data stream.

This option is available only if the client supports it. It is supported if it is listed in `cvs --help-options`. You can compile the command-line client to support it by using the `--enable-client` and `--enable-encryption` options to the `configure` script.

`-z N`
: Compress all network traffic by using the specified `gzip` compression level *N*. The compression levels range from `0` (no compression) to `9` (maximum compression). This option overrides settings in the `.cvsrc` file.

This option is available only if the client supports it. It is supported if it is listed in `cvs --help-options`. You can compile the command-line client to support it by using the `--enable-client` option to the `configure` script.

CVS

Common Subcommand Options

Many of the CVS subcommands (`add`, `commit`, and so on) share a large number of common options. They are described here.

`-d directory-name`
: Check out or update a sandbox into a directory called *directory-name* instead of using the repository directory name or the name designated in the `modules` file in the repository's `CVSROOT` directory. This is particularly useful when creating a second sandbox for a project.

CVS usually creates the same directory structure that the repository uses. However, if the `checkout` parameter contains only one file or directory and the `-d` option is used, CVS does not create any intervening directories. Use `-N` to prevent CVS from shortening the path.

`-D date`
: Run the subcommand on the latest revision of a file that is as old as or older than the date or time specified by `date`.

`-f`
: Use the latest (`HEAD`) revision of a file that is on the current branch or trunk if no revision matches a specified date or revision number. This option applies only if `-r` or `-D` is used.

-k *mode*
: Specify the keyword expansion mode to be *mode*. For cvs add, this option also sets the default keyword mode for the file. If you forget to set the default keyword mode with cvs add, you can do so later with cvs admin. The keyword-expansion modes are listed in the later section "Keywords and Keyword Modes."

-l
: Run the subcommand on the files in the local directory only. (Do not recurse into subdirectories.) See also -R.

-m *message*
: Use the specified *message* as the description of the newly added file or as the description of the change made.

-n
: Do not run any program listed in the modules file for this directory.

-N
: Do not shorten the path. CVS usually creates the same directory structure that the repository uses. However, if the checkout parameter contains only one file and the -d option is used, CVS does not create any intervening directories unless -N is also specified.

-r *revision*
: Run the subcommand on the specified *revision* or tag of a file. If this option refers to a branch, run the command on the latest (HEAD) revision of the branch.

-R
: Run the subcommand on the files in the local directory and all subdirectories and recurse down the subdirectories. This option is generally the default. See also -l.

Dot Files

In client/server mode, all the dot files other than .rhosts should be on the client computer. The .rhosts file should be in the user's home directory on the server computer.

These are the dot files in the sandbox directory:

.cvsignore
: Contains a list of files CVS should not process. The format is one or more lines, with whitespace-separated filenames or shell wildcard patterns matching files that CVS should ignore when producing informational messages, and during commit, update, or status operations. A single ! causes CVS to empty out its ignore list and start over again with subsequent filenames or patterns. The file may be checked into CVS.

.#*filename.revision*
: If a project file that is not fully synchronized with the repository is overwritten by CVS, the original file is stored as .#*filename.revision*, where *revision* is the BASE revision of the file.

These are the dot files in a user's home directory:

.cvsignore
: Contains a list of files CVS should not process. See the earlier description.

.cvspass
: Used in pserver remote-access mode. This file contains the user's password for each repository the user is logged into, stored in a simple form of

encoding. Be aware that the file is human-readable and that the passwords are easy to decrypt.

`.cvsrc`
: Contains a list of CVS commands and the options the user wants as default options for those commands.

`.cvswrappers`
: Contains a list of wrappers that affect how a file is stored. The wrappers include a pattern that CVS matches against filenames and a keyword-expansion mode that CVS applies to any file whose name matches the pattern.

`.rhosts`
: Used when connecting with `rsh`. This file should be in the user's home directory on the server machine, and it should contain the client's computer and username.

The `rsh` command is terribly, terribly insecure. You should avoid it completely; use `ssh` instead.

Environment Variables

Several environment variables affect CVS. Some are read only when CVS is the client, and some are read only when CVS is the server. When the repository resides on the local machine, both sets are read.

Client Environment Variables

The environment variables in the following list are read and used by the process that runs on the client computer and must be in the calling user's environment:

`CVS_CLIENT_LOG`
: Used for debugging CVS in client/server mode. If set, everything sent to the server is stored in the `$CVS_CLIENT_LOG.in` file, and everything received by the client is stored in `$CVS_CLIENT_LOG.out`.

`CVS_CLIENT_PORT`
: Used to set the port the client uses to connect to the CVS server in `kserver`, `gserver`, and `pserver` modes. By default, the client uses port 2401 (`gserver` and `pserver`) or port 1999 (`kserver`) to connect to the server.

`CVSIGNORE`
: A whitespace-separated list of filename patterns that should be ignored. See the description of the `.cvsignore` file, earlier in this chapter.

`CVSEDITOR, EDITOR, VISUAL`
: Used to set the editor CVS calls when it opens an editor for log messages. On Unix and GNU/Linux systems, the default editor is `vi`. Using CVSEDITOR is preferred over EDITOR and VISUAL, as other variables may be used by other programs.

CVS_PASSFILE
: Used to change the file CVS uses to store and retrieve the password in pserver remote-access mode. The default file is `$HOME/.cvspass`.

CVSREAD
: If set to 1, CVS tries to check out your sandbox in read-only mode. (CVS actually checks whether this variable is nonnull, so it works regardless of the setting. This behavior may change in the future.)

CVSROOT
: Contains the full pathname of the CVS repository. When you're working in a sandbox, this variable is not needed. If you're working outside a sandbox, either this variable must be present or the `-d` *`repository_path`* option must be used.

CVS_RSH
: Used to set the program CVS calls to connect to a remote repository in ext mode. The default program is `rsh`.

The `rsh` command is terribly, terribly insecure. You should avoid it completely; use `ssh` instead.

CVS_SERVER
: If connecting to a CVS server using `rsh`, this variable is used to determine which program is started on the server side. In ext and server modes, this defaults to cvs. When the repository is on the local system, this defaults to the path to the CVS client program.

CVSWRAPPERS
: May contain no more than one *wrapper*, as explained in the earlier section "CVS Wrappers."

HOME, HOMEPATH, HOMEDRIVE
: Used to determine where the user's home directory is, to enable CVS to locate its files. On Unix, GNU/Linux, and related systems, only HOME is used. On Windows systems, HOMEDRIVE and HOMEPATH are used. Some Windows operating systems (Windows NT, 2000, and XP) set these variables automatically. If yours doesn't, HOMEDRIVE should be set to the drive letter (e.g., `C:`) and HOMEPATH should be set to the path (e.g., `\home\arnold`).

PATH
: Used to locate any programs whose path is not compiled with the CVS program. This variable is still used, but it is less important now that the `rcs`, `diff`, and `patch` programs CVS uses are all distributed with CVS.

Server Environment Variables

The following variables are read when CVS is operating as the server (or when the repository is on the local system). They must be in the calling user's environment on the server computer.

`CVS_SERVER_SLEEP`
: Used only when debugging the server in client/server mode. This variable delays the start of the server process by CVS_SERVER_SLEEP seconds to allow the debugger to be attached to it.

`CVSUMASK`
: Used to set the default permissions of files in the repository. This variable may be added to the client code in a later version of CVS.

`PATH`
: Used to locate any programs whose path is not compiled with the CVS program. This variable is still used, but it is less important now that the `rcs`, `diff`, and `patch` programs CVS uses are all distributed with CVS.

`TMPDIR`
: Sets the temporary directory CVS stores data in. This variable defaults to `/tmp`.

  CVS creates temporary files with `mkstemp` (BSD 4.3), if possible. If `mkstemp` is not available when CVS is compiled, it tries `tempnam` (SVID 3), `mktemp` (BSD 4.3), or `tmpnam` (POSIX), in that order. If it uses `tmpnam`, it cannot use the TMPDIR environment variable and files are created in `/tmp`.

Keywords and Keyword Modes

CVS contains keywords that can be included in nonbinary project files. When CVS finds a keyword in a file it is checking out, it expands the keyword to provide metadata about the latest revision of the file. You can set keyword-expansion modes on a file to tell CVS whether (and how) to expand the keywords it finds.

Keyword-expansion modes also control line-ending conversion. Unix, Macintosh, and Windows operating systems use different sets of codes to signal the ends of lines. (GNU/Linux uses the same codes as Unix.) When you commit a file from an operating system that doesn't use Unix line endings, CVS converts the line endings to Unix style. If you are storing binary files, this conversion can corrupt the file. Use the `-kb` keyword-expansion mode to tell CVS not to convert line endings.

CVS keywords take the form:

```
$Keyword$
```

All keywords except `Log` expand to the format:

```
$Keyword: value$
```

These are the keywords and the information they show about the file they are in:

`Author`
: The username of the user who committed the last revision.

`Date`
: The date on which the last revision was committed, in UTC.

`Header`
: A header containing information about the file, including the author, date and revision number, path and filename of the RCS file (project file in the repository), file status, and whether the file is locked.

Id
: A header like the one given by the Header keyword, without the path of the RCS file.

Locker
: The username of the user who locked the file with cvs admin -l (empty if the file is not locked).

Log
: The commit messages, dates, and authors for the file. This keyword instructs CVS to store this information in the file itself. Any characters that prefix the keyword are also used to prefix log lines; this enables comment markers to be included automatically. Unlike most keywords, existing log expansions are not overwritten with the new ones; the new log expansions are merely prepended to the list.

  The Log keyword is best used at the end of a file, to avoid users having to go through all the log messages to get to the important parts of the file.

  This feature was inherited from RCS. As such, the log created by the Log keyword does not merge neatly when CVS merges a branch back to the trunk. If your file is likely to be branched and remerged, it is better to use the cvs log command than to store a log within the file.

The cvs log command displays all the information that the Log keyword provides.

Name
: The tag name the file was checked out with. This keyword can display a branch or provide a more meaningful identification of a revision than the revision number alone.

RCSfile
: The name of the RCS file (the project file in the repository).

Revision
: The CVS internal revision number of the file. This number is specific to the individual file and does not identify a stage within the project.

Source
: The name and path of the RCS file (the project file in the repository).

State
: The current state assigned to the current revision, set with cvs admin -s. See Chapter 7 in *Essential CVS*.

The keyword-expansion modes in the following list are used in commands and CVS wrappers to control keyword expansion and line-ending conversion. The syntax differs slightly for each use. In commands, you use the mode without a space between the option and the mode (e.g., -kb). In wrappers, you need a space and may need to quote (e.g., -k 'b').

b
: Inhibit keyword expansion and line-ending conversion. Use this keyword-expansion mode to signal that a file is binary. This option is needed because CVS can convert line endings from the form appropriate to the server to the

form appropriate to the client. This causes obvious problems when working with binary files.

`k` Generate only a keyword name, not a name and value. Use this option when merging different (nonbinary) versions of a file, to prevent keyword substitution from creating spurious merge errors. This option can corrupt binary files.

`o` Generate the version of a keyword string that was present just before the current file was last committed, rather than generating a version with the modifications of the last commit. This option is similar to `-kb`, but with line-ending conversion.

`v` Generate only the value of a keyword, rather than the name and value. This is most useful with `cvs export`, but do not use it for binary files. Once any keyword is removed from a file, further expansions are not possible unless the word is replaced.

`kv` Generate the name and value of a keyword. This is the default mode.

`kvl` Generate the name and value of a keyword and add the name of the locking user if the revision is locked with `cvs admin -l`.

Dates

In CVS, all dates and times are processed by a version of the GNU `getdate` function, which can translate dates and times given in several different formats. Case is always irrelevant when interpreting dates. Spaces are permitted in date strings, but in the command-line client a string with spaces should be surrounded by quotes. If a year is 0 to 99, it is considered to be in the twentieth century.

If a time is not given, midnight at the start of the date is assumed. If a time zone is not specified, the date is interpreted as being in the client's local time zone.

Legal Date Formats

The legal time and date formats for CVS are defined by the ISO 8601 standard and RFC 822 as amended by RFC 1123. Other formats can be interpreted, but CVS is designed to handle only these standards.

ISO 8601

The basic ISO 8601 date format is as follows:

year-month-day hours:*minutes*:*seconds*

All values are numbers with leading zeros to ensure that the correct number of digits are used. Hours are given in 24-hour time. This produces the structure `YYYY-MM-DD HH:MM:SS`, which is internationally acceptable and can be sorted easily. You can use a date, a time, or both.

If you're using ISO 8601 format with the hyphens, the full date is required in CVS. The `YYYYMMDD` date format is also acceptable and can be abbreviated to `YYYYMM` or `YYYY`.

The `HH` and `HH:MM` time formats are acceptable. Times can also be specified without the colon, so `HHMMSS` or `HHMM` are usable.

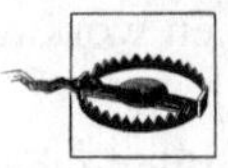

Be aware that `HHMM` may be misinterpreted as `YYYY`. Get into the habit of using separators.

In strict ISO 8601 format, a `T` is required between the date and the time, but CVS understands this format with or without the `T`. The ISO 8601 standard also states that a `Z` at the end of the string designates UTC (Universal Coordinated Time), but CVS does not recognize the use of `Z`.

RFC 822 and RFC 1123

RFCs 822 and 1123 define a precise time format:

```
[DDD ,] DD MMM YYYY HH:MM[:SS] ZZZ
```

These are the terms in the format:

DDD
: A three-letter day of the week.

DD
: A two-digit date of the month.

MMM
: A three-letter month.

YYYY
: The year (it must be a four-digit year).

HH
: Hours.

MM
: Minutes.

SS
: Seconds.

ZZZ
: The time zone (can be the text abbreviation, a military time zone, or an offset from UTC in hours and minutes).

Legal Date Keywords

CVS also allows short English phrases such as “last Wednesday” and “a month ago” to be used in placed of actual dates. Case is not significant, and CVS can understand plurals. These are the keywords it understands:

Month names
: `January`, `February`, `March`, `April`, `May`, `June`, `July`, `August`, `September`, `October`, `November`, and `December`

Month abbreviations
: `Jan`, `Feb`, `Mar`, `Apr`, `Jun`, `Jul`, `Aug`, `Sep`, `Sept`, `Oct`, `Nov`, and `Dec`

Days of the week
: `Sunday`, `Monday`, `Tuesday`, `Wednesday`, `Thursday`, `Friday`, and `Saturday`

Day abbreviations
: `Sun`, `Mon`, `Tue`, `Tues`, `Wed`, `Wednes`, `Thu`, `Thur`, `Thurs`, `Fri`, and `Sat`

Units of time
: `year`, `month`, `fortnight`, `week`, `day`, `hour`, `minute`, `min`, `second`, and `sec`

Relative times
: `tomorrow`, `yesterday`, `today`, and `now`

Meridian qualifiers
: `am`, `pm`, `a.m.`, and `p.m.`

Modifiers

`a`, `last`, `this`, `next`, and `ago`

Sequences

`first`, `third`, `fourth`, `fifth`, `sixth`, `seventh`, `eighth`, `ninth`, `tenth`, `eleventh`, and `twelfth` (`second` can't be used as a sequence term, because it is used as a time unit)

Time Zones

CVS understands time zones expressed in offsets from UTC, such as `+0700` (7 hours ahead) and `-1130` (11 hours, 30 minutes behind). The format for these time zones is `+HHMM` or `-HHMM`, where `+` means ahead of UTC and `-` means behind UTC. CVS also understands time-zone abbreviations and ignores case and punctuation when interpreting them.

Some of the time-zone abbreviations CVS recognizes are ambiguous. CVS recognizes only one meaning for each of the ambiguous time zones. However, which meaning is recognized may vary depending on your operating system, and on how CVS was configured when it was compiled.

Table 14-2 shows the valid civilian time-zone abbreviations for CVS. Table 14-3 shows military time-zone abbreviations that CVS recognizes.

Table 14-2. Civilian time-zone abbreviations

Abbrev.	Offset/name	Abbrev.	Offset/name
gmt	+0000 Greenwich Mean	met	-0100 Middle European
ut	+0000 Coordinated Universal Time	mewt	-0100 Middle European Winter
utc	+0000 Coordinated Universal Time	mest	Middle European Summer
wet	+0000 Western European	swt	-0100 Swedish Winter
bst	+0000 British Summer (ambiguous with Brazil Standard)	sst	Swedish Summer (ambiguous with South Sumatra)
wat	+0100 West Africa	fwt	-0100 French Winter
at	+0200 Azores	fst	French Summer
bst	+0300 Brazil Standard (ambiguous with British Summer)	eet	-0200 Eastern Europe, USSR Zone 1
gst	+0300 Greenland Standard (ambiguous with Guam Standard)	bt	-0300 Baghdad, USSR Zone 2
nft	+0330 Newfoundland	it	-0330 Iran
nst	+0330 Newfoundland Standard (ambiguous with North Sumatra)	zp4	-0400 USSR Zone 3
ndt	Newfoundland Daylight	zp5	-0500 USSR Zone 4
ast	+0400 Atlantic Standard	ist	-0530 Indian Standard
adt	Atlantic Daylight	zp6	-0600 USSR Zone 5
est	+0500 Eastern Standard	nst	-0630 North Sumatra (ambiguous with Newfoundland Summer)

Table 14-2. Civilian time-zone abbreviations (continued)

Abbrev.	Offset/name	Abbrev.	Offset/name
edt	Eastern Daylight	sst	-0700 South Sumatra, USSR Zone 6 (ambiguous with Swedish Summer)
cst	+0600 Central Standard	wast	-0700 West Australian Standard
cdt	Central Daylight	wadt	West Australian Daylight
mst	+0700 Mountain Standard	jt	-0730 Java
mdt	Mountain Daylight	cct	-0800 China Coast, USSR Zone 7
pst	+0800 Pacific Standard	jst	-0900 Japan Standard, USSR Zone 8
pdt	Pacific Daylight	cast	-0930 Central Australian Standard
yst	+0900 Yukon Standard	cadt	Central Australian Daylight
ydt	Yukon Daylight	east	-1000 Eastern Australian Standard
hst	+1000 Hawaii Standard	eadt	Eastern Australian Daylight
hdt	Hawaii Daylight	gst	-1000 Guam Standard, USSR Zone 9 (ambiguous with Greenland Standard)
cat	+1000 Central Alaska	nzt	-1200 New Zealand
ahst	+1000 Alaska-Hawaii Standard	nzst	-1200 New Zealand Standard
nt	+1100 Nome	nzdt	New Zealand Daylight
idlw	+1200 International Date Line West	idle	-1200 International Date Line East
cet	-0100 Central European		

Table 14-3. Military time-zone abbreviations

Name	Offset	Name	Offset	Name	Offset	Name	Offset	Name	Offset
a	+0100	f	+0600	l	+1100	q	-0400	v	-0900
b	+0200	g	+0700	m	+1200	r	-0500	w	-1000
c	+0300	h	+0800	n	-0100	s	-0600	x	-1100
d	+0400	i	+0900	o	-0200	t	-0700	y	-1200
e	+0500	k	+1000	p	-0300	u	-0800	z	0000

CVSROOT Variables

The administrative files in CVSROOT can use several types of variables: internal, environment, and shell variables. You can use these variables to pass parameters to the scripts in the scripting files, or you can use them as part of command-line templates.

The internal variables allow you to use information CVS stores about the currently running command. The environment variables are used to access information from the environment the command is running in, and the shell variables are used to access information about the shell.

Environment Variables in CVSROOT Files

Three environment variables are set when CVS runs commands or scripts from CVS administrative files:

`CVS_USER`
: This variable is meaningful only with the `pserver` access method. It refers to the CVS username provided in the leftmost field of the appropriate line in `CVSROOT/passwd`. If this username does not exist, the variable expands to an empty string.

`LOGNAME, USER`
: Both of these variables contain the username of the user calling the CVS process.

  In the `pserver` access method, the username is the third field of the line in `passwd`. If no username is there, the `CVS_USER` value is used.

Internal Variables in CVSROOT Files

The syntax for referencing a CVS internal variable is `${VARIABLE}`. The `$VARIABLE` syntax can also be used if the character immediately following the variable is neither alphanumeric nor an underscore (_).

These are the internal CVS variables:

`CVSROOT`
: The path to the repository root directory (not the path to the `CVSROOT` directory within the repository). This variable contains the path only, not any access method or host information.

`CVSEDITOR, EDITOR, VISUAL`
: The editor CVS is using. If you use the `-e` *`editor`* CVS option, CVS uses the editor you specify on the command line. If you don't use `-e`, CVS reads the environment variables and uses the first editor it finds. CVS uses CVSEDITOR by preference, then EDITOR, then VISUAL.

`USER`
: The username (on the server machine in client/server mode) of the user running CVS.

  With the `pserver` access method, this is the third field of the appropriate line in `passwd`. If no username is there, it is the name in the leftmost field.

CVS permits user-defined variables that can be passed to administrative files from the client. In the administrative files, reference such a variable with the syntax `${=VARIABLE}`. On the command line, use the `-s` *`variable=value`* CVS option to pass the variable to CVS. All strings that contain the `$` symbol, other than the variable references, are reserved for CVS internal use. There is no way to escape the `$` symbol.

Shell Variables in CVSROOT Files

Two shell variables are also used in the administrative files:

`~/`
: The home directory of the user calling the CVS process.

`~username`
: The home directory of the user identified as *username*.

CVS

Alphabetical Summary of Commands

Most of your interaction with CVS is through the various CVS subcommands. Even if you use a graphical client, most of the functions the client uses call the CVS subcommands.

Most subcommands have a shortened nickname that you can type instead of the longer subcommand name. These are called *command synonyms* in CVS jargon.

---

add

`cvs [cvs-options] add [-k mode] [-m message] files`

Add a file or directory to the repository. This command can also be used to undo an uncommitted file deletion or to restore a deleted file. You must commit any added files in order for the addition to fully take effect.

Synonyms: `ad`, `new`.

Standard subcommand options: `-k`, `-m`.

Example

```
$ cvs add Design.rtf
cvs server: scheduling file `Design.rtf' for addition
cvs server: use 'cvs commit' to add this file permanently
```

---

admin

`cvs [cvs-options] admin [options] [files ...]`

Use RCS commands on the repository copy of project files. This command is a frontend for a range of useful (though sometimes useless to CVS) RCS-based commands. Project files are stored in the repository in RCS format, so it is useful to have a way to use some of the RCS commands on the files directly.

Synonyms: `adm`, `rcs`.

Standard subcommand options: `-k`.

Options

`-ausernames`
: Append the comma-separated list of *usernames* to the RCS access list in the repository (RCS-format) copy of a file. This change to an RCS file has no effect on CVS. See also `-A` and `-e`.

`-Afilename`
: Append the RCS access list in *filename* to the access list of the files being operated on.This change to an RCS file has no effect on CVS. See also `-a` and `-e`.

`-b[revision]`
: Set the default branch of a file to the named branch revision; or, if no revision is named, set the default branch to the highest branch revision on the trunk. This option should be used very rarely in CVS; it is better to check out a sandbox as a branch sandbox with the `-r` option to `checkout` or `update`.

`-cstring`
: Set the RCS comment leader of a file to the specified *string*. This option is not used in CVS.

`-e[usernames]`
: Remove the comma-separated list of *usernames* from the RCS access list in the repository (RCS-format) copy of a file. If no list of *usernames* is provided, remove all names. This change to an RCS file has no effect on CVS. See also `-a` and `-A`.

`-i`
: Create and initialize an RCS file. This option isn't used in CVS (use `cvs add` instead), and it is not available in CVS 1.9.14 and later.

`-I`
: Run interactively. This option does not work in client/server-mode CVS and may be removed from later versions of CVS.

`-l[revision]`
: Lock the specified *revision* of a file so that another user cannot commit to it. If *revision* is omitted, CVS locks the latest revision on the current sandbox's branch or the trunk. To work with CVS, the lock requires a script such as the `rcslock` script in the `contrib` directory of the source. See *Essential CVS* for how to use this option. See also `-u`.

`-L`
: Set RCS locking for a file to strict, which means that the owner of the file must lock the file before committing. (This locking is done by the CVS code, and need not be done manually.) File locking must be set to strict for CVS to work properly; see also `-U`.

`-mrevision:message`
: Replace the log message of the designated *revision* of a file with the specified *message*.

`-ntagname[:[revision]]`
: Tag the designated *revision* or branch of a file with the *tagname*. If there is no *revision* and no colon, delete the tag; if there is a colon but no *revision*, tag the latest revision on the default branch, usually the trunk. If the *tagname* is already present in the file (and the operation isn't "delete"), this option prints an error and exits. See also `-N`.

  Generally, it is better to use `cvs tag` and `cvs rtag` to manipulate tags.

`-Ntagname[:[revision]]`
: Tag the designated *revision* or branch of a file with the *tagname*. If there is no *revision* and no colon, delete the tag; if there is a colon but no revision, tag the latest revision on the default branch, usually the trunk. If the *tagname* is already present in the file (and the operation isn't "delete"), this option moves the tag to the new revision. See also `-n`.

  Generally, it is better to use `cvs tag` and `cvs rtag` to manipulate tags.

`-orange`
: Delete the revisions specified in the *range*. The revisions given in the range can be revision numbers or tags, but be wary of using tags if multiple tags in a file denote the same revision.

CVS

There is no way to undo a cvs admin -o command.

The *range* can be any of the following:

revision1:*revision2*
: Delete revisions between *revision1* and *revision2*, including *revision1* and *revision2*.

revision1::*revision2*
: Delete revisions between *revision1* and *revision2*, excluding *revision1* and *revision2*.

revision:
: Delete *revision* and all newer revisions on the same branch (or the trunk).

revision::
: Delete all revisions newer than *revision* on the same branch (or the trunk).

:*revision*
: Delete *revision* and all older revisions on the same branch (or the trunk). This range does not delete the base revision of the branch or revision 1.1.

::*revision*
: Delete all revisions older then *revision* on the same branch (or the trunk). This range does not delete the base revision of the branch or revision 1.1.

revision
: Delete *revision*.

-q
: Run quietly, without printing diagnostics (redundant with cvs -q admin).

-s*state*[:*revision*]
: Set the *state* of the designated *revision* of a file, or set the last revision on the trunk or the current branch if no *revision* is listed. The *state* should be a string and is shown in the output of cvs log and by the Log and State keywords. The dead state is reserved for CVS internal use.

-t[*filename*]
: Write the contents of the file specified by *filename* to the description of each file listed in the command. The description is an RCS field, shown in cvs log output. This option deletes any existing description. If the *filename* is omitted, CVS seeks input from standard input, ending with a period (.) on a line by itself. See also -t-*string*.

-t-*string*
: Write the contents of the *string* to the description of each file listed in the command. The description is an RCS field, shown in cvs log output. This option deletes any existing description. See also -t.

-u[*revision*]
: Unlock the specified *revision* of a file so that another user can commit from that revision. If the *revision* is omitted, this option unlocks the latest revision on the current sandbox's branch or the trunk. This option requires a script such as the rcslock script in the contrib directory of the source. See *Essential CVS* for how to use this option. See also -l.

-U
: Set RCS locking for a file to nonstrict, which means that the owner of the file does not need to lock the file before committing. (This locking is done by the CVS code and need not be done manually.)

  File locking must be set to strict for CVS to work properly. This option should never be used on CVS-stored files. See also -L.

-V*N*
: Write an RCS file compatible with RCS version *N*. This option isn't used in CVS anymore, and it is not available in CVS 1.9.20 and later.

-x*suffix*
: Specify the *suffix* for the RCS file. This option is not used or available in CVS (all CVS files use ,v as the suffix).

Example

```
$ cvs admin -kb AcceptanceTest.doc
RCS file: /var/lib/cvs/wizzard/doc/AcceptanceTest.doc,v
done
```

annotate

cvs [*cvs-options*] annotate [*options*] [*files* ...]

Display a file or files with annotations showing the last editor and revision that changed each line of the file. If no files are supplied, the files in the current sandbox are shown. See also **rannotate**.

Synonym: ann.

Standard subcommand options: -D, -f, -l, -r, -R.

Option

-F
: Show annotations for binary files.

Example

```
$ cvs annotate Makefile

Annotations for Makefile
***************
1.2  (arnold     01-Sep-02): #
1.2  (arnold     01-Sep-02): # Wizzard project Makefile
1.2  (arnold     01-Sep-02): # A Robbins, 1 September 2002
```

checkout

cvs [*cvs-options*] checkout [*options*] *projects* ...

Create a new sandbox in the current working directory. This command can also be used to update an existing sandbox. See also **export** and **update**.

The *projects* argument to checkout may be one or more paths to directories within the repository, paths to files within the repository, or module names as specified in the modules file in the repository's CVSROOT directory. These paths must be separated by spaces.

When creating a new sandbox, the repository path must be specified by using the -d *repository_path* CVS option or the CVSROOT environment variable.

If you are creating a new sandbox inside an existing sandbox, the CVS/Root file of the current directory in the existing sandbox can provide a repository path. In most cases, having a sandbox inside a sandbox is needlessly confusing.

Synonyms: co, get.

Standard subcommand options: -d, -D, -f, -k, -l, -n, -N, -r, -R.

Options

-A
: Clear sticky tags, dates, and keyword-expansion modes from a project and replace the current files with the head of the trunk.

-c
: Display the contents of the modules file in the repository's CVSROOT directory. This option lists the modules in the current repository and the options applicable to those modules. See also -s.

checkout -c lists only those projects that have entries in the modules file.

-j *revision*[:*date*]
: Determine the changes between the revision the files in the sandbox are based on and the specified *revision* and merge those changes to the sandbox.

  If two -j options are used, determine the changes between the first -j revision and the second -j revision and merge those changes to the sandbox.

  The *date* can be used only if the revision designates a branch. *date* specifies the latest revision on that date.

-p
: Check out the listed files to the standard output, rather than to the filesystem.

-P
: Do not include empty directories in the sandbox.

-s
: Display the contents of the modules file in the repository's CVSROOT directory. This option lists the modules in the current repository and their status. See also -c.

Example

```
$ cvs -d cvs:/var/lib/cvs checkout wizzard
cvs server: Updating wizzard
U wizzard/Changelog
U wizzard/INSTALL
U wizzard/Makefile
```

commit

cvs [*cvs-options*] commit [*options*] [*files* ...]

Commit changes in a sandbox to the repository. Until a commit is run, changes such as modified, new, or removed files are not reflected in the repository. If no files are listed as arguments, CVS uploads all changes in the current sandbox.

Unless you use either the -m or -F options, commit invokes an editor to request a log message.

If there have been changes in the repository version of a file since it was last synchronized with the repository and the local version has also changed, you have a *conflict* and the file cannot be committed. You can try to commit the file again once you have updated it using cvs update or cvs checkout. The update will include an attempt to merge the file.

Synonyms: ci, com.

Standard subcommand options: -l, -m, -n, -r, -R.

Options

-f
: Force CVS to commit a file even if there have been no changes to the file. This option implies the -l option.

-F *logfile*
: Read a log message from the specified *logfile* rather than calling an editor.

Example

```
/home/arnold/cvs/wizzard$ cvs commit
cvs commit: Examining .
cvs commit: Examining doc
cvs commit: Examining lib
...
RCS file: /var/lib/cvs/wizzard/doc/Design.rtf,v
done
Checking in doc/Design.rtf;
/var/lib/cvs/wizzard/doc/Design.rtf,v  <--  Design.rtf
initial revision: 1.1
done
```

diff

cvs [*cvs-options*] diff [*format-options*] [*options*] [*files* ...]

Display the differences between two revisions of a file or files. By default, diff checks the sandbox copy against the revision in the repository that the sandbox copy was last synchronized with. If the *files* argument is a directory, all files under that directory are compared and files in subdirectories are also compared recursively. See also **rdiff**.

Synonyms: di, dif.

Standard subcommand options: -D, -k, -l, -r, -R.

The *format-options* determine how cvs diff displays any differences it finds. They operate in the same way as the options to the

GNU diff program. This includes full support for the line and group format options; see the entry for **diff** in Chapter 2.

Example

This is a simple example to show how CVS displays the difference between the current and repository revisions of the Makefile.

```
$ cvs diff Makefile
Index: Makefile
==============================
RCS file: /var/lib/cvs/wizzard/Makefile,v
retrieving revision 1.6
diff -r1.6 Makefile
25a26
>         rm -f lib/*.o
```

---

edit

cvs [*cvs-options*] edit [*options*] [*files* ...]

Mark a file as being edited by the current user. This command is used as part of the cvs watch family of commands. If a file is being watched, it is checked out to the sandbox with read permissions but not write permissions. The edit command sets the sandbox file as writable, notifies any watchers that the file is being edited, and sets the user as a temporary watcher to be notified if certain actions are performed on the file by other users. See also **editors**, **unedit**, **watch**, and **watchers**.

CVS does not notify you of your own changes.

You can unedit (set read-only and clear the temporary watch) a file with cvs unedit or cvs release, or by removing the file and recreating it with cvs update or cvs checkout.

CVS uses any script in the notify file in the repository's CVSROOT directory to notify the user of changes.

Synonyms: none.

Standard subcommand options: -l, -R.

Option

-a *action*
: Notify the user when the specified *action* occurs to the file. This setting acts as a temporary watch (see **watch**) on the file and is removed when the file is no longer being edited. Each -a designates one of the possible actions. The -a option can be repeated to designate multiple actions. The *action* may be any of the following:

  commit
  : Notify the user when someone else commits changes to the file.

`edit`
: Notify the user if someone else has run cvs edit on the file.

`unedit`
: Notify the user when the file is no longer being edited by someone else. This notification is triggered by the user running cvs unedit or cvs release or by the file being deleted and re-created with cvs update or cvs checkout.

`all`
: Notify the user of all of the previous actions.

`none`
: Notify the user of none of the previous actions.

---

editors

cvs [*cvs-options*] editors [-lR] [*files* ...]

Displays the list of people who have a current edit command for the file or files listed as parameters. If no files are listed, this command lists the editors for the files in the current directory and subdirectories. See also **edit**, **unedit**, **watch**, and **watchers**.

Synonyms: none.

Standard subcommand options: -l, -R.

Example

```
$ cvs editors Makefile
Makefile arnold Sat Oct 26 01:51:02 2002 GMT helit
/home/arnold/cvs/wizzard
```

---

export

cvs [*cvs-options*] export [*options*] *project*

Create a directory containing all directories and files belonging to a specified release of a project, with no CVS administrative files. It acts like a checkout or update for that specific point, but it does not produce the CVS administrative files. export requires the -r or -D command options. When exporting, the repository path must be specified by using the -d *repository_path* CVS option or the CVSROOT environment variable. See also **checkout** and **update**.

The argument to export can be a directory name or path within the repository, a filename or path within the repository, or a module name as specified in the modules file in the repository's CVSROOT directory.

You can imply the repository path by being in a sandbox, but exporting into a sandbox is not recommended.

Synonyms: exp, ex.

Standard subcommand options: -d, -D, -f, -k, -l, -n, -N, -r, -R.

Example

```
$ cvs -d cvs:/var/lib/cvs export -D now wizzard
cvs server: Updating wizzard
U wizzard/Changelog
U wizzard/INSTALL
U wizzard/Makefile
```

history

`cvs [cvs-options] history [options] [files ...]`

Display the information stored in the `history` file in the repository's `CVSROOT` directory. If that file does not exist or is not writable, the `history` command fails with an error. CVS writes to the `history` file during `checkout`, `export`, `commit`, `rtag`, `update`, and `release` operations.

Synonyms: `hi`, `his`.

Standard subcommand options: `-D`, `-r`.

The `-f`, `-l`, `-n`, and `-p` options for `cvs history` act differently than their normal uses in CVS.

Options

`-a` Show history data for all users. By default, CVS shows only the data for the calling user.

`-b` *string*
: Show data that is more recent than the newest record that contains the given *string* in the module name, filename, or repository path.

`-c` Report only commits—times when the repository was modified (equivalent to `-xAMR`).

`-e`
: Report on every record type. This option is equivalent to `-x` with every type specified.

`-f` *file*
: Show data for the specified *file*. This option can be repeated to show data for multiple files.

`-l` Show only the most recent commit to the repository.

`-m` *module*
: Show data for a particular *module*. CVS checks the `modules` file in the repository's `CVSROOT` directory and then searches the `history` file for files and directories that belong to the `module`.

`-n` *module*
: Like `-m`, but search only the `history` file for the specified *module* name.

`-o` Report on records of checkouts (equivalent to `-xO`).

`-p` *directory*
: Show records for a particular project *directory*. This option can be repeated to show records for several projects.

`-r` *revision*
: Show data as of, or more recent than, the *revision* or tag. CVS searches the repository's project files to determine the timestamp of the *revision*.

`-t` *tagname*
: Show data as of, or more recent than, the latest time a tag record with this *tagname* was stored in the `history` file by any user.

`-T` Report on records of tags (equivalent to `-xT`).

`-u` *username*
: Report on records for the specified *username*. This option can be repeated to search for multiple users.

`-w` Report on records of actions that match the current working directory.

`-x` *flag(s)*
: Extract records that match the given *flag* or *flags*. Any number of flags can be used with the `-x` option. `cvs history` extracts all records in the *history* file that match this option and all other options. The flags may be any of the following:

  `A` Report on records of files added to the repository.

  `C` Report on records of files that would have been updated in a sandbox, but where the files needed to be merged and there were conflicts in the merge.

  `E` Report on records of files exported from the repository.

  `F` Report on records of files that were released.

  `G` Report on records of files updated in a sandbox with a successful merge.

  `M` Report on records of files that were modified (a sandbox revision added to the repository).

  `O` Report on records of files that were checked out.

  `R` Report on records of files that were removed from the repository.

  `T` Report on records of files that were tagged with CVS `rtag`.

  `U` Report on records of files updated in a sandbox file with no merge required.

  `W` Report on records of files deleted from a sandbox during an update because they were no longer active in the repository.

`-z` *timezone*
: Produce output and convert times to the specified *timezone*. The time zone can be a recognized abbreviation such as `EST`, or it can be given as an offset of UTC. Time zones are listed in the earlier section "Time Zones."

Example

```
$ cvs history
O 2002-10-03 08:33 +0000 arnold wizzard/src =wizmain=  <remote>/*
O 2002-10-03 09:12 +0000 arnold wizzard     =wizmake=  <remote>/*
O 2002-10-03 09:12 +0000 arnold wizzard/src =wiztest=  <remote>/*
O 2002-10-25 08:58 +0000 arnold wizzard     =wizzard=  <remote>/*
```

import

cvs [*cvs-options*] import [*options*] *project-name vendor-tag release-tag*

Create a new project in the repository or manage *vendor branches*. To create a new project, lay out the project structure and any initial files. You can do this in a temporary directory, as CVS does not need the initial structure or files once the project has been imported. Change directories into the root directory of the new project, then run `cvs import`. You need to specify the repository path and provide a project name and two tags: a vendor tag and a release tag.

The *project-name* will become the project's root directory name. The tags are less critical; if you do not intend to use a vendor branch, a meaningless pair of tags such as `a1 b2` is sufficient. The tag names must conform to all the normal requirements for tags: they must start with a letter and can contain only alphanumeric characters, underscores (_), and hyphens (-). The `HEAD` and `BASE` tag names are reserved.

A *vendor branch* is a special branch that CVS provides to track third-party code that contributes to a project. If you use vendor branches, CVS uses the *vendor-tag* as a branch tag for the vendor branch, and it uses the *release-tag* to mark the current revisions of the vendor branch files.

Create a vendor branch by using `cvs import` to create the project. When you want to update to a new release from the vendor, use `cvs import` on the same project with the same vendor tag and a new release tag.

Test that you can `cvs checkout` the new project before removing the original files.

Synonyms: `im`, `imp`.

Standard subcommand options: `-k`, `-m`.

Options

`-b` *branch*

Import to the specified vendor *branch*. If you have more than one external supplier for a project, you may need to use two or more distinct vendor branches to manage the project. If you are using multiple vendor branches, use the `-b` option to specify which branch you are importing to. *branch* must be the branch number, not a tag, and CVS does not check that the branch number given with the option and the symbolic tag provided as the *vendor-tag* argument to the command correspond to the same branch.

`-d` When setting the timestamp on each imported file, use each file's last modification time rather than the current time.

`-I` *file*
: Ignore *file* when updating. `-I` can be used more than once. Use `-I !` to clear the list of ignored files.

`-W` *wrapper*
: Modify the import based on elements of each filename.

Example

```
$ cvs -d cvs:/var/lib/cvs import wizzard wizproject ver_0-1
...
No conflicts created by this import
```

init

`cvs [cvs-options] init`

Convert an existing directory into a CVS repository and create and populate the `CVSROOT` directory that contains the administrative files for a CVS repository.

CVS creates the final directory in the path if it does not already exist. Previous directories in the path must exist.

Synonyms: none.

Example

```
$ cvs -d /var/lib/cvsroot init
```

kserver

`cvs [cvs-options] kserver`

Run the repository-server end of a Kerberos 4 connection. The `cvs kserver` command must be called from `inetd` or an equivalent server daemon. See also **pserver**.

Synonyms: none.

log

`cvs [cvs-options] log [options] [files ...]`

Display information about the files in the current sandbox or the files specified as parameters. The information this command provides is part of the header section of the files in the repository. This command also provides information from the log messages created when files are imported or changes are committed.

With no options, `cvs log` displays all the information it has available. See also **rlog**.

Synonym: `lo`.

Standard subcommand options: `-l`.

CVS

Options

-b Display information about only the revisions on the default branch, normally the trunk.

-d *dates*
: Display information only on revisions checked in on or between the dates or times provided. Date and time formats are listed in the earlier section "Dates." More than one date range can be given; ranges must be separated by semicolons. Date ranges can be specified according to the following list:

  date1>date2, date2<date1
  : Select all revisions between the two dates.

  date1>=date2, date2<=date1
  : Select all revisions on or between the two dates.

  date>, <date
  : Select all revisions earlier than *date*.

  date>=, <=date
  : Select all revisions on or earlier than *date*.

  date<, >date
  : Select all revisions later than *date*.

  date<=, >=date
  : Select all revisions on or later than *date*.

  date
  : Select all revisions on *date*.

-h Print only the header information for a file, not the description, the log messages, or revision information.

-N Do not list the tags (the symbolic names).

-r[*revisions*]
: Provide information only on *revisions* in the ranges provided. More than one range can be given; ranges must be separated by commas. There must be no space between the -r and its argument. If no range is provided, the latest revision on the default branch, normally the trunk, is used.

  Ranges can be specified according to the following list:

  revision1:*revision2, revision1*::*revision2*
  : Select all revisions between *revision1* and *revision2*. The revisions must be on the same branch. With the double colon, CVS excludes *revision1*.

  :*revision,* ::*revision*
  : Select revisions from the start of the branch or trunk the *revision* is on, up to and including the *revision*.

  revision:, *revision*::
  : Select revisions from *revision* to the end of the branch or trunk the *revision* is on. With the double colon, CVS excludes the *revision*.

  branch
  : Select all revisions on *branch*.

branch1:*branch2*, *branch1*::*branch2*
: Select all revisions on both branches and any branches that split off from the two branches.

branch.
: Select the latest revision on *branch*. Note the trailing period.

-R Display the name of the repository copy of a file only.

-s *states*
: Display only revisions with states that match one of the *states* in the comma-separated list.

-S Do not display header information if there are no revisions to display.

-t Print only the header information and description, not the log messages or revision information.

-w[*usernames*]
: Display only revisions committed by the specified list of users. Provide the list of users as a comma-separated list. If no usernames are listed, the revisions committed by the current user are displayed. There can be no space between -w and its argument.

Example

```
$ cvs log
cvs server: Logging .

RCS file: /var/lib/cvs/wizzard/Changelog,v
Working file: Changelog
head: 1.1
branch:
locks: strict
access list:
symbolic names:
beta_0-1_branch: 1.1.0.2
beta_0-1_branch_root: 1.1
pre_beta_0-1: 1.1
keyword substitution: kv
total revisions: 1;     selected revisions: 1
description:
----------------------------
revision 1.1
date: 2002/08/31 13:37:56;  author: arnold;  state: Exp;
Creating a structure.
...
```

login

cvs [*cvs-options*] login

Log in to a CVS pserver session. This command is needed only with the pserver connection mode. See also **logout**.

Synonyms: none.

Example

```
$ acct=:pserver:arnold:password:@cvs.nosuch.net:/var/lib/cvs
$ cvs -d $acct login
Logging in to :pserver:arnold@cvs:2401/var/lib/cvs
```

---

logout

`cvs [cvs-options] logout`

Log out of a CVS pserver session. This command is needed only with the pserver connection mode. See also **login**.

Synonyms: none.

Example

```
$ cvs -d :pserver:arnold@cvs:/var/lib/cvs logout
Logging out of :pserver:arnold@cvs:2401/var/lib/cvs
```

---

pserver

`cvs [cvs-options] pserver`

Run the repository-server end of a password server or Kerberos 5 (via the GSS-API) connection. This command must be called from `inetd` or an equivalent server daemon. See also **kserver**.

Synonyms: none.

---

rannotate

`cvs [cvs-options] rannotate [options] files ...`

Displays files with annotations showing the last editor and revision that changed each line of each specified file. You can run `rannotate` without a sandbox, but you must have a repository specified if you do so. `rannotate` requires at least one filename, directory name, or module name from within the repository as an argument. See also **annotate**.

Synonyms: `ra`, `rann`.

Standard subcommand options: `-D`, `-f`, `-l`, `-r`, `-R`.

Option

`-F` Show annotations for binary files.

Example

```
$ cvs rannotate wizzard/Makefile

Annotations for wizzard/Makefile
***************
1.2  (arnold     01-Sep-02): #
1.2  (arnold     01-Sep-02): # Wizzard project Makefile
1.2  (arnold     01-Sep-02): # A Robbins, 1 September 2002
```

---

rdiff

`cvs [cvs-options] rdiff [options] projects ...`

Create output that can be redirected into a file and used with the GNU (or equivalent) `patch` program. The output goes to the standard output. `rdiff` operates directly from the repository and does not need to be used from a sandbox. It does require a filename, directory name, or module name as an argument, and you must specify one or two revisions or dates. If you specify one revision or date, `rdiff` calculates the differences between that date and the current (HEAD) revision. If two dates are specified, `rdiff` calculates the differences between the two. See also **diff**.

Synonyms: `pa`, `patch`.

Most people use `rdiff` to make a file to use with `patch`. If you're using a `patch` file that was created over more than one directory, you may need to use the `-p` option to `patch`, so that it can find all the appropriate directories.

Standard subcommand options: `-D`, `-f`, `-l`, `-r`, `-R`.

Options

`-c`
: Use `context` output format, with three lines of context around each change. This is the default format.

`-s`
: Create a summary change report rather than a patch, showing which files have changed with one line per file.

`-t`
: Produce a report on the two most recent revisions in a file. Do not use `-r` or `-D` with the `-t` option.

`-u`
: Use `unidiff` format instead of `context` format.

`-V` *`version`*
: This option is now obsolete, but it used to allow you to expand keywords according to the rules of the specified RCS *version*.

Example

```
$ cvs rdiff -r 1.5 wizzard/Makefile
Index: wizzard/Makefile
diff -c wizzard/Makefile:1.5 wizzard/Makefile:1.6
*** wizzard/Makefile:1.5      Thu Oct 17 08:50:14 2002
--- wizzard/Makefile          Thu Oct 17 10:01:12 2002
***************
*** 2,18 ****
  # Makefile for the Wizzard project
  # First created by A Robbins, 1 September 2002
  #
! # Current revision $Revision: 1.5 $
  # On branch $Name:  $ (not expanded if this is the trunk)
! # Latest change by
  # $Author: arnold $ on $Date: 2002/10/16 22:50:14 $
  #
  ##

  # Initial declarations
  #
  CC=gcc
! SUBDIRS = man doc src lib


  # Declaring phony targets
--- 2,18 ----
```

```
  # Makefile for the Wizzard project
  # First created by A Robbins, 1 September 2002
  #
! # Current revision $Revision: 1.6 $
  # On branch $Name:  $ (not expanded if this is the trunk)
! # Latest change by
  # $Author: arnold $ on $Date: 2002/10/17 00:01:12 $
  #
  ##

  # Initial declarations
  #
  CC=gcc
! SUBDIRS = man doc src lib test


  # Declaring phony targets
***************
...
```

release

cvs [*cvs-options*] release [-d] *directories* ...

Make a sandbox inactive. This command checks for uncommitted changes, removing any existing edit flags, and writes to the CVSROOT/history file that the sandbox has been released. You can use release on an entire sandbox or on one or more subdirectories.

Synonyms: re, rel.

Option

-d Delete the sandbox after it has been released.

Example

```
$ cvs -d cvs:/var/lib/cvs release wizzard
You have [0] altered files this repository.
Are you sure you want to release directory `wizzard': y
```

remove

cvs [*cvs-options*] remove [-flR] [*files* ...]

The remove command removes a file or directory from the repository. It can also be used to undo an uncommitted file addition.

Synonyms: rm, delete.

Standard subcommand options: -l, -R.

Option

-f Delete the files from the sandbox before removing them from the repository.

Example

```
$ cvs remove server.cc
cvs server: scheduling `server.cc' for removal
cvs server: use 'cvs commit' to remove this file permanently
```

rlog

`cvs [cvs-options] rlog [options] files ...`

The `rlog` command is a remote version of the `log` command. `rlog` works without a sandbox and requires a file, directory, or module name from the repository. See also **log**.

Synonym: `rl`.

Standard subcommand option: `-l`.

Options

`-b` Provide information only about the revisions or a file on the default branch, normally the highest branch on the trunk.

`-d` *dates*
: Provide information only on revisions of a file that were checked in on or between the dates or times provided. Date formats are listed in the earlier section "Dates." More than one date range can be given; ranges must be separated by semicolons. Date ranges are the same as for the `log` command; see **log**.

`-h` Print only the header information, not the description, log messages, or revision information.

`-N` Do not list the tags (the symbolic names).

`-r[`*revisions*`]`
: Provide information only on *revisions* in the ranges provided. More than one revision range can be given; ranges must be separated by commas. There must be no space between the `-r` and its argument. If no range is provided, the latest revision on the default branch, normally the trunk, is used. The possible values for *revisions* are the same as for `log`, see **log**.

`-R` Display the name of the repository copy of the file only.

`-s` *states*
: Display only revisions with states that match one of the *states* in the comma-separated list.

`-S` Do not display header information of a file if there are no revisions to display.

`-t` Print only the header information of a file and its description, not the log messages or revision information.

`-w[`*usernames*`]`
: Display only revisions committed by the *usernames* in the comma-separated list. If there are no usernames listed, the revisions committed by the current user are displayed. There can be no space between `-w` and its argument.

rtag

`cvs [cvs-options] rtag [options] tagname files ...`

Mark a revision of a single file with a meaningful name or mark a set of revisions of multiple files so that they can all be retrieved easily as a group. Tagnames must begin with a letter and may contain only alphanumeric characters, underscores (_), and hyphens (-). There are two tags reserved for CVS: the `BASE` and `HEAD` tags. See also **tag**.

The tag and rtag commands are also used to create branches.

The rtag command does not need to run from a sandbox, but it does need to have a revision or date specified. It also requires a filename, directory name, or module name given as a parameter.

Synonyms: rt, rfreeze.

Standard subcommand options: -D, -f, -l, -n, -r, -R.

Options

-a
: Clear a tag from files that have been removed from active development. Normally, removed files are not searched when tags are removed. This option works with the -d and -F options.

-b
: Create a branch off the designated *revision* (provided with -r), using the designated *tagname* as the branch name.

-B
: Allow -F and -d to act on branch tags. Back up the repository before you use this option, and be extremely careful. See Chapter 4 in *Essential CVS* before using this option.

-d
: Delete the specified tag.

-F
: Move the tag from the revision it currently refers to, to the revision specified in the rtag command.

Example

```
$ cvs -d cvs:/var/lib/cvs rtag -D now alpha_1-6 wizzard
cvs rtag: Tagging wizzard
cvs rtag: Tagging wizzard/doc
cvs rtag: Tagging wizzard/doc/design
cvs rtag: Tagging wizzard/doc/plan
...
```

---

server

cvs server

Runs the repository end of the CVS server using an internal version of the rsh program. The CVS client must also be able to use this internal version. This is used for the server access method. See also **kserver** and **pserver**.

Synonyms: none.

---

status

cvs [*cvs-options*] status [-vlR] [*files* ...]

Display information about files, such as the current working or base revision, the current revision in the repository, and whether the files are currently synchronized with the repository. With the -v option, status also shows the files' tags.

Synonyms: st, stat.

Standard subcommand options: -l, -R.

Option

-v
: Include information about tags.

Example

```
$ cvs status Makefile
=============================
File: Makefile                  Status: Locally Modified

Working revision:    1.6
Repository revision: 1.6     /var/lib/cvs/wizzard/
Makefile,v
Sticky Tag:          (none)
Sticky Date:         (none)
Sticky Options:      (none)
```

---

tag

`cvs [cvs-options] tag [options] tagname [files ...]`

Mark a revision of a single file with a meaningful name or mark a set of revisions of multiple files so that they can all be retrieved easily as a group. Tagnames must begin with a letter and may contain only alphanumeric characters, underscores (_), and hyphens (-). There are two tags reserved for CVS: the `BASE` and `HEAD` tags. See also **rtag**.

The `tag` and `rtag` commands are also used to create branches.

If no revision number or date is given to the `tag` command, this command tags based on the most recent revision in the repository that was synchronized with the current sandbox directory (i.e., the most recently updated, checked-out, or committed revision). This revision can be seen as the `working revision` in the `cvs status` command.

Synonyms: `ta`, `freeze`.

Standard subcommand options: `-D`, `-f`, `-l`, `-r`, `-R`.

Options

`-b`
Create a branch off the specified *revision*, using the specified *tagname* as the branch name.

`-c`
Check whether the sandbox copies of the specified *files* have been modified since they were last synchronized with the repository. If they have been modified, do not tag them and display an error. If they are unmodified, tag them with the specified *tagname*. This option is useful when tagging the current sandbox revisions.

`-d`
Delete the specified *tagname* from a file.

`-F`
Move the *tagname* from the revision it currently refers to, to the revision specified in the `tag` command.

Example

```
$ cvs tag alpha_1-5
cvs server: Tagging .
T Changelog
T INSTALL
T Makefile
T README
T TODO
...
```

unedit

```
cvs [cvs-options] unedit [-lR] [files ...]
```

Unmark a file as being edited by the current user. The cvs unedit command is used as part of the cvs watch family of commands. If a file is being watched, CVS writes it (when it is checked out) to the sandbox with read permissions but not write permissions. The unedit command notifies watchers that the file is no longer being edited, clears the temporary watch, sets the file as read-only, and restores the file to the repository revision that the sandbox copy was based on. See also **edit**, **editors**, **watch**, and **watchers**.

The script in the `notify` file in the repository's `CVSROOT` directory is used to notify the user of changes.

Synonyms: none.

Standard subcommand options: `-l`, `-R`.

update

```
cvs [cvs-options] update [options] [files ...]
```

Download changes from the repository to an existing sandbox. While doing this, `update` merges changes from the repository into changed files in the sandbox. See also **checkout** and **export**.

If `update` cannot merge repository changes with sandbox changes without losing data, it reports a conflict.

If `update` is not given any filenames or directory names as parameters, it acts on the current sandbox.

Synonyms: `up`, `upd`.

Standard subcommand options: `-D`, `-f`, `-k`, `-l`, `-r`, `-R`.

Options

`-A` Clear sticky tags, dates, and keyword-expansion modes and replace the current files in the sandbox with the head of the trunk.

`-C` Replace any file that has been changed locally with the revision from the repository that the local file was based on. The modified local file is saved as `.#`*`file.revision`* in the local sandbox directory.

`-d` Create any directories that are in the repository but not in the sandbox. By default, `update` works only on the directories that are currently in the sandbox and ignores any new directories.

`-I` *`file`*
: Ignore *file* when updating. `-I` can be used more than once. Use `-I !` to clear the list of ignored files.

`-j` *`revision`*`[:`*`date`*`]`
: Determine the changes between the revision the files in the sandbox are based on and the specified *revision* and merge the changes to the sandbox.

: If two `-j` options are used, determine the changes between the first `-j` *revision* and the second `-j` *revision* and merge those changes to the sandbox.

The *date* can be used only if the *revision* designates a branch. If *date* is used, it specifies the latest revision on (not before) that date.

-p
: Update the listed files, but write them to the standard output rather than to the filesystem. Do not change the sandbox.

-P
: Do not include empty directories in the sandbox.

-W *wrapper*
: Modify the update based on elements of each filename.

Example

```
$ cvs update
cvs server: Updating .
U wizzard/Changelog
U wizzard/INSTALL
U wizzard/Makefile
```

version

cvs [*cvs-options*] version

Display the version information for the current installation of CVS.

Synonyms: ve, ver.

Example

```
$ cvs version
Concurrent Versions System (CVS) 1.11.15 (client/server)
```

watch

cvs [*cvs-options*] watch *command* [*options*] [*files* ...]

Set files to be watched or add users to the file watch list. Users who are watching a file are notified via the script in the notify file in the repository's CVSROOT directory when other users perform specific actions. *Essential CVS* explains uses of the cvs watch family of commands. See also **edit**, **editors**, **unedit**, and **watchers**.

CVS does not notify you of your own changes.

Synonyms: none.

Standard subcommand options: -l, -R.

Commands

on *and* off
: The on and off subcommands control whether the file or files are marked as being watched. If a file is marked as being watched, CVS sets it as read-only when it is checked out of the repository. Without this read-only setting, developers might forget to use cvs edit when editing a file.

  If the argument is a directory, all current files in the directory and all new files added to that directory in the future are set as being watched.

CVS

The on and off subcommands set whether a file is watchable, but they do not set who is watching it; the add and remove subcommands set whether or not you are watching a file.

add *and* remove
Use the add and remove subcommands to set or remove files you want to watch. Use the -a option to specify which actions you want to be notified of.

Option

-a *action*
Notify the user when the designated actions occur to the file. Each -a designates one possible action. The -a option can be repeated to designate multiple actions. The -a option is usable only with the add and remove subcommands.

These are the possible actions:

commit
Notify the user when someone else commits changes to the file.

edit
Notify the user if someone else has run cvs edit on the file.

unedit
Notify the user when the file is no longer being edited by someone else. Notification occurs when cvs unedit or cvs release runs or when the file is deleted and re-created with cvs update or cvs checkout.

all
Notify the user in all of the previous cases.

none
Notify the user in none of the previous cases.

Examples

```
$ cvs watch on Makefile          Enable watching
$ cvs watch add Makefile         Add me to list of watchers
```

watchers

cvs [*cvs-options*] watchers [-lR] [*files* ...]

Displays the list of users who are watching the files listed as parameters. If no files are listed, this command lists the watchers for the files in the current directory and its subdirectories. See also **edit**, **editors**, **unedit**, and **watch**.

Standard subcommand options: -l, -R.

Example

```
$ cvs watchers Makefile
Makefile doppel edit unedit commit
arnold edit unedit commit
```

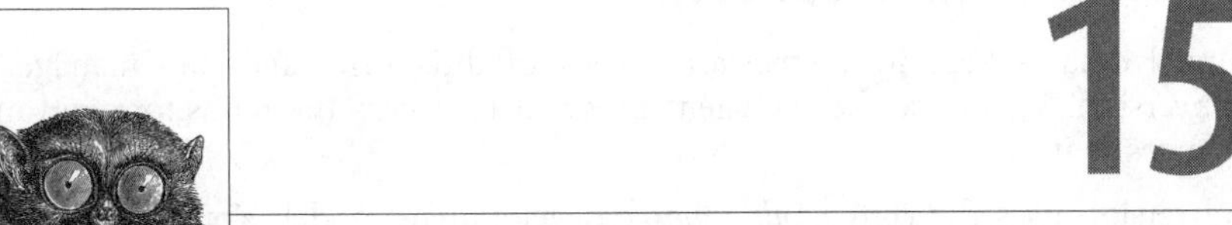

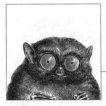

15 The Subversion Version Control System

The Subversion version control system is a powerful Open Source system for management of file and directory versions. Designed from the ground up to support distributed development, it offers many leading-edge features.

This chapter covers the following topics:

- Conceptual overview
- Obtaining Subversion
- Using Subversion: a quick tour
- The Subversion command line client: `svn`
- Repository administration: `svnadmin`
- Examining the repository: `svnlook`
- Providing remote access: `svnserve`
- Other Subversion components

Most of the material in this chapter is adapted from *Version Control with Subversion*, which is cited in the Bibliography. See that book for much more information on Subversion.

Conceptual Overview

Subversion is a version control system. It lets you track changes to an entire project directory tree. Every change made to the tree is recorded and can be retrieved.

Subversion is intended to be "a better CVS;" this is discussed in detail shortly. Subversion is purposely an Open Source project. If you want to participate, you can!

Basic Version Control Operations

Actual data is kept in a *repository*, a set of directories and files managed by Subversion. Users use the svn client program to access the repository and make changes to it.

Subversion uses the *copy-modify-merge* development model. You make a private copy of a given project in a *sandbox*. (This is often called *checking out* a copy.) Like CVS and unlike RCS, this private copy is not locked in the repository. You then make all the changes you like to the copy within the sandbox, without having to worry about what other developers are doing. As you work, you can compare your changes to the version you started with, as well as to the version currently in the repository. Once you're satisfied with the changes, you *commit* them, sometimes referred to as a *check-in*. (These terms come from RCS and CVS.)

In the event that another developer has modified part of a file that you were working on and checked it in, when you commit your changes Subversion notices, and indicates that a *conflict* exists. Conflicts are marked as such in the file, and Subversion creates pristine copies of the file as it exists in the repository and of the file as you modified it, so that you can do full comparisons. Once you have resolved the conflict, you tell Subversion about it, and then commit the final version.

Like CVS, Subversion lets you create a development *branch*, a separate stream of development versions. You can periodically merge changes from the main development stream (the *trunk*) into your branch, and also merge changes from your branch back into the trunk.

Finally, you can *tag* a particular copy of the project. For instance, when a project is ready for a release, you can create a snapshot of the project, and give it a descriptive tag that allows you to re-create the project tree exactly as it was for the release. This is particularly valuable for when you need to produce a bug fix for an older version of the project, or attempt to retrofit a fix or feature from current development into an older version.

Building a Better CVS

When discussing Subversion's features, it is often helpful to speak of them in terms of how they improve upon CVS's design. Subversion provides:

Directory versioning
: CVS only tracks the history of individual files, but Subversion implements a "virtual" versioned filesystem that tracks changes to whole directory trees over time. Files *and* directories are versioned.

True version history
: Since CVS is limited to file versioning, operations such as copies and renames—which might happen to files, but which are really changes to the contents of some containing directory—aren't supported in CVS. In CVS, you cannot delete a versioned file and then create a new file of the same name with different contents without inheriting the history of the old—perhaps completely unrelated—file. With Subversion, you can add, delete, copy, and

rename both files and directories. Every newly added file begins with a fresh, clean history all its own, even if the filename was previously used.

Atomic commits
: A collection of modifications either goes into the repository completely, or not at all. This allows developers to construct and commit changes as logical chunks, and prevents problems that can occur when only a portion of a set of changes is successfully sent to the repository.

Versioned metadata
: Each file and directory has a set of properties—keys and their values—associated with it. You can create and store any arbitrary key/value pairs. Properties are versioned over time, just like file contents.

Choice of network layers
: Subversion has an abstracted notion of repository access, making it easy to implement new network mechanisms. Subversion can plug into the Apache HTTP Server as an extension module. This gives Subversion a big advantage in stability and interoperability, and instant access to existing features provided by that server—authentication, authorization, wire compression, and so on. A more lightweight, standalone Subversion server process is also available. This server speaks a custom protocol that can be easily tunneled over SSH.

Consistent data handling
: Subversion expresses file differences using a binary differencing algorithm, which works identically on both text (human-readable) and binary (human-unreadable) files. Both types of files are stored equally compressed in the repository, and only the differences are transmitted in both directions across the network.

Efficient branching and tagging
: The cost of branching and tagging need not be proportional to the project size. Subversion creates branches and tags by simply copying the project, using a mechanism similar to a hard link. Thus these operations take only a very small, constant amount of time.

Hackability
: Subversion has no historical baggage; it is implemented as a collection of shared C libraries with well-defined APIs. This makes Subversion extremely maintainable and usable by other applications and languages.

Optimized around the network
: Disk storage continues to increase in size and speed and decrease in cost: disk space is cheap on today's systems. However, network connectivity has not kept pace; access to remote repositories is several orders of magnitude slower than local access. Thus the Subversion design is optimized to avoid connecting to the repository when possible. For example, in the working copy's administrative directory, `.svn`, Subversion maintains a pristine copy of each file as it was checked out of the repository. This makes it possible to produce the differences very quickly, with no need to contact the repository.

In addition, Subversion uses commands similar to those of CVS, making it straightforward to transfer your CVS habits to Subversion.

Converting a Repository from CVS to Subversion

A very effective way to learn Subversion if you already know CVS is to move your project from CVS to Subversion. The quickest way to accomplish this is to do a flat import into a Subversion repository from an exported CVS repository. However, this only gives you a "snapshot" of your repository; the revision history (changes, logs, tags, branches, etc.) are not kept.

Copying a repository while maintaining history is a difficult problem to solve. Nevertheless, a few tools exist that at least partially convert existing CVS repositories into new Subversion ones, such as `cvs2svn`, a Python script originally created by members of Subversion's own development community (see *http://cvs2svn.tigris.org/*), and Lev Serebryakov's RefineCVS (see *http://lev.serebryakov.spb.ru/refinecvs/*).

For an updated collection of links to known converter tools, visit the Links page of the Subversion web site, *http://subversion.tigris.org/project_links.html*.

Special File Properties

Subversion allows you to associate *properties* with files or directories. A property is just a keyword/value pair associated with the file. Subversion reserves property names starting with `svn:` for its own use. The special properties in Subversion 1.0 are:

`svn:author`
: The username of the person who committed a particular revision.

`svn:date`
: The date when the transaction for a revision was created.

`svn:eol-style`
: Different operating systems use different conventions to mark the end of lines in text files. Unix and its workalikes use a single ASCII line-feed character (LF) to end lines. MS Windows systems use a Carriage Return + Line Feed combination (CRLF), and older Macintosh systems use a single Carriage Return (CR). This can cause problems when a Windows user stores a new revision of the file: suddenly a Unix user who does a checkout sees a file with extraneous Carriage Return characters at the end of every line. The `svn:eol-style` attribute solves this problem. It should be set to one of the following values:

`CR`	Clients should always use CR line terminators, no matter what the native format is.
`CRLF`	Clients should always use CR-LF line terminators, no matter what the native format is.
`LF`	Clients should always use LF line terminators, no matter what the native format is.
`native`	Clients should use the native format when checking out files.

Subversion always stores files in normalized, LF-only format in the repository.

`svn:executable`
: Valid only for files, the mere presence of this property indicates that the file should be made executable when it's checked out or updated from the repository. It has no effect on filesystems, such as FAT-32 or NTFS, that don't have the concept of an execute bit.

`svn:externals`
: This property, when set on a directory under version control, allows you to specify other external repositories to use for particular local subdirectories. You set this property with `svn propset` or `svn propedit` (see the "svn Subcommands" section later in the chapter). The value is a multiline table of directories and fully-qualified Subversion URLs. For example:

```
$ svn propget svn:externals calc
third-party/sounds             http://sounds.red-bean.com/repos
third-party/skins              http://skins.red-bean.com/repositories/skinproj
third-party/skins/toolkit -r21 http://svn.red-bean.com/repos/skin-maker
```

Once set, anyone else who checks out a working copy will also get the third-party files checked out automatically.

`svn:ignore`
: A property containing a list of file patterns that certain Subversion operations will ignore. It should be set on directories, as needed. It works to filter unversioned files and directories out of commands like `svn status`, `svn add`, and `svn import`. It is similar to the `.cvsignore` file in CVS, and you can often import your `.cvsignore` with this command:

```
$ svn propset svn:ignore -F .cvsignore .
property 'svn:ignore' set on '.'
```

`svn:keywords`
: A list of keywords for which Subversion should perform *keyword expansion* when checking out the file. This is purposely similar to the same feature in RCS and CVS. However, Subversion only does keyword expansion when this property is set, and only for the keywords listed in the property's value. The list of recognized keywords is provided shortly.

`svn:log`
: The log message associated with the commit of a particular revision.

`svn:mime-type`
: An indication of the type of data stored in the file. In general, if it does not begin with `text/`, Subversion assumes that the file contains binary data. For updates, this causes Subversion to rename a modified working copy of the file with a `.orig` extension and replace the file with the current version from the repository. This prevents an attempt to perform a "merge" on data that can't be merged. This property also influences how the Subversion Apache module sets the HTTP `Content-type:` header.

`svn:realmstring`
: A specialized property that describes the "authentication realm" for a file in Subversion's cached copy of the authentication credentials. See Chapter 6 of *Version Control with Subversion* for more information.

Subversion defines the list of keywords available for substitution. That list contains the following five keywords, some of which have shorter aliases that you can also use:

`$LastChangedDate$`
: This keyword describes the last time the file was changed in the repository, and looks like `$LastChangedDate: 2002-07-22 21:42:37 -0700 (Mon, 22 Jul 2002) $`. It may be abbreviated as `Date`.

`$LastChangedRevision$`
: This keyword describes the last revision in which this file changed in the repository, and looks like `$LastChangedRevision: 144 $`. It may be abbreviated as `Revision` or `Rev`.

`$LastChangedBy$`
: This keyword describes the last user to change this file in the repository, and looks like `$LastChangedBy: joe $`. It may be abbreviated as `Author`.

`$HeadURL$`
: This keyword describes the full URL to the latest version of the file in the repository. It looks like `$HeadURL: http://svn.collab.net/repos/trunk/README $`. It may be abbreviated as `URL`.

`$Id$`
: This keyword is a compressed combination of the other keywords. Its substitution looks like `$Id: calc.c 148 2002-07-28 21:30:34Z sue $`, and is interpreted to mean that the file `calc.c` was last changed in revision 148 on the evening of July 28, 2002 by the user `sue`.

Obtaining Subversion

The Subversion project web site is *http://subversion.tigris.org/*. It contains links to project documentation, Frequently Asked Questions (FAQs), and project source code.

Some GNU/Linux systems come with Subversion available on the installation CDs. Thus, you may be able to install a pre-built binary for your system, or use a package manager to download and install it.

Subversion Releases

Subversion uses the "even/odd" release model. Even numbered point releases (1.0, 1.2, etc.) are considered to be *stable* releases. Such releases undergo change only to fix problems. New features are not added, and users can expect to use the software without problems. Odd numbered point releases (1.1, 1.3, etc.), on the other hand, are *development* versions. New features are added in such versions, they tend to undergo rapid change and evolution, and such releases may have bugs or problems that could cause loss of data. You should use an even-numbered release if stability and data preservation are important to you. Use an odd-numbered release only if it has a critical, must-have feature *and* if you are willing to live with the risks involved.

A View Down the Road

The one constant in the Open Source world is *change*. At the time of writing, Subversion 1.0 is the current released stable version. The first development release of Subversion 1.1 is also available. Along with a host of fixes and several new command-line options, the next version has the following interesting features:

Symbolic links may be versioned
: Unix-style symbolic links are stored in the repository as a regular file with a special attribute. The `svn` client knows how to store and extract symbolic links correctly on Unix-style systems.

Nondatabase repository back-end
: Repositories can be set up to store data in regular files, instead of requiring the use of Berkeley DB.

Better localization support
: The framework for localization of the Subversion code has been improved, with at least eight translations already available.

The Subversion web site's Roadmap page (*http://subversion.tigris.org/roadmap.html*) lists the following future development goals (you should recheck the web site; things will undoubtedly have changed):

Subversion 1.2 goals

- Optional locking (reserved checkouts)

Medium-term goals

- True rename support (not based on copy/delete)
- Merge tracking (describes a whole class of problems)
- Repository-level Access Control Lists (ACLs)*

Long-term goals

- SQL repository back-end
- Rewrite of working-copy library
- Broader WebDAV/deltaV compatibility†
- Pluggable client-side `diff` programs
- Progressive multilingual support

Source Code

The latest Subversion source is kept in a Subversion archive available from the main Subversion site. This leads to a so-called *bootstrapping* problem; you can't

* ACLs provide finer-grained access controls than the regular Unix user/group/other permissions mechanism. Many Unix systems support some form of ACLs, but in incompatible ways.

† WebDAV is short for "Web-based Distributed Authoring and Versioning," an extension to HTTP that makes read/write file resources available over the Web. Despite the "V" in the name, the original specification (RFC 2518) does not provide a model for version control; this is provided by DeltaV, described in RFC 3253. See *http://www.webdav.org* for more information.

Subversion

get Subversion unless you already have it. Fortunately, the developers make Subversion releases available as standalone tar archives that you can use to build your initial Subversion client. You can get these from the main web site, *http://subversion.tigris.org*. Once there, select the "Downloads" link. You may choose to download a binary distribution (Red Hat RPM file, Debian package, etc.), if one is available. This is the easiest road to take. Or you may choose to download source code and build your own. Building Subversion follows the general steps outlined in the section "Building Software," in Chapter 1.

Using Subversion: A Quick Tour

This section provides a very quick tour of using Subversion for version control. We start with the initial version of a project for importing into Subversion:

```
$ find /tmp/hello -print                    Show directory layout
/tmp/hello
/tmp/hello/branches                         Directory for branch development
/tmp/hello/tags                             Directory for tagged releases
/tmp/hello/trunk
/tmp/hello/trunk/hello.c                    Mainline development is done on the trunk
/tmp/hello/trunk/Makefile
/tmp/hello/trunk/README
```

The next steps are to create the repository and then to import the project into it:

```
$ svnadmin create /path/to/svnrepos
$ svn import /tmp/hello file:///path/to/svnrepos -m "initial import"
Adding         /tmp/hello/trunk
Adding         /tmp/hello/trunk/hello.c
Adding         /tmp/hello/trunk/Makefile
Adding         /tmp/hello/trunk/README
Adding         /tmp/hello/branches
Adding         /tmp/hello/tags

Committed revision 1.
```

Now that the project exists in Subversion, we check out a working copy into a sandbox underneath our home directory and start making changes:

```
$ cd                                        Move to home directory
$ svn checkout file:///path/to/svnrepos hello   Check out working copy
A  hello/trunk
A  hello/trunk/hello.c
A  hello/trunk/README
A  hello/trunk/Makefile
A  hello/branches
A  hello/tags
Checked out revision 1.

$ cd hello/trunk                            Change to sandbox
$ vi message.c hello.c Makefile             Make changes
3 files to edit
```

```
$ cat message.c                                  Show newly created file
const char message[ ] = "hello, world!";
$ make                                           Compile program and test it
cc    -c -o hello.o hello.c
cc    -c -o message.o message.c
cc -O hello.o message.o -o hello
$ hello
hello, world!
```

One of the most common operations is to compare the changed copy with the original. The result is in "unified diff" format, the equivalent of the regular `diff -u` command:

```
$ svn diff hello.c
Index: hello.c
===================================================================
--- hello.c     (revision 1)
+++ hello.c     (working copy)
@@ -1,7 +1,9 @@
 #include <stdio.h>

+extern const char message[ ];
+
 int main(void)
 {
-       printf("hello, world!\n");
+       printf("%s\n", message);
        return 0;
 }
```

Now that we're comfortable with the changes, we schedule the new file, `message.c`, for addition to the repository, and then we actually commit our changes:

```
$ svn add message.c                              Schedule message.c for addition
A        message.c
$ svn commit                                     Commit all the changes
Sending        trunk/Makefile
Sending        trunk/hello.c
Adding         trunk/message.c
Transmitting file data ...
Committed revision 2.
```

Finally, we can view *all* of our changes relative to the initial revision:

```
$ svn diff -r 1
Index: hello.c
===================================================================
--- hello.c     (revision 1)
+++ hello.c     (working copy)
@@ -1,7 +1,9 @@
 #include <stdio.h>

+extern const char message[ ];
+
 int main(void)
 {
```

```
-       printf("hello, world!\n");
+       printf("%s\n", message);
        return 0;
 }
Index: Makefile
===================================================================
--- Makefile    (revision 1)
+++ Makefile    (working copy)
@@ -1,2 +1,2 @@
-hello: hello.c
-       $(CC) -O $< -o $@
+hello: hello.o message.o
+       $(CC) -O hello.o message.o -o $@
Index: message.c
===================================================================
--- message.c   (revision 0)
+++ message.c   (revision 2)
@@ -0,0 +1 @@
+const char message[ ] = "hello, world!";
```

The Subversion Command Line Client: svn

The syntax for the Subversion command line client, `svn`, is:

`svn` [*options*] *subcommand* [*arguments*]

The *options* and *subcommand* may be provided in any order.

svn Options

While Subversion has different options for its subcommands, all options are global—that is, each option is guaranteed to mean the same thing regardless of the subcommand that you use it with. For example, `--verbose` (`-v`) always means "verbose output," no matter which subcommand you use it with.

`--auto-props`
: Enable auto-props, overriding the `enable-auto-props` directive in the `config` file.

`--config-dir` *dir*
: Read configuration information from the specified directory instead of the default location (`.subversion` in the user's home directory).

`--diff-cmd` *cmd*
: Use *cmd* as the external program to show differences between files. Normally, `svn diff` uses Subversion's internal `diff` engine, which provides unified diffs by default. To use an external `diff` program, use `--diff-cmd`. You can pass options to the `diff` program with the `--extensions` option (discussed later in this list).

`--diff3-cmd` *cmd*
: Use *cmd* as the external program to merge files.

`--dry-run`
: Pretend to run a command, but make no actual changes—either in the sandbox or in the repository.

`--editor-cmd` *cmd*
: Use *cmd* as the program for editing a log message or a property value. If not set, Subversion checks the environment variables SVN_EDITOR, VISUAL, and EDITOR, in that order, for the name of the editor to use.

`--encoding` *enc*
: Use *enc* as the encoding for the commit message. The default encoding is your operating system's native locale, and you should specify the encoding if your commit message is in any other encoding.

`--extensions` *args*, `-x` *args*
: Pass *args* to an external `diff` command when providing differences between files. To pass multiple arguments, enclose all of them in quotes (for example, `svn diff --diff-cmd /usr/bin/diff -x "-b -E"`). This option can be used *only* if you also pass the `--diff-cmd` option.

`--file` *filename*, `-F` *filename*
: Use the contents of *filename* for the specified subcommand.

`--force`
: Force a particular command or operation to run. There are some operations that Subversion prevents you from doing in normal usage, but you can pass this option to tell Subversion "I know what I'm doing as well as the possible repercussions of doing it, do it anyway." Use with caution.

`--force-log`
: Force a suspicious parameter passed to the `--message` (`-m`) or `--file` (`-F`) options to be accepted as valid. By default, Subversion produces an error if parameters to these options look like they might instead be targets of the subcommand. For example, if you pass a versioned file's path to the `--file` (`-F`) option, Subversion assumes that you've made a mistake, that the path was instead intended as the target of the operation, and that you simply failed to provide some other—unversioned—file as the source of your log message. To assert your intent and override these types of errors, pass the `--force-log` option to commands that accept log messages.

`--help`, `-h`, `-?`
: If used with one or more subcommands, show the built-in help text for each subcommand. If used alone, display the general client help text.

`--ignore-ancestry`
: Ignore ancestry when calculating differences (i.e., rely on path contents alone).

`--incremental`
: Print output in a format suitable for concatenation.

`--message` *message*, `-m` *message*
: Use *message* as the commit message. For example:

```
$ svn commit -m "They don't make Sunday."
```

Subversion

`--new` *arg*
: Use *arg* as the newer target when producing a diff.

`--no-auth-cache`
: Do not cache authentication information (e.g., username and password) in the Subversion administrative directories.

`--no-auto-props`
: Disable auto-props, overriding the `enable-auto-props` directive in the `config` file.

`--no-diff-deleted`
: Do not print differences for deleted files. The default behavior when you remove a file is for `svn diff` to print the same differences that you would see if you had left the file but removed all the content.

`--no-ignore`
: Show files in the status listing that would normally be omitted since they match a pattern in the `svn:ignore` property.

`--non-interactive`
: In the case of an authentication failure, or insufficient credentials, do not prompt for credentials (e.g., username or password). This is useful if you're running Subversion inside of an automated script where it's better to have Subversion fail instead of trying to prompt for more information.

`--non-recursive, -N`
: Stop a subcommand from recursing into subdirectories. Most subcommands recurse by default, but some subcommands—usually those that have the potential to remove or undo your local modifications—do not.

`--notice-ancestry`
: Pay attention to ancestry when calculating differences.

`--old` *arg*
: Use *arg* as the older target when producing a diff.

`--password` *pass*
: Use *pass* as the password for authentication on the command line—otherwise, if it is needed, Subversion prompts you for it.

`--quiet, -q`
: Print only essential information while performing an operation.

`--recursive, -R`
: Make a subcommand recurse into subdirectories. Most subcommands recurse by default.

`--relocate` *from to* [*path* ...]
: Used with the `svn switch` subcommand to change the location of the repository that your working copy references. This is useful if the location of your repository changes and you have an existing working copy that you'd like to continue to use. See **svn switch** for an example.

`--revision` *rev*, `-r` *rev*
Use *rev* as the revision (or range of revisions) for a particular operation. You can provide revision numbers, revision keywords, or dates (in curly braces), as arguments to the revision option. To provide a range of revisions, provide two revisions separated by a colon. For example:

```
$ svn log -r 1729
$ svn log -r 1729:HEAD
$ svn log -r 1729:1744
$ svn log -r {2001-12-04}:{2002-02-17}
$ svn log -r 1729:{2002-02-17}
```

The list of revision keywords is provided later in this section.

`--revprop`
Operate on a revision property instead of a Subversion property specific to a file or directory. This option requires that you also pass a revision with the `--revision` (`-r`) option.

`--show-updates, -u`
Display information about which files in your working copy are out-of-date. This doesn't actually update any of your files, it just shows you which files will be updated if you run `svn update`.

`--stop-on-copy`
Cause a Subversion subcommand that is traversing the history of a versioned resource to stop harvesting that historical information when it encounters a copy—that is, a location in history where that resource was copied from another location in the repository.

`--strict`
Use strict semantics, a notion that is rather vague unless talking about specific subcommands. See *Version Control with Subversion* for more information.

`--targets` *filename*
Retrieve the list of files to operate on from *filename* instead of listing all the files on the command line.

`--username` *name*
Use *name* as the username for authentication—otherwise, if it is needed, Subversion prompts you for it.

`--verbose, -v`
Print out as much information as possible while running any subcommand. This may result in Subversion printing out additional fields, detailed information about every file, or additional information regarding its actions.

`--version`
Print the client version info. This information not only includes the version number of the client, but also a listing of all repository access modules that the client can use to access a Subversion repository.

`--xml`
Print output in XML format.

The acceptable revision keywords for `--revision` are:

`BASE`
: The original unmodified version of the working copy. This keyword cannot refer to a URL.

`COMMITTED`
: The last revision, before or at `BASE`, at which an item actually changed. This keyword cannot refer to a URL.

`HEAD`
: The most recent revision in the repository.

`PREV`
: The revision just before that at which an item changed. Equivalent to `COMMITED` – 1. This keyword cannot refer to a URL.

Revision Date
: A date specification enclosed in curly braces, { and }, such as `{2002-02-17}`, `{15:30}`, `{"2002-02-17 15:30"}`, `{2002-02-17T15:30}`, or `{20020217T1530-0500}`. Full details are provided in *Version Control with Subversion*.

svn Subcommands

The `svn` command is the main user interface to Subversion. It works by accepting subcommands with arguments. The general form is:

svn *subcommand* [*options*] *arguments*

---

add

svn add *path* ...

Add files and directories to your working copy and schedule them for addition to the repository. They will be uploaded and added to the repository on your next commit. If you add something and change your mind before committing, you can unschedule the addition using `svn revert`.

Alternate Names:	None
Changes:	Working Copy
Accesses Repository:	No

Options

`--auto-props`	`--non-recursive (-N)`
`--config-dir` *dir*	`--quiet (-q)`
`--no-auto-props`	`--targets` *filename*

Examples

To add a file to your working copy:

```
$ svn add foo.c
A         foo.c
```

You can add a directory without adding its contents:

```
$ svn add --non-recursive otherdir
A         otherdir
```

blame

```
svn blame target ...
```

Show author and revision information in-line for the specified files or URLs. Each line of text is annotated at the beginning with the author (username) and the revision number for the last change to that line.

Alternate Names:	praise, annotate, ann
Changes:	Nothing
Accesses Repository:	Yes

Options

--config-dir *dir*	--password *pass*
--no-auth-cache	--revision *rev*, -r *rev*
--non-interactive	--username *user*

cat

```
svn cat target ...
```

Output the contents of the specified files or URLs. For listing the contents of directories, see **svn list**.

Alternate Names:	None
Changes:	Nothing
Accesses Repository:	Yes

Options

--config-dir *dir*	--password *pass*
--no-auth-cache	--revision *rev*, -r *rev*
--non-interactive	--username *user*

Examples

To view `readme.txt` in your repository without checking it out:

```
$ svn cat http://svn.red-bean.com/repos/test/readme.txt
This is a README file.
You should read this.
```

If your working copy is out of date (or if you have local modifications) and you want to see the `HEAD` revision of a file in your working copy, `svn cat` automatically fetches the `HEAD` revision when you give it a path:

```
$ cat foo.c
This file is in my local working copy
and has changes that I've made.

$ svn cat foo.c
Latest revision fresh from the repository!
```

Subversion

checkout

`svn checkout URL ... [path]`

Check out a working copy from a repository. If *path* is omitted, the basename of the URL is used as the destination. If multiple URLs are given, each one is checked out into a subdirectory of *path*, with the name of the subdirectory being the basename of the URL.

Alternate Names:	`co`
Changes:	Creates a working copy
Accesses Repository:	Yes

Options

`--config-dir` *dir*	`--password` *pass*
`--no-auth-cache`	`--quiet (-q)`
`--non-interactive`	`--revision` *rev*, `-r` *rev*
`--non-recursive (-N)`	`--username` *user*

Examples

Check out a working copy into a directory called `mine`:

```
$ svn checkout file:///tmp/repos/test mine
A  mine/a
A  mine/b
Checked out revision 2.
$ ls
mine
```

If you interrupt a checkout (or something else interrupts your checkout like loss of connectivity, etc.), you can restart it either by issuing the identical checkout command again, or by updating the incomplete working copy:

```
$ svn checkout file:///tmp/repos/test test
A  test/a
A  test/b
^C
svn: The operation was interrupted
svn: caught SIGINT

$ svn checkout file:///tmp/repos/test test
A  test/c
A  test/d
^C
svn: The operation was interrupted
svn: caught SIGINT

$ cd test
$ svn update
A  test/e
A  test/f
Updated to revision 3.
```

cleanup

```
svn cleanup [path ...]
```

Recursively clean up the working copy, removing locks and resuming unfinished operations. If you ever get a "working copy locked" error, run this command to remove stale locks and get your working copy into a usable state again.

If, for some reason, an svn `update` fails due to a problem running an external `diff` program (e.g., user input or network failure), pass the `--diff3-cmd` option to allow cleanup to complete any merging with your external `diff` program. You can also specify any configuration directory with the `--config-dir` option, but you should rarely need these options.

Alternate Names:	None
Changes:	Working copy
Accesses Repository:	No

Options:

`--config-dir` *dir*
`--diff3-cmd` *cmd*

commit

```
svn commit [path ...]
```

Send changes from your working copy to the repository. If you don't supply a log message with your commit by using either the `--file` or `--message` option, svn starts your editor for you to compose a commit message.

If you begin a commit and Subversion starts your editor to compose the commit message, you can still abort without committing your changes. To cancel your commit, just quit your editor without saving your commit message. Subversion prompts you to either abort the commit, continue with no message, or edit the message again.

Alternate Names:	`ci` (short for "check in," not co, which is short for "check out")
Changes:	Working copy, repository
Accesses Repository:	Yes

Options

`--config-dir` *dir*	`--non-interactive`
`--encoding` *enc*	`--non-recursive` (`-N`)
`--file` *file*, `-F` *file*	`--password` *pass*
`--force-log`	`--quiet` (`-q`)
`--message` *text*, `-m` *text*	`--targets` *filename*
`--no-auth-cache`	`--username` *user*

Examples

Commit a simple modification to a file with the commit message on the command line and an implicit target of your current directory ("."):

```
$ svn commit -m "added howto section."
Sending        a
Transmitting file data .
Committed revision 3.
```

To commit a file scheduled for deletion:

```
$ svn commit -m "removed file 'c'."
Deleting       c
Committed revision 7.
```

copy

`svn copy src dst`

Copy a file in a working copy or in the repository. *src* and *dst* can each be either a working copy (WC) path or a URL:

WC → WC
: Copy and schedule an item for addition (with history).

WC → URL
: Immediately commit a copy of WC to URL.

URL → WC
: Check out URL into WC, and schedule it for addition.

URL → URL
: Complete server-side copy. This is usually used to branch and tag.

You can only copy files within a single repository. Subversion does not support cross-repository copying.

Alternate Names:	cp
Changes:	Repository if destination is a URL Working copy if destination is a WC path
Accesses Repository:	If source or destination is in the repository, or if needed to look up the source revision number

Options

```
--config-dir dir              --no-auth-cache
--editor-cmd editor           --non-interactive
--encoding enc                --password pass
--file file, -F file          --quiet (-q)
--force-log                   --revision rev, -r rev
--message text, -m text       --username user
```

Examples

Copy an item within your working copy (just schedule the copy—nothing goes into the repository until you commit):

```
$ svn copy foo.txt bar.txt
A         bar.txt
$ svn status
A  +   bar.txt
```

Copy an item from the repository to your working copy (just schedule the copy—nothing goes into the repository until you commit):

```
$ svn copy file:///tmp/repos/test/far-away near-here
A         near-here
```

This is the recommended way to resurrect a dead file in your repository!

And finally, copying between two URLs:

```
$ svn copy file:///tmp/repos/test/far-away \
>          file:///tmp/repos/test/over-there -m "remote copy."
Committed revision 9.
```

This is the easiest way to "tag" a revision in your repository—just svn copy that revision (usually HEAD) into your tags directory.

```
$ svn copy file:///tmp/repos/test/trunk \
>          file:///tmp/repos/test/tags/0.6.32-prerelease \
>          -m "tag tree"
Committed revision 12.
```

delete

```
svn delete path ...
svn delete URL ...
```

Items specified by *path* are scheduled for deletion upon the next commit. Files (and directories that have not been committed) are *immediately* removed from the working copy. The command will not remove any unversioned or modified items; use the `--force` option to override this behavior.

Items specified by URL are deleted from the repository via an immediate commit. Multiple URLs are committed atomically.

Alternate Names:	`del`, `remove`, `rm`
Changes:	Working copy if operating on files Repository if operating on URLs
Accesses Repository:	Only if operating on URLs

Options

--config-dir *dir*	--no-auth-cache
--editor-cmd *editor*	--non-interactive
--encoding *enc*	--password *pass*
--file *file*, -F *file*	--quiet (-q)
--force-log	--targets *filename*
--force	--username *user*
--message *text*, -m *text*	

diff

```
svn diff [-r N[:M]] [--old old-tgt][--new new-tgt] [path ...]
svn diff -r N:M URL
svn diff [-r N[:M]] URL1[@N] URL2[@M]
```

Display the differences between two paths. The three different ways you can use svn diff are:

svn diff [-r *N*[:*M*]] [--old *old-tgt*] [--new *new-tgt*] [*path* ...]
: Display the differences between *old-tgt* and *new-tgt*. If *paths* are given, they are treated as relative to *old-tgt* and *new-tgt* and the output is restricted to differences in only those paths. *old-tgt* and *new-tgt* may be working copy paths or *URL*[@*rev*]. *old-tgt* defaults to the current working directory and *new-tgt* defaults to *old-tgt*. *N* defaults to BASE or, if *old-tgt* is a URL, to HEAD. *M* defaults to the current working version or, if *new-tgt* is a URL, to HEAD. svn diff -r *N* sets the revision of *old-tgt* to *N*, whereas svn diff -r *N*:*M* also sets the revision of *new-tgt* to *M*.

svn diff -r *N*:*M* *URL*
: A shorthand for svn diff -r *N*:*M* --old=*URL* --new=*URL*.

svn diff [-r *N*[:*M*]] *URL1*[@*N*] *URL2*[@*M*]
: A shorthand for svn diff [-r *N*[:*M*]] --old=*URL1* --new=*URL2*.

If *target* is a URL, then revisions *N* and *M* can be given either via the --revision option or by using "@" notation as described earlier.

If *target* is a working copy path, then the --revision option means:

--revision *N*:*M*
: The server compares *target*@*N* and *target*@*M*.

--revision *N*
: The client compares *target*@*N* against the working copy.

No --revision *option*
: The client compares the base and working copies of *target*.

If the alternate syntax is used, the server compares *URL1* and *URL2* at revisions *N* and *M* respectively. If either *N* or *M* are omitted, a value of HEAD is assumed.

By default, svn diff ignores the ancestry of files and merely compares the contents of the two files being compared. If you use --notice-ancestry, the ancestry of the paths in question is taken into consideration when comparing revisions (that is, if you run svn diff on two files with identical contents but different ancestry you will see the entire contents of the file as having been removed and added again).

Alternate Names:	di
Changes:	Nothing
Accesses Repository:	For obtaining differences against anything but the BASE revision in your working copy

Options

--config-dir *dir*	--non-recursive (-N)
--diff-cmd *cmd*	--notice-ancestry
--extensions *args*, -x *args*	--old *old-target*
--new *new-target*	--password *pass*
--no-auth-cache	--revision *rev*, -r *rev*
--no-diff-deleted	--username *user*
--non-interactive	

Examples

Compare BASE and your working copy:

```
$ svn diff COMMITTERS
Index: COMMITTERS
===========================================================
--- COMMITTERS  (revision 4404)
+++ COMMITTERS  (working copy)
...
```

See how your working copy's modifications compare against an older revision:

```
$ svn diff -r 3900 COMMITTERS
Index: COMMITTERS
===========================================================
--- COMMITTERS  (revision 3900)
+++ COMMITTERS  (working copy)
...
```

Use --diff-cmd *cmd* and -x to pass arguments directly to the external diff program:

```
$ svn diff --diff-cmd /usr/bin/diff -x "-i -b" COMMITTERS
Index: COMMITTERS
===========================================================
0a1,2
> This is a test
>
```

export

```
svn export [-r rev] URL [path]
svn export path1 path2
```

The first form exports a clean directory tree from the repository specified by *URL* (at revision *rev* if it is given, otherwise at HEAD)

Subversion

into *path*. If *path* is omitted, the last component of the *URL* is used for the local directory name.

The second form exports a clean directory tree from the working copy specified by *path1* into *path2*. All local changes are preserved, but files not under version control are not copied.

Alternate Names:	None
Changes:	Local disk
Accesses Repository:	Only if exporting from a URL

Options

`--config-dir` *dir*	`--password` *pass*
`--force`	`--quiet (-q)`
`--no-auth-cache`	`--revision` *rev*, `-r` *rev*
`--non-interactive`	`--username` *user*

help

`svn help [subcommand ...]`

Provide a quick usage summary. With *subcommand*, provide information about the given subcommand.

Alternate Names:	`?`, `h`
Changes:	Nothing
Accesses Repository:	No

Options

`--quiet (-q)`
`--version`

import

`svn import [path] URL`

Recursively commit a copy of *path* to *URL*. If *path* is omitted "." is assumed. Parent directories are created in the repository as necessary.

Alternate Names:	None
Changes:	Repository
Accesses Repository:	Yes

Options

`--auto-props`	`--no-auth-cache`
`--config-dir` *dir*	`--no-auto-props`
`--editor-cmd` *editor*	`--non-interactive`
`--encoding` *enc*	`--non-recursive (-N)`
`--file` *file*, `-F` *file*	`--password` *pass*
`--force-log`	`--quiet (-q)`
`--message` *text*, `-m` *text*	`--username` *user*

Examples

Import the local directory myproj into the root of your repository:

```
$ svn import -m "New import" myproj \
> http://svn.red-bean.com/repos/test
Adding         myproj/sample.txt
...
Transmitting file data .........
Committed revision 16.
```

Import the local directory myproj into trunk/vendors in your repository. The directory trunk/vendors need not exist before you import into it—svn import will recursively create directories for you:

```
$ svn import -m "New import" myproj \
> http://svn.red-bean.com/repos/test/trunk/vendors/myproj
Adding         myproj/sample.txt
...
Transmitting file data .........
Committed revision 19.
```

After importing data, note that the original tree is *not* under version control. To start working, you still need to svn checkout a fresh working copy of the tree.

info

svn info [*path* ...]

Print information about paths in your working copy, including:

- Path
- Name
- URL
- Revision
- Node Kind
- Last Changed Author
- Last Changed Revision
- Last Changed Date
- Text Last Updated
- Properties Last Updated
- Checksum

Alternate Names:	None
Changes:	Nothing
Accesses Repository:	No

Options

--config-dir *dir*
--recursive (-R)
--targets *filename*

list

```
svn list [target ...]
```

List each *target* file and the contents of each *target* directory as they exist in the repository. If *target* is a working copy path, the corresponding repository URL is used. The default *target* is ".", meaning the repository URL of the current working copy directory.

With `--verbose`, the following fields show the status of the item:

- Revision number of the last commit
- Author of the last commit
- Size (in bytes)
- Date and time of the last commit

Alternate Names:	`ls`
Changes:	Nothing
Accesses Repository:	Yes

Options

`--config-dir` *dir*	`--recursive` (`-R`)
`--no-auth-cache`	`--revision` *rev*, `-r` *rev*
`--non-interactive`	`--username` *user*
`--password` *pass*	`--verbose` (`-v`)

Examples

To see what files a repository has without downloading a working copy:

```
$ svn list http://svn.red-bean.com/repos/test/support
README.txt
INSTALL
examples/
...
```

Pass the `--verbose` option for additional information:

```
$ svn list --verbose file:///tmp/repos
     16 sue          28361 Jan 16 23:18 README.txt
     27 sue              0 Jan 18 15:27 INSTALL
     24 joe                Jan 18 11:27 examples/
```

log

```
svn log [path]
svn log URL [path ...]
```

The default target is the path of your current directory. If no arguments are supplied, `svn log` shows the log messages for all files and directories inside of (and including) the current working directory of your working copy. You can refine the results by specifying a path, one or more revisions, or any combination of the two. The default revision range for a local path is `BASE:1`.

If you specify a URL alone, svn log prints log messages for everything that the URL contains. If you add paths past the URL, only messages for those paths under that URL are printed. The default revision range for a URL is HEAD:1.

With --verbose, svn log also prints all affected paths with each log message. With --quiet, svn log does not print the log message body itself (this is compatible with --verbose).

Each log message is printed just once, even if more than one of the affected paths for that revision were explicitly requested. Logs follow copy history by default. Use --stop-on-copy to disable this behavior, which can be useful for determining branch points.

Alternate Names:	None
Changes:	Nothing
Accesses Repository:	Yes

Options

--config-dir *dir*	--revision *rev*, -r *rev*
--incremental	--stop-on-copy
--no-auth-cache	--targets *filename*
--non-interactive	--username *user*
--password *pass*	--verbose (-v)
--quiet (-q)	--xml

Examples

To see the log messages for all the paths that changed in your working copy, run svn log from the top (some long output lines have wrapped):

```
$ svn log
------------------------------------------------------------------------
r20 | joe | 2003-01-17 22:56:19 -0600 (Fri, 17 Jan 2003) | 1 line
Tweak.
------------------------------------------------------------------------
r17 | sue | 2003-01-16 23:21:19 -0600 (Thu, 16 Jan 2003) | 2 lines
...
```

If you don't have a working copy handy, you can log a URL:

```
$ svn log http://svn.red-bean.com/repos/test/foo.c
------------------------------------------------------------------------
r32 | sue | 2003-01-13 00:43:13 -0600 (Mon, 13 Jan 2003) | 1 line

Added defines.
------------------------------------------------------------------------
r28 | sue | 2003-01-07 21:48:33 -0600 (Tue, 07 Jan 2003) | 3 lines
...
```

If you run svn log on a specific path and provide a specific revision and get no output at all:

```
$ svn log -r 20
> http://svn.red-bean.com/untouched.txt
------------------------------------------------
```

then that just means that the path was not modified in that revision. If you log from the top of the repository, or know the file that changed in that revision, you can specify it explicitly:

```
$ svn log -r 20 touched.txt
------------------------------------------------
r20 | sue | 2003-01-17 22:56:19 -0600 (Fri, 17
Jan 2003) | 1 line

Made a change.
------------------------------------------------
```

merge

svn merge *sourceURL1*[@*N*] *sourceURL2*[@*M*] [*wcpath*]
svn merge -r *N*:*M* *source* [*path*]

In the first form, the source URLs are specified at revisions *N* and *M*. These are the two sources to be compared. The revisions default to HEAD if omitted.

In the second form, *source* can be a URL or working copy item, in which case the corresponding URL is used. This URL, at revisions *N* and *M*, defines the two sources to be compared.

wcpath is the working copy path that will receive the changes. If *wcpath* is omitted, a default value of "." is assumed, unless the sources have identical basenames that match a file within ".", in which case, the differences are applied to that file.

Unlike svn diff, this command takes the ancestry of a file into consideration when performing a merge operation. This is very important when you're merging changes from one branch into another and you've renamed a file on one branch but not the other.

Alternate Names:	None
Changes:	Working copy
Accesses Repository:	Only if working with URLs

Options

--config-dir *dir*	--non-interactive
--diff3-cmd *cmd*	--non-recursive (-N)
--dry-run	--password *pass*
--force	--quiet (-q)
--ignore-ancestry	--revision *rev*, -r *rev*
--no-auth-cache	--username *user*

Examples

Merge a branch back into the trunk (assuming that you have a working copy of the trunk, and that the branch was created in revision 250):

```
$ svn merge -r 250:HEAD \
>         http://svn.red-bean.com/repos/branches/my-branch
U  myproj/tiny.txt
U  myproj/thhgttg.txt
U  myproj/win.txt
U  myproj/flo.txt
```

If you branched at revision 23, and you want to merge changes from the trunk into your branch, you could do this from inside the working copy of your branch:

```
$ svn merge -r 23:30 file:///tmp/repos/trunk/vendors
U  myproj/thhgttg.txt
...
```

To merge changes to a single file:

```
$ cd myproj
$ svn merge -r 30:31 thhgttg.txt
U  thhgttg.txt
```

mkdir

```
svn mkdir path ...
svn mkdir URL ...
```

Create a directory with a name given by the final component of the *path* or URL. A directory specified by a working copy *path* is scheduled for addition in the working copy. A directory specified by a URL is created in the repository via an immediate commit. Multiple directory URLs are committed atomically. In both cases all the intermediate directories must already exist.

Alternate Names:	None
Changes:	Working copy; repository if operating on a URL
Accesses Repository:	Only if operating on a URL

Options

`--config-dir` *dir*	`--no-auth-cache`
`--editor-cmd` *editor*	`--non-interactive`
`--encoding` *enc*	`--password` *pass*
`--file` *file*, `-F` *file*	`--quiet (-q)`
`--force-log`	`--username` *user*
`--message` *text*, `-m` *text*	

move

```
svn move src dst
```

This command moves (renames) a file or directory in your working copy or in the repository.

This command is equivalent to an svn copy followed by svn delete.

WC → WC
: Move and schedule a file or directory for addition (with history).

URL → URL
: Complete server-side rename.

Subversion does not support moving between working copies and URLs. In addition, you can only move files within a single repository—Subversion does not support cross-repository moving.

Alternate Names:	`mv`, `rename`, `ren`
Changes:	Working copy; repository if operating on a URL
Accesses Repository:	Only if operating on a URL

Options

`--config-dir` *dir*	`--no-auth-cache`
`--editor-cmd` *editor*	`--non-interactive`
`--encoding` *enc*	`--password` *pass*
`--file` *file*, `-F` *file*	`--quiet` (`-q`)
`--force-log`	`--revision` *rev*, `-r` *rev*
`--force`	`--username` *user*
`--message` *text*, `-m` *text*	

propdel

```
svn propdel propname [path ...]
svn propdel propname --revprop -r rev [URL]
```

This removes properties from files, directories, or revisions. The first form removes versioned properties in your working copy, whereas the second removes unversioned remote properties on a repository revision.

Alternate Names:	`pdel`, `pd`
Changes:	Working copy; repository only if operating on a URL
Accesses Repository:	Only if operating on a URL

Options

`--config-dir` *dir*	`--recursive` (`-R`)
`--no-auth-cache`	`--revision` *rev*, `-r` *rev*
`--non-interactive`	`--revprop`
`--password` *pass*	`--username` *user*
`--quiet` (`-q`)	

Examples

Delete a property from a file in your working copy:

```
$ svn propdel svn:mime-type some-script
property 'svn:mime-type' deleted from 'some-script'.
```

Delete a revision property:

```
$ svn propdel --revprop -r 26 release-date
property 'release-date' deleted from repository revision '26'
```

propedit

svn propedit *propname path* ...
svn propedit *propname* --revprop -r *rev* [*URL*]

Edit one or more properties using your favorite editor. The first form edits versioned properties in your working copy, while the second edits unversioned remote properties on a repository revision.

Alternate Names:	pedit, pe
Changes:	Working copy; repository only if operating on a URL
Accesses Repository:	Only if operating on a URL

Options

--config-dir *dir*
--editor-cmd *editor*
--encoding *enc*
--no-auth-cache
--non-interactive
--password *pass*
--revision *rev*, -r *rev*
--revprop
--username *user*

propget

svn propget *propname* [*path* ...]
svn propget *propname* --revprop -r *rev* [*URL*]

Print the value of a property on files, directories, or revisions. The first form prints the versioned property of an item or items in your working copy, while the second prints the unversioned remote property on a repository revision.

Alternate Names:	pget, pg
Changes:	Working copy; repository only if operating on a URL
Accesses Repository:	Only if operating on a URL

Options

--config-dir *dir*
--no-auth-cache
--non-interactive
--password *pass*
--recursive (-R)
--revprop
--strict
--username *user*

proplist

```
svn proplist propname [path ...]
svn proplist propname --revprop -r rev [URL]
```

List all properties on files, directories, or revisions. The first form lists versioned properties in your working copy, while the second lists unversioned remote properties on a repository revision.

Alternate Names:	plist, pl
Changes:	Working copy; repository only if operating on a URL
Accesses Repository:	Only if operating on a URL

Options

`--config-dir` *dir*	`--recursive` (`-R`)
`--no-auth-cache`	`--revision` *rev*, `-r` *rev*
`--non-interactive`	`--revprop`
`--password` *pass*	`--username` *user*
`--quiet` (`-q`)	`--verbose` (`-v`)

Examples

You can use `svn proplist` to see the properties on an item in your working copy:

```
$ svn proplist foo.c
Properties on 'foo.c':
  svn:mime-type
  svn:keywords
  owner
```

But with the `--verbose` flag, `svn proplist` is extremely handy as it also shows you the values for the properties:

```
$ svn proplist --verbose foo.c
Properties on 'foo.c':
  svn:mime-type : text/plain
  svn:keywords : Author Date Rev
  owner : sue
```

propset

```
svn propset propname [propval] path ...
svn propset propname --revprop -r rev [propval] [URL]
```

Set *propname* to *propval* on files, directories, or revisions. The first example creates a versioned, local property change in the working copy, and the second creates an unversioned, remote property change on a repository revision. The new property value, *propval*, may be provided literally, or using the `-F` *valfile* option.

Alternate Names:	pset, ps
Changes:	Working copy; repository only if operating on a URL
Accesses Repository:	Only if operating on a URL

Options

--config-dir *dir*	--quiet (-q)
--encoding *enc*	--recursive (-R)
--file *file*, -F *file*	--revision *rev*, -r *rev*
--force	--revprop
--no-auth-cache	--targets *filename*
--non-interactive	--username *user*
--password *pass*	

Examples

Set the mimetype on a file:

```
$ svn propset svn:mime-type image/jpeg foo.jpg
property 'svn:mime-type' set on 'foo.jpg'
```

On a Unix system, if you want a file to have execute permission:

```
$ svn propset svn:executable ON somescript
property 'svn:executable' set on 'somescript'
```

By default, you cannot modify revision properties in a Subversion repository. Your repository administrator must explicitly enable revision property modifications by creating a hook named pre-revprop-change.

resolved

`svn resolved` *path* ...

Remove the “conflicted” state on working copy files or directories. This command does not semantically resolve conflict markers; it merely removes conflict-related artifact files and allows *path* to be committed again; that is, it tells Subversion that the conflicts have been “resolved.” Use it after you have resolved the conflict in the file.

Alternate Names:	None
Changes:	Working copy
Accesses Repository:	No

Options

--config-dir *dir*	--recursive (-R)
--quiet (-q)	--targets *filename*

Example

If you get a conflict on an update, your working copy will contain three additional files:

```
$ svn update
C  foo.c
Updated to revision 31.
$ ls
foo.c                      Merged version with conflict markers
foo.c.mine                 Original working copy version
foo.c.r30                  Unmodified BASE version
foo.c.r31                  Unmodified HEAD version
```

Subversion

Once you've resolved the conflict and `foo.c` is ready to be committed, run `svn resolved` to let your working copy know you've taken care of everything.

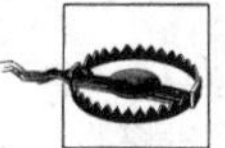

You *can* just remove the conflict files and commit, but `svn resolved` fixes up some bookkeeping data in the working copy administrative area in addition to removing the conflict files, so you should use this command.

revert

`svn revert` *`path ...`*

Revert any local changes to a file or directory and resolve any conflicted states. `svn revert` not only reverts the contents of an item in your working copy, but also any property changes. Finally, you can use it to undo any scheduling operations that you may have done (e.g., files scheduled for addition or deletion can be "unscheduled").

Alternate Names:	None
Changes:	Working copy
Accesses Repository:	No

Options

`--config-dir` *`dir`*	`--recursive (-R)`
`--quiet (-q)`	`--targets` *`filename`*

Examples

Discard changes to a file:

```
$ svn revert foo.c
Reverted foo.c
```

If you want to revert a whole directory of files, use the `--recursive` flag:

```
$ svn revert --recursive .
Reverted newdir/afile
Reverted foo.c
Reverted bar.txt
```

If you provide no targets to `svn revert`, it does nothing—to protect you from accidentally losing changes in your working copy, `svn revert` requires you to provide at least one target.

status

`svn status [`*`path ...`*`]`

Print the status of working copy files and directories. With no arguments, print only locally modified items (no repository access).

With `--show-updates`, add working revision and server out-of-date information. With `--verbose`, print full revision information on every item.

The first five columns in the output are each one character wide, and each column gives you information about different aspects of each working copy item.

The first column indicates that an item was added, deleted, or otherwise changed:

space	No modifications.
`A`	Item is scheduled for addition.
`D`	Item is scheduled for deletion.
`M`	Item has been modified.
`C`	Item is in conflict with updates received from the repository.
`X`	Item is related to an externals definition.
`I`	Item is being ignored (e.g., with the `svn:ignore` property).
`?`	Item is not under version control.
`!`	Item is missing (e.g., you moved or deleted it without using `svn`). This also indicates that a directory is incomplete (a checkout or update was interrupted).
`~`	Item is versioned as a directory, but has been replaced by a file, or vice versa.

The second column tells the status of a file's or directory's properties:

space	No modifications.
`M`	Properties for this item have been modified.
`C`	Properties for this item are in conflict with property updates received from the repository.

The third column is populated only if the working copy directory is locked:

space	Item is not locked.
`L`	Item is locked.

The fourth column is populated only if the item is scheduled for addition-with-history:

space	No history scheduled with commit.
`+`	History scheduled with commit.

The fifth column is populated only if the item is switched relative to its parent:

space	Item is a child of its parent directory.
`S`	Item is switched.

If you pass the `--show-updates` option, the out-of-date information appears in the eighth column:

space	The item in your working copy is up-to-date.
*	A newer revision of the item exists on the server.

The remaining fields are variable width and delimited by spaces. The working revision is the next field if the `--show-updates` or `--verbose` options are passed.

If the `--verbose` option is passed, the last committed revision and last committed author are displayed next.

The working copy path is always the final field, so it can include spaces.

Alternate Names:	`stat`, `st`
Changes:	Nothing
Accesses Repository:	Only if using `--show-updates`

Options

`--config-dir` *dir*	`--password` *pass*
`--no-auth-cache`	`--quiet` (`-q`)
`--no-ignore`	`--show-updates` (`-u`)
`--non-interactive`	`--username` *user*
`--non-recursive` (`-N`)	`--verbose` (`-v`)

Examples

To find out what changes you have made to your working copy:

```
$ svn status wc
 M     wc/bar.c
A  +   wc/qax.c
```

To find out what files in your working copy are out-of-date, pass the `--show-updates` option (this does *not* make any changes to your working copy). Here you can see that `wc/foo.c` has changed in the repository since we last updated our working copy:

```
$ svn status --show-updates wc
 M           965    wc/bar.c
       *     965    wc/foo.c
A  +         965    wc/qax.c
Status against revision:    981
```

`--show-updates` places an asterisk *only* next to items that are out of date (that is, items that will be updated from the repository if you run `svn update`). `--show-updates` does *not* cause the status listing to reflect the repository's version of the item.

And finally, the most information you can get out of the status subcommand:

```
$ svn status --show-updates --verbose wc
 M           965       938 sue       wc/bar.c
       *     965       922 joe       wc/foo.c
A  +         965       687 joe       wc/qax.c
             965       687 joe       wc/zig.c
Head revision:   981
```

switch

`svn switch URL [path]`

This subcommand updates your working copy to mirror a new URL—usually a URL that shares a common ancestor with your working copy, although not necessarily. This is the Subversion way to move a working copy to a new branch.

Alternate Names:	sw
Changes:	Working copy
Accesses Repository:	Yes

Options

```
--config-dir dir          --password pass
--diff3-cmd cmd           --quiet (-q)
--no-auth-cache           --relocate
--non-interactive         --revision rev, -r rev
--non-recursive (-N)      --username user
```

Examples

If you're currently inside the directory `vendors`, which was branched to `fixed`, and you'd like to switch your working copy to that branch:

```
$ svn switch http://svn.red-bean.com/repos/branches/fixed .
U  myproj/foo.txt
U  myproj/bar.txt
U  myproj/baz.c
U  myproj/qux.c
Updated to revision 31.
```

And to switch back, just provide the URL to the location in the repository from which you originally checked out your working copy:

```
$ svn switch http://svn.red-bean.com/repos/trunk/vendors .
U  myproj/foo.txt
U  myproj/bar.txt
U  myproj/baz.c
U  myproj/qux.c
Updated to revision 31.
```

You can just switch part of your working copy to a branch if you don't want to switch your entire working copy.

Sometimes an administrator might change the "base location" of your repository—in other words, the contents of the repository doesn't change, but the main URL used to reach the root of the repository does. For example, the hostname may change, or the URL schema, or perhaps just the path that leads to the repository. Rather than check out a new working copy, you can have the `svn switch` command "rewrite" the beginnings of all the URLs in your working copy. Use the `--relocate` command to do the substitution. No file contents are changed, nor is the repository contacted. It's similar to running a `sed` script over your working copy `.svn/` directories that runs `s/OldRoot/NewRoot/`.

```
$ cd /tmp
$ svn checkout file:///tmp/repos test
A  test/a
A  test/b
...

$ mv repos newlocation
$ cd test/

$ svn update
svn: Unable to open an ra_local session to URL
svn: Unable to open repository 'file:///tmp/repos'

$ svn switch --relocate \
> file:///tmp/repos file:///tmp/newlocation .
$ svn update
At revision 3.
```

update

`svn update [PATH ...]`

`svn update` brings changes from the repository into your working copy. If no revision is given, it brings your working copy up-to-date with the `HEAD` revision. Otherwise, it synchronizes the working copy to the revision given by the `--revision` option.

For each updated item, Subversion prints a line starting with a specific character reporting the action taken. These characters have the following meaning:

A	Added
C	Conflict
D	Deleted
G	Merged
U	Updated

A character in the first column signifies an update to the actual file, while updates to the file's properties are shown in the second column.

Alternate Names:	up
Changes:	Working copy
Accesses Repository:	Yes

If you want to examine an older revision of a single file, you may want to use svn cat.

Options

`--config-dir` *dir*	`--password` *pass*
`--diff3-cmd` *cmd*	`--quiet (-q)`
`--no-auth-cache`	`--revision` *rev*, `-r` *rev*
`--non-interactive`	`--username` *user*
`--non-recursive (-N)`	

Repository Administration: svnadmin

`svnadmin` is the administrative tool for monitoring and repairing your Subversion repository.

svnadmin Options

`--bdb-log-keep`
Disable automatic log removal of database log files. (Berkeley DB-specific)

`--bdb-txn-nosync`
Disable use of `fsync( )` when committing database transactions. (Berkeley DB-specific)

`--bypass-hooks`
Bypass the repository hook system.

`--clean-logs`
Remove unused Berkeley DB logs.

`--force-uuid`
By default, when loading data into a repository that already contains revisions, `svnadmin` ignores the UUID from the dump stream. This option causes the repository's UUID to be set to the UUID from the stream.

`--ignore-uuid`
By default, when loading an empty repository, `svnadmin` uses the UUID from the dump stream. This option causes that UUID to be ignored.

`--incremental`
Dump a revision only as a diff against the previous revision, instead of the usual full text.

`--parent-dir` *dir*
When loading a dumpfile, root paths at *dir* instead of `/`.

`--quiet`
Do not show normal progress—show only errors.

`--revision` *rev*, `-r` *rev*
Specify a particular revision to operate on.

svnadmin Subcommands

The `svnadmin` command creates and administers the repository. As such, it always operates on local paths, not on URLs.

create

`svnadmin create` *repos_path*

Create a new, empty repository at the path provided. If the provided directory does not exist, it is created for you.

Options

```
--bdb-log-keep
--bdb-txn-nosync
```

Example

Creating a new repository is just this easy:

```
$ svnadmin create /usr/local/svn/repos
```

deltify

`svnadmin deltify [-r` *lower*`[:`*upper*`]]` *repos_path*

`svnadmin deltify` exists in 1.0.x only due to historical reasons. This command is deprecated and no longer needed.

It dates from a time when Subversion offered administrators greater control over compression strategies in the repository. This turned out to be a lot of complexity for *very* little gain, and this "feature" was deprecated.

Options

`--quiet`
`--revision` *rev*, `-r` *rev*

dump

`svnadmin dump` *repos_path* `[-r` *lower*`[:`*upper*`]] [--incremental]`

Dump the contents of filesystem to standard output in a "dumpfile" portable format, sending feedback to standard error. Dump revisions *lower* rev through *upper* rev. If no revisions are given, dump all revision trees. If only *lower* is given, dump that one revision tree.

Options

`--incremental`
`--quiet`
`--revision` *rev*, `-r` *rev*

Examples

Dump your whole repository:

```
$ svnadmin dump /usr/local/svn/repos
SVN-fs-dump-format-version: 1
Revision-number: 0
* Dumped revision 0.
Prop-content-length: 56
Content-length: 56
...
```

Incrementally dump a single transaction from your repository:

```
$ svnadmin dump /usr/local/svn/repos -r 21 --incremental
* Dumped revision 21.
SVN-fs-dump-format-version: 1
Revision-number: 21
Prop-content-length: 101
Content-length: 101
...
```

help

`svnadmin help [subcommand ...]`

Provide a quick usage summary. With *subcommand*, provide information about the given subcommand.

Alternate Names: ?, h

hotcopy

`svnadmin hotcopy old_repos_path new_repos_path`

This subcommand makes a full "hot" backup of your repository, including all hooks, configuration files, and, of course, database files. If you pass the `--clean-logs` option, `svnadmin` performs a hotcopy of your repository, and then removes unused Berkeley DB logs from the original repository. You can run this command at any time and make a safe copy of the repository, regardless of whether other processes are using the repository.

Options

`--clean-logs`

list-dblogs

`svnadmin list-dblogs repos_path`

List Berkeley DB log files. Berkeley DB creates logs of all changes to the repository, allowing the repository to recover in the face of catastrophe. Unless you enable `DB_LOGS_AUTOREMOVE`, the log files accumulate, although most are no longer used and can be deleted to reclaim disk space.

list-unused-dblogs

`svnadmin list-unused-dblogs repos_path`

List unused Berkeley DB log files (see **svnadmin list-dblogs**).

Example

Remove all unused log files from a repository:

```
$ svnadmin list-unused-dblogs /path/to/repos | xargs rm
## disk space reclaimed!
```

load

`svnadmin load repos_path`

Read a "dumpfile"-formatted stream from standard input, committing new revisions into the repository's filesystem. Send progress feedback to standard output.

Options

```
--force-uuid          --parent-dir
--ignore-uuid         --quiet (-q)
```

Examples

This shows the beginning of loading a repository from a backup file (made, of course, with svn dump):

```
$ svnadmin load /usr/local/svn/restored < repos-backup
<<< Started new txn, based on original revision 1
     * adding path : test ... done.
     * adding path : test/a ... done.
...
```

Or, to load into a subdirectory:

```
$ svnadmin load --parent-dir new/subdir/for/project \
>   /usr/local/svn/restored < repos-backup
<<< Started new txn, based on original revision 1
     * adding path : test ... done.
     * adding path : test/a ... done.
...
```

lstxns

`svnadmin lstxns repos_path`

Print the names of all uncommitted transactions.

recover

`svnadmin recover repos_path`

Run this command if you get an error indicating that your repository needs to be recovered.

rmtxns

`svnadmin rmtxns repos_path txn_name ...`

Delete outstanding transactions from a repository.

Options

```
--quiet (-q)
```

Examples

Remove all uncommitted transactions from your repository, using svn lstxns to provide the list of transactions to remove:

```
$ svnadmin rmtxns /usr/local/svn/repos/ \
>          `svnadmin lstxns /usr/local/svn/repos/`
```

setlog

`svnadmin setlog repos_path -r revision file`

Set the log message on revision *revision* to the contents of *file*.

This is similar to using svn propset --revprop to set the svn:log property on a revision, except you can also use the option --bypass-hooks to avoid running any pre- or post-commit hooks, which is useful if the modification of revision properties has not been enabled in the pre-revprop-change hook.

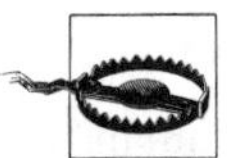

Revision properties are not under version control, so this command permanently overwrites the previous log message.

Options

```
--bypass-hooks
--revision rev, -r rev
```

Example

Set the log message for revision 19 to the contents of the file msg:

```
$ svnadmin setlog /usr/local/svn/repos/ -r 19 msg
```

verify

`svnadmin verify repos_path`

Run this command to verify the integrity of your repository. This iterates through all revisions in the repository by internally dumping all revisions and discarding the output.

Examining the Repository: svnlook

svnlook is a command-line utility for examining different aspects of a Subversion repository. It does not make any changes to the repository. svnlook is typically used by the repository hooks, but a repository administrator might find it useful for diagnostic purposes.

Since svnlook works via direct repository access (and thus can only be used on the machine that holds the repository), it refers to the repository with a path, not a URL.

If no revision or transaction is specified, svnlook defaults to the youngest (most recent) revision of the repository.

svnlook Options

Options in svnlook are global, just like in svn and svnadmin; however, most options only apply to one subcommand since the functionality of svnlook is (intentionally) limited in scope.

`--no-diff-deleted`
: Do not print differences for deleted files. The default behavior when a file is deleted in a transaction/revision is to print the same differences that you would see if you had left the file but removed all the content.

`--revision` *rev*, `-r` *rev*
: Examine revision number *rev*.

`--show-ids`
: Show the filesystem node revision IDs for each path in the filesystem tree.

`--transaction` *tid*, `-t` *tid*
: Examine transaction ID *tid*.

`--verbose`
: Show property values too for the property-related commands.

`--version`
: Display version and copyright information.

svnlook Subcommands

---

author

`svnlook author` *repos_path*

Print the author of a revision or transaction in the repository.

Options

```
--revision rev, -r rev
--transaction tid, -t tid
```

---

cat

`svnlook cat` *repos_path path_in_repos*

Print the contents of a file.

Options

```
--revision rev, -r rev
--transaction tid, -t tid
```

---

changed

`svnlook changed` *repos_path*

Print the paths that were changed in a particular revision or transaction, as well as an svn update-style status letter in the first column: A for added, D for deleted, and U for updated (modified).

Options

```
--revision rev, -r rev
--transaction tid, -t tid
```

Example

Show a list of all the changed files in revision 39 of a test repository:

```
$ svnlook changed -r 39 /usr/local/svn/repos
A   trunk/vendors/deli/
A   trunk/vendors/deli/chips.txt
A   trunk/vendors/deli/sandwich.txt
A   trunk/vendors/deli/pickle.txt
```

date

svnlook date *repos_path*

Print the datestamp of a revision or transaction in a repository.

Options

--revision *rev*, -r *rev*
--transaction *tid*, -t *tid*

diff

svnlook diff *repos_path*

Print GNU-style differences of changed files and properties in a repository. If a file has a nontextual svn:mime-type property, then the differences are explicitly not shown.

Options

--no-diff-deleted
--revision *rev*, -r *rev*
--transaction *tid*, -t *tid*

dirs-changed

svnlook dirs-changed *repos_path*

Print the directories that were themselves changed (property edits) or whose file children were changed.

Options

--revision *rev*, -r *rev*
--transaction *tid*, -t *tid*

help

svnlook help
svnlook -h
svnlook -?

Provide a quick usage summary. With *subcommand*, provide information about the given subcommand.

Alternate Names: ?, h

history

svnlook history *repos_path* [*path_in_repos*]

Print information about the history of a path in the repository (or the root directory if no path is supplied).

Options

--revision *rev*, -r *rev*
--show-ids

Example

This shows the history output for the path /tags/1.0 as of revision 20 in our sample repository.

```
$ svnlook history -r 20 /usr/local/svn/repos /tags/1.0 \
> --show-ids
REVISION   PATH <ID>
--------   ---------
      19   /tags/1.0 <1.2.12>
      17   /branches/1.0-rc2 <1.1.10>
      16   /branches/1.0-rc2 <1.1.x>
      14   /trunk <1.0.q>
...
```

info

svnlook info *repos_path*

Print the author, datestamp, log message size, and log message.

Options

--revision *rev*, -r *rev*
--transaction *tid*, -t *tid*

log

svnlook log *repos_path*

Print the log message.

Options

--revision *rev*, -r *rev*
--transaction *tid*, -t *tid*

propget

svnlook propget *repos_path propname path_in_repos*

List the value of a property on a path in the repository.

Alternate Names: pg, pget

Options

--revision *rev*, -r *rev*
--transaction *tid*, -t *tid*

Example

Show the value of the "seasonings" property on the file /trunk/sandwich in the HEAD revision:

```
$ svnlook pg /usr/local/svn/repos seasonings \
> /trunk/sandwich
mustard
```

proplist

svnlook proplist *repos_path path_in_repos*

List the properties of a path in the repository. With --verbose, show the property values too.

Alternate Names: pl, plist

Options

--revision *rev*, -r *rev*
--transaction *tid*, -t *tid*
--verbose (-v)

Examples

Show the names of properties set on the file /trunk/README in the HEAD revision:

```
$ svnlook proplist /usr/local/svn/repos /trunk/README
original-author
svn:mime-type
```

This is the same command as in the previous example, but this time showing the property values as well:

```
$ svnlook proplist --verbose /usr/local/svn/repos \
> /trunk/README
original-author : fitz
svn:mime-type : text/plain
```

tree

svnlook tree *repos_path*
[*path_in_repos*]

Print the tree, starting at *path_in_repos* (if supplied, at the root of the tree otherwise), optionally showing node revision IDs.

Options

--revision *rev*, -r *rev*
--show-ids
--transaction *tid*, -t *tid*

Example

This shows the tree output (with node-IDs) for revision 40 in our sample repository:

```
$ svnlook tree -r 40 /usr/local/svn/repos --show-ids
/ <0.0.2j>
 trunk/ <p.0.2j>
  vendors/ <q.0.2j>
```

```
deli/ <1g.0.2j>
 egg.txt <1i.e.2j>
 soda.txt <1k.0.2j>
 sandwich.txt <1j.0.2j>
```

uuid

`svnlook uuid` *`repos_path`*

Print the UUID for the repository. The UUID is the repository's *U*niversal *U*nique *ID*entifier. The Subversion client uses this identifier to differentiate between one repository and another.

youngest

`svnlook youngest` *`repos_path`*

Print the youngest revision number of a repository.

Providing Remote Access: svnserve

svnserve provides access to Subversion repositories using the svn network protocol. You can run svnserve either as a standalone server process, or you can have another process, such as inetd, xinetd, or sshd, start it for you.

Once the client has selected a repository by transmitting its URL, svnserve reads a file named conf/svnserve.conf in the repository directory to determine repository-specific settings such as what authentication database to use and what authorization policies to apply. The details are provided in *Version Control with Subversion*.

svnserve Options

Unlike the previous commands we've described, svnserve has no subcommands—svnserve is controlled exclusively by options.

`--daemon, -d`
: Run in daemon mode. svnserve backgrounds itself and accepts and serves TCP/IP connections on the svn port (3690, by default).

`--foreground`
: When used together with -d, this option causes svnserve to stay in the foreground. This option is mainly useful for debugging.

`--help, -h`
: Display a usage summary and exit.

`--inetd, -i`
: Use the standard input/standard output file descriptors, as is appropriate for a server running out of inetd.

`--listen-host=`*`host`*
: Listen on the interface specified by *host*, which may be either a hostname or an IP address.

`--listen-once, -X`
: Accept one connection on the svn port, serve it, and exit. This option is mainly useful for debugging.

`--listen-port=`*port*
: Listen on *port* when run in daemon mode.

`--root=`*root*`, -r=`*root*
: Set the virtual root for repositories served by svnserve to *root*. The pathnames in URLs provided by the client are interpreted relative to this root, and are not allowed to escape this root.

`--threads, -T`
: When running in daemon mode, spawn a thread instead of a process for each connection. The svnserve process still backgrounds itself at startup time.

`--tunnel, -t`
: Run in tunnel mode, which is just like the inetd mode of operation (serve one connection over standard input/standard output) except that the connection is considered to be pre-authenticated with the username of the current UID. This flag is selected by the client when running over a tunnelling agent such as ssh.

Other Subversion Components

Subversion creates the mod_dav_svn plug-in for use with the Apache 2.0 httpd web server. By running Apache 2.0 with mod_dav_svn, you can make your repository available via the HTTP protocol. Full details are provided in *Version Control with Subversion*, which is cited in the Bibliography. Two other commands are supplied with Subversion.

---

svndumpfilter

`svndumpfilter` *subcommand* `[`*options*`]` *paths* `...`

Filter out files from a repository dump for use in later repository restoration (see **svnadmin dump** and **svnadmin load**).

Subcommands

`exclude`	Exclude from the dump the files and directories named by *paths*. Everything else is left in the dump.
`help, h, ?`	Print a help message and exit.
`include`	Include in the dump only the files and directories named by *paths*. Everything else is excluded.

Options

`--drop-empty-revs`
: Remove empty revisions. Such a revision can be created when the original revision contained paths that were filtered out. This option removes such empty revisions from the dump.

`--preserve-revprops`
: If empty revisions are being kept, preserve their revision properties (such as log message, author, date, and so on).

Subversion

Otherwise, empty revisions contain only the original datestamp and a generated log message that the revision was dropped.

`--renumber-revs`
: If empty revisions are being dropped, subsequent revisions are renumbered, so that all revision numbers are contiguous.

Example

Dump the repository, then separate out its two components:

```
$ svnadmin dump /path/to/repos > dumpfile
* Dumped revision 0.
* Dumped revision 1.
* Dumped revision 2.
...

$ svndumpfilter include \
> client < dumpfile > client-dumpfile
$ svndumpfilter include \
> server < dumpfile > server-dumpfile
```

---

svnversion

`svnversion [options] path [URL]`

Produce a version number for the working copy in *path*. The *URL* is the pathname part of a Subversion URL used to tell if the *path* was switched (see **svn switch**).

The output is a single number if the working copy represents an unmodified, non-switched revision whose URL matches the supplied *URL*.

Options

`-c` Report "last changed" revision instead of the current revision.

`-n` Do not print the final newline.

16
The GNU make Utility

The make program is a long time mainstay of the Unix toolset. It automates the building of software and documentation based on a specification of dependencies among files; e.g., object files that depend upon program source files, or PDF files that depend upon documentation program input files. GNU make is the standard version for GNU/Linux and Mac OS X.

This chapter presents the following topics:

- Conceptual overview
- Command-line syntax
- Makefile lines
- Macros
- Special target names
- Writing command lines

For more information, see *Managing Projects with GNU make* and *GNU Make: A Program for Directing Recompilation*, both listed in the Bibliography.

The software download site for GNU make is *ftp://ftp.gnu.org/gnu/make/*.

Conceptual Overview

The make program generates a sequence of commands for execution by the Unix shell. It uses a table of file dependencies provided by the programmer, and with this information, can perform updating tasks automatically for the user. It can keep track of the sequence of commands that create certain files, and the list of files or programs that require other files to be current before they can be rebuilt correctly. When a program is changed, make can create the proper files with a minimum of effort.

Each statement of a dependency is called a *rule*. Rules define one or more *targets*, which are the files to be generated, and the files they depend upon, the *prerequisites* or *dependencies*. For example, `prog.o` would be a target that depends upon `prog.c`; each time you update `prog.c`, `prog.o` must be regenerated. It is this task that `make` automates, and it is a critical one for large programs that have many pieces.

The file containing all the rules is termed a *makefile*; for GNU `make`, it may be named `GNUmakefile`, `makefile` or `Makefile`, in which case `make` will read it automatically, or you may use a file with a different name and tell `make` about it with the `-f` option.

Over the years, different enhancements to `make` have been made by many vendors, often in incompatible ways. POSIX standardizes how `make` is supposed to work. Today, GNU `make` is the most popular version in the Unix world. It has (or can emulate) the features of just about every other version of `make`, and many Open Source programs require it.

This chapter covers GNU `make`. Commercial Unix systems come with versions derived from the original System V version; these can be used for bootstrapping GNU `make` if need be. On the x86 versions of Solaris 10, you can find GNU `make` in `/usr/sfw/bin/gmake`. It isn't available on the Sparc version, although it can be easily bootstrapped with the standard version of `make` in `/usr/ccs/bin`.

Command-Line Syntax

The `make` program is invoked as follows:

```
make [options] [targets] [macro definitions]
```

Options, targets, and macro definitions can appear in any order. The last assignment to a variable is the one that's used. Macro definitions are typed as:

```
name=string
```

or

```
name:=string
```

For more information, see the section "Creating and Using Macros," later in this chapter.

If no `GNUmakefile`, `makefile`, or `Makefile` exists, `make` attempts to extract the most recent version of one from either an RCS file, if one exists, or from an SCCS file, if one exists. Note though, that if a real makefile exists, `make` will not attempt to extract one from RCS or SCCS, even if the RCS or SCCS file is newer than the makefile.

Options

Like just about every other GNU program, GNU `make` has both long and short options. The available options are as follows:

`-b` Silently accepted, but ignored, for compatibility with other versions of `make`.

`-B, --always-make`
: Treat all targets as out of date. All targets are remade, no matter what the actual status is of their prerequisites.

`-C` *dir*, `--directory=`*dir*
: Change directory to *dir* before reading makefiles. With multiple options, each one is relative to the previous. This is usually used for recursive invocations of `make`.

`-d`
: Print debugging information in addition to regular output. This information includes which files are out of date, the file times being compared, the rules being used to update the targets, and so on. Equivalent to `--debug=a`.

`--debug[=`*debug-opt*`]`
: Print debugging information as specified by *debug-opt*, which is one or more of the following letters, separated by spaces or commas. With no argument, provide basic debugging.

`a`	All. Enable all debugging.
`b`	Basic. Print each target that is out of date, and whether or not the build was successful.
`i`	Implicit. Like basic, but include information about the implicit rules searched for each target.
`j`	Jobs. Provide information about subcommand invocation.
`m`	Makefiles. Enable basic debugging, and any of the other options, for description of attempts to rebuild makefiles. (Normally, `make` doesn't print information about its attempts to rebuild makefiles.)
`v`	Verbose. Like basic, but also print information about which makefiles were read, and which prerequisites did not need to be rebuilt.

`-e`, `--environment-overrides`
: Environment variables override any macros defined in makefiles.

`-f` *file*, `--file=`*file*, `--makefile=`*file*
: Use *file* as the makefile; a filename of - denotes standard input. `-f` can be used more than once to concatenate multiple makefiles. With no `-f` option, `make` first looks for a file named `GNUmakefile`, then one named `makefile`, and finally one named `Makefile`.

`-h`, `--help`
: Print a usage summary, and then exit.

`-i`, `--ignore-errors`
: Ignore error codes from commands (same as `.IGNORE`).

`-I` *dir*, `--include-dir=`*dir*
: Look in *dir* for makefiles included with the `include` directive. Multiple options add more directories to the list; `make` searches them in order.

`-j [`*count*`]`, `--jobs[=`*count*`]`
: Run commands in parallel. With no *count*, `make` runs as many separate commands as possible. (In other words, it will build all the targets that are independent of each other, in parallel.) Otherwise, it runs no more than *count* jobs. This can decrease the time it takes to rebuild a large project.

`-k`, `--keep-going`
: Abandon the current target when it fails, but keep working with unrelated targets. In other words, rebuild as much as possible.

`-l [load], --load-average[=load], --max-load[=load]`
: If there are jobs running and the system load average is at least *load*, don't start any new jobs running. Without an argument, clear a previous limit. The *load* value is a floating point number.

`-m`
: Silently accepted, but ignored, for compatibility with other versions of `make`.

`-n, --dry-run, --just-print, --recon`
: Print commands but don't execute (used for testing). `-n` prints commands even if they begin with `@` in the makefile.

: Lines that contain `$(MAKE)` are an exception. Such lines *are* executed. However, since the `-n` is passed to the subsequent `make` in the MAKEFLAGS environment variable, that `make` also just prints the commands it executes. This allows you to test out all the makefiles in a whole software hierarchy without actually doing anything.

`--no-print-directory`
: Don't print the working directory as `make` runs recursive invocations. Useful if `-w` is automatically in effect but you don't want to see the extra messages.

`-o file, --assume-old=file, --old-file=file`
: Pretend that *file* is older than the files that depend upon it, even if it's not. This avoids remaking the other files that depend on *file*. Use this in cases where you know that the changed contents of *file* will have no effect upon the files that depend upon it; e.g., changing a comment in a header file.

`-p, --print-data-base`
: Print macro definitions, suffixes, and built-in rules. In a directory without a makefile, use `env -i make -p` to print out the default variable definitions and built-in rules.

`-q, --question`
: Query; return 0 if the target is up to date; nonzero otherwise.

`-r, --no-builtin-rules`
: Do not use the default rules. This also clears out the default list of suffixes and suffix rules.

`-s, --quiet, --silent`
: Do not display command lines (same as `.SILENT`).

`-S, --no-keep-going, --stop`
: Cancel the effect of a previous `-k`. This is only needed for recursive `make` invocations, where the `-k` option might be inherited via the MAKEFLAGS environment variable.

`-t, --touch`
: Touch the target files, causing them to be updated.

`-v, --version`
: Print version, copyright, and author information, and exit.

`-w, --print-directory`
: Print the working directory, before and after executing the makefile. Useful for recursive `make` invocations. This is usually done by default, so it's rare to explicitly need this option.

`--warn-undefined-variables`
: Print a warning message whenever an undefined variable is used. This is useful for debugging complicated makefiles.

`-W` *file*, `--assume-new=`*file*, `--new-file=`*file*, `--what-if=`*file*
: Treat *file* as if it had just been modified. Together with `-n`, this lets you see what `make` would do if *file* were modified, without actually doing anything. Without `-n`, `make` pretends that the file is freshly updated, and acts accordingly.

Makefile Lines

Instructions in the makefile are interpreted as single lines. If an instruction must span more than one input line, use a backslash (\) at the end of the line so that the next line is considered a continuation. The makefile may contain any of the following types of lines:

Blank lines
: Blank lines are ignored.

Comment lines
: A number sign (#) can be used at the beginning of a line or anywhere in the middle. `make` ignores everything after the #.

Dependency lines
: One or more target names, a single- or double-colon separator, and zero or more prerequisites:

```
targets : prerequisites
targets :: prerequisites
```

In the first form, subsequent commands are executed if the prerequisites are newer than the target. The second form is a variant that lets you specify the same targets on more than one dependency line. (This second form is useful when the way you rebuild the target depends upon which prerequisite is newer.) In both forms, if no prerequisites are supplied, subsequent commands are always executed (whenever any of the targets are specified). For example, the following is invalid, since single-colon rules do not allow targets to repeated:

```
# PROBLEM: Single colon rules disallow repeating targets
whizprog.o: foo.h
        $(CC) -c $(CFLAGS) whizprog.o
        @echo built for foo.h

whizprog.o: bar.h
        $(CC) -c $(CFLAGS) whizprog.o
        @echo built for bar.h
```

In such a case, the last set of rules is used and make issues a diagnostic. However, double-colon rules treat the dependencies separately, running each set of rules if the target is out of date with respect to the individual dependencies:

```
# OK: Double colon rules work independently of each other
whizprog.o:: foo.h
        $(CC) -c $(CFLAGS) whizprog.o
        @echo built for foo.h

whizprog.o:: bar.h
        $(CC) -c $(CFLAGS) whizprog.o
        @echo built for bar.h
```

No tab should precede any *targets*. (At the end of a dependency line, you can specify a command, preceded by a semicolon; however, commands are typically entered on their own lines, preceded by a tab.)

Targets of the form *library*(*member*) represent members of archive libraries, e.g., libguide.a(dontpanic.o). Furthermore, both targets and prerequisites may contain shell-style wildcards (e.g., *.c). make expands the wildcard and uses the resulting list for the targets or prerequisites.

Suffix rules

These specify that files ending with the first suffix can be prerequisites for files ending with the second suffix (assuming the root filenames are the same). Either of these formats can be used:

```
.suffix.suffix:
.suffix:
```

The second form means that the root filename depends on the filename with the corresponding suffix.

Pattern rules

Rules that use the % character define a pattern for matching targets and prerequisites. This is a powerful generalization of the original make's suffix rules. Many of GNU make's built-in rules are pattern rules. For example, this built-in rule is used to compile C programs into relocatable object files:

```
%.o : %.c
        $(CC) -c $(CFLAGS) $(CPPFLAGS) $< -o $@
```

Each target listed in a pattern rule must contain only one % character. To match these rules, files must have at least one character in their names to match the %; a file named just .o would not match the above rule. The text that matches the % is called the *stem*, and the stem's value is substituted for the % in the prerequisite. (Thus, for example, prog.c becomes the prerequisite for prog.o.)

Conditional statements

Statements that evaluate conditions, and depending upon the result, include or exclude other statements from the contents of the makefile. More detail is given in the section "Conditional Input," later in this chapter.

Macro definitions

Macro definitions define variables: identifiers associated with blocks of text. Variable values can be created with either =, :=, or define, and appended to with +=. More detail is provided in the later section "Creating and Using Macros."

include *statements*

Similar to the C #include directive, there are three forms:

```
include file [file ...]
-include file [file ...]
sinclude file [file ...]
```

make processes the value of *file* for macro expansions before attempting to open the file. Furthermore, each *file* may be a shell-style wildcard pattern, in which case make expands it to produce a list of files to read.

The second and third forms have the same meaning. They indicate that make should try to include the named lines, but should continue without an error if a file could not be included. The sinclude version provides compatibility with other versions of make.

vpath *statements*

Similar to the VPATH variable, the vpath line has one of the following three forms:

```
vpath pattern directory ...      Set directory list for pattern
vpath pattern                    Clear list for pattern
vpath                            Clear all lists
```

Each *pattern* is similar to those for pattern rules, using % as a wildcard character. When attempting to find a prerequisite, make looks for a vpath rule that matches the prerequisite, and then searches in the directory list (separated by spaces or colons) for a matching file. Directories provided with vpath directives are searched *before* those provided by the VPATH variable.

Command lines

These lines are where you give the commands to actually rebuild those files that are out of date. Commands are grouped below the dependency line and are typed on lines that begin with a tab. If a command is preceded by a hyphen (–), make ignores any error returned. If a command is preceded by an at sign (@), the command line won't echo on the display (unless make is called with -n). Lines beginning with a plus (+) are always executed, even if -n, -q, or -t are used. This also applies to lines containing $(MAKE) or ${MAKE}. Further advice on command lines is given later in this chapter.

Special Dependencies

GNU make has two special features for working with dependencies.

Library dependencies

A dependency of the form -l*NAME* causes make to search for a library file whose name is either lib*NAME*.so or lib*NAME*.a in the standard library directories. This is customizable with the .LIBPATTERNS variable; see the later section "Macros with Special Handling" for more information.

Order-only prerequisites

When a normal prerequisite of a target is out of date, two things happen. First, the prerequisite (and its prerequisites, recursively) are rebuilt as needed. This imposes an *ordering* on the building of targets and prerequisites. Second, after the prerequisites are updated, the target itself is rebuilt using the accompanying commands. Normally, both of these are what's desired.

Sometimes, you just wish to impose an ordering, such that the prerequisites are themselves updated, but the target is not rebuilt by running its rules. Such *order-only* prerequisites are specified in a dependency line by placing them to the right of a vertical bar or pipe symbol, `|`:

```
target: normal-dep1 normal-dep2 | order-dep1 order-dep2
        command
```

Dependency lines need not contain both. I.e., you do not have to provide regular dependencies if there are order-only dependencies as well; just place the `|` right after the colon.

Here is an annotated example of an order-only dependency:

```
$ cat Makefile
all: target                        First target is default, point to real target

prereq0:                           How to make prereq0
        @echo making prereq0
        touch prereq0

prereq1:                           How to make prereq1
        @echo making prereq1
        touch prereq1

prereq2: prereq0                   prereq2 depends on prereq0
        @echo making prereq2
        touch prereq2

target: prereq1 | prereq2          How to make target
        @echo making target
        touch target
```

The order of creation is shown in Figure 16-1.

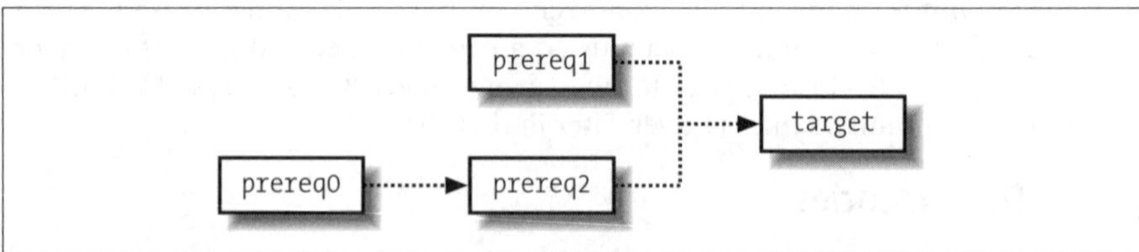

Figure 16-1. The order of creation

And here is the result of running `make`:

```
$ make
making prereq1
touch prereq1
```

```
making prereq0
touch prereq0
making prereq2
touch prereq2
making target
touch target
```

This is normal and as expected. Now, let's update one of the order-only prerequisites and rerun make:

```
$ touch prereq0
$ make
making prereq2
touch prereq2
```

Note that target was *not* rebuilt! Had the dependency on prereq2 been a regular dependency, then target itself would also have been remade.

Conditional Input

Conditional statements allow you to include or exclude specific lines based on some condition. The condition can be that a macro is or is not defined, or that the value of a macro is or is not equal to a particular string. The equivalence/nonequivalence tests provide three different ways of quoting the values. Conditionals may have an optional "else" part; i.e., lines that are used when the condition is *not* true. The general form is as follows:

```
ifXXX test
    lines to include if true
[ else
    lines to include if false ]
endif
```

(The square brackets indicate optional parts of the construct; they are not to be entered literally.) Actual tests are as follows:

Condition	Meaning
ifdef *macroname*	True if *macroname* is a macro that has been given a value.
ifndef *macroname*	True if *macroname* is a macro that has *not* been given a value.
ifeq (*v1*,*v2*) ifeq '*v1*' '*v2*' ifeq "*v1*" "*v2*"	True if values *v1* and *v2* are equal.
ifneq (*v1*,*v2*) ifneq '*v1*' '*v2*' ifneq "*v1*" "*v2*"	True if values *v1* and *v2* are not equal.

For example:

```
whizprog.o: whizprog.c
ifeq($(ARCH),ENIAC)      # Serious retrocomputing in progess!
        $(CC) $(CFLAGS) $(ENIACFLAGS) -c $< -o $@
else
        $(CC) $(CFLAGS) -c $< -o $@
endif
```

Macros

This section summarizes creating and using macros, internal macros, macro modifiers, macros with special handling, and text manipulation with macros and functions.

Creating and Using Macros

Macros (often called *variables*) are like variables in a programming language. In `make`, they are most similar to variables in the shell language, having string values that can be assigned, referenced, and compared.

Defining macros

GNU `make` provides multiple ways to define macros. The different mechanisms affect how `make` treats the value being assigned. This in turn affects how the value is treated when the macro's value is retrieved, or *referenced*. GNU `make` defines two types of variables, called *recursively expanded variables* and *simply expanded variables*, respectively. The various macro assignment forms are as follows:

name = *value*
: Create a recursively expanded variable. The value of *name* is the *verbatim text* on the right side of the `=`. If this value contains any references to other variable values, those values are retrieved and expanded when the original variable is referenced. For example:

```
bar = v1
foo = $(bar)          Value of bar retrieved when foo's value is referenced
...
x = $(foo)            x is assigned 'v1'
bar = v2
y = $(foo)            y is assigned 'v2'
```

name := *value*
: Create a simply expanded variable. The *value* is expanded completely, immediately at the time of the assignment. Any variable references in *value* are expanded then and there. For example:

```
bar = v1
foo := $(bar)         foo is assigned 'v1'
x = $(foo)            x is assigned 'v1'
bar = v2
y = $(foo)            y is still assigned 'v1'
```

A significant advantage of simply expanded variables is that they work like variables in most programming languages, allowing you to use their values in assignments to themselves:

```
x := $(x) other stuff
```

name += *value*
: Append *value* to the contents of variable *name*. If *name* was never defined, `+=` acts like `=`, creating a recursively defined variable. Otherwise, the result of `+=` depends upon the type of *name*. If *name* was defined with `=`, then *value* is

appended literally to the contents of *name*. However, if *name* was defined with `:=`, then `make` completely expands *value* before appending it to the contents of *name*.

name `?=` *value*
: Create recursively expanded variable *name* with value *value* only if *name* is not defined. Note that a variable that has been given an empty value is still considered to be defined.

```
define name
 ...
endef
```

Define a recursively expanded variable, similar to `=`. However, using `define`, you can give a macro a value that contains one or more newlines. This is not possible with the other assignment forms (`=`, `:=`, `+=`, `?=`).

Macro values

Macro values are retrieved by prefixing the macro name with a `$`. A plain `$` is enough for macros whose names are a single character, such as `$<` and `$@`. However, macro names of two or more characters must be enclosed in parentheses and preceded by a `$`. For example, `$(CC)`, `$(CPP)`, and so on.

Although it was not documented, the original V7 Unix version of `make` allowed the use of curly braces instead of parentheses: `${CC}`, `${RM}`, and so on.* All Unix versions and GNU `make` support this as well, and it is included in POSIX. This usage was particularly common in makefiles in the BSD distributions. There is no real reason to prefer one over the other, although long-time Unix programmers may prefer the parentheses form, since that is what was originally documented.

Exporting macros

By default, `make` exports variables to subprocesses only if those variables were already in the environment or if they were defined on the command line. Furthermore, only variables whose names contain just letters, digits, and underscores are exported, as many shells cannot handle environment variables with punctuation characters in their names. You can use the `export` directive to control exporting of specific variables, or all variables. The `unexport` directive indicates that a particular variable should *not* be exported; it cancels the effect of a previous `export` command. The command forms are as follows:

`export`
: By itself, the `export` directive causes `make` to export all alphanumerically named variables to the environment (where underscore counts as a letter too).

`export` *var*
: Export variable *var* to the environment. The variable will be exported even if its name contains nonalphanumeric characters.

* See the function `subst()` in *http://minnie.tuhs.org/UnixTree/V7/usr/src/cmd/make/misc.c.html*.

`export` *var* `=` *value*
`export` *var* `:=` *value*
`export` *var* `+=` *value*
`export` *var* `?` *value*

Perform the kind of assignment indicated by the given operator (as described earlier), and then export the variable to the environment.

`unexport` *var*

Do not export variable *var* to the environment. Cancels a previous `export` of *var* (for example, from a separate, included makefile).

Overriding command-line macros

Normally, when a macro is defined on the command line, the given value is used, and any value assigned to the macro within the makefile is ignored. Occasionally, you may wish to force a variable to have a certain value, or to append a value to a variable, no matter what value was given on the command line. This is the job of the `override` directive.

`override` *var* `=` *value*
`override` *var* `:=` *value*
`override` *var* `+=` *value*
`override` *var* `?` *value*
`override define` *name*
`...`
`endef`

Perform the kind of assignment indicated by the given operator (as described earlier), and then export the variable to the environment.

The example given in the GNU `make` documentation, *GNU Make: A Program for Directing Recompilation*, is forcing `CFLAGS` to always contain the -g option:

```
override CFLAGS += -g
```

Internal Macros

$? — The list of prerequisites that have been changed more recently than the current target. Can be used only in normal makefile entries—not suffix rules.

$@ — The name of the current target, except in makefile entries for making libraries, where it becomes the library name. (For `libguide.a(dontpanic.o)`, `$@` is `libguide.a`). Can be used both in normal makefile entries and in suffix rules.

$$@ — The name of the current target. Can be used only to the right of the colon in dependency lines. This is provided only for compatibility with System V `make`; its use is not recommended.

$< — The name of the current prerequisite that has been modified more recently than the current target.

$* — The name—without the suffix—of the current prerequisite that has been modified more recently than the current target. Should be used only in implicit rules or static pattern rules.

$% — The name of the corresponding `.o` file when the current target is a library module. (For `libguide.a(dontpanic.o)`, `$%` is `dontpanic.o`). Can be used both in normal makefile entries and in suffix rules.

$^ The list of prerequisites for the current target. For archive members, only the member name is listed. Even if a prerequisite appears multiple times in a dependency list for a target, it only appears once in the value of $^.

$+ Like $^, but prerequisites that appear multiple times in a dependency list for a target are repeated. This is most useful for libraries, since multiple dependencies upon a library can make sense and be useful.

$$ A literal $ for use in rule command lines: for example, when referencing shell variables in the environment or within a loop.

$| The order-only prerequisites for the current target.

Macro Modifiers

Macro modifiers may be applied to the built-in internal macros listed earlier, except for $$.

D The directory portion of any internal macro name. Valid uses are:

```
$(%D)     $(@D)
$(*D)     $$(@D)
$(<D)     $(^D)
$(?D)     @(+D)
```

F The file portion of any internal macro name. Valid uses are:

```
$(%F)     $(@F)
$(*F)     $$(@F)
$(<F)     $(^F)
$(?F)     @(+F)
```

Macros with Special Handling

`CURDIR`	The current working directory. Set by `make` but not used by it, for use in makefiles.
`.LIBPATTERNS`	Used for finding link library names as prerequisites of the form `-l`*`name`*. For each such prerequisite, `make` searches in the current directory, directories matching any `vpath` directives, directories named by the `VPATH` variable, `/lib`, `/usr/lib`, and *`prefix`*`/lib`, where *prefix* is the installation directory for GNU `make` (normally `/usr/local`). The default value of `.LIBPATTERNS` is `lib%.so lib%.a`. Thus `make` first searches for a shared library file, and then for a regular archive library.
`MAKE`	The full pathname used to invoke `make`. It is special because command lines containing the string `$(MAKE)` or `${MAKE}` are always executed, even when any of the `-n`, `-q`, or `-t` options are used.
`MAKECMDGOALS`	The targets given to `make` on the command line.
`MAKEFILE_LIST`	A list of makefiles read so far. The rightmost entry in the list is the name of the makefile currently being read.
`MAKEFILES`	Environment variable: `make` reads the whitespace-separated list of files named in it before reading any other makefiles.
`MAKEFLAGS`	Contains the flags inherited in the environment variable MAKEFLAGS, plus any command-line options. Used to pass the flags to subsequent invocations of `make`, usually via command lines in a makefile entry that contain `$(MAKE)`.
`MAKELEVEL`	The depth of recursion (sub-`make` invocation). Primarily for use in conditional statements so that a makefile can act in one way as the top-level makefile and in another way if invoked by another `make`.

MAKOVERRIDES	A list of the command-line variable definitions. MAKEFLAGS refers to this variable. By setting it to the empty string: `MAKEOVERRIDES =` You can pass down the command-line options to sub-makes but avoid passing down the variable assignments.
MAKESHELL	For MS-DOS only, the shell make should use for running commands.

MFLAGS	Similar to MAKEFLAGS, this variable is set for compatibility with other versions of make. It contains the same options as in MAKEFLAGS, but not the variable settings. It was designed for explicit use on command lines that invoke make. For example:
	`mylib:`
	`        cd mylib && $(MAKE) $(MFLAGS)`
	The use of MAKEFLAGS is preferred.

SHELL	Sets the shell that interprets commands. If this macro isn't defined, the default is /bin/sh. On MS-DOS, if SHELL not set, the value of COMSPEC is used; see also the MAKESHELL variable, earlier in this list.
SUFFIXES	The default list of suffixes, before make reads and processes makefiles.
.VARIABLES	A list of all variables defined in all makefiles read up to the point that this variable is referenced.
VPATH	Specifies a list of directories to search for prerequisites when not found in the current directory. Directories in the list should be separated with spaces or colons.

Text Manipulation with Macros and Functions

Standard versions of make provide a limited text manipulation facility:

`$(`*macro*`:`*s1*`=`*s2*`)`
: Evaluates to the current definition of `$(`*macro*`)`, after substituting the string *s2* for every occurrence of *s1* that occurs either immediately before a blank or tab, or at the end of the macro definition.

GNU make supports this for compatibility with Unix make and the POSIX standard. However, GNU make goes *far* beyond simple text substitution, providing a host of *functions* for text manipulation. The following list provides a brief description of each function.

`$(addprefix` *prefix*`,` *names* `...)`
: Generates a new list, created by prepending *prefix* to each of the *names*.

`$(addsuffix` *suffix*`,` *names* `...)`
: Generates a new list, created by appending *suffix* to each of the *names*.

`$(basename` *names* `...)`
: Returns a list of the *basename* of each of the *names*. The basename is the text up to but not including the final period.

`$(call` *var*`,` *param*`, ...)`
: The call function allows you to treat the value of a variable as a procedure. *var* is the *name* of a variable, not a variable reference. The *params* are assigned to temporary variables that may be referenced as `$(1)`, `$(2)`, and so on. `$(0)` will be the name of the variable. The value of *var* should reference the temporary values. The result of call is the result of evaluating *var* in this way. If *var* names a built-in function, that function is always called, even if a

make variable of the same name exists. Finally, `call` may be used recursively; each invocation gets its own `$(1)`, `$(2)`, and so on.

`$(dir` *`names ...`*`)`
: Returns a list of the *directory part* of each of the *names*. The directory part is all text, up to and including the final `/` character. If there is no `/`, the two characters `./` are used.

`$(error` *`text ...`*`)`
: Causes make to produce a fatal error message consisting of *text*.

`$(filter` *`pattern ..., text`*`)`
: Chooses the words in *text* that match any *pattern*. Patterns are written using `%`, as for the `patsubst` function.

`$(filter-out` *`pattern ..., text`*`)`
: Like `filter`, but selects the words that do *not* match the patterns.

`$(findstring` *`find, text`*`)`
: Searches *text* for an instance of *find*. If found, the result is *find*; otherwise, it's the empty string.

`$(firstword` *`names ...`*`)`
: Returns the first word in *names*.

`$(foreach` *`var, words, text`*`)`
: This function is similar to the `for` loop in the shell. It expands *var* and *words*, first. The result of expanding *var* names a macro. make then loops, setting *var* to each word in *words*, and then evaluating *text*. The result is the concatenation of all the iterations. The *text* should contain a reference to the variable for this to work correctly.

  If *var* is defined before the `foreach` is evaluated, it maintains the same value it had after the evaluation. If it was undefined before the `foreach`, it remains undefined afterwords. In effect, `foreach` creates a temporary, private variable named *var*.

`$(if` *`condition, then-text`*`[,` *`else-text`*`])`
: The *condition* is evaluated. If, after removing leading and trailing whitespace, the result is not empty, the condition is considered to be true, and the result of `if` is the expansion of the *then-text*. Otherwise, the condition is considered to be false, and the result is the expansion of *else-text*, if any. If there's no *else-text*, then a false condition produces the empty string. Only one or the other of *then-text* and *else-text* is evaluated.

`$(join` *`list1, list2`*`)`
: Produces a new list where the first element is the concatenation of the first elements in *list1* and *list2*, the second element is the concatenation of the second elements in *list1* and *list2*, and so on.

`$(notdir` *`names ...`*`)`
: Returns a list of the nondirectory part of each of the *names*. The nondirectory part is all the text after the final `/`, if any. If not, it's the entire *name*.

`$(origin variable)`
: Returns a string describing the origin of *variable*. Here, *variable* is a variable name (`foo`), not a variable reference (`$(foo)`). Possible return values are one of the following:

`automatic`	The variable is an automatic variable for use in the commands of rules, such as `$*` and `$@`.
`command line`	The variable was defined on the command line.
`default`	The variable is one of those defined by `make`'s built-in rules, such as `CC`.
`environment`	The variable was defined in the environment, and `-e` was *not* used.
`environment override`	The variable was defined in the environment, and `-e` *was* used.
`file`	The variable was defined in a makefile.
`override`	The variable was defined with an `override` command. See the earlier section "Overriding command-line macros."
`undefined`	The variable was never given a value.

`$(patsubst pattern, replacement, text)`
: Replaces words in *text* that match *pattern* with *replacement*. The *pattern* should use a `%` as a wildcard character. In *replacement*, a `%` acts as the placeholder for the text that matched the `%` in *pattern*. This is a general form of string substitution. For example, the traditional `OBJS = $(SRCS:.c=.o)` could instead be written `OBJS = $(patsubst %.c, %.o, $(SRCS))`.

`$(shell command)`
: Runs the shell command *command* and returns the output. `make` converts newlines in the output into spaces and removes trailing newlines. This is similar to \`...\` in the shell.

`$(sort list)`
: Returns a sorted copy of the words in *list*, with duplicates removed. Each word is separated from the next by a single space.

`$(subst from, to, text)`
: Replaces every instance of *from* in *text* with *to*.

`$(suffix names ...)`
: Returns a list of the suffixes of each *name*. The suffix is the final period and any following text. Returns an empty string for a *name* without a period.

`$(strip string)`
: Removes leading and trailing whitespace from *string* and converts internal runs of whitespace into single spaces. This is especially useful in conjunction with conditionals.

`$(warning text ...)`
: Causes `make` to produce a warning message consisting of *text*.

`$(wildcard pattern ...)`
: Creates a space-separated list of filenames that match the shell pattern *pattern*. (Note! Not a `make`-style `%` pattern.)

`$(word n, text)`
: Returns the *n*th word of *text*, counting from one.

`$(wordlist start, end, text)`
: Creates a new list consisting of the words *start* to *end* in *text*. Counting starts at one.

`$(words text)`
: Returns the number of words in *text*.

Special Target Names

`.DEFAULT:`	Commands associated with this target are executed if `make` can't find any makefile entries or suffix rules with which to build a requested target.
`.DELETE_ON_ERROR:`	If this target appears in a makefile, then for any target that `make` is rebuilding, if its command(s) exit with a nonzero status, `make` deletes the target.
`.EXPORT_ALL_VARIABLES:`	The mere existence of this target causes `make` to export all variables to child processes.
`.IGNORE:`	With prerequisites, ignore problems just for those files. For historical compatibility, with no prerequisites, ignore error returns from all commands. This is the same as the `-i` option.
`.INTERMEDIATE:`	Prerequisites for this target are treated as intermediate files, even if they are mentioned explicitly in other rules. (An intermediate file is one that needs to be built "along the way" to the real target. For example, making a `.c` file from a `.y` file, in order to create a `.o` object file. The `.c` file is an intermediate file.) This prevents them from being re-created, unless one of their prerequisites is out of date.
`.LOW_RESOLUTION_TIME:`	`make` notes that prerequisites for this target are updated by commands that only create low resolution timestamps (one second granularity). For such targets, if their modification time starts at the same second as the modification time of a prerequisite, `make` does not try to compare the sub-second time values, and does not treat the file as being out of date.
`.NOTPARALLEL:`	Prerequisites for this target are ignored. Its existence in a makefile overrides any `-j` option, forcing all commands to run serially. Recursive `make` invocations may still run jobs in parallel, unless their makefiles also contain this target.
`.POSIX:`	When this target exists, changing the `MAKEOVERRIDES` variable does *not* affect the `MAKEFLAGS` variable. (This is a rather specialized case.) This target also disables the special treatment of `$$@`, `$$(@D)`, and `$$(@F)`.
`.PHONY:`	Prerequisites for this target are marked as "phony." I.e., `make` always executes their rules, even if a file by the same name exists.
`.PRECIOUS:`	Files you specify for this target are not removed when you send a signal (such as interrupt) that aborts `make`, or when a command line in your makefile returns an error.
`.SECONDARY:`	Prerequisites of this target are treated like intermediate files, except that they are never automatically removed. With no prerequisites, all targets are treated as secondary.
`.SILENT:`	When given prerequisites, `make` will not print the commands for those prerequisites when they are rebuilt. Otherwise, for historical compatibility, when this target has no prerequisites, `make` executes all commands silently, which is the same as the `-s` option.
`.SUFFIXES:`	Suffixes associated with this target are meaningful in suffix rules. If no suffixes are listed, the existing suffix rules are effectively "turned off."

Writing Command Lines

Writing good, portable makefile files is a bit of an art. Skill comes with practice and experience. Here are some tips to get you started:

- Depending upon your locale, naming your file `Makefile` instead of `makefile` can cause it to be listed first with `ls`. This makes it easier to find in a directory with many files.
- Remember that command lines must start with a leading tab character. You cannot just indent the line with spaces, even eight spaces. If you use spaces, `make` exits with an unhelpful message about a "missing separator."
- Remember that `$` is special to `make`. To get a literal `$` into your command lines, use `$$`. This is particularly important if you want to access an environment variable that isn't a `make` macro. Also, if you wish to use the shell's `$$` for the current process ID, you have to type it as `$$$$`.
- Write multiline shell statements, such as shell conditionals and loops, with trailing semicolons and a trailing backslash:

  ```
  if [ -f specfile ] ; then \
  ... ; \
  else \
  ... ; \
  fi
  ```

  Note that the shell keywords `then` and `else` don't need the semicolon. (What happens is that `make` passes the backslashes and the newlines to the shell. The escaped newlines are not syntactically important, so the semicolons are needed to separate the different parts of the command. This can be confusing. If you use a semicolon where you would normally put a newline in a shell script, things should work correctly.)
- Remember that each line is run in a separate shell. This means that commands that change the shell's environment (such as `cd`) are ineffective across multiple lines. The correct way to write such commands is to keep the commands on the same line, separated with a semicolon. In the particular case of `cd`, separate the commands with `&&` in case the subdirectory doesn't exist or can't be changed to:

  ```
  cd subdir && $(MAKE)
  ...
  PATH=special-path-value ; export PATH ; $(MAKE)
  ```
- For guaranteed portability, always set `SHELL` to `/bin/sh`. Some versions of `make` use whatever value is in the environment for `SHELL`, unless it is explicitly set in the makefile.
- Use macros for standard commands. `make` already helps out with this, providing macros such as `$(CC)`, `$(YACC)`, and so on.
- When removing files, start your command line with `-$(RM)` instead of `$(RM)`. (The – causes `make` to ignore the exit status of the command.) This way, if the file you were trying to remove doesn't exist, and `rm` exits with an error, `make` can keep going.

- When running subsidiary invocations of make, typically in subdirectories of your main program tree, always use $(MAKE), and not make. Lines that contain $(MAKE) are always executed, even if -n has been provided, allowing you to test out a whole hierarchy of makefiles. This does not happen for lines that invoke make directly.
- Often, it is convenient to organize a large software project into subprojects, with each one having a subdirectory. The top-level makefile then just invokes make in each subdirectory. Here's the way to do it:

```
SUBDIRS = proj1 proj2 proj3
...
projects: $(SUBDIRS)
        for i in $(SUBDIRS); \
        do \
                echo ====== Making in $$i ; \
                ( cd $$i && $(MAKE) $(MAKEFLAGS) $@ ) ; \
        done
```

make

17
The GDB Debugger

The GNU Debugger, GDB, is the standard debugger on GNU/Linux and BSD systems, and can be used on just about any Unix system with a C compiler and at least one of several well-known object file formats. It can be used on other kinds of systems as well. It has a very rich feature set, making it the preferred debugger of many developers the world over.

This chapter covers the following topics:

- Conceptual overview
- Command-line syntax
- Initialization files
- GDB expressions
- The GDB text user interface
- Group listing of GDB commands
- Summary of `set` and `show` commands
- Summary of `info` command
- Alphabetical summary of GDB commands

For more information, see *Debugging with GDB: The GNU Source-Level Debugger*, listed in the Bibliography.

Conceptual Overview

A *debugger* is a program that lets you run a second program, which we will call the *debuggee*. The debugger lets you examine and change the state of the debuggee, and control its execution. In particular, you can *single-step* the program, executing one statement or instruction at a time, in order to watch the program's behavior.

Debuggers come in two flavors: *instruction-level debuggers*, which work at the level of machine instructions, and *source-level debuggers*, which operate in terms of your program's source code and programming language. The latter are considerably easier to use, and usually can do machine-level debugging if necessary. GDB is a source level debugger; it is probably the most widely applicable debugger (portable to the largest number of architectures) of any current debugger.

GDB itself provides two user interfaces: the traditional command-line interface (CLI) and a text user interface (TUI). The latter is meant for regular terminals or terminal emulators, dividing the screen into separate "windows" for the display of source code, register values, and so on.

GDB provides support for debugging programs written in C, C++, Objective C, Java,* and Fortran. It provides partial support for Modula-2 programs compiled with the GNU Modula-2 compiler and for Ada programs compiled with the GNU Ada Translator, GNAT. GDB provides some minimal support for debugging Pascal programs. The Chill language is no longer supported.

When working with C++ and Objective C, GDB provides *name demangling*. C++ and Objective C encode overloaded procedure names into a unique "mangled" name that represents the procedure's return type, argument types, and class membership. This ensures so-called *type-safe linkage*. There are different methods for name mangling, thus GDB allows you to select among a set of supported methods, besides just automatically demangling names in displays.

If your program is compiled with GCC (the GNU Compiler Collection), using the `-g3` and `-gdwarf-2` options, GDB understands references to C preprocessor macros. This is particularly helpful for code using macros to simplify complicated `struct` and `union` members. GDB itself also has partial support for expanding preprocessor macros, with more support planned.

GDB allows you to specify several different kinds of files when doing debugging:

- The *exec file* is the executable program to be debugged—i.e., your program.
- The optional *core file* is a memory dump generated by the program when it dies; this is used, together with the exec file, for post-mortem debugging. Core files are usually named `core` on commercial Unix systems. On BSD systems, they are named *program*`.core`. On GNU/Linux systems, they are named `core.`*PID*, where *PID* represents the process ID number. This lets you keep multiple core dumps, if necessary.
- The *symbol file* is a separate file from which GDB can read symbol information: information describing variable names, types, sizes, and locations in the executable file. GDB, not the compiler, creates these files if necessary. Symbol files are rather esoteric; they're not necessary for run-of-the-mill debugging.

* GDB can only debug Java programs that have been compiled to native machine code with GJC, the GNU Java compiler (part of GCC, the GNU Compiler Collection).

There are different ways to stop your program:

- A *breakpoint* specifies that execution should stop at a particular source code location.
- A *watchpoint* indicates that execution should stop when a particular memory location changes value. The location can be specified either as a regular variable name or via an expression (such as one involving pointers). If hardware assistance for watchpoints is available, GDB uses it, making the cost of using watchpoints small. If it is not available, GDB uses virtual memory techniques, if possible, to implement watchpoints. This also keeps the cost down. Otherwise, GDB implements watchpoints in software by single-stepping the program (executing one instruction at a time).
- A *catchpoint* specifies that execution should stop when a particular event occurs.

The GDB documentation and command set often use the word *breakpoint* as a generic term to mean all three kinds of program stoppers. In particular, you use the same commands to enable, disable, and remove all three.

GDB applies different statuses to breakpoints (and watchpoints and catchpoints). They may be *enabled*, which means that the program stops when the breakpoint is hit (or *fires*), *disabled*, which means that GDB keeps track of them but that they don't affect execution, or *deleted*, which means that GDB forgets about them completely. As a special case, breakpoints can be enabled only once. Such a breakpoint stops execution when it is encountered, then becomes disabled (but not forgotten).

Breakpoints may have conditions associated with them. When execution reaches the breakpoint, GDB checks the condition, stopping the program only if the condition is true.

Breakpoints may also have an *ignore count*, which is a count of how many times GDB should ignore the breakpoint when it's reached. As long as a breakpoint's ignore count is nonzero, GDB does not bother checking any condition associated with the breakpoint.

Perhaps the most fundamental concept for working with GDB is that of the *frame*. This is short for *stack frame*, a term from the compiler field. A stack frame is the collection of information needed for each separate function invocation. It contains the function's parameters and local variables, as well as *linkage* information indicating where return values should be placed and the location the function should return to. GDB assigns numbers to frames, starting at `0` and going up. Frame `0` is the innermost frame, i.e., the function most recently called.

GDB uses the *readline* library, as does the Bash shell, to provide command history, command completion, and interactive editing of the command line. Both Emacs and `vi` style editing commands are available.

Finally, GDB has many features of a programming language. You can define your own variables and apply common programming language operators to them. You can also define your own commands. Additionally, you can define special *hook* commands, user-defined commands that GDB executes before or after running a built-in command. (See the entry for **define** in the section "Alphabetical Summary of GDB Commands" for the details.) You can also create `while` loops and test conditions with `if` ... `else` ... `end`.

GDB is typically used to debug programs on the same machine (*host*) on which it's running. GDB can also be configured for *cross-debugging*, i.e., controlling a remote debuggee with a possibly different machine architecture (the *target*). Remote targets are usually connected to the host via a serial port or a network connection. Such use is rather esoteric and is therefore not covered here. See the GDB documentation for the full details.

Source Code Locations

GDB is the default debugger on GNU/Linux and BSD systems. It is usable on just about any modern Unix system, though, as well as many older ones. (However, if your system is really ancient, you may need to fall back to an older version of GDB.) Besides the command line and text user interfaces built in to GDB, there are other programs that provide GUI debuggers. Two of the more popular ones are `ddd` (the Data Display Debugger) and Insight. Both of these use GDB to provide the underlying debugging functionality. Source code URLs for these programs are listed in the following table.

Debugger	Location
`ddd`	*ftp://ftp.gnu.org/gnu/ddd/*
GDB	*ftp://ftp.gnu.org/gnu/gdb/*
Insight	*http://sources.redhat.com/insight/*

Command-Line Syntax

GDB is invoked as follows:

```
gdb [options] [executable [corefile-or-PID]]
gdb [options] --args executable [program args ...]
```

The `gdbtui` command is equivalent to `gdb --tui`; it invokes GDB with the Text User Interface. The TUI is described in the later section "The GDB Text User Interface."

GDB has both traditional short options and GNU-style long options. Long options may start with either one or two hyphens. The command-line options are as follows.

`--args`
: Pass on arguments after *executable* to the program being debugged.

`--async`, `--noasync`
: Enable/disable the asynchronous version of the command-line interface.

`-b` *baudrate*, `--baud` *baudrate*
: Set the serial port baud rate used for remote debugging.

`--batch`
: Process options and then exit.

`--cd` *dir*
: Change current directory to *dir*.

`-c` *file*, `--core` *file*
: Analyze the core dump *file*.

`-d` *dir*, `--directory` *dir*
: Search for source files in *dir*.

`-e` *file*, `--exec` *file*
: Use *file* as the executable.

`-f`, `--fullname`
: Output information used by the Emacs-GDB interface.

`--help`
: Print a usage and option summary and then exit.

`--interpreter` *interp*
: Select a specific interpreter/user interface. The command-line interface is the default, although there are other interfaces for use by frontend programs.

`-n`, `--nx`
: Do not read the `.gdbinit` file.

`-nw`, `--nowindows`
: Force the use of the command-line interface, even if a windows interface is available.

`-p` *pidnum*, `-c` *pidnum*, `--pid` *pidnum*
: Attach to running process *pidnum*.

`-q`, `--quiet`, `--silent`
: Do not print the version number on startup.

`-r`, `--readnow`
: Fully read symbol files on first access.

`-s` *file*, `--symbols` *file*
: Read symbols from *file*.

`--se` *file*
: Use *file* for both the symbol file and the executable file.

`--statistics`
: Print statistics about CPU time and memory usage after each command finishes.

`-t` *device*, `--tty` *device*
: Use *device* for input/output by the program being debugged.

`--tui`
: Use the Terminal User Interface (TUI).

`-x` *file*, `--command` *file*
: Execute GDB commands from *file*.

--version
: Print version information and then exit.

-w, --windows
: Force the use of a window interface if there is one.

--write
: Allow writing into the executable and core files.

Initialization Files

Two files are used to initialize GDB and the *readline* library, respectively.

The .gdbinit File

At startup, GDB reads its *initialization file*. This is a file of commands, such as option settings, that you tell GDB to run every time it starts up. The initialization file is named `.gdbinit` on Unix (BSD, Linux, etc.) systems. Some MS-Windows versions of GDB use `gdb.ini` instead. Empty lines (they do nothing) are allowed, and comments in initialization files start with a `#` and continue to the end of the line. GDB executes commands from initialization files and from the command line in the following order:

1. Commands in `$HOME/.gdbinit`. This acts as a "global" initialization; settings that should always be used go here.
2. Command-line options and operands.
3. Commands in `./.gdbinit`. This allows for option settings that apply to a particular program by keeping the file in the same directory as the program's source code.
4. Command files specified with the `-x` option.

You may use the `-nx` option to make GDB skip the execution of the initialization files.

The .inputrc File

Just like the Bash shell (see Chapter 4), GDB uses the *readline* library to provide command-line history and editing. You may use either `vi`- or Emacs-style commands for editing your command line. The *readline* library reads the file `~/.inputrc` to initialize its settings and options. The details are beyond the scope of this book; see the Bash and GDB documentation or the online Info system for the full story. Here is a sample `.inputrc` file:

```
set editing-mode vi                  Use vi editor commands
set horizontal-scroll-mode On        Scroll line left/right as cursor moves along it
control-h: backward-delete-char      Use ^H as backspace character
set comment-begin #                  For Bash, # starts comments
set expand-tilde On                  Expand ~ notation
"\C-r": redraw-current-line          Make ^R redraw the current input line
```

GDB Expressions

GDB can be thought of as a specialized programming language. It has variables and operators similar to those of C, and special features for debugging. This section looks at the different kinds of expressions that GDB understands.

The Value History

Every time you print a value with `print`, GDB saves the value in the *value history*. You can reference these saved values by their numeric place in the history, preceded with a `$`. GDB reminds you of this by printing `$n = val`. For example:

```
$ gdb whizprog
...
(gdb) print stopped_early
$1 = 0
(gdb) print whiny_users
$2 = TRUE
(gdb)
```

A plain `$` refers to the most recent value in the value history. This can save considerable typing. If you've just looked at a pointer variable, you can use:

```
(gdb) print *$
```

to print the contents of whatever the pointer is pointing to. `$$` refers to the next most recent value in the history, and `$$n` refers to the value *n* places from the end. (Thus, `$n` counts from the beginning, while `$$n` counts from the end.)

You can use `show values` to see the values in the history. Whenever GDB reloads the executable (rereads the symbol table), it clears the value history. This is because the value history may have contained pointers into the symbol table and such pointers become invalid when the symbol table is reloaded.

Convenience Variables and Machine Registers

GDB lets you create *convenience variables*. These are variables you can use to store values as you need them. Their names begin with a `$` and consist of alphanumeric characters and underscores. They should start with a letter or underscore. (Note that values in the value history have names that are numeric.) You might want to use a convenience variable as an array index:

```
(gdb) set $j = 0
(gdb) print data[$j++]
```

After these two commands, simply hitting the ENTER key repeats the last command, stepping through the array one element at a time.

GDB predefines several convenience variables. It also enables you to access the machine registers using predefined register names. Register names vary with machine architecture, of course, but there are four predefined registers available on every architecture. The following list summarizes the convenience variables and predefined registers. The last four entries in the list are the registers that are always available.

`$`	The most recent value in the value history.
`$`*n*	Item *n* in the value history.
`$$`	The next to last item in the value history.
`$$`*n*	Item *n* in the value history, counting from the end.
`$_`	The address last printed by the x command.
`$__`	The *contents* of the address last printed by the x command.
`$_exitcode`	The exit status that the debuggee returned when it exited.
`$bpnum`	The breakpoint number of the most recently set breakpoint.
`$cdir`	The compilation directory for the current source file, if one is recorded in the object file.
`$cwd`	The current working directory.
`$fp`	The frame pointer register.
`$pc`	The program counter register.
`$ps`	The processor status register.
`$sp`	The stack pointer register.

Special Expressions

GDB understands the syntax (types, operators, operator precedence) of the language being debugged. You can use the same syntax to enter expressions as you do to modify GDB convenience variables (such `$i++`). GDB also understands several special syntaxes that let you do things that are not in the target language, as follows:

Array constants
: You can create an array constant in the debuggee's memory by enclosing a list of element values in braces. For example, `{ 1, 2, 3, 42, 57 }`.

Array operator
: The `@` array operator prints all the elements of an array up to a given subscript. For example, if your program uses `malloc()` to allocate memory:

```
double *vals = malloc(count * sizeof(double));
```

you can print a single element using regular subscripting:

```
(gdb) print vals[3]
$1 = 9
```

However, you can access `vals[0]` through `vals[2]` with:

```
(gdb) print *vals@3
$2 = {0, 1, 4}
```

File resolution
: If you use the same variable name in several source files (for example, each one is `static`), you can specify which one you mean using *`file`*`::`*`variable`*. For example:

```
(gdb) print 'main.c'::errcount
$2 = 0
```

It is necessary to put `main.c` in single quotes to avoid ambiguity with the C++ `::` operator.

The GDB Text User Interface

GDB, in its default mode, shows its line-oriented heritage. When single stepping, it displays only one line of source code at a time. Graphical debuggers can show you much more, and indeed many programmers prefer a graphical debugger, if only for this reason. However, recent versions of GDB offer a *Text User Interface* (TUI), which uses the tried-and-true *curses* library to provide several "windows" on a regular terminal or terminal emulator, such as an `xterm`. This can be quite effective, especially since it allows you to do *everything* from the keyboard.

A number of set options and GDB commands are specific to the TUI. These are listed along with the rest of the set options and GDB commands in the later sections "Summary of set and show Commands" and "Alphabetical Summary of GDB Commands."

Unfortunately (as of GDB 6.3), the TUI is still immature; the author could not get several documented features to work. Thus this book doesn't provide detailed coverage of it. However, it should improve over time, and you should continue to evaluate it to see if it meets your needs.

Group Listing of GDB Commands

This section summarizes the GDB commands by task. Esoteric commands, such as those used by GDB's maintainers, or to cross-debug remote systems connected via serial port or a network, have been omitted.

Aliases for Other Commands

Alias	Short for...	Alias	Short for ..	Alias	Short for...
`bt`	`backtrace`	`f`	`frame`	`p`	`print`
`c`	`continue`	`fo`	`forward-search`	`po`	`print-object`
`cont`	`continue`	`gcore`	`generate-core-file`	`r`	`run`
`d`	`delete`	`h`	`help`	`s`	`step`
`dir`	`directory`	`i`	`info`	`share`	`sharedlibrary`
`dis`	`disable`	`l`	`list`	`si`	`stepi`
`do`	`down`	`n`	`next`	`u`	`until`
`e`	`edit`	`ni`	`nexti`	`where`	`backtrace`

Breakpoints

`awatch` Set an expression watchpoint.
`break` Set a breakpoint at a line or function.
`catch` Set a catchpoint to catch an event.
`clear` Clear a given breakpoint.
`commands` Specify commands to run when a breakpoint is reached.
`condition` Supply a condition to a particular breakpoint.
`delete` Delete one more breakpoints or auto-display expressions.

GDB

`disable`	Disable one or more breakpoints.
`enable`	Enable one or more breakpoints.
`hbreak`	Set a hardware assisted breakpoint.
`ignore`	Set the ignore-count of a particular breakpoint.
`rbreak`	Set a breakpoint for all functions matching a regular expression.
`rwatch`	Set a read watchpoint for an expression.
`tbreak`	Set a temporary breakpoint.
`tcatch`	Set a temporary catchpoint.
`thbreak`	Set a temporary hardware assisted breakpoint.
`watch`	Set an expression watchpoint.

Examining Data

`call`	Call a function in the program.
`delete display`	Cancel one or more expressions that have been set to display when the program stops.
`delete mem`	Delete a memory region.
`disable display`	Disable one or more expressions that have been set to display when the program stops.
`disable mem`	Disable a memory region.
`disassemble`	Disassemble a section of memory.
`display`	Print the value of an expression each time the program stops.
`enable display`	Enable one or more expressions that have been set to display when the program stops.
`enable mem`	Enable a memory region.
`inspect`	Same as `print`.
`mem`	Define attributes for a memory region.
`output`	Similar to `print`, but doesn't save the value in history and doesn't print a newline. For scripting.
`print`	Print the value of an expression.
`print-object`	Cause an Objective C object to print information about itself.
`printf`	Print values like the `printf` command.
`ptype`	Print the definition of a given type.
`set`	Evaluate an expression and save the result in a program variable.
`set variable`	Same as `set`, avoids conflict with GDB variables.
`undisplay`	Cancel one or more expressions that have been set to display when the program stops.
`whatis`	Print the data type of an expression.
`x`	Examine memory: `x/`*`fmt address`*. See the entry for **`x`** in the later section "Alphabetical Summary of GDB Commands."

Controlling and Examining Files

`add-symbol-file`
: Add symbols from a dynamically loaded file to GDB's symbol table.

`add-symbol-file-from-memory`
: Load the symbols from a dynamically loaded object file in the debuggee's memory.

`cd`
: Set the current directory for GDB and the debuggee.

`core-file`
: Specify a file to use as the core dump for memory and register contents.

`directory`
: Add a directory to the beginning of the source file search path.

`edit`
: Edit a file or function.

`exec-file`
: Specify a file to use as the executable.

`file`
: Specify the filename of the program to be debugged.

`forward-search`
: Search forward in the current source file for a regular expression, starting at the last line listed.

`generate-core-file`
: Create a core file from the current state of the debuggee.

`list`
: List a function or line.

`nosharedlibrary`
: Unload all shared object library symbols.

`path`
: Add one or more directories to the object file search path.

`pwd`
: Print the current directory.

`reverse-search`
: Search backward in the current source file for a regular expression, starting at the last line listed.

`search`
: Same as `forward-search`.

`section`
: Change the base address of a particular section in the exec file.

`sharedlibrary`
: Load shared object library symbols for files matching a regular expression.

`symbol-file`
: Load symbol table information from a specified executable file.

Running a Program

`advance`	Continue the program up to the given location.
`attach`	Attach to a process or file outside of GDB.
`continue`	Continue the program being debugged.
`detach`	Detach a previously attached process or file.
`finish`	Execute until selected stack frame returns.
`handle`	Specify how to handle a signal.
`interrupt`	Interrupt the execution of the debugged program.
`jump`	Continue program being debugged at specified line or address.

GDB

`kill`	Kill the program being debugged.
`next`	Execute the program's next statement.
`nexti`	Execute the program's next instruction.
`run`	Start the debugged program.
`signal`	Continue the program, giving it a specified signal.
`start`	Run the debugged program until the beginning of the main procedure. Useful for C++ where constructors run before `main()`.
`step`	Step the program until it reaches a different source line. Descends into called functions.
`stepi`	Step exactly one instruction.
`thread`	Switch between threads.
`thread apply`	Apply a command to a list of threads.
`thread apply all`	Apply a command to all threads.
`tty`	Set the terminal for future runs of the debuggee.
`unset environment`	Remove a variable from the debuggee's environment.
`until`	Execute until the program reaches a source line greater than the current one.

Examining the Stack

`backtrace`	Print a backtrace of all stack frames.
`down`	Select and print the stack frame called by the current one.
`frame`	Select and print a stack frame.
`return`	Make selected stack frame return to its caller.
`select-frame`	Select a stack frame without printing anything.
`up`	Select and print the stack frame that called the current one.

Status Inquiries

`info`	General command for showing information about the debuggee.
`macro`	Prefix for commands dealing with C preprocessor macros.
`show`	General command for showing information about the debugger.

Support Facilities

`apropos`	Search for commands matching a regular expression.
`complete`	List the command completions for the rest of the line.
`define`	Define a new command.
`document`	Document a user-defined command.
`dont-repeat`	Don't repeat this command. For use in user-defined commands.
`down-silently`	Same as the `down` command, but doesn't print messages.
`echo`	Print a constant string.
`else`	Provide a list of alternative commands for use with `if`.
`end`	End a list of commands or actions.
`help`	Print list of commands.
`if`	Execute nested commands once if the conditional expression is nonzero.
`make`	Run the `make` program using the rest of the line as arguments.
`quit`	Exit GDB.

`shell`	Execute the rest of the line as a shell command.
`source`	Read commands from a named file.
`up-silently`	Same as the up command, but doesn't print messages.
`while`	Execute nested commands while the conditional expression is nonzero.

Text User Interface Commands

`focus`	Change which window receives the keyboard focus.
`layout`	Change the layout of the windows in use.
`refresh`	Clear and redraw the screen.
`tui reg`	Change which registers are shown in the register window.
`update`	Update the source window.
`winheight`	Change the height of a particular window.

Frequently Used Commands

GDB offers a bewilderingly large number of commands, but most users can get by with just a small handful. Table 17-1 lists the ones that you are likely to use most often.

Table 17-1. The top dozen GDB commands

Command	Purpose	Examples
`backtrace`	Show call trace	`ba`
`break`	Set breakpoint at routine entry or at line number	`b main` `b parser.c:723`
`continue`	Continue from breakpoint	`cont`
`delete`	Remove breakpoint	`d 3`
`finish`	Step until end of routine	`fin`
`info breakpoints`	List current breakpoints	`i br`
`next`	Step to next statement and over routine calls	`ne`
`print`	Print expression	`print 1.0/3.0`
`run`	(Re)run program, optionally with arguments	`ru` `ru -u -o foo < data`
`step`	Step to next statement and into routines	`s`
`x`	Examine memory	`x/s *environ`
`until`	Continue execution until reaching a source line	`until` `until 2367`

Summary of set and show Commands

The set command accepts a large number of different parameters that control GDB's behavior. Many of the accepted parameters are rather esoteric. The show command displays the values of the same parameters as set accepts. This section summarizes the parameters and how they affect GDB.

GDB

For most of the options, set *option* and set *option* on are equivalent; they enable the option. Use set *option* off to disable the option.

annotate

```
set annotate level
show annotate
```

Set the annotation_level variable to *level*. GUI programs that call GDB as a subsidiary process use this variable.

architecture

```
set architecture architecture
show architecture
```

Set the architecture of target to *architecture*. Primarily used in cross-debugging.

args

```
set args
show args
```

Give the debuggee the argument list when you start it. The run command uses this list when it isn't given any arguments. See the entry for **run** in the later section "Alphabetical Summary of GDB Commands."

auto-solib-add

```
set auto-solib-add
show auto-solib-add
```

Automatically load symbols from shared libraries as needed. When set to off, symbols must be loaded manually with the sharedlibrary command.

auto-solib-limit

```
set auto-solib-limit megs
show auto-solib-limit
```

Limit the size of symbols from shared libraries that will be automatically loaded to *megs* megabytes. Not available on all systems.

backtrace

```
set backtrace limit count
show backtrace limit
set backtrace past-main
show backtrace past-main
```

The first syntax limits the number of stack frames shown in a backtrace to *count*. The default is unlimited. The second syntax controls whether GDB shows information about frames that precede the main( ) function. Such *startup* code is usually not of interest, thus the default is off.

breakpoint

```
set breakpoint pending val
show breakpoint pending
```

How GDB should handle breakpoint locations that can't be found (for example, if a shared library has yet to be loaded). Values are `on`, `off`, or `auto`. When *val* is `on`, GDB automatically creates a pending breakpoint. For `auto`, it asks you. For `off`, pending breakpoints are not created.

can-use-hw-watchpoints

```
set can-use-hw-watchpoints value
show can-use-hw-watchpoints
```

If nonzero, GDB uses hardware support for watchpoints, if the system has such support. Otherwise, it doesn't.

case-sensitive

```
set case-sensitive
show case-sensitive
```

Set whether GDB should ignore case when searching for symbols. This variable can be set to `on`, `off`, or `auto`. For `auto` the case sensitivity depends upon the language.

coerce-float-to-double

```
set coerce-float-to-double
show coerce-float-to-double
```

When calling a function that is not prototyped, if this variable is `on`, GDB coerces values of type `float` to type `double`. If the variable is `off`, `float`s are not coerced to `double` and prototyped functions receive `float` values as is.

commands

```
show commands [cmdnum]
show commands +
```

By default, show the last 10 commands in the command history. With a numeric *cmdnum*, show the 10 commands centered around *cmdnum*. The second syntax shows the 10 commands following those just printed.

complaints

```
set complaints limit
show complaints
```

When GDB encounters problems reading in symbol tables, it normally does not complain. By setting this variable, GDB produces up to *limit* complaints about each kind of problem it finds. The default is `0`, which creates no complaints. Use a large number to mean "unlimited."

confirm

```
set confirm
show confirm
```

GDB normally asks for confirmation before certain operations, such as deleting breakpoints. Set this value to `off` to disable confirmation. Do this only if you're really sure that you know what you're doing.

convenience

```
show convenience
```

Print a list of convenience variables used so far, along with their values. Can be abbreviated `show conv`.

copying

```
show copying
```

Display the GNU General Public License (GPL).

cp-abi

```
set cp-abi
show cp-abi
```

The Application Binary Interface (ABI) used for inspecting C++ objects. The default is `auto`, where GDB determines the ABI on its own. Other acceptable values are `gnu-v2` for g++ versions before 3.0, `gnu-v3` for g++ versions 3.0 and later, and `hpaCC` for the HP ANSI C++ compiler.

debug-file-directory

```
set debug-file-directory dir
show debug-file-directory
```

Look in *dir* for separate debugging information files. For use on systems where debugging information is not included in executable files.

demangle-style

```
set demangle-style style
show demangle-style
```

Choose the scheme used to convert a "mangled" name back into the original Objective C or C++ name. Available values for *style* are:

`arm`	Use the algorithm given in *The Annotated C++ Reference Manual* (see the Bibliography). The GDB documentation warns that this setting alone does not allow debugging of code produced by `cfront`.[a]
`auto`	GDB attempts to figure out the demangling style.
`gnu`	Use the same scheme as that of the GNU C++ compiler (g++). This is the default.
`hp`	Use the scheme of HP's ANSI C++ compiler, aCC.
`lucid`	Use the scheme from Lucid's C++ compiler, `lcc`.

[a] In practice this isn't likely to be an issue; `cfront`-based C++ compilers are no longer common.

directories

```
show directories
```

Print the current search path of directories that contain source files.

disassembly-flavor

```
set disassembly-flavor flavor
show disassembly-flavor
```

The current instruction set for printing machine-level instructions. This command is currently defined only for the Intel x86 architecture. The *flavor* is either `intel` or `att`; the default is `att`.

editing

```
set editing
show editing
```

Enable editing of command lines as they are typed.

environment

```
set environment variable[=value]
show environment [variable]
```

Set environment variable *variable* to optional *value* or to the empty string. With no *variable*, show the entire environment. Otherwise, show the value of the given *variable*.

exec-done-display

```
set exec-done-display
show exec-done-display
```

Enable notification of completion for asynchronous execution commands.

extension-language

```
set extension-language .ext lang
show extension-language
```

Associate filename extension *.ext* with programming language *lang*.

follow-fork-mode

```
set follow-fork-mode mode
show follow-fork-mode
```

Choose which process GDB should continue to debug when the debuggee creates a new process. The value of *mode* is `parent` if GDB should follow the parent, or `child` if GDB should follow the child.

gnutarget

```
set gnutarget format
show gnutarget
```

The current file format of the debuggee (core file, executable, `.o` file). The default is `auto`, and is probably best left that way.

height

```
set height count
show height
```

The number of lines GDB thinks are in a page. Use `0` to keep GDB from pausing.

history

```
set history feature
show history feature
```

Control different aspects of GDB's command history. Values and meanings for *feature* are as follows:

`set history expansion, show history expansion`
: Use `csh`-style `!` commands for history operations. The default is `off`.

`set history filename file, show history filename`
: Save the command history to *file*, and restore it from there upon startup. This overrides the default filename, which is taken from the value of the environment variable GDBHISTFILE if it is set. Otherwise, the default filename is `./.gdb_history`.

`set history save, show history save`
: Enable saving/restoring of the command history.

`set history size amount, show history size`
: Limit the number of saved history commands to *amount*.

input-radix

```
set input-radix base
show input-radix
```

The default input radix for entering numbers. Acceptable values for *base* are 8, 10, and 16. The value must be entered unambiguously (leading `0` for octal, leading `0x` or `0X` for hexadecimal), or in the current input radix.

language

```
set language lang
show language
```

Set the source language to *lang*. Normally, GDB is able to determine the source language from information in the executable file.

listsize

```
set listsize count
show listsize
```

The number of source lines GDB lists with the `list` command.

logging

```
set logging
set logging option value
show logging
```

With the usual on and `off` values, `set logging` enables and disables logging of GDB command output. With an *option* and *value*, the particular logging option is set to *value*.

Logging Options

`file`
: The file to which GDB logs command output. The default is `gdb.txt`.

`overwrite`
: If set, overwrite the log file each time. Otherwise GDB appends to it.

`redirect`
: If set, send output to the log file only. The default outputs to both the terminal and the log file.

max-user-call-depth

```
set max-user-call-depth limit
show max-user-call-depth
```

Set the maximum number of recursive calls to a user-defined command to *limit*. When the limit is exceeded, GDB assumes that the command has gone into infinite recursion and aborts with an error.

opaque-type-resolution

```
set opaque-type-resolution
show opaque-type-resolution
```

Resolve opaque `struct/class/union` types when loading symbols. That is, if one file uses a type opaquely (`struct foo` *), find the definition for that type in the file that defines it.

osabi

```
set osabi os-abi-type
show osabi
```

The Operating System/Application Binary Interface of the debuggee. The default is `auto`, which means GDB figures it out automatically. Use this if you need to override GDB's guess.

output-radix

```
set output-radix base
show output-radix
```

The default output radix for displaying numbers. Acceptable values for *base* are 8, 10, and 16. The value must be entered unambiguously (leading `0` for octal, leading `0x` or `0X` for hexadecimal), or in the current input radix.

overload-resolution

```
set overload-resolution
show overload-resolution
```

When calling an overloaded function from GDB, search for a function whose signature matches the types of the arguments.

pagination

```
set pagination
show pagination
```

Enable/disable pagination of output. Default is `on`.

paths

```
show paths
```

Display the current search path for executable programs (the PATH environment variable). This path is also used to find object files.

print

```
set print print-opt
show print print-opt
```

GDB lets you control the printing of many different aspects of the debuggee. Many of these options are enabled by typing either `set print` *`option-name`* or `set print` *`option-name`* `on`. Using `off` instead of `on` disables the particular printing option. You can use `show print` *`option-name`* to see if the option's printing setting is `on` or `off`. The values for *print-opt*, and descriptions of GDB's behavior when a particular *print-opt* is on, are presented in the following list.

`set print address, show print address`
: Include the program counter in stack frame information.

`set print array, show print array`
: Prettyprint arrays. This is easier to read but takes up more space. Default is `off`.

`set print asm-demangle, show print asm-demangle`
: Demangle C++/Objective C names, even in disassembly listings.

`set print demangle, show print demangle`
: Demangle C++/Objective C names in output.

`set print elements` *`count`*`, show print elements`
: Print no more than *count* elements from an array. The default is 200; a value of `0` means "unlimited."

`set print null-stop, show print null-stop`
: Stop printing array elements upon encountering one set to zero (ASCII NUL for character arrays, hence the name). Default is `off`.

`set print object, show print object`
: For a pointer, print the pointed-to object's actual type, which is derived from virtual function table information, instead of the declared type. The default is `off`, which prints the declared type.

`set print pascal_static-members`
`show print pascal_static-members`
Print Pascal static members.

`set print pretty`, `show print pretty`
Prettyprint structures, one element per line, with indentation to convey nesting.

`set print sevenbit-strings, show print sevenbit-strings`
Print 8-bit characters in strings as `\`*nnn*.

`set print static-members, show print static-members`
Print static members when displaying a C++ object.

`set print symbol-filename, show print symbol-filename`
When printing the symbolic form of an address, include the source filename and line number.

`set print union`, `show print union`
Print unions inside structures.

`set print vtbl`, `show print vtbl`
Prettyprint C++ virtual function tables. The default is `off`.

`set print max-symbolic-offset` *max*
`show print max-symbolic-offset`
When displaying addresses, only use the *symbol* + *offset* form if the offset is less than *max*. The default is `0`, which means "unlimited."

prompt

`set prompt` *string*
`show prompt`

Set GDB's prompt to *string*, or show the prompt string. The default prompt is `(gdb)`.

radix

`set radix` *base*
`show radix`

Set the input and output radixes to the same number. Acceptable values for *base* are 8, 10, and 16. The value must be entered unambiguously (leading `0` for octal, leading `0x` or `0X` for hexadecimal), or in the current input radix. See also **input-radix** and **output-radix**.

scheduler-locking

`set scheduler-locking`
`show scheduler-locking`

On some operating systems, control the scheduling of other threads (those not being traced) in the debuggee. The value is one of `on`, `off`, or `step`. If set to `off`, all threads run, with the chance that a different thread could pre-empt the debugger (hit a breakpoint, catch a signal, etc.). When set to `on`, GDB only allows the current thread to run. When set to `step`, the scheduler locks only during single-stepping operations.

GDB

solib-absolute-prefix

```
set solib-absolute-prefix path
show solib-absolute-prefix
```

Use *path* as the prefix for any absolute paths to shared libraries. This is mainly useful for cross-debugging, to find the target's shared libraries when debugging on a host.

solib-search-path

```
set solib-search-path path
show solib-search-path
```

Search the colon separated list of directories in *path* to find a shared library. GDB searches this path after trying `solib-absolute-prefix`. This too is mainly useful for cross-debugging.

step-mode

```
set step-mode
show step-mode
```

Set the mode of the `step` command. By default, `step` does not enter functions that lack debugging information. Setting this variable to `on` causes GDB to enter such functions, allowing you to examine the machine-level instructions.

stop-on-solib-events

```
set stop-on-solib-events
show stop-on-solib-events
```

Stop when a shared library event occurs. The most common such events are the loading and unloading of a shared library.

symbol-reloading

```
set symbol-reloading
show symbol-reloading
```

On systems that support automatic relinking (such as VxWorks), reload the symbol table when an object file has changed.

trust-readonly-sections

```
set trust-readonly-sections
show trust-readonly-sections
```

Believe that read-only sections will remain read-only. This allows GDB to fetch the contents from the object file, instead of from a possibly remote debuggee. This is useful primarily for remote debugging.

tui

```
set tui feature value
show tui feature
```

Set the TUI feature *feature* to *value*.

TUI Features

`set tui active-border-mode` *mode*
`show tui active-border-mode`

Choose/show the *curses* library attribute for the border of the active window. Available choices are `normal`, `standout`, `half`, `half-standout`, `bold`, and `bold-standout`.

`set tui border-kind` *kind*, `show tui border-kind`

Set/show the characters used to draw the border to one of the following:

`acs`	Draw borders using the Alternate Character Set (line drawing characters) if the terminal supports it.
`ascii`	Draw borders using the regular characters +, -, and |.
`space`	Draw borders using space characters.

`set tui border-mode` *mode*, `show tui border-mode`

Choose/show the *curses* library attribute for the border of the other, nonactive windows. Available choices are `normal`, `standout`, `half`, `half-standout`, `bold`, and `bold-standout`.

---

values

`show values [`*valnum*`]`
`show values +`

With no arguments, print the last 10 values in the value history (see the earlier section "The Value History"). With *valnum*, print 10 values centered around that value history item number. With +, print 10 more saved values following the one most recently printed.

---

variable

`set variable` *assignment*

Ensure that *assignment* actually affects a program variable instead of a GDB variable.

---

verbose

`set verbose`
`show verbose`

Enable display of informative messages during long operations. This reassures you that GDB is still alive.

---

version

`show version`

Show the current version of GDB.

---

warranty

`show warranty`

Display the "no warranty" provisions from the GNU General Public License (GPL).

watchdog

```
set watchdog seconds
show watchdog
```

Wait no more than *seconds* seconds for a remote target to finish a low-level stepping or continuation operation. If the timeout expires, GDB reports an error.

width

```
set width numchars
show width
```

Set the number of characters allowed in a line. Use a value of `0` to keep GDB from wrapping long lines.

write

```
set write
show write
```

Allow GDB to write into the executable and core files. The default is `off`.

Summary of the info Command

The `info` command displays information about the state of the debuggee (as opposed to `show`, which provides information about internal GDB features, variables and options). With no arguments, it provides a list of possible features about which information is available.

info ...	Information displayed
`address` *sym*	Information about where symbol *sym* is stored. This is either a memory address or a register name.
`all-registers`	Information about all registers, including floating-point registers.
`args`	Information about the arguments to the current function (stack frame).
`break` [*bpnum*]	Information about breakpoint *bpnum* if given, or about all breakpoints if not.
`breakpoints` [*bpnum*]	Same information as the `info break` command.
`catch`	Information on exception handlers active in the current frame.
`classes` [*regexp*]	Information about Objective-C classes that match *regexp*, or about all classes if *regexp* is not given.
`display`	Information about items in the automatic display list.
`extensions`	Information about the correspondence of filename extensions to source code programming languages.
`f` [*address*]	Same information as the `info frame` command.
`files`	Information about the current debugging target, including the current executable, core, and symbol files.
`float`	Information about the floating-point flags and registers.

info ...	Information displayed
`frame` [*address*]	With no argument, print information about the current frame. With an *address*, print information about the frame containing *address*, but do not make it the current frame.
`functions` [*regexp*]	With no argument, print the names and types of all functions. Otherwise, print information about functions whose names match *regexp*.
`handle`	The list of all signals and how GDB currently treats them.
`line` *line-spec*	The starting and ending address for the code containing the line specified by *line-spec*. See **list** for a description of *line-spec*. This sets the default address to the starting address for the given line, so that `x/i` may be used to examine instructions.
`locals`	Information about local variables (`static` or automatic) accessible from the current frame.
`macro` *macroname*	Show the definition and source location for the macro *macroname*.
`mem`	Information about memory regions and their attributes.
`proc` [*item*]	Information about the running debuggee. Available on systems that supply `/proc`. The optional *item* is one of: `mappings` for available address ranges and how they may be accessed, `times` for starting time and user and system CPU time, `id` for process ID information, `status` for general status of the process, or `all` for all of the above.
`program`	Information about the running debuggee, such as running or stopped, and the process ID.
`registers` [*reg* ...]	With no arguments, information about all machine registers except floating-point registers. Otherwise, information about the named registers.
`s`	Same information as the `info stack` command (which is the same as the `backtrace` command).
`scope` *address*	Information about variables local to the scope containing *address*, which can be a function name, source line, or absolute address preceded by *.
`selectors` [*regexp*]	Information about Objective-C selectors that match *regexp*, or about all selectors if *regexp* is not given.
`set`	Same as the `show` command with no arguments.
`share`	Same as the `info sharedlibrary` command.
`sharedlibrary`	Information about currently loaded shared libraries.
`signal`	Same as the `info handle` command.
`source`	Information about the source file, such as compilation directory, programming language, and debugging information.
`sources`	Information about all source files that have debugging information. The output is split into two lists: those whose information has already been read, and those whose information will be read when needed.
`stack`	Same information as the `backtrace` command.
`symbol` *address*	The name of the symbol (function, variable, etc.) stored at address *address*.
`target`	Identical to the `info files` command.
`terminal`	Current terminal modes settings.
`threads`	All the program's current threads.

GDB

info ...	Information displayed
`types [regexp]`	Information about types that match *regexp*, or about all types in the program if *regexp* is not given.
`variables [regexp]`	With no argument, print the names and types of all variables except for local variables. Otherwise, print information about variables whose names match *regexp*.
`watchpoints [wpnum]`	Information about watchpoint *wpnum*, or about all watchpoints if *wpnum* is not given.
`win`	The names and sizes of all displayed TUI windows.

Alphabetical Summary of GDB Commands

The following alphabetical summary of GDB commands includes all those that are useful for day-to-day debugging. Esoteric commands, such as those used by GDB's maintainers, or to cross-debug remote systems connected via serial port or a network, have been omitted.

Many of these commands may be abbreviated. The list of abbreviations is provided in the earlier section "Aliases for Other Commands."

---

add-symbol-file

```
add-symbol-file file addr [-readnow]
add-symbol-file file [-s section address ...]
```

Read additional symbol table information from *file*, which was dynamically loaded into the debuggee outside of GDB's knowledge. You must tell GDB the address at which it was loaded, since GDB cannot determine this on its own. The `-readnow` option is the same as for the `file` command; see **file** for more information. You may use `-s` to name the memory starting at *address* with the name *section*. You can provide multiple *section/address* pairs with multiple `-s` options.

---

advance

```
advance bp-spec
```

Continue executing until the program reaches *bp-spec*, which can have any value acceptable to the `break` command (see **break** for the details). This command is like the `until` command, but it does not skip recursive function calls, and the location doesn't have to be in the current frame.

---

apropos

```
apropos regex
```

Search through the built-in documentation for commands that match the regular expression *regex*. Multiple words constitute a single regular expression. GDB uses Basic Regular Expressions (see Chapter 7); however, it also ignores case when matching.

attach

`attach` *pid*

Attach to the running process *pid*, and use it to obtain information about in-memory data. You must have appropriate permission in order to attach to a running process.

awatch

`awatch` *expression*

Set a watchpoint to stop when *expression* is either read or written. (Compare **rwatch** and **watch**.)

backtrace

`backtrace [`*count*`]`

Print a full list of all stack frames. With a positive *count*, print only the innermost *count* stack frames. With a negative *count*, print only the outermost *count* stack frames.

Example

Show a backtrace upon hitting a breakpoint:

```
...
Breakpoint 1, do_print (tree=0x924f9e0) at builtin.c:1573
1573            struct redirect *rp = NULL;
(gdb) backtrace
#0  do_print (tree=0x924f9e0) at builtin.c:1573
#1  0x08087bef in interpret (tree=0x924f9e0) at eval.c:784
#2  0x08086b68 in interpret (tree=0x924f980) at eval.c:453
#3  0x08072804 in main (argc=2, argv=0xbfe41bd4) at main.c:584
```

break

```
break [bp-spec]
break bp-spec if condition
break bp-spec thread threadnum
break bp-spec thread threadnum if condition
```

Set a breakpoint. The first form sets an unconditional breakpoint; execution of the debuggee stops when the breakpoint is reached. The second form sets a conditional breakpoint: when the breakpoint is reached, GDB evaluates the *condition*. If the condition is true, execution stops. If it isn't, the program continues. In either case, *bp-spec* is one of the items given in the following section.

The third and fourth forms are similar to the first and second ones respectively; however, they work on individual threads of control running within the debuggee. They specify that GDB should stop the program only when the given thread *threadnum* reaches the point specified by *bp-spec*.

Breakpoint Specifications

The following list shows the different forms that the `break` command can take.

`break`
: Set a breakpoint at the next instruction in the current stack frame. If you are not in the innermost stack frame, control stops as soon as execution returns to that frame. This is like the `finish` command, except that `finish` doesn't leave a breakpoint set. In the innermost frame, GDB stops when the breakpoint is reached. This is most useful inside loop bodies.

`break` *`function`*
: Set a breakpoint at the first instruction of *function*.

`break` *`linenumber`*
: Set a breakpoint at line *linenumber* in the current file.

`break` *`file`*`:`*`line`*
: Set a breakpoint at line number *line* in source file *file*.

`break` *`file`*`:`*`function`*
: Set a breakpoint at function *function* in source file *file*.

`break +`*`offset`*
`break -`*`offset`*
: Set a breakpoint at *offset* lines forward (+*`offset`*) or backward (-*`offset`*) from where execution stopped in the current stack frame.

`break *`*`address`*
: Set a breakpoint at *address*. This is useful for parts of the object file that don't have debugging symbols available (such as inside shared libraries).

A breakpoint set at a line or statement stops when the first instruction in that statement is reached.

Example

Set a breakpoint in the `main( )` function:

```
$ gdb whizprog
GNU gdb 6.3
...
(gdb) break main
Breakpoint 1 at 0x80483c0: file whizprog.c, line 6.
```

---

call

`call` *`expression`*

Call a function within the debuggee. *expression* is a function name and parameter list. Non-`void` results are printed and saved in the value history.

---

catch

`catch` *`event`*

Place a catchpoint. Execution stops when the specified *event* occurs.

Catchpoint Events

`catch`
: A C++ exception is caught.

`exec`
: The program calls `execve()`. This is not implemented on all systems.

`fork`
: The program calls `fork()`. This is not implemented on all systems.

`throw`
: A C++ exception is thrown.

`vfork`
: The program calls `vfork()`. This is not implemented on all systems.

---

cd

`cd` *`dir`*

Change GDB's working directory to *dir*.

---

clear

`clear [`*`bp-spec`*`]`

Clear a breakpoint. The argument is the same as for the `break` command (see **break**).

---

commands

```
commands [bp]
... commands ...
end
```

Supply GDB commands that should run when the program stops at a given breakpoint. With no *bp*, the list of commands is associated with the most recent breakpoint, watchpoint, or catchpoint that was *set*, not the one that was most recently *executed*. To clear a list of commands, supply the `commands` keyword and follow it immediately with `end`.

Example

```
break myfunc if x > 42          Break myfunc if x > 42
commands                        List of commands
silent                          Don't print GDB commands
printf "x = %d\n", x            Print variable value
cont                            Continue execution
end                             End of command list
```

---

complete

`complete` *`prefix`*

Show possible command completions for *prefix*. This is intended for Emacs when running GDB in an Emacs buffer.

condition

```
condition bp
condition bp expression
```

Add or remove a condition to a given breakpoint. The first syntax removes any condition associated with breakpoint number *bp*. The second form adds *expression* as a condition for breakpoint number *bp*, similar to the `break ... if` command. See also **break**.

continue

```
continue [count]
```

Resume execution after stopping at a breakpoint. If supplied, *count* is an *ignore count*; see the entry for **ignore**.

Example

Set a breakpoint in `main()`. Once there, set another break point and then continue until the new breakpoint is reached.

```
(gdb) break main
Breakpoint 3 at 0x8071d2e: file main.c, line 209.
(gdb) run ...
Starting program: ...

Breakpoint 3, main (argc=2, argv=0xbff59f04) at main.c:209
209             const char *optlist = "+F:f:v:W;m:D";
(gdb) break do_print
Breakpoint 4 at 0x805b239: file builtin.c, line 1573.
(gdb) continue
Continuing.

Breakpoint 4, do_print (tree=0x91589e0) at builtin.c:1573
1573            struct redirect *rp = NULL;
```

core-file

```
core-file [filename]
```

With no argument, indicate that there is no separate core file. Otherwise, treat *filename* as the file to use as a core file; that is, a file containing a dump of memory from an executing program.

define

```
define commandname
... commands ...
end
```

Create a user-defined command named *commandname*. The series of *commands* makes up the definition of *commandname*. Whenever you type *commandname*, GDB executes the *commands*. This is similar to functions or procedures in regular programming languages. See also **document**.

Hooks

If *commandname* has the form hook-*command*, where *command* is a built-in GDB command, when you enter *command* GDB runs *commandname* before it runs *command*.

Similarly, if *commandname* has the form hookpost-*command*, then GDB runs the provided sequence of commands after *command* finishes. You thus have available both pre- and post-execution hook facilities.

Finally, for the purposes of providing hooks, GDB recognizes a pseudo-command named stop that "executes" every time the debuggee stops. This allows you to define a hook of the form hook-stop in order to execute a sequence of commands every time the program stops.

---

delete

```
delete [breakpoints] [range ...]
delete display dnums ...
delete mem mnums ...
```

For the first syntax, remove the given *range* of breakpoints, watchpoints, or catchpoints. With no arguments, delete all breakpoints. (GDB may prompt for confirmation depending upon the setting of set confirm.) The second syntax removes items from the automatic display list (created with display); see **display** for more information. The third syntax removes defined memory regions created with mem; see **mem** for more information.

---

detach

```
detach
```

Detach the debugger from the running process previously attached to with attach.

---

directory

```
directory [dirname ...]
```

Add *dirname* to the list of directories that GDB searches when attempting to find source files. The directory is added to the *front* of the search path. With no argument, clear the directory search path.

---

disable

```
disable [breakpoints] [range ...]
disable display dnums ...
disable mem mnums ...
```

With the first syntax, disable the breakpoints in *range*, or all breakpoints if these are not supplied. GDB remembers disabled breakpoints, but they do not affect execution of the debuggee. The second syntax disables item(s) *dnums* in the automatic display list; see **display** for more information. The third syntax disables item(s) *mnums* in the list of defined memory regions; see **mem** for more information.

disassemble

```
disassemble
disassemble pc-val
disassemble start end
```

Print a range of memory addresses as assembly code instructions. With no argument, print the entire current function. One argument is assumed to be a program counter value; the function containing this value is dumped. Two arguments specify a range of addresses to dump, from (and including) *start* up to (but not including) *end*.

display

```
display
display/format expression
```

Add *expression* (usually a variable or address) to the list of values that GDB automatically displays every time the debuggee stops. The *format* is one of the format letters accepted by the `x` command; see **x** for the full list. The trailing "/" and *format* immediately follow the `display` command. With no arguments, print the current values of the expressions on the display list.

document

```
document commandname
... text ...
end
```

Provide documentation for the user-defined command *commandname*. The documentation consists of the lines provided in *text*. After executing this command, `help` *commandname* displays *text*. See also **define**.

dont-repeat

```
dont-repeat
```

This command is designed for use inside user-defined commands (see **define**). It indicates that the user-defined command should not be repeated if the user presses ENTER.

down

```
down count
```

Move down *count* stack frames. Positive values for *count* move towards more recent stack frames. See also **frame** and **up**.

down-silently

```
down-silently count
```

Same as the `down` command, but don't print any messages. This is intended mainly for use in GDB scripts.

echo

```
echo strings ...
```

Print *strings*. You may use the standard C escape sequences to generate nonprinting characters. In particular, you should use `\n` for newline. Note: unlike the shell-level `echo` command, GDB's `echo` does *not* automatically supply a newline. You must explicitly request one if you want it.

edit

```
edit [line-spec]
```

Edit the lines in the source file as specified by *line-spec*. See **list** for values for *line-spec*. With no argument, edit the file containing the most recently listed line. This uses the value of $EDITOR as the editor, or ex if that environment variable is not set.

else

```
else
```

Provide an alternate list of commands to execute if the expression in an `if` is false. Terminate the commands with `end`. See **if**.

enable

```
enable [breakpoints] [range ...]
enable [breakpoints] delete range ...
enable [breakpoints] once range ...
enable display dnums ...
enable mem mnums ...
```

The first syntax enables breakpoints; either all breakpoints if no *range* is supplied, or just the given breakpoints. The second syntax enables the specified breakpoints so that they stop the program when they're encountered, but are then deleted. The third syntax enables the specified breakpoints so that they stop the program when encountered, but then become disabled. The fourth syntax enables items in the automatic display list that were previously disabled with `disable`; for more information see **display**. The fifth syntax enables items in the list of defined memory regions; for more information, see **mem**.

end

```
end
```

Terminate a list of commands provided with keywords `commands`, `define`, `document`, `else`, `if`, or `while`.

exec-file

```
exec-file [filename]
```

With no argument, discard all information about the executable file. Otherwise, treat *filename* as the file to execute. This command searches $PATH to find the file if necessary.

fg

```
fg [count]
```

An alias for `continue`; see **continue**.

file

```
file
file filename [-readnow]
```

The first syntax causes GDB to discard all its information on both the symbol file and the executable file. The second syntax treats *filename* as the file to be debugged; it is used both for symbol table information and as the program to run for the `run` command.

The `-readnow` option forces GDB to load symbol table information immediately instead of waiting until information is needed.

finish

```
finish
```

Continue execution until the current stack frame (function) is about to return. This is most useful when you accidentally step into a function (using `step`) that does not have debugging information in it (such as a library function).

focus

```
focus window
```

Change the focus to TUI window *window*. Acceptable values for *window* are `next`, `prev`, `src`, `asm`, `regs`, and `cmd`.

forward-search

```
forward-search regex
```

Search forward from the current line for a line that matches the regular expression *regex*, and print it.

frame

```
frame
frame frame-num
frame address
```

Select or print information about the current stack frame (function invocation). Frame zero is the innermost (most recent) stack frame. With no arguments, print the current stack frame. With a *frame-num*, move to that frame. This is the most common kind of argument. An *address* argument may be used to select the frame at the given address. This is necessary if the chaining of stack frames has been damaged by a bug. Some architectures may require more than one *address*.

Example

Move up the call stack toward an older function:

```
(gdb) where
#0  do_print (tree=0x83579e0) at builtin.c:1573
#1  0x08087bef in interpret (tree=0x83579e0) at eval.c:784
#2  0x08086b68 in interpret (tree=0x8357980) at eval.c:453
#3  0x08072804 in main (argc=2, argv=0xbfeb8584) at main.c:584
(gdb) frame 2
#2  0x08086b68 in interpret (tree=0x8357980) at eval.c:453
453                     (void) interpret(tree->rnode);
```

generate-core-file

`generate-core-file [`*`file`*`]`

Generate a core file from the state of the debuggee. With *file*, send the core dump to *file*. Otherwise, use a file named `core.`*`PID`*.

handle

`handle `*`signal keywords ...`*

Set GDB up to handle one or more signals. The *signal* may be a signal number, a signal name (with or without the `SIG` prefix), a range of the form *low–high*, or the keyword `all`. The *keywords* are one or more of the following:

`ignore`	Ignore the signal; do not let the program see it.
`noignore`	Same as the `pass` command.
`nopass`	Same as the `ignore` command.
`noprint`	Do not print a message when the signal arrives.
`nostop`	Do not stop the program when the signal arrives; let the debuggee receive it immediately.
`pass`	Pass the signal on through to the program.
`print`	Print a message when the signal arrives.
`stop`	Stop the program when the signal arrives. Normally, only "error" signals such as `SIGSEGV` stop the program.

hbreak

`hbreak `*`bp-spec`*

Set a hardware-assisted breakpoint. The argument is the same as for the `break` command (see **break**, earlier in this list). This command is intended for EEPROM/ROM code debugging; it allows you to set a breakpoint at a location without changing the location. However, not all systems have the necessary hardware for this.

help

`help [`*`command`*`]`

With no arguments, print a list of subtopics for which help is available. With *command*, provide help on the given GDB command or group of commands.

if

```
if expression
... commands1 ...
[ else
... commands2 ... ]
end
```

Conditionally execute a series of commands. If *expression* is true, execute *commands1*. If an else is present and the expression is false, execute *commands2*.

ignore

```
ignore bp count
```

Set the ignore count on breakpoint, watchpoint, or catchpoint *bp* to *count*. GDB does not check conditions as long as the ignore count is positive.

inspect

```
inspect print-expressions
```

An obsolete alias for the print command. See **print** for more information.

info

```
info [feature]
```

Display information about *feature*, which concerns the state of the debuggee. With no arguments, provide a list of features about which information is available. Full details are provided in the section "Summary of the info Command," earlier in this chapter.

jump

```
jump location
```

Continue execution at *location*, which is either a *line-spec* as for the list command (see **list**), or a hexadecimal address preceded by a *.

The continue command resumes execution where it stopped, while jump moves to a different place. If the *location* is not within the current frame, GDB asks for confirmation since GDB will not change the current setup of the machine registers (stack pointer, frame pointer, etc.).

kill

```
kill
```

Kill the process running the debuggee. This is most useful to force the production of a core dump for later debugging.

layout

```
layout layout
```

Change the layout of the TUI windows to *layout*. Acceptable values for *layout* are:

`asm`	The assembly window only.
`next`	The next layout.
`prev`	The previous layout.
`regs`	The register window only.
`split`	The source and assembly windows.
`src`	The source window only.

The command window is always displayed.

list

```
list function
list line-spec
```

List lines of source code, starting at the beginning of function *function* (first form), or centered around the line defined by *line-spec* (second form). Pressing the ENTER key repeats the last command; for `list`, this shows successive lines of source text. A *line-spec* can take one of the forms shown below.

Line Specifications

`list` *`number`*
: List lines centered around line *number*.

`list` *`+offset`*
`list` *`-offset`*
: List lines centered around the line *offset* lines after (first form) or before (second form) the last line printed.

`list` *`file`*`:`*`line`*
: List lines centered around line *line* in source file *file*.

`list` *`file`*`:`*`function`*
: List lines centered around the opening brace of function *function* in source file *file*. This is necessary if there are multiple functions of the same name in different source files.

`list` *`*address`*
: List lines centered around the line containing *address*, which can be an expression.

`list` *`first,last`*
: List the lines from *first* to *last*, each of which may be any of the previous forms for a *line-spec*.

`list` *`first,`*
: List lines starting with *first*.

GDB

`list ,last`
: List lines ending with *last*.

`list +`
`list -`
: List the lines just after (first form) or just before (second form) the lines just printed.

macro

```
macro expand expression
macro expand-once expression
macro define macro body
macro define macro(args) body
macro undefine macro
```

Work with C preprocessor macros. As of GDB 6.3, not all of these are implemented.

`macro expand` *expression*
: Display the result of macro expanding *expression*. The results are *not* evaluated, thus they don't need to be syntactically valid. `expand` may be abbreviated `exp`.

`macro expand-once` *expression*
: Expand only those macros whose names appear in *expression* instead of fully expanding all macros. `expand-once` may be abbreviated `exp1`. *Not implemented as of GDB 6.3.*

`macro define` *macro body*
`macro define` *macro(args) body*
: Define a macro named *macro* with replacement text *body*. As in C and C++, the first form defines a symbolic constant, while the second form defines a macro that accepts arguments. *Not implemented as of GDB 6.3.*

`macro undefine` *macro*
: Remove the definition of the macro named *macro*. This works only for macros defined with `macro define`; you cannot undefine a macro in the debuggee. *Not implemented as of GDB 6.3.*

make

```
make [args]
```

Run the `make` program, passing it *args*. Equivalent to the shell `make` *args* command. This is useful for rebuilding your program while remaining within GDB.

mem

```
mem start-addr end-addr attributes ...
```

Define a *memory region*, i.e., a portion of the address space starting at *start-addr* and ending at *end-addr* that has particular *attributes*.

Memory Access Attributes

ro	Memory is read-only.
rw	Memory is read-write.
wo	Memory is write-only.
8, 16, 32, 64	GDB should use memory accesses of the specified width in bits. This is often needed for memory-mapped device registers.

next

`next [count]`

Run the next statement. Unlike `step`, a function call is treated as a simple statement; single-stepping does not continue inside the called function. With a *count*, run the next *count* statements. In any case, execution stops upon reaching a breakpoint or receipt of a signal. See also **step**.

nexti

`nexti [count]`

Run the next machine instruction. Otherwise, this is similar to the `next` command in that single-stepping continues *past* a called function instead of into it.

nosharedlibrary

`nosharedlibrary`

Unload all shared libraries from the debuggee.

output

```
output expression
output/format expression
```

Print expression, completely unadorned. No newlines are added, nor is the value preceded by the usual `$n =`. Neither is the value added to the value history. With "`/`" and *format*, output the expression using *format*, which is the same as for the `print` command; see **print**.

path

`path dir`

Add directory *dir* to the front of the PATH environment variable.

print

`print [/format] [expression]`

Print the value of *expression*. If the first argument is "`/`" and *format*, use the *format* to print the expression. Omitting *expression* prints the previous expression, allowing you to use a different format to see the same value. The allowed *format* values are a subset of the *format* items for the `x` command; see also **x**, later in this section.

Print Formats

a	Print the value as an address. The address is printed as both an absolute (hexadecimal) address, and as an offset from the nearest symbol.
c	Print the value as a character constant.
d	Print the value as a signed decimal integer.
f	Print the value as a floating point number.
o	Print the value as an octal integer.
t	Print the value as a binary integer (t stands for "two").
u	Print the value as an unsigned decimal integer.
x	Print the value as a hexadecimal integer.

Example

Print a wide character value as a regular character:

```
(gdb) print tmp->sub.val.wsp
$2 = (wchar_t *) 0x99f0910
(gdb) print/c *$2
$3 = 97 'a'
```

print-object

`print-object` *`object`*

Cause the Objective C object *object* to print information about itself. This command may only work with Objective C libraries that define the hook function `_NSPrintForDebugger()`.

printf

`printf` *`format-string, expressions ...`*

Print *expressions* under control of the *format-string*, as for the C library *printf*(3) function. GDB allows only the simple, single-letter escape sequences (such as `\t` and `\n`) to appear in *format-string*.

ptype

```
ptype
ptype expression
ptype type-name
```

Print the full definition of a type. This differs from `whatis`, in that `whatis` only prints type names, while `ptype` gives a full description.

With no argument (the first syntax), print the type of the last value in the value history. This is equivalent to `ptype $`. With *expression* (the second syntax), print the type of *expression*. Note that the *expression* is not evaluated. No operators with side effects (such as ++, or a function call) execute. The third syntax prints the type of *type-name*, which is either the name of a type or one of the keywords `class`, `enum`, `struct`, or `union`, followed by a tag. See also **whatis**.

pwd

`pwd`

Print GDB's current working directory.

quit

`quit`

Exit GDB.

rbreak

`rbreak` *regexp*

Set breakpoints on all functions matching the regular expression *regexp*. The regular expression syntax used is that of `grep` (i.e., Basic Regular Expressions, see Chapter 7). This is useful for overloaded functions in C++.

refresh

`refresh`

Redraw and refresh the screen for the TUI. See the earlier section "The GDB Text User Interface" for more information.

return

`return [`*expression*`]`

Cause the current stack frame to return to its caller. If provided, *expression* is used at the return value. GDB pops the current stack frame and any below it (functions it called) from the execution stack, causing the returning frame's caller to become the current frame. Execution does *not* resume; the program remains stopped until you issue a `continue` command.

reverse-search

`reverse-search` *regex*

Search backwards from the current line for a line that matches the regular expression *regex*, and print it.

run

`run [`*arguments*`]`

Run the debuggee, optionally passing it *arguments* as the command-line arguments. GDB also supports simple I/O redirections (<, >, >>); pipes are not supported. GDB remembers the last-used *arguments*; thus a plain `run` command restarts the program with these same arguments. (Use `set args` to clear or change the argument list.)

The debuggee receives the arguments you give to the `run` command, the environment as inherited by GDB and modified by `set environment`, the current working directory, and the current standard input, standard output, and standard error (unless redirected).

rwatch

`rwatch` *`expression`*

Set a watchpoint to stop when *expression* is read. (Compare **awatch** and **watch**.)

search

`search` *`regex`*

An alias for `forward-search`. See **forward-search** for more information.

section

`section` *`sectname address`*

Change the base address of *sectname* to *address*. This is a last-ditch command, used when the executable file format doesn't contain data on section addresses or if the data in the file is wrong.

select-frame

```
select-frame
select-frame frame-num
select-frame address
```

Same as the `frame` command, except that it does not print any messages. See **frame** for more information.

set

`set [`*`variable`*`]`

Change the setting either of GDB variables or variables in the debuggee. See the earlier section "Summary of set and show Commands" for more information.

sharedlibrary

`sharedlibrary [`*`regexp`*`]`

With no argument, load all the shared libraries required by the program or core file. Otherwise, load only those files whose names match *regexp*.

shell

`shell [`*`command args`*`]`

Run the shell command *command* with arguments *args* without leaving GDB. With no arguments, start an interactive subshell.

Example

Run grep to find the definition of a macro:

```
510             return tmp_number((AWKNUM) len);
(gdb) shell grep tmp_number *.h
whizprog.h:#define   tmp_number(x)   mk_number((x), TEMP)
(gdb)
```

show

```
show [variable]
```

Show the setting of internal GDB variables. See the earlier section "Summary of set and show Commands" for more information.

signal

```
signal sig
```

Continue the program running, and immediately send it signal *sig*. *sig* may be either a signal number or a signal name. The signal number `0` is special: if the program stops due to receipt of a signal, sending signal `0` resumes it without delivering the original signal.

silent

```
silent
```

Don't print breakpoint-reached messages. Use this command inside a commands list; see **commands**.

source

```
source file
```

Read and execute the commands in *file*. The commands are not printed as they are read, and an error in any one command terminates execution of the file. When executing a command file, commands that normally ask for confirmation do not do so, and many commands that would otherwise print messages are silent.

step

```
step [count]
```

Run the next statement. This differs from the `next` command in that if the next statement is a function call, `step` steps into it and continues single-stepping in the called function. However, `next` calls the function without stepping into it. With a *count*, step through *count* statements. In any case, execution stops upon reaching a breakpoint or receipt of a signal. See also **next**.

stepi

```
stepi [count]
```

Run the next machine instruction. Otherwise, this is similar to the `step` command in that single-stepping continues into a called function. With a *count*, step through *count* instructions.

symbol-file

```
symbol-file
symbol-file filename [-readnow]
```

With no argument, discard all symbol table information. Otherwise, treat *filename* as the file to get symbol table information from, and as the file to execute. This command searches $PATH to find the file if necessary. The `-readnow` option has the same meaning as for the `file` command; see **file** for more information.

tbreak

`tbreak bp-spec`

Set a temporary breakpoint. The argument is the same as for the `break` command (see **break**, earlier in this list). The difference is that once the breakpoint is reached, it is removed.

tcatch

`tcatch event`

Set a temporary catchpoint. The argument is the same as for the `catch` command (see **catch**, earlier in this list). The difference is that once the catchpoint is reached, it is removed.

thbreak

`thbreak bp-spec`

Set a temporary hardware-assisted breakpoint. The argument is the same as for the `hbreak` command (see **hbreak**, earlier in this list).

thread

```
thread threadnum
thread apply [threadnum | all] command
```

The first form makes *threadnum* the current thread, i.e., the one that GDB works with. The second form lets you apply *command* to either the specific thread *threadnum* or to all threads.

tty

`tty device`

Set the debuggee's input and output to *device* (typically the device file for a terminal).

tui

`tui reg regkind`

For the TUI, update the register window to display the register set *regkind*.

Register Sets

The following are the acceptable values for *regkind*.

`float`	The floating-point registers.
`general`	The general purpose registers.
`next`	The "next" register group. Predefined register groups are `all`, `float`, `general`, `restore`, `save`, `system`, and `vector`.
`system`	The system registers.

undisplay

```
undisplay dnums ...
```

Remove display items *dnums* from the automatic display list. See **display** for more information.

unset

```
unset environment variable
```

Remove environment variable *variable* from the environment passed to the debuggee.

until

```
until [location]
```

Continue execution until it reaches the next source line after the current line. This is most useful for reaching the line after the end of a loop body. Without a *location*, `until` uses single-stepping to reach the next source line. With a *location*, it uses an internal breakpoint to reach the next source line; this is much faster. The *location* may be any form acceptable to the `break` command; see **break** for more information.

Example

Use `until` to skip through the entire execution of a loop:

```
$ nl -ba foo.c                   Show source file
     1  #include <stdio.h>
     2
     3  int main(void)
     4  {
     5      int i;
     6
     7      for (i = 1; i <= 10; i++)
     8              printf("i = %d\n", i);
     9
    10      printf("all done: i = %d\n", i);
    11  }
$ gcc -g foo.c -o foo            Compile it
$ gdb foo                        Run GDB
GNU gdb 6.3
...

(gdb) break main                 Set breakpoint
Breakpoint 1 at 0x8048358: file foo.c, line 7.
(gdb) run                        Start it running
Starting program: /tmp/foo

Breakpoint 1, main () at foo.c:7
7       for (i = 1; i <= 10; i++)
(gdb) next                       Next statement
8               printf("i = %d\n", i);
```

```
(gdb)                                   ENTER repeats 'next'
i = 1
7           for (i = 1; i <= 10; i++)
(gdb)                                   Same
8               printf("i = %d\n", i);
(gdb)                                   Same
i = 2
7           for (i = 1; i <= 10; i++)
(gdb) until 9                           Finish up the loop
i = 3
i = 4
i = 5
i = 6
i = 7
i = 8
i = 9
i = 10
main ( ) at foo.c:10
10          printf("all done: i = %d\n", i);
(gdb) continue                          Finish program
Continuing.
all done: i = 11

Program exited with code 021.
(gdb) quit
```

up

`up` *`count`*

Move up *count* stack frames. Positive values for *count* move towards less recent stack frames. See also **frame** and **down**.

up-silently

`up-silently` *`count`*

Same as the up command, but don't print any messages. Intended mainly for use in GDB scripts.

update

`update`

For the TUI, update the source window and the current execution point.

watch

`watch` *`expression`*

Set a watchpoint to stop when *expression* is written. (Compare **awatch** and **rwatch**.)

whatis

`whatis [expression]`

With no argument, print the type of the last value in the value history. This is equivalent to `whatis $`. With *expression*, print the type of *expression*. Note that the *expression* is not evaluated. No operators with side effects (such as ++, or a function call) execute. See also **ptype**.

where

`where [count]`

Identical to the `backtrace` command; see **backtrace** for more information.

while

```
while expression
... commands ...
end
```

Repeatedly execute a series of commands. As long as *expression* is true, execute *commands*.

winheight

`winheight win ±amount`

For the TUI, change the height of window *win* by *amount*. Using + increases the height; using – decreases it. The window name *win* may be one of `asm`, `cmd`, `regs`, or `src`.

x

`x [[/NFU] addr]`

Examine the data at *address*. Subsequent `x` commands without an address move forward in memory according to the values for *N*, *F*, and *U*.

The *N* value is a repeat count, for example, to examine a given number of instructions. The *F* value is a format, indicating how to print the data. The *U* value is the unit size in bytes of the items to be displayed.

GDB stores the address printed by the `x` command in the `$_` convenience variable. It stores the *contents* of the address in the `$__` convenience variable.

Format Values

`a`	Print the value as an address. The address is printed as both an absolute (hexadecimal) address and as an offset from the nearest symbol.
`c`	Print the value as a character constant.
`d`	Print the value as a signed decimal integer.
`f`	Print the value as a floating point number.
`i`	Print the value as a machine instruction.
`o`	Print the value as an octal integer.

s	Print the value as a NUL-terminated string.
t	Print the value as a binary integer (t stands for "two").
u	Print the value as an unsigned decimal integer.
x	Print the value as a hexadecimal integer.

Unit Size Values

b	Bytes.
g	Giant words, i.e., 8 bytes.
h	Halfwords, i.e., 2 bytes.
w	Words, i.e., 4 bytes.

18

Writing Manual Pages

The man command prints the online "manual page" for commands, system calls, functions, devices and file formats. Developers creating new software also need to create manual pages for their programs. This in turn requires a basic understanding of the Unix troff text-processing program and the *man* macro package.

This chapter presents the following topics:

- Introduction
- Overview of nroff/troff
- Alphabetical summary of the *man* macros
- Predefined strings
- Names used internally by the *man* macros
- Sample document

Introduction

The standard Unix text-processing tools are nroff and troff. They are not What You See Is What You Get (WYSIWYG) word-processors. Rather, they are *text processing* programs, where the input consists of a mixture of text to be formatted and special commands that instruct the programs how to format the text.

troff is for output devices such as typesetters and high resolution laser printers that can handle variable-width fonts and different character sizes. nroff is for simpler devices where all characters have the same width, such as terminals or line printers. Both programs accept the same set of commands; thus, carefully prepared input may be used with both programs to produce reasonable results. The original troff program worked for only one specific typesetter. The modern version, known as "device independent troff," or ditroff, can be tuned via specific drivers to work on multiple output devices.

Different commercial versions of Unix come with different versions of the troff suite. GNU/Linux and BSD systems all use GNU troff (groff), which is an excellent, full-featured implementation of ditroff and all the troff preprocessors. The Internet starting point for groff is *http://www.gnu.org/software/groff/groff.html*. We recommend downloading and building it if you intend to do serious troff-based typesetting work.*

Knowledge of nroff and troff was once an integral part of a Unix wizard's claims to Unix mastery. Over time though, they have been superseded for daily document preparation, either by WYSIWYG programs, or by TEX and LATEX. More information about troff in general is available from *http://www.troff.org/*.

However, one important task where knowledge of troff is still handy is the writing of manual pages (for the man command) to accompany software. This chapter introduces the subset of the troff command and feature set that is useful for writing manual pages, and then describes the *man* macros, concluding with a sample manual page. See also the *Writing Manual Pages* appendix in *Classic Shell Scripting*, cited in the Bibliography.

The canonical reference for nroff/troff is *Bell Labs Computing Science Technical Report #54, Troff User's Manual*, by J.F. Ossanna and B.W. Kernighan. It is available in PostScript from *http://cm.bell-labs.com/cm/cs/cstr/54.ps.gz*. You should read it if you plan to do any serious work in nroff/troff (such as writing or modifying macro packages). This document explains the ideas of diversions, environments, fields, registers, strings, and traps. The online Info documentation for groff explains the GNU-specific extensions that it supplies.

Overview of nroff/troff

This section is condensed from the material on troff from the third edition of this book. It covers features available in all versions of nroff and troff, and focuses on those features necessary for writing manual pages.

Command-Line Invocation

nroff and troff are invoked from the command line as follows:

```
nroff [options] [files]
troff [options] [files]
```

Although both formatters support a plethora of options, the following two are the most important for everyday use.

-m*name*

Prepend a macro file to input *files*. Historically, one of /usr/lib/tmac/tmac.*name* or /usr/share/lib/tmac/tmac.*name* were the locations of the macros for *name*. Solaris uses /usr/share/lib/tmac/*name*. GNU troff uses something like /usr/

* groff is written in C++, so you may need a C++ compiler. In this case, you may first need to bootstrap g++, the GNU C++ compiler from GCC (the GNU Compiler Collection).

local/share/groff/*x.y.z*/tmac/*name*.tmac. The actual location and filename(s) vary among different Unix systems.

-T*name*
: Prepare output designed for printer or typesetter *name*. For device names, see your specific documentation or a local expert. GNU troff provides both PostScript and TeX DVI output.

Example

Format a manual page for printing using groff:

```
$ groff -man /usr/share/man/man1/awk.1 | lpr
```

Conceptual Overview

This section provides a brief overview of how to prepare input for nroff and troff. It presents the following topics:

- Requests and macros
- Common requests
- Specifying measurements
- Requests that cause a line break
- Embedded formatting controls

Requests and macros

Formatting is specified by embedding brief codes (called *requests*) into the text source file. These codes act as directives to nroff and troff when they run. For example, to center a line of text, type the following code in a file:

```
.ce
This text should be centered.
```

When formatted, the output appears centered:

```
                This text should be centered.
```

There are two types of formatting codes:

- *Requests*, which provide the most elementary instructions
- *Macros*, which are predefined combinations of requests

Requests, also known as *primitives*, allow direct control of almost any feature of page layout and formatting. Macros combine requests to create a total effect. In a sense, requests are like statements, and macros are like functions.

All nroff/troff requests are two-letter lowercase names. Macros are usually upper- or mixed-case names. GNU troff removes the two-character restriction on the length of names.

Specifying measurements

With some requests, the numeric argument can be followed by a scale indicator that specifies a unit of measurement. The valid indicators and their meanings are listed in the following table. Note that all measurements are internally converted to basic units (this conversion is shown in the last column). A basic unit is the smallest possible size on the printer device. The device resolution (e.g., 600 dots per inch) determines the size of a basic unit. Also, *T* specifies the current point size, and *R* specifies the device resolution.

Scale indicator	Meaning	Equivalent unit	# of basic units
`c`	Centimeter	0.394 inches	$R / 2.54$
`i`	Inch	6 picas or 72 points	R
`m`	Em	*T* points	$R \times T / 72$
`n`	En	0.5 em	$R \times T / 144$
`p`	Point	1/72 inch	$R / 72$
`P`	Pica	1/6 inch	$R / 6$
`u`	Basic unit		1
`v`	Vertical line space		(Current value of line spacing in basic units)
None	Default		

It is worth noting that *all* numbers in `nroff`/`troff` are stored internally using integers. This applies even to apparently fractional values in commands such as:

```
.sp .5
```

which spaces down one-half of the current vertical spacing.

An "em" is the width of the letter "m" in the current font and point size. An "en" is the width of the letter "n" in the current font and point size. Note that in `nroff`, an "em" and an "en" are the same—the width of one character.

Requests that cause a line break

A *line break* occurs when `nroff`/`troff` writes the current output line, even if it is not completely filled. Most requests can be interspersed with text without causing a line break in the output. The following requests cause a break:

```
.bp   .ce   .fi   .in   .sp
.br   .cf   .fl   .nf   .ti
```

If you need to prevent these requests from causing a break, begin them with the "no break" control character (normally `'`) instead of a dot (.). For example, `.bp` flushes the current output line and starts a new page immediately. However, `'bp` starts a new page, with the current output line not being written until it is full.

Embedded formatting controls

In addition to requests and macros, which are written on their own separate lines, you may also have formatting controls embedded within your text lines. These typically provide the following capabilities:

General formatting

Considerable formatting control is available, such as switching fonts (\f), changing point sizes (\s), computing widths (\w), and many other things. For example:

```
This text is in \fIitalic\fR, but this is in roman.
This text is \s-2VERY SMALL\s0 but this text is not.
```

Special characters

Predefined special typesetting characters, such as the bullet symbol \(bu (•), the left hand \(lh (☜), and the right hand \(rh (☞).

Strings

User-defined sequences of characters, like macros, but usable inline. For example:

```
.\" define a shorthand for UNIX
.ds UX  the \s-1UNIX\s0 Operating System
...
Welcome to \*(UX.
While \*(UX may appear daunting at first,
it is immensely powerful. ...
```

Number registers

Like variables in programming languages, number registers store numeric values that can be printed in a range of formats (decimal, roman, etc.). Number registers hold integer values; fractional values are converted into the corresponding number of basic units. Number registers can be set to auto-increment or auto-decrement, and are particularly useful when writing macro packages, for managing automatic numbering of headings, footnotes, figures, and so on. For example:

```
.nr Cl 0 1  \" Chapter Level
.de CH
.bp
\\n+(Cl. \\$1 \\$2 \\$3
..
```

This creates a macro that uses register Cl as the "chapter level." The first three arguments to the macro (represented in the macro body by \\$1 etc.) become the chapter title. The extra backslashes are needed inside the macro definition to prevent too-early evaluation.

Comments in nroff/troff begin with \". Lines beginning with . that contain an unknown request are ignored. In general, don't put leading whitespace on your text lines. This causes a break, and nroff and troff honor the leading whitespace literally.

Outline of Useful Requests

The following is a list of the requests that you may see in manual pages, or that were mentioned earlier in the chapter.

.ad	Adjust margins.	.ls	Line spacing (e.g., single-spaced).
.bp	Begin a new page.	.na	Don't adjust margins.
.br	Break the output line.	.ne	Keep lines on same page if there's room.

`.ce`	Center lines.	`.nf`	Don't fill lines.
`.cf`	Copy raw file to output.	`.nr`	Define a number register.
`.de`	Define a macro.	`.po`	Change page offset.
`.ds`	Define a string.	`.ps`	Set point size.
`.fi`	Fill lines.	`.so`	Go to a file, then return.
`.fl`	Flush output buffer.	`.sp`	Output blank spacing.
`.ft`	Set font.	`.ta`	Define tab settings.
`.in`	Indent.	`.ti`	Indent next line (temporary indent).
`.ll`	Set line length.	`.vs`	Set vertical spacing for lines.

Useful Escape Sequences

This partial list of `troff` escape sequences provides those that are most useful.

Sequence	Effect
`\\`	Prevent or delay the interpretation of `\`.
`\e`	Printable version of the current escape character (usually `\`).
`\-`	– (minus sign in the current font).
`\.`	Period (dot).
`\`*`space`*	Unpaddable space-size space character.
`\`*`newline`*	Concealed (ignored) newline.
`|`	1/6-em narrow space character (zero width in `nroff`).
`\^`	1/12-em half-narrow space character (zero width in `nroff`).
`\&`	Nonprinting, zero-width character.
`\"`	Beginning of comment.
`\$`*n*	Interpolate macro argument $1 \leq n \leq 9$.
`\(`*xx*	Character named *xx*. See the following section "Special Characters."
`\*`*x* or `\*(`*xx*	Interpolate string *x* or *xx*.
`\f`*x* or `\f(`*xx* or `\f`*n*	Change to font named *x* or *xx* or to position *n*. If *x* is `P`, return to the previous font.
`\n`*x*, `\n(`*xx*	Interpolate number register *x* or *xx*.
`\n+`*x*, `\n+(`*xx*	Interpolate number register *x* or *xx*, applying auto-increment.
`\n-`*x*, `\n-(`*xx*	Interpolate number register *x* or *xx*, applying auto-decrement.
`\s`*n*, `\s±`*n*	Change point size to *n* or increment by *n*. For example, `\s0` returns to previous point size.
`\s(`*nn*, `\s±(`*nn*	Just like `\s`, but allow unambiguous two-character point sizes (`ditroff` only).
`\w'`*`string`*`'`	Interpolate width of *string* in basic units.

Special Characters

Table 18-1 lists the special characters that reside in the standard fonts. `troff` includes a large number of other characters that we have not described here, since they are mostly for typesetting mathematics.

Table 18-1. Characters in the standard fonts

Input	Char	Character name	Input	Char	Character name
'	’	Close quote	\(hy	-	Hyphen
`	‘	Open quote	\(bu	•	Bullet
\(em	—	Em-dash (width of “m”)	\(sq	❑	Square
\(en	–	En-dash (width of “n”)	\(rg	®	Registered
\-	–	Minus in current font	\(co	©	Copyright
-	-	Hyphen			

Alphabetical Summary of man Macros

Brian Kernighan describes the reason for macro packages very pithily:

> Since bare `troff` is unusable by humans, a race of gods now gone created macro packages for mortals to use.

Today, the *man* macros are the most widely used macro package. They are used for writing program manual pages for the online manual, accessed via the `man` command.

As many as six arguments may be given for all the macros that change fonts or produce a heading. The seventh and later arguments are ignored. Use double quotes around multiple words to get longer headings.

The `.TS`, `.TE`, `.EQ`, and `.EN` macros are not defined by the *man* macros. Because `nroff` and `troff` ignore unknown requests, you can still use them in your manpages; `tbl` and `eqn` work with no problems.

.B

`.B [`*`text ...`*`]`

Set the arguments in the bold font, with a space between each argument. If no arguments are supplied, the next input line is set in bold.

.BI

`.BI` *`barg iarg ...`*

Set alternating *barg* in bold and *iarg* in italic, with no intervening spaces.

.BR

`.BR` *`barg rarg ...`*

Set alternating *barg* in bold and *rarg* in roman, with no intervening spaces.

.DT

`.DT`

Reset the tab stops to their defaults, every 1/2 inch.

.HP

```
.HP [indent]
tag text
```

Start a paragraph with a "hanging" indent, one where a tag sits out to the left side. The optional *indent* is how far to indent the paragraph. The tag text follows on the next line. See the example under **.TP**.

.I

```
.I [text ...]
```

Set the arguments in the italic font, with a space between each argument. If no arguments are supplied, the next input line is set in italic.

.IB

```
.IB iarg barg ...
```

Set alternating *iarg* in italic and *barg* in bold, with no intervening spaces.

.IP

```
.IP tag [indent]
```

Start a paragraph with a hanging indent, one where a tag sits out to the left side. Unlike `.HP` and `.TP`, the *tag* is supplied as an argument to the macro. The optional *indent* is how far to indent the paragraph.

Example

```
.IP 1.
The first point is ...
.IP 2.
The second point is ...
```

.IR

```
.IR iarg rarg ...
```

Set alternating *iarg* in italic and *rarg* in roman, with no intervening spaces.

.LP

```
.LP
```

Start a new paragraph. Just like `.PP`.

.P

```
.P
```

Start a new paragraph. Just like `.PP`.

.PD

```
.PD [distance]
```

Set the interparagraph spacing to *distance*. With no argument, reset it to the default. Most useful to get multiple tags for a paragraph.

Example

Show that two options do the same thing:

```
.PP
.I Whizprog
accepts the following options.
.TP \w'\fB\-\^\-help\fP'u+3n
.PD 0
.B \-h
.TP
.PD
.B \-\^\-help
Print a helpful message and exit.
```

.PP

`.PP`

Start a new paragraph. This macro resets all the defaults, such as point size, font, and spacing.

.RB

`.RB` *rarg barg ...*

Set alternating *rarg* in roman and *barg* in bold, with no intervening spaces.

.RE

`.RE`

End a relative indent. Each `.RE` should match a preceding `.RS`. See **.RS** for an example.

.RI

`.RI` *rarg iarg ...*

Set alternating *rarg* in roman and *iarg* in italic, with no intervening spaces.

.RS

`.RS [`*indent*`]`

Start a relative indent. Each successive `.RS` increases the indent. The optional *indent* is how far to indent the following text. Each `.RS` should have an accompanying `.RE`.

Example

```
.PP
There are a number of important points to remember.
.RS
.IP 1.
The first point is ...
.IP 2.
The second point is ...
...
.RE
Forget these at your own risk!
```

.SB

`.SB` *`arg ...`*

Set arguments in bold, using a smaller point size, separated by spaces.

.SH

`.SH` *`arg ...`*

Section header. Start a new section, such as `NAME` or `SYNOPSIS`. Use double quotes around multiple words for longer headings.

.SM

`.SM` *`arg ...`*

Set arguments in roman, using a smaller point size, separated by spaces.

.SS

`.SS` *`arg ...`*

Subsection header. Start a new subsection. Use double quotes around multiple words for longer headings.

.TH

`.TH` *`title section date ...`*

Title heading. This is the first macro of a manpage, and sets the header and footer lines. The *title* is the name of the manpage. The *section* is the section the manpage should be in (a number, possibly followed by a letter). The *date* is the date the manpage was last updated. Different systems have different conventions for the remaining arguments to this macro. For Solaris, the fourth and fifth arguments are the left-page footer and the main (center) header.

Example

```
.TH WHIZPROG 1L "April 1, 2007"
.SH NAME
whizprog \- do amazing things
...
```

.TP

`.TP [`*`indent`*`]`
`tag text`

Start a paragraph with a hanging indent, one where a tag sits out to the left side. The optional *indent* is how far to indent the paragraph. The tag text follows on the next line. See also the example under **.PD**.

Example

```
.TP .2i
1.
The first point is ...
.TP .2i
2.
The second point is ...
```

Predefined Strings

The following strings are predefined by the *man* macros; of these, only R and S are documented.

String	Effect in troff	Effect in nroff
*(lq	`` (“)	"
*(rq	'' (”)	"
*R	\(rg (®)	(Reg.)
*S	Restore default point size	Restore default point size

Internal Names

The Solaris *man* macros use a number of macro, string, and number register names that begin with], }, and). Such names should be avoided in your own files.

The number registers D, IN, LL, P, X, d, m, and x are used internally by the Solaris *man* macros. Using .nr D 1 before calling the .TH macro generates pages with different even and odd footers.*

Sample Document

The output of this sample document is shown in Figure 18-1.

```
.TH WHIZPROG 1 "April 1, 2007"
.SH NAME
whizprog \- do amazing things
.SH SYNOPSIS
.B whizprog
[
.I options
] [
.I files
\&... ]
.SH DESCRIPTION
.I Whizprog
is the next generation of really
.B cool
do-it-all programs. ...
.SH OPTIONS
.PP
.I Whizprog
accepts the following options.
.TP \w'\fB\-\^\-level\fP'u+3n
.PD 0
.B \-h
```

* This information was gleaned by examining the actual macros. It is not documented, so Your Mileage May Vary.

```
.TP
.PD
.B \-\^\-help
Print a helpful message and exit.
.TP
.BI \-\^\-level " level"
Set the level for the
.B \-\^\-stun
option.
.TP
.B \-\^\-stun
Stun the competition, or other beings, as needed. ...
.SH SEE ALSO
.IR "Whizprog \- The Be All and End All Program" ,
by J. Programmer.
.PP
.IR wimpprog (1)
.SH FILES
.B /dev/phaser
.br
.B /dev/telepath
.SH CAVEATS
.PP
There are a number of important points to remember.
.RS
.IP 1.
Use
.B \-\^\-help
to get help.
.IP 2.
Use
.B \-\^\-stun
with care.  ...
.RE
Forget these at your own risk!
.SH BUGS
The
.B \-\^\-stun
option currently always uses
.BR "\-\^\-level 10" ,
making it rather dangerous.
.SH AUTHOR
J. Programmer,
.B jp@wizard-corp.com
```

WHIZPROG(1) WHIZPROG(1)

NAME

whizprog – do amazing things

SYNOPSIS

whizprog [*options*] [*files* ...]

DESCRIPTION

Whizprog is the next generation of really **cool** do-it-all programs. ...

OPTIONS

Whizprog accepts the following options.

–h
––help Print a helpful message and exit.

––level *level*
Set the level for the **––stun** option.

––stun Stun the competition, or other beings, as needed. ...

SEE ALSO

Whizprog – The Be All and End All Program, by J. Programmer.

wimpprog(1)

FILES

/dev/phaser
/dev/telepath

CAVEATS

There are a number of important points to remember.

1. Use **––help** to get help.
2. Use **––stun** with care. ...

Forget these at your own risk!

BUGS

The **––stun** option currently always uses **––level 10**, making it rather dangerous.

AUTHOR

J. Programmer, **jp@wizard-corp.com**

April 1, 2007 1

Figure 18-1. Output of sample document

IV

References

Part IV contains an Appendix of ISO 8859-1 (Latin-1) characters and a Unix Bibliography.

ISO 8859-1 (Latin-1) Character Set

This appendix presents the set of ISO 8859-1 (Latin-1) characters, along with their equivalent values in decimal, octal, and hexadecimal. This character set suffices for English and languages that can be written using just the English alphabet, plus the major Western European languages. The lower half of this set of characters is identical to traditional ASCII. Table A-1 shows nonprinting characters; it's useful when you need to represent nonprinting characters in some printed form, such as octal. For example, the `echo` and `tr` commands let you specify characters using octal values of the form *\nnn*. Also, the `od` command can display nonprinting characters in a variety of forms.

Table A-2 shows printing characters. This table is useful when using the previous commands, but also when specifying a range of characters in a pattern-matching construct. The characters from decimal 128–159 are not used in Latin-1.

Table A-1. Nonprinting characters

Decimal	Octal	Hex	Character	Remark
0	000	00	CTRL-@	NUL (Null prompt)
1	001	01	CTRL-A	SOH (Start of heading)
2	002	02	CTRL-B	STX (Start of text)
3	003	03	CTRL-C	ETX (End of text)
4	004	04	CTRL-D	EOT (End of transmission)
5	005	05	CTRL-E	ENQ (Enquiry)
6	006	06	CTRL-F	ACK (Acknowledge)
7	007	07	CTRL-G	BEL (Bell)
8	010	08	CTRL-H	BS (Backspace)
9	011	09	CTRL-I	HT (Horizontal tab)
10	012	0A	CTRL-J	LF (Linefeed)
11	013	0B	CTRL-K	VT (Vertical tab)

Table A-1. Nonprinting characters (continued)

Decimal	Octal	Hex	Character	Remark
12	014	0C	CTRL-L	FF (Formfeed)
13	015	0D	CTRL-M	CR (Carriage return)
14	016	0E	CTRL-N	SO (Shift out)
15	017	0F	CTRL-O	SI (Shift in)
16	020	10	CTRL-P	DLE (Data link escape)
17	021	11	CTRL-Q	DC1 (XON)
18	022	12	CTRL-R	DC2
19	023	13	CTRL-S	DC3 (XOFF)
20	024	14	CTRL-T	DC4
21	025	15	CTRL-U	NAK (Negative acknowledge)
22	026	16	CTRL-V	SYN (Synchronous idle)
23	027	17	CTRL-W	ETB (End transmission blocks)
24	030	18	CTRL-X	CAN (Cancel)
25	031	19	CTRL-Y	EM (End of medium)
26	032	1A	CTRL-Z	SUB (Substitute)
27	033	1B	CTRL-[	ESC (Escape)
28	034	1C	CTRL-\	FS (File separator)
29	035	1D	CTRL-]	GS (Group separator)
30	036	1E	CTRL-^	RS (Record separator)
31	037	1F	CTRL-_	US (Unit separator)
127	177	7F		DEL (Delete or rubout)

Table A-2. Printing characters

Decimal	Octal	Hex	Character	Remark
32	040	20		Space
33	041	21	!	Exclamation point
34	042	22	"	Double quote
35	043	23	#	Number sign
36	044	24	$	Dollar sign
37	045	25	%	Percent sign
38	046	26	&	Ampersand
39	047	27	'	Apostrophe
40	050	28	(	Left parenthesis
41	051	29	)	Right parenthesis
42	052	2A	*	Asterisk
43	053	2B	+	Plus sign
44	054	2C	,	Comma
45	055	2D	–	Hyphen
46	056	2E	.	Period
47	057	2F	/	Slash

Table A-2. Printing characters (continued)

Decimal	Octal	Hex	Character	Remark
48	060	30	0	
49	061	31	1	
50	062	32	2	
51	063	33	3	
52	064	34	4	
53	065	35	5	
54	066	36	6	
55	067	37	7	
56	070	38	8	
57	071	39	9	
58	072	3A	:	Colon
59	073	3B	;	Semicolon
60	074	3C	<	Left angle bracket
61	075	3D	=	Equal sign
62	076	3E	>	Right angle bracket
63	077	3F	?	Question mark
64	100	40	@	At sign
65	101	41	A	
66	102	42	B	
67	103	43	C	
68	104	44	D	
69	105	45	E	
70	106	46	F	
71	107	47	G	
72	110	48	H	
73	111	49	I	
74	112	4A	J	
75	113	4B	K	
76	114	4C	L	
77	115	4D	M	
78	116	4E	N	
79	117	4F	O	
80	120	50	P	
81	121	51	Q	
82	122	52	R	
83	123	53	S	
84	124	54	T	
85	125	55	U	
86	126	56	V	
87	127	57	W	
88	130	58	X	

Table A-2. Printing characters (continued)

Decimal	Octal	Hex	Character	Remark
89	131	59	Y	
90	132	5A	Z	
91	133	5B	[	Left square bracket
92	134	5C	\	Backslash
93	135	5D	]	Right square bracket
94	136	5E	^	Caret
95	137	5F	_	Underscore
96	140	60	`	Back quote
97	141	61	a	
98	142	62	b	
99	143	63	c	
100	144	64	d	
101	145	65	e	
102	146	66	f	
103	147	67	g	
104	150	68	h	
105	151	69	i	
106	152	6A	j	
107	153	6B	k	
108	154	6C	l	
109	155	6D	m	
110	156	6E	n	
111	157	6F	o	
112	160	70	p	
113	161	71	q	
114	162	72	r	
115	163	73	s	
116	164	74	t	
117	165	75	u	
118	166	76	v	
119	167	77	w	
120	170	78	x	
121	171	79	y	
122	172	7A	z	
123	173	7B	{	Left curly brace
124	174	7C	|	Vertical bar
125	175	7D	}	Right curly brace
126	176	7E	~	Tilde
160	240	A0		Non-breaking space
161	241	A1	¡	Inverted exclamation
162	242	A2	¢	Cent sign

Table A-2. Printing characters (continued)

Decimal	Octal	Hex	Character	Remark
163	243	A3	£	Pound sign (British currency)
164	244	A4	¤	Currency sign
165	245	A5	¥	Yen sign
166	246	A6	¦	Broken bar
167	247	A7	§	Section symbol
168	250	A8	¨	Umlaut or diaeresis
169	251	A9	©	Copyright symbol
170	252	AA	ª	Feminine ordinal
171	253	AB	«	Left angle quotes
172	254	AC	¬	Logical not symbol
173	255	AD	-	Soft hyphen
174	256	AE	®	Registered trademark symbol
175	257	AF	¯	Spacing macron
176	260	B0	°	Degree sign
177	261	B1	±	Plus-minus
178	262	B2	²	Superscript 2
179	263	B3	³	Superscript 3
180	264	B4	´	Spacing acute
181	265	B5	µ	Micro sign
182	266	B6	¶	Paragraph symbol
183	267	B7	•	Middle dot
184	270	B8	¸	Spacing cedilia
185	271	B9	¹	Superscript 1
186	272	BA	º	Masculine ordinal
187	273	BB	»	Right angle quotes
188	274	BC	1/4	One-fourth
189	275	BD	1/2	One-half
190	276	BE	3/4	Three-fourths
191	277	BF	¿	Inverted question mark
192	300	C0	À	A with grave accent
193	301	C1	Á	A with acute accent
194	302	C2	Â	A with circumflex
195	303	C3	Ã	A with tilde
196	304	C4	Ä	A with umlaut
197	305	C5	Å	A with ring accent
198	306	C6	Æ	AE ligature
199	307	C7	Ç	C with cedilia
200	310	C8	È	E with grave accent
201	311	C9	É	E with acute accent
202	312	CA	Ê	E with circumflex
203	313	CB	Ë	E with umlaut

Table A-2. Printing characters (continued)

Decimal	Octal	Hex	Character	Remark
204	314	CC	Ì	I with grave accent
205	315	CD	Í	I with acute accent
206	316	CE	Î	I with circumflex
207	317	CF	Ï	I with umlaut
208	320	D0	Ð	Eth (Icelandic)
209	321	D1	Ñ	N with tilde
210	322	D2	Ò	O with grave accent
211	323	D3	Ó	O with acute accent
212	324	D4	Ô	O with circumflex
213	325	D5	Õ	O with tilde
214	326	D6	Ö	O with umlaut
215	327	D7	×	Multiplication sign
216	330	D8	Ø	O with slash
217	331	D9	Ù	U with grave accent
218	332	DA	Ú	U with acute accent
219	333	DB	Û	U with circumflex
220	334	DC	Ü	U with umlaut
221	335	DD	Ý	Y with acute accent
222	336	DE	Þ	Thorn (Icelandic)
223	337	DF	ß	Sharp s
224	340	E0	à	a with grave accent
225	341	E1	á	a with acute accent
226	342	E2	â	a with circumflex
227	343	E3	ã	a with tilde
228	344	E4	ä	a with umlaut
229	345	E5	å	a with ring accent
230	346	E6	æ	ae ligature
231	347	E7	ç	c with cedilia
232	350	E8	è	e with grave accent
233	351	E9	é	e with acute accent
234	352	EA	ê	e with circumflex
235	353	EB	ë	e with umlaut
236	354	EC	ì	i with grave accent
237	355	ED	í	i with acute accent
238	356	EE	î	i with circumflex
239	357	EF	ï	i with umlaut
240	360	F0	ð	eth (Icelandic)
241	361	F1	ñ	n with tilde
242	362	F2	ò	o with grave accent
243	363	F3	ó	o with acute accent
244	364	F4	ô	o with circumflex

Table A-2. Printing characters (continued)

Decimal	Octal	Hex	Character	Remark
245	365	F5	õ	o with tilde
246	366	F6	ö	o with umlaut
247	367	F7	÷	Division sign
248	370	F8	Ø	o with slash
249	371	F9	ù	u with grave accent
250	372	FA	ú	u with acute accent
251	373	FB	û	u with circumflex
252	374	FC	ü	u with umlaut
253	375	FD	ý	y with acute accent
254	376	FE	þ	thorn (Icelandic)
255	377	FF	ÿ	y with umlaut

Bibliography

Many books have been written about Unix and related topics. It would be impossible to list them all, nor would that be very helpful. In this chapter, we present the "classics"—those books that the true Unix wizard has on his or her shelf. (Alas, some of these are now out of print; thus only older Unix wizards have them.)

Because Unix has affected many aspects of computing, you will find books listed here on things besides just the Unix operating system itself.

This chapter presents:

- Unix descriptions and programmer's manuals
- Unix internals
- System and network administration
- Programming with the Unix mindset
- Programming languages
- TCP/IP networking
- Software development
- Emacs
- Standards
- O'Reilly books

Unix Descriptions and Programmer's Manuals

1. *The Bell System Technical Journal*, Volume 57 Number 6, Part 2, July–August 1978. AT&T Bell Laboratories, Murray Hill, NJ, USA. ISSN 0005-8580. A special issue devoted to Unix, by the creators of the system.
2. *AT&T Bell Laboratories Technical Journal*, Volume 63 Number 8, Part 2, October 1984. AT&T Bell Laboratories, Murray Hill, NJ, USA. Another special issue devoted to Unix.

These two volumes were republished as:

3. *UNIX System Readings and Applications*, Volume 1, Prentice Hall, Englewood Cliffs, NJ, USA, 1987. ISBN 0-13-938532-0.
4. *UNIX System Readings and Applications*, Volume 2, Prentice Hall, Englewood Cliffs, NJ, USA, 1987. ISBN 0-13-939845-7.
5. *UNIX Time-sharing System: UNIX Programmers Manual*, Seventh Edition, Volumes 1, 2A, 2B. Bell Telephone Laboratories, Inc., January 1979.

   These are the reference manuals (Volume 1), and descriptive papers (Volumes 2A and 2B) for the landmark Seventh Edition Unix system, the direct ancestor of all current commercial Unix systems.

   They were reprinted by Holt Rinehart & Winston, but are now long out of print. However, they are available online from Bell Labs in `troff` source, PDF, and PostScript formats. See *http://plan9.bell-labs.com/7thEdMan*.
6. *UNIX Research System: Programmer's Manual, Tenth Edition*, Volume 1, AT&T Bell Laboratories, M.D. McIlroy and A.G. Hume editors, Holt Rinehart & Winston, New York, NY, USA, 1990. ISBN 0-03-047532-5.
7. *UNIX Research System: Papers, Tenth Edition*, Volume 2, AT&T Bell Laboratories, M.D. McIlroy and A.G. Hume editors, Holt Rinehart & Winston, New York, NY, USA, 1990. ISBN 0-03-047529-5.

   These are the manuals and papers for the Tenth Edition Unix system. Although this system was not used much outside of Bell Labs, many of the ideas from it and its predecessors were incorporated into various versions of System V. The manuals make interesting reading, in any case.
8. *4.4BSD Manuals*, Computing Systems Research Group, University of California, Berkeley. O'Reilly Media, Inc., Sebastopol, CA, USA, 1994. ISBN 1-56592-082-1. Out of print.

   The manuals for 4.4BSD.
9. Your Unix programmer's manual. One of the most instructive things you can do is read your manual from front to back.* (This is harder than it used to be, as Unix systems have grown.) It is easier to do if your Unix vendor makes printed copies of its documentation available. Otherwise, start with the Seventh Edition manual, and then read your local documentation as needed.
10. *A Quarter Century of Unix*, Peter H. Salus. Addison-Wesley, Reading, MA, USA, 1994. ISBN 0-201-54777-5.

    A delightful book that tells the history of Unix, from its inception up to the time the book was written. It reads like a good novel, except that it's all true!
11. *Linux and the Unix Philosophy*, Mike Gancarz. Digital Press, Bedford, MA, USA, 2003. ISBN 1-55558-273-7.

* One summer, while working as a contract programmer, I spent my lunchtimes reading the manual for System III (yes, that long ago) from cover to cover. I don't know that I ever learned so much in so little time.

Unix Internals

The dedicated Unix wizard knows not only how to use his or her system, but how it works.

1. *Lions' Commentary on UNIX 6th Edition, with Source Code*, John Lions. Peer-To-Peer Communications LLC, Charlottesville, VA, USA, 2005. ISBN 1-57398-013-7. *http://www.peerllc.com/*.

   This classic work provides the source code for the Sixth Edition Unix kernel, with a complete exegesis of it. It set the standard for clear exposition of operating system internals.

2. *The Design of the UNIX Operating System*, Maurice J. Bach. Prentice Hall, Englewood Cliffs, NJ, USA, 1986. ISBN 0-13-201799-7.

   This book very lucidly describes the design of System V Release 2, with some discussion of important features in System V Release 3, such as STREAMS and the filesystem switch.

3. *The Magic Garden Explained: The Internals of Unix System V Release 4: An Open Systems Design*, Berny Goodheart, James Cox, and John R. Mashey. Prentice Hall, Englewood Cliffs, NJ, USA, 1994. ISBN 0-13-098138-9.

4. *Unix Internals: The New Frontiers*, Uresh Vahalia. Prentice Hall, Englewood Cliffs, NJ, USA, 1996. ISBN 0-13-101908-2.

5. *Solaris Internals: Core Kernel Architecture*, Jim Mauro and Richard McDougall. Prentice Hall PTR, Upper Saddle River, NJ, USA, 2000. ISBN 0-13-022496-0.

6. *UNIX(R) Systems for Modern Architectures: Symmetric Multiprocessing and Caching for Kernel Programmers*, Curt Schimmel. Addison-Wesley, Reading, MA, USA, 1994. ISBN 0-201-63338-8.

7. *The Design and Implementation of the 4.3BSD UNIX Operating System*, Samuel J. Leffler, Marshall Kirk McKusick, Michael J. Karels and John S. Quarterman. Addison-Wesley, Reading, MA, USA, 1989. ISBN 0-201-06196-1.

   This book describes the 4.3BSD version of Unix. Many important features found in commercial Unix systems first originated in the BSD Unix systems, such as long filenames, job control, and networking.

8. *The Design and Implementation of the 4.4 BSD Operating System*, Marshall Kirk McKusick, Keith Bostic, Michael J. Karels, and John S. Quarterman. Addison Wesley Longman, Reading, MA, USA, 1996. ISBN 0-201-54979-4.

   This book is an update of the previous one, for 4.4BSD, the last Unix system released from UCB. To quote from the publisher's description, the book "details the major changes in process and memory management, describes the new extensible and stackable filesystem interface, includes an invaluable chapter on the new network filesystem, and updates information on networking and interprocess communication."

9. *The Design and Implementation of the FreeBSD Operating System*, Marshall Kirk McKusick and George V. Neville-Neil. Addison-Wesley, Reading, MA, USA, 2005. ISBN 0-201-70245-2.

   An update of the previous book, focusing on the FreeBSD operating system. It presents the state of current BSD operating system technology.

10. *Linux Kernel Development*, Second Edition, Robert Love. Novell Press, Que Publishing, Indianapolis, IN, USA, 2005. ISBN 0-672-32720-1.
11. *Understanding the Linux Kernel*, Second Edition, Daniel P. Bovet, and Marco Cesati. O'Reilly Media, Inc., Sebastopol, CA, USA, 2002. ISBN 0-596-00213-0.
12. *Linux Device Drivers*, Third Edition, Jonathan Corbet, Alessandro Rubini, and Greg Kroah-Hartman. O'Reilly Media, Inc. Sebastopol, CA, USA, 2005. ISBN 0-596-00590-3

System and Network Administration

Unix system administration is a complicated topic in its own right. In these days of single-user workstations, even regular users also have to understand basic system administration tasks. Besides managing the system (users, filesystems, accounting), administrators also have to understand TCP/IP network administration.

1. *UNIX System Administration Handbook*, Third Edition, Evi Nemeth, Garth Snyder, Scott Seebass, and Trent R. Hein. Prentice Hall PTR, Upper Saddle River, NJ, USA, 2000. ISBN 0-13-020601-6.
2. *Linux Administration Handbook*, Evi Nemeth, Garth Snyder, and Trent R. Hein. Prentice Hall PTR, Upper Saddle River, NJ, USA, 2002. ISBN 0-13-008466-2.

   A revision of the previous book focused on GNU/Linux.
3. *Essential System Administration*, Third Edition, Æleen Frisch. O'Reilly Media, Inc., Sebastopol, CA, USA, 2002. ISBN 0-596-00343-9.
4. *DNS and BIND*, Fouth Edition, Paul Albitz and Cricket Liu. O'Reilly Media, Inc., Sebastopol, CA, USA, 2001. ISBN 0-596-00158-4.
5. *TCP/IP Network Administration*, Third Edition, Craig Hunt. O'Reilly Media, Inc., Sebastopol, CA, USA, 2002. ISBN 0-596-00297-1.
6. *Linux Network Administrator's Guide*, Third Edition, Tony Bautts, Terry Dawson, and Gregor N. Purdy. O'Reilly Media, Inc. Sebastopol, CA, USA, 2005. ISBN 0-596-00548-2.

Programming with the Unix Mindset

Any book written by Brian Kernighan deserves careful reading, usually several times. The first two books present the Unix "toolbox" programming methodology. They will help you learn how to "think Unix." The third book continues the process, with a more explicit Unix focus. The fourth and fifth are about programming in general, and also very worthwhile.

1. *Software Tools*, Brian W. Kernighan and P. J. Plauger. Addison-Wesley, Reading, MA, USA, 1976. ISBN 0-201-03669-X.

   A wonderful book* that presents the design and code for programs equivalent to Unix's `grep`, `sort`, `ed`, and others. The programs use RATFOR (Rational FORTRAN), a preprocessor for FORTRAN with C-like control structures.

* One that changed my life forever.

2. *Software Tools in Pascal*, Brian W. Kernighan and P. J. Plauger. Addison-Wesley, Reading, MA, USA, 1981. ISBN 0-201-10342-7.

   A translation of the previous book into Pascal. Still worth reading; Pascal provides many things that FORTRAN does not.

3. *The Unix Programming Environment*, Brian W. Kernighan and Rob Pike. Prentice Hall, Englewood Cliffs, NJ, USA, 1984. ISBN 0-13-937699-2 (hardcover), 0-13-937681-X (paperback).

   This books focuses explicitly on Unix, using the tools in that environment. In particular, it adds important material on the shell, `awk`, and the use of `lex` and yacc. See *http://cm.bell-labs.com/cm/cs/upe*.

4. *The Elements of Programming Style*, Second Edition, Brian W. Kernighan and P. J. Plauger. McGraw-Hill, New York, NY, USA, 1978. ISBN 0-07-034207-5.

   Modeled after Strunk & White's famous *The Elements of Style*, this book describes good programming practices that can be used in any environment.

5. *The Practice of Programming*, Brian W. Kernighan and Rob Pike. Addison Wesley Longman, Reading, MA, USA, 1999. ISBN 0-201-61586-X.

   Similar to the previous book, with a somewhat stronger technical focus. See *http://cm.bell-labs.com/cm/cs/tpop*.

6. *The Art of UNIX Programming*, Eric S. Raymond. Addison-Wesley, Reading, MA, USA, 2003. ISBN 0-13-124085-4.

   We don't agree with everything the author says, but this book is still worth reading.

7. *Writing Efficient Programs*, Jon Louis Bentley. Prentice Hall, Englewood Cliffs, NJ, USA, 1982. ISBN 0-13-970251-2 (hardcover), 0-13-970244-X (paperback).

   Although not related to Unix, this is an excellent book for anyone interested in programming efficiently.

8. *Programming Pearls*, Second Edition, Jon Louis Bentley. Addison-Wesley, Reading, MA, USA, 2000. ISBN 0-201-65788-0.

9. *More Programming Pearls: Confessions of a Coder*, Jon Louis Bentley. Addison-Wesley, Reading, MA, USA, 1988. ISBN 0-201-11889-0.

   These two excellent books, to quote Nelson H. F. Beebe, "epitomize the Unix mindset, and are wonderful examples of little languages, algorithm design, and much more." These should be on every serious programmer's bookshelf.

10. *Advanced Programming in the UNIX Environment*, Second Edition, W. Richard Stevens and Stephen Rago. Addison-Wesley, Reading, MA, USA, 2005. ISBN 0-201-43307-9.

    A thick but excellent work on how to use the wealth of system calls in modern Unix systems.

11. *Linux Programming by Example: The Fundamentals*, Arnold Robbins. Prentice Hall PTR, Upper Saddle River, NJ, USA, 2004. ISBN 0-13-142964-7.

    This book is more selective than the one by Stevens and Rago, focusing on the core systems calls and library functions used by most standard applications. Wherever possible, it uses example code from both V7 Unix and GNU software for demonstration.

12. *Advanced UNIX Programming*, Second Edition, Marc J. Rochkind, Addison-Wesley, Reading, MA, USA, 2004. ISBN 0-13-141154-3.

Programming Languages

A number of important programming languages were first developed under Unix. Note again the books written by Brian Kernighan.

1. *The C Programming Language*, Brian W. Kernighan and Dennis M. Ritchie. Prentice Hall, Englewood Cliffs, NJ, USA, 1978. ISBN 0-13-110163-3.

   The original "bible" on C. Dennis Ritchie invented C and is one of the two "fathers" of Unix. This edition is out of print.

2. *The C Programming Language*, Second Edition, Brian W. Kernighan and Dennis M. Ritchie. Prentice Hall, Englewood Cliffs, NJ, USA, 1988. ISBN 0-13-110362-8.

   This revision of the original covers the 1990 version of Standard C. It retains and improves upon the high qualities of the first edition. See *http://cm.bell-labs.com/cm/cs/cbook*.

3. *C: A Reference Manual*, Fifth Edition, Samuel P. Harbison III and Guy L. Steele. Prentice Hall, Upper Saddle River, NJ, USA, 2002. ISBN 0-13-089592-X.

   An excellent discussion of the details for those who need to know. This edition covers everything from the original, pre-Standard C, through the 1999 version of Standard C.

4. *The C++ Programming Language*, Special Third Edition, Bjarne Stroustrup. Addison-Wesley, Reading, MA, USA, 2000. ISBN 0-201-70073-5.

   The definitive statement on C++ by the language's inventor and the ANSI C++ committee chair. See *http://www.awl.com/cseng/titles/0-201-70073-5/*.

5. *The C++ Standard Library—A Tutorial and Reference*, Nicolai M. Josuttis. Addison-Wesley, Reading, MA, USA, 1999. ISBN 0-201-37926-0.

6. *C++ Primer*, Third Edition, Stanley B. Lippman and Josée Lajoie. Addison Wesley Longman, Reading, MA, USA, 1998. ISBN 0-201-82470-1.

   This is an excellent introduction to C++. See *http://www.awl.com/cseng/titles/0-201-82470-1/*.

7. *The Annotated C++ Reference Manual*, Margaret A. Ellis and Bjarne Stroustrup. Addison-Wesley, Reading, MA, USA, 1990. ISBN 0-201-51459-1.

   The first attempt to rigorously define the C++ language. This book became one of the base documents for the ANSI C++ standardization committee. It is now of mostly historical interest. See *http://www.awl.com/cseng/titles/0-201-51459-1/*.

8. *The Java Programming Language*, Third Edition, Ken Arnold, James Gosling and David Holmes. Addison-Wesley, Reading, MA, USA, 2000. ISBN 0-201-70433-1.

   This book is intended for learning Java. The first two authors are two of the designers of the language.

9. *The Java Language Specification*, Second Edition, James Gosling, Bill Joy, Guy L. Steele Jr. and Gilad Bracha. Addison-Wesley, Reading, MA, USA, 2000. ISBN 0-201-31008-2.

10. *The AWK Programming Language*, Alfred V. Aho, Brian W. Kernighan, and Peter J. Weinberger. Addison-Wesley, Reading, MA, USA, 1987. ISBN 0-201-07981-X.

    The original definition for the awk programming language. Extremely worthwhile. See *http://cm.bell-labs.com/cm/cs/awkbook*.

11. *Effective awk Programming*, Third Edition, Arnold Robbins. O'Reilly Media, Inc., Sebastopol, CA, USA, 2001. ISBN 0-596-00070-7.

    A more tutorial treatment of awk that covers the POSIX standard for awk. It also serves as the user's guide for gawk.

12. *Tcl and the Tk Toolkit*, John K. Ousterhout. Addison-Wesley, Reading, MA, USA, 1994. ISBN 0-201-63337-X.

    The first book on Tcl/Tk. this book is now out of date, although it was written by the creator of Tcl/Tk.

13. *Practical Programming in Tcl & Tk*, Fourth Edition, Brent B. Welch, Ken Jones, and Jeffry Hobbs. Prentice Hall PTR, Upper Saddle River, NJ, USA, 2003. ISBN 0-13-038560-3

14. *Effective Tcl/Tk Programming: Writing Better Programs in Tcl and Tk*, Mark Harrison and Michael J. McLennan. Addison-Wesley, Reading, MA, USA, 1997. ISBN 0-201-63474-0.

15. *The New Kornshell Command and Programming Language*, Morris I. Bolsky and David G. Korn. Prentice Hall, Englewood Cliffs, NJ, USA, 1995. ISBN 0-13-182700-6.

    The definitive work on the Korn shell, by its author.

16. *Hands-On KornShell 93 Programming*, Barry Rosenberg. Addison Wesley Longman, Reading, MA, USA, 1998. ISBN 0-201-31018-X.

17. *Compilers—Principles, Techniques, and Tools*, Alfred V. Aho and Ravi Sethi and Jeffrey D. Ullman. Addison Wesley Longman, Reading, MA, USA, 1986. ISBN 0-201-10088-6.

    This is the famous "dragon book" on compiler construction. It provides much of the theory behind the operation of lex and yacc.

TCP/IP Networking

The books by Comer are well-written; they are the standard descriptions of the TCP/IP protocols. The books by Stevens are also very highly regarded.

1. *Internetworking with TCP/IP Volume 1: Principles, Protocols, and Architecture*, Fourth Edition, Douglas E. Comer. Prentice Hall, Upper Saddle River, NJ, USA, 2000. ISBN 0-13-018380-6.

2. *Internetworking With TCP/IP Volume 2: ANSI C Version: Design, Implementation, and Internals*, Third Edition, Douglas E. Comer and David L. Stevens. Prentice Hall, Englewood Cliffs, NJ, USA, 1998. ISBN 0-13-973843-6.

3. *Internetworking With TCP/IP Volume 3: Client-Server Programming and Applications: Linux/Posix Sockets Version*, Second Edition, Douglas E. Comer, David L. Stevens, Marshall T. Rose, and Michael Evangelista. Prentice-Hall, Englewood Cliffs, NJ, USA, 2000. ISBN 0-13-032071-4.

4. *TCP/IP Illustrated, Volume 1: The Protocols*, W. Richard Stevens. Addison Wesley Longman, Reading, MA, USA, 1994. ISBN 0-201-63346-9.
5. *TCP/IP Illustrated, Volume 2: The Implementation*, W. Richard Stevens and Gary R. Wright. Addison Wesley Longman, Reading, MA, USA, 1995. ISBN 0-201-63354-X.
6. *TCP/IP Illustrated, Volume 3: TCP for Transactions, HTTP, NNTP, and the Unix Domain Protocols*, W. Richard Stevens. Addison Wesley Longman, Reading, MA, USA, 1996. ISBN 0-201-63495-3.
7. *Unix Network Programming, Volume 1: The Sockets Networking API*, Third Edition W. Richard Stevens, Bill Fenner and Andrew M. Rudoff. Addison-Wesley, Reading, MA, USA, 2003. ISBN 0-13-141155-1.
8. *Unix Network Programming, Volume 2: Interprocess Communications*, Second Edition, W. Richard Stevens. Prentice Hall PTR, Upper Saddle River, NJ, USA, 1998. ISBN 0-13-081081-9.

Software Development

1. *Applying RCS and SCCS*, Don Bolinger and Tan Bronson. O'Reilly Media, Inc., Sebastopol, CA, USA, 1995. ISBN 1-56592-117-8.
2. *Open Source Development with CVS*, Third Edition, Karl Fogel and Moshe Bar. Paraglyph Press, Phoenix, AZ, USA, 2003. ISBN 1932111816.

   This book is available online: see *http://cvsbook.red-bean.com/*.
3. *Essential CVS*, Jennifer Vesperman. O'Reilly Media, Inc., Sebastopol, CA, USA, 2003. ISBN 0-596-00459-1.
4. *Version Control With Subversion*, Ben Collins-Sussman, Brian W. Fitzpatrick and C. Michael Pilato. O'Reilly Media, Inc., Sebastopol, CA, USA, 2004. ISBN 0-596-00448-6.
5. *GNU Make: A Program for Directing Recompilation*, Richard M. Stallman, Roland McGrath, and Paul D. Smith. The Free Software Foundation, Cambridge, MA, USA, 2004. ISBN 1-882114-83-3.
6. *Managing Projects with GNU make*, Third Edition, Robert Mecklenburg, Andy Oram, and Steve Talbott. O'Reilly Media, Inc., Sebastopol, CA, USA, 2005. ISBN 0-596-00610-1.
7. *Debugging with GDB: The GNU Source-Level Debugger*, Richard M. Stallman, Roland Pesch, Stan Shebs, et al. The Free Software Foundation, Cambridge, MA, USA, 2002. ISBN 1-882114-88-4.
8. *The Cathedral and the Bazaar*, Eric S. Raymond, O'Reilly Media, Inc., Sebastopol, CA, USA, 2001. ISBN 0-596-00131-2 (hardback), 0-596-00108-8 (paperback).

Emacs

1. *GNU Emacs Manual, for Version 21*, Fifteenth Edition, Richard M. Stallman. The Free Software Foundation, Cambridge, MA, USA, 2002. ISBN 1-882114-85-X.
2. *An Introduction to Programming in Emacs Lisp*, Revised Second Edition, Robert J. Chassell. The Free Software Foundation, Cambridge, MA, USA, 2004. ISBN 1-882114-56-6
3. *GNU Emacs Lisp Reference Manual* (in two volumes), Bil Lewis, Dan LaLiberte, Richard Stallman, and the GNU Manual Group. The Free Software Foundation, Cambridge, MA, USA, 2000. ISBN 1-882114-73-6. Out of print.
4. *Learning GNU Emacs*, Third Edition, Debra Cameron, James Elliott, and Marc Loy. O'Reilly Media, Inc., Sebastopol, CA, USA, 2005. ISBN 0-596-00648-9.
5. *Writing GNU Emacs Extensions*, Bob Glickstein. O'Reilly Media, Inc., Sebastopol, CA, USA, 1997. ISBN 1-56592-261-1.
6. *GNU Emacs: UNIX Text Editing and Programming*, Michael A. Schoonover, John S. Bowie, and William R. Arnold. Addison-Wesley, Reading, MA, USA, 1992. ISBN 0-201-56345-2.

Standards

There are a number of "official" standards for the behavior of portable applications among Unix and Unix-like systems. The first entry is the current POSIX standard. The rest are the formal standards for the C and C++ programming languages.

1. *IEEE Standard 1003.1-2004: Standard for information Technology—Portable Operating System Interface (POSIX®)*. IEEE, New York, NY, USA, 2004.

   This is the POSIX standard. It combines both the system call interface standard and the shell and utilities standard in one document. The standard consists of several volumes: *Base Definitions* (Volume 1), *System Interfaces* (Volume 2), *Shell and Utilities* (Volume 3), and *Rationale* (Volume 4).

   The standard may be ordered from *http://www.standards.ieee.org* on CD-ROM (Product number SE95238, ISBN 0-7381-4049-X) or as PDF (Product number SS95238, ISBN 0-7381-4048-1).
2. X3 Secretariat: *Standard—The C Language*. X3J11/90-013. ISO Standard ISO/IEC 9899. Computer and Business Equipment Manufacturers Association. Washington DC, USA, 1990.
3. *International Standard: Programming Languages—C*. ISO Standard ISO/IEC 9899:1999(E). Information Technology Industry Council, Washington DC, USA, 1999.

   These two documents are the 1990 and 1999 standards for the C language. It generally takes five or more years from when a language standard is published until compilers for that version become widely available.

4. X3 Secretariat: *International Standard—The C++ Language*. X3J16-14882. Information Technology Council (NSITC). Washington DC, USA, 1998.

   This is the initial standard for the C++ programming language, used by most C++ compilers as of this writing.

5. *International Standard: Programming Languages—C++*. ISO Standard ISO/IEC 14882-2003. Information Technology Industry Council, Washington DC, USA, 2003.

   A revision of the previous document.

O'Reilly Books

Here is a list of O'Reilly Media books cited throughout this book. There are, of course, many other O'Reilly books relating to Unix. See *http://www.oreilly.com/catalog*.

1. *Advanced Perl Programming*, Second Edition, Simon Cozens. O'Reilly Media, Inc., Sebastopol, CA, USA, 2005. ISBN 0-596-00456-7
2. *Checking C Programs with lint*, Ian F. Darwin. O'Reilly Media, Inc., Sebastopol, CA, USA, 1988. ISBN 0-937175-30-7.
3. *Classic Shell Scripting*, Arnold Robbins and Nelson H.F. Beebe. O'Reilly Media, Inc., Sebastopol, CA, USA, 2005. ISBN 0-596-00595-4.
4. *Learning Perl*, Third Edition, Randal L. Schwartz and Tom Phoenix. O'Reilly Media, Inc., Sebastopol, CA, USA, 2001. ISBN 0-596-00132-0.
5. *Learning the bash Shell*, Third Edition, Cameron Newham and Bill Rosenblatt. O'Reilly Media, Inc., Sebastopol, CA, USA, 2005. ISBN 0-596-00965-8.
6. *Learning the Korn Shell*, Second Edition, Bill Rosenblatt and Arnold Robbins. O'Reilly Media, Inc., Sebastopol, CA, USA, 2002. ISBN 0-596-00195-9.
7. *Learning Python*, Second Edition, Mark Lutz and David Ascher. O'Reilly Media, Inc., Sebastopol, CA, USA, 2003. ISBN: 0-596-00281-5.
8. *Learning the Unix Operating System*, Fifth Edition, Jerry Peek, Grace Todino, and John Strang. O'Reilly Media, Inc., Sebastopol, CA, USA, 2001. ISBN 0-596-00261-0.
9. *Learning the vi Editor*, Sixth Edition, Linda Lamb and Arnold Robbins. O'Reilly Media, Inc., Sebastopol, CA, USA, 1998. ISBN 1-56592-426-6.
10. *lex & yacc*, Second Edition, John Levine, Tony Mason, and Doug Brown. O'Reilly Media, Inc., Sebastopol, CA, USA, 1992. ISBN 1-56592-000-7.
11. *Linux in a Nutshell*, Fifth Edition, Ellen Siever, Aaron Weber, Stephen Figgins, Robert Love, and Arnold Robbins. O'Reilly Media, Inc., Sebastopol, CA, USA, 2005. ISBN 0-596-00482-6.
12. *Mac OS X Panther in a Nutshell*, Second Edition, Jason McIntosh, Chuck Toporek, and Chris Stone. O'Reilly Media, Inc., Sebastopol, CA, USA, 2004. ISBN 0-596-00606-3.
13. *Mastering Regular Expressions*, Second Edition, Jeffrey E. F. Friedl. O'Reilly Media, Inc., Sebastopol, CA, USA, 2002. ISBN 0-596-00289-0.

14. *PGP: Pretty Good Privacy*, Simson Garfinkel. O'Reilly Media, Inc., Sebastopol, CA, USA, 1994. ISBN 1-56592-098-8.

15. *Programming Perl*, Third Edition, Larry Wall, Tom Christiansen, and Jon Orwant. O'Reilly Media, Inc., Sebastopol, CA, USA, 2000. ISBN 0-596-00027-8.

16. *Programming Python*, Second Edition, Mark Lutz. O'Reilly Media, Inc., Sebastopol, CA, USA, 2001. ISBN: 0-596-00085-5.

17. *sed & awk*, Second Edition, Dale Dougherty and Arnold Robbins. O'Reilly Media, Inc., Sebastopol, CA, USA, 1997. ISBN 1-56592-225-5.

18. *SSH, The Secure Shell, The Definitive Guide*, Second Edition, Daniel J. Barrett, Richard E. Silverman, and Robert G. Byrnes. O'Reilly Media, Inc., Sebastopol, CA, USA, 2005. ISBN: 0-596-00895-3.

19. *Using csh & tcsh*, Paul DuBois. O'Reilly Media, Inc., Sebastopol, CA, USA, 1995. ISBN 1-56592-132-1.

Index

Symbols

We'd like to hear your suggestions for improving our indexes. Send email to *index@oreilly.com*.

A

B

C

D

E

F

G

H

I

J

K

L

M

N

O

P

Q

R

S

T

U

V

W

X

Y

Z

About the Author

Arnold Robbins, an Atlanta native, is a professional programmer and technical author. He is also a happy husband, the father of four very cute children, and an amateur Talmudist (Babylonian and Jerusalem). Since late 1997, he and his family have been living in Israel.

Arnold has been working with Unix systems since 1980, when he was introduced to a PDP-11 running a version of Sixth Edition Unix. His experience also includes multiple commercial Unix systems, from Sun, IBM, HP, and DEC. He has been working with GNU/Linux systems since 1996, and for this book was introduced to the joys of the Macintosh. (iTunes is now his current favorite "killer app.")

Arnold has also been a heavy awk user since 1987, when he became involved with gawk, the GNU project's version of awk. As a member of the POSIX 1003.2 balloting group, he helped shape the POSIX standard for awk. He is currently the maintainer of gawk and its documentation.

In previous incarnations he has been a systems administrator and a teacher of Unix and networking Continuing Education classes. He has also had more than one poor experience with start-up software companies, which he prefers not to think about anymore. These days he writes high-end Command and Control–related software for a leading Isreali software compnay. One day he hopes to put up his own web site at *http://www.skeeve.com*.

O'Reilly has been keeping him busy; he is author and/or coauthor of these best-selling titles: *Learning the vi Editor*, *Effective awk Programming*, *sed & awk*, *Classic Shell Scripting*, and several pocket references.

Colophon

Our look is the result of reader comments, our own experimentation, and feedback from distribution channels. Distinctive covers complement our distinctive approach to technical topics, breathing personality and life into potentially dry subjects.

The animal on the cover of *Unix in a Nutshell*, Fourth Edition, is a tarsier, a nocturnal mammal related to the lemur. Its generic name, Tarsius, is derived from the animal's very long ankle bone, the tarsus. The tarsier is a native of the East Indies jungles from Sumatra to the Philippines and Sulawesi, where it lives in the trees, leaping from branch to branch with extreme agility and speed.

A small animal, the tarsier's body is only 6 inches long, followed by a 10-inch tufted tail. It is covered in soft brown or grey silky fur, has a round face, and huge eyes. Its arms and legs are long and slender, as are its digits, which are tipped with rounded, fleshy pads to improve the tarsier's grip on trees. Tarsiers are active only at night, hiding during the day in tangles of vines or in the tops of tall trees. They subsist mainly on insects, and though very curious animals, tend to be loners.

Colleen Gorman was the production editor and the copyeditor for *Unix in a Nutshell*, Fourth Edition. Genevieve d'Entremont and Mary Brady provided quality control. Ellen Troutman wrote the index.

Edie Freedman designed the cover of this book. The cover image is a 19th-century engraving from the Dover Pictorial Archive. Karen Montgomery produced the cover layout with Adobe InDesign CS using Adobe's ITC Garamond font. The back cover illustration is by J.D. "Illiad" Frazer.

David Futato designed the interior layout. This book was converted by Keith Fahlgren to FrameMaker 5.5.6 with a format conversion tool created by Erik Ray, Jason McIntosh, Neil Walls, and Mike Sierra that uses Perl and XML technologies. The text font is Linotype Birka; the heading font is Adobe Myriad Condensed; and the code font is LucasFont's TheSans Mono Condensed. The illustrations that appear in the book were produced by Robert Romano, Jessamyn Read, and Lesley Borash using Macromedia FreeHand MX and Adobe Photoshop CS. The tip and warning icons were drawn by Christopher Bing. This colophon was written by Michael Kalantarian.

Related Titles from O'Reilly

Unix Administration

Classic Shell Scripting

DNS & BIND, *4th Edition*

DNS & BIND Cookbook

Essential System Administration, *3rd Edition*

Essential System Administration Pocket Reference

Postfix: The Definitive Guide

qmail

sendmail, *3rd Edition*

sendmail Cookbook

System Performance Tuning, *2nd Edition*

The Unix CD Bookshelf, *Version 3.0*

Unix Backup & Recovery

Unix Basics

GNU Emacs Pocket Reference

Learning GNU Emacs, *2nd Edition*

Learning the bash Shell, *3rd Edition*

Learning the Korn Shell

Learning the Unix Operating System, *5th Edition*

Learning the vi Editor, *6th Edition*

sed & awk Pocket Reference, *2nd Edition*

sed & awk, *2nd Edition*

Unix in a Nutshell, *4th Edition*

Using csh & tcsh

Unix Tools

BSD Hacks

CVS Pocket Reference, *2nd Edition*

Effective awk Programming, *3rd Edition*

Essential CVS

GDB Pocket Reference

lex & yacc, *2nd Edition*

Managing Projects with make, *2nd Edition*

Practical PostgreSQL

The Complete FreeBSD, *4th Edition*

Unix Power Tools, *3rd edition*

Version Control with Subversion

Writing GNU Emacs Extensions

Our books are available at most retail and online bookstores.

To order direct: 1-800-998-9938 • *order@oreilly.com* • *www.oreilly.com*

Online editions of most O'Reilly titles are available by subscription at *safari.oreilly.com*

Keep in touch with O'Reilly

Download examples from our books

To find example files from a book, go to: *www.oreilly.com/catalog* select the book, and follow the "Examples" link.

Register your O'Reilly books

Register your book at *register.oreilly.com*
Why register your books? Once you've registered your O'Reilly books you can:

- Win O'Reilly books, T-shirts or discount coupons in our monthly drawing.
- Get special offers available only to registered O'Reilly customers.
- Get catalogs announcing new books (US and UK only).
- Get email notification of new editions of the O'Reilly books you own.

Join our email lists

Sign up to get topic-specific email announcements of new books and conferences, special offers, and O'Reilly Network technology newsletters at:

elists.oreilly.com

It's easy to customize your free elists subscription so you'll get exactly the O'Reilly news you want.

Get the latest news, tips, and tools

www.oreilly.com

- "Top 100 Sites on the Web"—PC Magazine
- CIO Magazine's Web Business 50 Awards

Our web site contains a library of comprehensive product information (including book excerpts and tables of contents), downloadable software, background articles, interviews with technology leaders, links to relevant sites, book cover art, and more.

Work for O'Reilly

Check out our web site for current employment opportunities:

jobs.oreilly.com

Contact us

O'Reilly Media, Inc.
1005 Gravenstein Hwy North
Sebastopol, CA 95472 USA
Tel: 707-827-7000 or 800-998-9938
(6am to 5pm PST)
Fax: 707-829-0104

Contact us by email

For answers to problems regarding your order or our products:
order@oreilly.com

To request a copy of our latest catalog:
catalog@oreilly.com

For book content technical questions or corrections: **booktech@oreilly.com**

For educational, library, government, and corporate sales: **corporate@oreilly.com**

To submit new book proposals to our editors and product managers:
proposals@oreilly.com

For information about our international distributors or translation queries:
international@oreilly.com

For information about academic use of O'Reilly books:
adoption@oreilly.com
or visit:
academic.oreilly.com

For a list of our distributors outside of North America check out:
international.oreilly.com/distributors.html

Order a book online

www.oreilly.com/order_new

Our books are available at most retail and online bookstores.
To order direct: 1-800-998-9938 • *order@oreilly.com* • *www.oreilly.com*
Online editions of most O'Reilly titles are available by subscription at *safari.oreilly.com*